Peace and War

UNITED STATES FOREIGN POLICY

1931-1941

UNITED STATES GOVERNMENT PRINTING OFFICE

WASHINGTON : 1943

DEPARTMENT OF STATE

PUBLICATION 1983

For sale by the
Superintendent of Documents
Government Printing Office
Washington, D.C.

PRICE, $2.00 (CLOTH)

FOREWORD

On January 2, 1943 the Department of State released a publication entitled "Peace and War: United States Foreign Policy, 1931–1941", containing references to a number of documents concerning the conduct of the foreign relations of the United States during that ten-year period. It was stated at the time that these documents would be published later. They are accordingly published herein, together with a reprint of the publication released on January 2. The present publication presents a record of policies and acts by which the United States sought to promote conditions of peace and world order and to meet the world-wide dangers resulting from Japanese, German, and Italian aggression.

July 1, 1943

CONTENTS

CONTENTS

CONTENTS

CONTENTS

DOCUMENTS

CONTENTS

CONTENTS

CONTENTS

CONTENTS

CONTENTS

CONTENTS

CONTENTS

CONTENTS

CONTENTS

CONTENTS

CONTENTS

CONTENTS

⟫⟫ I ⟪⟪

THE FATEFUL DECADE

THE FATEFUL decade, 1931–1941, began and ended with acts of violence by Japan. It was marked by the ruthless development of a determined policy of world domination on the part of Japan, Germany, and Italy.

In 1931 Japan seized Manchuria. Two years later Germany withdrew from the Disarmament Conference and began rearming. In 1934 Japan gave notice of termination of the Washington Treaty for the Limitation of Naval Armament.

In 1935 Italy invaded Ethiopia. In 1936 Hitler tore up the Treaty of Locarno and fortified the demilitarized Rhineland Zone. In 1937 Japan again attacked China. In 1938 Hitler occupied Austria and dismembered Czechoslovakia. During the first half of 1939 Hitler completed the destruction of Czechoslovakia and seized Memel, while Italy invaded Albania.

In September 1939 Hitler struck at Poland, and during the two years that followed almost all of the countries of Europe were plunged or dragged into war. In 1940 Japan with threats of force entered French Indochina. Finally, on December 7, 1941, Japan launched an armed attack on the United States, followed immediately by declarations of war against the United States on the part of Japan, of Germany, of Italy, and of their satellites.

In the face of these multiplying instances of treaty-breaking, of violence, and of open warfare, the United States followed a policy the successive stages of which are summed up here.

During the years preceding the outbreak of war in Europe in 1939, the Government of the United States directed much of its energies toward an improvement of international relations and thus toward prevention of a break-down of world peace. In his inaugural address of March 4, 1933 President Roosevelt dedicated the United States to the Policy of the Good Neighbor—"the neighbor who resolutely respects himself and, because he does so, respects the rights of others—the neighbor who respects his obligations and respects the sanctity of his agreements in and with a world of neighbors". The Government of the United States advocated and applied the Good Neighbor Policy in the Western Hemisphere and everywhere in the world.

After the strain and confusion of the depression years, that policy bore its first fruit at the Seventh International Conference of American States, held in December 1933 at Montevideo, which ushered in a new era of inter-American friendship and solidarity, and through

1

the adoption by this country, in June 1934, of the reciprocal-trade-agreements program. During the ensuing years the Government of the United States strove, by word and by deed, to make its contribution toward staying the rapidly proceeding deterioration of international political relations and toward building an economic foundation of enduring world peace.

After September 1939, when the forces of aggression and conquest burst all bounds, this Government sought in every practicable way to prevent the spread of conflict, while at the same time intensifying its efforts to carry out George Washington's admonition to place the country "on a respectable defensive posture". With the collapse of France in June 1940, with the appearance of Nazi legions on the shores of Western Europe, with Hitler's "blitz" attack on Britain and his openly proclaimed bid for control of the Atlantic, which paralleled Japan's drive for mastery of the western Pacific area, the United States took measures of self-defense by giving aid to nations resisting aggression and by greatly accelerating this nation's military, naval, and air rearmament program.

The documents, and the comments which here follow, set forth various acts and measures taken by the Government of the United States in the presence of mounting dangers to our national security. They should be read in the light of certain basic factors which necessarily affect the conduct of this country's foreign relations.

The conduct of the foreign relations of the United States is a function of the President, acting usually through the Secretary of State. The powers of the Executive in this field are very broad and sweeping. Yet the President and the Secretary of State have by no means entire freedom in matters of foreign policy. Their powers may be defined or circumscribed by legislation—or by lack thereof. They must closely approximate the prevailing views of the country. In the conduct of foreign relations they must interpret and implement not a particular point of view in the country but the point of view of the nation as a whole.

Another factual limitation is that our foreign policy, like the foreign policy of any other country, must at all times take into consideration the policies, circumstances, and reactions of other governments and peoples. Action deemed desirable by the United States may be wholly impracticable if it does not harmonize with policies of other governments whose cooperation is necessary, or if such action would excite substantial enmity or effective opposition on the part of other nations or would isolate this country at a time when close cooperation with other governments is essential.

2

In the history of our country situations have arisen in which the Executive, with wide access to many sources of information from abroad, has known of or foreseen developments in foreign relations of which the public had not yet become aware. In such cases the President and the Secretary of State have exercised such executive powers as they possess and have endeavored to explain to the public the forces at work and the probable course of events and to outline the policies which need be pursued in the best interest of the United States. In such cases, if and as legislation has been needed, the executive branch of the Government has as soon as practicable asked of the Congress legislation to make possible the pursuit of the proposed policies.

During a large part of the period with which this volume deals, much of public opinion in this country did not accept the thesis that a European war could vitally affect the security of the United States or that an attack on the United States by any of the Axis powers was possible. In this respect it differed from the President and the Secretary of State, who early became convinced that the aggressive policies of the Axis powers were directed toward an ultimate attack on the United States and that, therefore, our foreign relations should be so conducted as to give all possible support to the nations endeavoring to check the march of Axis aggression.

Our foreign policy during the decade under consideration necessarily had to move within the framework of a gradual evolution of public opinion in the United States away from the idea of isolation expressed in "neutrality" legislation and toward realization that the Axis design was a plan of world conquest in which the United States was intended to be a certain, though perhaps ultimate, victim, and that our primary policy therefore must be defense against actual and mounting danger. This was an important factor influencing the conduct of our foreign relations. Of determining importance also was another factor, namely, that in many nations outside the United States a similar complacency of view had originally prevailed and likewise was undergoing a gradual modification.

The pages which follow show the slow march of the United States from an attitude of illusory aloofness toward world-wide forces endangering America to a position in the forefront of the United Nations that are making common cause against an attempt at world conquest unparalleled alike in boldness of conception and in brutality of operation.

3

JAPANESE CONQUEST
OF MANCHURIA 1931–1932

Attack of September 18, 1931

ON SEPTEMBER 18, 1931 Japan launched an attack on Manchuria. Within a few days Japanese armed forces had occupied several strategic points in South Manchuria.

The United States Minister to China reported to Secretary of State Stimson, in a telegram dated September 22, his opinion that this was "an aggressive act by Japan", apparently long-planned, and carefully and systematically put into effect. Minister Johnson found no evidence that it was the result of accident or the act of minor and irresponsible officials. He was convinced that the Japanese military operation in Manchuria "must fall within any definition of war" and that this act of aggression had been deliberately accomplished in "utter and cynical disregard" of Japan's obligations under the Kellogg-Briand Pact of August 27, 1928 for the renunciation of war as an instrument of national policy. (1)[1]

On September 22 Secretary Stimson informed Japanese Ambassador Debuchi at Washington that the responsibility for determining the course of events with regard to liquidating the situation in Manchuria rested largely upon Japan, "for the simple reason that Japanese armed forces have seized and are exercising *de-facto* control in South Manchuria". (2)

Meanwhile, the League of Nations was deliberating on the Manchuria situation. Secretary Stimson instructed the United States Consul at Geneva to inform the Secretary General of the League of Nations, in a communication dated October 5, 1931, that it was most desirable that the League in no way relax its vigilance and in no way fail to assert all its pressure and authority toward regulating the action of China and Japan. Secretary Stimson stated further that this Government, acting independently, would "endeavor to reinforce what the League does" and would make clear its keen interest in the matter and its awareness of the obligations of the disputants in the Kellogg-Briand Pact and the Nine-Power Treaty, "should a time arise when it would seem advisable to bring forward these obligations". (3)

The United States Government, in identic notes of October 20, 1931 to China and Japan, called attention to their obligations under

---

[1] The numbers within parentheses refer to the numbers of the supporting documents, 1 to 271, beginning with p. 155.

the Kellogg-Briand Pact. This Government expressed the hope that the two nations would refrain from measures which might lead to war and that they would agree upon a peaceful method for resolving their dispute "in accordance with their promises and in keeping with the confident expectations of public opinion throughout the world". (4)

"Non-Recognition" Policy

The Japanese Government professed a desire to continue friendly relations with China and denied that it had territorial designs in Manchuria. However, Japanese military operations continued. By the end of 1931 Japan had destroyed the last remaining administrative authority of the Government of the Chinese Republic in South Manchuria, as it existed prior to September 18 of that year. The United States Government notified the Chinese and Japanese Governments on January 7, 1932 that it could not admit the legality of any situation *de facto* nor did it intend to recognize any treaty or agreement entered into between these Governments which might impair the treaty rights of the United States or its citizens in China; that it did not intend to recognize "any situation, treaty, or agreement" which might be brought about by means contrary to the obligations of the Kellogg-Briand Pact. In pursuance of this policy the puppet government established by Japanese arms in Manchuria a few weeks later has not been recognized by the United States. (5)

After the hostilities between Japan and China had spread to the Shanghai area early in 1932 the Japanese Government asked that the United States extend its good offices for stopping hostilities. Thereupon, the United States made a proposal on February 2 containing the following points: cessation of all acts of violence on both sides; no further preparation for hostilities; withdrawal of both Chinese and Japanese combatants in the Shanghai area; protection of the International Settlement at Shanghai by the establishment of neutral zones; and upon acceptance of the foregoing, prompt negotiations to settle all outstanding controversies between Japan and China with the aid of neutral observers or participants. The same proposal was made to Japan and China by the British, French, and Italian Governments. The Chinese Government promptly accepted the proposal; the Japanese Government, while accepting some of the points, rejected flatly the second and fifth points, and consequently the proposal came to no avail. (6)

In February 1932 Secretary of State Stimson proposed to the British Government that the United States and British Governments issue a joint statement invoking the Nine-Power Treaty and the Kellogg-Briand Pact in the Far Eastern controversy, making clear that the two Governments considered these treaties as fully binding and declaring that they would not recognize as valid any situation created in violation of these treaties. (8)

In a letter of February 23, 1932 to Senator Borah, Chairman of the Senate Committee on Foreign Relations, Secretary Stimson said that the situation which had developed in China could not be reconciled with the obligations set forth in the Nine-Power Treaty and the Kellogg-Briand Pact. He referred to the statement of the United States Government of January 7 and said that if a similar policy were followed by the other governments of the world, an effective bar would be placed on the legality of any title or right sought to be obtained by pressure or treaty violation and that eventually such action would lead to restoration to China of the rights and titles of which China had been deprived. (9)

The British Government did not adopt the specific suggestion made by Secretary Stimson. Later it introduced in the Assembly of the League of Nations a resolution which was unanimously adopted; this resolution of March 11, 1932 stated in part: "it is incumbent upon the members of the League of Nations not to recognize any situation, treaty or agreement which may be brought about by means contrary to the Covenant of the League of Nations or to the Pact of Paris."

Ambassador Grew's Report on Japanese Military Spirit

The United States Ambassador to Japan, Joseph C. Grew, reported to Secretary Stimson on August 13, 1932 the growing dangers in the existing situation. Ambassador Grew said that in Japan the deliberate building up of public animosity against foreign nations in general and the United States in particular was doubtless for the purpose of strengthening the hand of the military in its Manchuria venture in the face of foreign opposition. He stated that the Japanese military machine had been "built for war", felt prepared for war, and would "welcome war"; that it had never yet been beaten and possessed unlimited self-confidence. (10)

After consolidating their position in Manchuria the Japanese military forces proceeded, early in January 1933, to extend the boundaries of the new puppet state by the occupation of the province of Jehol in North China. The Japanese Ambassador, in a conversation of January 5 with Secretary Stimson, stated that Japan had no territorial ambition south of the Great Wall. The Secretary reminded the Ambassador that a year previously the latter had said that Japan had no territorial ambitions in Manchuria. The Ambassador replied that no Japanese Cabinet which advocated a compromise on the Manchuria question could survive in Japan and that the Manchuria incident must be regarded as closed. Secretary Stimson said that this Government had come to the conclusion that another war such as the World War might destroy our civilization; therefore, we were "determined to support the peace machinery which would render such a recurrence impossible". (11)

Condemnation of Japanese Aggression

Meanwhile, the League of Nations had been considering the report of the Lytton Commission which had been appointed by the League to make an investigation of the situation in Manchuria. The Commission reported that the military operations of the Japanese in Manchuria could not be regarded as measures of legitimate self-defense; that the regime which the Japanese had set up there disregarded the wishes of the people of Manchuria and was not compatible with the fundamental principles of existing international obligations. The League Assembly adopted this report on February 24, 1933, and the Japanese delegation thereupon walked out of the Assembly. In a letter of February 25 to the Secretary General of the League of Nations, Secretary Stimson stated that the United States was in substantial accord with the findings and conclusions of the League. (12)

On March 27, 1933 Japan gave notice of its intention to withdraw from the League.

In the spring of 1933, in connection with proposed legislation to authorize the President under certain conditions to apply embargoes on the export of arms from the United States, consideration was given to the possibility of an arms embargo against Japan. In a statement made on behalf of Secretary of State Hull to the Senate Committee on Foreign Relations, May 17, 1933, it was emphasized that the United States Government concurred "in general in the findings of the Lytton Commission which place the major responsibility upon Japan for the international conflict now proceeding in China". In this statement concerning the proposed legislation, Secretary Hull said that it was not the intention of this Government to use the authority as a means of restoring peace between China and Japan. He said that an arms embargo would not be an effective means of restoring peace in this instance; that Japan was an important producer of arms with industries sufficiently developed to supply its own needs; that China was dependent upon her importation of these commodities; that an arms embargo applied to both China and Japan would, therefore, militate against China and in favor of Japan; that an embargo directed against Japan alone would probably result in the seizure by the Japanese of arms intended for China, thus ultimately decreasing China's supply of arms and increasing Japan's supply. The Secretary stated that this Government would not be disposed to take any action which would favor the military operations of the Japanese. Further, he said that we would not under any circumstances agree to participate in an international embargo of this kind unless we had secured substantial guaranties from the Governments of all the great powers which would insure against the effects of any retaliatory measures which the Japanese might undertake. (16)

The proposed arms-embargo legislation was not enacted. (See pp. 23–24.)

DISARMAMENT DISCUSSIONS 1932–1934

Statement of February 1932

THE FIRST General Conference for the Limitation and Reduction of Armaments assembled at Geneva in February 1932.

At the Washington Conference of 1922 the principle of limitation had been established by treaty for capital ships of the United States, France, Great Britain, Italy, and Japan; at the London Naval Conference of 1930 this principle was extended to other types of warships of the United States, Great Britain, and Japan. Prior to the opening of the General Disarmament Conference in 1932, these were the principal steps taken by the nations of the world to lighten the burden of large armies and navies.

At the beginning of this conference Ambassador Hugh Gibson, speaking for the United States delegation, said that civilization was threatened by the burden and dangers of the gigantic machinery of warfare then being maintained. He recalled that practically all the nations of the world had pledged themselves not to wage aggressive war. Therefore, he said, the conference should devote itself to the abolition of weapons devoted primarily to aggressive war. Among the points advocated by Ambassador Gibson were the following: Special restrictions for tanks and heavy mobile guns, which were considered to be arms peculiarly for offensive operations; computation of the number of armed forces on the basis of the effectives necessary for the maintenance of internal order plus some suitable contingent for defense; abolition of lethal gases and bacteriological warfare; effective measures to protect civilian populations against aerial bombing; abolition of submarines; prolonging the existing naval agreements concluded at Washington and London; proportional reduction from the figures laid down in the Washington and London agreements. (7)

Proposal of May 16, 1933

For more than a year the Conference at Geneva struggled with the tremendous problems involved—without making substantial progress. President Roosevelt made an effort in May 1933 to inject new life into the Conference. In a message of May 16 to the heads of 54 governments he stated that if all nations would agree to eliminate entirely from possession and use the weapons which make possible a successful attack, defenses automatically would become impregnable and the frontiers and independence of every nation would become secure. Therefore, he said, the ultimate objective of the Conference must be "complete elimination of all offensive weapons". His specific proposals were: Through a series of steps the weapons of offensive warfare should be eliminated; the first definite step should be taken at once; while these steps were being taken no nation should increase existing armaments over and above the limitations of treaty obligations; subject to existing treaty rights no nation should send any armed force of whatsoever nature across its own borders. (15)

Ten days before this message was sent, President Roosevelt had made clear to Dr. Schacht of Germany, President of the Reichsbank, who was in Washington as a special representative of the German Government, that the United States would insist that Germany remain *in statu quo* in armament and that we would support every possible effort to have the offensive armament of every other nation brought down to the German level. The President intimated as strongly as possible that we regarded Germany as the "only possible obstacle" to a disarmament treaty; that he hoped Dr. Schacht would give this point of view to Hitler. (14)

Statement of May 22, 1933

One of the complications arising from the Disarmament Conference was that France felt that it could not agree to reduce armaments unless the United States and Great Britain would join with France and other nations in a system of collective security to enforce compliance on the part of Germany of provisions for arms limitation and reduction. It was argued that if League states took measures against an aggressor nation, there was no assurance that the United States would not interfere with these measures. In an effort to meet this objection and difficulty, Norman H. Davis, Chairman of the United States delegation at Geneva, stated to the Conference in an address of May 22, 1933 that the United States was ready not only to do its part toward the substantive reduction of armaments but that if this were effected by general international agreement, the United States was prepared to contribute in other ways to the organization of peace. In particular we were willing to consult other states in case of a threat to peace, with the view to averting conflict. Furthermore, in the event that the states, in conference, determined that a state had been guilty of a breach of the peace in violation of its international obligations and took measures against the violator, then the United States, if it concurred in the judgment rendered as to the responsible and guilty party, would refrain from any action tending to defeat this collective effort for a restoration of peace. (17)

A few days later the Senate Committee on Foreign Relations rejected a proposal, urged by the Secretary of State, which would have permitted this Government to join with other governments in an arms embargo against an aggressor nation. (See p. 24.)

During a conversation on October 9, 1933 Secretary of State Hull discussed with the German Ambassador at Washington, Hans Luther, the question of disarmament. The Secretary said that the purpose of the United States was the promotion of general disarmament; that the theory of this Government was that we should "wage a steady contest for the disarmament of the heavily armed nations, rather than become parties to a plan for others to proceed to rearm". (19)

A plan was considered by the Disarmament Conference for certain immediate steps of disarmament and for progressive limitation and reduction of armaments. France proposed that instead of agreeing to steps being taken immediately and progressively there should be a period of trial in which to test German good faith. Germany refused to accept this proposal. On October 14, 1933 Germany withdrew from the Disarmament Conference and on the same day gave notice of withdrawal from the League of Nations.

Consul General Messersmith at Berlin reported to the Department of State a month later that Germany would "fight shy of all conferences" on disarmament but would make constant professions of a will for peace and a desire to cooperate. He said that in the meantime Germany would go on rearming, as this was what Germany wanted to do and would do; that while all sorts of protestations might be made with regard to the reduction of armaments by other countries, what Germany was interested in was not so much the other countries' cutting down their armaments as having on its part a free hand, or rather time, to go ahead and rearm. (21)

The Conference continued at Geneva, without substantial progress. Twenty-seven months after its opening, Chairman Norman H. Davis of the United States delegation made an address to the Conference surveying the disarmament situation. In this address of May 29, 1934 Mr. Davis summarized as follows the attitude and policy of the United States: "We are prepared to cooperate in every practicable way in efforts to secure a general disarmament agreement and thus to help promote the general peace and progress of the world. We are furthermore willing, in connection with a general disarmament convention, to negotiate a universal pact of non-aggression and to join with other nations in conferring on international problems growing out of any treaties to which we are a party. The United States will not, however, participate in European political negotiations and settlements and will not make any commitment whatever to use its armed forces for the settlement of any dispute anywhere. In effect, the policy of the United States is to keep out of war, but to help in every possible way to discourage war." (34)

Japanese Denunciation of Naval Treaty of 1922

At the end of 1934 the Japanese Government gave notice of intention to terminate the Washington Naval Treaty of 1922. In a statement made on December 29, 1934 Secretary Hull said that this notice was a source of genuine regret, as he believed that the existing treaties had safeguarded the rights and promoted the collective interests of all the signatories. (39)

⟫ I V ⟪

WARNINGS OF DANGER 1933–1935

Secretary Hull's Conversation With the German Ambassador

ON NOVEMBER 2, 1933, in a conversation between Secretary of State Hull and German Ambassador Luther on the related questions of disarmament and world peace, the Secretary said that "the outlook in Europe at this distance for disarmament or for peace" did not appear very encouraging; that "a general war during the next two to ten years seemed more probable than peace"; that this country "had exerted itself in every way possible in support of the latter [peace] and against the possible recurrence of the former [war]", but that frankly he felt discouraged.

The German Ambassador quoted Hitler's statement to the effect that Germany would not seek the restoration of Alsace-Lorraine, and that in his opinion this should quiet French apprehension. He added that the Saar question was an entirely separate one. (20)

Consul General Messersmith's Report From Berlin

The United States Consul General at Berlin, George S. Messersmith, who had been at that post since 1930, reported frequently to the Department of State during this period on the menace inherent in the Nazi regime. Mr. Messersmith expressed the view, in a letter of June 26, 1933 to Under Secretary of State Phillips, that the United States must be exceedingly careful in its dealings with Germany as long as the existing Government was in power, as that Government had no spokesmen who could really be depended upon and those who held the highest positions were "capable of actions which really outlaw them from ordinary intercourse". He reported that some of the men who were running the German Government were "psychopathic cases"; that others were in a state of exaltation and in a frame of mind that knew no reason; and that those men in the party and in responsible positions who were really worthwhile were powerless because they had to follow the orders of superiors who were suffering from the "abnormal psychology" prevailing in Germany. "There is a real revolution here and a dangerous situation", he said.

Consul General Messersmith reported further that a martial spirit was being developed in Germany; that everywhere people were seen drilling, including children from the age of five or six to persons well into middle age; that a psychology was being developed that the whole world was against Germany, which was defenseless before the world; that people were being trained against gas and airplane attacks; and that the idea of war from neighboring countries was constantly harped upon. He emphasized that Germany was headed in directions which could only carry ruin to it and create a situation "dangerous to world peace". He said we must recognize that while Germany at that time wanted peace, it was by no means a peaceful country or one looking forward to a long period of peace; that the German Government and its adherents desired peace ardently for the time being because they needed peace to carry through the changes in Germany which they wanted to bring about. What they wanted to do was to make Germany "the most capable instrument of war that there has ever existed". (18)

Consul General Messersmith reported from Berlin five months later, in a letter of November 23, 1933 to Under Secretary Phillips, that the military spirit in Germany was constantly growing and that innumerable measures were being taken to develop the German people into a hardy, sturdy race which would "be able to meet all comers". He said that the leaders of Germany had no desire for peace unless it was a peace in complete compliance with German ambitions; that Hitler and his associates really wanted peace for the moment, but only to have a chance to prepare for the use of force if it were found essential; and that they were preparing their way so carefully that the German people would be with them when they wanted to use force and when they felt that they had the "necessary means to carry through their objects". (21)

President Roosevelt's Address of December 28, 1933

In an address delivered at Washington on December 28, 1933 President Roosevelt stated that the blame for the danger to peace was not in the world population but in the political leaders of that population. He said that probably 90 percent of the people in the world were content with the territorial limits of their respective nations and were willing further to reduce their armed forces if every other nation would agree to do the same thing. He said that back of the threat to world peace were the fear and possibility that the other 10 percent might go along with a leadership seeking territorial expansion at the expense of neighbors and unwilling to reduce armament or stop rearmament even if everybody else agreed to non-aggression and to arms reduction. He believed that if the 10 percent could be persuaded "to do their own thinking and not be led", we would have permanent peace throughout the world. (24)

Acting Commercial Attaché Miller's Report on the Nazis

Consul General Messersmith transmitted to the Department of State on April 21, 1934 a report by Acting Commercial Attaché Douglas Miller on the situation in Germany. The Consul General noted that the conclusions of the Attaché had been arrived at independently and that they accorded entirely with his own appraisal of the situation.

Mr. Miller stated that the fundamental purpose of the Nazis "is to secure a greater share of the world's future for the Germans, the expansion of German territory and growth of the German race until it constitutes the largest and most powerful nation in the world, and ultimately, according to some Nazi leaders, until it dominates the entire globe". He expressed the view that the German people were suffering from a traditional inferiority complex, smarting from their defeat in the war and the indignities of the post-war period, disillusioned in their hopes of a speedy return to prosperity along traditional lines, and inflamed by irresponsible demagogic slogans and flattered by the statement that their German racial inheritance gave them inherent superior rights over other peoples. As a result the German people, who were "politically inept and unusually docile", had to a large measure adopted the Nazi point of view for the time being.

The most important objective of the Nazis, according to Mr. Miller's analysis, was to retain absolute control of the German people. This control, he said, had been gained by making irresponsible and extravagant promises; by the studied use of the press, the radio, public meetings, parades, flags, uniforms; and finally by the use of force. He said that the Nazis were at heart belligerent and aggressive; that although they desired a period of peace for several years in which to rearm and discipline their people, the more completely their experiments succeeded "the more certain is a large-scale war in Europe some day".

Mr. Miller warned that we must not place too much reliance on Nazi public statements designed for consumption abroad, which breathed the spirit of good-will and peace and asserted the intention of the Government to promote the welfare of the German people and good relations with their neighbors. The real emotional drive behind

15

the Nazi program, he said, was not so much love of their own country
as dislike of other countries. The Nazis would never be content in
merely promoting the welfare of the German people; they desired to
be feared and envied by foreigners and "to wipe out the memory of 1918
by inflicting humiliations in particular upon the French, the Poles,
the Czechs and anybody else they can get their hands on". Hitler
and the other Nazi leaders had capitalized on the wounded inferiority
complex of the German people and had magnified their own bitter
feelings "into a cult of dislike against the foreign world which is
past the bounds of ordinary good sense and reason". Mr. Miller
emphasized that the Nazis were building a tremendous military machine, physically very poorly armed, but morally aggressive and
belligerent. The control of this machine was in the hands of "narrow,
ignorant and unscrupulous adventurers who have been slightly
touched with madness from brooding over Germany's real or imagined
wrongs". Mr. Miller stated that the Nazis were determined to secure
more power and more territory in Europe; that they would certainly
use force if these were not given to them by peaceful means. (27)

Reported German-Japanese Entente

Throughout this period indications were received by this Government from various sources that Germany and Japan were drawing
together in closer relations. The two countries were in similar situations in that each had left the League of Nations and each was already
engaged in preparing militarily and otherwise a program of national
expansion. In May 1934 the United States Military Attaché in
Berlin, Lieutenant Colonel Wuest, reported that evidence was accumulating which tended "to show the existence of unusually close and
friendly relations between Germany and Japan even to the extent of a
possible secret alliance". This report stated further that these friendly relations between the two countries were dependent entirely upon
self-interest; that the Germans usually expressed themselves to the
effect that "we are encouraging close and friendly relations with
Japan because it is to our advantage to do so but we must never
forget that we are white people and they are not". (32)

Shortly thereafter, United States Consul Geist at Berlin reported
to the Department of State that the German Government was bent on
recovering Germany's military prestige and then seeing what could be
obtained from the rest of the world. He said that German rearmament was concentrated upon power in the air and motorization of
attacking forces; that the young Nazis were enthusiastic with regard

to military prospects; that they spoke of gas war, bacteriological war, and the use of death-dealing rays; that they boasted that airplanes would not pass the German frontiers; and that they had fantastic ideas about Germany's invincibility in "the next war".

Mr. Geist emphasized that the youth of Germany were being inculcated with an unprecedented, conscious, and deliberate love of militarism; that one of the amazing things of modern history was that the government of a great power should definitely teach children to cherish ideas of valor, heroism, and self-sacrifice, "unrelieved by any of the virtues which modern civilization has come to place above brute force". The Consul said that war might not be imminent but it was difficult to foresee "how the bellicose spirit here can be restrained and directed into permanent channels of peace towards the end of this present decade". (36)

Addresses by Secretary Hull

In an address at Washington, May 5, 1934, Secretary of State Hull warned of the dangers in the international situation. He said that dictatorships had sprung up suddenly in place of democracies; that nations everywhere were narrowing their vision, their policies, and their programs; that each was undertaking more and more to visualize only itself and to live by itself; that numerous nations were "feverishly arming", taxing their citizens beyond the limit of ability to pay, and in many ways were developing a military spirit which might lead to war. He warned that it "would be both a blunder and a crime for civilized peoples to fail much longer to take notice of present dangerous tendencies".

Secretary Hull stated that international cooperation to promote understanding, friendship, and reciprocal benefits and conditions of peace was indispensable to the progress of civilization; that these international relationships had been practically abandoned; and that the entire political, economic, social, and moral affairs of most parts of the world were in a chaotic condition. The Secretary said that every Christian nation had an obligation to itself and to humanity to promote understanding, friendship, and peace. The civilization of the time was amply capable of meeting the unprecedented challenge which existing conditions offered and which must be met successfully unless the world was to be threatened with "another period of long night—such as the Dark Ages". He appealed to every individual to awaken and come to a realization of the problems and difficulties facing all and of the necessity for real sacrifice of time and service. (30)

In another address of June 11, 1934 at Williamsburg, Virginia, Secretary Hull again warned of international dangers. He said that abroad there was reason "for the gravest apprehension"; that armaments were being increased; that the theory seemed to be abandoned that nations like individuals should live as neighbors and friends. He stated that the Government of the United States was striving to the utmost to make its fullest contribution to the maintenance of peace and civilization. (35)

Relations With Japan—1934

The Japanese Minister for Foreign Affairs, Koki Hirota, in a message delivered to Secretary Hull on February 21, 1934, stated that no question existed between the United States and Japan which was fundamentally incapable of amicable solution and emphasized that Japan had no intention whatsoever of making trouble with any other power. (25)

Secretary Hull replied on March 3, 1934 that it was the fixed intention of the United States to rely in the prosecution of its national policies upon pacific processes; that if there should arise any controversy between the United States and Japan, this Government would be prepared to examine the position of Japan in a spirit of amity and of desire for peaceful and just settlement. He expressed the hope that it might be possible for all countries interested in the Far East to approach every question arising between or among them in such spirit and manner that these questions might be regulated or resolved with injury to none and with definite and lasting advantage to all. (26)

Despite this encouraging exchange of views, there occurred almost immediately thereafter significant indications of an attitude inconsistent therewith on the part of the Japanese Government with regard to the rights and interests in China of other countries. These indications included a statement by Mr. Amau, spokesman of the Japanese Foreign Office. On April 29, 1934, in accordance with instructions from Washington, Ambassador Grew presented to the Japanese Foreign Minister a note stating that the relations of the United States with China, with Japan, and with other countries were governed by the generally accepted principles of international law and the provisions of treaties to which the United States was a party; that treaties could lawfully be modified or terminated only by processes prescribed or recognized or agreed upon by the parties to them; that no nation could, without the assent of the other nations concerned, rightfully endeavor to make conclusive its will in situations where there were involved the rights, the obligations, and the legitimate interests of other sovereign states; that the United States sought to be duly considerate of the rights, obligations, and legitimate interests of other countries, and it expected on the part of other governments due consideration of the rights, obligations, and legitimate interests of the United States. (29)

In a conversation four days earlier the Japanese Foreign Minister had assured Ambassador Grew that Japan had no intention whatever of seeking special privileges in China, of encroaching on the territorial and administrative integrity of China, or of creating difficulties for the *bona-fide* trade of other countries with China; and that Japan would take no action in China purposely provocative to other countries. In reply, Ambassador Grew had said to the Foreign Minister that the Government and people of the United States would be less impressed by statements of policy than by more concrete evidence. (28)

On May 16, 1934 Secretary Hull had a general conversation with Japanese Ambassador Saito, one of many conversations in which the Secretary endeavored to convince the Japanese that their best interests lay in following policies of peace. Citing the commercial and military possibilities brought about by the remarkable advance in aviation, he said that twenty years ago no human being could have visualized the amazing changes that were taking place in every part of the world; that amidst these amazing changes the more highly civilized nations had correspondingly greater responsibilities and duties, from the standpoint both of their own progress and well-being and of that of the world. He expressed the belief that no highly civilized nation could let the people of other countries undergo a steady state of decline and even collapse without that civilized nation itself being drawn down in the vortex. He said that this meant that Japan and the United States, for their own self-preservation and for their world responsibility, should exhibit the utmost breadth of view and the most profound statesmanship. (31)

Three days later the Secretary talked again with the Japanese Ambassador. During the conversation the Ambassador repeated the formula which his Government had been putting forward publicly for some weeks to the effect that Japan had a superior and special function in connection with the preservation of peace in eastern Asia. The Secretary felt it desirable to bring to the Japanese Ambassador's attention the clear implications contained in the Japanese formula of the intention on the part of Japan to exercise an overlordship over neighboring nations and territories. Accordingly, he inquired why the Ambassador's Government "singled out" the formula of Japan's claim to superior and special interests in "eastern Asia" and of her superior rights and duties in connection with the preservation of peace there; whether this formula had ulterior or ultimate implications partaking of the nature of an "overlordship of the Orient". The Ambassador protested that this was not the meaning intended.

The Secretary said to the Ambassador that there was universal talk about armaments on a steadily increasing scale, and that Japan and Germany were the two countries considered chiefly responsible for this talk. He said that if the world understood the absence of any Japanese intentions of overlordship or other unwarranted interference by the Ambassador's Government, Japan "would not be the occasion for armament discussion in so many parts of the world". (33)

A comprehensive appraisal of the situation in Japan was sent to the Secretary of State by Ambassador Grew in a despatch of December 27, 1934. The Ambassador reported that things were being constantly said and written in Japan to the effect that Japan's destiny was to subjugate and rule the world. He said that the aim of certain elements in the Army and Navy, the patriotic societies, and the intense nationalists throughout the country was "to obtain trade control and eventually predominant political influence in China, the Philippines, the Straits Settlements, Siam and the Dutch East Indies, the Maritime Provinces and Vladivostok, one step at a time, as in Korea and Manchuria, pausing intermittently to consolidate and then continuing as soon as the intervening obstacles can be overcome by diplomacy or force". With such dreams of empire cherished in Japan, and with a Japanese Army and Navy capable of "taking the bit in their own teeth and running away with it", we would be "reprehensibly somnolent", Ambassador Grew warned, if we were to trust to the security of treaty restraints or international comity to safeguard our own interests.

Continuing, the Ambassador said that there was a "swashbuckling temper" in the country, largely developed by military propaganda, which could lead Japan during the next few years to any extreme unless the saner minds in the Government were able to cope with it and to restrain the country from national suicide. He referred to the extreme sensitiveness of the Japanese people which, he said, arose out of a marked inferiority complex manifested "in the garb of an equally marked superiority complex, with all its attendant bluster, chauvinism, xenophobia and organized national propaganda". He characterized as "thoroughly mistaken" the idea that a great body of liberal thought lying just beneath the surface since 1931 would be sufficiently strong to emerge and, with a little foreign encouragement, assume control. The liberal thought was there, he stated, but it was inarticulate and largely impotent and probably would remain so for some time to come.

The Ambassador said that unless we were prepared to subscribe to the "Pax Japonica" in the Far East, we should rapidly build up our Navy to treaty strength, and when the Washington Naval Treaty expired we should continue "regardless of cost" to maintain the existing naval ratios with Japan; that Japan's naval policy had been formulated on a premise that the United States would never build up to treaty strength. He reported that almost half of the Japanese national budget for 1935-36 was for the Army and Navy.

Finally, the Ambassador declared, it would be "criminally short-sighted" to discard from calculations the possibility of eventual war with Japan; the best possible way to avoid it would be adequate preparation, as "preparedness is a cold fact which even the chauvinists, the military, the patriots and the ultra-nationalists in Japan, for all their bluster concerning 'provocative measures' in the United States, can grasp and understand". (38)

Defeat of Proposed Adherence to World Court

On January 16, 1935 President Roosevelt sent a message to the Senate, asking that the latter advise and consent to membership of the United States in the World Court. In his message the President said that such action would in no way diminish or jeopardize the sovereignty of the United States. He declared further that at this juncture, when every act was of moment to the future of world peace, the United States had an opportunity "once more to throw its weight into the scale in favor of peace". On January 29, 1935 the resolution of adherence was voted on by the Senate but failed of passage. (40)

Warnings February–June 1935

Secretary Hull, in an address on February 16, 1935 at New York, said that the enormous speeding up of trade and communications made futile any endeavor to induce the United States again to withdraw into "splendid isolation". Our policies must of necessity be those of a great power; we could not, even if we would, "fail profoundly to affect international relations". The Secretary said that there had been a time when the ocean meant, or could mean, a certain degree of isolation; but that modern communication had ended this forever.

In this address Secretary Hull listed four pillars of a sound peace structure: first, the renunciation of war as an instrument of national policy; second, a promise of non-aggression; third, consultation in the event of a threat to peace; and fourth, non-interference on our part with measures of constraint brought against a deliberate violator of peace. In mentioning these peace pillars the Secretary emphasized that they might "readily crumble were they to be built on the shifting foundations of unrestricted and competitive armaments". Therefore, he said, the United States insisted that a real limitation and reduction of armament must be an essential concomitant of a peace program. (43)

Mr. Messersmith, who had been appointed Minister to Austria in 1934, continued to send to the Department of State reports on the situation in Germany. In February 1935 he reported that the Nazis had their eyes on Memel, Alsace-Lorraine, and the eastern frontier; that they nourished just as strongly the hope to get the Ukraine for the surplus German population; that Austria was a definite objective; and that absorption or hegemony over the whole of southeastern Europe was a definite policy. A few weeks later he reported a conversation with William E. Dodd, United States Ambassador to Germany, in which they had agreed that no faith whatsoever could be placed in the Nazi regime and its promises, that what the Nazis were after was "unlimited territorial expansion", and that there was probably in existence a German-Japanese understanding, if not an alliance. (41, 44)

During a conversation with German Ambassador Luther on March 28, 1935, Secretary Hull questioned the Ambassador regarding the reported objectives of Germany with respect to Austria, Czechoslovakia, Memel, and the Polish Corridor. The Ambassador denied each reported objective and insisted that his Government favored peace. The Secretary said that the German Government then had the greatest opportunity in two generations to make a remarkable showing of leadership with a program that would gradually bring Western Europe to normal political, social, and peace relations. He said that nations could either take this course or could continue more or less aloof from each other with misunderstanding of each other's motives, purposes, and objectives; the result of the latter would be that each country would go forward and "arm to the teeth" so that at some stage a local incident might ignite the spark that would start a conflagration disastrous in ultimate effect to western civilization. (45)

In an address on June 12, 1935 Secretary Hull warned that there were ominous tendencies in the world. He referred to the reckless, competitive building up of armaments which if unchecked would result in national bankruptcies and consequent inevitable inflation together with the utter destruction of such national stability as had thus far been achieved. He said that the world could not extricate itself from this relentless circle if it did not stop its extravagant military expenditures; that the continuation of the armament race would "again plunge the world into disaster." (46)

In an address of a few days later the Secretary said that any clash abroad would dislocate the progress of recovery in the United States and that this country could not, in the long run, avoid the disastrous effects of such a clash. He could not, therefore, assure the people of the United States that they were immune from the effects of a possible conflict by being far removed from its locus or that they could "look without concern on the darkening clouds around the magic circle of the United States". (47)

Proposed Arms Embargo

In a letter of April 5, 1933 to the appropriate committees of Congress, Secretary of State Hull asked that Congress enact legislation authorizing the application of arms embargoes under certain conditions. A similar proposal had been strongly urged upon Congress early in 1933 by President Hoover and Secretary of State Stimson.

The terms of the legislation advocated by Secretary Hull were that whenever the President found that the shipment of arms or munitions of war might promote or encourage the employment of force in a dispute or conflict between nations and, after securing the cooperation of such governments as the President deemed necessary and after making proclamation thereof, it should be unlawful to export any arms or munitions of war from the United States to any country designated by the President. This proposal would have authorized cooperation by the United States in an arms embargo against an aggressor nation.

In supporting the proposed legislation Secretary Hull said that it would be exercised by any President "to the sole end of maintaining the peace of the world and with a due and prudent regard for our national policies and national interests". He said that the special circumstances of each particular case which might arise would dictate what action, if any, would be taken, but the authority to act on terms of equality with other governments should be left to the discretion of the Executive. The Secretary said further that this Government should no longer be left in the position of being unable to join with other governments in preventing the supply of arms for use in an international conflict when it was exercising its diplomacy and the whole weight of our national influence and prestige to prevent or put an end to that conflict. Finally, he said that the enactment of the proposed legislation "would strengthen the position cf this Government in its international relations and would enable us to cooperate more efficiently in efforts to maintain the peace of the world". (13)

In a statement made on behalf of Secretary Hull to the Senate Committee on Foreign Relations, May 17, 1933, it was declared that in certain cases this Government might concur in the opinion of the rest of the world in fixing the responsibility for a conflict upon an aggressor nation; that in such cases an international embargo on the shipment of arms to one party to the conflict might be deemed an equitable and effective method of restoring peace; that this method, nevertheless, "would certainly not be adopted by this Government without such effective guarantees of international cooperation as would safeguard us against the danger of this country's being involved in the conflict as a result of such action". (16)

Late in May the arms-embargo resolution, which had already been passed by the House of Representatives, was reported by the Senate Committee on Foreign Relations to the Senate with an amendment that any embargo established under it be applied impartially to all belligerents. Secretary Hull stated on May 29 that such an amendment was not in accord with the views of the President and of himself. The amended resolution was subsequently passed by the Senate but was not enacted.

Neutrality Legislation

In 1935 there developed considerable public support in the United States for an embargo on the export of arms to belligerents as a means of keeping the United States out of war. This support was based on the fallacious concept that the entrance of the United States into the World War in 1917 had been brought about by the sale of arms to belligerents. Under the influence of this concept and with the shadow of a new European war on the horizon the Congress passed a joint resolution in August 1935 providing that upon the outbreak or during the progress of war between or among two or more foreign states "the President shall proclaim such fact, and it shall thereafter be unlawful to export arms, ammunition, or implements of war" from the United States to any belligerent country. This legislation also contained provisions for the licensing of arms exports, the prohibition of the carriage by United States vessels of arms to belligerent states, and the restriction of travel by United States citizens on vessels of belligerent states. This joint resolution, known as the Neutrality Act, was signed by President Roosevelt on August 31, 1935. In signing it the President said he had done so "because it was intended as an expression of the fixed desire of the Government and the people of the United States to avoid any action which might involve us in war". However, he said that the "inflexible" arms-embargo provisions "might drag us into war instead of keeping us out"; that no Congress and no Executive could foresee all possible future situations. (49, 50)

A few months later Secretary Hull, in referring to the Neutrality Act, warned that to assume that by placing an embargo on arms we were making ourselves secure from dangers of conflict with belligerent countries was "to close our eyes to manifold dangers in other directions". He said further that every war presented different circumstances and conditions which might have to be dealt with differently; that, therefore, there were apparent difficulties inherent in any effort to lay down by legislative enactment "inelastic rules or regulations to be applied to every situation that may arise"; that the Executive should not be unduly or unreasonably handicapped; that discretion could wisely be given the President. (57)

Montevideo Conference

The Seventh International Conference of American States assembled in December 1933 at Montevideo, Uruguay. There the Good Neighbor Policy set forth by President Roosevelt on March 4, 1933 was given concrete expression. In an address before the Conference on December 15, 1933 Secretary Hull expressed confidence that each of the American nations wholeheartedly supported the Good Neighbor Policy—that each earnestly favored "the absolute independence, the unimpaired sovereignty, the perfect equality, and the political integrity of each nation, large or small, as they similarly oppose aggression in every sense of the word".

The Secretary stated that peace and economic rehabilitation must be "our objective" and avoidance of war "our supreme purpose"; that he believed profoundly that the American nations during the coming years would "write a chapter of achievement in the advancement of peace that will stand out in world history". He said that "while older nations totter under the burden of outworn ideas, cling to the decayed and cruel institution of war, and use precious resources to feed cannon rather than hungry mouths, we stand ready to carry on in the spirit of that application of the Golden Rule by which we mean the true good-will of the true good neighbor".

The Secretary asked that this be made the beginning of a new era, "a great renaissance in American cooperative effort to promote our entire material, moral, and spiritual affairs and to erect an edifice of peace that will forever endure"; that suspicion, misunderstanding, and prejudice be banished from every mind and genuine friendship for and trust in each other be substituted; that actions rather than mere words be the acid test of the conduct and motives of each nation; and that each country demonstrate by its every act and practice the sincerity of its purpose and the unselfishness of its relationship as a neighbor.

Finally, the Secretary said it was in this spirit that the Government and people of the United States expressed their "recognition of the common interests and common aspirations of the American nations" and joined with them "in a renewed spirit of broad cooperation for the promotion of liberty under law, of peace, of justice, and of righteousness". (22)

At Montevideo the 21 American republics agreed upon principles for peaceful international relations, in a convention on the rights and duties of states. This convention, of December 26, 1933, contained provisions that: No state has the right to intervene in the internal or external affairs of another; the primary interest of states is the conservation of peace; differences of any nature which arise between states should be settled by recognized pacific methods; and territorial acquisitions or special advantages obtained by force or other measures of coercion should not be recognized. Ratification of this convention was approved by the United States Senate on June 15, 1934; the convention was proclaimed by the President on January 18, 1935. (23)

Acting in the spirit and on the basis of the principles of the Good Neighbor Policy, the Montevideo Conference attempted to bring to an end the conflict between Bolivia and Paraguay which had broken out in 1932 as a result of a long-standing boundary dispute. Through the efforts of the Conference and a League of Nations commission a temporary armistice was brought about in December 1933. However, hostilities were soon resumed. The American nations continued persistent efforts to end the war, and in June 1935 Argentina, Brazil, Chile, Peru, Uruguay, and the United States succeeded in bringing about a termination of hostilities. As a result of an arbitral award delivered by representatives of these six countries, final settlement of the dispute was reached in 1938.

National Defense

In 1933 the enlisted strength of the United States Army was 115,-000 men. As a result of reductions in governmental expenditures the War Department appropriation act of March 4, 1933 provided only $270,000,000 for the military activities of the Army—a sharp reduction from the amount made available for similar purposes during the previous year. General Douglas MacArthur, Chief of Staff, stated in his annual report of 1933 that successive reductions in appropriations had seriously injured the equipment and training of the Army. He said that the strength of the Army in personnel and equipment and its readiness for employment were "below the danger line".

In 1934 General MacArthur recommended a program of expansion for the Army; the accomplishment of this program, he said, would still leave us far behind all other major powers but would at least offer the United States "a justified assurance in freedom from attack or, at the worst, from extreme consequences in the event of attack".

The War Department appropriation act of April 1935 authorized an increase of the Army to 165,000 enlisted men. In his report of 1935 General MacArthur said that measures had been undertaken to procure additional airplanes, motorized vehicles, tanks, and artillery, in most of which the Army's supplies had become obsolete or inadequate.

By 1933 the United States Navy, in up-to-date ships, had fallen far below the tonnage allowed by treaty. In that year President Roosevelt allocated funds from the National Industrial Recovery Act for the purpose of constructing and equipping 32 naval vessels. The Secretary of the Navy reported in 1933 that no such building program had been undertaken by this country since 1916; that of the signatories to the naval treaties we alone had not undertaken an orderly building program designed to bring the Navy up to treaty strength. He recommended an orderly annual naval building and replacement program which would "shortly give this country a treaty navy". He stated that the United States continued to strive for a reduction of armament by agreement but that the time had come when we could no longer afford to lead in disarmament by example. Other powers had not followed such a policy, he said, with the result that the United States found its relative naval strength seriously impaired. He said that our weakened position jeopardized the cause of peace, "because balanced armament fortifies diplomacy and is an important element in preserving peace and justice, whereas undue weakness invites aggressive, war-breeding violation of one's rights".

During 1934 the Vinson Naval Bill was enacted, authorizing the construction of ships up to the limits of the Washington and London Naval Treaties.

V

ITALIAN CONQUEST
OF ETHIOPIA 1935–1936

Italian Preparations for War

ON SEPTEMBER 28, 1934 the United States Ambassador at Rome, Breckinridge Long, reported to the Secretary of State that rumors were current that Italy contemplated war against Ethiopia and was making extensive preparations to this end. Ambassador Long said he was convinced that preparations of an unusual sort were under way; he considered it quite possible that these preparations related to Ethiopia. A few months later, February 14, 1935, he reported to the Secretary of State that there were indications of general preparation for an extensive campaign in Ethiopia. The Ambassador reported that factories for the manufacture of trucks, tanks, and artillery at and around Milan were working day and night; that supplies and military forces were moving clandestinely; that concerted effort was being made to prevent any information getting out as to the size or general nature of shipments; that troop movements were at night; that embarkation was proceeding from several cities; that he had received reports that 30,000 troops had left Naples, and that the movement under way contemplated the use in Ethiopia of 200,000 or 300,000 troops; and that all of these movements were being camouflaged by the use of the regular merchant marine without using war vessels. (37, 42)

Italian preparations continued in the spring and summer and the danger of war became acute. Secretary Hull called in Italian Ambassador Rosso on July 10, 1935 to discuss the situation. He informed the Ambassador that the United States was deeply interested in the preservation of peace in all parts of the world. He emphasized the increasing concern of this Government in the situation arising out of Italy's dispute with Ethiopia and expressed the earnest hope that a peaceful means might be found to arrive at a mutually satisfactory solution of the problem. (52)

On August 18, 1935 President Roosevelt sent a personal message to Premier Mussolini of Italy, stating that the Government and people of the United States felt that failure to arrive at a peaceful settlement of this dispute and a subsequent outbreak of hostilities would be a world calamity the consequences of which would adversely affect the interests of all nations. (48)

Ambassador Long cabled the Secretary of State on September 10, 1935 that there remained no vestige of doubt that Italy was irrevo-

cably determined to proceed in Africa. The Ambassador reported
that the entire population, both military and civilian, was in complete accord with Mussolini's policies; that the press in every issue
gave expression of the national determination to proceed to war
and not to tolerate interference from any source. There was every
indication of a carefully prepared, well-calculated, "hard, cold, and
cruel" prosecution of preconceived plans by the use of an army and
navy which were almost fanatic in their idolatry of and devotion
to one man and which were worked up to an emotional pitch unique
in modern times. Ambassador Long expressed the view that the
situation was fraught with dangers for the future as well as for
the present. (51)

A few days later he pointed out in a despatch to the Secretary of
State that the long period of friendly cooperation between Italy
and Great Britain had come to an end; he feared that it would be
generations before the situation could be cured. The Ambassador
said that any estimate of future possibilities must be based on one
of two alternatives: first, that sufficient force would be applied to
stop Italy's adventure and to impose upon it a definite defeat by
arms or, second, that Italy would be successful in attaining its objectives in Ethiopia. In the latter case, he said, there would be
nothing but trouble in the future; for if the venture were successful,
Italy would be emboldened to proceed to others. Ambassador Long
declared that Italy must either be defeated "now" and prevented
from realizing its ambitions in East Africa, "or the trouble will
continue on through for a generation as an additional irritation to
European politics and an additional menace to world peace". (53)

On September 12, 1935 Secretary Hull made a public statement of
the attitude of this Government. He said that the United States
desired peace; that we believed international controversies could and
should be settled by peaceful means; that a threat of hostilities anywhere would be a threat to the political, economic, and social interests
of all nations; and that armed conflict in any part of the world
would have adverse effects in every part of the world. He stated that
all nations had the right to ask that any and all issues between
nations be resolved by pacific means; that every nation had the right
to ask that no other nation subject it to the hazards and uncertainties that must inevitably accrue to all from resort to arms by any
two. In conclusion, the Secretary said that this Government asked
the parties in dispute to "weigh most solicitously" the pledge given in
the Kellogg-Briand Pact, which was made by the signatories for the

purpose of safeguarding peace and sparing the world the incalculable losses and human suffering that inevitably follow in the wake of war. (52)

Outbreak of War

During this period of threatening hostilities the League of Nations was endeavoring to prevent the outbreak of war. The Italian Government, however, refused to be deterred from carrying out its plan for conquest. On October 3, 1935 Italian armed forces invaded Ethiopia.

With the outbreak of war between Italy and Ethiopia President Roosevelt, in accordance with provisions of the Neutrality Act, issued proclamations putting into effect an embargo on the export of arms, ammunition, and implements of war to the two belligerent nations and restrictions on travel by United States citizens on vessels of the belligerents. Upon issuing these proclamations on October 5, 1935, the President stated that "any of our people who voluntarily engage in transactions of any character with either of the belligerents do so at their own risk". (54)

The League of Nations, after deciding that Italy had violated its obligations under the Covenant, recommended to its members a number of commercial and financial sanctions against Italy. While sanctions were under consideration, it was reported that the League might ask non-League countries to participate. Thereupon the Secretary of State instructed the United States representatives at Geneva, on October 9, 1935, that he considered it advisable for the League to understand that definite measures had already been taken by the United States in accordance with our own limitations and policies; that these measures included the restriction of commercial and financial transactions with the belligerents; and that we desired to follow our course independently, in the light of developing circumstances. A week later the Secretary again sent instructions explaining the attitude of the United States toward cooperation with other governments or with the League of Nations in relation to the Italian-Ethiopian conflict. He declared that the United States was acting on its own initiative with respect to the war and that its actions had preceded those of other governments. He said that the major policy of the United States was to keep from becoming involved in war; that, however, this Government was "keeping thoroughly alive its definite conviction" that it had an obligation to contribute to the cause of peace in every practical way consistent with this policy. (55, 56)

Secretary Hull, in a radio address on November 6, 1935, stated the position of the United States on the general subject of peace. He conceived it to be our duty and in the interests of our country and of humanity not only to remain aloof from disputes and conflicts with which we had no direct concern, but also to use our influence in any appropriate way to bring about the peaceful settlement of international differences. He said that our own interests and our duty as a great power forbade that we sit idly by and watch the development of hostilities with a feeling of self-sufficiency and complacency when by the use of our influence, short of becoming involved in the dispute, we might "prevent or lessen the scourge of war". (57)

During this period there was an increase in the export from the United States to Italy of war materials which did not come within the category of "arms, ammunition, and implements of war". There was no statutory authority for stopping these exports. In a statement of November 15, 1935 Secretary Hull said that the people of the United States were entitled to know that considerably increasing amounts of oil, copper, trucks, tractors, scrap iron, and scrap steel, which were essential war materials, were being exported for war purposes. He said that this class of trade was directly contrary to the policy of the Government of the United States. (60)

Secretary Hull's Conversation With the Italian Ambassador

Under instructions from his Government, Italian Ambassador Rosso called on the Secretary of State on November 22, 1935. The Ambassador referred to the various statements of the United States Government on the war between Italy and Ethiopia, especially the Secretary's statement of November 15, and said that although these statements applied formally and theoretically to both contending parties, it was well known that their practical result would be actually to impair the freedom of trade only with respect to Italy. The Ambassador said further that the statement of November 15 was contrary to the letter and spirit of the treaty of 1871 between the United States and Italy which accorded freedom of commerce and navigation to each contracting party; that the limitation on freedom cf commerce envisaged by the statement of November 15 would constitute an "unfriendly act".

The Secretary replied emphatically that these trading incidents complained of by the Italian Government were trivial compared with the real problems and deep concern which the war caused the United States; that the Ambassador must realize the resulting awful repercussions that made their immediate appearance in remote parts of the world, and which would give the United States and other nations unimaginable troubles for a generation. The Secretary said that this Government was immensely concerned with the possible spread of war to other countries at almost any time with serious consequences. He said that it was deplorable to see Italy moving forward with a war which it must realize threatened to create terrific problems and conditions so far-reaching that the imagination could not grasp their possibilities. He inquired why these considerations were not in the mind of the Italian Government before it went to war. He reiterated his surprise that Italy was upbraiding this Government because we showed our deep concern and were striving in every possible way to keep entirely out of the war.

The Secretary took up the Italian complaint that the United States had violated the treaty of 1871 and said that, with both Italy and the United States signatory to the Kellogg-Briand Pact, it was not possible to understand how Italy could go to war and announce to the United States that regardless of this pact we must supply Italy with materials of war or be guilty of an unfriendly act. The Secretary said that the people of the United States were convinced that Italy was under most solemn obligation to keep the peace, and it was incomprehensible to them to find Italy contending that to be neutral the United States must furnish war supplies.

In this long conversation the Secretary endeavored to impress upon the Ambassador that the United States and other peace-loving nations were greatly pained to see their traditional friends, the Italian people, involved in this war in spite of numerous peace treaties and despite the awful menace to the peace of the world. (61)

Italy continued the conquest of Ethiopia. By the spring of 1936 Italian military forces had overrun most of Ethiopia and on May 5 Addis Ababa, the capital, fell to the invader. Shortly thereafter, on June 20, the United States terminated the application of the Neutrality Act to the conflicting parties.

The United States never recognized Italian sovereignty over Ethiopia.

VI

DEVELOPING DANGERS 1936–1937

Warnings by President Roosevelt and Secretary Hull

THROUGHOUT 1935 the world peace structure had continued to deteriorate. In Europe, Germany swept away the disarmament provisions of the Versailles Treaty when in March Hitler announced the existence of a German air force and the reestablishment of conscription. In the Far East, Japan was increasing its military and naval strength and undertaking limited military actions for extending domination over China. At the end of the year Italian armies were advancing steadily into Ethiopia.

It was against this background that President Roosevelt delivered his Armistice Day address on November 11, 1935. He made clear that in foreign policy the primary purpose of the United States was to avoid being drawn into war; that we sought also in every practicable way to promote peace and to discourage war. He said that jealousies between nations continued, armaments were increasing, national ambitions were disturbing world peace and, most serious of all, confidence in the sacredness of international contracts was declining; we could not and must not hide our concern for grave world dangers, we could not "build walls around ourselves and hide our heads in the sand", we must go forward with all our strength to strive for international peace. He declared that aggression on the part of the United States was an impossibility; that defense against aggression by others was our accepted policy; and that the measure of defense would be solely the amount necessary to safeguard the United States against the armaments of others. In conclusion, he said that the more greatly others decreased their armaments, the more quickly and surely would we decrease ours. (58)

In an address to Congress on January 3, 1936 President Roosevelt warned that developments in international affairs had resulted in a situation which might lead to the "tragedy of general war". He said that nations seeking expansion had reverted to belief in the law of the sword, to the fantastic conception that they alone were chosen to fulfil a mission and that all the other human beings in the world must learn from and be subject to them.

The President in this address summarized the foreign policy of the United States: We sought earnestly to limit world armaments and to attain the peaceful solution of disputes among nations; we sought by every legitimate means to exert our moral influence against discrimination, intolerance, and autocracy, and in favor of freedom of expression, equality before the law, religious tolerance, and popular rule; in the field of commerce we undertook to encourage a more reasonable interchange of the world's goods; in the field of international finance we had, so far as we were concerned, put an end to dollar diplomacy; we followed a twofold neutrality policy toward nations engaging in wars not of immediate concern to the Americas; that is, we declined to encourage the prosecution of war by permitting belligerents to obtain arms from the United States and sought to discourage the export to belligerent nations of abnormal quantities of other war materials. Finally, the President said that if peace continued to be threatened by those who sought selfish power, the United States and the rest of the Americas could play but one role: through a well-ordered neutrality to do nothing to encourage war; through adequate defense to avoid embroilment and attack; and through example and all legitimate encouragement and assistance to persuade other nations "to return to the days of peace and goodwill". (64)

In line with the policy enunciated by the President of restricting the export to belligerents of abnormal quantities of war materials, which had been urged by the Government since the beginning of the war between Italy and Ethiopia, a "neutrality" bill containing such a provision was introduced in Congress in January 1936. Secretary of State Hull, in supporting this proposal before the Senate Committee on Foreign Relations, emphasized that a neutral should not "deliberately help to feed the fires and flames of war" by delivering essential materials to belligerents, thus helping "not only to carry on war but to prolong it indefinitely". This proposal was not adopted by the Congress.

By a joint resolution approved February 29, 1936 the Neutrality Act of 1935 was amended to prohibit persons in the United States from making loans or extending credits to belligerents. Upon signing this joint resolution President Roosevelt referred to the fact that the "high moral duty" which he had urged on our people of restricting their exports of essential war materials to either belligerent to approximately the normal peacetime basis had not been the subject of legislation. Nevertheless, he said, it was clear that greatly to exceed that basis "would serve to magnify the very evil of war which we seek to prevent". Therefore, the President renewed the appeal to the people of the United States "that they so conduct their trade with belligerent nations that it cannot be said that they are seizing new opportunities for profit or that by changing their peacetime trade they give aid to the continuation of war". (68, 69)

The United States Minister to Switzerland, Hugh Wilson, had reported to Secretary Hull in November 1935 that the states of Europe, while fully realizing and apprehensive of the dangers inherent in Italy's course in Ethiopia, had no real fear of Italy; that, however, they were "profoundly afraid of Germany". In a letter of January 1936 Mr. Wilson reported to the Secretary that while three months earlier the thoughts of European statesmen were concentrated on Africa, now the minds of these men were fixed on the intensity of the rearmament of Germany. He said that there was indisputable evidence of the magnitude and intensity of German military preparations; that while there might be a question as to the exact stage of the development of this preparation, there was no doubt that it was on a scale to cause alarm. The idea was becoming prevalent, he said, "that German rearmament on this scale and in this tempo can be designed only for the purposes of aggression". (59, 66)

During a conversation of January 22, 1936 with the British Ambassador, Sir Ronald Lindsay, Secretary Hull said that "the most incomprehensible circumstance in the whole modern world is the ability of dictators, overnight almost, to stand 35 million Italians and 65 million Germans on their heads and so dominate their mental processes that they arise the next morning and insist on being sent to the first-line trenches without delay". (65)

Less than two months later, Hitler struck a blow at the peace of Europe. In flagrant violation of the Locarno Pact he proceeded in March 1936 to occupy and fortify the demilitarized Rhineland. This action was taken despite the fact that two years previously Hitler had said that after the solution of the Saar question the German Government was ready to accept not only the letter but also the spirit of the Locarno Pact.

Civil Conflict in Spain

Another threat to peace occurred in July 1936 with the outbreak of a civil conflict in Spain. The attitude of this Government toward the conflict was based squarely on the consistent policy of the United States of promoting peace and at the same time avoiding involvement in war situations. All acts and utterances of this Government in relation to the conflict were directed toward the attainment of these controlling objectives. In line with these objectives, this Government in August 1936 declared a policy of strict non-interference in the struggle and announced that the export of arms from the United States to Spain would be contrary to this policy. In line also with these objectives, the Congress of the United States four months later passed, by a unanimous vote of the Senate and by a vote of 406 to 1 in the House of Representatives, a joint resolution prohibiting export of arms to the contending factions in Spain. (73, 75, 81)

Shortly after the beginning of the conflict in Spain it became evident that several of the principal powers of Europe were projecting themselves into the struggle through the furnishing of arms and war materials and other aid to the contending sides, thus creating real danger of a spread of the conflict into a European war. In an effort to remedy this menacing situation, a committee was set up in London, by agreement of the European governments, to carry out a concerted policy of non-intervention and to put an end to export of arms to Spain.

As the Spanish civil conflict continued, and as the European non-intervention agreement was flagrantly violated, the policy of non-interference pursued by the United States aroused criticism from partisans in this country of one or the other of the contending factions in Spain. There was a feeling in some quarters that our policy should be changed. This Government, however, was convinced that—in the light of growing complications and in view of its thoroughly unsatisfactory experience during 1935 in endeavoring to preserve peace in the Italo-Ethiopian situation—a change in its policy with regard to Spain would in no way serve the cause of peace but on the contrary would create for this country a serious risk of military involvement. Consequently the policy announced by the Executive and unanimously adopted by the Congress was pursued by the United States throughout the period of the Spanish civil conflict. (107)

Addresses by President Roosevelt and Secretary Hull

On August 14, 1936 President Roosevelt delivered an address at Chautauqua, New York, in which he declared that the United States had sought steadfastly to assist international movements to prevent war. The President said that we shunned political commitments which might entangle the United States in foreign wars; that we avoided connection with the political activities of the League of Nations but had cooperated wholeheartedly in the social and humanitarian work at Geneva. He said that we were not isolationists "except in so far as we seek to isolate ourselves completely from war";

that we must remember that so long as war existed there would be some danger that even the nation most ardently desiring peace might be drawn into war; and that no matter how well we were supported by neutrality legislation, we must remember that no laws could be provided to cover every contingency. (74)

In an address delivered at Washington on September 7, 1936 Secretary of State Hull gave pointed warning of the threat to peace which was mounting throughout the world. He said that in all history the weight of the responsibility of governments and peoples to preserve the peace had never been so great. He warned that if war came it would be fought not alone by uniformed armies and navies, but by the entire populations of the countries involved; that airplanes, poison gas, and other modern fighting equipment would make the world a "veritable inferno". He believed that a general war would set loose forces that would be beyond control; that these forces might bring about a virtual destruction of modern political thought and possibly a shattering of our civilization.

The one hope of the world, he said, was that governments and peoples might fully realize the solemn responsibility resting upon all of them and that realistic envisaging of the inevitable consequences would "prevent their flying at each other's throats". (76)

In an address of the following week, Secretary Hull dealt with the criticism that the United States declined to depart from its traditional policy and join with other governments in collective arrangements carrying the obligation of employing force, if necessary, in case disputes with other countries brought them into war. He declared that we could not accept that responsibility, which carried with it direct participation in the political relations of the whole world, because current experience indicated how uncertain was the possibility that we could vitally influence the policies or activities of other countries from which war might come. He said that the statesmen of the world should continue their effort to effect security by arrangements which would prove more durable than those which had been broken. (77)

Japanese Expansion and Attitude

Late in 1935 Japan attempted to promote a so-called "autonomy movement" in North China, with a view to detaching the northern provinces from the rest of China and bringing them under Japanese domination. Secretary of State Hull took notice of this situation in a public statement of December 5, 1935. He called attention to the interests of the United States involved in that area and to the treaty rights and obligations of the several powers there. He declared that political disturbances and pressures gave rise to uncertainty and tended to produce economic and social dislocations which made difficult the enjoyment of treaty rights and the fulfilment of treaty obligations.

In this statement the Secretary emphasized the importance "in this period of world-wide political unrest and economic instability that governments and peoples keep faith in principles and pledges". He declared that the United States respected the treaties to which it was a party and bespoke respect by all nations for treaties solemnly entered into. (62)

During a conversation of December 23, 1935 with a member of the staff of the United States Embassy in Tokyo, Mr. Saburo Kurusu, a high Japanese Foreign Office official, stated that Japan was destined to be the leader of the oriental civilization and would in course of time be the "boss" of a group comprising "China, India, the Netherlands East Indies, etc." Mr. Kurusu said that while Japan led the oriental civilization, the United States would lead the occidental civilization; that the two countries must not fight, as that would be suicidal. He said that Great Britain was "degenerating" and that the Russians were dreamers and never would "amount to anything". Mr. Kurusu went on to say that he opposed Japan's "hypocritical attitude" toward treaties for collective security; that he was critical of his own country for signing agreements which could not be carried out if Japan wanted to progress in the world. (63)

London Naval Conference

At the London Naval Conference of 1935-36 Japan endeavored to have substituted for the 5-5-3 ratio of the naval treaties of 1922 and 1930 a "common upper limit" for all powers. This proposal would have established a uniform maximum level for fleets of all nations without taking into consideration their respective needs and responsibilities. None of the other states represented could accept this proposal even as a basis for negotiation. The United States opposed the Japanese proposal, according to a statement by Chairman Norman H. Davis of the United States delegation, on the ground that "equal security" had been achieved under the Washington and London Naval Treaties and that, owing to the difference in relative needs and vulnerability, "naval parity would give to Japan naval superiority". Japan withdrew from the Conference and as a result no quantitative naval limitation treaty was concluded. Despite the departure of the Japanese representatives from the Conference, the United States, Great Britain, and France concluded a treaty of qualitative naval limitation on March 25, 1936. The treaty provided, however, that if the national security of a contracting party should be menaced by naval construction by powers outside the scope of the treaty, it could depart from the qualitative limits. (71)

At the time of the signature of the treaty, Chairman Davis of the United States delegation and British Foreign Secretary Eden exchanged letters declaring that there would be no competitive naval building between the two countries and that the principle of parity would be maintained as between their Fleets. Subsequently Japan was approached by the British Government and asked to give assurances that it would adhere in practice to the qualitative limits laid down in the 1936 treaty. Japan declined to give such assurances. Japan's attitude marked the death knell, for the period under consideration, of naval limitation among the great powers.

The United States and Great Britain later invoked the "escalator" clause of the treaty and undertook increased naval building programs.

German-Japanese Anti-Comintern Pact

The Secretary of State discussed the Far Eastern situation on June 12, 1936 with the Japanese Ambassador to Great Britain, Shigeru Yoshida. The Ambassador said that the people of the United States should recognize the rapidly growing population of Japan and the absolute necessity for more territory for their existence. He said that there was misunderstanding and misapprehension on the part of the people of the United States concerning Japanese movements in and about China; that Japanese armaments were not intended for war against any particular country, especially not the United States, but that Japanese naval officials were always undertaking to create additional vacancies and additional room for promotion. This was not convincing to Secretary Hull. He replied that the impression among people in the United States was that Japan sought economic domination, first of eastern Asia, and then of other areas such as it might see fit to dominate; that this would mean political as well as military domination in the end.

The Secretary said that there was no reason why countries like the United States, Great Britain, and Japan could not in an amicable spirit and with perfect justice and fairness agree to abide by the world-wide principle of equality in commercial and industrial affairs, and each country solemnly agree not to resort to force in connection with the operation of this rule of equality. He felt that governments should be able to sit down together and in a spirit of fair-dealing confer and collaborate without ceasing until they found a way for amicable and reasonable adjustment; that this would eliminate 90 percent of the occasions for friction between nations. (72)

On November 25, 1936 Japan openly associated itself with Germany by the signature of the Anti-Comintern Pact, whereby the two countries agreed to exchange information on the activities of the Communist International and to consult and collaborate on the necessary preventive measures. While there had been signs for some time of a gradual *rapprochement* of these two states, this was the first open indication of their common designs in foreign policy. It foreshadowed the parallel courses of aggression which Germany and Japan were to follow during the coming years.

In connection with this agreement, Ambassador Grew reported from Tokyo on December 4, 1936 that the Japanese Foreign Office had denied categorically the existence of an understanding in regard to military matters or Japanese participation in a Fascist bloc. He stated, however, that foreign diplomatic representatives in Tokyo in general were of the opinion that the Japanese and German General Staffs had concluded a secret military understanding. (78)

Inter-American Peace Conference

Representatives of the American republics assembled in conference at Buenos Aires in December 1936. This conference had been suggested by President Roosevelt early in the year for the purpose of determining how the maintenance of peace among the American republics might best be safeguarded. The President felt that steps in this direction would advance the cause of world peace in as much as the agreements which might be reached would supplement and reinforce the efforts of the League of Nations and of other peace agencies seeking to prevent war. (67)

In an address at Buenos Aires on December 5, 1936 Secretary Hull said that the primary purpose of the conference was to "banish war from the Western Hemisphere". He believed that every country must play its part in determining whether the world would slip back toward war and savagery or whether it would maintain and advance the level of civilization and peace. He said that the American republics could not remain unconcerned by the grave and threatening conditions in many parts of the world; that it was now absolutely clear that each nation in any part of the world was concerned with peace in every part of the world.

The Secretary enumerated in this address eight principles for a comprehensive peace program: 1. Peoples must be educated for peace; each nation must make itself safe for peace. 2. Frequent conferences between representatives of nations and intercourse between their peoples are essential. 3. The consummation of five well-known peace agreements will provide adequate machinery. 4. In the event of war there should be a common policy of neutrality. 5. The nations should adopt commercial policies to bring each that prosperity upon which enduring peace is founded. 6. Practical international cooperation is essential to restore indispensable international relationships. 7. International law should be reestablished, revitalized, and strengthened; armies and navies are no permanent substitute for its great principles. 8. Faithful observance of undertakings between nations is the foundation of international law, and rests upon moral law, the highest of all law. (79)

The American republics at this conference agreed upon a convention for the maintenance, preservation, and reestablishment of peace, which contained a procedure for consultation among the signatories. The conference also approved a declaration stating that every act susceptible of disturbing the peace of America affects each and every one of the republics and justifies the initiation of the procedure of consultation provided for in the above-mentioned convention; that territorial conquest is proscribed, and consequently no acquisition made through violence shall be recognized; that intervention by one state in the internal or external affairs of another is condemned; that forcible collection of pecuniary debts is illegal; that any difference or dispute between the American nations shall be settled by the methods of conciliation, or unrestricted arbitration, or through operation of international justice. (80)

In a conversation with Italian Ambassador Suvich a few months later, on July 6, 1937, the Secretary of State reviewed at length the increasingly critical world situation and cited the Buenos Aires peace program as an example for the rest of the world. He said that the program contained a practicable set of principles and policies as the single alternative to the disastrous course of affairs in Europe. He said that the only foundations which Europe presented for restoring international order were the "narrowest, cut-throat, trouble-breeding methods of trading and a wild, runaway race in armaments"; that this was in striking contrast with the program of the 21 American republics, which provided a solid and permanent foundation for a stable structure of business, of peace, and of government. The Secretary said that the single question was whether the civilized nations would wait until it was too late before proclaiming and pursuing this practical and constructive course. The American nations had offered this program and were "pleading to all other civilized nations to embrace it and give it support without a day's delay". Never before, he said, had there been such an opportunity for some important country in Europe to furnish leadership with just this sort of program. When the Italian Ambassador said that the time was not propitious for such a program, the Secretary replied that if each nation waited until the time was exactly right from its standpoint, the time would never become propitious.

Referring to the dangerous situation in Europe, the Secretary remarked that another war or a deep-seated economic panic would be utterly destructive of everything worthwhile in the western world—and yet absolutely nothing was being done in the way of permanent planning for peace and general stability. There were, he continued, probably four million wage-earners in Germany engaged in armament production; relative numbers in other countries were likewise engaged; within another 18 months, when the resources of most countries necessary for further increased armaments were exhausted, it would not be humanly possible to find other gainful and productive employment for all the millions of these wage-earners. And yet, "with the roar of the economic and the military Niagara below, now within distinct hearing, and with the certain knowledge that the happening of either catastrophe would be fatal, nations are drifting and drifting and drifting with no broad or permanent or peaceful planning".

The United States, Secretary Hull said, while taking every precaution to keep aloof from political and military involvements abroad, strongly felt that each civilized country had the unshirkable responsibility of making a real contribution to promote peace. The Secretary declared that the United States and the other American nations were behind the broad program to which he had referred and were looking "longingly" to leading countries in Europe to offer a similar contribution to peace and economic well-being. (84)

National Defense

President Roosevelt stated the policy of the Government toward national defense in a letter of April 20, 1936 to the Daughters of the American Revolution. He said that it was the aim of the Government "to make our national defense efficient and to keep it adequate"; that what was necessary for adequate defense was not always the same and was bound to change with changing conditions; that if this were a disarming world our needs obviously would be proportionally decreasing; that he regretted that the world of the time was not a disarming world; and that our defense forces were "on a stronger peace-time basis than before", and it was our purpose to keep them that way.

The President said that we would press continually for limitation of armament by international agreement and that if this should fail, we would not increase our own armament unless other powers by increasing theirs made increase by us necessary to our national safety. (70)

In an address delivered at New York on September 15, 1936 Secretary Hull stated that the defense forces of the United States had been substantially increased; that this appeared essential in the face of the universal increase of armaments elsewhere and the disturbed conditions of the world; that "we would not serve the cause of peace" if we had inadequate means of self-defense; and that we must be sure that in our desire for peace we would not appear weak and unable to resist the imposition of force or to protect our just rights. (77)

President Roosevelt, on January 8, 1937, announced that he had directed the Navy Department to proceed with the construction of two replacement battleships. This was the first battleship construction to be undertaken by the United States since the Washington Naval Treaty of 1922. (82)

Throughout this period the United States Army was proceeding with an expansion program which increased its enlisted strength from 118,000 in 1935 to 158,000 in 1937. Notwithstanding this increase, the Secretary of War said in his annual report of 1937 that the Army was not keeping pace with the enormous expansions in the military establishments of other leading powers and recommended that it be further strengthened.

→≫ VII ≪←

JAPANESE ATTACK ON CHINA 1937

Marco Polo Bridge Incident

ON JULY 7, 1937 a clash occurred between Chinese and Japanese troops near Peiping in North China. When this clash was followed by indications of intensified military activity on the part of Japan, Secretary of State Hull urged upon the Japanese Government a policy of self-restraint. In a conversation of July 12 with Japanese Ambassador Saito, Secretary Hull elaborated upon the futility of war and its awful consequences, emphasizing the great injury to the victor as well as to the vanquished in case of war. He said that a first-class power like Japan not only could afford to exercise general self-restraint but that in the long run it was far better that this should characterize the attitude and policy of the Japanese Government; that he had been looking forward to an early period when Japan and the United States would have opportunity for world leadership with a constructive program like that proclaimed by the American republics at Buenos Aires in December 1936 for the purpose of restoring and preserving stable conditions of business and of peace. (85)

Secretary Hull's Statement of Principles

On July 16, 1937, a few days after the beginning of Japan's undeclared war on China, Secretary Hull issued a statement of fundamental principles of international policy. The Secretary stated that any situation in which armed hostilities were in progress or were threatened was a situation wherein rights and interests of all nations either were or might be seriously affected. Therefore, he felt it a duty to make a statement of this Government's position in regard to international problems and situations with respect to which this country felt deep concern. He said that the following principles were advocated by the United States: maintenance of peace; national and international self-restraint; abstinence from use of force in pursuit of policy; abstinence from interference in the internal affairs of other nations; adjustment of problems in international relations by processes of peaceful negotiation and agreement; faithful observance of international agreements; modification of provisions of treaties, when need therefor arises, by orderly processes carried out in a spirit of mutual helpfulness and accommodation; respect by all nations for the rights of others and performance by all nations of established obligations; revitalization and strengthening of international law; promotion of economic security and stability the world over; lowering or removing of excessive barriers of international trade; effective equality of commercial opportunity and application of the principle of equality of treatment; and limitation and reduction of armament. The Secretary stated that the United States avoided entering into alliances or entangling commitments but believed in cooperative effort by peaceful and practical means in support of the above-stated principles. (86)

This statement of fundamental principles of international policy was sent to the other governments of the world for comment. The reply from Germany was that the Reich Government had taken note with due interest of Secretary Hull's statement; that the Reich Government's "basic principle is, as is generally known, directed toward the regulation of international relations by pacific agreement and hence coincides with the ideas developed by the Secretary of State". The reply from Italy was that the Fascist Government "appreciates at their high value the principles enunciated by Secretary of State Hull"; that it favored everything which conduced to the pacification and to the political and economic reconstruction of the world; and that, therefore, it regarded with sympathy every initiative which tended to achieve that end by means of the limitation of armaments, by means of economic understanding among nations, non-intervention in the internal affairs of other countries, and any other means which might then or in the future appear responsive to this objective. The Japanese Government replied that it expressed concurrence with the principles contained in the statement by Secretary Hull; that it believed that the objectives of those principles would only be attained, in their application to the Far Eastern situation, by a full recognition and practical consideration of the actual particular circumstances of that region.

Offer of Good Offices

Secretary Hull called in Chinese Ambassador Wang and Japanese Ambassador Saito on July 21, 1937 and in separate conversations with them emphasized that the United States Government was ready and would gladly do anything short of mediation—which would require the agreement of both parties in advance—to contribute in a fair and impartial way toward composing the matters of controversy between China and Japan. The Secretary said that when two nations comprising 500,000,000 people were engaged in a controversy in which general hostilities appeared imminent the United States could not help feeling great concern. He said that it was in the light of this situation and of the "intense desire" of the United States for peace everywhere that he conferred with them; that he thus approached each Government in a spirit of friendliness and impartiality in an earnest effort to contribute something to the cause of peace. He expressed the opinion that a war would result in irreparable harm to all countries involved and would prove "utterly disastrous" to human welfare and progress. (87)

On August 10, 1937 the United States Ambassador to Japan, under instructions from the Secretary of State, offered informally to the Japanese Government the good offices of the United States toward the settlement of the controversy between Japan and China. This offer contemplated the providing of neutral ground where Japanese and Chinese representatives might meet to negotiate and the giving of assistance in adjusting difficulties that might develop during negotiations. Japan did not respond to this offer; consequently the United States Government felt that there would be no useful purpose in making a similar approach to the Chinese Government. (88)

Meanwhile, the China "incident" had developed into large-scale military operations as Japan poured men and engines of war into China. On August 23, 1937 the Department of State issued a statement declaring that the issues and problems which were of concern to the United States in the existing situation in the Pacific area went "far beyond merely the immediate question of protection of the nationals and interests of the United States"; that the conditions prevailing in that area were intimately connected with and had a direct and fundamental relationship to the general principles of policy made public on July 16. In this statement it was declared further that the existence of serious hostilities anywhere was a matter of concern to all nations; that without attempting to pass judgment on the merits of the controversy, the United States appealed to the parties to refrain from war; that the United States considered applicable throughout the world, in the Pacific area as elsewhere, the principles set forth in the statement of July 16; and that that statement embraced the principles embodied in the Washington Conference treaties and the Kellogg-Briand Pact.

The Department stated that from the beginning of the controversy in the Far East the United States had urged upon both Japan and China the importance of refraining from hostilities and of maintaining peace; that the United States had been participating constantly in consultation with interested governments, directed toward peaceful adjustment; that this Government did not believe in political alliances or entanglements, nor in extreme isolation; that this Government did believe in international cooperation for the purpose of seeking through pacific means the achievement of the objectives set forth in the statement of July 16. (89)

On September 2, 1937 the Secretary of State sent a telegram to Ambassador Grew in Japan summarizing the attitude of the United States toward the conflict between China and Japan. The Secretary stated that the course of the United States as pursued during recent years in regard to the Far East had been animated partly by the thought of encouraging Japanese and Chinese efforts at developing toward each other and toward the world attitudes of real cooperativeness. The situation produced by the hostilities going on between China and Japan permitted, he said, little hope of any such attitude being reciprocally developed by those two countries in the near future. He doubted that those in control of Japanese policies valued appreciably the friendship of other nations or efforts made by the United States and other nations to cultivate good-will, confidence, and stability. Public opinion in the United States, he said, had been outraged by the methods and strategy employed by the combatants, particularly by the Japanese military, and had become gradually more critical of Japan; in addressing authorities of either side he did not intend to call names or make threats; however, he wished the Japanese Government to understand fully that the United States looked with thorough disapproval upon the current manifestation of Japanese foreign policy and upon the methods employed by the Japanese military in pursuit of that policy. He asked the Ambassador to suggest to Japanese officials that Japan, by the course it was pursuing, was destroying the good-will of the world and was laying up for itself among the people of the world a liability of "distrust, suspicion, popular antipathy, and potential ostracism", the liquidation of which would take many, many years of benevolent endeavor by Japan. (90)

A year later, in a conversation with the Canadian Minister, Secretary Hull said that since August 1937 he had proceeded on the theory that "Japan definitely contemplates securing domination over as many hundreds of millions of people as possible in eastern Asia and gradually extending her control through the Pacific islands to the Dutch East Indies and elsewhere, thereby dominating in practical effect that one-half of the world". (111)

On September 14, 1937 the President issued a statement to the effect that the question of applying the Neutrality Act remained *in statu quo;* that merchant vessels owned by the Government of the United States would not be permitted to transport to China or Japan any arms, ammunition, or implements of war; and that any other merchant vessel flying the American flag which attempted to transport such articles to China or Japan would do so at its own risk. (91)

On September 28, 1937 the Secretary of State sent instructions to Minister Harrison in Switzerland for the Minister's background information in connection with the activities of the League of Nations in the dispute between China and Japan. The Secretary said that the United States had been approached on several occasions by other governments with suggestions for joint action; that while the United States believed in and wished to practice cooperation it was not prepared to take part in joint action, though it would consider the possibility of taking parallel action. In general, the Secretary felt that spontaneous and separate action on parallel lines was more likely to serve effectively the attainment of the objectives sought. The Secretary said that the Japanese military operations had increased in intensity; that China had affirmed a willingness to resort to conciliation; that the Japanese had announced, however, their intention to destroy the Chinese will and capacity to resist and to overthrow the existing Chinese Government. He said that the Sino-Japanese situation definitely concerned the world as a whole; that no longer did the questions involved relate merely to specific provisions of particular treaties being violated; that they were questions of international law, of humanity, of war and of peace. The Secretary said that the United States in action taken thus far had gone further than any other nation or group of nations in making efforts calculated to strengthen general principles of world peace and world security. Therefore, he felt that other nations might well direct their efforts toward going as far as or farther than the United States had gone. (92)

President Roosevelt's "Quarantine" Address

In a significant address delivered at Chicago on October 5, 1937, President Roosevelt dwelt at length on the tense condition of international affairs. He declared that the political situation in the world was one to cause grave concern and anxiety; that the existing reign of terror and international lawlessness had reached the stage where the very foundations of civilization were seriously threatened.

He warned that no one should imagine that America would escape from this or that the Western Hemisphere would not be attacked. He called for a concerted effort by the peace-loving nations in opposition to the actions that were creating international anarchy and instability.

The President declared that isolation or neutrality afforded no escape and that international anarchy jeopardized the security of every nation, large or small. He cited the spreading of the "epidemic of world lawlessness", and drew the parallel that in case of an epidemic of physical disease the community joins in a "quarantine" of the patients in order to protect the health of the community against the spread of the disease. War, he said, is a "contagion" and can engulf states remote from the original scene of hostilities. We were determined, he continued, to keep out of war, we were adopting measures to minimize the risk, yet we could not insure ourselves against war's disastrous effects and the dangers of involvement. The President called upon the peace-loving nations to express their will for peace to the end that nations tempted to violate their agreements and the rights of others would desist. He concluded with: "America hates war. America hopes for peace. Therefore, America actively engages in the search for peace." (93)

On October 6, 1937 the Assembly of the League of Nations adopted a report stating that the Japanese action in China was a violation of Japan's treaty obligations. On the same day the Department of State issued a statement that the action of Japan in China was inconsistent with the principles which should govern the relations between nations and was contrary to the Nine-Power Treaty of February 6, 1922 regarding the principles and policies to be followed in matters concerning China, and contrary to the Kellogg-Briand Pact. (94)

Brussels Conference

In November 1937 the United States participated with 18 other nations in a Conference held at Brussels to consider "peacable means" for hastening the end of the conflict between China and Japan. This Conference was held in accordance with a provision of the Nine-Power Treaty of 1922.

The instructions given by President Roosevelt and Secretary Hull to United States delegate Norman H. Davis stated that the first objective of the foreign policy of the United States was national security, and that consequently we sought to keep peace and promote the maintenance of peace; that we believed in cooperative effort for the preservation of peace by pacific and practicable means; that this country as a signatory to the Kellogg-Briand Pact had renounced war as an instrument of national policy; and that "public opinion in the United States has expressed its emphatic determination that the United States keep out of war". Mr. Davis was instructed to keep in mind the interest of the United States in peace in the Pacific and in the Far East as evidenced by the Washington Conference treaties, the statements relating to foreign policy made by the President in his Chicago address of October 5, and this Government's statement of October 6 on the controversy between China and Japan. In the view of this Government the primary function of the Conference was "to provide a forum for constructive discussion, to formulate and suggest possible bases of settlement, and to endeavor to bring the parties together through peaceful negotiation".

It was emphasized to the United States delegate that if we were to avoid an ultimate serious clash with Japan, some practical means must be found to check Japanese conquest and to make effective the collective will of the powers which desired the settlement of international controversies by peaceful means; that the Conference might be an agency for bringing to bear upon Japan every moral pressure directed toward bringing about a change in Japanese attitude and policy. Finally, the delegate was to "observe closely the trend of public opinion in the United States and take full account thereof". (95)

Japan refused to participate in the Conference, maintaining that its dispute with China was outside the purview of the Nine-Power Treaty. On November 15 the Conference adopted a declaration affirming that the representatives of 15 states considered the conflict between China and Japan to be of concern to all countries parties to the Nine-Power Treaty and the Kellogg-Briand Pact. In the presence of this difference between the views of the Conference and the Japanese Government, the Conference considered that there was no opportunity at the time for carrying out its terms of reference so far as they related to bringing about peace by agreement. (96)

In a declaration, dated November 24, 1937, the Conference stated that it strongly reaffirmed the principles of the Nine-Power Treaty; that it believed that a satisfactory settlement between China and Japan could not be achieved by direct negotiation between the parties to the conflict alone and that an acceptable agreement could be achieved only by consultation with other powers principally concerned; that it strongly urged that hostilities be suspended and resort be had to peaceful processes; that the Conference deemed it advisable temporarily to suspend its sittings; that the conflict remained, however, a matter of concern to all the powers assembled at Brussels; and that the Conference would be called together again when it was considered that deliberations could be advantageously resumed. (97)

The United States delegate reported at the conclusion of the Conference that it had demonstrated the "unwillingness of Japan to resort to methods of conciliation" and that the Japanese continued to insist that the issues between Japan and China were exclusive to those two countries whereas the Conference powers, with the exception of Italy, affirmed that the situation was of concern to all members of the family of nations. (100)

"Panay" Incident

On December 12, 1937 the Government and people of the United States were deeply shocked by the news of the bombing and destruction by Japanese aircraft of the United States gunboat *Panay* and three United States merchant vessels on the Yangtze River in China. The bombing and machine-gunning of the crews and passengers resulted in loss of life to citizens of the United States. This Government immediately sent a note to the Japanese Government stating that the United States vessels involved were on the Yangtze River "by uncontested and incontestable right", that they were flying the American flag, and that they were engaged in legitimate and appropriate business. The Government of the United States requested and expected of the Japanese Government "a formally recorded expression of regret, an undertaking to make complete and comprehensive indemnifications; and an assurance that definite and specific steps have been taken which will insure that hereafter American nationals, interests and property in China will not be subjected to attack by Japanese armed forces or unlawful interference by any Japanese authorities or forces". (98)

This note was sent to Japan on the evening of December 13. On December 14 the United States Ambassador to Japan received a note from the Japanese Minister for Foreign Affairs stating that the Japanese Government regretted "most profoundly" the damage to these vessels and the casualties among the personnel; that it desired to present "sincere apologies"; that it would make indemnifications for all the losses; that it would deal "appropriately" with those responsible for the incident; and that it had already issued "strict orders to the authorities on the spot with a view to preventing the recurrence of a similar incident". Finally, the Japanese Government expressed the "fervent hope" that the friendly relations between Japan and the United States would not be affected by this "unfortunate affair". The Japanese Government later made full indemnification in accordance with the request of the United States. (99)

The overwhelming endorsement given by the people of the United States to the manner in which the *Panay* incident was settled attested to their earnest desire to keep the United States out of war.

→»» VIII «←←

EUROPEAN CRISIS 1938

United States Rearmament

As 1937 drew to a close the situation in the world became increasingly threatening. The hostilities between China and Japan raged with growing intensity; in Europe, Spain was torn by a civil struggle which threatened to turn into a general continental war. In November 1937 Italy joined Germany and Japan in the Anti-Comintern Pact. Meanwhile, Germany, arming at a feverish pace, was causing grave apprehension as to its intentions toward the European political structure.

During this period there developed considerable public support in the United States for the adoption of a constitutional amendment requiring a popular vote as prerequisite to a declaration of war by the Congress. Both President Roosevelt and Secretary of State Hull at various times expressed their strong opposition to this proposal. On January 6, 1938 the President wrote to the Speaker of the House of Representatives that such an amendment "would cripple any President in his conduct of our foreign relations" and "would encourage other nations to believe that they could violate American rights with impunity". Secretary Hull on January 8 warned that the proposal would impair the ability of the Government to safeguard the peace of the people of the United States. On January 10 the proposal was voted on by the House of Representatives but was rejected by the close vote of 209 to 188. (101, 102)

President Roosevelt recommended to Congress, in a special message of January 28, 1938, the strengthening of our national defense. The President reported with deep regret that armaments were increasing "at an unprecedented and alarming rate". He called attention to the ominous fact that at least one fourth of the world's population was involved in "merciless devastating conflict" in spite of the fact that most people in most countries wished to live at peace. As Commander in Chief of the Army and Navy, the President deemed it his constitutional duty to report to the Congress that the national defense of the United States was, in the light of the increasing armaments of other nations, inadequate for purposes of national security and therefore required increase. The President said that "adequate defense" meant that for the protection not only of our coasts but also of our communities far removed from the coasts, we must keep any potential enemy many hundreds of miles away from our continental limits. We could not assume, he stated, that our defense would be limited to one ocean and one coast and that the others would certainly be safe. "Specifically and solely because of the piling up of additional land and sea armaments in other countries" the President recommended to Congress that authorizations be granted for substantial increases in military and naval armament. Included were recommendations for increasing by 20 percent the existing naval building program and for appropriations to lay down two additional battleships and two additional cruisers during 1938. (104)

The President's proposals for military and naval rearmament were debated in Congress during the spring of 1938. Doubt was expressed in some quarters that the proposed naval increases were really necessary for the defense of the United States, and several Senators and Representatives voiced the suspicion that the contemplated naval increases were based on an agreement for naval cooperation with some other power, such as Great Britain. Secretary of State Hull took cognizance of these ideas in a letter to a member of Congress on February 10, 1938. He stated categorically his opinion that the proposed naval program was needed for the defense of the United States. Referring to the desire of the people and Government of the United States to keep out of war, he said that those who, with a full sense of responsibility, were advocating this program, were doing so in the belief that its adoption would contribute to achieving this desire. Secretary Hull pointed out that the Navy, even with the proposed increases, would not be able to embark upon offensive or aggressive operations overseas.

The Secretary also declared that the proposed program did not contemplate naval cooperation with any other power in the world; that the policy of the United States was to avoid both extreme internationalism and extreme isolation; that, while avoiding alliances and entangling commitments, it was advisable to confer and exchange information with other governments having common objectives and, when practicable, to proceed on parallel lines. Finally, the Secretary said that if every peaceful nation insisted on remaining aloof from every other peaceful nation and on pursuing a policy of armament limitation without reference to relative armaments, the inevitable consequences would be to encourage and even to assist nations inclined to play lawless roles. (105)

The President's proposals for military and naval rearmament were substantially adopted by the Congress.

By July 1, 1938 Secretary of War Woodring was able to report encouraging improvements in the military establishment. He declared, however, that there were still deficiencies in organization, equipment, and personnel that required correction. The Chief of Staff of the Army, General Malin Craig, pointed out at the same time that the Regular Army ranked only eighteenth among the standing armies of the world.

German Occupation of Austria

During this period Secretary Hull was proceeding on the theory that Germany was "bent on becoming the dominating colossus of continental Europe", as he later said during a conversation with the Canadian Minister. (111)

The Secretary conferred with German Ambassador Dieckhoff on January 14, 1938. He told the Ambassador that the supreme issue of the time was whether the principles underlying the structure of international law and order should be preserved or whether the doctrine of force, militarism, and aggression and destruction of all international law and order should prevail. He said that all nations could with perfect consistency join in support of the former alternative no matter what their form of government. The Secretary said that this program contemplated that the road to permanent peace was based upon these principles which in turn rested upon the solid foundation of economic readjustment. (103)

On March 11, 1938 Hitler sent his armed forces into Austria and on March 13 proclaimed the union of Germany and Austria. This action was taken in violation of Hitler's declaration of three years earlier that Germany had neither the intention nor the wish to annex Austria.

Secretary Hull's Address of March 17

The Secretary of State in an address at Washington, March 17, 1938, declared that the momentous question was whether the doctrine of force would once more become enthroned or whether the United States and other peaceful nations would work unceasingly to preserve law, order, morality, and justice as the bases of civilized international relations.

The Secretary said that the United States might, if it chose, turn its back on the whole problem and decline the responsibility of contributing to its solution. But he warned of what such a choice would involve. It would mean a voluntary abandonment of some of the most important things that had made us great; an abject retreat before the forces which we had consistently opposed throughout our whole national history. Our security would be menaced as other nations came to believe that through fear or unwillingness we did not propose to protect our legitimate interests abroad, but intended to abandon them at the first sign of danger. The sphere of all of our international relations would shrink until we stood practically alone among the nations, "a self-constituted hermit state". We would find it necessary to reorganize our entire social and economic structure, which would mean lower living standards, regimentation, and wide-spread economic distress.

All this, the Secretary said, would be done in order to avoid war. But, he asked, would this policy give any such assurance? He believed that reason and experience definitely pointed to the contrary. We might seek to withdraw from participation in world affairs, "but we cannot thereby withdraw from the world itself". Isolation, he declared, "is not a means to security; it is a fruitful source of insecurity".

Secretary Hull emphasized that for the sake of our own best interests we must maintain our influence in world affairs and our participation in efforts toward world progress and peace. Only by making our reasonable contribution to a firm establishment of a world order based on law "can we keep the problem of our own security in true perspective, and thus discharge our responsibility to ourselves". (106)

Increased Tension in Europe

The months following the seizure of Austria saw a new wave of tension sweep over Europe. It soon became evident that Hitler, his appetite whetted for further conquests, was casting covetous eyes toward the Sudetenland in Czechoslovakia. Meanwhile, the ruthless and barbarous persecution of minorities which the Nazis had imposed in Germany was drastically put into effect in Austria.

On July 7, 1938 Secretary Hull talked with the German Ambssador about the European situation. He told the Ambassador that this Government had been earnestly hoping that the German Government would reach a stage where it would decide to support the program of peace and orderly progress which the United States had been striving to keep alive and to advance. The Secretary said that there was only one alternative course—the course of force, militarism, and territorial aggression with all the accompanying hurtful and destructive practices; that this course was leading the world inevitably backward instead of forward and would sooner or later bring on a general war. (110)

Throughout the summer of 1938 the tension between Germany and Czechoslovakia mounted. Germany launched a "war of nerves" against the latter, and it became evident that Hitler was bent on securing his territorial designs on the Sudetenland, even at the risk of a general war. By the middle of September the crisis was nearing a climax, and all over Europe armies were put on a war footing. The British Government tried to halt the threatened catastrophe when Prime Minister Chamberlain went to Germany for several conferences with Hitler, but this effort appeared fruitless as the latter remained inexorable in his demands upon Czechoslovakia.

In the midst of this tension, President Roosevelt early on September 26 sent a personal message to the heads of the Governments of Czechoslovakia, France, Germany, and Great Britain. The President stated that the fabric of peace on the continent of Europe and possibly throughout the rest of the world was in immediate danger; that the consequences of its rupture were incalculable. He said that the supreme desire of the American people was to live in peace, but in the event of a general war they faced the fact that no nation could escape some measure of its consequences. Referring to the Kellogg-Briand Pact and other instruments for the pacific settlement of disputes, he said that whatever might be the differences in the controversies at issue he was persuaded that there was no problem so difficult or so pressing for solution that it could not be justly solved by resort to reason rather than by resort to force. The President said that so long as negotiations continued there would remain the hope that reason and the spirit of equity might prevail and that the world might thereby escape the madness of a new resort to war. On behalf of the people of the United States and for the sake of humanity everywhere, he appealed for the continuance of negotiations looking to a peaceful, fair, and constructive settlement of the questions at issue. (112)

Later on September 26 President Roosevelt received replies from the Governments of Czechoslovakia, France, and Great Britain assuring him of their desire to avoid recourse to force and of their willingness to search for a peaceful solution. On the same day the President received a reply from Chancelor Hitler which made it clear that if the Sudetenland were not handed over to Germany, Hitler would endeavor to take it by force.

On September 27 Secretary Hull sent urgent instructions to our diplomatic representatives throughout the world to express the opinion of this Government that no step should be overlooked that might possibly contribute to the maintenance of peace and that if the governments to which they were accredited would send messages to Germany and Czechoslovakia emphasizing the supreme importance of a peaceful settlement of the dispute, the cumulative effect of such an expression of opinion might possibly contribute to the preservation of peace. (113)

In a message of September 27 to Premier Mussolini the President asked whether the latter would extend his help in the continuation of the efforts to arrive at an agreement by negotiation rather than by resort to force. (114)

President Roosevelt on September 27 sent a second appeal to Hitler for the continuance of negotiations until a fair and constructive solution was reached. The President reminded Hitler that negotiations were still open; that they could be continued if he would give the word. Should the need for supplementing them become evident, the President believed that nothing stood in the way of widening their scope into a conference of all the nations directly interested in the controversy. The President said that such a meeting might be held at once in a neutral country in Europe and would offer an opportunity for this and correlated questions to be solved in a spirit of justice and fair dealing. The President concluded his appeal with the statement that "the conscience and the impelling desire of the people of my country demand that the voice of their Government be raised again and yet again to avert and to avoid war". (115)

On September 28, 1938 the German Ambassador called on the Secretary of State. The Secretary referred to the impression created that Hitler was seeking "general dominion by force". The Ambassador hastily denied that Hitler had world ambitions. The Secretary again referred to the question of acquiring dominion generally over territory, and the Ambassador denied again that Germany had such territorial ambitions. (116)

Munich

At literally the "eleventh hour", when almost all hope of preventing a general European war had vanished, the heads of government of Great Britain, France, Germany, and Italy agreed to meet at Munich, in a last-minute effort to avoid war. They reached an agreement on September 29, 1938 that the Sudetenland of Czechoslovakia be handed over to Germany.

On the next day Secretary Hull, by way of warning against any assumption that the Munich agreement insured peace or was based on sound principles, and of emphasizing the necessity for the nations of the world to redouble their efforts on behalf of maintaining peace based on such principles, made a statement as follows:

"As to immediate peace results, it is unnecessary to say that they afford a universal sense of relief. I am not undertaking to pass upon the merits of the differences to which the Four-Power Pact signed at Munich on yesterday related. It is hoped that in any event the forces which stand for the principles governing peaceful and orderly international relations and their proper application should not relax, but redouble, their efforts to maintain these principles of order under law, resting on a sound economic foundation." (117)

A month after the Munich crisis, which had brought Europe closer to a general war than it had been since the guns were stilled in November 1918, Secretary of State Hull made another urgent appeal for a return to the ways of peace. In an address on November 1, 1938 the Secretary warned that the world was at a crossroads but that its power of choice was not lost. One of the roads ahead, he said, was that of increased reliance on armed force as an instrument of national policy, which meant the sacrifice of individual well-being, a regimentation of national life, and a lowering of material, cultural, and spiritual standards. If the nations continued along this road, he declared, they would be marching toward the final catastrophe of a new world war, "the horror and destructiveness of which pass human imagination". The other road, he said, was that of reliance on peaceful processes and the rule of law and order in personal and international relations, with the result that vast productive forces would be released for the advancement of mankind and the human mind enabled to turn once more to the arts of peace.

In this address Secretary Hull expressed his conviction that without economic security and well-being there could be no social or political stability in national life, and that without economic, social, and political stability within nations there could be no peaceful and orderly relations among nations. He declared that the withdrawal by a nation from orderly trade relations with the rest of the world inevitably leads to regimentation of all phases of national life, to the suppression of human rights, and frequently to preparation for war and a provocative attitude toward other nations. (119)

Return of United States Ambassador From Germany

During the autumn of 1938 German persecution of the Jews, which had been severe for some time, became increasingly violent and profoundly shocked the people of the United States. On November 15 President Roosevelt stated that he could "scarcely believe that such things could occur in a twentieth-century civilization". As an expression of the condemnation by the people and Government of the United States, the President ordered Ambassador Hugh Wilson to return from Germany at once. (120)

Lima Conference

With wars and rumors of wars in Europe and Asia, the American republics, at peace with the world, continued their efforts to advance the principles of international law and order and to protect themselves from dangers outside the Western Hemisphere. They had taken definite steps in this direction at Montevideo in 1933 and at Buenos Aires in 1936. They assembled again in December 1938 at Lima.

At the Lima conference the 21 American republics agreed upon a "Declaration of the Solidarity of America", which stated in effect: They reaffirmed their continental solidarity and their purpose to collaborate in the maintenance of its underlying principles; faithful to these principles and to their absolute sovereignty, they reaffirmed their decision to maintain and defend them against all foreign intervention or activity that might threaten; they proclaimed their common concern and their determination to make effective their solidarity in case the peace, security, or territorial integrity of any American republic should be threatened; and in order to facilitate consultation, the Foreign Ministers of the American republics agreed to meet whenever it was deemed desirable. (121)

The 21 republics also issued a "Declaration of American Principles" calling for pacific settlement of international differences, proscription of force as an instrument of national or international policy, proscription of intervention; respect for treaties and international law, peaceful collaboration and intellectual interchange among nations, economic reconstruction, and international cooperation. (122)

⇢⟩⟩ IX ⟨⟨⇠

EUROPEAN WAR 1939

United States Rearmament

IN HIS ANNUAL message to Congress on January 4, 1939, President Roosevelt declared that while a threatened war had been averted, it had become increasingly clear that peace was not assured; that throughout the world there were undeclared wars, military and economic, and threats of new aggression, military and economic. The President said that storms from abroad directly challenged three institutions indispensable to Americans: religion, democracy, and international good faith. He warned of what might happen to the United States if new philosophies of force were to encompass the other continents and invade our own; and that we could not afford "to be surrounded by the enemies of our faith and our humanity".

The President declared that the world had grown so small and weapons of attack so swift that no nation could be safe so long as any single powerful nation refused to settle its grievances at the council table. He said that acts of aggression must not be allowed to pass without effective protest; that there were "many methods short of war, but stronger and more effective than mere words" of bringing home to aggressor governments the sentiments of our people. He spoke critically of neutrality legislation that might actually give aid to the aggressor and deny it to the victim. (124)

Eight days later the President, in a special message to Congress, called for immediate steps to strengthen the defense of the United States. He asked Congress to appropriate, "with as great speed as possible", more than half a billion dollars for Army and Navy equipment, particularly for military and naval aircraft. These planes, he said, would considerably strengthen the air defense of continental United States, Alaska, Hawaii, Puerto Rico, and the Canal Zone. The President likewise recommended the training of additional air pilots and urged that steps be taken to prepare industry for quantity production of war materials. These recommendations, which the President characterized as "a minimum program for the necessities of defense", were substantially enacted into law. (125)

For several years agencies of this Government had been studying the problem of the acquisition of stock-piles of strategic and critical materials not produced in the United States or produced here in quantities below national requirements. These stock-piles were to be for use in case of national emergency.

Secretary of State Hull discussed the problem in a letter of October 21, 1938 to the President. He said that events of the past few weeks had shown clearly the wisdom of adequate handling of the problem of strategic raw materials "with all possible despatch"; that these events indicated how disturbed sources of supply would be in any general war; and that there were insufficient supplies in the United States of a number of raw materials which would be of great strategic importance in the event of a general war, whether or not the United States were involved. The Secretary said further that the Department of State concurred in the view of the War and Navy Departments that it was "highly desirable to adopt a national policy with respect to this problem and to secure early and effective action by Congress"; that it was felt that there should be no further delay in initiating steps which would make available adequate supplies of the materials which were of the most critical importance. (118)

The President approved the recommendation, and there was later enacted, on June 7, 1939, legislation stating that it was the policy of Congress to provide for the acquisition of stocks of "certain strategic and critical materials being deficient or insufficiently developed to supply the industrial, military, and naval needs of the country for common defense . . . in times of national emergency". This legislation authorized the appropriation of $100,000,000, which was gradually appropriated for the purpose.

One hundred thousand tons of rubber were brought into this country as a result of an agreement between the United States and Great Britain, dated June 23, 1939, providing for the delivery by the United States of cotton in return for rubber.

Invasion of Czechoslovakia and Albania

In Europe the uneasy calm that had followed the Munich settlement was soon to be broken. A few days before the signing of the Munich Pact Hitler had promised that once the Sudetenland problem was solved Germany had no more territorial claims in Europe; at the time of the Munich settlement he had said that he was ready to guarantee the new frontiers of Czechoslovakia.

In flagrant disregard of these pledges, German troops invaded and occupied Czechoslovakia on March 14, 1939, thus completing the absorption of that country. Acting Secretary of State Welles, on

March 17, condemned this "temporary extinguishment of the liberties of a free and independent people" and declared that world peace and the very structure of modern civilization were being threatened by acts of "wanton lawlessness and of arbitrary force". (126)

Within a month after Hitler's invasion of Czechoslovakia the forces of aggression struck again. In emulation of the ruthless tactics of his German partner, Mussolini, on Good Friday, April 7, 1939, sent his Fascist legions into Albania and after a few days of military and political maneuvering established Italian control over that country. This "forcible and violent invasion" was condemned by Secretary Hull as a threat to world peace. (127)

These two blows at the world peace structure awoke Europe to a full sense of the danger which threatened it. They were followed by feverish diplomatic and military activity. Great Britain and France pledged assistance to Poland, Greece, and Rumania in the event that the independence of those nations should be threatened by aggression. Diplomatic interchanges began among Great Britain, France, and Russia, with a view to establishing a common front against further aggression.

President Roosevelt's Appeal to Hitler and Mussolini

At this point President Roosevelt addressed personal messages to Hitler and Mussolini in an appeal for the maintenance of peace. The President reminded the European dictators, in messages of April 14, 1939, that hundreds of millions of people throughout the world were living in constant fear of a new war or series of wars; that in such an event all the world—victors, vanquished, and neutrals—would suffer. He said that he could not believe that the world was, of necessity, such a "prisoner of destiny"; he believed, on the contrary, that the leaders themselves had the power to liberate their peoples from the impending disaster.

Accordingly the President asked the dictators if they were willing to give assurances that their armed forces would not attack or invade any of the independent nations of Europe and the Near East. If such assurances were forthcoming, the President said, two important problems would promptly be discussed in peaceful surroundings, and in the discussions the United States would take part. These problems were relief from the crushing burden of armaments and the opening up of international trade on terms of equality for all nations.

The President said that "heads of great governments in this hour are literally responsible for the fate of humanity in the coming years"; that "history will hold them accountable for the lives and the happiness of all". (128)

Neither Hitler nor Mussolini replied directly to President Roosevelt. However, in an address, Hitler said that Germany's neighbors knew that Germany had no aggressive intentions against them; that all states bordering on Germany had received much more binding assurances than those requested by the President.

In an address of April 25, 1939 Secretary of State Hull made a strong plea against resort to war for settling international differences. He declared that there could be no controversy between nations impossible of settlement by the peaceful processes of friendly adjustment. The Secretary said that the world contained ample resources to enable all nations to enjoy economic prosperity and spiritual advancement; that no single nation held a monopoly of material resources, nor was any nation excluded from participation in the means of advancement of mankind unless it excluded itself by adopting a policy of isolation or of armed aggrandizement. Furthermore, no nation could prosper without access to the resources of the entire world, but such access was possible only on the basis of peaceful international cooperation.

Secretary Hull said that he could not believe that any nation had entered irrevocably upon the road to war; that the road to peaceful adjustment still lay open, and he hoped that "at the present fateful juncture of history, all nations will decide to enter upon this road". Yet so long as some nations continued to arm for conquest, all other nations were confronted with the "tragic alternatives of surrender or armed defense". He said that the United States hoped for a fair negotiated peace before rather than after the "senseless arbitrament of war"; that the United States was prepared to make its contribution to world peace. However, if our hopes were doomed to disappointment we were equally prepared to defend successfully our national interests and our cherished institutions. He said that, terrible as are the realities and consequences of war, "sooner or later conditions arise in which peaceful and peace-loving nations prefer armed defense to subjection and slavery". (129)

Neutrality Legislation

It has been mentioned that President Roosevelt in his address to Congress on January 4, 1939 criticized neutrality legislation which might actually give aid to the aggressor and deny it to the victim. This neutrality legislation, enacted in 1935 and amended in 1936 and 1937, contained as its principal feature a rigid embargo on the export of arms to belligerents. (83)

By 1939 it was clear that the arms-embargo provision was exerting an injurious effect on the world peace structure. Germany, which had been furiously arming since the Nazis came to power in 1933, had become the strongest military power in Europe. Great Britain, France, and other states which feared they were to be the next objects of Nazi aggression were rearming swiftly, but their late start handicapped them in attempting to overtake a heavily armed Germany. Accordingly, they turned to the arms industry in the United States as a source of supply, especially for aircraft in which German numerical superiority was particularly marked. With the arms-embargo provision of the Neutrality Act on the statute books this source of supply would be cut off as soon as war should break out. The advantages accruing to Germany from this arms-embargo legislation were thus clear.

In a letter of May 27, 1939 to the appropriate committees of Congress, Secretary Hull urged removal of the arms embargo, and at the same time suggested other provisions to prevent the loss of American lives and American property by belligerent action. The Committee on Foreign Affairs of the House of Representatives reported out a bill substantially in line with the program outlined in this letter. However, in the House of Representatives an arms-embargo provision was inserted in the bill, which passed the House on June 30. On the following day Secretary Hull urged again the adoption of the proposal of May 27, which he considered not only best calculated to keep the United States out of war in the event that war came, but also, "what is all important at this time, best calculated to make a far greater contribution than could the present law or its equivalent toward the discouragement of the outbreak of war". (130, 131)

The Senate Committee on Foreign Relations, on July 11, 1939, decided by a close vote to defer action on neutrality legislation until the next session of Congress. Three days later, President Roosevelt strongly recommended to Congress that in the light of world conditions it was highly advisable that Congress should enact the neutrality legislation without delay. With the President's message to Congress there was transmitted a statement by Secretary Hull urging enactment of the program proposed on May 27. The Secretary said further that peace was so precious and war so devastating that the people of the United States and their Government must not fail to make a just and legitimate contribution to the preservation of peace. In the grave conditions then existing in the world, Secretary Hull believed that the first great step toward keeping the United States out of war was to use our influence so as to make a major war less likely.

The Secretary made clear that those who supported the elimination of the arms embargo were convinced that the embargo played into the hands of the nations which had taken the lead in building up their fighting power. The arms embargo worked directly against the interests of the peace-loving nations, the Secretary said, especially those which did not possess their own munitions plants. It meant, he said, that if any country was disposed toward conquest and devoted its energies and resources to establish itself as a superior fighting power, that country might be more tempted to try the fortunes of war if it knew that less well-prepared opponents would be shut off from supplies. (133)

On July 18 a statement was issued by President Roosevelt and Secretary Hull that failure to take action "would weaken the leadership of the United States in exercising its potent influence in the cause of preserving peace among other nations in the event of a new crisis in Europe between now and next January". No further action, however, was taken on neutrality legislation by Congress at that session. (134)

August Crisis

Meanwhile the crisis in Europe was growing more and more acute. In April 1939 Hitler had followed up his absorption of Czechoslovakia with demands on Poland for the return of Danzig and for concessions in the Polish Corridor. Despite a clear warning from Great Britain and France that aggression against Poland meant war, Hitler exercised strong diplomatic pressure on Poland and undertook military concentrations near the Polish frontier. It was clear that he was bent on securing his demands by force if necessary, even though a world war might result.

On August 21, 1939 the situation was rendered even more critical by the announcement in Berlin that Germany and Russia had agreed to sign a non-aggression treaty. President Roosevelt at this juncture again launched an appeal to the European states to keep the peace. He sent a personal message to the King of Italy on August 23, referring to his suggestion of April 14 for an understanding that no armed forces should attack or invade the territory of any other independent nation, and that this being assured, discussions be undertaken to effect progressive relief from the burden of armaments and to open avenues of international trade. President Roosevelt said that if it were possible for the Italian Government to formulate proposals for a pacific solution of the existing crisis along these lines, the earnest sympathy of the United States would be assured. The President concluded his appeal with the statement that the Government of Italy and the Government of the United States could advance the ideals of Christianity; that the "unheard voices of countless millions of human beings ask that they shall not be vainly sacrificed again". (136)

On the following day the President appealed directly to Hitler and to the President of Poland. He asked that the Governments of Germany and Poland agree to settle their controversy either by direct negotiation, by arbitration, or by conciliation through a third party. He also asked that each refrain from any positive act of hostility against the other. In his message to Hitler the President declared that the American people were as one in their opposition to military conquest and domination and in rejecting the thesis that any ruler or any people had the right to achieve their objectives by plunging countless millions into war when such objectives, so far as they were just and reasonable, could be satisfied through processes of peaceful negotiation. (137, 138)

Poland replied immediately and favorably to the President's message, and on August 25 President Roosevelt sent a second message to Hitler conveying to him the Polish reply. The President pointed out that Poland was willing to solve its controversy with Germany by direct negotiation or by conciliation. He declared to Hitler that "countless human lives can be yet saved and hope may still be restored that the nations of the modern world may even now construct a foundation for a peaceful and a happier relationship if you and the Government of the German Reich will agree to the pacific means of settlement accepted by the Government of Poland". (139)

The only official German reply to the President's messages was a note from the German Embassy delivered at the Department of State on the afternoon of September 1, after the German invasion of Poland had already begun. The note stated that Chancelor Hitler had left nothing untried for a friendly settlement but that owing to the attitude of the Polish Government all these endeavors were without result. (141)

War

In the face of Hitler's determination to proceed with his plan of conquest all efforts at peace failed. On the early morning of September 1, 1939 Hitler sent his military forces into Poland. Two days later France and Great Britain, in compliance with their obligations to Poland, declared war on Germany. The Nazi aggressors had at last brought Europe into a new and terrible armed conflict.

On the evening of September 3, 1939 President Roosevelt delivered a radio address in which he outlined the position of the United States with respect to the European war. He pointed out that the unfortunate events of recent years had been based on force or threat of force, and said that America should seek for humanity a final peace which would eliminate so far as possible the use of force between nations. He warned that although it was easy for us to say that conflicts taking place thousands of miles from the Western Hemisphere did not seriously affect the Americas, we were forced to realize that every word that came through the air, every ship that sailed the sea, every battle fought, did affect the future of America. The President said that the safety of the United States was bound up with the safety of the Western Hemisphere and the adjacent seas; that we must keep war from our firesides by keeping war from coming to the Americas. The President said that this nation would remain a neutral nation, but he could not ask that every American remain neutral in thought as well. He said that even a neutral had a right to take account of facts; that even a neutral could not be asked "to close his mind or his conscience". In conclusion, the President said that so long as it remained within his power to prevent it, there would be "no blackout of peace in the United States". (142)

The President took steps at once to prepare the Nation to meet the shock of war. On September 5 he proclaimed the neutrality of the United States and, in accordance with the provisions of the Neutrality Act, placed an embargo on the shipment of arms to the belligerents. A few days later he proclaimed a limited national emergency and issued orders for increasing the Army, the Navy, and the Marine Corps.

The President summoned Congress to convene in extra session on September 21. In an address to the Congress he recommended that the arms embargo be repealed and that our citizens and our ships be kept out of dangerous areas in order to prevent controversies that might involve the United States in war. Public opinion in the United States rallied in support of this program. After a few weeks of debate there was enacted into law on November 4 substantially the program of May 27, with the addition of provisions prohibiting the arming of United States merchant vessels engaged in foreign trade and prohibiting such vessels from carrying cargoes to belligerent ports. With the repeal of the arms embargo, large shipments of aircraft and other implements of war, much of which had been ordered by Great Britain and France before the outbreak of war, could be shipped to Europe for use in defense against Nazi aggression. (143, 145)

Panamá Conference

In accordance with agreements reached at the Buenos Aires and Lima Conferences which provided for consultation in the event of a menace to the peace of the Americas, the Foreign Ministers of the American republics met at Panamá following the outbreak of war in Europe in September 1939. This meeting was held in order that the American states might consult together regarding measures to preserve their neutrality, to protect so far as possible their economic and commercial interests from dislocation arising from the war, and to keep war away from the American Continent.

Under Secretary of State Welles, who represented the United States at the meeting, declared in an address on September 25, 1939 that the war in Europe constituted "a potential menace to the wellbeing, to the security, and to the peace of the New World". He said that however much the American republics might desire to insulate themselves from the war's effects, such insulation could be only relative; that there was an overwhelming will on the part of peoples everywhere for peace based on renunciation of force, on justice, and on equality; and that the expression of that will might well be facilitated by the action of the American republics. (144)

The Panamá meeting demonstrated in a moment of grave emergency the strong understanding and solidarity among the American republics. Steps taken at the meeting included the establishment of an Inter-American Financial and Economic Advisory Committee to study and recommend measures to cushion the shock of war on the inter-American economy; a declaration setting forth uniform standards of neutral conduct; and the Declaration of Panamá, in which the waters adjacent to the American Continent were declared "of inherent right" to be free from the commission of hostile acts by non-American belligerent nations.

➤➤➤ X ⋘⋘

EUROPEAN WAR 1940

President Roosevelt's Address to Congress January 3

IN HIS ADDRESS to Congress on January 3, 1940, President Roosevelt
recalled his repeated warnings that the daily lives of citizens of the
United States would, of necessity, feel the shock of events on other
continents. He said that the overwhelming majority of our people
continued in their hope and expectation that this country would not
become involved in military participation in the war. There was a
vast difference, however, between keeping out of war and "pretending
that this war is none of our business". The President said that the
future world would be "a shabby and dangerous place to live in" if
it were ruled by force in the hands of a few. He declared that we
must look ahead and see the possibilities for our children if the rest
of the world should come to be dominated by concentrated force
alone; if a large part of the world were forbidden to worship God and
were "deprived of the truth which makes men free"; if world trade
were controlled by any nation or group of nations which set up that
control through military force.

President Roosevelt declared further that while other peoples had
the right to choose their own form of government the people of the
United States believed that such choice "should be predicated on certain freedoms which we think are essential everywhere"; that we
knew that we ourselves would never be wholly safe at home unless
other governments recognized these freedoms. (146)

Visit of Under Secretary Welles to Europe

After the German armies had crushed military resistance in Poland
in September 1939, the European war entered into a period of comparative inactivity as the opposing forces maintained positions behind
their respective fixed fortifications. This inactivity continued during
the winter of 1939–40.

The United States Government took advantage of this period to
endeavor to ascertain whether there was any possibility whatever at
that time for the establishment of a just and lasting peace in Europe.
On February 9, 1940 the White House announced that Under Secretary of State Welles would proceed to Europe for the purpose of
reporting to the President and the Secretary of State on conditions
there; that he would visit Italy, France, Germany, and Great Britain

71

but would not be authorized to make any proposals or commitments in the name of the Government. Mr. Welles arrived in Europe at the end of February and during the following three weeks conferred with the heads of governments as well as with other prominent statesmen in the four countries.

On March 29, following the return of Mr. Welles to the United States, President Roosevelt said that "even though there may be scant immediate prospect for the establishment of any just, stable and lasting peace in Europe", the information obtained by Mr. Welles would be of great value to this Government in the general conduct of its foreign relations as well as in a future peace settlement. (147)

German Invasion of Denmark and Norway

The military inactivity of the winter of 1939–40 came to an abrupt end when on April 9, 1940 German troops invaded Denmark, without opposition, and Norway, where their invasion was contested. On April 13 President Roosevelt denounced this latest instance of German aggression. He emphasized this Government's disapprobation of such "unlawful exercise of force". If civilization was to survive, he said, the rights of smaller nations to independence, to their territorial integrity, and to their unimpeded opportunity for self-government must be respected by their more powerful neighbors. (148)

The British and French Governments immediately sent military forces to Norway to assist the Norwegians against the German invasion. Despite this, the better-prepared German armies pushed the allies back, and in a few weeks Germany was in military control of Norway.

Efforts To Keep Italy out of the War

At the beginning of the war in Europe, Italy, although a military ally of Germany, had announced that it would not take part in the war. During the following spring, however, there were indications that Italy might soon become a participant. President Roosevelt therefore decided to appeal to Mussolini to prevent the war from spreading further. On April 29, 1940 he sent a message to Mussolini stating that a further extension of the area of hostilities would necessarily have far-reaching and unforeseeable consequences not only in Europe, but also in the Near East and the Far East, in Africa, and in the three Americas. The President said that no one could predict with assurance, should such a further extension take place, what the ultimate result might be, or foretell what nations might eventually find it imperative to enter the war in their own defense. The President said further that because of the geographic position of the United States we had a panoramic view of the existing hostilities in Europe; that he saw no reason to anticipate that any one nation, or any one combination of nations, could successfully undertake to dominate either the continent of Europe or much less a greater part of the world. The President concluded his appeal with an expression of the hope that the powerful influence of Italy and of the United States might yet be exercised, when the appropriate opportunity was presented, "in behalf of the negotiation of a just and stable peace which will permit of the reconstruction of a gravely stricken world". (151)

The United States Ambassador to Italy, William Phillips, read the President's message to Mussolini during a conversation on May 1. Mussolini replied orally to the following effect: Peace in Europe could not be considered without a recognition of the conditions which had come about as a consequence of the war; Germany could not be beaten; Poland had been defeated by Germany and the latter would permit the creation of a new independent Polish state; Germany was also willing that a new Czechoslovak state be reestablished; he hoped that the necessity of a "new geography" would be foreseen by the President; a new map of Europe must come into being. Mussolini went on to say that the political problem which then made a peaceful Europe impossible must be liquidated; that this must be done before the economic problems could be disposed of. He also referred generally to Italy's aspirations in a reconstituted Europe and said that Italy's position as a "prisoner within the Mediterranean" was intolerable. (152)

A direct reply from Mussolini to the President was delivered to the latter by the Italian Ambassador on the following day. The reply was to the effect that the non-belligerency of Italy had effectively assured peace for 200,000,000 people; that Germany and Italy were opposed to a further extension of the conflict; that no peace was possible unless the fundamental problems of Italian liberty were solved; that as for repercussions which extension of the war would have on the three Americas, Italy had never concerned herself with the relations of the other American republics among themselves or with the United States and expected "reciprocity" so far as European affairs were concerned; and that when conditions permitted, and always based upon recognition of accomplished facts, Italy was ready to contribute toward a better world order. (153)

President Roosevelt sent another message to Mussolini, shortly after Belgium and the Netherlands were invaded by Germany, mentioning reports that Mussolini contemplated early entrance into the war. In this message of May 14, 1940 the President appealed to Mussolini to "stay wholly apart from any war". He said that the forces of slaughter, forces which denied God, forces which sought to dominate mankind by fear rather than by reason seemed to be extending their conquest against 100,000,000 human beings who had no desire but peace. He reminded Mussolini that the latter had it in his hands to stay the spread of the war to another group of 200,000,000 people. The President said that if this war should extend throughout the world it would pass beyond the control of the heads of states and would encompass the "destruction of millions of lives and the best of what we call the liberty and culture of civilization". (155)

Mussolini replied on May 18 that "Italy is and intends to remain allied with Germany", and that "Italy cannot remain absent at a moment in which the fate of Europe is at stake". (158)

On May 26 President Roosevelt in a third message to Mussolini referred to the Italian desire to obtain readjustments with regard to Italy's position and said that if Mussolini were willing to inform the President of the specific desires of Italy in this regard, he would communicate them to Great Britain and France. This would be done with the understanding that if an agreement were arrived at it would involve an assurance to the President by the French and British Governments that the agreement would be faithfully executed at the end of the war and that those Governments would welcome Italian participation at any eventual peace conference with a status equal to that of the belligerents; Mussolini would in a similar fashion assure the President that the claims of Italy would be satisfied by the execution of this agreement and that the agreement so reached would avoid the possibility of Italy's entering the war. (159)

Ambassador Phillips was not permitted to deliver this message to Mussolini in person. The Ambassador discussed it with the Italian Foreign Minister who, with the approval of Mussolini, said that Italy could not accept the President's proposal; that Mussolini was resolved to fulfil his obligations under the alliance with Germany; that Mussolini desired to keep his freedom of action and was not disposed to engage in any negotiations which "would not be in accordance with the spirit of Fascism"; and that "any attempt to prevent

Italy from fulfilling her engagements is not well regarded". The Foreign Minister informed Ambassador Phillips that Italy would enter the war "soon". (160)

On May 30 President Roosevelt sent still another appeal to Mussolini. He warned the Italian dictator that if the war in Europe should be extended through the entrance of Italy, direct interests of the United States would be immediately and prejudicially affected. He reminded Mussolini of the historic and traditional interests of the United States in the Mediterranean. He said that this Government had never asserted any political interests in Europe, but had asserted its clearly defined economic interests; that through the extension of the war to the Mediterranean region the legitimate interests of the people of the United States would be gravely curtailed; and that such a possibility "cannot be viewed with equanimity". The President declared that the further extension of the war as the result of Italian participation would at once result in an increase in the rearmament program of the United States and in a redoubling of the efforts of the Government of the United States to facilitate in every practical way the securing within the United States by the allied powers of all the supplies which they might require. In conclusion, he spoke of his desire to promote profitable commercial relations between the United States and Italy, as well as a friendly understanding of their respective policies and interests. (161)

Mussolini replied to the President on June 1 through his Foreign Minister. Mussolini confirmed the Foreign Minister's statement that the decision to enter the war had already been taken. He said it was "of no concern to him" that the entry of Italy into the war would mean the redoubling of American efforts to help the allies. Finally, he said he preferred not to receive any "further pressure" from the President; this would only "stiffen his attitude". (164)

German Invasion of the Low Countries

Meanwhile on May 10, 1940, despite repeated statements by Hitler that he would not violate the neutrality of Belgium, Luxembourg, and the Netherlands, those three countries were treacherously attacked. On the same day President Roosevelt said, in an address at Washington to the Pan American Scientific Congress, that "we are shocked and angered" by this tragic news. He declared that we had come to the reluctant conclusion that a continuance of these processes of armed force presented a definite challenge to the type of civilization to which all in the three Americas had been accustomed. He said it was a mistaken idea that the American republics were wholly safe—physically, economically, and socially—from the impact of the attacks on civilization in other parts of the world. (154)

The British and French immediately sent troops to the assistance of Belgium and the Netherlands. Nevertheless, with overwhelming superiority in aviation and tanks, the Germans quickly overpowered the Belgian and Netherlands armies. The British and French troops who had gone to their assistance had no alternatives but retreat or surrender, and in the last week of May began the heroic withdrawal from Dunkirk which left Hitler in complete mastery of the Low Countries.

The German armies then turned to drive against Paris. With superiority in weapons the Nazis relentlessly pushed their attacks until on June 10 they were almost at the gates of Paris. On that day Italy declared war against France and Great Britain.

United States Aid to Opponents of Force

President Roosevelt in an address of June 10, 1940 at Charlottesville, Virginia, declared that we as a nation—and likewise all the other American nations—were convinced that "military and naval victory for the gods of force and hate would endanger the institutions of democracy in the western world" and that all of our sympathies were with those nations that were giving their lifeblood in combat against these forces. He stated that two obvious and simultaneous courses would be followed: "We will extend to the opponents of force the material resources of this nation and, at the same time, we will harness and speed up the use of those resources in order that we ourselves in the Americas may have equipment and training equal to the task of any emergency and every defense."

The President stated in this address that Italy had now chosen to fulfil its promises to Germany; that in so doing it had manifested disregard for the rights and security of other nations and had evidenced its unwillingness to find peaceful means for satisfaction of what it believed to be its legitimate aspirations; that "the hand that held the dagger has struck it into the back of its neighbor". (165)

In line with the policy of extending aid to the opponents of force, the Government of the United States took immediate steps to send to the British and French large quantities of aircraft, rifles, field artillery, machine-guns, and ammunition.

French Appeal to the United States

On June 10, 1940 the French Premier, Paul Reynaud, made a direct appeal to the President for increased aid, at the same time expressing gratitude for the decision of the United States to send assistance in aviation and arms. The Premier said that the French would fight in front of Paris; would fight behind Paris; would close themselves in one of their provinces to fight and if driven out of it would establish themselves in North Africa to continue the fight, and if necessary, in French possessions in America. He urgently requested the President to declare publicly that the United States would give the allies aid and material support by all means "short of an expeditionary force". (166)

President Roosevelt replied on June 13 that the Government of the United States was doing everything in its power to make available to the allied governments the material they urgently required and that our efforts to do still more were being redoubled; we were doing this because of our faith in and our support of the ideals for which the allies were fighting. The President said he was particularly impressed by the Premier's declaration that France would continue to fight on behalf of democracy, although it meant slow withdrawal, even to North Africa and across the Atlantic. He said it was important to remember that the French and British Fleets continued to have mastery of the Atlantic and other oceans and that vital materials from the outside world were necessary to maintain all armies. (167)

The French Premier sent another message to the President on June 14, 1940, the day on which German troops entered Paris. The Premier said that "at the most tragic hour" of its history France must choose whether to continue resistance or ask for an armistice. He warned that the defeat of Great Britain appeared possible if not probable. The Premier said that the only chance of saving France, and through her to save Great Britain, was to throw into the balance "this very day the weight of American power". Finally, the Premier said that if the President could not give to France in the hours to come the certainty that the United States would enter the war within a very short time, "the fate of the world will change". "Then," he said, "you will see France go under like a drowning man and disappear after having cast a last look towards the land of liberty from which she awaited salvation." (168)

President Roosevelt replied on the following day. He repeated emphatically that the Government of the United States had made it possible for the allied armies to obtain, during the weeks that had just passed, airplanes, artillery, and munitions of many kinds, and that so long as the allied governments continued to resist, this Government would redouble its efforts in that direction. He believed it was possible to say that every passing week would see additional war supplies on the way to the allied nations. The President said that in accordance with our policy not to recognize the results of conquests of territory acquired through military aggression, the United States would not consider as valid any attempts to infringe by force the independence and territorial integrity of France.

President Roosevelt assured the Premier that so long as the French people continued a defense of their liberty, so long would they rest assured that war supplies would be sent to them from the United States in ever-increasing quantities and kinds. He said, however, that these statements did not carry any implication of military commitments, that only Congress could make such commitments. (169)

Fall of France

On June 17 the French Cabinet, headed by the new Premier, Marshal Pétain, asked for the terms of an armistice with Germany.

On that day President Roosevelt sent a message to the French Government regarding the disposition of the French Fleet. He said that should the French Government, before concluding an armistice with the Germans, fail to see that the Fleet was kept out of the hands of France's opponents, the French Government would be pursuing a policy which would fatally impair the preservation of the French Empire and the eventual restoration of French independence. Furthermore, the President said, should the French Government fail to take steps to prevent the French Fleet from being surrendered to Germany, "the French Government will permanently lose the friendship and good-will of the Government of the United States". (170)

On the following day, June 18, the United States Government received from the French Government a categorical assurance that the French Fleet would "never be surrendered to the enemy". (171)

Monroe Doctrine

Immediately following the French request for the terms of an armistice with Germany, the Governments of Italy, Germany, France, Great Britain, and the Netherlands were informed by this Govern-

78

ment that in accordance with the traditional policy of the United States relating to the Western Hemisphere the United States would not recognize any transfer, and would not acquiesce in any attempt to transfer, any geographic region of the Western Hemisphere from one non-American power to another non-American power. (172)

In connection with this subject, Secretary Hull stated on July 5, 1940 that the "Monroe Doctrine is solely a policy of self-defense, which is intended to preserve the independence and integrity of the Americas". The Secretary said that its purpose was to prevent aggression in this hemisphere by any non-American power, and likewise to make impossible any further extension to this hemisphere of any non-American system of government imposed from without; that it contained within it "not the slightest vestige of any implication, much less assumption, of hegemony on the part of the United States". The Secretary said further that the Monroe Doctrine did not resemble policies which appeared to be arising in other parts of the world, which policies were alleged to be similar to the Monroe Doctrine, but which in reality seemed to be only "the pretext for the carrying out of conquest by the sword, of military occupation, and of complete economic and political domination by certain powers of other free and independent peoples". (175)

XI

DEFENSE MEASURES
OF THE UNITED STATES 1940

President Roosevelt's Request for 50,000 Planes

IN JANUARY 1940, when the European war was still in a period of lull, President Roosevelt asked Congress for a national defense appropriation of $1,800,000,000. By the middle of the following May, the rapid development of military events in Europe impelled him to request further appropriations for national defense. In an address to Congress on May 16, 1940, he said that the brutal force of modern offensive war had been loosed in all its horror; that new and swift and deadly powers of destruction had been developed which were wielded by men who were ruthless and daring; that no old defense was so strong that it required no further strengthening and no attack was so unlikely or impossible that it might be ignored. The President said that we had had before us over and over again the lesson that nations not ready and unable to get ready found themselves overrun by the enemy; that so-called impregnable fortifications no longer existed; that an effective defense required the equipment to attack an aggressor on his route "before he can establish strong bases within the territory of American vital interests".

The President said to Congress that he should like to see the United States "geared up to the ability to turn out at least 50,000 planes a year"; furthermore, he believed "that this Nation should plan at this time a program that would provide us with 50,000 military and naval planes". He made a request for $1,000,000,000 to procure the essential equipment for a larger and thoroughly rounded-out Army, to replace or modernize Army or Navy equipment, to increase production facilities for everything needed for the Army or Navy, and to speed up to a 24-hour basis all Army and Navy contracts. In making this request the President reminded Congress that our ideal and our objective still was peace. Nevertheless, we stood ready "not only to spend millions for defense but to give our service and even our lives for the maintenance of our American liberties". (156)

In a message to Congress on May 31 President Roosevelt made an additional request for appropriations of over a billion dollars for national defense and asked for authority to call the National Guard and the necessary Reserve personnel into active military service. He declared that "the almost incredible events of the past two weeks in the European conflict, particularly as a result of the use of aviation and mechanized equipment", necessitated further increases in our military program. No one could foretell the future, he said, but American defense must be made more certain so long as the possibility existed that not one or two continents but all continents might be involved in a world-wide war. He again emphasized the necessity for expansion of facilities for the production of munitions. (163)

These requests for appropriations were promptly met by the Congress, as also was the President's request of July 10 for $5,000,000,000 more for the rearmament program. The President's request for authority to call the National Guard and Reserve personnel into active military service was granted in a resolution approved August 27, 1940. However, the legislation provided that the personnel ordered into active Federal service under this authority should "not be employed beyond the limits of the Western Hemisphere except in the territories and possessions of the United States, including the Philippine Islands".

Secretary Hull's Address of June 20

Secretary of State Hull delivered an address on June 20, 1940, describing in unmistakable terms the existing danger to peaceful nations. He said that there were at work in the world forces which sprang from "godless and soulless lust for power which seeks to hold men in physical slavery and spiritual degradation and to displace a system of peaceful and orderly relations among nations by the anarchy of wanton violence and brute force". Never before, he said, had these forces flung so powerful a challenge to freedom and civilized progress; never before had there been a more desperate need for freedom-loving men and nations to gather into an unconquerable defensive force every element of their spiritual and material resources, every ounce of their moral and physical strength. The Secretary said that no more vital test had ever confronted the American people; that difficult and dangerous days were ahead; and that our national independence and cherished institutions were not immune from the challenge of the lust for power that already stalked so much of the earth's surface. We could successfully meet this challenge, he declared, if we retained unimpaired an unshakable faith in the everlasting worth of freedom and honor, of truth and justice, of intellectual and spiritual integrity, and an immutable determination to give our all, if necessary, for the preservation of our way of life. (173)

Habana Conference

The rapid developments in the European war during May and June 1940 resulted in increased danger to the peace, security, and welfare of the American Continent. In order to prepare to meet this danger the Foreign Ministers of the American republics assembled at Habana in July. There they consulted regarding measures with respect to three sets of problems: the possibility of the transfer of sovereignty of certain islands and regions in the Americas from one non-American state to another non-American state; the threat of subversive activities in the American nations directed from outside the continent; and the grave economic difficulties and dislocations resulting from the war.

At Habana there was formulated an arrangement for the provisional administration by an inter-American organization of any non-American possession in the Americas in case of a danger of change in its sovereignty. It was agreed that each of the 21 republics would take measures to prevent subversive activities directed from abroad against the internal life of the American republics and would exchange information regarding such activities. The Inter-American Financial and Economic Advisory Committee, which had been provided for at Panamá in 1939, was instructed to cooperate with each of the republics in the study of possible measures for increasing domestic consumption of its own exportable surpluses, to provide increased markets among the American nations for these surpluses, and to create instruments for the temporary storing, financing, and handling of any such commodities and for their orderly marketing.

At this meeting the representatives of the 21 American republics declared "that any attempt on the part of a non-American State against the integrity or inviolability of the territory, the sovereignty or the political independence of an American State shall be considered as an act of aggression against the States which sign this declaration". (177)

Shortly after the Conference, on August 6, 1940, Secretary Hull, who represented the United States, said it was strongly believed at Habana that "the military and other sinister activities on the part of some nations in other large areas of the world present real possibilities of danger to the American republics". He said it was universally recognized that a threat to any important part of the Americas meant a threat to each and all of the American nations; that it was therefore agreed that full and adequate preparations for continental defense could not be taken too soon. (178)

"We Cannot Pursue Complacently the Course of Our Customary Normal Life"

In his statement of August 6 Secretary Hull warned that vast forces of lawlessness, conquest, and destruction were moving across the earth "like a savage and dangerous animal at large" and that by their very nature those forces would not stop unless and until they recognized that there existed unbreakable resistance. He expressed the firm conviction that what was taking place in many areas of the earth was a relentless attempt to transform the civilized world into a world in which lawlessness, violence, and force would reign supreme as they did a thousand years ago.

The Secretary said that "the one and only sure way" for our nation to avoid being drawn into serious trouble or actual war and to command respect for its rights and interests abroad, was for our people to become thoroughly conscious of the possibilities of danger and "to make up their minds that we must continue to arm, and to arm to such an extent that the forces of conquest and ruin will not dare make an attack on us or on any part of this hemisphere". To this end, the Secretary stated, each citizen must be ready and willing for real sacrifice of time and of substance, and for hard personal service; in the face of terrific problems and conditions "we cannot pursue complacently the course of our customary normal life". (178)

Exchange of Destroyers for Bases

An important step for the defense of the Western Hemisphere was taken early in September 1940 when an agreement between the United States and Great Britain was concluded whereby Great Britain received fifty over-age United States destroyers, and the United States acquired the right to lease naval and air bases in Newfoundland, in British Guiana, and in the islands of Bermuda, the Bahamas, Jamaica, St. Lucia, Trinidad, and Antigua. President Roosevelt reported to Congress that this agreement was not in any way inconsistent with our status of peace; that it was not a threat against any nation; that it was "an epochal and far-reaching act of preparation for continental defense in the face of grave danger". The President said that the value to the Western Hemisphere "of these outposts of security is beyond calculation". He considered them essential to the protection of the Panama Canal, Central America, the northern portion of South America, the Antilles, Canada, Mexico, and our Eastern and Gulf seaboards. This Government later announced that the resulting facilities at these bases would be made available to all American republics for the common defense of the hemisphere. (179, 180)

During this month the United States took another important step for national defense. On September 16, 1940 was enacted the Selective Service and Training Act. For the first time in its history the United States adopted compulsory military training of manpower when the Nation was not at war. The act included a provision that persons inducted into the land forces should not be employed beyond the Western Hemisphere except in United States territories and possessions.

Treaty of Alliance Between Germany, Italy, and Japan

In 1934 and 1935 reports had reached this Government that Japan and Germany were contemplating or had consummated some sort of an agreement for joint action. In 1936 those powers had joined together publicly in the Anti-Comintern Pact. A year later Italy had become a party to this agreement. During the next three years it had become clear to the world that these three countries were pursuing a common pattern of aggression in both Europe and the Far East. On September 11, 1940, in a conversation with French Ambassador Henry-Haye, Secretary Hull declared that for several years the United States had pursued the fixed policy of basing all utterances and action on the assumption that "Hitler was out to become the ruthless and utterly destructive conqueror of Europe, and that the Japanese military clique was bent on the same course in the Pacific area from Hawaii to Siam". (181)

On September 27, 1940 Germany, Italy, and Japan signed a far-reaching treaty of alliance. In that treaty it was provided that Japan recognized and respected the leadership of Germany and Italy in the establishment of a new order in Europe; that Germany and Italy recognized and respected the leadership of Japan in the establishment of a new order in Greater East Asia; and that the three countries would assist one another with all political, economic, and military means when one of the powers was attacked by a power not then involved in the European war or in the Chinese-Japanese conflict. The last of these provisions obviously was aimed directly at the United States.

On the day the alliance was announced Secretary Hull said that its consummation did not substantially alter a situation which had existed for several years, that the agreement had been in process of conclusion

84

for some time, and that the announcement merely made clear to all a relationship which had long existed in effect. (184)

In a conversation on September 30 with the British Ambassador, Secretary Hull declared that the three-power alliance had come about primarily because of "Hitler's effort to divert attention from his failure to invade Great Britain and to preserve his prestige by a sensational announcement of something that already existed". The Secretary said it was certain that Japan would assume that, whether or not the United States and Great Britain had definite agreements in regard to naval and air bases in the Pacific including Singapore, the special relations between these two countries were such that they could overnight easily establish cooperative relations for the mutual use of all these bases. The relations among Germany, Italy, and Japan, each having a common objective of conquering certain areas of the world and each pursuing identical policies of force, devastation, and seizure, had been during recent years on the "basis of complete understanding and of mutual cooperation" for all practical purposes.

The Secretary emphasized to the Ambassador that the special desire of this Government was to see Great Britain succeed in the war and that its acts and utterances with respect to the Pacific area would be more or less affected by the question what course would most effectively and legitimately aid Great Britain in winning the war. (185)

Secretary Hull's Address of October 26

In an address of October 26, 1940 Secretary of State Hull warned that all peaceful nations were gravely menaced because of the plans and acts of a small group of national rulers who had succeeded in transforming their peoples into forceful instruments for wide-spread domination by conquest. The Secretary said that we were in the presence not of local or regional wars, but of an "organized and determined movement for steadily expanding conquest". The rulers of the aggressor nations, he said, had repudiated and violated in every essential respect the long-accepted principles of peaceful and orderly international relations; they adhered to no geographic lines, and they fixed no time-limit on their program of invasion and destruction; they cynically disregarded every right of neutral nations; they had as a fixed objective the securing of control of the high seas; they threatened peaceful nations with the direst consequences if these nations did not remain acquiescent while the conquerors were seizing the other continents and most of the seven seas. "Let no one comfort himself with the delusion that these are mere excesses or exigencies of war," the

Secretary continued, "to be voluntarily abandoned when fighting ceases."

The appalling tragedy of the world's situation, the Secretary said, lay in the fact that peacefully disposed nations had failed to recognize in time the true nature of the aims and ambitions which actuated the rulers of the heavily arming nations. Recoiling from the mere contemplation of the possibility of another wide-spread war, he said, the people of the peaceful nations had permitted themselves to be lulled into a false sense of security by the assurances made by these rulers that their aims were limited. The first need for all nations still masters of their own destiny was to create for themselves, as speedily and as completely as possible, "impregnable means of defense". This was the "staggering lesson of mankind's recent experience". As an important means of strengthening our own defense and of preventing attack on any part of the Western Hemisphere, the United States was affording all feasible facilities for the obtaining of supplies by nations which, while defending themselves against barbaric attack, were checking the spread of violence and thus reducing the danger to us. Under our "inalienable right of self-defense", he said, we intended to continue this to the greatest possible extent.

The Secretary admonished that nothing could be more dangerous for our nation "than for us to assume that the avalanche of conquest could under no circumstances reach any vital portion of this hemisphere". He stated that oceans gave the nations of this hemisphere no guaranty against the possibility of economic, political, or military attack from abroad; that oceans are barriers but they are also highways; that barriers of distance are merely barriers of time. Should the would-be conquerors gain control of other continents, the Secretary said, they would next concentrate on perfecting their control of the seas, of the air over the seas, and of the world's economy. They might then be able with ships and with planes to strike at the communication lines, the commerce, and the life of this hemisphere, and "ultimately we might fin 1 ourselves compelled to fight on our own soil, under our own skies, in defense of our independence and our very lives". (188)

President Roosevelt's "Arsenal of Democracy" Address

In an address of December 29, 1940 President Roosevelt stated that the Nazi masters of Germany had made it clear that they intended not only to dominate all life and thought in their own country but also to enslave the whole of Europe and then to use the resources of

Europe to dominate the rest of the world. The United States, he said, had no right or reason to encourage talk of peace until the day should come when there was a clear intention on the part of the aggressor nations to abandon all thought of dominating or conquering the world. Although some of our people liked to believe that wars in Europe and Asia were of no concern to us, the President said, it was a matter of most vital concern to us that European and Asiatic war-makers should not gain control of the oceans which lead to the Western Hemisphere. If Great Britain went down, the Axis powers would control the continents of Europe, Asia, Africa, and Australia, and the high seas, and would then be in a position to bring enormous military and naval resources against this hemisphere. It was no exaggeration to say that all of us in the Americas "would be living at the point of a gun—a gun loaded with explosive bullets, economic as well as military".

There was danger ahead, the President warned, danger against which we must prepare. We were planning our own defense with the utmost urgency, and in it we must "integrate the war needs of Britain and the other free nations resisting aggression". He had, he said, set up a more effective organization to direct our efforts to increase our production of munitions. American industrial genius, unmatched throughout the world in the solution of production problems, had been called upon to bring its resources and talents into action. Manufacturers of peacetime articles were now making instruments of war. But, he said, all our present efforts were not enough. We must have more ships, more guns, more planes; we must be the great "arsenal of democracy". (193)

XII

RELATIONS WITH JAPAN 1938–1940

Principles of United States Policy

IN OUR RELATIONS with Japan the United States Government sought constantly and consistently to protect this country's nationals and rights, and to uphold the principles of peaceful and orderly international conduct which Japan was violating by its attack on China. At the same time, in keeping with overwhelming public sentiment, this Government endeavored to prevent the development of a situation which would be likely to involve the United States in hostilities. It consistently protested against and declined to give assent to actions on the part of and situations brought about by Japanese authorities or agents in China in violation of treaties and international law and through the unwarranted use of force. While resolved not to compromise the principles of United States policy—much less abandon those principles—it sought to avoid closing the door to such chance as there might be, however small, for peaceful negotiation of differences and general pacific settlement.

Throughout this period the United States Government had under active consideration various ways and means which might be used to induce Japan to renounce its policies and programs of conquest and domination through the use of force or threat of force. Among other methods, this Government frequently had under consideration the question of applying economic pressure—advocated in many quarters as a means of checking Japanese aggression. It was the opinion of the responsible officials of the Government, including the highest military and naval authorities, that adoption and application of a policy of imposing embargoes upon strategic exports to Japan would be attended with serious risk of retaliatory action of a character likely to lead to this country's becoming involved in war. Practically all realistic authorities have been agreed that imposition of substantial economic sanctions or embargoes against any strong country, unless that imposition be backed by show of superior force, involves serious risk of war.

The President and the heads of the Army and the Navy and the Department of State were in constant consultation throughout this period in regard to all aspects of the military and diplomatic situation confronting the United States. They knew that Germany and Italy were arming in Europe, as Japan had armed in the Far East, preparatory to resorting to force to achieve objectives of expansion. They realized that, with the outbreak in 1939 of war in Europe, the fall in June 1940 of France, and the conclusion in September 1940 of the Tripartite Pact, danger of war in the western Pacific was progressively increasing. They realized also that Axis preparations were virtually complete and that this country and similarly minded countries were far behind parity with offsetting preparations. They were in agreement that prevailing public opinion in this country and, with the imminence of and finally the outbreak of war in Europe, the comparative military unpreparedness of this country were such as to render it inadvisable to risk, by resort to drastic economic measures against Japan, involvement in war. Even before the common objectives of Germany, Italy, and Japan were formalized in the Tripartite Pact, this Government had to consider that if the United States became involved in war there might easily arise the problem of defense in both oceans—and to meet that problem this country was not adequately prepared.

The foregoing were the principal considerations which determined this Government's course with regard to proposed use of economic pressures.

"Moral Embargoes"

Throughout this period there was wide-spread bombing of Chinese civilians by the Japanese. This practice aroused great indignation in the United States. It also adversely affected American nationals in China. The Secretary of State on June 11, 1938 condemned the practice and its "material encouragement". On July 1, 1938 the Department of State notified aircraft manufacturers and exporters that the United States Government was strongly opposed to the sale of airplanes and aeronautical equipment to countries whose armed forces were using airplanes for attack on civilian populations. In 1939 this "moral embargo" was extended to materials essential to airplane manufacture and to plans, plants, and technical information for the production of high-quality aviation gasoline. These measures resulted in the suspension of the export to Japan of aircraft, aeronautical equipment, and other materials within the scope of the moral embargoes. As Japanese purchases in the United States of "arms, ammunition, and implements of war", other than aircraft and aeronautical equipment, were relatively unimportant, these operated ultimately to stop the export of arms to Japan. (108, 109)

This Government also, beginning in 1938, adopted and put into effect a policy of informally discouraging the extension of credit by United States nationals to Japan.

United States Protest December 31, 1938

As the conflict between Japan and China developed, interferences with the rights and interests of the United States and its nationals by Japanese or Japanese-sponsored agents in China became more and more frequent. The Government of the United States on many occasions protested to the Japanese Government against these interferences. In a note presented December 31, 1938 the United States declared that these interferences were not only "unjust and unwarranted" but also "counter to the provisions of several binding international agreements, voluntarily entered into" to which the United States and Japan were parties. The note stated that the people and Government of the United States could not assent to the establishment of a regime "which would arbitrarily deprive them of the long-established rights of equal opportunity and fair treatment". In reply to Japan's claim that it was establishing a "new order based on genuine international justice throughout East Asia" it was stated that the United States did not admit there was warrant for any one power to prescribe the terms and conditions of a "new order" in areas not under its sovereignty. Finally the note declared that the United States could not assent to the abrogation of any of its rights and obligations by the arbitrary action of any other country, but was always ready to discuss proposals based on justice and reason for the resolving of problems by the processes of free negotiation and new commitment on the part of all parties directly concerned. (123)

Notice of Termination of Commercial Treaty With Japan

As evidence accumulated of the endangering of American lives, the destruction of American property, and the violation of American rights and interests by Japanese authorities or Japanese-sponsored agents in China, and after diplomatic representations had failed to effect a substantial alleviation of the situation, further consideration was given to the possibility of commercial retaliation against Japan. It was felt that the 1911 commercial treaty between the United States and Japan was not affording adequate protection to American commerce either in Japan or in Japanese-occupied portions of China, while at the same time the operation of the most-favored-nation clause of the treaty was a bar to the adoption of retaliatory measures against Japanese commerce. Consequently, in July 1939 this Government gave notice of termination of that treaty at the end of the six-month period prescribed by the treaty. That termination removed the legal obstacle to an embargo by the United States upon the shipment of materials to Japan. (135)

Secretary Hull's Conversations With the Japanese Ambassador

Secretary of State Hull in a conversation with the Japanese Ambassador on July 10, 1939 said that while the present interests and rights of the United States in the Far East were highly important, the serious question was whether all of China and the Pacific islands skirting it were to be "Manchurianized" by Japan, with international law destroyed and treaty observance abolished and all other nations excluded from that half of the world.

In connection with the Ambassador's suggestion for possible co-operation of the United States and Japan to compose the threatening dangers in Europe, the Secretary said that the single test of this Gov ernment in dealing with other governments was the question of peace, that we considered the preservation of peace so supremely important to the future of all nations that we drew the line between, on the one hand, honest, law-abiding, peaceful countries and peoples, without reference to their form of government, and on the other, those who were flaunting law and order and threatening military conquest without limit as to time or extent. He said that we would work in a friendly spirit with every peaceful nation to promote and preserve peace and that, while we had no alliances with any nation, we would keep thoroughly armed and prepared to take care of our interests and rights; that we had made every kind of plea to European countries for the peaceful settlement and adjustment of their relations and we had indicated our readiness to cooperate in every feasible plan to restore international trade and finance. Notwithstanding these earnest pleas, he said, nations could not but take notice that Japan herself was engaged in military operations for purposes of conquest; this situation might well now have an ending if Japan were to exercise its fullest influence along with the United States and other countries in efforts to stop threatening military conquest in other parts of the world.

The Japanese Ambassador made no particular comment on the Secretary's remarks except to state that there had been reports in the United States that Japan might enter into a military pact with Germany and Italy, whereas the truth was that Japan had no idea of doing so; that Japan, because of its proximity to and difficulties with Russia had been interested in the anti-Comintern policy of certain European states and in working with them against Bolshevism. (132)

A few weeks later, at a time when the outbreak of war in Europe was imminent, Secretary Hull again talked with the Japanese Ambassador. In this conversation, on August 26, 1939, five days after the announcement that Germany and Russia had agreed to sign a non-aggression treaty, the Ambassador said that his Government had decided to abandon any further negotiations with Germany and Italy relative to closer relations under the Anti-Comintern Pact. He said that the change in affairs in Europe made this course manifest.

The Secretary said that the United States had made representations over and over again in protest against Japanese actions which had conflicted with principles and policies of the United States. The Japanese Government had given assurances time after time that it would respect the principles involved, but over and over Japanese authorities had immediately committed other acts in disregard of them. The United States, the Secretary said, wished to have amicable relations with every other country in the world; our policy was a policy of "live and let live"; we sought nowhere any special position. The world was being given new object lessons in the futility of policies wherein nations planned to take advantage of other nations by the use of armed force in disregard of legal and moral principles and generally accepted axioms of friendly international intercourse. In conclusion, the Secretary said that the future of United States-Japanese relations was largely in the hands of Japan; that our permanent policy was one of friendliness and fair-dealing toward all nations. (140)

Status of Netherlands Indies

The outbreak of war in Europe in September 1939 naturally affected and complicated the situation in the Pacific. In April 1940 the Japanese Minister for Foreign Affairs made a statement expressing concern on the part of his Government for the maintenance of the *status quo* of the Netherlands Indies. On April 17 Secretary Hull stated that the Netherlands Indies were an important factor in the commerce of the whole world; that they produced considerable portions of the world's supplies of important commodities, such as rubber, quinine, and copra; that many countries, including the

United States, depended substantially upon them for these commodities. Intervention in the domestic affairs of the Netherlands Indies or any alteration of their *status quo* by other than peaceful processes would, the Secretary said, "be prejudicial to the cause of stability, peace, and security not only in the region of the Netherlands Indies but in the entire Pacific area". (149)

Three days later, in a conversation with the Japanese Ambassador, the Secretary stated that there was no more resemblance between our Monroe Doctrine and the so-called Monroe Doctrine of Japan than there was between black and white. Our Monroe Doctrine, he said, contemplated only steps for our physical safety, while Japan's doctrine was seemingly applicable to all other purposes and objectives including economic, political, and social objectives. (150)

In a conversation with the Japanese Ambassador on May 16, 1940, at the time when the German armies were smashing through Belgium and the Netherlands, the Secretary remarked that it appeared more and more evident that no country was safe from aggressive intervention by force in one way or another and that the only thing a nation could do was to "arm to the teeth" and be ready for any serious interference with its rights and interests by military force or threat of force. However, he continued, this Government was striving for peace year in and year out and our constant desire was to promote and preserve peace both with other countries and among other countries.

The Secretary then brought to the attention of the Ambassador a report from Tokyo which indicated that Japanese newspapers were emphasizing some supposed special interests of Japan in the Netherlands Indies. The Secretary said it seemed very surprising that Japan, after endeavoring to spread itself over the huge Republic of China, might not be content unless it extended itself to take in the great archipelago comprising the East Indies, presumably with a view to shutting out all equality of trade opportunities among nations. The Ambassador replied that his Government was satisfied with the Netherlands Indies situation and had no plans or purposes to proceed there. (157)

Instruction to Ambassador Grew

On May 30, 1940, in a telegram to Ambassador Grew in Japan, Secretary of State Hull reviewed the world situation in the light of recent developments in the European war. He said that the United States was going forward strenuously with plans and production which soon would greatly increase our military strength. Whatever the results of the European war, he said, the United States would probably in a relatively short time be more powerful militarily and better-organized in the economic field than it had been for many years. He was convinced that a general international deterioration could be checked only by determined and enlightened resistance by nations which desired that principles of law, order, justice, and national sovereignty should survive and principles of economic freedom prevail. He referred to reports that the Japanese were considering whether they would throw in their lot with Germany, which was committed to the use of force for purposes of conquest, or would give their support to the principles advocated by the United States and many other nations. He emphasized the necessity of making clear that the United States had not modified nor would it modify its opposition to policies of attempting to achieve international objectives by use of force, whether on the part of Japan or of any other nation. (162)

On June 28, 1940 the Secretary of State discussed the Far Eastern situation with the British Ambassador and the Australian Minister. In discussing possible steps to oppose Japanese aggression in the Far East, the Secretary declared that the United States had been exerting economic pressure on Japan for a year; that the United States Fleet was stationed in the Pacific; and that everything possible was being done "short of a serious risk of actual military hostilities" to keep the Japanese situation stabilized. This course, he added, was the best evidence of the intentions of the United States in the future. In regard to a possible settlement between Japan and China, he set forth two points; first, that for such a settlement the principles underlying Japanese policy would have to be negatived or at least seriously modified; second, that properties or interests of China must not be offered to Japan, or in other words that peace must not be made with Japan at the expense of China or of the principles of international policy to which the United States was committed. (174)

Temporary Closing of the Burma Road

In the middle of July 1940 reports became current that the British Government, at the instance of the Japanese Government, would prohibit temporarily the movement of certain commodities through Burma into China. On July 16, Secretary of State Hull, in reply to inquiries by press correspondents in regard to these reports, made comment that the United States Government had a "legitimate interest in the keeping open of arteries of commerce in every part of the world" and considered that action such as this, if taken, "would constitute unwarranted interpositions of obstacles to world trade". On July 18 the foreshadowed restrictions were, under the provisions of a British-Japanese agreement, imposed by British authorities for a period of three months. Upon expiration of the term of the agreement under reference, those restrictions were lifted by the British authorities at midnight, October 17, 1940. (176)

Report From Ambassador Grew

The United States Ambassador in Japan cabled to the Secretary of State on September 12, 1940 that whatever the intentions of the existing Japanese Government, there could be no doubt that the military and other elements in Japan saw in the world situation a "golden opportunity" to carry their dreams of expansion into effect; that the German victories, "like strong wine", had gone to their heads; that they had believed implicitly until recently in Great Britain's defeat; that they had argued that the war would probably be ended in a quick German victory and that Japan's position in Greater East Asia should be consolidated while Germany was still agreeable; and that, although carefully watching the actions of the United States, they had discounted effective opposition on our part.

However, the Ambassador went on, a gradual change could now be sensed, as it was beginning to be seen by the Japanese that Germany might not defeat Great Britain after all. The Japanese saw Great Britain and the United States steadily drawing closer together in mutual defense measures. Furthermore, it was beginning to be questioned in Japan whether even a victorious Germany would not furnish a new hazard to their program of expansion. There was also an uncertain factor in their calculations regarding the future attitude of Russia. The Ambassador said that until the world situation, particularly the position of the United States, became clearer, Japan's "nibbling policy" appeared likely to continue.

Referring to the question of "sanctions", the Ambassador warned that the probability must be contemplated that drastic embargoes on such important products as oil would be interpreted in Japan as sanctions, and that some form of retaliation might and probably would follow. The risks, he said, would depend on the "do or die" temper of the Japanese Army and Navy should they impute to the United States the responsibility for the failure of their plans for expansion. The retaliation, he said, would probably be some sudden stroke by that Navy or Army without the prior authority or knowledge of the Government. Japan was, he said, one of the predatory powers; having submerged all ethical and moral sense, it had become unashamedly and frankly opportunist, seeking at every turn to profit through the weakness of others. He believed that United States interests in the Pacific were definitely threatened by Japan's policy of southward expansion. Japan, he said, had been deterred from taking greater liberties with our interests only because it respected our potential power; also, it had trampled upon our rights in exact ratio to the strength of its conviction that the people of the United States would not permit that power to be used. If, the Ambassador said, we could by firmness preserve the *status quo* in the Pacific until Great Britain should be successful in the European war, it would be impossible for the opportunist philosophy in Japan to keep the upper hand; then it might be possible to undertake a readjustment of the whole Pacific problem on an equitable basis. Until there was in Japan a complete regeneration of thought, he said, nothing but a show of force coupled with the determination that force would be used if necessary could effectively contribute to such an outcome and to the future security of the United States. (182)

Japanese Penetration Into Indochina

Even before the French-German armistice was signed in June 1940 the Japanese militarists began to exert pressure on French Indochina. Throughout the summer of 1940 this pressure continued. On September 22, following a Japanese ultimatum involving a threat of force, a military agreement concluded between the French and Japanese authorities provided for Japan's use of three airdromes and for the transit, in case of operations against China, of Japanese troops. Notwithstanding this agreement, Japanese forces attacked Indochina and occupied several strategic points there. On September 23 Secretary of State Hull, referring to these events in Indochina, declared that it seemed obvious that the *status quo* there was being upset "under duress"; he repeated that the United States disapproved and deprecated such procedures. (183)

On September 27, 1940 announcement was made of the conclusion of the treaty of alliance between Germany, Italy, and Japan containing a threat against the United States. (See p. 84.)

Restrictions on Exports to Japan

The "moral embargoes" of 1938 and 1939, referred to previously, brought about the cessation of the export to Japan of airplanes, aeronautic equipment, and certain other materials. As the rearmament program in the United States gained momentum and required more and more available strategic materials, this Government gradually adopted measures, legislative and administrative, which resulted in a steady decline of export to Japan of such materials. The Export Control Act of July 2, 1940 authorized the President, in the interest of national defense, to prohibit or curtail the export of basic war materials. Under that act, licenses were refused for the export to Japan of aviation gasoline and most types of machine tools, beginning in August 1940. After it was announced in September that the export of iron and steel scrap would be prohibited, Japanese Ambassador Horinouchi protested to Secretary Hull on October 8, 1940 that this might be considered an "unfriendly act". The Secretary told the Ambassador that it was really "amazing" for the Japanese Government, which had been violating in the most aggravating manner American rights and interests throughout most of China, to question the fullest right of this Government to impose such an embargo. To go further and call it an "unfriendly act", the Secretary said, was still more amazing in the light of Japan's conduct in disregarding all law, treaty obligations, and other rights and privileges and the safety of Americans, while proceeding to an ever-increasing extent to seize territory by force. The Ambassador replied that he very much regretted the differences between Japan and the United States and that strife between them would be extremely tragic for both. Secretary Hull agreed that such an occurrence would be exceedingly unfortunate but added that this Government had been extremely patient. The Secretary went on to say that we stood for law and order and treaty observance and justice, along with genuine friendliness between the two countries; that it was clear now, however, that those dominating the external policy of Japan were, "as we here have believed for some years, bent on the conquest by force of all worthwhile territory in the Pacific Ocean area without limit as to extent in the south and in southern continental areas of that part of the world". Furthermore, we and all other nations were expected by Japan to sit perfectly quiet and be cheerful and agreeable, but static, while most of Asia was "Manchurianized", which would render practically impossible all reasonable or satisfactory relations so far as other nations were concerned, and would result ultimately in correspondingly lower levels of existence for the people of most of Asia.

The Secretary reiterated that it was unheard-of for a country engaged in aggression and seizure of another country, contrary to all law and treaty provisions, to turn to a third nation and seriously insist that the latter would be guilty of an unfriendly act if it did not cheerfully provide some of the necessary implements of war to aid the aggressor nation in carrying out its policy of invasion. The Secretary made clear to the Ambassador this Government's view that Germany and Japan were undertaking to subjugate both of their respective areas of the world and to place them on an international order and a social basis resembling that of eight centuries ago. (186)

Despite the Japanese protest, a total embargo on the export of iron and steel scrap to destinations other than countries of the Western Hemisphere and Great Britain went into effect on October 16, 1940.

The effect of United States policy in regard to exports to Japan was that by the winter of 1940–41 shipment had ceased of many strategic commodities including arms, ammunition, and implements of war, aviation gasoline and many other petroleum products, machine tools, scrap iron, pig iron, iron and steel manufactures, copper, lead, zinc, aluminum, and a variety of other commodities important to war effort.

⇻⇻ XIII ⇺⇺

EUROPEAN WAR 1941

The Four Freedoms

IN HIS ADDRESS to Congress on January 6, 1941 President Roosevelt declared that "at no previous time has American security been as seriously threatened from without as it is today". The democratic way of life was being directly assailed "by arms, or by secret spreading of poisonous propaganda" in every part of the world. The President said that the assault had blotted out the whole pattern of democratic life in an appalling number of independent nations and that the assailants were still on the march threatening other nations, great and small. Armed defense of democratic existence was being waged on four continents; if that defense failed, all the population and all the resources of Europe, Asia, Africa, and Australasia would be dominated by the conquerors.

The President defined our national policy as follows: We were committed to an all-inclusive national defense; we were committed to full support of resolute peoples everywhere who were resisting aggression and were thereby keeping war away from our hemisphere; and we were committed to the proposition that principles of morality and considerations for our own security would "never permit us to acquiesce in a peace dictated by aggressors and sponsored by appeasers".

President Roosevelt said that we looked forward to a world founded upon four essential human freedoms: Freedom of speech and expression; freedom of every person to worship God in his own way; freedom from want—which meant economic understandings that would secure to every nation a healthy peacetime life for its inhabitants; freedom from fear—which meant a world-wide reduction of armaments to such a point that no nation would be in a position to commit an act of physical aggression against any neighbor. These four essential human freedoms constituted a definite basis for the kind of world attainable in our own time and generation, the kind of world which is "the very antithesis of the so-called new order of tyranny which the dictators seek to create with the crash of a bomb". (194)

The President's budget message of this month, January 1941, called for the expenditure of approximately $11,000,000,000 for the national-defense program. This raised to $28,000,000,000 the estimated outlay for the defense program inaugurated in May 1940.

Lend-Lease Act

Early in January 1941 there was introduced in Congress a bill to enable the Government to furnish aid to nations whose defense was deemed by the President to be vital to the defense of the United States. Both Houses of Congress held extensive public hearings on the bill. Secretary Hull made a statement before the House Committee on Foreign Affairs on January 15 in support of the bill. In this statement the Secretary declared that it had become increasingly apparent that mankind was face to face with an organized, ruthless, and implacable movement of steadily-expanding conquest; that we were in the presence of forces which were not restrained by considerations of law or principles of morality; that these forces had no fixed limits for their program of conquest; that they had spread over large areas on land and were desperately struggling to seize control of the oceans as an essential means of achieving and maintaining the conquest of other continents. The Secretary stated that control of the high seas by law-abiding nations "is the key to the security of the Western Hemisphere"; that should such control be gained by the Axis powers, the danger to the United States "would be multiplied manyfold". The most serious question for the United States, the Secretary said, was whether the control of the high seas would pass into the hands of powers bent on a program of unlimited conquest.

The Secretary felt that on no other question of public policy were the people of the United States so nearly unanimous and so emphatic as they were on that of the imperative need, in our own most vital interest, to give Great Britain and other victims of attack the maximum of material aid in the shortest possible space of time. This was so because it was clear that such assistance to those resisting attack was a vital part of our national self-defense. The bill before the Committee, he said, known as the Lend-Lease bill, provided for machinery which would enable the United States to make the most effective use of our resources for our own needs and for those whom, in our own self-defense, we were determined to aid. The Secretary expressed the belief that this bill would make it possible for us to allocate our resources in ways best calculated to provide for the security of the United States and of this continent. (195)

The Lend-Lease bill became law with the signature of the President on March 11, 1941. Immediately thereafter the President requested an appropriation of $7,000,000,000 to accomplish the objectives of the act, and that appropriation was speedily made. (200)

In an address on March 15 President Roosevelt stated that the decision embodied in the Lend-Lease Act ended the urging that we get along with the dictators and ended the compromise with tyranny and the forces of oppression. When our production output was in full swing, he said, the democracies of the world would be able to prove that dictators could not win. The time element he considered of "supreme importance". Every plane, every other instrument of war, old and new, which we could spare would be sent overseas; the great task of the day, the deep duty which rested upon us, was to "move products from the assembly lines of our factories to the battle lines of democracies—Now!"

The President said that the Nazi forces were not asking mere modifications in colonial maps or in minor European boundaries; that they openly sought the destruction of all elective systems of government on every continent—including our own; that they sought to establish systems of government based on the regimentation of all human beings by a handful of individual rulers who had seized power by force.

The nation, he said, was calling for the sacrifice of some privileges but not for the sacrifice of fundamental rights. Referring to the four freedoms set forth in his January address, the President said that they might not be immediately attainable throughout the world but "humanity does move towards those ideals through democratic processes". If we failed and democracy were superseded by slavery, "then those four freedoms or even the mention of them will become forbidden things".

There was no longer any doubt, he said, that our people recognized the seriousness of the international situation. That was why they had demanded and obtained "a policy of unqualified, immediate, all-out aid for Britain, Greece, China, and for all the governments in exile whose homelands are temporarily occupied by the aggressors". Aid would be increased, he emphasized, "and yet again increased", until total victory had been won. (201)

In instructions shortly thereafter to United States diplomatic missions in several neutral European countries, the Secretary of State said that every effort should be made to see that this authoritative statement by the President of our position was circulated as widely as possible. He said a salutary effect on public and official opinion in countries which had not been drawn directly into the war, would result from a forceful, continuous presentation of the position of the United States and of the scope of our national effort and determination to resist aggression. Such a presentation also would be of great assistance in counteracting totalitarian propaganda. The missions were to stress that we were absolutely convinced that the forces of aggression would be defeated. It had been made abundantly clear by our people and Government, the Secretary said, that we intended to play our part in resistance against the forces of aggression. Therefore, it was incumbent upon every representative of the United States and upon every United States citizen abroad to reflect "the absolute determination" of the United States to "see this thing through". (205)

Invasion of Greece and Yugoslavia

In October 1940 Italy had launched an unprovoked and ruthless attack on Greece. While the neutrality of the United States was proclaimed in the ensuing war between Greece and Italy, Minister MacVeagh at Athens was instructed on November 16 to inform the Greek Government that this action should be construed in no way as being an indication of any lessening of the sympathy of the United States for Greece in its conflict with Italy. In December 1940 President Roosevelt in a message to the King of Greece expressed the deep impression which had been made upon all free peoples by the courage and steadfastness of the Greek nation and assured him that, in line with our policy of furnishing aid to nations defending themselves against aggression, steps were being taken to extend such aid to Greece. (191)

Despite numerical superiority of the Italian forces the brave resistance of the Greeks was successful during the following months. By the beginning of 1941 the Italian forces were retreating into Albania. Meanwhile, the German Government was preparing to join the Italian attack on Greece and at the same time attempting to coerce Yugoslavia into adhering to the Tripartite Pact.

On February 9, 1941 Secretary Hull sent a message to our Minister to Yugoslavia making clear the position of the United States with respect to the developing world situation. The Secretary referred to the President's statement that "we are planning our own defense with the utmost urgency and in its vast scale we must integrate the war needs of Britain". This position, he said, continued to be the keystone of the national-defense policy of the United States; we were convinced that Great Britain would win. War-material production in the United States had been undertaken on a vast scale to meet the requirements of the British and would continue ever increasingly until the final victory. (197)

A week later, on February 14, President Roosevelt sent a message to the Yugoslav Government, expressing his conviction that any victory on behalf of the predatory powers, even if only in the diplomatic field, would pave the way for fresh demands accompanied by threats of force against the very independence of the nation thus menaced. He called attention to the Lend-Lease bill before Congress which would authorize the President to supply war materials to nations victims of aggression or threatened with aggression. (198)

The constant pressure exercised by Hitler on Yugoslavia resulted in the adherence by the Yugoslav Government on March 25, 1941 to the Axis Tripartite Pact. However, this act was promptly repudiated by the government formed in Yugoslavia as a result of an anti-Axis *coup d'état* on the following day. Hitler's legions thereupon prepared to march on Yugoslavia. It was at this point that the Secretary of State, on April 5, 1941, sent instructions to the United States Ministers in Bulgaria, Hungary, and Rumania, which countries had already adhered to the Axis Tripartite Pact. In these instructions the Secretary asked the Ministers to use their good offices to the end that the governments to which they were accredited might understand how support given acts of aggression against Yugoslavia was bound to be regarded in the United States. The Secretary emphasized that our every effort was being exerted under existing law to assist the nations which were defending their integrity and independence against aggression. (203)

On the following day, April 6, the German armies launched an attack on Yugoslavia and Greece. On that day Secretary Hull said that in line with its policy of assisting those nations defending themselves against aggression, this Government was proceeding as speedily as possible to send military and other supplies to Yugoslavia. (204)

Despite stout resistance, the German armies, supported by their Italian, Hungarian, and Bulgarian satellites, overran a large part of Yugoslavia and Greece.

Greenland Agreement

The Department of State announced on April 10, 1941 the signing on the day before of an agreement regarding Greenland. This agreement recognized that as a result of the European war there was danger that Greenland might be converted into a point of aggression against nations of the American Continent, and accepted the responsibility on behalf of the United States of assisting Greenland in the maintenance of its existing status. The agreement, after explicitly recognizing Danish sovereignty over Greenland, granted to the United States the right to locate and construct airplane landing fields and facilities for the defense of Greenland and of the American Continent. In announcing this agreement the Department stated that the United States had no thought "save that of assuring the safety of Greenland and the rest of the American Continent, and Greenland's continuance under Danish sovereignty"; that it was recognized that so long as Denmark remained under German occupation the Government in Denmark could not exercise the Danish sovereign powers over Greenland under the Monroe Doctrine. The agreement was signed by the Secretary of State and by the Danish Minister in Washington, acting as representative of the King of Denmark in his capacity as Sovereign of Greenland, and with the concurrence of the Governors of Greenland.

The Department announced that this step was taken in furtherance of the traditional friendliness between Denmark and the United States; that the policy of the United States was that of defending for Denmark her sovereignty over Greenland so that she might have a full exercise of it as soon as the German invasion of Denmark was ended. Accordingly the agreement provided that as soon as the war was over and the danger had passed, the two Governments should promptly consult as to whether the arrangements made by this agreement should continue or should then cease. (206)

Secretary Hull's Address of April 24

In an address on April 24, 1941 Secretary Hull stated that unfortunately many people failed to grasp the nature of the world-wide crisis and its meaning to our own country. Too many people assumed, he said, that the present struggle was merely an ordinary regional war and that when it came to an end the victorious nations would collect indemnities but otherwise leave the defeated nations more or less as they were before the conflict began. This assumption, he said, would prove "entirely erroneous" if the aggressors should win the war; the would-be conquerors proposed to take unto themselves the territory, the sovereignty, and the possessions of every conquered nation; they proposed to make the people of each nation into serfs—"to extinguish their liberties, their rights, their law, and their religion".

The Secretary declared that the aggressors not only did not wish peace but literally did not believe in it; that behind the deceptive protection of the word "peace" they accumulated vast striking forces;

they infiltrated shock troops disguised as peaceful travelers and businessmen; they set up organizations for spying, sabotage, and propaganda; they endeavored to sow hatred and discord; they used every tool of economic attack, bribery, and corruption to weaken the countries with which they were at "peace" until a military movement could easily complete the task of subjugation. Peace of that type was nothing more than a "trap" into which many nations had fallen in earlier phases of this movement for world conquest when its true nature had not been understood.

The Secretary warned that it made a "fateful difference" to us who won this war—the difference whether we would stand with our backs to the wall with the other four continents against us and the high seas lost, alone defending the last free territories on earth, or whether we would keep our place in an orderly world. Those who felt that a British defeat would not matter to us overlooked the fact that the resulting delivery of the high seas to the invader would create colossal danger to our own national defense and security. The breadth of the sea might give us a little time but it did not give us safety. Safety could only come from our ability, in conjunction with other peace-loving nations, "to prevent any aggressor from attaining control of the high seas".

Some people contended, he said, that our country need not resist until the armed forces of the invader should have crossed the border of this hemisphere. To him this merely meant that there would be no resistance by the hemisphere, including the United States, until the invading countries had acquired complete control of the other four continents and of the high seas, and thus had obtained every possible strategic advantage. This he considered an "utterly short-sighted and extremely dangerous view"; events had shown beyond question that the safety of this hemisphere and of this country called for "resistance wherever resistance will be most effective".

With reference to the question whether aid to freedom-loving nations and a vigorous policy of defending our interests would irritate some aggressor into attacking us, the Secretary said that no nation would attack us merely because it was our policy to defend ourselves; aggressors were not going to let us alone merely because we attempted to placate them. In the philosophy of the conquerors an attack was justified whenever and wherever it looked easy and convenient and served their purposes; there was no possible safeguarding of our security except by "solid strength". He declared that the best and only way of allaying the fears and doubts of those in anxiety was for us "to rise in our might and proceed as one man in the Herculean task of equipping this nation to the fullest for its self-defense". (207)

Unlimited National Emergency

On May 27, 1941 President Roosevelt proclaimed the existence of an "unlimited national emergency", and in a radio address on the same day he outlined the policy of the United States in the light of developments in the world situation. In this address the President declared that our whole program of aid for the democracies had been "based on a hard-headed concern for our own security and for the kind of safe and civilized world in which we wish to live"; that every dollar of material we sent helped to keep the dictators away from our own hemisphere; that every day they were held off gave us time to build more guns and tanks and planes and ships.

The President warned of the conditions which would exist should Hitler be victorious in the war: Germany would set up puppet governments of its own choosing, wholly subject to its own will; the dictatorships would force the enslaved peoples of their Old World conquests into a system they were then organizing—to build a naval and air force intended to obtain mastery of the Atlantic and the Pacific; an economic stranglehold would be fastened upon the nations of the Western Hemisphere; the American laborer would have to compete with slave labor in the rest of the world, and trade unions would become "historical relics"; the American farmer would face obvious disaster and complete regimentation; the whole fabric of business, manufacturing, mining, and agriculture would be mangled and crippled; a permanent conscription of our manpower would be necessary, and our resources would be permanently poured into armaments. We did not accept and we would not permit this Nazi "shape of things to come".

The Axis powers could never achieve their objective of world domination, the President said, "unless they first obtain control of the seas". If they failed to gain control of the seas they were "certainly defeated". The President then described the dangerous situation in the "battle of the Atlantic". He revealed that the rate of Nazi sinkings of merchant ships was more than three times as high as the capacity of British shipyards to replace those ships; the rate was more than twice the combined British and American output of merchant ships at that time. This peril could be met, he said, by speeding up and increasing our great shipbuilding program and by helping to cut down the losses on the high seas. He announced that we had extended our patrol in North and South Atlantic waters; that we were adding steadily more and more ships to that patrol. The purpose of these ships and planes was to "warn of the presence of attacking raiders, on the sea, under the sea, and above the sea".

The President summed up our national policy as follows: We would actively resist wherever necessary and with all our resources every attempt by Hitler to extend his domination to the Western Hemisphere; we would actively resist his every attempt to gain control of the seas; we would insist upon the vital importance of keeping Hitlerism away from any point in the world which could be used and would be used as a base of attack against the Americas; we would give every possible assistance to Great Britain and all countries which, like Great Britain, were resisting Hitlerism or its equivalent with force of arms; our patrols were helping to insure delivery of the needed supplies to Great Britain, and all additional measures necessary to deliver the goods would be taken.

We in the Americas would decide for ourselves, the President said, whether and when and where our American interests were attacked or our security threatened. We were placing our armed forces in strategic military posts and would not hesitate to use them to repel attack. In conclusion, the President repeated the words of the signers of the Declaration of Independence: "With a firm reliance on the protection of Divine Providence, we mutually pledge to each other our lives, our fortunes, and our sacred honor". (210)

Policy Toward France

The policy of the United States toward France in its broad aspects was based primarily on steady opposition to German aggression. After the fall of France and the conclusion of the French-German armistice this policy was specifically directed toward (1) denial of the French Fleet and French naval and air bases to the Axis powers; (2) closest practicable cooperation with the French people for the purpose of aiding them to keep alive their aspirations for liberty and democracy and to attain their earliest possible liberation from their conquerors; and (3) constant exertion of influence against French collaboration, voluntary or involuntary, with Hitler and Hitlerism. Another vital consideration was the need of keeping the French people reminded that their commitments under the terms of the French-German armistice strictly defined the limits to which they, the French, were obligated as regards Germany.

The first fruit of continuing contact with the French Government was its pledge given on June 18, 1940, and repeated subsequent to the French-German armistice, that the French Fleet would "never be surrendered to the enemy". (187, 189, 192)

On November 4, 1940, following indications of French collaboration with Germany, Secretary of State Hull conferred with French Ambassador Henry-Haye. The Secretary declared that "we propose to be on our guard" with respect to acts of the Vichy Government, inspired by Foreign Minister Laval, that were intended to aid the military activities of Hitler, such as the supplying of naval and air bases, or other help given by French military or naval forces. He said that while this Government recognized the unfortunate situation of France as a "captive nation" it maintained that the French Government had no justification to render the slightest military aid to Germany. The Secretary referred to what he called the "extreme pro-German plans" of Laval and said that there could be no appeasement of Hitler, that Hitler would do what he pleased with all of his captive nations regardless of whether they offered him gifts and other considerations. He declared that the United States was too much concerned with possible future attacks by Hitler to acquiesce in the slightest degree in acts of the French Government that would aid Hitler in wider conquests, particularly in the direction of the Western Hemisphere. (190)

In June 1941, when Germany was exercising increasing pressure upon the French Government at Vichy in order to obtain assistance from that Government in the conduct of the war, Secretary Hull, in a statement of June 5, reviewed the policy of the United States with respect to France. Throughout our history, the Secretary said, we had been sympathetic to the true aspirations of France; we had fought beside France; France's cause had been our cause; the principles of free representative government by the people had been the bases of the democratic institutions of both countries. We had, he said, consistently conveyed to the French Government our understanding of the difficulty of their position and our determination to be of every assistance we could in solving their problems for the ultimate benefit of the French people. We had made clear to the French Government that the basic policy of the United States was to aid Great Britain in her defense against the same forces of conquest which had invaded and were subjugating France. We had aided in the furnishing of foodstuffs for unoccupied France, and children's supplies were now being distributed through the American Red Cross. We had collaborated in safeguarding the welfare and maintaining the integrity of the French possessions in the Western Hemisphere. In cooperation with the French Government we had helped in supplying commodities urgently needed for the economic stability of French North Africa. The Vichy Government had been assured that the United States had no interest in any territories of the French Empire other than their preservation for the French people.

It had been the determined policy of this Government, the Secretary said, to continue friendly and helpful cooperation with France in the existing difficult situation in which French action was restricted and limited by the terms of the armistices with Germany and Italy. It seemed scarcely believable, he said, that the French Government should adopt a policy of collaboration with other powers for the purpose of aggression and oppression; such action would not only be yielding priceless rights and interests beyond the requirements of a harsh armistice, but would at once place France in substantial political and military subservience and would also make France in part an instrument of aggression; this could only be "utterly inimical to the just rights of other countries, to say nothing of its ultimate effects on the liberties, the true interests, and the welfare of the people of France". (211)

Despite the collapse of resistance in France in June 1940 a number of French soldiers and sailors had continued to maintain the struggle against Germany on land and sea under the name of the "Free French". Portions of the French colonial empire rallied to their support. The Government of the United States entered into working arrangements with the Free French authorities in control of such territories, and a Free French delegation was established at Washington. In November 1941, President Roosevelt, finding that the defense of territory under control of Free French authorities was vital to the defense of the United States, directed that Lend-Lease aid be extended to them. This aid was given in such forms as the repair of naval vessels in American shipyards and the supply of tanks and other munitions to land forces.

The "Robin Moor"

In a message to the Congress on June 20, 1941 the President reported that on May 21 a German submarine had sunk an American merchant vessel, the *Robin Moor*, in the South Atlantic Ocean, while the vessel was on the high seas *en route* to South Africa. The vessel had been sunk within 30 minutes from the time of the first warning; it was sunk without provision for the safety of the passengers and crew, who were left afloat in small lifeboats from two to three weeks until they were accidentally discovered and rescued by friendly vessels. He said that the "total disregard shown for the most elementary principles of international law and humanity brands the sinking of the *Robin Moor* as the act of an international outlaw"; that the United States held Germany responsible for this "outrageous and indefensible sinking"; that full reparation for the losses and damages suffered by American nationals would be expected from the German Government. This Government, the President continued, could only assume that Germany hoped, through the commission of such acts of cruelty, to intimidate the United States and other nations into a course of non-resistance to German plans of universal conquest. He said that the United States would not be intimidated, nor would it acquiesce in the plans of the German leaders for world domination. (212)

German Attack on Russia

In the winter of 1940–41 this Government received reports that Germany intended to attack the Soviet Union, despite the existence of the German-Russian non-aggression pact. This information was conveyed by Under Secretary Welles to the Soviet Ambassador early in 1941. On March 20, 1941 Mr. Welles informed the Ambassador that this Government had additional information in confirmation of the report that Germany intended to attack the Soviet Union. (202)

Hitler's treacherous attack on the Soviet Union occurred on June 22, 1941, when Germany launched an offensive along a front extending from the Baltic Sea to the Black Sea. In a public statement on the following day Acting Secretary Welles stated that to the leaders of the German Reich solemn pledges such as non-aggression pacts were "but a symbol of deceit, and constitute a dire warning on the part of Germany of hostile and murderous intent"; that to the German Government the very meaning of the word "honor" was unknown. The Acting Secretary said that the immediate issue presenting itself to the people of the United States was whether Hitler's plan for universal conquest and for the ultimate destruction of the remaining free democracies was to be successfully halted and defeated. He said that in the opinion of this Government any defense against Hitlerism, any rallying of the forces opposing Hitlerism, from whatever sources they might spring, would hasten the eventual downfall of the German leaders and would therefore redound to the benefit of our own defense and security. Finally, the Acting Secretary declared, "Hitler's armies are today the chief dangers of the Americas". (214)

110

Agreement With Iceland

President Roosevelt announced to the Congress on July 7, 1941 that in accordance with an understanding reached with the Prime Minister of Iceland, forces of the United States had arrived in Iceland in order to supplement, and eventually to replace, the British forces which had been stationed there to insure the adequate defense of that country. The President said that the United States could not permit the occupation by Germany of strategic outposts in the Atlantic, to be used as air or naval bases for eventual attack against the Western Hemisphere; that we had no desire to see any change in the existing sovereignty of those regions; that assurance that such outposts in our defense frontier remain in friendly hands was the very foundation of our national security and of the national security of every independent nation in the New World. It was imperative, therefore, that the approaches between the Americas and those strategic outposts should remain open and free from all hostile activity or threat. As Commander in Chief the President had issued orders to the Navy that all necessary steps be taken to insure the safety of communications in the approaches between Iceland and the United States, as well as on the seas between the United States and all other strategic outposts. This Government, the President said, would insure the adequate defense of Iceland with full recognition of the independence of Iceland as a sovereign state. He had given assurance to the Prime Minister of Iceland that the American forces sent there would in no way interfere with the internal and domestic affairs of that country, and that immediately upon the termination of the international emergency all American forces would be at once withdrawn, leaving the people of Iceland and their Government in full and sovereign control of their own territory. (216)

Atlantic Charter

President Roosevelt and Prime Minister Churchill met at sea in August 1941. At this conference they examined the whole problem of the supplying of munitions of war, as provided by the Lend-Lease Act, for the armed forces of the United States and for the countries actively engaged in resisting aggression. Deeming it "right to make known certain common principles in the national policies of their respective countries on which they base their hopes for a better future for the world", they agreed on the joint declaration of August 14, 1941 which has become known as the "Atlantic Charter", as this conference took place on the Atlantic Ocean:

"First, their countries seek no aggrandizement, territorial or other;

"Second, they desire to see no territorial changes that do not accord with the freely expressed wishes of the peoples concerned;

"Third, they respect the right of all peoples to choose the form of government under which they will live; and they wish to see sovereign rights and self-government restored to those who have been forcibly deprived of them;

"Fourth, they will endeavor, with due respect for their existing obligations, to further the enjoyment by all States, great or small, victor or vanquished, of access, on equal terms, to the trade and to the raw materials of the world which are needed for their economic prosperity;

"Fifth, they desire to bring about the fullest collaboration between all nations in the economic field with the object of securing, for all, improved labor standards, economic advancement, and social security;

"Sixth, after the final destruction of the Nazi tyranny, they hope to see established a peace which will afford to all nations the means of dwelling in safety within their own boundaries, and which will afford assurance that all the men in all the lands may live out their lives in freedom from fear and want;

"Seventh, such a peace should enable all men to traverse the high seas and oceans without hindrance;

"Eighth, they believe that all of the nations of the world, for realistic as well as spiritual reasons, must come to the abandonment of the use of force. Since no future peace can be maintained if land, sea or air armaments continue to be employed by nations which threaten, or may threaten, aggression outside of their frontiers, they believe, pending the establishment of a wider and permanent system of general security, that the disarmament of such nations is essential. They will likewise aid and encourage all other practicable measures which will lighten for peace-loving peoples the crushing burden of armaments."

In reporting this joint declaration to the Congress the President said that it presented a goal which was "worthwhile for our type of civilization to seek". The declaration was so clear-cut, he said, that it was difficult to oppose it in any major particular without automatically admitting a willingness to accept compromise with Nazi-ism or to agree to a world peace which would give to Nazi-ism domination over large numbers of conquered nations. The President pointed out that the declaration included, of necessity, "the world need for freedom of religion and freedom of information". (229)

This Government has frequently expressed its view that after hostilities have ended, the nations contributing to the defeat of the common enemy should join together in an effort to restore peace and order on the basis of the general principles laid down in the Atlantic Charter; that meanwhile we expect a continuation of discussions between the several governments looking to the fullest possible agreement on basic policies and to later arrangements at the proper time; and that, above all, there must not be any "secret agreements".

Aid to Russia

On August 15, 1941 a joint message from President Roosevelt and Prime Minister Churchill was delivered to Joseph Stalin, President of the People's Commissars of the Union of Soviet Socialist Republics. In this message the President and the Prime Minister said that they had consulted together as to how best their two countries could help the Soviet Union; that they were cooperating to provide the Soviet Union with the very maximum of supplies most urgently needed; that many shiploads had left already for the Soviet Union and more would leave in the immediate future. In order that all concerned might be in a position to arrive at speedy decisions as to the apportionment of joint resources, they suggested that a meeting of representatives of the three Governments be held at Moscow. Realizing how vitally important to the defeat of Hitlerism was "the brave and steadfast resistance of the Soviet Union", they felt that they must act "quickly and immediately in this matter on planning the program for the future allocation of our joint resources." The conference was agreed to and was held in Moscow shortly thereafter. (227)

Battle of the Atlantic

By September 1941 the Axis war against shipping had resulted in several incidents that clearly demonstrated the grave menace to the vital interests of the United States. Two United States - owned merchant ships under the flag of Panama, the *Sessa* and the *Montana*, had been torpedoed and sunk while carrying cargoes to Iceland, where the United States had established a defense outpost. A United States merchant ship *en route* to Suez, the *Steel Seafarer*, had been sunk in the Red Sea by a German aircraft. On September 4 the United States destroyer *Greer* had been attacked by a German submarine while carrying mail to Iceland.

On September 11, 1941, in a radio address, President Roosevelt de-

113

nounced these "acts of international lawlessness" as a manifestation of the Nazi design to abolish the freedom of the seas and to acquire the domination of the seas for themselves. It would be unworthy, he said, for a great nation to exaggerate an isolated incident but it would be "inexcusable folly to minimize such incidents in the face of evidence which makes it clear that the incident is not isolated, but part of a general plan"; for with the control of the seas by the Nazis the way could become clear for their next step—domination of the United States and the Western Hemisphere by force. Under Nazi control of the seas no merchant ship of the United States or of any other American republic would be free to carry on any peaceful commerce, "except by the condescending grace of this foreign and tyrannical power". To be ultimately successful in world mastery, Hitler knew that he must get control of the seas, that he must first destroy the bridge of ships which we were building across the Atlantic, over which we would continue to roll the implements of war "to help destroy him and all his works in the end". He must wipe out our patrol on sea and in the air, and he must silence the British Navy. The President said that the United States Navy was "an invincible protection" only if the British Navy survived; that if the world outside the Americas fell under Axis domination, the shipbuilding facilities which the Axis powers would then possess in all of Europe, in the British Isles, and in the Far East would be two or three times greater than all the shipbuilding facilities and possibilities of all the Americas. Even if the United States threw all its resources into such a situation, seeking to double and even redouble the size of our Navy, the Axis powers, in control of the rest of the world, "would have the manpower and the physical resources to outbuild us several times over".

Generation after generation, the President said, America had fought for the freedom of the seas, which meant that "no nation has the right to make the broad oceans of the world, at great distances from the actual theater of land war, unsafe for the commerce of others". The President stated that no act of violence or intimidation would keep us from maintaining intact two bulwarks of defense: our line of supply to Hitler's enemies and the freedom of our shipping on the high seas. We would "keep open the line of legitimate commerce in these defensive waters". We had sought no shooting war with Hitler and did not seek it "now", but we did not want peace so much that we were willing to pay for it by permitting him to attack our naval or merchant vessels when they were on legitimate business.

President Roosevelt declared that the very presence of Axis submarines or raiders in any waters which America deemed vital to its defense constituted an attack. In these waters, the President said, "American naval vessels and American planes will no longer wait until Axis submarines lurking under the water, or Axis raiders on the surface of the sea, strike their deadly blow—first". Our naval and air patrol operating over a vast expanse of the Atlantic Ocean would protect all merchant ships engaged in commerce in our defensive waters. It was no act of war on our part when we decided to protect the seas which were vital to American defense; the aggression was not ours. The President warned that from then on, if German or Italian vessels of war entered the waters the protection of which was necessary for American defense, they would do so "at their own peril". The sole responsibility rested upon Germany; there would be "no shooting" unless Germany continued to seek it.

Finally, the President said that he had no illusions about the gravity of this step; that he had not taken it hurriedly or lightly; that it was the result of many months of constant thought and anxiety and prayer; that in the protection of the nation it could not be avoided. (235)

Revision of the Neutrality Act

Ships of the United States and of other American republics continued to be sunk in the Atlantic Ocean by Nazi submarines. In view of this situation and in view of the fact that the Neutrality Act of 1939 prohibited the arming of United States merchant ships engaged in foreign commerce and prevented United States merchant ships from carrying cargoes to belligerent ports, it became increasingly difficult to obtain shipping for the carriage of Lend-Lease supplies to Great Britain and to other nations whose defense was considered vital to the defense of the United States.

On October 9, 1941 the President asked Congress to modify the Neutrality Act. In his message the President said that the act had been passed at a time when few people visualized the true magnitude of the Nazi attempt to dominate the world; that it required a complete reconsideration in the light of known facts. He recommended the repeal of section 6, which prohibited the arming of United States flagships engaged in foreign commerce. He said that the practice of arming merchant ships for defense had never been prohibited by international law; that there was now an imperative need to equip United States merchant vessels with arms. He declared that we were faced with modern pirates of the sea who were destroying defenseless ships without warning and without provision for the safety of the passengers and crews; that our merchant vessels were sailing the seas on missions connected with the defense of the United States; that it was not just for the crews of these vessels to be denied the means of defending their lives and their ships. Although the arming of merchant vessels did not guarantee their safety, the President said, it certainly added to their safety. He emphasized that the arming of our ships was a matter of "immediate necessity, and extreme urgency".

The President then said that there were other phases of the Neutrality Act to which he hoped Congress would give earnest and early attention. While most of the vital Lend-Lease goods were being delivered, many of them were being sunk; as we approached full production requiring the use of many ships being built, it would be increasingly necessary to deliver our goods under our own flag. We could not and should not depend on the strained resources of our friends to deliver our goods "nor should we be forced to masquerade American-owned ships behind the flags of our sister republics". By keeping our ships out of the ports of our own friends we were inviting control of the seas by the aggressors. The President asked that Congress carry out the true intent of the Lend-Lease Act by making it possible for the United States to help deliver the articles to those who were in a position effectively to use them. It was our duty as never before, he said, to extend more and more assistance and ever more swiftly to Great Britain, to Russia, and to all peoples fighting slavery; we would not let Hitler prescribe the waters of the world on which our ships might travel. We could not permit the affirmative defense of our rights to be annulled by sections of the Neutrality Act "which have no realism in the light of unscrupulous ambition of madmen". (242)

Shortly after the President's delivery of this message, Secretary Hull made a statement before the Senate Committee on Foreign Relations in support of the proposal for modifying the Neutrality Act of 1939. At the outset of this statement of October 21 he said: The "paramount principle of national policy is the preservation of the safety and security of the nation"; the "highest right flowing from that principle is the right of self-defense"; this right "must now be invoked"; the key to that defense under existing conditions was to prevent Hitler from gaining control of the seas.

The Secretary reaffirmed that Hitler and his satellites were seeking to control the seas, particularly to sever the sea lanes which linked the United States "to the remaining free peoples". He believed, he said, that an indispensable part of our policy must be resolute self-defense on the high seas and that this called especially for protection of shipping on open sea lanes. When American ships were being "wantonly and unlawfully attacked with complete disregard of life and property" it was absurd to forego any legitimate measures that might be helpful toward self-defense. One of the greatest mistakes we could possibly make would be to base our policy upon an assumption that we were secure when, if the assumption should prove erroneous, the consequence thereof would "lay us completely open to hostile invasion". (243)

The Congress passed, and the President approved on November 17, 1941, a joint resolution repealing sections 2, 3, and 6 of the Neutrality Act of 1939, thereby permitting United States vessels to be armed and to carry cargoes to belligerent ports anywhere. (249)

"We Americans Have Cleared Our Decks and Taken Our Battle Stations"

Meanwhile, on October 17, 1941 the United States destroyer *Kearny* had been attacked and hit by a torpedo from a Nazi submarine and eleven men of the Navy were killed. President Roosevelt said in an address on October 27 that we had wished to avoid shooting but the shooting had begun and "history has recorded who fired the first shot". The purpose of Hitler's attack was, he said, to frighten the American people off the high seas; if our national policy were to be dominated by the fear of shooting, then all of our ships and those of the other American republics would have to be tied up in home harbors. Naturally we rejected that "absurd and insulting suggestion". Each day we were producing and providing more and more arms for the men who were fighting on actual battlefronts; it was this nation's will that these vital arms and supplies of all kinds should neither be locked up in American harbors nor sent to the bottom of the sea; it was the nation's will that "America shall deliver the goods". He emphasized that the orders to the United States Navy "to shoot on sight" were still in effect.

The forward march of Hitler and of Hitlerism could be stopped, the President said, and would be stopped; we were pledged to pull our own oar in the destruction of Hitlerism; when we had helped to end the curse of Hitlerism we would help to establish "a new peace which will give to decent people everywhere a better chance to live and prosper in security and in freedom and in faith".

The President concluded his address with a statement that in the face of this newest and greatest challenge "we Americans have cleared our decks and taken our battle stations"; we stood ready "in the defense of our nation and the faith of our fathers to do what God has given us the power to see as our full duty". (244)

117

DISCUSSIONS WITH JAPAN 1941
PEARL HARBOR

Secretary Hull's Statement on Japanese Aggression, January 15

SECRETARY HULL discussed Japan's actions in the Far East, on January 15, 1941, at a hearing of the Foreign Affairs Committee of the House of Representatives on the Lend-Lease bill. The Secretary recounted the various steps in Japan's program of expansion, including the conquest of Manchuria, the denunciation of the naval treaty of 1922, the intensified construction of military and naval armaments, and the large-scale military operations against China which had begun in July 1937. He said it was clear that "Japan has been actuated from the start by broad and ambitious plans for establishing herself in a dominant position in the entire region of the Western Pacific"; that Japan's leaders had openly declared their intention to achieve and maintain that position by force of arms and thus to make themselves masters of an area containing almost one half of the entire population of the world.

The Secretary said that notwithstanding the course which Japan had followed during recent years, the United States Government had made repeated efforts to persuade Japan that its best interests lay in the development of friendly relations with the United States and with other countries which believed in orderly and peaceful international processes. (195)

Report That Japan Might Attack Pearl Harbor

Ambassador Grew reported to the Department of State on January 27, 1941 that one of his diplomatic colleagues had told a member of the Embassy staff that there were reports from many sources, including a Japanese source, that Japanese military forces planned a surprise mass attack at Pearl Harbor in case of "trouble" with the United States. (196)

Arrival of Ambassador Nomura

Shortly thereafter the new Japanese Ambassador, Admiral Nomura, presented his credentials to President Roosevelt, and on March 8, 1941 Secretary Hull had his first extended conversation with the Ambassador. The Secretary pointed out that the efforts of the United States to bring about organization of the world along liberal commercial lines had been impeded by movements of military conquest in various parts of the world. He inquired of the Ambassador whether the military groups in control of the Japanese Government could possibly expect the United States "to sit absolutely quiet while two or three nations before our very eyes organized naval and military forces and went out and conquered the balance of the earth, including the seven seas and all trade routes and the other four continents". The Secretary inquired further what would countries like the United States gain by remaining complacent in the face of a movement to substitute force and conquest for law and justice. The Ambassador sought to minimize the view that such military conquest was in the mind of his Government, and he said that embargoes by the United States were of increasing concern to Japan and that he did not believe there would be any further military movements by the Japanese Government unless compelled by the policy of increasing embargoes on the part of the United States. Secretary Hull replied that this was a matter entirely in the hands of the Japanese Government because Japan had taken the initiative in military expansion and seizure of territory, thereby creating an increasing concern on the part of the United States and other countries as to the full extent of Japan's contemplated conquests by force. He referred to the terms of the Tripartite Pact and to public declarations of Hitler and of Japanese Foreign Minister Matsuoka that their countries were out to establish by military force a new world order under their control. The Secretary said that, whatever interpretation the Ambassador might give these statements and military activities in harmony with them, the people of the United States had become thoroughly aroused and viewed with most serious concern the German and Japanese movements to take charge of the seas and the other continents for their own arbitrary control and pecuniary profit at the expense of the welfare of all of the victims of such a course. He said that these apprehensions would remain so long as Hitler continued his "avowed course of unlimited conquest and tyrannical rule and so long as the Japanese Army and Navy increase their occupation by force of other and distant areas". (199)

Exploratory Conversations

Meanwhile, reports had been received in the United States that elements in the Japanese Government and certain private groups in Japan would welcome negotiations between the two Governments looking toward a settlement of the issues between the United States and Japan.

President Roosevelt and Secretary of State Hull well realized the probability that Japan had already gone so far in a policy of conquest that it would be impossible to persuade her to stop. Nevertheless, entertainment of even a faint hope that there might be worked out a fair and peaceful settlement in the Far Eastern area impelled this Government to agree to participate in exploratory conversations in order to ascertain whether there was sufficient agreement on basic issues to warrant entry upon more formal negotiations. Furthermore, there was the desirability of guarding against Japanese advances upon the relatively weak defenses of United States territory in the western Pacific and of territory of friendly nations in that area.

Accordingly, in the spring of 1941 the Secretary of State and the Japanese Ambassador began a series of conversations in which they discussed the issues between the two countries. In a conversation on May 11 Secretary Hull told Ambassador Nomura that if Japan really desired a settlement of the Pacific situation on a basis of peace and friendliness, there should be no serious difficulty. The Secretary inquired why it was that Japan persisted in using the slogan "New Order in Greater East Asia" unless Japan was using it as a cloak to continue her policy of conquest by force. He repeated that we were profoundly convinced that Hitlerism would prove not only a "scourge" to other parts of the world, as it had in Europe, but that it would be applied to Japan herself just as quickly as it had been applied to countries in Europe which had trusted Hitler. The Ambassador said that it would be "an incalculable loss to both Japan and the United States, as well as to civilization, if our two countries should become engaged in war". The Secretary rejoined that unless the civilization of the world was to run the great risk of being destroyed by Hitler, the united efforts of nations like Japan, the United States, and Great Britain would be required to shape the course of the world in a different direction. He said that steps looking toward the gradual development of basic programs for both the transition and the post-war periods could not be taken too soon. He re-emphasized that the United States was determined that Hitler should not get control of the seas, and that we should feel obliged to resist indefinitely such effort on Hitler's part. Since Hitler had avowed his movement to be one for world control, the United States did not, he said, propose to commit suicide as so many countries in continental Europe had done, by trusting Hitler and waiting until it was too late to resist; we proposed to resist when and where such resistance would be most

120

effective, whether within our own boundaries, on the high seas, or in aid of such countries as Great Britain. (208)

Japanese Proposal of May 12

On the following day, May 12, 1941, the Japanese Ambassador handed to the Secretary of State, as under instruction from his Government, a proposal for a general settlement between the United States and Japan. This proposal served to reveal authoritatively for the first time what the Japanese Government had in mind as a basis for agreement.

The proposal contained in the beginning a statement expressing the hope that "our nations may establish a just peace in the Pacific". It stated that the Tripartite Pact was "defensive and designed to prevent the nations which are not at present directly affected by the European war from engaging in it". It included an undertaking by the United States forthwith to "request the Chiang Kai-shek regime to negotiate peace with Japan". The Japanese stated that the United States would be expected also to "discontinue her assistance to the Chiang Kai-shek regime" in case the latter should decline to enter into such negotiations. They explained also that Japan's attitude toward China would include the principles of neighborly friendship; no annexations and no indemnities; independence of "Manchukuo"; mutual respect of sovereignty and territories; "withdrawal of Japanese troops from Chinese territory in accordance with an agreement to be concluded between Japan and China"; and joint defense against communism, which would involve the right of Japan to station troops in Chinese territory. The Japanese proposal contained also a mutual undertaking by the United States and Japan that each would supply the commodities which the other required; a mutual undertaking that steps would be taken to bring about resumption of normal trade relations between the two countries; and an undertaking by the United States that as "Japanese expansion in the direction of the southwestern Pacific area is declared to be of peaceful nature, American cooperation shall be given in the production and procurement of natural resources (such as oil, rubber, tin, nickel) which Japan needs". The proposal also contained an undertaking that the United States and Japan should "jointly guarantee the independence of the Philippine Islands on the condition that the Philippine Islands shall maintain a status of permanent neutrality". (209)

United States Proposal of June 21

Although the Japanese Ambassador constantly professed his Government's desire to adopt peaceful courses and although the general provisions of the Japanese proposal of May 12 contained affirmations of Japan's peaceful intent, the Japanese Government insisted upon maintaining its alignment with the Axis, insisted upon the stationing of an unspecified number of Japanese troops in large areas of China for an indefinite period, refused to commit itself to a policy precluding the retention by Japan of a preferential economic position in China and in the western Pacific, and refused to commit itself unreservedly to a general policy of peace. It was felt by the United States Government that an explicit understanding on these points was necessary in view of Japan's current course and in view of repeated affirmations by many responsible Japanese officials, including Foreign Minister Matsuoka, of Japan's determination to pursue a policy of cooperation with its Axis partners.

The Secretary of State, on June 21, 1941, handed to the Japanese Ambassador a document containing a comprehensive statement of the attitude of the United States. This included a proposal of the following points: 1. Affirmation by both Governments that their national policies were directed toward the foundation of a lasting peace and the inauguration of a new era of reciprocal confidence and cooperation between the two peoples. 2. A suggested formula that the "Government of Japan maintains that the purpose of the Tripartite Pact was, and is, defensive and is designed to contribute to the prevention of an unprovoked extension of the European war" and that the "Government of the United States maintains that its attitude toward the European hostilities is and will continue to be determined solely and exclusively by considerations of protection and self-defense". (For an explanation of the United States concept of self-defense, the Japanese, in a separate statement, were referred to Secretary Hull's address of April 24, 1941; see p. 104.) 3. A suggestion by the United States to China that China and Japan enter into negotiations, provided that Japan first communicate to and discuss with the United States the general terms which Japan contemplated proposing to China. 4. Mutual assurances by the United States and Japan that each would supply the other with such commodities as were required and were available and that steps would be taken to resume normal trade relations between the two countries. 5. Provision for cooperation between the two countries toward obtaining non-discriminatory access by peaceful means to supplies of natural resources which each needed. 6. A mutual affirmation that the basic policy of each country was one of peace throughout the Pacific area and a mutual disclaimer of territorial designs there. 7. A provision that Japan declare its willingness to negotiate with the United States, at such time as the latter might desire, with a view to concluding a treaty for the neutralization of the Philippine Islands, when Philippine independence should have been achieved. (213)

Report of Japanese Plan To Attack Russia

On June 22, 1941 Hitler launched his invasion of Russia. Several days later, on July 4, a message was sent by this Government to the Japanese Prime Minister referring to reports which were being received from varied sources that Japan had decided to attack Russia. The message stated that such military conquest and aggression would destroy our hope that peace in the Pacific might not be disturbed anew but rather might be reinforced; that it was our sincere hope that such reports were incorrect; and that assurances to this effect by the Japanese Government would be appreciated. (215)

The Japanese reply of July 8, 1941 was to the effect that prevention of the European war from spreading to the regions of Greater East Asia and preservation of peace in the Pacific area had always been the sincere and genuine desire of the Japanese Government; that the Japanese Government had not so far considered the possibility of joining the hostilities against the Soviet Union. (217)

Japanese Occupation of Southern Indochina

Even before this time the United States Government had received reports that a Japanese military movement into southern Indochina was imminent. This Government brought these reports to the attention of the Japanese Ambassador at Washington, pointing out the inconsistency between such a military movement and the discussions which were then proceeding looking toward the conclusion of an agreement for peace in the Pacific. About July 22, as a result of pressure exerted by Axis authorities upon the Vichy Government, Japan was granted by the French the right to maintain troops and establish air and naval bases in southern Indochina. In explanation of this action the Japanese Ambassador informed Acting Secretary of State Welles on July 23 that Japan must be assured of an uninterrupted source of supply of rice and raw materials and other foodstuffs, whose flow to Japan might be obstructed by Chinese and DeGaullist activities in southern Indochina; and that the step taken was a safeguard against a policy of encircling Japan on which the latter believed certain powers were intent. The Acting Secretary replied that any agreement which might have been concluded between the French Government at Vichy and Japan could only have resulted from pressure exerted on Vichy by Germany; therefore, it was our judgment that this agreement could only be looked upon as offering assistance to Germany's policy of world domination and conquest. He pointed out that the conclusion of the agreement which had been under discussion by the Secretary of State and the Ambassador would bring about a far greater measure of economic security to Japan than she could gain by occupation of Indochina. He said further that the policy of the United States was the opposite of an encirclement policy or of any policy which would be a threat to Japan; that Japan was not menaced by the policy of Great Britain and if an agreement had been concluded, Great Britain, the British Dominions, China, and the Netherlands would have joined the United States and Japan in support of the underlying principles stood for by the United States; that the United States could only regard the action of Japan as constituting notice that Japan intended to pursue a policy of force and conquest, and must assume that Japan was taking the last step before proceeding on a policy of expansion and conquest in the region of the South Seas. Finally, the Acting Secretary said that in these circumstances the Secretary of State—with whom he had talked a few minutes before—could not see any basis for pursuing further the conversations in which the Secretary and the Ambassador had been engaged. (218)

On the following day, July 24, 1941, the Acting Secretary, Mr. Welles, stated to the press that the Japanese Government was giving clear indication that it was determined to pursue an objective of expansion by force or threat of force; that there was no apparent valid ground upon which the Japanese Government would be warranted in occupying Indochina or establishing bases in that area as measures of self-defense; that there was not the slightest ground for belief that the United States, Great Britain, or the Netherlands had any territorial ambitions in Indochina or had been planning any moves which could be regarded as threats to Japan; that this Government could only conclude that the action of Japan was undertaken because of the estimated value to Japan of bases in that region primarily for purposes of further movements of conquest in adjacent areas. The Acting Secretary went on to say that these Japanese actions endangered the use of the Pacific by peaceful nations; that these actions tended to jeopardize the procurement by the United States of essential materials such as tin and rubber, which were necessary in our defense program; and that the steps which Japan was taking endangered the safety of other areas of the Pacific, including the Philippine Islands. (219)

On the afternoon of that same day, July 24, 1941, President Roosevelt received the Japanese Ambassador. The President told the Ambassador that the new move by Japan in Indochina created an exceedingly serious problem for the United States. The President said that the Japanese Government surely could not have the slightest belief that China, Great Britain, the Netherlands, or the United States had any territorial designs on Indochina or were in the slightest degree providing any real threats of aggression against Japan. This Government consequently could only assume that the occupation of Indochina "was being undertaken by Japan for the purpose of further offense".

The President then made a proposal that if the Japanese Government would refrain from occupying Indochina with its military and naval forces, or, had these steps actually been commenced, if the Japanese Government would withdraw such forces, the President would do everything within his power to obtain from the Governments of China, Great Britain, the Netherlands, and of course the United States, a binding declaration, provided Japan would make a similar commitment, to regard Indochina as a neutralized area. This would imply that the powers concerned would not undertake any military act of aggression against Indochina and would not exercise any military control within or over Indochina. The President would further endeavor to procure from the other interested powers a guaranty that so long as the existing emergency continued, the local French authorities in Indochina would remain in control of the territory. If these steps were taken, the President said, Japan would be given binding proof that no other power had any hostile designs on Indochina and that Japan would be afforded the fullest and freest opportunity of assuring for itself a source of food supplies and other raw materials which—according to Japan's accounts—Japan was seeking to secure.

The President then said that it was believed in the United States that such policies as Japan was pursuing were due to German pressure upon Japan; that the Japanese Government did not understand as clearly as we that Hitler was bent upon world domination; that if Germany succeeded in defeating Russia and dominating Europe and Africa, Germany thereafter would turn her attention to the Far East and to the Western Hemisphere; and that it was entirely possible that after some years the Navies of Japan and of the United States would be cooperating against Hitler as a common enemy.

In the course of this conversation the President reminded the Japanese Ambassador that the United States had been permitting oil to be exported from the United States to Japan; that this had been done because we realized that if these oil supplies had been shut off or restricted the Japanese Government and people would have used this as an incentive or pretext for moving down upon the Netherlands Indies in order to assure themselves of a greater oil supply; that the United States had been pursuing this policy primarily for the purpose of doing its utmost to preserve peace in the Pacific region; that our citizens were unable to understand why, at a time when they were asked to curtail their use of gasoline, the United States should be permitting oil supplies to go to Japan when Japan had given every indication of pursuing a policy of force and conquest in conjunction with the policy of world conquest and domination being carried on by Hitler. The President said that if Japan attempted to seize oil supplies by force in the Netherlands Indies, the latter would undoubtedly resist, the British would immediately come to their assistance, and war would then result. In view of our own policy of assisting Great Britain, "an exceedingly serious situation would immediately result". The President stated that with these facts in mind oil had up to this time been permitted to be shipped from the United States to Japan, notwithstanding the bitter criticism leveled against the administration. (220)

President Roosevelt discussed this question in an informal talk at the White House on July 24. He explained the essential necessity, from the standpoint of our own defense and of that of Great Britain, of preventing war from breaking out in the South Pacific. He said that if oil supplies from the United States had been cut off, Japan probably would have attacked the Netherlands Indies to obtain oil and war would have resulted; that the policy of the United States in allowing oil to go to Japan had succeeded in keeping war out of the South Pacific, "for our own good, for the good of the defense of Great Britain, and the freedom of the seas". (221)

Freezing of Japanese Assets in the United States

The Japanese move into southern Indochina, in disregard of the entire spirit underlying the exploratory conversations, was unmistakably an overt and flagrant act of aggression. Japan's constant expansion of its military position in the southwest Pacific had already substantially imperiled the security of the United States along with that of other powers. By this further expansion of its field of aggression Japan virtually completed the encirclement of the Philippine Islands and placed its armed forces within striking distance of vital trade routes. This created a situation in which the risk of war became so great that the United States and other countries concerned were confronted no longer with the question of avoiding such risk but from then on with the problem of preventing a complete undermining of their security. In these circumstances the Government of the United States decided at that point, as did certain other governments especially concerned, that discontinuance of trade with Japan had become an appropriate, warranted, and necessary step—as a warning to Japan and as a measure of self-defense.

On July 26, 1941 President Roosevelt issued an Executive order freezing Japanese assets in the United States. This order brought under control of the Government all financial and import and export trade transactions in which Japanese interests were involved, and the effect of this was to bring about very soon the virtual cessation of trade between the United States and Japan. (222)

Japanese Proposal of August 6

Notwithstanding the President's proposal of July 24 for the neutralization of Indochina, Japanese forces continued to move into southern Indochina. Not until August 6 was a reply received to the President's proposal. On that day the Japanese Ambassador presented a counter-proposal, according to which his Government would undertake not further to station its troops in the southwestern Pacific areas, except French Indochina; would withdraw the troops then stationed in French Indochina after settlement of the "China incident"; would guarantee the neutrality of the Philippine Islands "at an opportune time"; and would cooperate with the United States in the production and procurement of such natural resources as were required by the United States. According to this counter-proposal, the United States on its part would suspend its "military measures" in the southwestern Pacific areas and, upon the successful conclusion of the conversations, would advise the Governments of Great Britain and of the Netherlands to take similar steps; would cooperate with the Japanese Government in the production and procurement of natural resources required by Japan in the southwestern Pacific areas; would take steps necessary for restoring normal trade relations between the

United States and Japan; would use its good offices for the initiation of direct negotiations between the Japanese Government and "the Chiang Kai-shek regime" for the purpose of a speedy settlement of the China incident; and would recognize a special status for Japan in French Indochina, even after the withdrawal of Japanese troops from that area. On presenting this proposal the Japanese Ambassador explained that the Japanese measures taken in Indochina were absolutely necessary "to prevent from getting beyond control the Japanese public opinion which had been dangerously aroused because of the successive measures taken by the United States, Great Britain and Netherlands East Indies against Japan". (223)

The Japanese counter-proposal disregarded the President's suggestion for the neutralization of Indochina and attempted to take full advantage—military, political, and economic—of the Japanese *fait accompli* in occupying southern Indochina. On August 8, 1941 the Secretary of State informed the Japanese Ambassador that Japan's counter-proposal could not be considered as responsive to the President's proposal. The Ambassador then inquired whether it might be possible to arrange for a meeting of the responsible heads of the two Governments to discuss means of adjusting relations between the two countries. (224, 225)

United States - British Collaboration

During a conversation between Secretary Hull and the British Ambassador on August 9, 1941 the Secretary referred to the Japanese plan "to invade by force the whole of the Indian Ocean and the islands and continents adjacent thereto, isolating China, sailing across probably to the mouth of the Suez Canal, to the Persian Gulf oil area, to the Cape of Good Hope area, thereby blocking by a military despotism the trade routes and the supply sources to the British". The Secretary said that this broad military occupation would perhaps be even more damaging to British defense in Europe than any other step short of a German crossing of the Channel; that this Government visualized these broad conditions and the problems of resistance which they presented; that the activities of the United States in the way of discouraging this Japanese movement and of resistance would be more or less affected by the British defensive situation in Europe and hence by the number of United States naval vessels and other United States aid that might be needed by Great Britain at the same time. The Secretary said that in the event of further Japanese movements south this Government and the British Government should naturally have a conference at once; this Government would then be able to determine more definitely and in detail its position as to resistance. (226)

During the August 1941 conference between President Roosevelt and Prime Minister Churchill of Great Britain the situation in the Far East was discussed, and it was agreed that the United States and Great Britain should take parallel action in warning Japan against new moves of aggression. It was agreed also that the United States should continue its conversations with the Japanese Government and by such means offer Japan a reasonable and just alternative to the course upon which that country was embarked.

Warning to Japan

President Roosevelt and Secretary Hull conferred with the Japanese Ambassador on August 17. The President handed the Ambassador a document stating that notwithstanding the efforts of the United States to reach a sound basis for negotiations between the two countries for the maintenance of peace with order and justice in the Pacific, the Government of Japan had continued its military activities and its disposals of armed forces at various points in the Far East and had occupied Indochina with its military, air, and naval forces. Therefore, the statement continued, the Government of the United States "finds it necessary to say to the Government of Japan that if the Japanese Government takes any further steps in pursuance of a policy or program of military domination by force or threat of force of neighboring countries, the Government of the United States will be compelled to take immediately any and all steps which it may deem necessary toward safeguarding the legitimate rights and interests of the United States and American nationals and toward insuring the safety and security of the United States".

The President also handed Ambassador Nomura a document in reply to a request which the Ambassador had made of the Secretary of State for a resumption of conversations and to the Ambassador's suggestion, advanced on August 8, that President Roosevelt and the Japanese Prime Minister meet with a view to discussing means for an adjustment in relations between the United States and Japan. In this document it was stated that in case Japan desired and was in a position to suspend its expansionist activities, to readjust its position, and to embark upon a peaceful program for the Pacific along the lines of the program and principles to which the United States was committed, the Government of the United States would be prepared to consider resumption of the informal exploratory discussions. It was also stated that before renewal of the conversations or proceeding with plans for a meeting of the heads of the two Governments, it would be helpful if the Japanese Government would furnish a clearer statement of its present attitude and plans. The President said to the Ambassador that "we could not think of reopening the conversations" if the Japanese Government continued its movement of force and conquest. (228)

Proposed Meeting of President Roosevelt and Prime Minister Konoye

Ten days later Prime Minister Konoye of Japan sent to President Roosevelt a message which was delivered by the Japanese Ambassador on August 28, 1941, urging that a meeting between President Roosevelt and himself be arranged as soon as possible for a frank exchange of views. The Prime Minister said in this message that the idea of continuing preliminary informal conversations and of having their conclusion confirmed by the responsible heads of the two Governments did not meet the need of the existing situation, which was developing swiftly and which might produce unforeseen contingencies; that he considered it, therefore, of urgent necessity that the heads of the two Governments meet first to discuss from a broad standpoint all important problems between Japan and the United States covering the entire Pacific area. (230)

Accompanying the Prime Minister's message was a statement by the Japanese Government giving assurances that Japan was seeking a program for the Pacific area consistent with the principles to which the United States Government had long been committed. However, the statement contained qualifications to the following effect: The Japanese Government was prepared to withdraw its troops from Indochina "as soon as the China incident is settled or a just peace is established in East Asia"; Japan would take no military action against the Soviet Union so long as the Soviet Union remained faithful to the Soviet-Japanese neutrality treaty and did "not menace Japan or Manchukuo or take any action contrary to the spirit of the said treaty"; the Japanese Government had no intention of using, "without provocation", military force against any neighboring nation.

In a conversation with Secretary Hull on the same day, Ambassador Nomura said that the Prime Minister would probably proceed to the proposed meeting in a Japanese warship and would probably be assisted by a staff of officials from the Foreign Office, the Army, the Navy, and the Japanese Embassy at Washington. The Ambassador thought that the inclusion of Japanese Army and Navy representatives would be "especially beneficial in view of the responsibility which they would share for the settlement reached". He said his Government was very anxious that the meeting be held at the earliest possible moment in view of the efforts of a "third country" and "fifth-columnists in Japan" to disturb Japanese-American relations.

In the same conversation Secretary Hull pointed out to the Ambassador the desirability of reaching an agreement in principle on the main issues prior to a meeting of President Roosevelt and the Japanese Prime Minister. He said that should such a meeting be a failure the consequences would be serious and that, therefore, its purpose should be the ratification of essential points agreed upon in advance. (231)

In a reply of September 3 to the Prime Minister's message President Roosevelt stated that he was very desirous of collaborating with the Prime Minister; that he could not avoid taking cognizance of indications in some quarters of Japan of concepts which seemed capable of raising obstacles to successful collaboration between the President and the Prime Minister; that in these circumstances precaution should be taken toward insuring that the proposed meeting prove a success, by endeavoring to enter immediately upon preliminary discussions of the fundamental and essential questions on which agreement was sought; that these questions involved practical application of the principles fundamental to the achievement and maintenance of peace. The President repeated the four principles regarded by this Government as the foundation upon which relations between nations should properly rest: respect for the territorial integrity and the sovereignty of each and all nations; support of the principle of non-interference in the internal affairs of other countries; support of the principle of equality, including equality of commercial opportunity; non-disturbance of the *status quo* in the Pacific except as the *status quo* might be altered by peaceful means. (232)

On September 6 Ambassador Grew reported by telegram that Prime Minister Konoye had said that from the beginning of the informal conversations in Washington he had had the warmest support of the responsible Japanese Army and Navy leaders. The Prime Minister also said that the Minister of War had agreed to have a full general accompany the Prime Minister to the conference; that the Navy had agreed to send a full admiral; and that the Army and Navy vice Chiefs of Staff and other high officers who were in full sympathy with the Prime Minister's aims would also go. (233)

In considering the Japanese proposal for a meeting between President Roosevelt and the Japanese Prime Minister this Government took into consideration that during the exploratory conversations up to this time Japan had evidenced an intention to continue its program of aggression and domination in the Far East. This Government had in mind that the Prime Minister, Prince Konoye, who would attend the meeting, had headed the Japanese Government in 1937 when Japan attacked China; that he had proclaimed and given publicity to the basic principles which the Japanese Government presumably would insist upon in any peace agreement with China; that the Japanese Government had shown in the "treaty" which Japan had concluded in November 1940 with the Japanese puppet regime at Nanking how it proposed to apply these principles. This "treaty" contained provisions that Japan should, "in order to carry out the defence against communistic activities through collaboration of the two countries, station required forces in specified areas of Mengchiang and of North China for the necessary duration"; that China should "recognize that Japan may, in accordance with previous practices or in order to preserve the common interests of the two countries, station for a required duration its naval units and vessels in specified areas within the territory of the Republic of China"; that "while considering the requirements of China, the Government of the Republic of China shall afford positive and full facilities to Japan and Japanese subjects" with respect to the utilization of resources.

This Government also had in mind that the military element in Japan, which would be heavily represented at the proposed conference, had been responsible for carrying on Japan's program of aggression since 1931 and that the Japanese military leaders had caused the Japanese Government to maintain in the conversations a rigid attitude and position.

Furthermore, if the proposed meeting accomplished no more than the endorsement of general principles, the Japanese Government would be free to make its own interpretation of those principles in their actual application. If the meeting ended without agreement the Japanese military leaders would be in a position to represent to their country that the United States was responsible for the failure of the meeting.

In view of all these factors, this Government could not but feel that there was scant hope that the Japanese Government could be persuaded to undergo a change of attitude and that in any case it was essential to determine in advance of a meeting between the responsible heads of the two Governments whether there was in fact any basis for agreement.

Japanese Proposal of September 6

On September 6, 1941 the Japanese Ambassador handed to the Secretary of State a revised proposal. In that proposal it was stated that: 1. Japan would not make any military advance from French Indochina against any adjoining areas, and likewise would not, "without any justifiable reason", resort to military action against any regions lying south of Japan. 2. The attitudes of Japan and the United States toward the European war would be "decided by the concepts of protection and self-defense, and, in case the United States should participate in the European war, the interpretation and execution of the Tripartite Pact by Japan shall be independently decided". (The Japanese Ambassador said that the formulae contained in points 1 and 2 represented the maximum that Japan could offer at that time.) 3. Japan would "endeavor to bring about the rehabilitation of general and normal relationship between Japan and China, upon the realization of which Japan is ready to withdraw its armed forces from China as soon as possible in accordance with the agreements between Japan and China". 4. The economic activities of the United States in China would "not be restricted so long as pursued on an equitable basis". 5. Japanese activities in the southwestern Pacific area would be carried on by peaceful means and in accordance with the principle of non-discrimination in international commerce, and Japan would cooperate in the production and procurement by the United States of needed natural resources in the said area. 6. Japan would take measures necessary for the resumption of normal trade relations between Japan and the United States. On its part the United States would undertake: to "abstain from any measures and actions which will be prejudicial to the endeavour by Japan concerning the settlement of the China Affair" (Ambassador Grew was informed by the Japanese Foreign Minister that this point referred to United States aid to Chiang Kai-shek); to reciprocate Japan's commitment expressed in point 5 referred to above; to "suspend any military measures" in the Far East and in the southwestern Pacific area; and to reciprocate immediately Japan's commitment expressed in point 6 above. (234)

Some of the Japanese provisions were equivocal and ambiguous and some indicated a disposition by the Japanese Government to narrow down and limit the application of the fundamental principles with which the Japanese professed in the abstract to agree. The revised proposals were much narrower than would have been expected from the assurances given in the statement communicated to President Roosevelt on August 28.

On September 6 Ambassador Grew reported that it had been revealed in his talk with Prince Konoye on that day that the Prime Minister and therefore the Japanese Government wholeheartedly subscribed to the four points considered by the United States Government essential as a basis for satisfactory reconstruction of United States - Japanese relations. These had been set out in President Roosevelt's reply of September 3 to the Prime Minister's message. However, the Japanese Minister for Foreign Affairs informed Ambassador Grew some time later that although Prince Konoye had "in principle" accepted the four points, the Prime Minister had indicated that some adjustment would be required in applying them to actual conditions.

Throughout September 1941 the Japanese Government continued to urge upon the United States an early meeting between the President and the Japanese Prime Minister. On September 23 the Japanese Ambassador told Secretary Hull that such a meeting would have a psychological effect in Japan by setting Japan on a new course; that it would counteract the influence of pro-Axis elements in Japan and provide support for the elements desiring peaceful relations with the United States. During a conversation with Secretary Hull on September 29 the Ambassador said that if the proposed meeting should not take place it might be difficult for the Konoye regime to stay in office and that if it fell it was likely to be followed by a less moderate government. The Ambassador handed to Secretary Hull a paper expressing the views of the Japanese Government on the proposed meeting. In this it was stated that the meeting would "mark an epochal turn for good in Japanese-American relations"; that should the meeting not take place there might never be another opportunity and the repercussions might be "most unfortunate". It stated that the ship to carry the Prime Minister was ready; that his suite, including a full general and a full admiral, had been privately appointed; that the party was prepared to depart at any moment. Finally, it stated that any further delay in arranging for the meeting would put the Japanese Government in a "very delicate position" and again emphasized that there was urgent necessity for holding the meeting at the earliest possible date. (237, 239)

The reply of the United States to the Japanese proposal of September 6, 1941 was contained in a statement made by Secretary Hull to the Japanese Ambassador on October 2. After reviewing the progress of the course of the conversations thus far, the Secretary stated that a clear-cut manifestation of Japan's intention in regard to the withdrawal of Japanese troops from China and French Indochina would be most helpful in making known Japan's peaceful intentions and Japan's desire to follow courses calculated to establish a sound basis for future stability and progress in the Pacific area. The Secretary said that the United States Government had welcomed the suggestion for a meeting of the heads of the two Governments, but while desiring to proceed with arrangements as soon as possible, felt that clarification of certain principles was necessary to insure the success of the meeting. He remarked that from what the Japanese Government had indicated, it contemplated a program in which the basic principles put forward by the United States would in their application be circumscribed by qualifications and exceptions. Secretary Hull asked whether, in view of these circumstances, the Japanese Government felt that the proposed meeting would be likely to contribute to the advancement of the high purposes which the two Governments mutually had in mind. He repeated the view of the United States that renewed consideration of the fundamental principles would be helpful in seeking a meeting of minds on the essential questions and laying a firm foundation for the meeting.

The Japanese Ambassador, after reading this statement, expressed the fear that his Government would be disappointed, because of its earnest desire to hold the meeting. Secretary Hull replied that we had no desire to cause any delay but felt there should be a meeting of minds on the essential points before the meeting between the President and the Prime Minister was held. (240, 241)

The conversations between the Secretary of State and the Japanese Ambassador at Washington continued, but the issues between the Governments appeared no nearer settlement. The chief questions on which agreement seemed impossible were Japanese obligations to Germany and Italy under the Tripartite Pact; the question of adherence by Japan to a basic course of peace; and the terms of settlement of the conflict between Japan and China, particularly the matter of the evacuation of Japanese troops from China. In regard to the last point this Government throughout the negotiations maintained that any settlement involving China must provide fully for the sovereignty and territorial integrity of that country; otherwise there would be no prospect of stable peace in the Pacific area. With reference to the Tripartite Pact, there was implicit throughout the discussions a Japanese threat that if the United States should become involved in war with Germany the Japanese Government, in accordance with the terms of the pact, would make war on the United States.

Ambassador Grew's Report That War Might Be "Inevitable"

In a telegram of November 3, 1941 Ambassador Grew reported to the Department of State on the current situation in Japan. He warned against acceptance of any theory that the weakening and final exhaustion of Japanese financial and economic resources would result shortly in Japan's collapse as a militarist nation. He pointed out that despite severe cuts in industrial output, the loss of most of Japan's commerce, and the depletion of national resources, such a collapse had not occurred; but instead there was being drastically prosecuted the integration of Japanese national economy. Events so far, he said, had given no support for the view that war in the Far East could best be averted by imposition of commercial embargoes. He said that considering the temper of the people of Japan it was dangerously uncertain to base United States policy on a view that the imposition of progressive and rigorous economic measures would probably avert war; that it was the view of the Embassy that war would not be averted by such a course.

The Ambassador said it was his purpose to insure against the United States becoming involved in war with Japan through any misconception of Japanese capacity to plunge into a "suicidal struggle" with us. Although reason, he said, would dictate against such a happening, our own standards of logic could not be used to measure Japanese rationality. While we need not be overly concerned by the "bellicose" utterances of the Japanese press, it would be short-sighted to underestimate the obvious preparations of Japan; it would be short-sighted also if our policy were based on a belief that these preparations amounted merely to saber rattling. Finally, he warned of the possibility of Japan's adopting measures with dramatic and dangerous suddenness which might make inevitable a war with the United States. (245)

Four days later, on November 7, Secretary Hull stated at a Cabinet meeting that relations between Japan and the United States were extremely critical and that there was "imminent possibility" that Japan might at any time start a new military movement of conquest by force. It thereupon became the consensus of the Cabinet that the critical situation might well be emphasized in speeches in order that the country would, if possible, be better prepared for such a development. Accordingly, Secretary of the Navy Knox delivered an address

136

on November 11, 1941 in which he stated that we were not only confronted with the necessity of extreme measures of self-defense in the Atlantic, but we were "likewise faced with grim possibilities on the other side of the world—on the far side of the Pacific"; that the Pacific no less than the Atlantic called for instant readiness for defense. On the same day Under Secretary of State Welles, carrying out the Cabinet suggestion in an address, stated that beyond the Atlantic a sinister and pitiless conqueror had reduced more than half of Europe to abject serfdom and that in the Far East the same forces of conquest were menacing the safety of all nations bordering on the Pacific. The waves of world conquest were "breaking high both in the East and in the West", he said, and were threatening, more and more with each passing day, "to engulf our own shores". He warned that the United States was in far greater peril than in 1917; that "at any moment war may be forced upon us". (247, 248)

On November 17 Ambassador Grew cabled from Tokyo that in calling attention to the necessity for vigilance against sudden Japanese naval or military attack in regions not then involved in the Chinese-Japanese conflict, he considered it probable that the Japanese would make use of every possible tactical advantage, including surprise and initiative. The Ambassador said that in Japan there was an extremely effective control over military information and that as a consequence it was unlikely that the Embassy would be able to give substantial warning. (250)

Kurusu Sent to Washington

Early in November the Japanese Government informed this Government that it desired to send Mr. Saburo Kurusu to Washington to assist Ambassador Nomura in the conversations. This Government at once responded favorably and, upon request by the Japanese Government, facilitated Mr. Kurusu's journey by arranging that priority passage be given him and his secretary on a United States trans-Pacific plane and that the scheduled departure of the plane from Hong Kong be delayed until Mr. Kurusu could reach Hong Kong from Tokyo.

President Roosevelt and Secretary Hull conferred with Ambassador Nomura and Mr. Kurusu on November 17. It soon became clear in the course of this and subsequent conversations that Mr. Kurusu had brought no new material or plans or proposals.

During this conversation of November 17 the President expressed the desire of the United States to avoid war between the two countries and to bring about a fair and peaceful settlement in the Pacific area; he accepted a statement of the Japanese Ambassador that this was also the desire of Japan. The President stated that, from the long-range point of view, there was no occasion for serious differences between the United States and Japan.

Secretary Hull said that any settlement for the Pacific area would not be taken seriously while Japan was still "clinging" to the Tripartite Pact; that since Hitler had announced that he was out for unlimited-invasion objectives and had started on a march across the earth, the United States had been in danger and this danger had grown with each passing week; that the United States recognized the danger and was proceeding with self-defense before it was too late; that the United States felt the danger so profoundly that it had committed itself to the expenditure of many billions of dollars in self-defense.

The Secretary said the belief in this country was that the Japanese formula for a new order in greater East Asia was but another name for a program to dominate all of the Pacific area politically, economically, socially, and otherwise, by military force; that this would include the high seas, the islands, and the continents, and would place every other country at the mercy of arbitrary military rule just as the Hitler program did in Europe and the Japanese program did in China.

Mr. Kurusu reiterated that ways must be found to work out an agreement to avoid trouble between the two countries and said that all the way across the Pacific "it was like a powder keg". Referring to the relations of Japan and Germany, he said that Germany had not up to then called upon Japan to fight. (251)

Secretary Hull conferred again with the Japanese Ambassador and Mr. Kurusu on November 18. The Secretary said that we were trying to make a contribution to the establishment of a peaceful world, based on law and order; that this was what we wanted to work out with Japan; that we had nothing to offer in the way of bargaining except our friendship. He said that the present situation was exceptionally advantageous for Japan to put her factories to work in producing goods needed by peaceful countries, if only the Japanese people could get war and invasion out of mind; that it would be difficult for him to cause this Government to go far in removing the embargo unless it were given reason to believe that Japan was definitely started on a peaceful course and had renounced purposes of conquest.

Mr. Kurusu expressed the belief that the two Governments should now make efforts to achieve something to tide over the present abnormal situation. He suggested that perhaps after the termination of the Sino-Japanese conflict it might be possible to adopt a more liberal policy but said that he was unable to promise anything on the part of his Government.

Ambassador Nomura emphasized that the situation in Japan was very pressing and that it was important to arrest further deterioration of the relations between the two countries. He suggested that if this situation could now be checked an atmosphere would develop when it would be possible to move in the direction of the courses which this Government advocated.

Our people did not trust Hitler, the Secretary said, and we felt that it was inevitable that Hitler would eventually, if successful, get around to the Far East and "double-cross" Japan. He cited the instance when Germany, after concluding an anti-Comintern pact with Japan, had surprised Japan later by entering into a non-aggression pact with Russia, and finally had violated the non-aggression pact by attacking Russia. The Secretary expressed great doubt that any agreement between the United States and Japan, while Japan at the same time had an alliance with Hitler, would carry the confidence of our people. He considered the Tripartite Pact inconsistent with the establishment of an understanding. He said that frankly he did not know whether anything could be done in the matter of reaching a satisfactory agreement with Japan; that we could go so far but rather than go beyond a certain point it would be better for us "to stand and take the consequences".

Mr. Kurusu replied that he could not say that Japan would abrogate the Tripartite Pact but intimated that Japan might do something to "outshine" it. He said that Japan would not be a "cat's-paw" for Germany; that Japan had entered into the Tripartite Pact in order to use the pact for its own purposes and because it felt isolated; that the situation in Japan was very pressing and that it was important to arrest a further deterioration of relations between the two countries; that our freezing regulations had caused impatience in Japan and a feeling that Japan had to fight while still in a position to fight. (252)

Japanese Proposal of November 20

On November 20 Ambassador Nomura and Mr. Kurusu presented to the Secretary of State a proposal comprising mutual commitments: to make no armed advance into regions of southeastern Asia and the southern Pacific area excepting French Indochina (where Japanese troops were then stationed), to cooperate with a view to "securing the acquisition of those . . . commodities which the two governments need in Netherlands East Indies", and to undertake "to restore their commercial relations to those prevailing prior to the freezing of the assets"; commitments by the United States to undertake to supply Japan "a required quantity of oil" and "to refrain from such measures and actions as will be prejudicial to the endeavors for the restoration of general peace between Japan and China" (which, the Japanese orally explained, meant that the Government of the United States was to discontinue its aid to the Chinese Government); and a commitment by Japan to undertake to withdraw its troops then in Indochina either upon restoration of peace between Japan and China or upon "the establishment of an equitable peace in the Pacific area" and "upon the conclusion of the present arrangement" to remove to northern Indochina the troops that it then had in southern Indochina (which would have left Japan free to increase its armed forces in Indochina to whatever extent it might desire). (254)

During a conversation on that same day with the Japanese Ambassador and Mr. Kurusu, Secretary Hull said that Japan could at any moment put an end to the existing situation by deciding upon an "all out" peaceful course; that at any moment Japan could bring to an end what Japan chose to call "encirclement".

The Secretary said the people of the United States believed that the purposes underlying our aid to China were the same as those underlying our aid to Great Britain and that there was a partnership between Hitler and Japan aimed at enabling Hitler to take charge of one half of the world and Japan the other half. The existence of the Tripartite Pact and the continual harping of Japan's leaders upon slogans of the Nazi type, the Secretary said, served to strengthen this belief; what was needed was the manifestation by Japan of a clear purpose to pursue peaceful courses. He said that our people desired to avoid a repetition in East Asia of what Hitler was doing in Europe; that our people opposed the idea of a "new order" under military control.

In this conversation the Japanese representatives reiterated that their Government was really desirous of peace and that Japan had "never pledged itself to a policy of expansion". Secretary Hull remarked that the Chinese "might have an answer to that point". When Mr. Kurusu declared that Japan could not abrogate the Tripartite Pact, the Secretary observed that Japan did not take a similar view of the Nine-Power Treaty. Mr. Kurusu replied to the effect that the latter treaty was twenty years old and "outmoded". (253)

During a conversation on November 22 the Secretary of State informed the Japanese Ambassador and Mr. Kurusu that he had called in representatives of certain other governments concerned in the Far East and that there had been a discussion of the question whether there could be some relaxation of freezing; that there was a general feeling that the matter could be settled if the Japanese could give some evidence of peaceful intentions. The Secretary said that if the United States and other countries should see Japan pursuing a peaceful course there would be no question about Japan's obtaining all the materials she desired. (255)

United States Memorandum of November 26

In all of the various formulae which the Japanese Government offered in succession during the course of the conversations statements of pacific intent were qualified and restricted. As each proposal was explored it became clear that Japan did not intend to budge from the fundamental objectives of its military leaders. Japan manifested no disposition to renounce its association with Hitlerism. It insisted that its obligations under the Tripartite Pact—a direct threat to this country—would be fulfilled by Japan. Japan was willing to affirm its adherence to the principle of non-discrimination in international commercial relations, but refused to relinquish in practice the preferential position which it had arrogated to itself in all areas under Japanese occupation. Japan insisted on obtaining in its hostilities with China a victor's peace and on having our assent thereto. Japan refused to make practical application of the principle of non-interference in the internal affairs of other countries. It was steadily adding to its armed establishment in Indochina; and it insisted upon continuing to maintain its armed forces in large areas of China for an indefinite period—clearly indicating an intention to achieve a permanent control there.

It was thus evident that it was illusory any longer to expect that a general agreement would be possible. It was also clearly apparent that the Japanese were attempting to maneuver the United States into either accepting the limited Japanese proposals or making some sort of an agreement which would serve only the ends of Japan, and that without trying to solve basic questions they were seeking to evade serious consideration of an equitable broad-gauge settlement such as had been under discussion in the earlier stages of the conversations. A clear manifestation was given by the Japanese Government that it would not desist from the menace which it was creating to the United States, to the British Empire, to the Netherlands Indies, to Thailand, and to China by the presence of large and increasing bodies of Japanese armed forces in Indochina.

The Government of the United States still felt obliged, however, to leave no avenue unexplored which might conceivably cause Japan to choose a better course. Moreover, if the Japanese proposal of November 20 was indeed Japan's "last word", it was obviously desirable that record of the United States Government's position before, at the beginning of, throughout, and at the end of the conversations be made crystal clear. Therefore, toward possibly keeping alive conversations looking toward inducing Japan to choose the pathway of restraint, and toward making its position utterly clear, this Government formulated a new statement.

On November 26, 1941 the Secretary of State handed to the Japanese Ambassador and Mr. Kurusu a proposed basis for agreement between the United States and Japan. In a statement accompanying the proposal it was said that the United States earnestly desired to afford every opportunity for the continuation of discussions with the Japanese Government; that the Japanese proposals of November 20 conflicted in some respects with the fundamental principles to which each Government had declared it was committed; that the United States believed that these proposals were not likely to contribute to insuring peace in the Pacific area; and that further effort should be made to resolve the divergent views. With this object in mind, the United States was offering for the consideration of Japan a plan of a broad but simple settlement covering the entire Pacific area as one practical exemplification of a program which this Government envisaged as something to be worked out during future conversations.

The proposal contained mutual affirmations that the national policies of the two countries were directed toward peace throughout the Pacific area, that they had no territorial designs or aggressive intentions in that area, and that they would give active support to the following fundamental principles: inviolability of territorial integrity and sovereignty of each and all nations; non-interference in the internal affairs of other countries; equality, including equality of commercial opportunity and treatment; and reliance upon international cooperation and conciliation for the prevention and pacific settlement of controversies. There was also provision for mutual pledges to support and apply in their economic relations with each other and with other nations and peoples certain enumerated liberal principles.

The proposal contemplated the following mutual commitments: to endeavor to conclude a multilateral non-aggression pact among the governments principally concerned in the Pacific area; to endeavor to conclude among the principally interested governments an agreement to respect the territorial integrity of Indochina and not to seek or accept preferential economic treatment therein; not to support any government in China other than the National Government of the Republic of China with its capital temporarily at Chungking; to relinquish extraterritorial and related rights in China and to obtain the agreement of other governments now enjoying such rights to give up those rights; to negotiate a trade agreement based upon reciprocal most-favored-nation treatment; to remove freezing restrictions imposed by each country on the funds of the other; to agree upon a plan for the stabilization of the dollar-yen rate; to agree that no agreement which either had concluded with any third power or powers should be interpreted by it in a way to conflict with the fundamental purpose of this proposed agreement; and to use their influence to cause other governments to adhere to the basic political and economic principles provided for in this proposed agreement.

The proposal envisaged a situation in which there would be no foreign armed forces in French Indochina or in China. Withdrawal of the last armed forces of the United States from China was then in progress and had almost been completed and withdrawal of British armed forces from China had already been completed. Accordingly there was suggested one unilateral commitment, an undertaking by Japan that she would "withdraw all military, naval, air and police forces from China and from Indochina".

After the Japanese representatives had read the document, Mr. Kurusu said that when this proposal of the United States was reported to the Japanese Government, that Government would be likely to "throw up its hands"; that this response to the Japanese proposal could be interpreted as tantamount to the end of the negotiations. The Japanese representatives then asked whether they could see the President. (256, 257, 258)

President Roosevelt, with Secretary Hull present, received Ambassador Nomura and Mr. Kurusu on November 27. The President stated that people in the United States wanted a peaceful solution of all matters in the Pacific area; that he had not given up yet, although the situation was serious. He said that this Government had been very much disappointed by the continued expressions of opposition by Japanese leaders to the fundamental principles of peace and order. This attitude on the part of the Japanese leaders had created an atmosphere, both in the United States and abroad, which had added greatly to the difficulty of making mutually satisfactory progress in the conversations.

The President called attention to the fact that this Government had been very patient in dealing with the whole Far Eastern situation; that we were prepared to continue to be patient if Japan's course of action permitted continuance of such an attitude on our part. He said that this country could not bring about any substantial relaxation in its economic restrictions unless Japan gave some clear manifestation of peaceful intent. If that occurred we could take some steps of a concrete character designed to improve the general situation.

The Secretary said everyone knew that the Japanese slogans of "co-prosperity", "new order in East Asia", and the "controlling influence" in certain areas were all terms to express in a camouflaged manner the policy of force and conquest by Japan and the domination by military agencies of the political, economic, social, and moral affairs of each of the populations conquered. As long as the Japanese moved in that direction and continued to increase their military and other relations with Hitler through such instruments as the Anti-Comintern Pact and the Tripartite Pact, no real progress could be made toward a peaceful solution. During this conference the Japanese representatives had little to say except to express their disappointment at the small progress made thus far. (259)

"Japan May Move Suddenly"

On November 25 and on November 28, at meetings of high officials of this Government, Secretary Hull emphasized the critical nature of the relations of this country with Japan. He stated that there was practically no possibility of an agreement being achieved with Japan; that in his opinion the Japanese were likely to break out at any time with new acts of conquest by force; and that the matter of safeguarding our national security was in the hands of the Army and the Navy. The Secretary expressed his judgment that any plans for our military defense should include an assumption that the Japanese might make the element of surprise a central point in their strategy and also might attack at various points simultaneously with a view to demoralizing efforts of defense and of coordination for purposes thereof.

On November 29, 1941, Secretary Hull conferred with the British Ambassador. The Secretary said that "the diplomatic part of our relations with Japan was virtually over and that the matter will now go to the officials of the Army and Navy". He said further that it would be "a serious mistake for our country and other countries interested in the Pacific situation to make plans of resistance without including the possibility that Japan may move suddenly and with every possible element of surprise and spread out over considerable areas and capture certain positions and posts before the peaceful countries interested in the Pacific would have time to confer and formulate plans to meet these new conditions; that this would be on the theory that the Japanese recognize that their course of unlimited conquest now renewed all along the line probably is a desperate gamble and requires the utmost boldness and risk". (260)

Reported Japanese Troop Movements

Secretary Hull conferred with the Japanese Ambassador and Mr. Kurusu on December 1. The Secretary said that in the current discussions we had to take into account the bellicose utterances emanating from Tokyo. He emphasized that we did not propose to go into partnership with Japan's military leaders; that he had not heard one whisper of peace from them, "only bluster and bloodcurdling threats". The Japanese representatives said that statements of Japanese officials were taken more seriously in the United States than was warranted; that these statements were misquoted in the press.

The Secretary said that this Government had no idea of trying to bluff Japan and that he saw no occasion for Japan's trying to bluff us; he emphasized that "there is a limit beyond which we cannot go".

He made clear that this Government was anxious to help settle the China affair if a settlement could be reached in accordance with the basic principles discussed in the conversations, and that under such circumstances we would be glad to offer our good offices. He said that under existing circumstances, while Japan was bound in the Tripartite Pact, Japan might just as well ask us to cease aiding Britain as to cease aiding China. The United States would give Japan all the materials it wanted, he said, if Japan's military leaders would only show that Japan intended to pursue a peaceful course.

The Secretary observed that Japanese troops in Indochina constituted a menace to the South Seas area; that the stationing of these troops in Indochina was making it necessary for the United States and its friends to keep large numbers of armed forces immobilized in East Asia; that in this way Japan's acts were having the effect of aiding Hitler. He called attention to reports of heavy Japanese troop movements in Indochina, stating that we could not be sure what the Japanese military leaders were likely to do. The Secretary said that we could not "sit still" while these developments were taking place; that we would not allow ourselves to be driven out of the Pacific. He said that there was no reason for conflict between the United States and Japan; that Japan did not have to use a sword to gain "a seat at the head of the table".

The Ambassador said the Japanese people believed that the United States wanted to keep Japan fighting with China and to keep Japan strangled; that the Japanese people were faced with the alternatives of surrendering to the United States or of fighting. Mr. Kurusu said that the Japanese Government had directed him to inquire what was the ultimate aim of the United States in the conversations and to request that the United States Government make "deep reflection of this matter". (261)

Meanwhile, this Government received reports of continued Japanese troop movements to Indochina. In a communication of December 2, handed to the Japanese Ambassador by Under Secretary Welles, President Roosevelt inquired regarding these reports and asked to be informed of the actual reasons for these steps. The President stated that the stationing of increased Japanese forces in Indochina seemed to imply the intention to utilize these forces for further aggression; that such aggression might be against the Philippine Islands, the Netherlands Indies, Burma, Malaya, or Thailand. (262)

On December 5 the Japanese Ambassador handed to Secretary Hull a reply which stated that as Chinese troops had recently shown frequent signs of movements along the northern frontier of French Indochina bordering on China, Japanese troops, with the object mainly of taking precautionary measures, had been reinforced to a certain extent in the northern part of French Indochina; that as a natural sequence of this step, certain movements had been made among the troops stationed in the southern part of the said territory; and that an exaggerated report had been made of these movements.

In a conversation which followed with the Japanese Ambassador and Mr. Kurusu, the Secretary said that he had been under the impression that Japan had been moving forces into northern Indochina for the purpose of attacking China from there; that he had never heard before that these troop movements were for the purpose of defense against Chinese attack.

Ambassador Nomura said that the Japanese were alarmed over the increasing naval and military preparations of the "ABCD powers"; that the United States blamed Japan for its move into Indochina but that if Indochina were controlled by other powers it would be a menace to Japan. Mr. Kurusu said that if an agreement could be reached on temporary measures, we could proceed with the exploration of fundamental solutions; that what was needed immediately was a temporary expedient.

The Secretary said that we could solve matters without delay if the Japanese Government would renounce its policy of force and aggression. He added that we were not looking for trouble but that at the same time "we were not running away from menaces". (263)

President Roosevelt's Message to the Emperor of Japan

Despite the completely unsatisfactory Japanese reply with respect to its operations in Indochina, the United States Government still felt that every possible effort for peace should be exhausted. President Roosevelt on December 6 telegraphed to Tokyo a personal message to the Emperor of Japan in which he stated that developments were occurring in the Pacific area which threatened to deprive the United States and Japan and all humanity of the beneficial influence of the long peace between the two countries, and that these developments contained "tragic possibilities". The President said that we had hoped that the peace of the Pacific could be consummated in such a way that many diverse peoples could exist side by side without fear of invasion, that unbearable burdens of armaments could be lifted, and that all peoples would resume commerce without discrimination against or in favor of any nation. In seeking these great objectives both Japan and the United States "should agree to eliminate any form of military threat". The President said further that during recent weeks it had become clear to the world that Japanese military, naval, and air forces had been sent to southern Indochina in such large numbers as to create a reasonable doubt that this continued concentration in Indochina was defensive in its character; that the people of the Philippines, of the Netherlands Indies, of Malaya, and of Thailand were asking themselves whether these Japanese forces were preparing or intending to make attack in one or more of these many directions; that none of these peoples could sit either indefinitely or permanently "on a keg of dynamite". Finally, the President said that he was addressing the Emperor in the fervent hope that the Emperor might give thought to ways of dispelling the darkening clouds; that both he and the Emperor had "a sacred duty to restore traditional amity and prevent further death and destruction in the world". (264)

Pearl Harbor

On Sunday, December 7, 1941, at 7:50 a.m. Honolulu time (1:20 p.m. Washington time) the Japanese Government brought discussions to an end with the surprise attack upon the United States at Pearl Harbor. One hour after that attack had begun, and while Japanese planes were sowing death and destruction in Hawaii, and simultaneously were attacking the United States and Great Britain in the Far East, Ambassador Nomura and Mr. Kurusu called on Secretary Hull at the Department of State and handed him a memorandum. In that memorandum the Japanese Government stated that the United States had "resorted to every possible measure to assist the Chungking regime so as to obstruct the establishment of a general peace between Japan and China" and had "attempted to frustrate Japan's aspiration to the ideal of common prosperity in cooperation with these regions"; that in the negotiations the United States had "failed to display in the slightest degree a spirit of conciliation"; that the United States had "made known its intention to continue its aid to Chiang Kai-shek"; that it "may be said to be scheming for the extension of the war"; that it was engaged "in aiding Great Britain and preparing to attack, in the name of self-defense, Germany and Italy, two powers that are striving to establish a new order in Europe"; that the demands of the United States for the "wholesale evacuation of troops" from China and for unconditional application of the principle of non-discrimination in international commerce "ignored the actual conditions of China, and are calculated to destroy Japan's position as the stabilizing factor of East Asia"; that the United States proposal of November 26 "ignores Japan's sacrifices in the four years of the China affair, menaces the Empire's existence itself and disparages its honour and prestige"; that obviously it was the intention of the United States "to conspire with Great Britain and other countries to obstruct Japan's efforts toward the establishment of peace through the creation of a new order in East Asia"; and finally, that "in view of the attitude of the American Government" the Japanese Government "cannot but consider that it is impossible to reach an agreement through further negotiations".

Upon reading this memorandum, Secretary Hull said to the Japanese representatives: "I have never seen a document that was more crowded with infamous falsehoods and distortions—infamous falsehoods and distortions on a scale so huge that I never imagined until today that any Government on this planet was capable of uttering them." (265)

Several hours after the beginning of the Japanese attack Ambassador Grew was informed by the Japanese Foreign Minister that the above-described memorandum, which had been delivered at Washington, was desired by the Emperor to be regarded as the Emperor's reply to the President's message. At the same time, however, the

Japanese Foreign Minister made an oral statement to the Ambassador also "as a reply" from the Emperor to the President to the effect that the establishment of peace "in the Pacific, and consequently of the world, has been the cherished desire of His Majesty for the realization of which he has hitherto made the Government to continue its earnest endeavors". (266)

At 11 a.m. December 8, Tokyo time (9 p.m. December 7, Washington time) the United States Embassy at Tokyo received a communication from the Japanese Foreign Minister, dated December 8, 1941, informing the Ambassador "that there has arisen a state of war between Your Excellency's country and Japan beginning today". (269)

War With Japan, Germany, and Italy

The Japanese attack of December 7 on territory of the United States aroused our entire nation. On the morning of December 8 President Roosevelt asked the Congress to declare the existence of a state of war between the United States and Japan. Both Houses of Congress acted immediately with but one dissenting vote. At 4:10 p.m. on the afternoon of December 8 the President approved a joint resolution providing that the state of war between the United States and the Government of Japan which had been "thrust upon the United States is hereby formally declared"; and that the President was authorized and directed to employ the entire naval and military forces of the United States and the resources of the Government to carry on war against Japan; and that, to bring the conflict to a successful termination, "all of the resources of the country are hereby pledged by the Congress of the United States". (267, 268)

In a radio address of the following day, December 9, President Roosevelt stated that Germany and Japan were conducting their military and naval operations in accordance with a joint plan, which plan considered all peoples and nations not helping the Axis powers as common enemies of each and every one of the Axis powers. The President said that Germany and Italy, regardless of any formal declaration of war, "consider themselves at war with the United States at this moment just as much as they consider themselves at war with Britain and Russia"; that we expected to "eliminate" the danger from Japan but it would "serve us ill" if we accomplished that and found the rest of the world dominated by Hitler and Mussolini.

The President said further that we were in the midst of war "not for conquest, not for vengeance, but for a world in which this nation, and all that this nation represents, will be safe for our children"; we "are going to win the war and we are going to win the peace that follows". (270)

On December 11, 1941 Germany and Italy declared war on the United States. On that day the Congress passed with no dissenting vote, and the President approved, resolutions formally declaring the existence of a state of war between the United States and Germany and between the United States and Italy. (271, 272, 273)

➤➤ X V ◄◄

UNITED NATIONS

SHORTLY AFTER WAR came to the United States this Government proposed that the nations arrayed against the Axis powers join together in a declaration pledging cooperation in the prosecution of the war and agreeing not to make a separate armistice or peace with the enemies. As a result, there was signed at Washington such a declaration, dated January 1, 1942, by representatives of the following Governments: United States of America, United Kingdom of Great Britain and Northern Ireland, Union of Soviet Socialist Republics, China, Australia, Belgium, Canada, Costa Rica, Cuba, Czechoslovakia, Dominican Republic, El Salvador, Greece, Guatemala, Haiti, Honduras, India, Luxembourg, Netherlands, New Zealand, Nicaragua, Norway, Panama, Poland, South Africa, and Yugoslavia. It is open to adherence by "other nations which are, or which may be, rendering material assistance and contributions in the struggle for victory over Hitlerism". During 1942 it was adhered to by Mexico, the Commonwealth of the Philippines, and Ethiopia.

This document, "Declaration by United Nations", states that the signatory Governments subscribe to a common program of purposes and principles embodied in the Atlantic Charter and are "convinced that complete victory over their enemies is essential to defend life, liberty, independence and religious freedom, and to preserve human rights and justice in their own lands as well as in other lands, and that they are now engaged in a common struggle against savage and brutal forces seeking to subjugate the world". Each signatory pledges itself "to employ its full resources, military or economic, against those members of the Tripartite Pact and its adherents with which such government is at war"; and "to cooperate with the Governments signatory hereto and not to make a separate armistice or peace with the enemies". (274)

DOCUMENTS
1 – 271

793.94/1838

1

The Minister in China (Johnson) to the Secretary of State

[Telegram]

PEIPING, September 22, 1931—8 p.m.
[Received September 23—9:20 a.m.[1]]

625. My 615, September 21, 2 p.m., referring to Nanking's appeal to us[2] under the Kellogg Pact,[3] also my 614, September 21, noon.

I desire to place on record the following as my personal reaction to events described in my telegram above referred to and to the responsibilities of powers signatory to Kellogg Pact in relation thereto.

1. According to all information available to me here, I am driven to the conclusion that the forceful occupation of all strategic points in South Manchuria, including the taking over and operation of public utilities, banks, and in Mukden at least the functions of civil government, is an aggressive act by Japan apparently long planned and when decided upon most carefully and systematically put into effect. I find no evidence that these events were the result of accident nor were they the acts of minor and irresponsible officials.

2. By article 1 of the Kellogg Treaty the high contracting parties, among which is Japan, renounce war "as an instrument of national policy in their relations with one another." By article 2 they agree "that the settlement or solution of all disputes all [*or*] conflicts of whatever nature or of whatever origin they may be, which may arise among them, shall never be sought except by pacific means."

3. It is my conviction that the steps taken by Japan in Manchuria must fall within any definition of war and certainly may not be considered as a pacific means of settling a dispute with China, a nation also adherent to the treaty.

4. The treaty providing for the renunciation of war as a national policy was a solemn undertaking on the part of the nations of the West and those nations now stand at the bar of the nations of the East to answer for their sincerity.

---

[1] Telegram in two sections.
[2] For text of the note of September 21, 1931, from the Chinese Government to the United States Government, see *Conditions in Manchuria*, S. Doc. 55, 72d Cong., 1st sess. (Washington, Government Printing Office, 1932), p. 3.
[3] Department of State Treaty Series No. 796.

5. It seems to me necessary that the powers signatory to the Kellogg Treaty owe it to themselves and to the world to pronounce themselves in regard to this Japanese act of aggression which I consider to have been deliberately accomplished in utter and cynical disregard of obligations which Japan as a nation shares with the other signatories of that pact.

JOHNSON

2

793.94/1868

Memorandum Handed by the Secretary of State to the Japanese Ambassador (Debuchi)

[WASHINGTON,] September 22, 1931.

Without going into the background, either as to the immediate provocation or remote causes or motivation, it appears that there has developed within the past four days a situation in Manchuria which I find surprising and view with concern. Japanese military forces, with some opposition at some points by Chinese military forces, have occupied the principal strategic points in South Manchuria, including the principal administrative center, together with some at least of the public utilities. It appears that the highest Chinese authority ordered the Chinese military not to resist, and that, when news of the situation reached Tokyo, but after most of the acts of occupation had been consummated, the Japanese Government ordered cessation of military activities on the part of the Japanese forces. Nevertheless, it appears some military movements have been continuously and are even now in process. The actual situation is that an arm of the Japanese Government is in complete control of South Manchuria.

The League of Nations has given evidence of its concern. The Chinese Government has in various ways invoked action on the part of foreign governments, citing its reliance upon treaty obligations and inviting special reference to the Kellogg Pact.

This situation is of concern, morally, legally and politically to a considerable number of nations. It is not exclusively a matter of concern to Japan and China. It brings into question at once the meaning of certain provisions of agreements, such as the Nine-Powers Treaty of February 6, 1922, and the Kellogg-Briand Pact.

The American Government is confident that it has not been the intention of the Japanese Government to create or to be a party to the creation of a situation which brings the applicability of treaty provisions into consideration. The American Government does not wish to be hasty in formulating its conclusions or in taking a position. However, the American Government feels that a very unfortunate situation exists, which no doubt is embarrassing to the Japanese Government. It would seem that the responsibility for determining the course of events with regard to the liquidating of this situation rests largely upon Japan, for the simple reason that Japanese armed forces have seized and are exercising *de facto* control in South Manchuria.

It is alleged by the Chinese, and the allegation has the support of circumstantial evidence, that lines of communication outward from Manchuria have been cut or interfered with. If this is true, it is unfortunate.

It is the hope of the American Government that the orders which it understands have been given both by the Japanese and the Chinese Governments to their military forces to refrain from hostilities and further movements will be respected and that there will be no further application of force. It is also the hope of the American Government that the Japanese and the Chinese Governments will find it possible speedily to demonstrate to the world that neither has any intention to take advantage, in furtherance of its own peculiar interests, of the situation which has been brought about in connection with and in consequence of this use of force.

What has occurred has already shaken the confidence of the public with regard to the stability of conditions in Manchuria, and it is believed that the crystallizing of a situation suggesting the necessity for an indefinite continuance of military occupation would further undermine that confidence.

H[ENRY] L. S[TIMSON]

3

793.94/2013

The Secretary of State to the Consul at Geneva (Gilbert)

[Telegram : Paraphrase]

WASHINGTON, October 9, 1931—6 p. m.

73. Consulate's 162, October 8 [7], 5 p. m. A memorandum in writing containing the following message from me dated as of October 5, 1931, may be handed by you to Sir Eric Drummond. This he may feel free to communicate confidentially to the Council members.

"I believe that our cooperation in the future handling of this difficult matter should proceed along the course which has been followed ever since the first outbreak of the trouble fortunately found the Assembly and Council of the League of Nations in session. The Council has deliberated long and earnestly on this matter and the Covenant of the League of Nations provides permanent and already tested machinery for handling such issues as between States members of the League. Both the Chinese and Japanese have presented and argued their cases before the Council and the world has been informed through published accounts with regard to the proceedings there. The Council has formulated conclusions and outlined a course of action to be followed by the disputants; and as the said disputants have made commitments to the Council, it is most desirable that the League in no way relax its vigilance and in no way fail to assert all the pressure and authority within its competence towards regulating the action of China and Japan in the premises.

On its part the American Government acting independently through its diplomatic representatives will endeavor to reinforce what the League does and will make clear that it has a keen interest in the matter and is not oblivious to the obligations which the disputants have assumed to their fellow signatories in the Pact of Paris as well as in the Nine Power Pact should a time arise when it would seem advisable to bring forward those obligations. By this course we avoid any danger of embarrassing the League in the course to which it is now committed."

STIMSON

4

793.94/2245a

The Secretary of State to the Chargé in Japan (Neville)

[Telegram]

WASHINGTON, October 20, 1931—2 p. m.

200. Please deliver to the Minister for Foreign Affairs immediately, as a note, the text which follows. Inform him that an identical note is being communicated by the American Minister to China to the Chinese Acting Minister for Foreign Affairs.

Text:

"The Government and people of the United States have observed with concern the events of the last month in Manchuria. When the difference between Japan and China came to a head on September 19th one of the parties to the dispute referred the matter to the League of Nations and since that time the American Government by representations through diplomatic channels, has steadily cooperated with the League in its efforts to secure a peaceful settlement. A threat of war, wherever it may arise, is of profound concern to the whole world and for this reason the American Government, like other Governments, was constrained to call to the attention of both disputants the serious dangers involved in the present situation.

This Government now desires, as do other signatories of the Treaty for the Renunciation of War, particularly to call to the attention of the Japanese and the Chinese Governments the obligations which they voluntarily assumed when they became parties to that Treaty, especially the obligations of Article II, which reads:

'The High Contracting Parties agree that the settlement or solution of all disputes or conflicts of whatever nature or of whatever origin they may be, which may arise among them, shall never be sought except by pacific means.'

The American Government takes this occasion again to express its earnest hope that Japan and China will refrain from any measures which might lead to war and that they will find it possible in the near future to agree upon a method for resolving by peaceful means, in accordance with their promises and in keeping with the confident expectations of public opinion throughout the world, the issues over which they are at present in controversy."

STIMSON

5

793.94/3437a

The Secretary of State to the Ambassador in Japan (Forbes)

[Telegram]

WASHINGTON, January 7, 1932—noon.

7. Please deliver to the Foreign Office on behalf of your Government as soon as possible the following note:

"With the recent military operations about Chinchow, the last remaining administrative authority of the Government of the Chinese Republic in South Manchuria, as it existed prior to September 18th, 1931, has been destroyed. The American Government continues confident that the work of the neutral commission recently authorized by the Council of the League of Nations will facilitate an ultimate solution of the difficulties now existing between China and Japan. But in view of the present situation and of its own rights and obligations therein, the American Government deems it to be its duty to notify both the Imperial Japanese Government and the Government of the Chinese Republic that it cannot admit the legality of any situation *de facto* nor does it intend to recognize any treaty or agreement entered into between those Governments, or agents thereof, which may impair the treaty rights of the United States or its citizens in China, including those which relate to the sovereignty, the independence, or the territorial and administrative integrity of the Republic of China, or to the international policy relative to China, commonly known as the open door policy; and that it does not intend to recognize any situation, treaty or agreement which may be brought about by means contrary to the covenants and obligations of the Pact of Paris of August 27, 1928, to which Treaty both China and Japan, as well as the United States, are parties."

State that an identical note is being sent to the Chinese government.

STIMSON

6

793.94/3902d

The Secretary of State to the Ambassador in Japan (Forbes)

[Telegram]

WASHINGTON, February 1, 1932—3 p. m.

34. You will please arrange to call on the Minister for Foreign Affairs at 6 o'clock evening, Tokyo time, February 2d, to deliver to him a note the text of which follows:

You will say to the Minister for Foreign Affairs by way of introduction that you have conveyed to the American Government his request made at your conference with him on January 31 to the effect "that he requested that the United States use its good offices to induce the Chinese troops not to bring up further reenforcements and to withdraw the troops now in Shanghai to a safe distance to avoid clashes." You will say that your Government has given earnest consideration to this request and in response suggests to the Japanese Government the following proposal for such cessation of hostilities. You will say that the same proposal is being submitted to the Chinese Government. You will then read him the following note and leave with him a copy of it.

"PROPOSAL OF THE POWERS FOR CESSATION OF CONFLICT

1. Cessation of all acts of violence on both sides forthwith on the following terms.
2. No further mobilization or preparation whatever for further hostilities between the two nations.
3. Withdrawal of both Japanese and Chinese combatants from all points of mutual contact in the Shanghai area.
4. Protection of the International Settlement by the establishment of neutral zones to divide the combatants. These zones to be policed by neutrals. The arrangements to be set up by the Consular authorities.
5. Upon acceptance of these conditions prompt advances to be made in negotiations to settle all outstanding controversies between the two nations in the spirit of the Pact of Paris and the Resolution of the League of Nations of December 9 [*10*], without prior demand or reservation and with the aid of neutral observers or participants."

The British Government is sending the British Ambassador similar instructions. The British Government is proposing to the French and the Italian Governments that they take similar action. In the event that those Governments decide favorably within time to make possible this presentation by their Ambassadors of like representations at the same time, you will be informed either through the Department or through your British colleague. Confer with the British Ambassador and arrange that you and he make your calls at the same time.

STIMSON

7

Press Releases, vol. VI, p. 147

Address Delivered by the Honorable Hugh S. Gibson, of the United States Delegation, at the General Disarmament Conference, Geneva, February 9, 1932

[Extracts]

The United States enters the first world conference on the limitation and reduction of armaments with the determination to leave nothing undone to achieve substantial progress.

The people of the United States have during the past generation played a useful and leading part in the movement for the limitation and reduction of arms. The Washington Conference of 1922 made the first concrete contribution in voluntary limitation. It met the then existing problem of armament at its most acute, its most threatening, and its most conspicuous point, and by a restriction of naval armament among the powers who found themselves setting an unhappy example, made a long and decisive stride in the direction demanded by world opinion. Our people at that conference sacrificed, if not a real predominance, at least a potential predominance in weight and strength for warfare. The American people have been proud of the contribution which they made to that pact of temperate conduct and common sense. In the London Naval Conference of 1930 the principle of limitation established for capital ships at the Washington meeting was enlarged to cover the whole field of equipment for warfare at sea by the three most heavily armed of the nations, and some progress was made toward including the two other powers most concerned. We enter the Conference to-day with the practicability of the limitation upon arms established, with the demand for it augmented by general pride and satisfaction in the achievement already made, and with the United States again willing to play its appropriate part in further progress. The American Delegation is prepared to consider any form of military limitation and reduction which promises real progress toward the feeling of international security, protection against surprise, and restraint on the use of arms for purposes of aggression.

The burden and dangers of the gigantic machinery of warfare which are now being maintained in times of peace have reached a point where they threaten civilization itself. For two years past the people of every race have been confronted with an economic crisis from which no nation has been free. All the governments of the world have faced reduction of income, unsettled budgets, and dangers to the very stability of government itself. The United States, while seriously affected by these difficulties, has suffered somewhat less severely than many of the other nations. It is to-day able to maintain the burden of armaments as readily as any of the nations, but it views that burden as unnecessary and inexcusable. No one will doubt the political instability of the world, of which these arms are not alone the effect but also the cause. No one will doubt that they not only contribute to the economic debacle but that they threaten the peace of the world. Our American people look upon the statesmanship which permits the continuance of existing conditions as nothing less than failure. The time has gone by when the peoples of the world will long permit the continuance of this failure.

There is a feeling sometimes expressed that the convictions of the

United States in this field, the faith of our people in an orderly and stable régime among the nations, and our conviction that the very existence of armaments unbalances the equilibrium, are a product of our geographical isolation and of our lack of experience of and exposure to the rivalries and strains of the European Continent. In answer, the American people point to the fact that the system of competitive armament, of alliances and cross alliances which has existed for centuries in Europe has failed to maintain peace and seems indeed to have been provocative of war, the results of which are such that victors and vanquished are victims alike. Furthermore, the altered conditions of international relationships, the development of communication and transport within the last generation to a point where the whole world is knit together by strands of commerce, finance, and intimate contact, have to-day produced new international relationships which are utterly inconsistent with the older methods and formulas. America is convinced that the world should not go on to new movements and new tasks hampered by the garments of an older régime, and that the problem is only how promptly and smoothly mankind will cast aside the weapons and traditions of the old.

The American Delegation has not attempted to formulate and submit any comprehensive plan for overcoming all of the obstacles that exist in the way of achieving a general limitation and reduction in armaments. In the first place, we do not desire to raise new questions which increase the points of difference and thus delay taking the forward steps which could otherwise be taken. In the second place, we do not believe the human mind is capable of so projecting itself into the future as to devise a plan which will adequately provide for all future developments and contingencies.

Since practically all the nations of the world have now pledged themselves not to wage aggressive war, we believe this Conference should and can successfully devote itself to the abolition of weapons which are devoted primarily to aggressive war, and we are prepared to give earnest and sympathetic consideration to any plans or proposals which seem to furnish a practicable and sound basis upon which we may effect a general limitation and reduction of armaments and establish a more healthy and peaceful state of affairs. It is my purpose to-day to lay before you certain points which the American Delegation advocates. Let me say that this list is not exclusive and contains merely some of the thoughts which we feel will carry on some of the purposes of the Conference.

1. The American Government advocates consideration of the draft convention as containing the outlines for a convenient basis for discussion, while expressing its entire willingness to give full consideration to any supplementary proposals calculated to advance the end we all seek.

2. We suggest the possibility of prolonging the existing naval agreements concluded at Washington and London, and we advocate completing the latter as soon as possible by the adherence of France and Italy.

3. We advocate proportional reduction from the figures laid down in the Washington and London agreements on naval tonnage as soon as all parties to the Washington agreement have entered this framework.

4. We advocate, as we long have done, the total abolition of submarines.

5. We will join in formulating the most effective measures to protect civilian population against aerial bombing.

6. We advocate the total abolition of lethal gases and bacteriological warfare.

7. We advocate, as I have already stated, the computation of the number of armed forces on the basis of the effectives necessary for the maintenance of internal order plus some suitable contingent for defense. The former are obviously impossible of reduction; the latter is a question of relativity.

8. We agree in advocating special restrictions for tanks and heavy mobile guns; in other words, for those arms of a peculiarly offensive character.

9. We are prepared to consider a limitation of expenditure on material as a complementary method to direct limitation, feeling that it may prove useful to prevent a qualitative race, if and when quantitative limitation has been effected.

8

793.94/4161A

The Secretary of State to the Minister in Switzerland (*Wilson*)

[Telegram]

FEBRUARY 12, 1932—2 p.m.

11. Reference Department's 9, February 12, noon. There follows the text of a draft concerning which I have just talked with Sir John Simon. Please deliver a copy to Sir John before he leaves Geneva, explaining that this is merely a rough draft; that I shall be working further on it; that I shall welcome his comments and suggestions.

"To the nations who are either signatories or adherents of the so-called Nine Power Treaty 'regarding principles and policies to be followed in matters concerning China':

"The (blank) Governments, signatories of the Nine-Power Treaty, pursuant to Article seventh thereof, desire to communicate to their fellow signatories and adherents to this Treaty their views as to certain matters which have recently occurred within the territory of the Republic of China.

"I. This Treaty was concluded in 1922 in the city of Washington at a conference, participated in by many powers, at which the policy of these powers towards the Republic of China was fully discussed and the attitude which they should hereafter adopt towards the Republic of China was set forth in this treaty. The treaty represented the culmination of a policy towards China which had been developed between these powers for many years, known as the Open Door policy. In the first article of that Treaty the Contracting Powers, other than China, agreed:

"'1. To respect the sovereignty, the independence, and the territorial and administrative integrity of China.

"'2. To provide the fullest and most unembarrassed opportunity to China to develop and maintain for herself an effective and stable government.'

"The Treaty thus represents a carefully developed and matured international policy intended to afford to the people of China the fullest possible opportunity of developing, without molestation, their sovereignty and independence among the nations of the world, according to the modern and enlightened standards believed now to maintain among the peoples of this earth. It was known that China was in the process of developing the free institutions of a self-governing Republic after her recent revolution from an autocratic form of government; that she would require many years of both economic and political effort to that end, and that the process would necessarily be a very long one. The Treaty was thus a deliberate covenant of self-denial among the signatory powers of all acts of aggression which were calculated to interfere with that development. But it was believed, and a study of the Treaty reveals that faith, that only by such a process of development could the fullest interests, not only of China but of all nations having intercourse with her, best be served.

"II. Six years later the general policy upon which the Nine-Power Treaty was based received a powerful reinforcement in the execution, by substantially all the nations of the world, of the Pact of Paris. These two treaties represent successive steps taken for the purpose of aligning the conscience and public opinion of the world in favor of a system of orderly development by the law of nations, including the settlement of all controversies by the methods of justice and peace instead of by arbitrary force. The program for the protection of China from outside aggression is an essential part of any such development. The signatories and the adherents of the Nine-Power Treaty rightly felt that the orderly and peaceful development of the four hundred millions of people inhabiting China was necessary to the peaceful welfare of the people of the entire world and that no program for the welfare of the world as a whole could afford to neglect the protection of the development of China.

"III. Although they have withheld adverse judgment pending the investigation which is to be made by the commission appointed by the League of Nations under the resolution of December 9, the nations of the world have watched with apprehension the events in Manchuria which have taken place during recent months. This apprehension was based upon the tragic experience of the last two decades which have made manifest the fact that in case of war no nation is immune from the danger of becoming involved in the conflict, however remote in its inception. The recent spread of these disturbances in Manchuria to the area of Shanghai, involving as it does the direct threat of danger to the interests of many nations, is further powerful evidence of this fact.

"IV. The rapid development of events in Shanghai seems to the (blank) Governments to give full cause for the deepest apprehension of all nations who have been interested in the policy of the two treaties to which we have referred. It is unnecessary to attempt to analyze the origin of the controversy or to apportion the blame between the two nations which unhappily are involved. For it is clear beyond peradventure that a situation has now developed which can not under any circumstances be reconciled with the covenants and the obligations of these two treaties and which is wholly abhorrent to the enlightened purpose for which they were conceived. There is now assembled in the port of Shanghai a Japanese force including over forty vessels of war and reenforced by a large expeditionary force of land troops. The very size of such an expedition is not only disproportionate to its avowed objective of protecting life and property in the city of Shanghai but is in itself provocative of counter-violence. Military airplanes have been bombing areas densely populated by helpless civilians of a nation with whom their operators are not ostensibly at war. Many miles away from the city where the alleged violence against Japanese nationals occurred, the Japanese Government is now engaged in military operations on a large scale. It is inconceivable that if the leaders of these two nations had been fully and equally imbued with the purpose underlying these treaties and had been adequately mindful of the covenants therein such a situation could have been allowed to develop or that at some stage a solution of their controversies could not have been otherwise achieved.

"V. The effect of this development of violence has been to threaten the very existence of the treaties themselves. This has been shown by the following occurrences which have greatly accentuated the concern of the (blank) Governments:

"(1) In rejecting a recent proffer of good offices from the British, the American and the French Governments submitted at the request of Japan, the Japanese Government has taken the position that it would not consent to the participation even as observers of any third nations in the discussions of questions arising between Japan and China in regard to that portion of China known as Manchuria. This would seem to deny to any other power even a signatory of the Nine-Power Treaty the right to participate even as an observer in negotiations involving rights and obligations comprised within that Treaty.

"(2) Again on February 8, 1932, the Foreign Office of the Japanese Government at Tokyo issued to the press of the world a suggested proposal that there should be created a system of 'demilitarized zones' around the principal commercial cities of China, out of which the forces of the Government of China should be excluded. The representative of the Japanese Foreign Office in advancing this proposal frankly affirmed that it was contrary to the Nine-Power Treaty but asserted that ten years' trial had proved that treaty to be ineffective.

"VI. The (blank) Governments do not concede that the Nine-Power Treaty is ineffective or inoperative or that it is to be discarded. They do not concede that such a situation as has arisen in Shanghai is inevitable, provided the covenants of the Nine-Power Treaty and the Pact of Paris are faithfully observed by those who have covenanted to observe them. They are unwilling to consent that the enlightened policy which has heretofore marked the efforts of the nations of the earth towards China and towards each other should be repudiated or abandoned without their most earnest reprobation. They do not intend to forego their legitimate prerogative, in view of their treaty rights and obligations, to participate together with the other powers concerned in any negotiations whereby those rights and obligations and the policies which they represent may be affected. They take this occasion to express these views in order that there may be no misunderstanding. They avail themselves of the opportunity afforded by the terms of Article seven of the Nine-Power Treaty to express frankly and without reserve their views upon these occurrences at Shanghai and their belief that if the covenants and policies of the Nine-Power Treaty and the Pact of Paris be allowed to be repudiated or repealed, the loss to all the nations of the world will be immeasurable. For this reason they further notify their fellow signatories and adherents to those treaties that they for themselves and each of them do not propose to recognize as valid any treaty, agreement, arrangement or situation which may be entered into or created in China by means of acts or policies which are in violation of the covenants of those treaties."

STIMSON

9

500.A4D/203

The Secretary of State to the Chairman of the Committee on Foreign Relations (Borah), United States Senate

[WASHINGTON,] February 23, 1932.

MY DEAR SENATOR BORAH:

You have asked my opinion whether, as has been sometimes recently suggested, present conditions in China have in any way indicated that the so-called Nine Power Treaty has become inapplicable or ineffective or rightly in need of modification, and if so, what I considered should be the policy of this Government.

This Treaty, as you of course know, forms the legal basis upon which now rests the "Open Door" policy towards China. That policy, enunciated by John Hay in 1899, brought to an end the struggle among various powers for so-called spheres of interest in China which was threatening the dismemberment of that empire. To accomplish this Mr. Hay invoked two principles (1) equality of commercial opportunity among all nations in dealing with China, and (2) as necessary to that equality the preservation of China's territorial and administrative integrity. These principles were not new in the foreign policy of America. They had been the principles upon which it rested in its dealings with other nations for many years. In the case of China they were invoked to save a situation which not only threatened the future development and sovereignty of that great Asiatic people, but also threatened to create dangerous and constantly increasing rivalries between the other nations of the world. War had already taken place between Japan and China. At the close of that war three other nations intervened to prevent

Japan from obtaining some of the results of that war claimed by her. Other nations sought and had obtained spheres of interest. Partly as a result of these actions a serious uprising had broken out in China which endangered the legations of all of the powers at Peking. While the attack on those legations was in progress, Mr. Hay made an announcement in respect to this policy as the principle upon which the powers should act in the settlement of the rebellion. He said

"The policy of the government of the United States is to seek a solution which may bring about permanent safety and peace to China, preserve Chinese territorial and administrative entity, protect all rights guaranteed to friendly powers by treaty and international law, and safeguard for the world the principle of equal and impartial trade with all parts of the Chinese Empire."

He was successful in obtaining the assent of the other powers to the policy thus announced.

In taking these steps Mr. Hay acted with the cordial support of the British Government. In responding to Mr. Hay's announcement, above set forth, Lord Salisbury, the British Prime Minister expressed himself "most emphatically as concurring in the policy of the United States."

For twenty years thereafter the Open Door policy rested upon the informal commitments thus made by the various powers. But in the winter of 1921 to 1922, at a conference participated in by all of the principal powers which had interests in the Pacific, the policy was crystallized into the so-called Nine Power Treaty, which gave definition and precision to the principles upon which the policy rested. In the first article of that Treaty, the contracting powers, other than China, agreed

1. To respect the sovereignty, the independence and the territorial and administrative integrity of China.
2. To provide the fullest and most unembarrassed opportunity to China to develop and maintain for herself an effective and stable government.
3. To use their influence for the purpose of effectually establishing and maintaining the principle of equal opportunity for the commerce and industry of all nations throughout the territory of China.
4. To refrain from taking advantage of conditions in China in order to seek special rights or privileges which would abridge the rights of subjects or citizens of friendly states, and from countenancing action inimical to the security of such states.

This Treaty thus represents a carefully developed and matured international policy intended, on the one hand, to assure to all of the contracting parties their rights and interests in and with regard to China, and on the other hand, to assure to the people of China the fullest opportunity to develop without molestation their sovereignty and independence according to the modern and enlightened standards believed to maintain among the peoples of this earth. At the time this Treaty was signed, it was known that China was engaged in an attempt to develop the free institutions of a self-governing republic after her recent revolution from an autocratic form of government; that she would require many years of both economic and political effort to that end; and that her progress would necessarily be slow. The Treaty was thus a covenant of self-denial among the signatory powers in deliberate renunciation of any policy of aggression which might tend to interfere with that development. It was believed—and the whole history of the development of the "Open Door" policy reveals that faith—that only by such a process, under the protection of such an agreement, could the fullest interests not only of China but of all nations which have intercourse with her best be served.

In its report to the President announcing this Treaty, the American Delegation, headed by the then Secretary of State, Mr. Charles E. Hughes, said [5]

"It is believed that through this Treaty the 'Open Door' in China has at last been made a fact."

During the course of the discussions which resulted in the Treaty,[6] the Chairman of the British delegation, Lord Balfour, had stated that

"The British Empire delegation understood that there was no representative of any power around the table who thought that the old practice of 'spheres of interest' was either advocated by any government or would be tolerable to this conference. So far as the British Government were concerned, they had, in the most formal manner, publicly announced that they regarded this practice as utterly inappropriate to the existing situation."

At the same time the representative of Japan, Baron Shidehara, announced the position of his Government as follows:

"No one denies to China her sacred right to govern herself. No one stands in the way of China to work out her own great national destiny."

The Treaty was originally executed by the United States, Belgium, the British Empire, China, France, Italy, Japan, the Netherlands

---

[5] See *Foreign Relations*, 1922, vol. II, pp. 306, 345.

[6] For minutes of the Committee on Pacific and Far Eastern Questions, see *Conference on the Limitation of Armament, November 12, 1921–February 6, 1922* (Washington, 1922), pp. 862–1567.

and Portugal. Subsequently it was also executed by Norway, Bolivia, Sweden, Denmark and Mexico. Germany has signed it but her parliament has not yet ratified it.

It must be remembered also that this Treaty was one of several treaties and agreements entered into at the Washington Conference by the various powers concerned, all of which were interrelated and interdependent. No one of these treaties can be disregarded without disturbing the general understanding and equilibrium which were intended to be accomplished and effected by the group of agreements arrived at in their entirety. The Washington Conference was essentially a disarmament conference, aimed to promote the possibility of peace in the world not only through the cessation of competition in naval armament but also by the solution of various other disturbing problems which threatened the peace of the world, particularly in the Far East. These problems were all interrelated. The willingness of the American Government to surrender its then commanding lead in battleship construction and to leave its positions at Guam and in the Philippines without further fortification, was predicated upon, among other things, the self-denying covenants contained in the Nine Power Treaty, which assured the nations of the world not only of equal opportunity for their Eastern trade but also against the military aggrandizement of any other power at the expense of China. One cannot discuss the possibility of modifying or abrogating those provisions of the Nine Power Treaty without considering at the same time the other promises upon which they were really dependent.

Six years later the policy of self-denial against aggression by a stronger against a weaker power, upon which the Nine Power Treaty had been based, received a powerful reinforcement by the execution by substantially all the nations of the world of the Pact of Paris, the so-called Kellogg Briand Pact. These two treaties represent independent but harmonious steps taken for the purpose of aligning the conscience and public opinion of the world in favor of a system of orderly development by the law of nations including the settlement of all controversies by methods of justice and peace instead of by arbitrary force. The program for the protection of China from outside aggression is an essential part of any such development. The signatories and adherents of the Nine Power Treaty rightly felt that the orderly and peaceful development of the 400,000,000 of people inhabiting China was necessary to the peaceful welfare of the entire world and that no program for the welfare of the world as a whole could afford to neglect the welfare and protection of China.

The recent events which have taken place in China, especially the hostilities which having been begun in Manchuria have latterly been extended to Shanghai, far from indicating the advisability of any modification of the treaties we have been discussing, have tended to bring home the vital importance of the faithful observance of the covenants therein to all of the nations interested in the Far East. It is not necessary in that connection to inquire into the causes of the controversy or attempt to apportion the blame between the two nations which are unhappily involved; for regardless of cause or responsibility, it is clear beyond peradventure that a situation has developed which cannot, under any circumstances, be reconciled with the obligations of the covenants of these two treaties, and that if the treaties had been faithfully observed such a situation could not have arisen. The signatories of the Nine Power Treaty and of the Kellogg-Briand Pact who are not parties to that conflict are not likely to see any reason for modifying the terms of those treaties. To them the real value of the faithful performance of the treaties has been brought sharply home by the perils and losses to which their nationals have been subjected in Shanghai.

That is the view of this Government. We see no reason for abandoning the enlightened principles which are embodied in these treaties. We believe that this situation would have been avoided had these covenants been faithfully observed, and no evidence has come to us to indicate that a due compliance with them would have interfered with the adequate protection of the legitimate rights in China of the signatories of those treaties and their nationals.

On January 7th last, upon the instruction of the President, this Government formally notified Japan and China that it would not recognize any situation, treaty or agreement entered into by those governments in violation of the covenants of these treaties, which affected the rights of our Government or its citizens in China. If a similar decision should be reached and a similar position taken by the other governments of the world, a caveat will be placed upon such action which, we believe, will effectively bar the legality hereafter of any title or right sought to be obtained by pressure or treaty violation, and which, as has been shown by history in the past, will eventually lead to the restoration to China of rights and titles of which she may have been deprived.

In the past our Government, as one of the leading powers on the Pacific Ocean, has rested its policy upon an abiding faith in the future of the people of China and upon the ultimate success in dealing with them of the principles of fair play, patience, and mutual goodwill. We appreciate the immensity of the task which lies before her statesmen

172

in the development of her country and its government. The delays in her progress, the instability of her attempts to secure a responsible government, were foreseen by Messrs. Hay and Hughes and their contemporaries and were the very obstacles which the policy of the Open Door was designed to meet. We concur with those statesmen, representing all the nations, in the Washington Conference who decided that China was entitled to the time necessary to accomplish her development. We are prepared to make that our policy for the future.

Very sincerely yours,

HENRY L. STIMSON

10

894.00/434–½

The Ambassador in Japan (Grew) to the Secretary of State

TOKYO, August 13, 1932.
[Received August 27.]

DEAR MR. SECRETARY:

The outburst in Japan against your speech before the Council on Foreign Relations [8] savors distinctly of a tempest in a teapot if not of a guilty conscience on the part of the Japanese, for we now understand that the speech was merely an academic discussion of a hypothetical case, while the Japanese took it as a specific charge of guilt. Unfortunately I was unable to take any steps to mitigate the effect here, because neither the text of the speech nor a resumé of its substance and intentions have reached me, and by the time the text arrives from Shanghai the incident will presumably be closed. However that may be, the Foreign Office has used the speech deliberately to pour fuel on the temporarily quiescent flames of public animosity against the United States. I say deliberately, because the violent Japanese press reaction was based not on the press despatches from the United States but on the Foreign Office's inflammatory interpretation of Debuchi's cabled account, and this interpretation was given to the Japanese press a day before it was released to the foreign correspondents.

This situation reminds me strongly of the efforts of the German Government, by calumniating foreign nations, to build up a public war psychology in 1914, the effort being repeated whenever some new venture, such as the indiscriminate submarine warfare, was about to be launched. Here in Japan the deliberate building up of public ani-

---

[8] Delivered August 8, 1932. For text, see *Foreign Affairs*, Special Supplement (October, 1932), vol. X, no. 1.

mosity against foreign nations in general and the United States in particular has doubtless a similar purpose—to strengthen the hand of the military in its Manchurian venture in the face of foreign, and especially American, opposition. I believe that on the part of the Japanese it is a sign of weakness, not of strength. The internal economic and financial situation in Japan is serious and may become desperate. The plight of the farmers is very bad, many industries are at low ebb, unemployment is steadily increasing. The yen is falling and prices have not yet risen proportionately. Money cannot be obtained from abroad; I was recently told, although I cannot vouch for the reliability of the information, that the Government had tried without success to obtain loans from England, France and Holland in turn. It will become increasingly difficult to obtain domestic loans. This situation is not critical, but it may become so when the ability of the National Bank of Japan to absorb domestic bonds comes to an end. Meanwhile millions of yen are being squandered to support the Manchurian venture, of which the eventual economic advantage is highly problematical, and when the full purport of these expenses becomes known to the people, in their own serious deprivation, there is no telling what effect it will create. I believe that a steadily increasing anxiety exists among the Government and the thinking men of the country outside of the hot-headed military clique which refuses to face these facts. It seems to be primarily this military element— vocalized by such men as Shiratori [9]—who believe that the best way to obscure these facts is to work the public into a patriotic and nationalistic fervor by representing foreign nations, particularly the United States, as trying to thwart Japan's efforts for alleged self-preservation.

Such a national temper is always dangerous. The German military machine, supported by a carefully nurtured public war psychology, took the bit in its teeth and overrode all restraining influences in 1914. The Japanese military machine is not dissimilar. It has been built for war, feels prepared for war and would welcome war. It has never yet been beaten and possesses unlimited self confidence. I am not an alarmist but I believe that we should have our eyes open to all possible future contingencies. The facts of history would render it criminal to close them.

In this connection the enclosed memorandum prepared by the Embassy,[10] which will be incorporated in a despatch, may be found significant.

Respectfully yours,

JOSEPH C. GREW

---

[9] Toshio Shiratori, Director of the Bureau of Intelligence, Japanese Foreign Office. [10] Not printed.

11

793.94/5709

Memorandum by the Secretary of State Regarding a Conversation With the Japanese Ambassador (Debuchi)

[WASHINGTON,] January 5, 1933.

The Japanese Ambassador came in with the remark that he regretted that his presence seemed to coincide with a new outbreak of war. He said that he was without instructions from his Government but that from the information he received this affair at Shanhaikwan was a local incident, provoked by a minor outbreak of Chinese against the Japanese there, and that when the Japanese who had sought permission to bring troops in to stabilize the situation approached the Gate of the City they were shot at and a Lieutenant and several soldiers killed. He said that the news he got from Ambassador Muto,[11] who is also General, indicated that some troops of the Japanese had now been withdrawn and there was reason to be hoped that unless there was further provocation in Jehol by Chang Hsueh-liang the matter would be controlled. He said that in any event Japan had no territorial ambition south of the Great Wall. I reminded the Ambassador that a year ago he had told me Japan had no territorial ambitions in Manchuria. He became flustered and said that that was so but the situation had changed greatly. At any rate, he could now assure me that they had no such ambitions in North China. He said further that in Japan he thought that matters were progressing; that Saito was getting better control, and he regarded this incident at Shanhaikwan as a test incident as to whether the military elements still remained in control or whether the civil government had regained its position.

I reminded the Ambassador that just before he went away he told me that the Japanese Government was in the control of a group of younger officers, none of them of a higher rank than a Lieutenant-Colonel, and I said to him that he must recognize that as long as that situation lasted I could not regard Japan as a normal Government and must make my own conclusions as to information coming from her. He said he remembered that situation but he found that when he got back to Japan it had somewhat changed and that Saito was getting into better control and that, as he expressed it, this incident at Shanhaikwan he regarded as a test of whether that was so. But he said he must in all frankness tell me that no Japanese

---

[11] Nobuyuki Muto, Japanese Ambassador in "Manchukuo".

Cabinet which advocated a compromise of the "Manchukuo" question could survive in Japan; that must be regarded as a closed incident. I told the Ambassador that in that case I could see, on my part, no other course than for Japan to get out of the League of Nations and the Kellogg Pact. I went over the situation of the basic policy of this Government and the rest of the world and Europe, arising out of the Great War which had brought us to the conclusion that another war might destroy our civilization and which had made us determined to support the peace machinery which would render such a recurrence impossible. We recognized that Japan had a right to live her own way, provided she did not break treaties which she had made, and that if she was determined to lead a life differently from what we were determined to do I saw no other way but for her to withdraw from the associations and treaties which we proposed to abide by.

H[ENRY] L. S[TIMSON]

12

793.94Commission/837

The Secretary of State to the Minister in Switzerland (*Wilson*)

[Telegram]

WASHINGTON, February 25, 1933—6 p. m.

78. Your 125, February 24, 7 p. m. Communicate to Drummond as a letter from me under today's date the following:

"There has been communicated to me the text of your letter of February 24, 1933, transmitting to me a copy of the report of the Committee of Nineteen as adopted by the Assembly of the League of Nations on this day.

I note your request that I communicate to you as soon as possible the reply of the Government of the United States.

In response to that request I have the honor to state the views of the American Government as follows:

In the situation which has developed out of the controversy between China and Japan, the purpose of the United States has coincided in general with that of the League of Nations, the common objective being maintenance of peace and settlement of international disputes by pacific means. In pursuance of that objective, while the League of Nations has been exercising jurisdiction over a controversy between two of its members, the Government of the United States has endeavored to give support, reserving to itself independence of judgment with regard to method and scope, to the efforts of the League on behalf of peace.

The findings of fact arrived at by the League and the understanding of the facts derived by the American Government from reports made to it by its own representatives are in substantial accord. In the light of its findings of fact, the Assembly of the League has formulated a measured statement of conclusions. With those conclusions the American Government is in general accord. In their affirmations respectively of the principle of non-recognition and their attitude in regard thereto the League and the United States are on common ground. The League has recommended principles of settlement. In so far as appropriate under the treaties to which it is a party, the American Government expresses its general endorsement of the principles thus recommended.

The American Government earnestly hopes that the two nations now engaged in controversy, both of which have long been in friendly relationship with our own and other peoples, may find it possible, in the light of the now clear expression of world opinion, to conform their policies to the need and the desire of the family of nations that disputes between nations shall be settled by none but pacific means."

2. The text of Drummond's letter to me and my reply are being released to the press here for publication in the Sunday morning papers. I hope that Drummond also will release the texts.

STIMSON

13

811.113/280A

The Secretary of State to the Chairman of the Committee on Foreign Affairs (McReynolds), House of Representatives

APRIL 5, 1933.

MY DEAR MR. MCREYNOLDS:

I have given careful consideration to H.J. Res. 93 [12] and I am strongly of the opinion that this legislation should be enacted. I should greatly appreciate it, therefore, if you could find it possible to urge favorable action on this resolution. I hope that you will be able to succeed in having it passed in the form in which it was reported out

---

[12] Joint Resolution To prohibit the exportation of arms or munitions of war from the United States under certain conditions:

"Resolved by the Senate and House of Representatives of the United States

of the Committee on Foreign Affairs and without the amendment which was introduced in the House when this legislation was being considered on the recommendation of the last administration—an amendment which would weaken its force and narrow its applicability.

The authority, which the passage of this resolution would confer upon the Executive, would be exercised by any Chief Magistrate of the United States to the sole end of maintaining the peace of the world and with a due and prudent regard for our national policies and national interests. The special circumstances of each particular case which may arise would dictate what action, if any, would be taken in that case, but the authority to act on terms of equality in cooperation with other governments when the occasion arises, should be left to the discretion of the Executive Branch of the Government which is charged, under the Constitution, with the conduct of our foreign relations. In justice to the firm convictions of the American people and to its own dignity, this Government should no longer be left in the position of being unable to join the other governments of the world in preventing the supply of arms and munitions for use in an international conflict when it is exercising its diplomacy and the whole weight of our national influence and prestige to prevent or put an end to that conflict. The enactment of this legislation would strengthen the position of this Government in its international relations and would enable us to cooperate more efficiently in efforts to maintain the peace of the world.

I am writing to Senator Pittman asking him to support this legislation in the Senate.

Sincerely yours,

CORDELL HULL

Footnote 12—Continued.

of America in Congress assembled, That whenever the President finds that in any part of the world conditions exist such that the shipment of arms or munitions of war from countries which produce these commodities may promote or encourage the employment of force in the course of a dispute or conflict between nations, and, after securing the cooperation of such governments as the President deems necessary, he makes proclamation thereof, it shall be unlawful to export, or sell for export, except under such limitations and exceptions as the President prescribes, any arms or munitions of war from any place in the United States to such country or countries as he may designate, until otherwise ordered by the President or by Congress.

"SEC. 2. Whoever exports any arms or munitions of war in violation of section 1 shall, on conviction, be punished by a fine not exceeding $10,000 or by imprisonment not exceeding two years, or both."

14

500.A15A4/1848

President Roosevelt to the Secretary of State

[WASHINGTON,] May 6, 1933.

I talked this afternoon with Dr. Schacht [12a] for one half hour and made it perfectly clear that the United States will insist that Germany remain in status quo in armament and that we would support every possible effort to have the offensive armament of every other nation brought down to the German level. We discussed only land armament and not naval. I intimated as strongly as possible that we regard Germany as the only possible obstacle to a Disarmament Treaty and that I hoped Dr. Schacht would give this point of view to Hitler as quickly as possible.

You might consider whether it is worthwhile bringing this to the attention of Davis.[12b]

F.D.R.

15

Press Releases, vol. VIII, p. 348

Message of President Roosevelt to the Congress, May 16, 1933

To the Congress:

For the information of the Congress I am sending herewith a message that I have addressed this morning to the sovereigns and presidents of those nations participating in the Disarmament Conference and the World Monetary and Economic Conference.[13]

I was impelled to this action because it has become increasingly evident that the assurance of world political and economic peace and

---

[12a] Hjalmer Schacht, President of the Reichsbank.

[12b] Norman H. Davis, Chairman of the United States Delegation, General Disarmament Conference, Geneva, Switzerland.

[13] The message of the President to the heads of the nations participating in the World Economic Conference and the Disarmament Conference was cabled direct to the sovereigns and presidents of the following nations: Albania, Argentina, Austria, Belgium, Brazil, Colombia, Bolivia, Bulgaria, Chile, China, Costa Rica, Cuba, Czechoslovakia, Denmark, Dominican Republic, Ecuador, Egypt, Estonia, Ethiopia, Finland, France, Germany, Great Britain, Greece, Guatemala, Haiti, Honduras, Hungary, Iraq, Italy, Japan, Latvia, Lithuania, Luxembourg, Mexico, Netherlands, Nicaragua, Norway, Panama,

stability is threatened by selfish and short-sighted policies, actions and threats of actions.

The sincere wish for this assurance by an overwhelming majority of the nations faces the danger of recalcitrant obstruction by a very

---

Footnote 13—Continued.

Paraguay, Persia, Peru, Poland, Portugal, Rumania, Russia, Siam, Spain, Sweden, Switzerland, Turkey, Uruguay, Venezuela, Yugoslavia.

The message follows:

"A profound hope of the people of my country impels me, as the head of their government, to address you and, through you, the people of your nation. This hope is that peace may be assured through practical measures of disarmament and that all of us may carry to victory our common struggle against economic chaos.

"To these ends the nations have called two great world conferences. The happiness, the prosperity, and the very lives of the men, women and children who inhabit the whole world are bound up in the decisions which their governments will make in the near future. The improvement of social conditions, the preservation of individual human rights, and the furtherance of social justice are dependent upon these decisions.

"The World Economic Conference will meet soon and must come to its conclusions quickly. The world can not await deliberations long drawn out. The Conference must establish order in place of the present chaos by a stabilization of currencies, by freeing the flow of world trade, and by international action to raise price levels. It must, in short, supplement individual domestic programs for economic recovery, by wise and considered international action.

"The Disarmament Conference has labored for more than a year and, as yet, has been unable to reach satisfactory conclusions. Confused purposes still clash dangerously. Our duty lies in the direction of bringing practical results through concerted action based upon the greatest good to the greatest number. Before the imperative call of this great duty, petty obstacles must be swept away and petty aims forgotten. A selfish victory is always destined to be an ultimate defeat. The furtherance of durable peace for our generation in every part of the world is the only goal worthy of our best efforts.

"If we ask what are the reasons for armaments, which, in spite of the lessons and tragedies of the World War, are today a greater burden on the peoples of the earth than ever before, it becomes clear that they are two-fold: First, the desire, disclosed or hidden, on the part of Governments to enlarge their territories at the expense of a sister nation. I believe that only a small minority of Governments or of peoples harbor such a purpose. Second, the fear of nations that they will be invaded. I believe that the overwhelming majority of peoples feel obliged to retain excessive armaments because they fear some act of aggression against them and not because they themselves seek to be aggressors.

"There is justification for this fear. Modern weapons of offense are vastly stronger than modern weapons of defense. Frontier forts, trenches, wire entanglements, coast defenses—in a word, fixed fortifications—are no longer impregnable to the attack of war planes, heavy mobile artillery, land battleships called tanks, and poison gas.

"If all nations will agree wholly to eliminate from possession and use the small minority, just as in the domestic field the good purposes of a majority in business, labor or in other cooperative efforts are often frustrated by a selfish few.

The deep-rooted desire of Americans for better living conditions and for the avoidance of war is shared by mass humanity in every country. As a means to this end, I have in the message to the various nations, stressed the practical necessity of reducing armaments. It is high time for us and for every other nation to understand the sim-

---

Footnote 13—Continued.

weapons which make possible a successful attack, defenses automatically will become impregnable, and the frontiers and independence of every nation will become secure.

"The ultimate objective of the Disarmament Conference must be the complete elimination of all offensive weapons. The immediate objective is a substantial reduction of some of these weapons and the elimination of many others.

"This Government believes that the program for immediate reduction of aggressive weapons, now under discussion at Geneva, is but a first step toward our ultimate goal. We do not believe that the proposed immediate steps go far enough. Nevertheless, this Government welcomes the measures now proposed and will exert its influence toward the attainment of further successive steps of disarmament.

"Stated in the clearest way, there are three steps to be agreed upon in the present discussions:

"First, to take, at once, the first definite step toward this objective, as broadly outlined in the MacDonald Plan.

"Second, to agree upon time and procedure for taking the following steps.

"Third, to agree that while the first and the following steps are being taken, no nation shall increase its existing armaments over and above the limitations of treaty obligations.

"But the peace of the world must be assured during the whole period of disarmament and I, therefore, propose a fourth step concurrent with and wholly dependent on the faithful fulfillment of these three proposals and subject to existing treaty rights:

"That all the nations of the world should enter into a solemn and definite pact of non-aggression: That they should solemnly reaffirm the obligations they have assumed to limit and reduce their armaments and, provided these obligations are faithfully executed by all signatory powers, individually agree that they will send no armed force of whatsoever nature across their frontiers.

"Common sense points out that if any strong nation refuses to join with genuine sincerity in these concerted efforts for political and economic peace, the one at Geneva and the other at London, progress can be obstructed and ultimately blocked. In such event the civilized world, seeking both forms of peace, will know where the responsibility for failure lies. I urge that no nation assume such a responsibility, and that all the nations joined in these great conferences translate their professed policies into action. This is the way to political and economic peace.

"I trust that your government will join in the fulfillment of these hopes.

"FRANKLIN D. ROOSEVELT"

ple fact that the invasion of any nation, or the destruction of a national sovereignty, can be prevented only by the complete elimination of the weapons that make such a course possible today.

Such an elimination will make the little nation relatively more secure against the great nation.

Furthermore, permanent defenses are a nonrecurring charge against governmental budgets while large armies, continually rearmed with improved offensive weapons, constitute a recurring charge. This, more than any other factor today is responsible for governmental deficits and threatened bankruptcy.

The way to disarm is to disarm. The way to prevent invasion is to make it impossible.

I have asked for an agreement among nations on four practical and simultaneous steps:

First, that through a series of steps the weapons of offensive warfare be eliminated;

Second, that the first definite step be taken now;

Third, that while these steps are being taken no nation shall increase existing armaments over and above the limitations of treaty obligations;

Fourth, that subject to existing treaty rights no nation during the disarmament period shall send any armed force of whatsoever nature across its own borders.

Our people realize that weapons of offense are needed only if other nations have them and they will freely give them up if all the nations of the world will do likewise.

In the domestic field the Congress has labored in sympathetic understanding with me for the improvement of social conditions, for the preservation of individual human rights, and for the furtherance of social justice.

In the message to the nations which I herewith transmit I have named the same objectives. It is in order to assure these great human values that we seek peace by ridding the world of the weapons of aggression and attack.

FRANKLIN D. ROOSEVELT

THE WHITE HOUSE,
  May 16, 1933.

16

811.113/297

Memorandum by the Secretary of State [14] to the Committee On Foreign Relations, United States Senate, May 17, 1933

[Extract]

It is impossible to foresee all the circumstances under which the President might exercise the authority granted by this Resolution. In many cases of threatened or actual international conflict an embargo on the export of arms placed by other nations not involved in the conflict would be of little or no avail in preventing or putting an end to that conflict. In such cases, the President would obviously take no action. In other cases, an international embargo on the shipment of arms and munitions to both parties to the conflict might be an effective means of preserving or restoring peace. It is conceivable that in certain cases the matured opinion of this Government might accord with the opinion of the rest of the world in fixing the responsibility for a conflict upon an aggressor nation. In such cases, an international embargo on the shipment of arms and munitions to one party to the conflict might be deemed an equitable and effective method of restoring peace. This method nevertheless would certainly not be adopted by this Government without such effective guarantees of international cooperation as would safeguard us against the danger of this country's being involved in the conflict as a result of such action. In a case of this kind, this Government would naturally take into careful consideration the international law of neutrality taking into account the definite, although perhaps as yet undefined, effect of the Kellogg-Briand Pact and other treaties designed to prevent war upon the concept of neutrality.

It has been urged by some that action by the President pursuant to this Resolution might result in involving this country in war. If a President were disposed to stir up conflicts with other countries, he would have, under the authority already conferred upon him many simpler and more expeditious means of doing so than by the use of an arms embargo. This is a peace measure and it would be used to promote peace.

It is natural that this Resolution, although it was originally proposed in pursuance of the development of the peace policy of this

[14] Presented orally by Joseph C. Green, Division of Western European Affairs, Department of State, to the Senate Committee on Foreign Relations, May 17, 1933, at a hearing on H.J. Res. 93, 73d Cong., 1st sess. (see doc. 13).

Government and without reference to specific cases, should be considered with reference to the cases of actual international conflict existing at the present time.

If this legislation were enacted, this Government would be disposed, in cooperation with other governments, to place immediately an embargo on the shipment of arms to Paraguay and Bolivia. The information in our possession leads us to believe that a request from other powers for our cooperation would be forthcoming and that international cooperation could be obtained to a degree sufficient to en_:re the complete stoppage of shipments of arms to those countries. As neither country is a producer of arms or munitions of war, such action would tend to bring about a cessation of the hostilities now being carried on between them.

Efforts are now in progress to put an end to the conflict between Colombia and Peru. Both Governments are members of the League of Nations. The Council of the League has submitted to these Governments a proposal for the settlement of the differences between them. The Government of Colombia has accepted this proposal. The Government of Peru still has this proposal under consideration. The question of an arms embargo in this case does not, therefore, arise at this time. The action if any which this Government might be disposed to take in this case pursuant to the proposed legislation would depend upon the unpredictable conditions which may exist in the future.

It has never been the intention and is not now the intention of this Government to use the authority which would be conferred upon the Executive by this Resolution as a means of restoring peace between China and Japan. An embargo on arms and munitions of war would not be an effective means of restoring peace in this case. Japan is an important producer of arms and munitions of war. Her industry is sufficiently developed to supply her present and probable future needs. China is dependent upon her importation of these commodities. An embargo on the exportation of arms and munitions to both China and Japan would, therefore, militate against China and in favor of Japan. An embargo directed against Japan alone would probably result in a Japanese blockade of Chinese ports, in the seizure by the Japanese of arms and munitions intended for China, and thus its ultimate effects would probably be to decrease China's supply of arms and increase, by virtue of seizures, Japan's supply. As this Government concurs in general in the findings of the Lytton Commission which place the major responsibility upon Japan for the international conflict now proceeding in China, this Government would not be disposed to take any action which would favor the military operations of the Japanese. From the information in our possession, it would appear that this view of the situation is shared by the principal powers members of the League of Nations. We do not, therefore, envisage the probability of proposals by the League or by its principal members to this Government to cooperate with them in an embargo on the shipment of arms and munitions to Japan. Should such proposals be made, we would not be disposed to give them favorable consideration, and we would not under any circumstances agree to participate in an international embargo of this kind unless we had secured substantial guarantees from the governments of all of the great powers which would ensure us against the effects of any retaliatory measures which the Japanese might undertake. In brief, this Government does not expect to take any action of this nature in connection with this case; if any action is taken it will certainly be taken with a due and prudent regard for American interests and in particular for our paramount interest of remaining free from any entanglements which would involve this country in a foreign war. One of the most important reasons for the passage of this Resolution at this time is, however, connected with the present situation in the Far East. There is danger that if this legislation is not enacted, certain European governments may find it to their interest to make it appear that this Government is responsible, by virtue of its not being in a position to cooperate, for a failure on their part to proceed with the imposition of sanctions to which they are committed by reason of their membership in the League of Nations. Thus they would make this country appear in the eyes of many of their nationals and of a large section of public opinion in this country to bear the onus of their failure to make effective the peace machinery which they have built up. If the Resolution is passed, it would no longer be possible for them to make the excuse that their failure to come to an agreement among themselves in regard to a course of action was due to the fact that we were not in a position to cooperate with them if requested to do so. Under these circumstances, failure on their part to take action would manifestly be due solely to their own inability to reach an agreement on the basis of which to request our cooperation, and the facts of the situation would be obvious to all the world; they could attribute no responsibility or blame to us.

It is not our policy to have this Government posing before the world as a leader in all the efforts to prevent or put an end to wars but on the other hand it is not our policy to lag behind the other nations of the world in their efforts to promote peace. The passage of this

Resolution is necessary in order that this Government may keep pace with other Governments of the world in this movement.

17

Press Releases, vol. VIII, p. 387

Address Delivered by the Honorable Norman H. Davis, Chairman of the United States Delegation, at the General Disarmament Conference, Geneva, May 22, 1933

The initiative taken by the President of the United States in communicating directly with the heads of states participating in the Economic and Disarmament Conferences was prompted by the pressing need for concerted and decisive action to solve the interrelated problems with which these two conferences must deal.

The Disarmament Conference has reached the moment for definite decisions. We must face the issue; we must now determine whether the nations of the world propose to go forward with progressive disarmament or revert to the pre-war system of unrestrained competition in armaments with all the continuance of the international suspicion and fear which this will involve.

At the end of the World War the peoples of all states and their leaders resolved that the suicidal armament policy of the preceding decades must be changed. They were convinced that this policy had been one of the contributing factors which brought about the war. Hence a new policy regarding armaments was incorporated as a fundamental part of the peace settlement. This policy, adopted to prevent a future race in armaments, was based on the principle that armaments are a matter of general concern and that the time had passed when each state should be the sole judge of its armaments.

To carry out this conception, provision was made for the disarmament of the defeated powers, and at the same time a decision was taken unprecedented in history whereby the victorious states voluntarily assumed an obligation to reduce their own armaments.

As a first step the peace treaties reduced the armaments of Germany and her allies with a view to rendering impossible any aggression on their part. In fact, the theory behind these treaties was that the military forces of the disarmed powers should be fixed on the basis of the maintenance of internal order and the necessary policing of frontiers, but no more. The whole purpose of these provisions was to guarantee that the armies of Germany and her former allies should thenceforth stay at home.

It would neither have been just nor wise, nor was it intended, that the Central Powers should be subject for all time to a special treatment in armaments. There is and has been a corresponding duty on the part of the other powers, parties to peace treaties, that by successive stages they too would bring their armaments down to a level strictly determined by the needs of self-defense. While the United States is not bound by the provisions or the implications of those treaties, I have no hesitancy in saying that it is the will of our people, interpreted by President Roosevelt, to join with the other powers in disarming down to that level, and we are prepared to exert our influence to bring this about, not by theoretical statements of good intentions but by decisive and progressive reduction of armaments through international agreement.

The present situation admits of no further delay. The states of the world must either go forward in good faith to carry out in all its implications the disarmament policy which they adopted in 1919 or we must recognize frankly that this policy has been abandoned and reconcile ourselves to reverting to a race in competitive armament. If the latter course is taken, the consequences are inevitable. Sooner or later there will be the break-down of the peace machinery which has been so laboriously built up since 1918, and the world will be swept into another war.

The immediate result of a failure here would be a set-back to economic recovery, which depends upon such mutual confidence between nations as will permit a real collaboration in the task of restoring international trade and the freer movement of goods. This is impossible in a situation clouded by the fear of war. National budgets which should be devoted to productive and social ends are burdened with excessive and wasteful expenditures for armament. This leads in turn to an almost unbearable load of taxation on all our peoples.

If we thus candidly face the situation, there is really no alternative for a sane world to consider. It is inconceivable that the responsible leaders of any country in the world could hesitate over this issue. We cannot shirk the duty which this choice imposes upon us. We cannot safely delay taking effective steps to reduce armaments to a purely defensive basis.

As far as the position of the United States is concerned, we are frank to recognize that we have a simpler problem to meet than have many of the European powers. Fears and apprehensions based on historical and racial grounds have led to the maintenance of large armaments in Europe. These large armaments have caused resentment, particularly in the less-armed countries. The resulting political tension has in turn reacted to keep up the general level of armaments. We are not unaware of the difficulties which lie in the way of reduction in armaments here. It is our very detachment from this situation which gives us hope that we may exert a helpful influence toward the realization of our common objective. But we are prepared to aid in other ways than through exerting our influence, and I shall take this opportunity to show what we are prepared to do.

As regards the level of armaments, we are prepared to go as far as the other states in the way of reduction. We feel that the ultimate objective should be to reduce armaments approximately to the level established by the peace treaties; that is, to bring armaments as soon as possible through successive stages down to the basis of a domestic police force.

In particular, as emphasized by President Roosevelt, we are prepared to join other nations in abolishing weapons of an aggressive character, which not only are the more costly to construct and maintain but at present are those most likely to lead to a breach of the peace. To cut the power of offense and remove the threat of surprise attack would do more than anything else to lessen the danger of a war. Almost a year ago the American Government submitted a proposal along these lines. This proposal, which received the approval of a large number of states, was not acceptable to certain states and was therefore not adopted. A few weeks ago the British Prime Minister submitted a detailed proposal which embodies many of the features of the American plan of last year. As the British proposal represents a real measure of disarmament, we accept it whole-heartedly as a definite and excellent step toward the ultimate objective. We therefore are prepared to give our full support to the adoption of this plan.

In addition I wish to make it clear that we are ready not only to do our part toward the substantive reduction of armaments but, if this is effected by general international agreement, we are also prepared to contribute in other ways to the organization of peace. In particular, we are willing to consult the other states in case of a threat to peace, with a view to averting conflict. Further than that, in the event that the states, in conference, determine that a state has been guilty of a breach of the peace in violation of its international obligations and take measures against the violator, then, if we concur in the judgment rendered as to the responsible and guilty party, we will refrain from any action tending to defeat such collective effort which these states may thus make to restore peace.

Finally, we believe that a system of adequate supervision should be formulated to insure the effective and faithful carrying out of any measure of disarmament. We are prepared to assist in this formulation and to participate in this supervision. We are heartily in sympathy with the idea that means of effective, automatic, and continuous supervision should be found whereby nations will be able to rest assured that as long as they respect their obligations with regard to armaments the corresponding obligations of their neighbors will be carried out in the same scrupulous manner.

The Disarmament Conference has already formulated measures for the establishing of a permanent disarmament commission. The powers now proposed for this commission may well be reinforced. The commission will have many important duties, but none more essential than that of effectively supervising the fulfillment of the treaty.

We recognize that the ultimate objective in disarmament must be attained by stages, but we believe that the time for the next and decisive step is long overdue and cannot be further postponed.

Virtually all the nations of the world have entered upon the solemn obligation of the Briand-Kellogg Pact to renounce war as an instrument of national policy and to settle their disputes only by pacific means. If we are to keep faith with these obligations, we must definitely make up our minds to settle our disputes around a conference table instead of preparing to settle them on the battlefield. It was with such a thought that the President proposed an undertaking by the nations that, subject to existing treaty rights, armed forces should not be sent across national frontiers. In the long run, we may come to the conclusion that the simplest and most accurate definition of an aggressor is one whose armed forces are found on alien soil in violation of treaties.

There have been two main obstacles to disarmament. One was the apprehension that Germany proposed to rearm; the other, the reluctance of the armed powers of Europe in the present state of the world to take a real step in disarmament.

If at this decisive point any nation should fail to give conclusive evidence of its pacific intentions and insist upon the right to rearm, even though the other powers take effective and substantial steps toward disarmament, then the burden of responsibility for the failure of the Disarmament Conference, with the incalculable consequences of such a failure, would rest on the shoulders of that nation. The problem with which we are faced cannot be solved if one nation insists on rearming while the others disarm. The result inevitably would be another race in armaments.

As regards the action of the other powers, we are not unaware in the United States of the political difficulties which still lie in the way of the reduction of European armaments. We recognize the legitimate claim which any state has to safeguard its security. But we are firmly convinced that in the long run this security can best be achieved through a controlled disarmament by which the military strength of the most heavily armed nations is progressively reduced to a level such as that provided for in the peace treaties. To the extent that armaments create political tension, they in themselves constitute a menace to peace and may jeopardize the security of the very nations which maintain them.

If we take a long step in the direction of disarmament today and agree by stages to achieve our ultimate objective, we can meet any legitimate claim of the powers bound by the peace treaties and at the same time effectively help to insure peace.

A few days ago the Conference met a serious obstacle to further progress in its detailed examination of the British plan. Since then there has been an appreciable change. The recent speech by the German Chancelor before the Reichstag clarifying the German attitude and policy with regard to disarmament and endorsing the proposal of President Roosevelt has been most helpful. This, and also the subsequent announcement made here by our colleague, Herr Nadolny, of Germany's acceptance of the British plan as the basis of the future convention, have so altered the situation as to justify us in assuming that we can now resume our consideration of this plan with real hope of agreement. Our present agenda is a consideration of the chapters on war material. It was understood that other related subjects might be introduced, and my colleagues may feel that I have made wide use of the latitude thus given me. But in closing my remarks, and to bring our discussion back to the concrete question before us, I desire to state that the American delegation accepts the chapter on material and expresses the hope that the other delegations will join in this acceptance and that the way may thus be cleared for an immediate decision on the concrete proposals in this chapter.

This conference is not only a disarmament conference. It is an emergency conference of a world in a state of political uncertainty and economic depression. The next weeks will bring the decisive test. It will require courage and statesmanship to meet this test, but the failure to do so will go far to shatter any hope of world organization for peace. As far as the United States is concerned, our abilities and our incentive to collaborate whole-heartedly in the continuing task of helping to maintain world peace depend in large measure upon the results achieved here in disarmament. President Roosevelt's message is a clear indication of the fact that the United States will exert its full power and influence and accept its just share of responsibility to make the results in disarmament definite, prompt, and effective.

The results of success here and now would bring benefits beyond all calculation. It would give new confidence and hope—confidence that governments can still govern and leaders lead; hope that a definite step in disarmament having at last been taken, economic recovery will be hastened and the millions in all countries who are only asking for the opportunity to work will have restored to them the possibility of living in peace and of earning their daily bread. If by a great act of faith each and every nation will now summon the courage to take a decisive step in general disarmament, conditions throughout the world will so improve that we can henceforth face the future with a real feeling of security and confidence. With the alternative to success in mind, we cannot allow ourselves to fail.

18

862.00/3415

The Consul General at Berlin (Messersmith) to the Under Secretary of State (Phillips)

[Extracts]

BERLIN, June 26, 1933.

DEAR MR. PHILLIPS:

I think the Department must be exceedingly careful in its dealings with Germany as long as the present Government is in power as it has no spokesman who can really be depended upon, and those who hold the highest positions are capable of actions which really outlaw them from ordinary intercourse.

I think we must recognize that while the Germany of to-day wants peace, it is by no means a peaceful country or one looking forward to a long period of peace. The present German Government and its adherents desire peace ardently for the present because they need peace to carry through the changes in Germany which they want to bring about. What they want to do, however, definitely is to make Germany the most capable instrument of war that there has ever existed. The Minister of Education, speaking yesterday, said that a Spartan spirit must be developed among the German youth. Wherever one goes in Germany one sees people drilling, from children of five and six on, up to those well into middle age. A psychology is being developed that the whole world is against Germany and that it lies defenseless before the world. People are being trained against gas attacks, against airplane attacks, and the idea of war and danger from one's neighbors is constantly harped upon. I wish it were really possible to make our people at home understand, for I feel that they should understand it, how definitely this martial spirit is being developed in Germany. If this Government remains in power for another year and carries on in the same measure in this direction, it will go far towards making Germany a danger to world peace for years to come.

This is a very disjointed and incoherent letter. I am dictating it under pressure as I wish to catch the courier pouch. What I do want to say really is that for the present this country is headed in directions which can only carry ruin to it and will create a situation here dangerous to world peace. With few exceptions, the men who are running this Government are of a mentality that you and I cannot understand. Some of them are psychopathic cases and would ordinarily be receiving treatment somewhere. Others are exalted and in a frame of mind that knows no reason. The majority are woefully ignorant and unprepared for the tasks which they have to carry through every day. Those men in the party and in responsible positions who are really worth-while, and there are quite a number of these, are powerless because they have to follow the orders of superiors who are suffering from the abnormal psychology prevailing in the country. It is impossible for us to talk about tariffs or monetary policy or any of these major matters with a Germany whose leaders do not think in any sense along the lines that we do. While their representatives are talking at London and seem to be just like everybody else, the most phantastic experiments on financial or economic lines are being definitely considered in their home country. Dr. Luther may talk bravely and fairly about Germany in the United States, but he can't tell what he knows, and even if he would, there is a great deal that he does not know. There is a real revolution here and a dangerous situation.

Very sincerely yours,

GEORGE S. MESSERSMITH

19

500.A15A4/2280

Memorandum by the Secretary of State Regarding a Conversation With the German Ambassador (Luther)

[Extract]

[WASHINGTON,] October 9, 1933.

The German Ambassador called and I stated to him that the one primary and paramount purpose and matter of consideration of the United States Government was the promotion of general disarmament. I said that, naturally, any organized movement for this purpose could not logically contemplate a modified program by which some governments might proceed to rearm; that the theory of my government was that we should wage a steady contest for the disarmament of the heavily armed nations, rather than become parties to a plan for others to proceed to rearm; that this viewpoint had no reference to countries or populations anywhere in particular.

C[ORDELL] H[ULL]

20

500.A15A4Personnel/1251

Memorandum by the Secretary of State Regarding a Conversation With the German Ambassador (Luther)

[WASHINGTON,] November 2, 1933.

After talking with me on another matter, the German Ambassador turned to the subject of the return of Norman Davis from the Disarmament Conference at Geneva. I said, "Yes, Mr. Davis is returning for a conference." The Ambassador inquired as to whether and when he would return to Geneva. I replied that my government was naturally deeply interested in the cause of world peace and hence in the cause of disarmament to the extent that it was strictly in harmony with world peace movements. I stated that this broad policy of world disarmament attracted our sympathy and support to the extent that it would be calculated to advance and improve conditions of world peace. I said that speaking individually and not even to be bound individually after I conferred with Norman Davis, the outlook in Europe at this distance for disarmament or for peace did not appear very encouraging. I added that a general war during the next two to ten years seemed more probable than peace; that my country had exerted itself in every way possible in support of the latter and against the possible recurrence of the former, but that frankly I felt somewhat discouraged, speaking still for myself individually. The Ambassador then quoted Hitler's statement to the effect that Germany would not seek the restoration of Alsace-Lorraine and that in his opinion this should quiet French apprehension. He added that the Saar question was an entirely separate one.

C[ORDELL] H[ULL]

21

862.00/3417

The Consul General at Berlin (Messersmith) to the
Under Secretary of State (Phillips)

[Extracts]

BERLIN, November 23, 1933.

DEAR MR. PHILLIPS:

In spite of the way in which the feelings of the German people have been whipped up by this new Government I do not believe that the majority of the German people yet desire war, but there is certainly no great desire for peace. Everything that is being done in the country to-day has for its object to make the people believe that Germany is threatened vitally in every aspect of its life by outside influences and by other countries. Everything is being done to use this feeling to stimulate military training and exercises, and innumerable measures are being taken to develop the German people into a hardy, sturdy race which will be able to meet all comers. The military spirit is constantly growing. It cannot be otherwise. The leaders of Germany to-day have no desire for peace unless it is a peace which the world makes at the expense of complete compliance with German desires and ambitions. Hitler and his associates really and sincerely want peace for the moment, but only to have a chance to get ready to use force if it is found finally essential. They are preparing their way so carefully that there is not in my mind any question but that the German people will be with them when they want to use force and when they feel that they have the necessary means to carry through their objects.

Just what Germany will do on the disarmament question I think it is too early to definitely predict, but that she has a definite aim which she will go after unswervingly, we can take for granted. She will fight shy of all conferences, but will make constant overtures all around and constant protestations of a desire to cooperate and of a will for peace. Germany will particularly embarrass France by protestations of her willingness to do all sorts of things, with the hope of making trouble between France and England and the United States. It will I believe be exceedingly difficult to pin her down to anything. In the meantime she will go on rearming. This is what she wants to do and will do. Germany may make all sorts of protestations with regard to the reduction of armaments by other countries, but what she is interested in is not so much the other countries cutting down their armaments, as having a free hand or rather time to go ahead and rearm herself.

Cordially and sincerely yours,

GEORGE S. MESSERSMITH

22

Press Releases, vol. IX, p. 343

Statement [15] by the Secretary of State at the Seventh International Conference of American States, Montevideo, December 15, 1933

MR. CHAIRMAN AND MEMBERS OF THE COMMITTEE: I arise to say that the Delegation of the United States of America is in the heartiest accord with the very timely and vitally important resolution offered by the able Minister of Foreign Affairs of Argentina, Dr. Saavedra Lamas. The beneficial benefits of this proposal on peace will be far-reaching. Their stimulating influence will extend beyond this hemisphere and to the uttermost parts of the earth. They will bring cheer and hope to the struggling and discouraged forces of peace everywhere.

May I express what is in the mind of every delegate, that our grateful appreciation of this outstanding service of Dr. Saavedra Lamas will most appropriately climax a series of splendid services to the cause of peace which he has rendered. Let me also thank the heads of each delegation with whom I have conferred during past

---

[15] In seconding Dr. Saavedra Lamas' proposal that all nations represented at the Conference give their adherence to the existing peace conventions since the Gondra treaty, signed in 1923.

days for their prompt and most valuable cooperation in support of this proposal.

The passage of this resolution and the agreement to attach from 12 to 20 signatures of governments to the five peace pacts or agencies thus far unsigned by them is not a mere mechanical operation. The real significance is the deep and solemn spirit of peace which pervades the minds and hearts of every delegate here and moves each to undertake a wise and effective step to promote conditions of peace at this critical stage. The adoption of this resolution and the agreement to sign these five splendid peace instruments will thoroughly strengthen the peace agencies of the 21 American states and make peace permanently secure in this hemisphere. This wholesale affixing of signatures to five treaties through conference action within itself thoroughly vindicates the policy of international conference.[16]

I desire most heartily to second the motion to report this resolution favorably. I desire also to say that the United States is ready to affix its signature to the Argentine anti-war pact, and I venture at the same time to express the earnest hope that representatives of all other governments present will aid in a great service to peace by signifying at this time their willingness to affix on behalf of their governments their signatures on any of these five treaties which they have not yet signed.

Universal peace has been the chief aim of civilization. Nations fail or succeed according to their failure or success in this supreme undertaking. I profoundly believe that the American nations during the coming years will write a chapter of achievement in the advancement of peace that will stand out in world history.

It is in these inspiring circumstances that I and my associates have come to the Conference here in Montevideo. We come too for the reason that the people and the Government of the United States feel the keenest interest in this Conference and have the strongest

---

[16] The five treaties and conventions referred to by Mr. Hull in the above statement are the following:

Kellogg-Briand Peace Pact (Pact of Paris), signed in Paris in 1928.

Argentine Anti-War Pact, signed at Rio de Janeiro, October 10, 1933.

Treaty To Avoid or Prevent Conflicts Between American States (Gondra treaty), signed at the Fifth Pan American Conference, Santiago, Chile, in 1923.

General Treaty of Inter-American Conciliation, signed at Washington, January 5, 1929.

General Treaty of Inter-American Arbitration, signed at Washington, January 5, 1929.

desire to contribute to its success. We come because we share in common the things that are vital to the entire material, moral, and spiritual welfare of the people of this hemisphere and because the satisfactory development of civilization itself in this Western World depends on cooperative efforts by all the Americas. No other common aspiration could so closely draw peoples together. We can have no other objective than these. Our common hopes and responsibilities, chaperoned by common sense and initiative, beckon to all of us. We sense a yearning here for a spirit of fine cooperative endeavor. We know too that in this great region the future possibilities of which no man dare calculate the world is being given another chance to right itself. By pooling all our resources in an unselfish spirit we shall undertake to meet the test of service to ourselves and to humanity and make the most of the spacious opportunities that lie ahead. We know when we survey our assets that we have the foundations in this part of the world laid for the greatest civilization of all the past—a civilization built upon the highest moral, intellectual, and spiritual ideals.

Indeed, while older nations totter under the burden of outworn ideas, cling to the decayed and cruel institution of war, and use precious resources to feed cannon rather than hungry mouths, we stand ready to carry on in the spirit of that application of the Golden Rule by which we mean the true good will of the true good neighbor.

It is really a very old and universal though sometimes neglected rule of conduct, this revitalized policy. It is, however, the real basis of that political liberty for which your own great heroes fought and which is our greatest common heritage. It is high time for the world to take new heed of it and to restore its ancient and potent meaning.

I am gratified to say that I have already found much of this spirit among the distinguished leaders with whom I have talked here in Montevideo. They all keenly realize the crisis that has been thrust upon the New World. The Old World looks hopefully in this direction, and we must not disappoint that hope. Today Europe staggers under the load of bristling armaments paid for out of treasuries depleted by the clogging of trade channels. Our common ties with them redouble our desire to offer our best in the molding of a new world order. We have the opportunity and the duty to carry on. We have a belt of sanity on this part of the globe. We are as one as to the objective we seek. We agree that it is a forward-looking enterprise which brings us here, and we must make it a forward-moving enterprise.

Peace and economic rehabilitation must be our objective. The avoidance of war must be our supreme purpose. Most gratifying is the practical appeal which your leaders are making to bring about an end to the bloody conflict between two of our sister republics, the one small and remaining exception to our hopes and ideals for enduring peace in this hemisphere. This is a blot on our civilization which we must erase. I grant with all my heart that with the end of that conflict war as an instrument for settling international disputes will have lost its last foothold in this hemisphere.

In its own forward-looking policy the administration at Washington has pledged itself, as I have said, to the policy of the good neighbor. As President Roosevelt has defined the good neighbor, he "resolutely respects himself and, because he does so, respects the rights of others". We must think, we must speak, we must act this part.

I am safe in the statement that each of the American nations whole-heartedly supports this doctrine—that every nation alike earnestly favors the absolute independence, the unimpaired sovereignty, the perfect equality, and the political integrity of each nation, large or small, as they similarly oppose aggression in every sense of the word.

May I for a moment direct attention to the significance of this broad policy as my country is steadily carrying it into effect under the Roosevelt administration, the extent and nature of which should be familiar to each of the nations here represented. My Government is doing its utmost, with due regard to commitments made in the past, to end with all possible speed engagements which have been set up by previous circumstances. There are some engagements which can be removed more speedily than others. In some instances disentanglement from obligations of another era can only be brought about through the exercise of some patience. The United States is determined that its new policy of the New Deal—of enlightened liberalism—shall have full effect and shall be recognized in its fullest import by its neighbors. The people of my country strongly feel that the so-called right of conquest must forever be banished from this hemisphere, and most of all they shun and reject that so-called right for themselves. The New Deal indeed would be an empty boast if it did not mean that.

Let us in the broad spirit of this revitalized policy make this the beginning of a great new era, of a great renaissance in American cooperative effort to promote our entire material, moral, and spiritual affairs and to erect an edifice of peace that will forever endure. Let each American nation vie with the other in the practice of the policy of the good neighbor. Let suspicion, misunderstanding, and prejudice be banished from every mind and genuine friendship for and trust in each other and a singleness of purpose to promote the welfare of all be substituted. Let each nation welcome the closest scrutiny by the others of the spirit and manner in which it carries out the policy of the good neighbor. Let actions rather than mere words be the acid test of the conduct and motives of each nation. Let each country demonstrate by its every act and practice the sincerity of its purposes and the unselfishness of its relationships as a neighbor.

It is in this spirit that the Government and the people of the United States express their recognition of the common interests and common aspirations of the American nations and join with them in a renewed spirit of broad cooperation for the promotion of liberty under law of peace, of justice, and of righteousness.

23

Treaty Series No. 881

Rights and Duties of States—Convention Signed at Montevideo, December 26, 1933

BY THE PRESIDENT OF THE UNITED STATES OF AMERICA

A PROCLAMATION

WHEREAS a convention on rights and duties of States was adopted by the Seventh International Conference of American States at Montevideo, Uruguay, and signed on December 26, 1933, by plenipotentiaries of the United States of America with a reservation which the delegation of the United States of America had presented to the plenary session of the conference on December 22, 1933, and by plenipotentiaries of Honduras, El Salvador, Dominican Republic, Haiti, Argentina, Venezuela, Uruguay, Paraguay, Mexico, Panama, Guatemala, Brazil with a reservation, Ecuador, Nicaragua, Colombia, Chile, Peru with a reservation, and Cuba, the English and Spanish texts of which convention are word for word as follows:

CONVENTION ON RIGHTS AND DUTIES OF STATES

The Governments represented in the Seventh International Conference of American States:

Wishing to conclude a Convention on Rights and Duties of States, have appointed the following Plenipotentiaries:

[Here follow the names of plenipotentiaries.]

Who, after having exhibited their Full Powers, which were found to be in good and due order, have agreed upon the following:

ARTICLE 1

The state as a person of international law should possess the following qualifications: *a*) a permanent population; *b*) a defined territory; *c*) government; and *d*) capacity to enter into relations with the other states.

ARTICLE 2

The federal state shall constitute a sole person in the eyes of international law.

ARTICLE 3

The political existence of the state is independent of recognition by the other states. Even before recognition the state has the right to defend its integrity and independence, to provide for its conservation and prosperity, and consequently to organize itself as it sees fit, to legislate upon its interests, administer its services, and to define the jurisdiction and competence of its courts.

The exercise of these rights has no other limitation than the exercise of the rights of other states according to international law.

ARTICLE 4

States are juridically equal, enjoy the same rights, and have equal capacity in their exercise. The rights of each one do not depend upon the power which it possesses to assure its exercise, but upon the simple fact of its existence as a person under international law.

ARTICLE 5

The fundamental rights of states are not susceptible of being affected in any manner whatsoever.

ARTICLE 6

The recognition of a state merely signifies that the state which recognizes it accepts the personality of the other with all the rights and duties determined by international law. Recognition is unconditional and irrevocable.

ARTICLE 7

The recognition of a state may be express or tacit. The latter results from any act which implies the intention of recognizing the new state.

ARTICLE 8

No state has the right to intervene in the internal or external affairs of another.

ARTICLE 9

The jurisdiction of states within the limits of national territory applies to all the inhabitants.

Nationals and foreigners are under the same protection of the law and the national authorities and the foreigners may not claim rights other or more extensive than those of the nationals.

ARTICLE 10

The primary interest of states is the conservation of peace. Differences of any nature which arise between them should be settled by recognized pacific methods.

ARTICLE 11

The contracting states definitely establish as the rule of their conduct the precise obligation not to recognize territorial acquisitions or special advantages which have been obtained by force whether this consists in the employment of arms, in threatening diplomatic representations, or in any other effective coercive measure. The territory of a state is inviolable and may not be the object of military occupation nor of other measures of force imposed by another state directly or indirectly or for any motive whatever even temporarily.

ARTICLE 12

The present Convention shall not affect obligations previously entered into by the High Contracting Parties by virtue of international agreements.

ARTICLE 13

The present Convention shall be ratified by the High Contracting Parties in conformity with their respective constitutional procedures. The Minister of Foreign Affairs of the Republic of Uruguay shall transmit authentic certified copies to the governments for the aforementioned purpose of ratification. The instrument of ratification shall be deposited in the archives of the Pan American Union in Washington, which shall notify the signatory governments of said deposit. Such notification shall be considered as an exchange of ratifications.

ARTICLE 14

The present Convention will enter into force between the High Contracting Parties in the order in which they deposit their respective ratifications.

ARTICLE 15

The present Convention shall remain in force indefinitely but may be denounced by means of one year's notice given to the Pan American Union, which shall transmit it to the other signatory governments. After the expiration of this period the Convention shall cease in its effects as regards the party which denounces but shall remain in effect for the remaining High Contracting Parties.

ARTICLE 16

The present Convention shall be open for the adherence and accession of the States which are not signatories. The corresponding instruments shall be deposited in the archives of the Pan American Union which shall communicate them to the other High Contracting Parties.

In witness whereof, the following Plenipotentiaries have signed this Convention in Spanish, English, Portuguese and French and hereunto affix their respective seals in the city of Montevideo, Republic of Uruguay, this 26th day of December, 1933.

RESERVATIONS

The Delegation of the United States of America, in signing the Convention on the Rights and Duties of States, does so with the express reservation presented to the Plenary Session of the Conference on December 22, 1933, which reservation reads as follows:

The Delegation of the United States, in voting "yes" on the final vote on this committee recommendation and proposal, makes the same reservation to the eleven articles of the project or proposal that the United States Delegation made to the first ten articles during the final vote in the full Commission, which reservation is in words as follows:

"The policy and attitude of the United States Government toward every important phase of international relationships in this hemisphere could scarcely be made more clear and definite than they have been made by both word and action especially since March 4. I have no disposition therefore to indulge in any repetition or rehearsal of these acts and utterances and shall not do so. Every observing person must by this time thoroughly understand that under the Roosevelt Administration the United States Government is as much opposed as any other government to interference with the freedom, the sovereignty, or other internal affairs or processes of the governments of other nations.

"In addition to numerous acts and utterances in connection with the carrying out of these doctrines and policies, President Roosevelt, during recent weeks, gave out a public statement expressing his disposition to open negotiations with the Cuban Government for the purpose of dealing with the treaty which has existed since 1903. I feel safe in undertaking to say that under our support of the general principle of non-intervention as has been suggested, no government need fear any intervention on the part of the United States under the Roosevelt Administration. I think it unfortunate that during the brief period of this Conference there is apparently not time within which to prepare interpretations and definitions of these fundamental terms that are embraced in the report. Such definitions and interpretations would enable every government to proceed in a uniform way without any difference of opinion or of interpretations. I hope that at the earliest possible date such very important work will be done. In the meantime in case of differences of interpretations and also until they (the proposed doctrines and principles) can be worked out and codified for the common use of every government, I desire to say that the United States Government in all of its international associations and relationships and conduct will follow scrupulously the doctrines and policies which it has pursued since March 4 which are embodied in the different addresses of President Roosevelt since that time and in the recent peace address of myself on the 15th day of December before this Conference and in the law of nations as generally recognized and accepted."

The delegates of Brazil and Peru recorded the following private vote with regard to article 11: "That they accept the doctrine in principle but that they do not consider it codifiable because there are some countries which have not yet signed the Anti-War Pact of Rio de Janeiro of which this doctrine is a part and therefore it does not yet constitute positive international law suitable for codification".

[Here follow signatures.]

AND WHEREAS the said convention, as signed, was duly ratified by the United States of America, and the instrument of ratification of the United States of America embracing the aforesaid reservation made by its delegation at the conference, as follows:

[Here follows text of the reservation made by the delegation of the United States of America, printed above.]
was deposited with the Pan American Union on July 13, 1934,

AND WHEREAS, the said convention has been duly ratified also by the Dominican Republic, whose ratification thereof was deposited with the Pan American Union on December 26, 1934, on which day the convention, pursuant to a provision in Article 14 thereof, entered into force between the United States of America and the Dominican Republic;

Now, THEREFORE, be it known that I, Franklin D. Roosevelt, President of the United States of America, have caused the said convention to be made public to the end that the same and every article and clause thereof may be observed and fulfilled with good faith by the United States of America and the citizens thereof subject to the reservation aforesaid.

IN TESTIMONY WHEREOF, I have hereunto set my hand and caused the Seal of the United States of America to be affixed.

DONE at the city of Washington this eighteenth day of January, in the year of our Lord one thousand nine hundred and thirty-[SEAL] five and of the Independence of the United States of America the one hundred and fifty-ninth.

FRANKLIN D. ROOSEVELT

By the President:
> CORDELL HULL
> *Secretary of State.*

24

Press Releases, vol. IX, p. 380

Address Delivered by President Roosevelt at Washington, December 28, 1933

"Comprehension must be the soil in which shall grow all the fruits of friendship." Those words, used by President Wilson in the Mobile speech in 1913, can well serve as a statement of policy by the Government of the United States. That policy applies equally to a comprehension of our internal problems and our international relations.

Woodrow Wilson was a teacher, and when he used the word "comprehension" he meant it not in terms of the statesmen and political leaders and business executives and financial kings; he meant it rather in its application to the peoples of the world, who are constantly going to school to learn simple truths in order that they and their neighbors can live their lives more safely, more happily, more fully.

In every continent and in every country Woodrow Wilson accelerated comprehension on the part of the people themselves. It is, I believe, true that the events of the past 10 months have caused a greater interest in government, the problems of government, and the purposes of government than in any similar period in our history; and yet this recent interest and comprehension would have been impossible for the American people had they not had from Woodrow Wilson the original stimulus and the original understanding of which he spoke 20 years ago.

In that speech in Mobile, President Wilson first enunciated the definite statement "that the United States will never again seek one additional foot of territory by conquest." The United States accepted that declaration of policy. President Wilson went further, pointing out with special reference to our Latin American neighbors that material interests must never be made superior to human liberty.

Nevertheless, and largely as a result of the convulsion of the World War and its after effects, the complete fruition of that policy of unselfishness has not in every case been obtained. And in this we, all of us, have to share the responsibility.

I do not hesitate to say that if I had been engaged in a political campaign as a citizen of some other American republic, I might have been strongly tempted to play upon the fears of my compatriots of that republic by charging the United States of North America with some form of imperialistic desire for selfish aggrandizement. As a citizen of some other republic I might have found it difficult to believe fully in the altruism of the richest American republic. In particular, as a citizen of some other republic, I might have found it hard to approve of the occupation of the territory of other republics, even as a temporary measure.

It therefore has seemed clear to me as President that the time has come to supplement and to implement the declaration of President Wilson by the further declaration that the definite policy of the United States from now on is one opposed to armed intervention.

The maintenance of constitutional government in other nations is not a sacred obligation devolving upon the United States alone. The maintenance of law and the orderly processes of government in this hemisphere is the concern of each individual nation within its own borders first of all. It is only if and when the failure of orderly processes affects the other nations of the continent that it becomes their concern; and the point to stress is that in such an event it becomes the joint concern of a whole continent in which we are all neighbors.

It is the comprehension of that doctrine—a comprehension not by the leaders alone but by the peoples of all the American republics, that has made the conference now concluding its labors in Montevideo such a fine success. A better state of feeling among the neighbor nations of North and Central and South America exists today than at any time within a generation. For participation in the bringing about of that result we can feel proud that so much credit belongs to the Secretary of State of the United States, Cordell Hull.

In the wider world field a chain of events has led, of late, away from rather than towards the ultimate objectives of Woodrow Wilson.

The superficial observer charges this failure to the growth of the spirit of nationalism. But in so doing he suggests a nationalism in its narrower, restrictive sense, and a nationalism of that kind supported by the overwhelming masses of the people themselves in each nation.

I challenge that description of the world population today.

The blame for the danger to world peace lies not in the world population but in the political leaders of that population.

The imagination of the masses of world population was stirred, as never before, by President Wilson's gallant appeal to them—to those masses—to banish future war. His appeal meant little to the imagination or the hearts of a large number of the so-called statesmen who gathered in Paris to assemble a treaty of so-called peace in 1919. I saw that with my own eyes and heard that with my own ears. Political profit, personal prestige, national aggrandizement attended the birth of the League of Nations, and handicapped it from its infancy by seeking their own profit and their own safety first.

Nevertheless, through the League directly, or through its guiding motives indirectly, the states of the world have groped forward to find something better than the old way of composing their differences.

The League has provided a common meeting place; it has provided machinery which serves for international discussion; and in very many practical instances it has helped labor and health and commerce and education, and, last but not least, the actual settlement of many disputes great and small among nations great and small.

Today the United States is cooperating openly in the fuller utilization of the League of Nations machinery than ever before.

I believe that I express the views of my countrymen when I state that the old policies, alliances, combinations, and balances of power have proved themselves inadequate for the preservation of world peace. The League of Nations, encouraging as it does the extension of nonaggression pacts, of reduction of armament agreements, is a prop in the world peace structure.

We are not members and we do not contemplate membership. We

are giving cooperation to the League in every matter which is not primarily political and in every matter which obviously represents the views and the good of the peoples of the world as distinguished from the views and the good of political leaders, of privileged classes, or of imperialistic aims.

If you figure the world's population at approximately one billion and a half people, you will find it safe to guess that at least 90 percent of all of them are today content with the territorial limits of their respective nations and are willing further to reduce their armed forces tomorrow if every other nation in the world will agree to do the same thing. Back of the threat to world peace lies the fear and perhaps even the possibility that the other 10 percent of the people of the world may go along with a leadership which seeks territorial expansion at the expense of neighbors and which under various pleas in avoidance are unwilling to reduce armament or stop rearmament even if everybody else agrees to nonaggression and to arms reduction.

If this 10 percent can be persuaded by the other 90 percent to do their own thinking and not be led, we will have practical peace, permanent peace, real peace throughout the world. Our own country has reduced the immediate steps to this greatest of objectives to practical and reasonable terms.

I have said to every nation in the world something to this effect:

1. Let every nation agree to eliminate over a short period of years, and by progressive steps, every weapon of offense in its possession and to create no additional weapons of offense. This does not guarantee a nation against invasion unless you implement it with the right to fortify its own border with permanent and nonmobile defenses; and also with the right to assure itself through international continuing inspection that its neighbors are not creating nor maintaining offensive weapons of war.

2. A simple declaration that no nation will permit any of its armed forces to cross its own borders into the territory of another nation. Such an act would be regarded by humanity as an act of aggression and as an act, therefore, that would call for condemnation by humanity.

3. It is clear, of course, that no such general agreement for the elimination of aggression and of the weapons of offensive warfare would be of any value to the world unless every nation, without exception, entered into the agreement by

solemn obligation. If, then, such an agreement were signed by a great majority of the nations on the definite condition that it would go into effect only when signed by all the nations, it would be a comparatively easy matter to determine which nations in this enlightened time are willing to go on record as belonging to the small minority of mankind which still believes in the use of the sword for invasion of and attack upon their neighbors.

I did not make this suggestion until I felt assured, after a hard-headed practical survey, that the temper of the overwhelming majority of all men and women in my own country, as well as those who make up the world's population, subscribes to the fundamental objective I have set forth and to the practical road to that objective. The political leaders of many of these peoples interpose and will interpose argument, excuse, befogging amendment—yes, and even ridicule. But I tell them that the men and women they serve are so far in advance of that type of leadership that we could get a world accord on world peace immediately if the people of the world spoke for themselves.

Through all the centuries and down to the world conflict of 1914 to 1918, wars were made by governments. Woodrow Wilson challenged that necessity. That challenge made the people who create and who change governments think. They wondered with Woodrow Wilson whether the people themselves could not some day prevent governments from making war.

It is but an extension of the challenge of Woodrow Wilson for us to propose in this newer generation that from now on war by governments shall be changed to peace by peoples.

25

711.94/908

Informal and Personal Message From the Japanese Minister For Foreign Affairs (Hirota) to the Secretary of State [17]

To THE HONORABLE
    THE SECRETARY OF STATE.

It is a significant fact that ever since Japan and the United States opened their doors to each other exactly eighty years ago, the two countries have always maintained a relationship of friendliness and cordiality.

---

[17] Handed to the Secretary of State by the Japanese Ambassador, February 21, 1934.

It is a matter for gratification to both our countries that they produce very few commodities which represent conflicting interests in their foreign trade, that each supplies what the other wants, that they are good customers of each other's products, and that they are strengthening their relation of interdependence year after year.

I firmly believe that viewed in the light of the broad aspect of the situation and studied from all possible angles, no question exists between our two countries that is fundamentally incapable of amicable solution. I do not doubt that all issues pending between the two nations will be settled in a satisfactory manner, when examined with a good understanding on the part of each of the other's position, discussed with an open mind and in all frankness, and approached with a spirit of coöperation and conciliation.

I can state with all emphasis at my command that the Japanese nation makes it its basic principle to collaborate in peace and harmony with all nations and has no intention whatever to provoke and make trouble with any other Power.

It is the sincere desire of Japan that a most peaceful and friendly relation will be firmly established between her and her great neighbor across the Pacific, the United States. And to this end I have been exerting my best efforts since I took the post of Foreign Minister.

I am happy, therefore, to avail myself of the occasion of the arrival in your country of Mr. Saito, the new Ambassador, to lay before you, through him, Mr. Secretary, my thoughts as to the necessity of promoting our traditional friendship as above.

I hope and believe that the desire of the Japanese Government in this respect will be reciprocated by a full support and countenance on the part of your Government.

26

711.94/908

Informal and Personal Message From the Secretary of State To the Japanese Minister for Foreign Affairs (Hirota)[18]

To His Excellency
  The Minister for Foreign Affairs of Japan.

Mr. Saito, the new Ambassador of Japan to the United States, has delivered to me the personal and informal message which you have been so good as to send me.

---

[18] Handed to the Japanese Ambassador by the Secretary of State, March 3, 1934, 12:30 p. m.

The cordial sentiments which you express in this message I highly appreciate and reciprocate.

I have not failed to note, with gratification, Your Excellency's effort to foster friendly relations with other powers. In all such effort I am sure that you realize that you may rely upon me for the fullest possible measure of cooperation.

You express the opinion that viewed in the light of the broad aspects of the situation and studied from all possible angles no question exists between our two countries that is fundamentally incapable of amicable solution. I fully concur with you in that opinion. Further, I believe that there are in fact no questions between our two countries which if they be viewed in proper perspective in both countries can with any warrant be regarded as not readily susceptible to adjustment by pacific processes. It is the fixed intention of the American Government to rely, in prosecution of its national policies, upon such processes. If unhappily there should arise in the future any controversy between our two countries, the American Government will be prepared, as I believe it always has been in the past, to examine the position of Japan in a spirit of amity and of desire for peaceful and just settlement, with the confident expectation that the Japanese Government will be prepared to examine the position of the United States in the same spirit.

You refer to the gratifying fact that in the field of trade the interests of our two countries are not in conflict and commercial ties are being constantly strengthened. I perceive every reason to anticipate that the United States and Japan will continue to develop their reciprocal trade with benefit to both countries and, where there may be competition, with constant reciprocal good will.

You state emphatically that Japan has no intention whatever to provoke and make trouble with any other power. I receive this statement with special gratification and I am glad to take this opportunity to state categorically that the United States on its part has no desire to create any issues and no intention to initiate any conflict in its relations with other countries.

In the light of these facts I feel that I should also avail myself of this opportunity to express my earnest hope that it may be possible for all of the countries which have interests in the Far East to approach every question existing or which may arise between or among them in such spirit and manner that these questions may be regulated or resolved with injury to none and with definite and lasting advantage to all.

I shall of course be glad to receive through the Ambassador of Japan to the United States or the Ambassador of the United States to Japan any suggestions calculated to maintain and to increase that friendliness and cordiality which have constantly marked since the conclusion of our first treaty the relations between our two countries. You may count upon my earnest desire to favor any measure or steps which may be practicable toward this end and toward fostering at the same time relations of peace, good will and general benefit among all members of the Family of Nations.

CORDELL HULL

27

862.00/3421

The Appointed Minister to Austria (Messersmith) to the Under Secretary of State (Phillips)

BERLIN, April 21, 1934.

DEAR MR. PHILLIPS:

In my last letter I mentioned that Miller,[19] the Acting Commercial Attache, was preparing a resume of the economic and financial situation for the Embassy as part of the background information to be presented to Mr. Child on his expected arrival here. As I anticipated, it is a very excellent review of certain aspects of the situation here and I am sending a copy to you now as I feel sure it will be of interest to you and to others in the Department.

He has avoided, as was of course proper, in his review a discussion of the political factors in the local situation, but these have been pretty well brought out in my recent letters to you. The review is interesting because it brings out some of the major details on which my own conclusions expressed to you have been based. The review may be particularly interesting to you in the Department when I say that Miller's conclusions have been entirely independently arrived at and in no way influenced by my own, and yet it will be apparent that we are very much in accord in our appraisal of the situation. . . .

Cordially and faithfully yours,

GEORGE S. MESSERSMITH

[Enclosure: Extracts]

APRIL 17, 1934

MEMORANDUM TO THE EMBASSY

MAIN PURPOSE OF NAZIS

The fundamental purpose is to secure a greater share of the world's future for the Germans, the expansion of German territory and

---

[19] Douglas Miller.

growth of the German race until it constitutes the largest and most powerful nation in the world, and ultimately, according to some Nazi leaders, until it dominates the entire globe.

The German people suffering from a traditional inferiority complex, smarting from their defeat in the war and the indignities of the post-war period, disillusioned in their hopes of a speedy return to prosperity along traditional lines, inflamed by irresponsible demagogic slogans and flattered by the statement that their German racial inheritance gives them inherent superior rights over other peoples, have to a large measure adopted the National Socialist point of view for the time being.

ECONOMIC AIMS

There are two other purposes subsidiary to the main purpose. Germany is to be made the economic center of a self-sustaining territorial block whose dependent nations in Central and Eastern Europe will look to Berlin for leadership. This block is to be so constituted that it can defy wartime blockade and be large enough to give the peoples in it the benefits of free trade now enjoyed by the 48 American States. In accordance with this purpose, an agricultural self-sufficiency program has been adopted, foreign foodstuffs are being rigorously excluded or the imported supply secured in increasing quantities from Central and Southeastern Europe. A hereditary peasantry has been set up, firmly attached to the soil through the prohibition of the sale or mortgaging of the peasants' land or crops. An increasing number of commodities have been placed under Government monopolies with fixed prices to consumers and producers, the principle of the numerus clausus or fixed number of persons engaged in any occupation has been increasingly adopted. The National Socialist conception of the correct or Government-fixed price instead of the price fixed by supply and demand has been introduced.

SOCIAL AIMS

The second subsidiary purpose is the welding of all individuals in the present and future Greater Germany into a homogeneous racial family, gladly obedient to the will of its leader, with class and cultural differences inside the country eliminated, but a sharp line drawn between Germans and the foreign world outside. In carrying out this purpose, the Jews are to be entirely eliminated, the Slavic or eastern elements in the population to be minimized and eventually bred out of the race. A national religion is in process of organization; trade unions, political parties and all social, political, cultural, trade or other organizations not affiliated with the National Socialist party, have been abolished, the individual's rights have been largely taken away. In the future the nation is to count for everything, the individual for nothing. Germany is to engage in a gigantic struggle with the rest of the world to grow at the expense of its neighbors. The German population owes the nation the patriotic duty of supporting it and bringing forward all necessary sacrifices to reach the common goal.

RETENTION OF POWER

To these long-distance objectives must be added the fourth and most important purpose of all, namely to retain control at all costs. The National Socialist party may compromise on distant objectives, if necessary, but cannot compromise on a question of retaining its absolute hold on the German people. This control had been gained by making most irresponsible and extravagant promises; by the studied use of the press, the radio, public meetings, parades, flags, uniforms, and all methods of working on popular psychology and finally by the use of force. This control once lost, could never be regained. It is absolutely necessary for the party to continue to make a show of success and to keep popular enthusiasm and fanaticism alive. There must be no open criticism or grumbling, even discussion of the future form of the State, the form in which industry is to be organized, or the laws regarding the hereditary peasantry is prohibited. Since the German public is politically inept and unusually docile, the Nazi movement has been able to dominate the situation for the past year, but the hard facts of the economic situation are beginning to be felt by the more intelligent Germans, particularly bankers, business men, professional men and persons who have touch with the outside world.

DANGER OF WAR

The Nazis are not satisfied with the existing map of Europe. They are at heart belligerent and aggressive. True, they desire nothing more than a period of peace for several years in which they can gradually re-arm and discipline their people. This period may be 5 years, 10 years, or longer, but the more completely their experiments succeed the more certain is a large-scale war in Europe some day.

NAZIS WANT TO WIPE OUT 1918

In estimating the aims and purposes of the National Socialist movement, we must not make the mistake of putting too much reliance on public statements designed for consumption abroad which breathe the spirit of good peace and will and assert the intention of

213

the Government to promote the welfare of the German people and good relations with their neighbors. Nor should we imagine that the present Government leaders will feel and act as we would in their circumstances, namely think only of Germany's welfare. The real emotional drive behind the Nazi program is not so much love of their own country as dislike of other countries. The Nazis will never be content in merely promoting the welfare of the German people. They desire to be feared and envied by foreigners and to wipe out the memory of 1918 by inflicting humiliations in particular upon the French, the Poles, the Czechs and anybody else they can get their hands on.

A careful examination of Hitler's book and his public speeches reveals the fact that he cannot be considered as absolutely sane and normal on this subject. The same is true of many other Nazi leaders. They have capitalized the wounded inferiority complex of the German people, and magnified their own bitter feelings into a cult of dislike against the foreign world which is past the bounds of ordinary good sense and reason. Let us repeat this fact and let it sink in, the National Socialist movement is building a tremendous military machine, physically very poorly armed, but morally aggressive and belligerent. The control of this machine lies in the hands of narrow, ignorant and unscrupulous adventurers who have been slightly touched with madness from brooding over Germany's real or imagined wrongs, as well as the slights and indignities thrown in their own individual way as they attempted to organize the movement. Power of this kind concentrated in hands like these is dangerous. The Nazis are determined to secure more power and more territory in Europe. If this is voluntarily given to them by peaceful means, well and good, but if not, they will certainly use force. That is the only meaning behind the manifold activities of the movement in Germany today.

28

793.94/6606

The Ambassador in Japan (Grew) to the Secretary of State

[Telegram : Paraphrase]

TOKYO, April 25, 1934—1 p. m.
[Received April 25—9 : 55 a.m.]

75. This morning I had an interview with the Foreign Minister. Mr. Hirota referred, on his own initiative, to the subject of the Amau

statement regarding the attitude of Japan toward foreign assistance to China, and said that he wished to clarify that statement to me in confidence. He told me that under questioning by newspaper men, Amau had given out the statement without his knowledge or approval, and that the world had received a wholly false impression of Japanese policy, that Japan had no intention whatever of seeking special privileges in China, of encroaching upon the territorial and administrative integrity of China, or of creating difficulties for the bona fide trade of other countries with China. Various foreign activities have tended to disturb peaceful conditions in China, and Japan is naturally very much interested in those peaceful conditions owing to her nearness to China. But that does not mean that there is any intention or desire on the part of Japan to claim a privileged position in derogation of the rights and responsibilities to which the signatories of the Nine-Power Treaty are entitled. The policy of Japan is complete observance and support of the provisions of the Nine-Power Treaty in every respect.

The insistence by the Chauvinists upon a more aggressive foreign policy, Mr. Hirota said, makes his position difficult. For his own part he is trying to follow the policy of the Emperor, with whom he is constantly in touch, and is seeking to achieve with all countries, and especially with the United States, relations of friendliness. He intends to do his best to bring to a successful conclusion the negotiations with Russia for the purchase of the Chinese Eastern Railway. If that controversy can be settled, there should be better relations between Russia and Japan, which would in turn tend to induce better relations between China and Japan. This whole constructive policy of the Emperor and the Government would obviously be impeded if Japan should now seek special privileges in China. Mr. Hirota said that he has managed thus far to satisfy both the Liberals and the Chauvinists, and that, since he has the Emperor's support, he will continue resolutely in his course even though that should mean his own death. He added also that the Minister of War supports him fully.

Mr. Hirota went on to say that attempts are constantly being made by certain foreign influences, through the press and by other means, to make trouble for Japan. It was his earnest hope that the United States Government should have a perfect understanding of his attitude toward Amau's statement, but he requested that his remarks to me be treated as confidential since his position was difficult. In conclusion, the Minister said that our Government may rest assured that Japan will take no action in China purposely provocative to other countries or contrary to the terms or spirit of the Nine-Power Treaty.

I do not question the sincerity of the Minister's remarks as reported above. Nevertheless I made the observation that the Government and people of the United States would be less impressed by statements of policy than by more concrete evidence.

I was told by the Minister that a similar explanation will be made to you by Saito. The Minister is to receive the British Ambassador at 3 o'clock.

Rumors are reported in the United Press that the Department will instruct me to ask for a clarification of the statement by Amau. Unless I receive supplementary instructions, however, I shall assume that the present telegram answers the Department's inquiry.

GREW

29

793.94/6625a

The Secretary of State to the Ambassador in Japan (Grew)

[Telegram]

WASHINGTON, April 28, 1934—7 p.m.

59. (1) Please call as soon as possible upon the Minister for Foreign Affairs and, under instruction from your Government, deliver to him an *aide memoire*, as follows:

"Recent indications of attitude on the part of the Japanese Government with regard to the rights and interests of Japan and other countries in China and in connection with China have come from sources so authoritative as to preclude their being ignored. Due consideration being given to the circumstances under which these indications have appeared and to their substance, it seems necessary and desirable that the American Government, adhering to the tradition of frankness that has prevailed in relations between it and the Government of Japan, reaffirm the position of the United States with regard to questions of rights and interests involved.

The relations of the United States with China are governed, as are our relations with Japan and our relations with other countries, by the generally accepted principles of international law and the provisions of treaties to which the United States is a party. In international law, in simple justice, and by virtue of treaties, the United States has with regard to China certain rights and certain obligations. In addition, it is associated with China or with Japan or with both, together with certain other countries, in multilateral treaties relating to rights and obligations in the Far East, and in one great multilateral treaty to which practically all the countries of the world are parties.

Entered into by agreement, for the purpose of regulating relations between and among nations, treaties can lawfully be modified or be terminated—but only by processes prescribed or recognized or agreed upon by the parties to them.

In the international associations and relationships of the United States, the American Government seeks to be duly considerate of the rights, the obligations and the legitimate interests of other countries, and it expects on the part of other governments due consideration of the rights, the obligations and the legitimate interests of the United States.

In the opinion of the American people and the American Government, no nation can, without the assent of the other nations concerned, rightfully endeavor to make conclusive its will in situations where there are involved the rights, the obligations and the legitimate interests of other sovereign states.

The American Government has dedicated the United States to the policy of the good neighbor. To the practical application of that policy it will continue, on its own part and in association with other governments, to devote its best efforts."

(2) Report delivery immediately by telegraph.[20]

(3) Thereafter, we expect to make text public here at our convenience.

Hull

30

Press Releases, vol. X, p. 273

Address Delivered by the Secretary of State at Washington, May 5, 1934

[Extracts]

There are innumerable demands both new and important which in this crisis rest upon the educational agencies of the Nation. The late war was supposed to have been waged to make the world safe for democracy. It is paradoxical to observe that since the war political systems on which representative or popular government has rested have been toppling over in every part of the world, while dictator-

---

[20] Message was delivered on April 29.

ships have sprung up overnight in their stead. Nations everywhere are steadily narrowing their vision, their policies, and their program. Each is undertaking more and more to visualize only itself, to live by itself, and to arm conceivably to defend itself against any and all aggressors. Individual cooperation to promote community interests and community welfare is indispensable to human progress. International cooperation to promote understanding, friendship, and vast and varied reciprocal benefits and conditions of peace is equally indispensable to the progress of civilization. These international relationships have been practically abandoned.

Most standards of conduct, both individual and international, have been seriously neglected and impaired. In its chief fundamental respects, civilization since the war has been on the decline. The entire political, economic, social, and moral affairs of most parts of the world are unquestionably in a more or less chaotic condition. They present an unprecedented challenge, especially to the parents, the schools, and the churches.

There are more opportunities for the present young generation than is generally believed. It would be folly, however, for all to fail to recognize that the world is living more in an iron than in the so-called "golden age". The youth may as well realize that they face a world of stress and responsibilities far more difficult and complex than any during recent generations. More of study and of time and of effort will be required of those who lead and plan than is generally imagined. The task must be approached with vision, energy, and resolution, and in many respects with a pioneering and self-sacrificing spirit.

The United States is in a position to render valuable service to the world in the existing exigency. In my judgment, this Nation will continue as in recent months to offer wise, sound, and efficient leadership with suitable programs for political, economic, social, and moral rehabilitation. If in this we should later fail, to whom would our and other countries look to perform this indispensable role? We must revive some of the spirit of hardihood and determination which sustained those who came to this continent, conquered the wilderness, and erected our marvelous free institutions. It becomes all-important to this end that the Nation restore its humanitarian, moral, and spiritual values. I repeat that we are not living amidst conditions where an easy, soft, and flabby existence is possible, as it has seemed at times in the recent past.

Today numerous nations are feverishly arming. They are taxing all of their citizens beyond the limit of ability to pay, and in many ways developing a military spirit which, regardless of present motives of self-defense, may probably lead to war, unless past human experience is to be reversed. Every Christian nation owes it to itself and to humanity to preach and promote understanding, friendship, and peace.

While there are no signs of immediate war anywhere, it is true that seriously volcanic conditions exist in many parts of the world. Peace stabilization is all-important at this stage. It would be both a blunder and a crime for civilized peoples to fail much longer to take notice of present dangerous tendencies which negative every idea of friendliness and of the spirit of the good neighbor.

Economic structures of most countries have been hopelessly undermined and must be restored under sound methods. The American people in this respect must realize that the World War destroyed hundreds of billions of physical wealth; that following the war the people in every country seemingly became obsessed with the one idea of materialism. To get rich or to secure money by the most direct method, regardless of ethics or law or decency, and to spend it for purposes of luxury, amusement, and pastime, became the all-absorbing passion. The result was the wildest runaway experience in the inflation of credit and securities in all human experience. From a combination of policies and methods, either short-sighted or narrow or selfish, the processes of exchange and distribution broke down, and the general world collapse of 1929 resulted. Conditions more or less chaotic have since characterized nearly all phases of affairs of both individuals and nations. Normal thinking and sane practical acting have been almost the exception rather than the rule. There is still a striking lack of enthusiasm for the restoration of those high standards of morals, of good fellowship, and of friendship which normally prevail and should prevail between both individuals and countries.

Let no one, however, become unduly pessimistic. The civilization of the present age, in my judgment, is amply capable of meeting the unprecedented challenge which existing conditions offer, and which must be successfully met unless the world is to be threatened with another period of long night—such as the Dark Ages. My appeal, therefore, is for every individual to awaken and come to a realization of the problems and difficulties facing all alike, and of the necessity for real sacrifices of time and service on the part of the individual in aiding his Government to effect a solution. I know we shall succeed in this epochal task, and that the educational institutions of our country can be relied upon to play their full part.

31

711.94/970–½

Memorandum by the Secretary of State Regarding a Conversation With the Japanese Ambassador (Saito)

[Extracts]

[WASHINGTON,] May 16, 1934.

In accordance with his personal request made of me prior to the middle of April for a confidential and purely informal conversation about affairs as they exist between his Government and the Government of the United States, I met the Japanese Ambassador at my apartments in the Carlton Hotel by appointment this morning.

I remarked that we were living in a highly civilized age, and that my country, for example, was exerting every effort as rapidly as possible to condemn, repudiate, and discard any and every practice, policy, or utterance that might be reasonably calculated to give just or reasonable grounds of complaint to any other people or country; that it was our attitude to condemn and abandon just as rapidly as possible a number of practices towards different Latin American countries which had given rise to friction, misunderstanding, and illwill between our country and those affected; that human progress and civilization called for just such reforms and that this was the way my government and my people felt; and that we had no notion of turning back to those irritating and trouble-breeding methods which at times my government had applied to different countries in Latin America.

I commented further, at the same time emphasizing that I was only offering this comment in the form of an inquiry which at present did not call for an answer, on the grave crisis in almost every conceivable way through which the world was passing; and remarked that some months ago an American citizen stepped into an aeroplane and sailed away, but that inside of eight days after flying around the world and over Japan, the Ambassador's own country, this same American alighted back at the station in the United States from which he had started; that formerly, and until very recently, England, for example, had felt herself isolated and secure from any ordinary interference with the Channel between her and Western Europe, whereas it was now patent that a fleet of 2000 bombing planes, probably carrying explosives of infinitely more powerful force than any heretofore used, could with perfect ease and convenience fly from many of the capitals of Western Europe to London, blow that city off the map, and return within a few hours time to their base. I said that twenty years ago no human being with the wildest stretch of imagination could have visualized the smallest part of the amazing changes that had taken place in every part of the world during this period, and that only the Lord could begin to visualize the even more startling changes that might reasonably take place during the next twenty years; that amidst these amazing changes the more highly civilized nations had correspondingly greater responsibilities and duties, both from the standpoint of their own progress and well-being and that of the world, that could not be dodged or evaded; and that no notion need for a moment be entertained that my country, or his, or any other one country, no matter how highly civilized, could securely keep itself above the much lower level of world affairs, leaving them and all of the people of other countries to undergo a steady state of decline and even collapse, without that civilized nation itself being drawn down in the vortex.

I stated that this meant that since there were no two more highly civilized countries than Japan and the United States, their own self-preservation, as well as their world responsibility, called for the utmost breadth of view and the profoundest statesmanship that their biggest and ablest statesmen could offer; that, faced with these unprecedented problems and conditions, it was all-important that his statesmen and mine should be broad-gauged enough to understand each other's problems and conditions, as well as those of the world, and to have the disposition and the will to deal with them in such capable manner as would avoid misunderstanding or material differences and promote both national and world progress; and that in no other way could countries like Japan and the United States, which were at present the trustees of the greatest civilization in history, make such showing as would give them a creditable place in the future history of the world. I said that, of course, Great Britain and other countries had their wonderful civilization, which I was not even remotely minimizing, but that Great Britain in particular was at present, and would be perhaps for some time to come, deeply engrossed with the serious and dangerous political, economic, and peace problems in Western Europe.

I repeated from time to time that I was only commenting in a general and inquiring way, and the Ambassador indicated his agreement with my utterances without elaborating upon them. I further commented in the way of professed inquiry that in all of these circumstances—together with another important circumstance, which was that Japan with her 65 million people was surrounded by over a billion of the world's population which was living chiefly in a very primitive condition, and that the economic, social, and political rehabilitation of all these peoples involved vast needs of capital and of other phases of material cooperation, with the result that these needs were and would be so vast that no one country could supply them within a number of generations—I was wondering, therefore, as to just how rapidly Japan would deem it either necessary or wise to expand with her commerce. I left the implication broad enough to include political and other kinds of expansion. I then elaborated just a little further about the huge undertaking that would be involved, and said that in the meantime nobody could predict what would be happening to the world in an infinite number of ways which would call for the utmost cooperation on the part of civilized nations.

C[ordell] H[ull]

32

762.94/44

Memorandum by the United States Military Attaché,
Berlin, May 17, 1934

[Extracts]

For sometime past evidence has been accumulating which tends to show the existence of unusually close and friendly relations between Germany and Japan even to the extent of a possible secret alliance. Japan has apparently taken the more active part in establishing these relations but she has met with a ready response from Germany, especially from the Nazi Government. The beginning of this relationship antedates the coming of the Nazi Government into power but owing to the friendship of the previous German Government for Russia and China its development was limited until the Nazis came in.

One factor in the situation stands out quite clearly and that is that these friendly relations have no personal basis whatever but are dependent entirely upon self interest. One can hardly conceive of the Japs developing any genuine brotherly feeling towards an occidental people and the Germans do not hesitate to speak freely to an American on their own attitude. They usually express themselves to the effect that "we are encouraging close and friendly relations with Japan because it is to our advantage to do so but we must never forget that we are white people and they are not".

HUGH W. ROWAN,
Capt., C.W.S.,
Assistant Military Attaché.

JACOB W. S. WUEST,
Lt. Colonel, A.C.,
Military Attaché.

33

793.94/6763

Memorandum by the Secretary of State Regarding a Conversation With the Japanese Ambassador (Saito)

[WASHINGTON,] May 19, 1934.

The Japanese Ambassador called and promptly drew out an elaborate telegram which he said was from Foreign Minister Hirota in Tokyo to him. He first remarked that Hirota desired to extend his appreciation of the friendly spirit in which I sent the statement to him on April 28, 1934, and which was delivered by United States Ambassador Grew. He added that Ambassador Grew had stated to Minister Hirota at the time that the United States Government did not expect any reply. The Japanese Ambassador then proceeded practically to read the telegram, although appearing more or less to be speaking orally. He retained the telegram which was in his language. At its conclusion, I inquired if it was virtually a restatement of the statement during the latter part of April of his Government to Sir John Simon in the London Foreign Office. He replied that it was. I then stated that I had kept perfectly quiet while Japanese officials all the way from Tokyo to Geneva on April 17th, and for many days following, were reported as giving out to the press the views and policies of the Japanese Government touching certain international phases relating to the Orient; that at the conclusion of these different statements I felt, in order not to be misunderstood here or anywhere, that I should in a respectful and friendly spirit offer a succinct but comprehensive restatement of rights, interests, and obligations as they related to my country primarily and as they related to all countries signatory to the Nine-Power Treaty, the Kellogg Pact, and international law as the same applied to the Orient.

I then inquired whether the Japanese Government differed with any of the fundamental phases of the statement I sent to the Japanese Foreign Minister on the 28th day of April, 1934? The Ambassador replied that it did not differ, that his Government did agree to the fundamentals of my note or statement, but that his Government did feel that it had a special interest in preserving peace and order in China. He then repeated the same formula that his government had been putting out for some weeks about the superior duty or function of his government to preserve peace and of its special interests in the peace situation in—to quote his words—"Eastern Asia". I remarked that, as Hirota wrote me, I saw no reason whatever why our two countries should not, in the most friendly and satisfactory way to each, solve every question or condition that existed now or that might arise in the future. I then said that, in my opinion, his country could conduct its affairs in such a way that it would live by itself during the coming generations, or that it might conduct its affairs even more profitably and at the same time retain the perfect understanding and the friendship of all civilized nations in particular; that my hope and prayer was that all the civilized nations of the world, including Japan, should work together and in a perfectly friendly and understanding way so as to promote to the fullest extent the welfare of their respective peoples and at the same time meet their duties to civilization and to the more backward populations of the world; and that my Government would always be ready and desirous of meeting his Government fully half-way in pursuing these latter objectives.

I then remarked that I would be entirely frank by saying that just now there was considerable inquiry everywhere as to just why his government singled out the clause or formula about Japan's claiming superior and special interests in the peace situation in "Eastern Asia" and her superior rights or duties in connection with the preservation of peace there; and that many were wondering whether this phrase or formula had ulterior or ultimate implications partaking of the nature of an overlordship of the Orient or a definite purpose to secure preferential trade rights as rapidly as possible in the Orient or "Eastern Asia"—to use the Japanese expression. The Ambassador commenced protesting that this was not the meaning contemplated or intended. I said it would be much simpler and easier if when the national of any other government engaged in some act in the Orient which Japan might reasonably feel would affect her unsatisfactorily, to bring up the individual circumstance to the proper government, instead of issuing a blanket formula which would cause nations everywhere to inquire or surmise whether it did not contemplate an overlordship of the Orient and an attempt at trade preferences as soon as possible. The Ambassador again said that this so-called formula about the superior interests of Japan in preserving peace, etc., did not contemplate the interference or domination or overlordship such as I had referred to.

I stated that to-day there was universal talk and plans about armaments on a steadily increasing scale and that Japan and Germany were the two countries considered chiefly responsible for that talk; that, of course, if the world understood the absence of any overlordship intentions or other unwarranted interference by his government, as the Ambassador stated them to me, his country would not be the occasion for armament discussion in so many parts of the world; and that this illustrated what I had said at the beginning of our conversation that nations should make it a special point to understand each other, and the statesmen of each country should be ready at all times to correct or explain any trouble-making rumors or irresponsible or inaccurate statements calculated to breed distrust and misunderstanding and lukewarmness between nations. I went on to say that it was never so important for the few existing civilized countries of the world to work whole-heartedly together; and that this action of course would, more fully than any other, promote the welfare of the people of each and also would best preserve civilization. I emphasized again that it would be the height of folly for any of the civilized nations to pursue any line of utterances or professed policies that would engender a feeling of unfairness or treaty violation or other unsatisfactory reaction in the important nations who might have both rights and obligations in a given part of the world such as the Orient. I said that in this awful crisis through which the world was passing, debtors everywhere were not keeping faith with creditors in many instances; that sanctity of treaties, in Western Europe especially, was being ignored and violated; that this was peculiarly a time when our civilized countries should be especially vigilant to observe and to preserve both legal and moral obligations; and that my country especially felt that way, not only on its own account but for the sake of preserving the better and the higher standards of both individual and national conduct everywhere.

I remarked that my Government, apart from its general treaty obligations, was only interested in the equality of trade rights in the Orient as in every part of the world and also its obligations and rights under the law of nations; that what little trade we had in the Orient we naturally desired to conduct on this basis of equality, even though it might be less in the future than now. Then I remarked that if these treaties which imposed special obligations on my government in the Orient were not in existence that, while interested in peace in all parts of the world, my government would also be interested in equality of trade rights.

I inquired whether his government had any disposition to denounce and get rid of these treaties in whole or in part, and said that to ignore or violate them would be embarrassing to my government, and that this would relieve it of any possibilities of such embarrassment. I said that I was not remotely suggesting in the matter. He replied that his government was not disposed to denounce and abrogate these treaties. He said that they felt obliged to get out of the League of Nations on account of certain considerations which their membership created. I then inquired of him whether his government abandoned membership on account of difficulties arising from the fact that Japan was a member of the League or whether it was due to Japan being a signatory to the Versailles Treaty. I did not get a complete answer to this.

The Ambassador then stated that in any preliminary naval conversations that might soon take place, his government would be opposed to discussing any Far Eastern political or similar questions or conditions and that only the purely naval side should be taken up. He said that political and all other phases of the subject were discussed at the Washington Conference and his government was opposed to a repetition of this. I offered no comment.

C[ORDELL] H[ULL]

34

Press Releases, vol. X, p. 330

Statement by the Honorable Norman H. Davis, Chairman of the United States Delegation to the General Disarmament Conference, at a Meeting of the General Commission of the Conference, at Geneva, May 29, 1934

(1) Twenty-seven months and more have passed since we met, in high hopes, to frame a general disarmament convention. No one foresaw a short or easy negotiation; the difficulties were more apparent than the solution; but the goal was so clear and the need for agreement so vital and so pressing that we confidently expected success. Now we meet once again but with hopes dimmed. One great power has chosen to withdraw from the Conference; parallel and private conversations have not smoothed out the principal diffi-

culties nor given the results we hoped for; certain powers are talking not in terms of reduction of armaments but in terms of mere limitation, and others of actual increase. In this confused situation, we can well ask ourselves: "Whither are we going?"

(2) Notwithstanding the inherent difficulties it is, I believe, the consensus of opinion of the delegates to this Conference that disarmament is a problem susceptible of a practical solution if the nations most vitally concerned will only cooperate in the proper spirit to that end.

(3) As a result of thorough studies and discussions here, a remarkable and considerable measure of accord has actually been reached with respect to the technical aspects of armaments and the kind of a disarmament convention that would be effective. Nevertheless, other questions and considerations have intervened which have not only prevented a general agreement but which now actually threaten the failure of the Conference.

(4) Every nation here has the same basic thought, how to remove the menace and lighten the burden of competitive armaments without reducing its security. It is somewhat difficult for anxious public opinions of countries which have armed primarily because of fear to realize that the apparent sacrifice of national defense involved in reduction of armaments may be fully compensated for by an increase of security along other lines. It is nevertheless the view of the American Government that such a compensatory advantage would be in fact obtainable through a mutual reduction and limitation of armaments in accordance with the revised draft convention that was accepted a year ago as the basis of our negotiations.

(5) Reduced to its simplest terms, there are two ways and only two conceivable ways to achieve security. The first is by overwhelming superiority in armament, coupled perhaps with reinsurance in the form of alliances; but this system has led first to a race in armaments and then to a war, from which we have not yet recovered and from a repetition of which we might never recover. Arms certainly did not prevent the World War, nor did they save either victor or vanquished from the terrible consequences of that war. The other way is to increase the power of defense and decrease the power of attack—in other words, to reduce the chances of a successful campaign of aggression—by a progressive abolition of those types of weapons peculiarly suitable for invasion, namely, heavy mobile artillery, tanks, and bombing planes. This method of disarmament, besides avoiding the complexities incident to limitation and reduction, which is solely numerical, constitutes a realistic aid to peace not only

through reducing the sum total of means of war but more particularly by doing away with the very instruments which are indispensable for successful aggression and by giving supremacy to fortifications and other means of defense. In fact, this method was accepted by the Conference in the resolution of July 23, 1932.

(6) Such is the choice. For its part, the American Government earnestly and sincerely believes that only by following the second path—that of disarmament—can the peace and progress of the world and the national security of each country be truly promoted. Unfortunately there is at present a distinct tendency in Europe toward the old policy of political alignments accompanied by an uncontrolled race in armaments which, if persisted in, will recreate the conditions which preceded the World War. Those who are today pursuing that policy, rather than one which promotes good will and increases security through a reduction of armaments, are inviting a terrible risk for the future.

(7) The United States has repeatedly stated in unequivocal terms its belief in the value and efficacy of a drastic reduction of armaments and its willingness to join with other powers in bringing armaments down to a level to be determined by the needs of actual self-defense. On May 22, 1933, in support of the draft convention which had been submitted to the Conference by the British Delegation, I outlined, with the approval of the President, the views of the United States Government on disarmament, its willingness to join in a decisive and progressive reduction of armaments through international agreement, and the extent to which it was prepared to cooperate to that end. It was with a view of helping indirectly to meet a given situation (in the event that the European powers should find it necessary or desirable to supplement a general convention by special regional agreements applicable to Europe) that I made on behalf of the United States Government this very considered statement of what its policy in certain circumstances would be. At that time it was our understanding that if the United States would be willing to adopt, subject to the conditions indicated, a policy that would not hamper the possible organization of European peace, it would be possible to conclude an agreement for a reduction and limitation of armaments along the lines of the draft convention then under consideration.

(8) In fact, President Roosevelt has authorized me to summarize the attitude and policy of the United States as follows: We are prepared to cooperate in every practicable way in efforts to secure a general disarmament agreement and thus to help promote the gen-

eral peace and progress of the world. We are furthermore willing, in connection with a general disarmament convention, to negotiate a universal pact of nonaggression and to join with other nations in conferring on international problems growing out of any treaties to which we are a party. The United States will not, however, participate in European political negotiations and settlements and will not make any commitment whatever to use its armed forces for the settlement of any dispute anywhere. In effect, the policy of the United States is to keep out of war, but to help in every possible way to discourage war.

(9) We have no new cures to offer. We suggested in the proposals of President Hoover in June 1932 a percentage cut covering all types of armaments. We suggested at that time a method of computing effectives to reach a basis of internal police requirements which was regarded by nearly all the powers as the only proposal which promised a fair and reasonable solution of this difficult question. A year later President Roosevelt, in his message to the chiefs of state, suggested the abolition of weapons of invasion and, to make this more effective, a pact of nonaggression, and then the establishment of an effective system of supervision and control. We are willing to go further and work out by international agreement an effective system for the regulation of the manufacture of and traffic in arms and munitions of war. Let me quote one paragraph from a recent message to Congress by President Roosevelt on this subject:

"It is my earnest hope that the representatives of the nations who will reassemble at Geneva on May 29 will be able to agree upon a convention containing provisions for the supervision and control of the traffic in arms even more far-reaching than those which were embodied in the convention of 1925. Some suitable international organization must and will take such action. The peoples of many countries are being taxed to the point of poverty and starvation in order to enable governments to engage in a mad race in armament which, if permitted to continue, may well result in war. This grave menace to the peace of the world is due in no small measure to the uncontrolled activities of the manufacturers and merchants of engines of destruction, and it must be met by the concerted action of the peoples of all nations."

The people of the United States are aroused at the evils which are being revealed in the production and traffic of munitions of war. The American people and Government are convinced that by some means the production and traffic in engines of death, and the profits resulting therefrom, must be controlled or eliminated. Those who have a sordid financial interest in fomenting international suspicion and discord, which in turn increases the demand for what they have to sell, must be put in a position in which they do not have the power or the incentive to do so much evil. If we are to foment international good will and stability we must take effective steps to control or suppress the forces which have a material interest in fomenting mistrust and discord. My Government is ready to join in measures for suppressing this evil, and is prepared to negotiate in connection with disarmament a treaty that would deal drastically with this problem.

(10) We will stand ready to advance along any constructive lines. Even where our arms are already limited, we are prepared to agree upon further reductions. Thus, in the matter of naval armaments, although we have felt it necessary to build up approximately to the treaty limits, largely in replacement ships, we are none the less willing to join the other interested powers in a substantial proportionate reduction of naval tonnage. In fact, our efforts remain directed toward disarmament in all branches and not toward either truce or rearmament.

(11) The Disarmament Conference recessed on the 16th of October last in order that there might be given an opportunity to carry on diplomatic negotiations with the view of reconciling the divergent views which stood in the way of agreement. Unfortunately these negotiations did not result in agreement, and they have now been terminated. On the other hand, they have served a necessary and useful purpose in clarifying the fundamental differences and issues. I feel, therefore, that in taking the initiative in these negotiations the British Government has rendered a real service. Nevertheless the termination of these parallel efforts brings us face to face with an emergency situation demanding a grave decision. We must determine whether our efforts shall result in a controlled disarmament, or in a mere limitation of armaments at a level so high as to be of doubtful value and effect, or in an uncontrolled race in armaments which would be disastrous. Surely no nation represented here wishes to take the responsibility for a failure of the Conference or to face the consequences of a failure. Let us therefore go back to the last stage in our negotiations where a general agreement was in sight, namely, to June 8 last year, when the British draft convention was accepted by all nations, including Germany, as the basis of the future convention. In doing so we may of course have due regard for subsequent contributions that may have been made toward agreement. If Germany desires a disarmament convention, which surely

must be the case, then I cannot easily believe that she would not be willing to resume negotiations on the basis to which she previously agreed.

The negotiations of the past 6 months were terminated by the demand that bilateral discussions be discontinued and that the work be brought back to Geneva. Very good. We are back in Geneva. I for one am glad to be here. I have stated the views of my Government, and I think every one here would consider it timely if all would explain their positions. The issue cannot be avoided. I am unshaken in my belief that with a real spirit of cooperation we can still achieve success.

35

Press Releases, vol. X, p. 374

Address Delivered by the Secretary of State at Williamsburg, Virginia, June 11, 1934

[Extract]

There are problems of vital importance to this and all other nations and to civilization itself which demand closer consideration by each citizen. The founders of our institutions, knowing the horrors of almost constant war in the Old World, were resolved, to the extent that might be possible, to save the New World from the most terrible scourge to which mankind is subjected. Washington led the Revolution in order that men should be free, but he led in the effort to weld into a more perfect union the States that then existed and those to be created, in order to insure harmony instead of discord and thus eliminate the causes of war. It is easy to imagine what would be the almost certain condition in this portion of the Western World had that effort not been successful. It is also easy to imagine how far less peaceful this hemisphere would be if, under the leadership of Monroe, who was one of Washington's soldiers and one of his successors in the Presidency, there had been no agreement, which is to remain effective for all time, to close the Great Lakes, the boundary between the United States and Canada, to warlike activities, and no emphatic proclamation through Monroe looking to our necessary self-defense.

At this moment, while on this side of the ocean there is a relatively peaceful condition, and neighborly and friendly ties among the nations are stronger and more genuine than ever before, we are obliged to feel deep concern that across the water, notwithstanding the terrible havoc and wreckage wrought by the war that began 20 years ago, and notwithstanding that the inventions of science will make future wars more terrible, there is so much reason for the gravest apprehension. Regardless of the fact that preparation for war but too often makes war inevitable, and the fact that preparation places a grievous burden on the people, armaments are being momentarily increased, and in practice the theory seems to be abandoned that nations, like individuals, should live not as potential enemies, but as neighbors and friends. Our Government has a duty to perform, and it is performing it. Supported by an overwhelming public sentiment, the Government, within the limitations necessary to be observed, is striving to the utmost to make its full contribution to the maintenance of peace and civilization. Without any question of its earnestness and fidelity, it is pursuing every method within its province to discourage and minimize armed conflict.

I wish to refer briefly to another problem belonging to the class I have just indicated, having both foreign and domestic aspects. In recent years a dangerous conception has become too prevalent, a strange economic conception that a nation can live to itself and virtually dispense with customary international relations. It is significant that none of the statesmen who made history in the period before and during the Revolution, and during a long later period were connected with the Federal Government, had any thought that this country could or should lead a self-contained existence. All of the evidence is directly to the contrary. They were devoted to their own land, but even though communication was slow with other lands, they completely realized that it was not possible for this country to develop without commercial, social, and cultural relations with Europe. They of course barred the possibility of political relationship. It is for the purpose of returning to the older conception which they held that it has just been decided by Congress that the Executive shall have authority to negotiate trade agreements with other nations, it being expected that by this method there can be effected a substantial expansion of international commercial dealings, and markets opened that in recent years have been to a large extent fenced about by insurmountable barriers. I can have no argument with any who may be actuated by mere partisanship in opposing that policy. But I would invite such opponents as are not thus controlled to tell me, if they are now fearful of the possibilities of the limited and temporary regimentation of business, what relief they expect to find in any other direction; and should they be unable to give a specific reply, I would suggest to them that their opposition might prove disastrous, should the continuance of such international relations as now impede commerce force further regimentation.

I shall not detain you by prolonging observations which might, but could not on an occasion of this character properly be elaborated; but I must not close without a reference to the spirit which should animate every citizen as we pass through an ordeal of extreme and unprecedented difficulty. A feeling of fear or despair would be dangerous and perhaps fatal. Those of the earlier days to whom I have alluded tolerated no such feeling, but in the bitterest hours displayed the utmost faith, courage, and patience; and had they not been supremely hopeful, they could not have been either courageous, faithful, or patient. To emphasize this, let me quote the striking language of James Bryce—the final words of his great work on "Modern Democracies": "Hope often disappointed but always renewed is the anchor by which the ship carries democracy and its fortunes will have to ride out the latest storm, as it has ridden out many storms . . . democracy will never perish until after hope has expired."

Not dismayed by the enormous difficulties now being encountered, or by the overturn of some of the democracies that were in existence when war swept the world, it is for us to face the future with unabated hope that our democratic system as created by the fathers shall lose none of its strength and vigor in this time or in the years to come.

36

862.00/3425–½

The Consul at Berlin (Geist) to the Chief of the Division of Western European Affairs (Moffat), Department of State

BERLIN, September 15, 1934.

DEAR MR. MOFFAT:

. . . With regard to the German public, observers are generally unanimous in the belief that the German nation, while anxiously regarding the present state of affairs, is content to be led on the political paths marked out for it by the National-Socialist Government. The National-Socialists have so strongly organized their position and so completely dominate the situation, that there is little possibility that anything serious will happen within the councils of the party or among the leaders of the Government. It is apparent that such men as von Neurath have agreed that the only hope for Germany's regaining her position in the world is along the lines laid down by the present regime, namely that Germany must first of all recover her military prestige, and then it may be seen what can be obtained from the rest of the world. They hope to be in a position to assert themselves on the basis of their military strength, which of course is a dangerous and a disquieting outlook. Mr. Goering is known to have said a short time ago that after the 1st of April 1935 nobody will have anything to say in the air, and from reports which I get I am convinced that the German rearmament is concentrating upon two points; first, power in the air, and second, motorization of any attacking forces. There is nothing conservative or traditional in their present policy. Many of the young Nazis are enthusiastic with regard to the military prospects. They speak of gas war, of bacteriological war, of the use of death-dealing rays. They boast that airplanes will not pass the German frontiers. Their ideas of Germany's invincibility and Germany's power in "the next war" are really phantastic. It is to be concluded, however, from these remarks that a good deal of lively talking is going on in the Nazi circles and they are really thrilled in contemplating Germany's future tremendous victory over her enemies.

It is a significant fact in estimating the present situation in Germany, that into the youth is being inculcated an unprecedented, conscious and deliberate love of militarism and all that it stands for. It is one of the amazing things of modern history that the Government of a great power should definitely teach its children to cherish ideas of valor, heroism, self-sacrifice, unrelieved by any of the virtues which modern civilization has come to place above brute force. Primarily owing to the international political situation and the disposition of the great powers in Europe to consolidate a defense position, war may not be imminent, but it is very difficult to foresee how the bellicose spirit here can be restrained and directed into permanent channels of peace towards the end of this present decade. . . .

Very sincerely yours,

RAYMOND H. GEIST

37

765.84/54

The Ambassador in Italy (Long) to the Secretary of State

No. 734   ROME, September 28, 1934.
                               [Received October 11.]
SIR:

I have the honor to refer to my despatch No. 721 of September 21, 1934, enclosing a Memorandum of conversations in connection with Italy's relations with Abyssinia, and to enclose herewith the copy of a Memorandum of another conversation on the same subject.[21]

---

[21] Not printed.

There have been current in Italy—in all parts of Italy—for some time rumors to the effect that Italy contemplated warlike activity there. These rumors are generally to the following effect: that the Ministries of War, Air, Marine, Finance and Colonies were cooperating; that they had agreed upon an expenditure of two billion lire; that the Treasury had made provision for it in its budget; that military reinforcements specifically and variously stated to amount to 100,000 men, 200,000 men, and 250,000 men had been allocated for transfer there; that large and varying quantities of supplies, equipment, had been or were being or were about to be sent; that tanks, air bombs, machine guns, barbed wire, airplanes, hangars, small tanks, small bore artillery, horses and mules had been and were being sent.

It was specifically reported that on September 26th there would be sent to Eritrea or Somalia a large military expedition. I wrote each Consul at a seaport and asked him to watch his harbor and the movement there on that date. Naples reported 200 mules and 20 armored cars had left the week before but no shipments on the 26th. It also reported the rumor that 100,000 men had sailed from Brindisi September 24th but the Consul General agrees that the rumor is fantastic. Naples also reports that on or about the first of September the S.S. *Caffaro* of the Tirrenan Line sailed for its regular run down the east coast of Africa with 4000 tons of munitions of war and 30 or 40 army ambulances on deck.

Trieste reported that "several weeks ago" all local shipping companies were instructed to advise the Captain of the Port when any of their ships finished discharging cargo and any space was free. Also that the three vessels of the Lloyd Triestino Line, the *Himalaya*, *Tergestea*, and *Fujiyama*, on the Far Eastern run, all of which touch at Massaua, received instructions in August to include Taranto as a port of call. There is no commercial cargo to be loaded there. I would like to send someone to Taranto to spend a week or more for observation purposes, but an officer of the American Government would not be a proper person to send.

Trieste also reports an order for 500,000 sun helmets to have been recently placed in Milan and the rumor that France has granted a war loan of 5,000,000 francs.

It is also reported General Badoglio is to command the expeditionary forces.

Leghorn reported that everything was normal there and at Pisa except the ubiquitous rumors about Italy's preparations for Abyssinian war.

Genoa reported that the S.S. *Dandolo*, sailing September 26th for Port Said, Suez, Massaua, and Indian ports, is leaving with little cargo, including a number of large cases very possibly containing a couple of hangars and airplane spare parts, as well as two or three hundred boxes, small and very heavy, marked "Wire Nails", apparently of Swiss origin and addressed to Bassorah and Madras; that "It is reported that the S.S. *Francesco Crispi*, which sailed September 5th from Massaua, etc., and the *Giuseppe Mazzini* on her last voyage for the same ports, carried hangars as part of their cargoes. It is rumored that the S.S. *Caffaro* and *Casaregis* are expected to embark locomotives, rolling stock, ammunition and Red Cross supplies at Naples. According to rumors which have been going around Genoa for the past three or four weeks, the 'banana boats', which used to make their outward voyages quite empty, are now leaving this port with good cargoes of airplanes, hangars, motor trucks and munitions, said to be intended for Massaua. It is stated by sources believed to be reliable that the Fiat Company is manufacturing a large number of small motor lorries, all to be shipped to Massaua and Italian Somalia."

That preparations of an unusual sort are under way as regards the Italian East African Colonies of Eritrea and Italian Somalia is fairly well established in my mind. That they relate to Abyssinia I accept as quite possible. However, I do not think the Italians will begin an unprovoked attack against Abyssinia. They may try to arrange a "defensive" war, or may be so "provoked" by "depredations" or by "unruly tribes" as to start a punitive expedition which will gradually develop into a penetration. Or they may, as I think most likely, try to stir up dissension in the ranks of Ras Taffari and help one of his opponents with the idea of placing on the throne a successful rival who will receive the protection of Italy . . .

Respectfully yours,

BRECKINRIDGE LONG

38

500.A15A5/372

The Ambassador in Japan (Grew) to the Secretary of State

No. 1102.   TOKYO, December 27, 1934.
                                          [Received January 16, 1935.]
SIR:

Now that the London Naval Conversations have terminated, I should like to convey to the Department various thoughts in this general connection to which the Department may desire to give consideration if and when the conversations are renewed or a naval conference convoked. I shall be contributing little that is new, for most of the facts and opinions set forth herein have already been brought to the Department's attention in previous reports. Furthermore the attitude, policy and action of our delegation in London, as directed by the Government and as revealed in the various summaries of developments telegraphed to this Embassy on October 25 and 31, November 22 and December 10, and in certain press reports, have indicated a sound comprehension of the situation in the Far East as it exists today. The firm stand of our Government and delegation to maintain the present naval ratios intact in the face of Japanese intransigence, as well as their decision that the action of the Japanese Government in denouncing the Washington Naval Treaty automatically created a new situation in which the conversations must be suspended *sine die*, leaving the Japanese to return home empty handed, were especially gratifying to those of us who have watched the developments in London from this angle. The purpose of this despatch is therefore mainly to summarize and to place my views in concise form on record for the future.

The thought which is uppermost in my mind is that the United States is faced, and will be faced in future, with two main alternatives. One is to be prepared to withdraw from the Far East, gracefully and gradually perhaps, but not the less effectively in the long run, permitting our treaty rights to be nullified, the Open Door to be closed, our vested economic interests to be dissolved and our commerce to operate unprotected. There are those who advocate this course, and who have advocated it to me personally, on the ground that any other policy will entail the risk of eventual war with Japan. ... In their opinion, "the game is not worth the candle" because the United States can continue to subsist comfortably even after relinquishing its varied interests in the Far East, thereby eliminating the risk of future war.

The other main alternative is to insist, and to continue to insist, not aggressively yet not the less firmly, on the maintenance of our legitimate rights and interests in this part of the world and, so far as practicable, to support the normal development of those interests constructively and progressively.

There has already been abundant indication that the present Administration in Washington proposes to follow the second of these alternatives. For purposes of discussion we may therefore, I assume, discard the hypothesis of withdrawal and examine the future outlook with the assurance that our Government has not the slightest intention of relinquishing the legitimate rights, vested interests, non-discriminatory privileges for equal opportunity and healthful commercial development of the United States in the Far East.

In following this second and logical course, there should be and need be nothing inconsistent, so far as our own attitude is concerned, with the policy of the good neighbor. The determination to support and protect our legitimate interests in the Far East can and should be carried out in a way which, while sacrificing no point of principle, will aim to restrict to a minimum the friction between the United States and Japan inevitably arising from time to time as a result of that determination.

The administration of that policy from day to day becomes a matter of diplomacy, sometimes delicate, always important, for much depends on the method and manner of approach to the various problems with which we have been, are, and will continue to be faced. With the ultra-sensitiveness of the Japanese, arising out of a marked inferiority complex which manifests itself in the garb of an equally marked superiority complex, with all its attendant bluster, chauvinism, xenophobia and organized national propaganda, the method and manner of dealing with current controversies assume a significance and importance often out of all proportion to the nature of the controversy. That the Department fully appreciates this fact has been amply demonstrated by the instructions issued to this Embassy since the present Administration took office, and it has been our endeavor to carry out those instructions, or to act on our own initiative when such action was called for, with the foregoing considerations constantly in view.

But behind our day to day diplomacy lies a factor of prime importance, namely national support, demonstrated and reinforced by national preparedness. I believe that a fundamental element of that preparedness should be the maintenance of the present naval ratios in principle and the eventual achievement and maintenance of those ratios, so far as they apply to Japan, in fact. With such a background, and only with such a background, can we pursue our diplomacy with any confidence that our representations will be listened to or that they will lead to favorable results. General Douglas MacArthur, Chief of Staff of the United States Army, was recently reported in the press as saying: "Armies and navies, in being efficient, give weight to the peaceful words of statesmen, but a feverish effort to create them when once a crisis is imminent simply provokes attack". We need thorough preparedness not in the interests of war but of peace.

It is difficult for those who do not live in Japan to appraise the present temper of the country. An American Senator, according to reports, has recently recommended that we should accord parity to Japan in order to avoid future war. Whatever the Senator's views may be concerning the general policy that we should follow in the Far East, he probably does not realize what harm that sort of public statement does in strengthening the Japanese stand and in reinforcing the aggressive ambitions of the expansionists. The Japanese press of course picks out such statements by prominent Americans and publishes them far and wide, thus confirming the general belief in Japan that the pacifist element in the United States is preponderantly strong and in the last analysis will control the policy and action of our Government. Under such circumstances there is a general tendency to characterize our diplomatic representations as bluff and to believe that they can safely be disregarded without fear of implementation. It would be helpful if those who share the Senator's views could hear and read some of the things that are constantly being said and written in Japan, to the effect that Japan's destiny is to subjugate and rule the world (sic), and could realize the expansionist ambitions which lie not far from the surface in the minds of certain elements in the Army and Navy, the patriotic societies and the intense nationalists throughout the country. Their aim is to obtain trade control and eventually predominant political influence in China, the Philippines, the Straits Settlements, Siam and the Dutch East Indies, the Maritime Provinces and Vladivostok, one step at a time, as in Korea and Manchuria, pausing intermittently to consolidate and then continuing as soon as the intervening obstacles can be overcome by diplomacy or force. With such dreams of empire cherished by many, and with an army and navy capable of taking the bit in their own teeth and running away with it regardless of the restraining influence of the saner heads of the Government in Tokyo (a risk which unquestionably exists and of which we have already had ample evidence in the Manchurian affair), we would be reprehensibly somnolent if we were to trust to the security of treaty restraints or international comity to safeguard our own interests or, indeed, our own property.

I may refer here to my despatch No. 608 of December 12, 1933, a re-reading of which is respectfully invited because it applies directly to the present situation. That despatch reported a confidential conversation with the Netherlands Minister, General Pabst, a shrewd and rational colleague with long experience in Japan, in which the Minister said that in his opinion the Japanese Navy, imbued as it is with patriotic and chauvinistic fervor and with a desire to emulate the deeds of the Army in order not to lose caste with the public, would be perfectly capable of descending upon and occupying Guam at a moment of crisis or, indeed, at any other moment, regardless of the ulterior consequences. I do not think that such an insane step is likely, yet the action of the Army in Manchuria, judged from the point of view of treaty rights and international comity, might also have been judged as insensate. The important fact is that under present circumstances, and indeed under circumstances which may continue in future (although the pendulum of chauvinism throughout Japanese history has swung to and fro in periodic cycles of intensity and temporary relaxation) the armed forces of the country are perfectly capable of over-riding the restraining control of the Government and of committing what might well amount to national "hara-kiri" in a mistaken conception of patriotism.

When Japanese speak of Japan's being the "stabilizing factor" and the "guardian of peace" of East Asia, what they have in mind is a Pax Japonica with eventual complete commercial control, and, in the minds of some, eventual complete political control of East Asia. While Ambassador Saito may have been misquoted in a recent issue of the Philadelphia Bulletin as saying that Japan will be prepared to fight to maintain that conception of peace, nevertheless that is precisely what is in the minds of many Japanese today. There is a swashbuckling temper in the country, largely developed by military propaganda, which can lead Japan during the next few years, or in the next few generations, to any extremes unless the saner minds in the Government prove able to cope with it and to restrain the country from national suicide.

The efficacy of such restraint is always problematical. Plots against the Government are constantly being hatched. We hear, for instance, that a number of young officers of the 3rd Infantry Regiment and students from the Military Academy in Tokyo were found on November 22 to have planned to assassinate various high members of the Government, including Count Makino, and that students of the Military Academy were confined to the school area for a few days after the discovery of that plot, which had for its object the placing in effect at once of the provisions of the now celebrated "Army pamphlet" (see despatch No. 1031 of November 1, 1934). A similar alleged plot to attack the politicians at the opening of the extraordinary session of the Diet—another May 15th incident—is also said to have been discovered and nipped in the bud. Such plots aim to form a military dictatorship. It is of course impossible to substantiate these rumors, but they are much talked about and it is unlikely that so much smoke would materialize without some fire. I wish that more Americans could come out here and live here and gradually come to sense the real potential risks and dangers of the situation instead of speaking and writing academically on a subject which they know nothing whatever about, thereby contributing ammunition to the Japanese military and extremists who are stronger than they have been for many a day. The idea that a great body of liberal thought lying just beneath the surface since 1931 would be sufficiently strong to emerge and assume control with a little foreign encouragement is thoroughly mistaken. The liberal thought is there, but it is inarticulate and largely impotent, and in all probability will remain so for some time to come.

At this point I should like to make the following observation. From reading this despatch, and perhaps from other reports periodically submitted by the Embassy, one might readily get the impression that we are developing something of an "anti-Japanese" complex. This is not the case. One can dislike and disagree with certain members of a family without necessarily feeling hostility to the family itself. For me there are no finer people in the world than the type of Japanese exemplified by such men as . . . and a host of others. I am rather inclined to place . . . in the same general category; if he could have his way unhampered by the military I believe that he would steer the country into safer and saner channels. One of these friends once sadly remarked to us: "We Japanese are always putting our worst foot foremost, and we are too proud to explain ourselves." This is profoundly true. Theirs has been and is a "bungling diplomacy". They habitually play their cards badly. Amau's statement of April 17 was a case in point. The declaration of the oil monopoly in Manchuria at this particular juncture, thereby tending to drive Great Britain into the other camp at a moment when closer Anglo-Japanese cooperation was very much in view, was another. While it is true that the military and the extremists are primarily responsible for the "bungling diplomacy" of Japan, the Japanese as a race tend to be inarticulate, more at home in action than with words. The recent negotiations in Batavia amply illustrated the fact that Japanese diplomats, well removed from home influences and at liberty to choose their own method and manner of approach, are peculiarly insensitive to the unhappy effects of arbitrary pronouncements. They have learned little from the sad experience of Hanihara. But the military and the extremists know little and care little about Japan's relations with other countries, and it is the desire of people like Shiratori, Amau and other Government officials to enhance their own prestige at home and to safeguard their future careers by standing in well with the military that brings about much of the trouble. Perhaps we should be grateful that they so often give their hand away in advance.

But all this does not make us less sympathetic to the better elements in Japanese life or in any sense "anti-Japanese". Japan is a country of paradoxes and extremes, of great wisdom and of great stupidity, an apt illustration of which may be found in connection with the naval conversations; while the naval authorities and the press have been stoutly maintaining that Japan cannot adequately defend her shores with less than parity, the press and the public, in articles, speeches and interviews, have at the same time been valiantly boasting that the Japanese Navy is today stronger than the American Navy and could easily defeat us in case of war. In such an atmosphere it is difficult, very difficult, for a foreigner to keep a detached and balanced point of view. We in the Embassy are making that effort, I hope with success, and in the meantime about all we can do is to keep the boat from rocking dangerously. Constructive work is at present impossible. Our efforts are concentrated on the thwarting of destructive influences.

Having placed the foregoing considerations on record, I have less hesitation in reiterating and emphasizing with all conviction the potential dangers of the situation and the prime importance of American national preparedness to meet it. As a nation we have taken the lead in international efforts towards the restriction and reduction of armaments. We have had hopes that the movement would be progressive, but the condition of world affairs as they have developed during the past twelve years since the Washington Conference has not afforded fruitful ground for such progress. Unless we are prepared to subscribe to a "Pax Japonica" in the Far East, with all that this movement, as conceived and interpreted by Japan, is bound to entail, we should rapidly build up our navy to treaty strength, and if and when the Washington Naval Treaty expires we should continue to maintain the present ratio with Japan regardless of cost, a peace-time insurance both to cover and to reduce the risk of war. In the meantime every proper step should be taken to avoid or to offset the belligerent utterances of jingoes no less than the defeatist statements of pacifists in the United States, many of which find their way into the Japanese press, because the utterances of the former tend to enflame public sentiment against our country, while the statements of the latter convey an impression of American weakness, irresolution and bluff.

My own opinion, although it can be but guesswork, is that Japan will under no circumstances invite a race in naval armaments, and that having found our position on the ratios to be adamant, further propositions will be forthcoming within the next two years before the Washington Treaty expires, or before our present building program is fully completed. When the United States has actually completed its naval building program to treaty limits, then, it is believed, and probably not before then, Japan will realize that we are in earnest and will seek a compromise. We believe that Japan's naval policy has been formulated on the premise that the United States would never build up to treaty strength, a premise which has been strengthened in the past by the naval policy of the past two Administrations, by the apparent strength of the pacifist element in the United States, and more recently by the effects of the depression.

While it is true that Japan, by sedulously forming and stimulating public opinion to demand parity with the United States in principle if not in fact, has burned her bridges behind her, nevertheless the Japanese leaders are past-masters at remoulding public opinion in the country by skillful propaganda to suit new conditions. Once convinced that parity is impossible, it is difficult to believe that she will allow matters to come to a point where competitive building becomes unavoidable. With a national budget for 1935–1936 totalling 2,193,-414,289 yen, of which about 47% is for the Army and Navy, and with an estimated national debt in 1936 of 9,880,000,000 yen, nearly equal to the Cabinet Bureau of Statistics estimate of the national income for 1930, namely 10,635,000,000 yen; with her vast outlay in Manchuria, her already heavily taxed population and the crying need of large sections of her people for relief funds, it is difficult to see how Japan could afford to embark upon a program of maintaining naval parity with the United States and Great Britain.

Having registered our position firmly and unequivocally, we can now afford to await the next move on the part of Japan. I believe that it will come.

So far as we can evaluate here the proceedings of the recent preliminary naval conversations in London, I am of the opinion that the most important and the most valuable result issuing therefrom has been the apparent tendency towards closer Anglo-American cooperation in the Far East. If we can count in future—again as a direct result of Japan's "bungling diplomacy"—on a solid and united front between the United States and Great Britain in meeting Japan's flaunting of treaty rights and her unrestrained ambitions to control East Asia, the future may well assume a brighter aspect for all of us.

Theodore Roosevelt enunciated the policy "Speak softly but carry a big stick". If our diplomacy in the Far East is to achieve favorable results, and if we are to reduce the risk of an eventual war with Japan to a minimum, that is the only way to proceed. Such a war may be unthinkable, and so it is, but the spectre of it is always present and will be present for some time to come. It would be criminally short-sighted to discard it from our calculations, and the best possible way to avoid it is to be adequately prepared, for preparedness is a cold fact which even the chauvinists, the military, the patriots and the ultra-nationalists in Japan, for all their bluster concerning "provocative measures" in the United States, can grasp and understand. The Soviet Ambassador recently told me that a prominent Japanese had said to him that the most important factor in avoiding a Japanese attack on the Maritime Provinces was the intensive Soviet military preparations in Siberia and Vladivostok. I believe this to be true, and again, and yet again, I urge that our own country be adequately prepared to meet all eventualities in the Far East.

The Counselor, the Naval Attaché and the Military Attaché of this Embassy, having separately read this despatch, have expressed to me their full concurrence with its contents both in essence and detail.

Respectfully yours,

JOSEPH C. GREW

39

Press Releases, vol. XII, p. 3

Statement by the Secretary of State, December 29, 1934

The American Government has today received the Japanese Government's notice of intention to terminate the Washington Naval Treaty. We of course realize that any nation has the right not to renew a treaty; also that any movement toward disarmament, to be successful, must rest on agreements voluntarily entered into. This notification is none the less a source of genuine regret to us, believing as we do that the existing treaties have safeguarded the rights and promoted the collective interests of all of the signatories.

The recent conversations at London, which have been carried on in a spirit of friendship and good will, have revolved around the question whether a movement of international cooperation and disarmament can rest on the principle of equality of armament rather than on the principle of equality of security. Each nation naturally desires—and we stand unalterably for that view—to be on a basis of absolute equality with other nations in the matter of national security.

Experience teaches that conditions of peace or measures of disarmament cannot be promoted by the doctrine that all nations, regardless of their varying and different defensive needs, shall have equality of armaments. What has been achieved up to the present time toward insuring conditions of peace has been based on a community of objective, a community of conception of the general interest, and a community of effort. The treaties thus far concluded have involved no invasion of the sovereign rights of the participating governments, and they have provided, with all proper respect for such sovereign rights, that the armaments of the participating nations be established by voluntary undertaking on a proportionate basis.

Notice of intention to terminate the Washington Naval Treaty does not mean that that treaty ceases to be in effect as of the date of notification: the provisions of that treaty remain in force until the end of 1936. There consequently remains a period of 2 years within which the interested nations may consider the situation that would be created by the abandonment of the naval treaties; and the American Government is ready to enter upon negotiations whenever it appears that there is prospect of arrival at a mutually satisfactory conclusion which would give further effect to the desire of the American Government and the American people—and, it is believed, that of the other governments and peoples concerned—that the nations of the world shall not be burdened by avoidable or extravagant expenditures on armament.

The question presented when the Washington treaties were negotiated, and which prompted each delegation to the signing and each country to the ratifying of those treaties, was that of promoting peace through disarmament and cooperative effort along certain defined lines. The objectives then and there envisaged are still fundamental among the objectives of the foreign policy of the United States. To this high purpose the people of this country, in a spirit of sincere friendship toward all other peoples, will continue unswervingly to devote their own efforts, and earnestly invoke like efforts on the part of others.

40

Press Releases, vol. XII, p. 27

Message of President Roosevelt to the Senate, January 16, 1935

The movement to make international justice practicable and serviceable is not subject to partisan considerations. For years, Republican and Democratic administrations and party platforms alike have advocated a court of justice to which nations might voluntarily bring their disputes for judicial decision.

To give concrete realization to this obviously sound and thoroughly American policy, I hope that at an early date the Senate will advise and consent to the adherence by the United States to the protocol of signature of the Statute of the Permanent Court of International Justice, dated December 16, 1920, the protocol for the revision of the Statute of the Permanent Court of International Justice, dated September 14, 1929, and the protocol for the accession of the United States of America to the protocol of signature of the Statute of the Permanent Court of International Justice, dated September 14, 1929, all of which were submitted to the Senate December 10, 1930.

I urge that the Senate's consent be given in such form as not to defeat or to delay the objective of adherence.

The sovereignty of the United States will be in no way diminished or jeopardized by such action. At this period in international relationships, when every act is of moment to the future of world peace, the United States has an opportunity once more to throw its weight into the scale in favor of peace.

FRANKLIN D. ROOSEVELT

THE WHITE HOUSE,
January 16, 1935.

41

863.00/1168

The Minister in Austria (Messersmith) to the Under Secretary Of State (Phillips)

[Extract]

VIENNA, February 8, 1935.

DEAR MR. PHILLIPS:

There is no use in having any illusions as to what Hitler and the Party want. They have their eyes on Memel, Alsace-Lorraine and the Eastern frontier. They nourish just as strongly the hope to get the Ukraine for the surplus German population and to get the fertile lands which Germany "must have". Austria is a definite objective, with absorption or hegemony over the whole of Southeastern Europe definite policy. As long as Hitler and National Socialism remain in power in Germany, Europe will have to deal with these aspirations, pacts or no pacts. With the present regime out of the way the danger is lessened and the field of ambition more restricted, but it would be illusory to believe that the danger of Germany to European peace is definitely eliminated. The only thing that can hold Germany in line is a concert of the powers so close and definite that Germany's policy will be reoriented. The danger to Europe can still be averted, for the German people, although warlike, have shown themselves docile under strong leadership. Probably in no other country in Europe could a Government have done with its people what this present one has done with Germany in the past two years. Germany can be led into being a good neighbor and into being a bad one, depending on her Government.

Cordially and sincerely yours,

G. S. Messersmith

42

765.84/161

The Ambassador in Italy (Long) to the Secretary of State
[Telegram : Paraphrase]

Rome, February 14, 1935—7 p. m.
[Received February 14—3 : 40 p. m.]

No. 72. My 69, February 13. All information recently obtained points to a more general preparation for an extensive campaign in Abyssinia than has been indicated by the Italian Government in its various announcements. Supplies and military forces are moving clandestinely. Concerted effort is being made to prevent any information getting out as to the size or general nature of shipments. Movements are being made by night and troops called up are kept in barracks and denied freedom.

I have been informed today from sources deemed to be reliable that 30,000 troops have left the port of Naples; that the movement now under way contemplates the use in Ethiopia of some 200,000 or 300,000 troops; and that the troops which are now or have recently been in Tripoli, and thus have had tropical experience, are being moved to Ethiopia and are being replaced by the newly formed forces from Italy.

It is learned from another trustworthy source that the *communiqué* of the Italian Government mentioned in my No. 65, February 11, 5 p. m., was misleading in that the class of 1911, though ostensibly called in sufficient numbers to bring the divisions to war strength, was actually called to form these divisions as the regiments comprising them had already left clandestinely for unknown destinations by the time the *communiqué* had been issued.

Mechanical, motor and air service specialists are being called from the reserves and from the militia of the classes as far back as 1895 and 1893. Factories for the manufacture of trucks, tanks and artillery at and around Milan are working day and night shifts.

Principal movements consist of motor, air and light artillery and, in addition to Naples, embarkation is proceeding from Venice, Messina, Ancona and probably from Leghorn. Supplies are leaving from Genoa, Venice and Trieste, as well as from Naples.

All of these movements are being camouflaged by the use of regular merchant marine without the use of war vessels. The Navy has not participated. If it were to do so, either as carrier or as convoy, it would advertise the movement. Moreover in the absence of an Abyssinian Navy, there is no need for protection and the passage of regular merchant ships through Suez would cause no comment nor evoke criticism, even should the authorities there be disposed to object.

Press stories justifying Italy's action under Paris, London and Geneva date lines, which are reprinted in full or in part in the Italian press, are preparing public opinion, but there has not been a single story under any Italian date line or a single editorial comment on this subject in any Italian newspaper, which constitutes an unusual departure from the established custom.

LONG

43

Department of State pub. 701

Address Delivered by the Secretary of State at New York,
February 16, 1935

MR. PRESIDENT, MEMBERS AND GUESTS OF THE CANADIAN SOCIETY OF New York: I am delighted to be with you on this occasion of your annual dinner and to be able to join you in extending a sincere welcome to Prime Minister Bennett and, through him, greetings of my fellow citizens to the people of your great Dominion. May I also take advantage of this opportunity to extend our greetings to the people of the entire British Commonwealth of Nations, with whom we share a heritage of profound devotion to the causes of international peace, justice, and fair dealing.

Your society, Mr. President, has a long and distinguished record. I am impressed with its purposes as set forth in your constitution: "To interpret Canadian nationalism, to further goodwill between English speaking peoples, to promote social intercourse among Canadians in New York and to provide relief for Canadians in need of assistance." I am confident that the work of your society has contributed to the happy state of the relations which subsist between our countries.

The United States and Canada probably have as many and as strong ties and associations as any other two countries in the world. The reasons for this are clear. Geography, naturally, is the prime factor, but we cannot underestimate our common origin and traditions. Furthermore, commerce between the United States and Canada is greater than that between any other two nations in the world. In addition, our peoples are closely interrelated. For example, citizens of the Dominion have achieved distinction in almost every walk of life in the United States. Jacob Gould Schurman, Margaret Anglin, Franklin K. Lane, Edward Johnson, and Sir William Osler are some of the names in a list that could be extended almost indefinitely. It has, in fact, been said that one of the surest prospects of attaining success in the United States is the possession of a Canadian grandmother. We have sent to Canada a large number of sturdy pioneers who have contributed a great deal to the building of your institutions and the widening of your activities. This exchange of numberless individuals, each of whom can be a messenger of understanding, is a circumstance which has assisted greatly in the development of our friendship.

Even between the best of friends there can be misunderstanding. The United States and Canada have frequently found themselves in disagreement over particular cases. But our countries have nevertheless a record for the speedy and amicable settlement of any differences, of which both may be proud, and in the background of any particular disagreement there has always been a quiet, firm realization that nothing must be allowed to stand in the way of our enduring friendship.

With reference to our economic relations, a few weeks ago announcement was made of forthcoming negotiations between our Governments looking to the conclusion of a trade agreement. It is my earnest hope that in these negotiations it will be possible to remove many of the obstacles, costly to both countries, which have interfered with their trade.

It is natural that on such an occasion as this I should think not only of our relations with Canada but of the nature of our general foreign policy.

It is often assumed that a nation's foreign policy is or can be altogether determined by the Government of the moment. This is true in fact only within certain very definite limits which greatly restrict the field of choice. I am thinking not merely of historical traditions and conventions which put a brake on the whims of statesmen and insure a certain continuity of foreign policy, or of the obvious fact that each country's policy is affected and to some extent motivated by that of other countries. What I have in mind rather are such external factors as size and resources, geographical location, and technical developments, which constitute the framework within which a nation's foreign policy must evolve and assume its formal characteristics.

The interaction of these factors is particularly interesting. Thus it would seem at first blush unlikely that a small nation with few or undeveloped resources can be in a position to play a major role in international affairs. Yet such is the influence of location that such a nation may conceivably counteract and even cancel the supposed disadvantage of relative smallness. We are all acquainted with the part played in former centuries by several small maritime communities along the Mediterranean. It would manifestly be impossible for a land-locked country, whatever its resources, to become a nation of seafarers. Access to the sea, however, is not the only consideration applicable to a small state, as shown by the history of many countries—for instance, Switzerland, whose foreign policy is fixed very largely by its central location in the heart of Europe, as well as by its control of the principal Alpine passes. It was this position which in part helped Switzerland to maintain her neutrality during the World War. The influence, finally, of technical developments on foreign policy is most clearly evident in connection with the rapid evolution of the means of communication which has brought country after country into the current of world affairs and made any attempted policy of isolation and pure nationalism increasingly obsolete and impracticable.

Let us consider the effect of some of these elements on American foreign policy. All of them have conspired to force the United States out of its earlier preoccupation with domestic matters into an increasingly active participation in international affairs. The enormous speeding up of trade and communications under the influence of technical discovery and advancement condemns to futility any endeavor to induce this nation again to withdraw into "splendid isolation". Our policies must of necessity be those of a so-called "great power". We cannot, even if we would, fail profoundly to affect international relations; our choice is of the various ways of affecting them which are open to a nation situated as we are. It would be hard to deny that we are so placed that we could, if that were our intention, engage in a policy of imperialistic expansion and aggression to the detriment of others. The alternative course open to us is to make our influence felt through a policy of political, economic, and cultural cooperation to the advantage of all and in an atmosphere of trust and peace. The latter is our policy, a policy so accurately described by the President as that of the "good neighbor". But this policy is not a simple alternative to that of force, arbitrarily chosen for the immediate future and liable to be discarded again at any time. Every day, on the contrary, makes it more evident that President Roosevelt's policy is in consonance with the pivotal factors I have touched upon, and the merit of its adoption lies not least in the recognition that it is both the better course, from an ideal humanitarian point of view, and the wiser course, in the interests of the United States as well as of other countries. The good-neighbor policy thus meets the requirements of every reasonable test of history. It is in harmony with the great need of the modern world and with the particular needs of a modern United States in this modern world.

While the present foreign policy of the United States represents, in its fundamental principles, a consistent whole, it operates differently in relation to different parts of the world, in line with basic geographic factors. Aside from the common bond created through community of language, traditions, and cultural heritage, the nature of our northern frontier, as I have said, has made of Canada and the United States outstanding examples of good neighbors for over a century. Our two countries, including Alaska, have the longest common boundaries anywhere on the globe. We are inevitably the most neighborly of neighbors, and a foreign policy on the part of either country which attempted to fly in the face of this fact would be suicidal, not to say impossible. Thus, out of a circumstance of geography has grown a sense of trust and mutual security which it would be hard to duplicate.

Looking southward, we must not be misled by the boundary lines of the map. Mexico may at one time have been our only southern neighbor, but the growth of trade and communications has steadily enlarged the number of our neighbors in the south. If our immediate neighborhood a few years past might appropriately be considered as having included only the Central American and Caribbean republics, the airplane and the coming inter-American highway are making neighbors of all countries in the Western Hemisphere.

I realize only too well that neighbors can be estranged even when race and language should make them brothers, and of this the present war in the Chaco is a ghastly reminder. Undoubtedly some of the states to the south in the past viewed the growing proximity of the United States with misgiving, and I cannot but admit that there have been occasions when our words and actions gave some justification to their fears. Today these suspicions are happily vanishing, and I believe the time is at hand when the American republics will be convinced not only that the good-neighbor policy is being carried out in practice, but also that in strictly observing it the President, with magnificent foresight, has adopted a course which the future progress of our two continents makes imperative. The truth is that cooperation is proving itself profitable in every way. The most recent instance is our reciprocity treaty with Cuba, which, in the few months of its operation, has worked wonders both in the economic and in the political spheres. If the Platt Amendment was symbolical of an early epoch in our inter-American relations, its recent abandonment is an emphatic symbol of a new era in which it becomes our manifest destiny to enter into ever closer relations of free and voluntary collaboration for the furtherance of the prosperity of each and the peace of all.

Thus far I have not dealt with our relations east and west, or what might be called our transoceanic policies. Here again, there is no break in unity but merely an adaptation to the very different geographical and historical situation. The fundamental element is the ocean, the Atlantic on the east, the Pacific on the west. There was a time when the ocean meant, or could mean, a certain degree of isolation. Modern communication has ended this forever; but necessarily a gap remains, and with it the difference in perspective. Seen from the distance of this hemisphere, the manifold boundary lines on the map of Europe become blurred and Europe emerges as an entity. We have no direct concern with the political and economic controversies of the European states. We have time and again expressly disassociated ourselves from these disputes. Nevertheless, we are deeply interested in the peace and stability of Europe as a whole, and have therefore taken part in a number of multilateral efforts to achieve this purpose.

The most outstanding instance is the Disarmament Conference, which, by concentrating on land and air armaments, deals with an issue of primary importance to Europe. Although believing that the limitation and reduction of armaments in itself tends to increase confidence and security—a view which has been amply confirmed by our experience on our northern borders—we are compelled to recognize that rampant suspicion and hostility between nations, based on long-standing political and economic differences, constitute a barrier to effective action. This is particularly true on the European Continent, still smarting under the ravages of the World War. Hence, our basic policy of not intervening in individual European disputes has not prevented us from encouraging, proposing, and offering to participate in measures of a universal nature designed on the one hand to forward general political appeasement and on the other to facilitate general disarmament. Thus, in his well-known message of May 16, 1933, to the heads of states, President Roosevelt, after reaffirming and amplifying the disarmament proposals designed to strengthen security through abolishing aggressive land weapons, suggested the conclusion of a general nonaggression pact in which each country would agree not to send any armed forces of whatsoever nature across its frontiers. Six days later Mr. Norman Davis, representing us at Geneva, made a further contribution in the form of an offer that the United States, subject to an effective disarmament agreement, would be willing to consult with other states in case of a threat to peace, with a view to averting conflict; and that, moreover, the United States would not take steps to hinder any collective action which the other states might decide to take against an aggressor, provided the United States should independently concur in their decision as to the identity of the aggressor.

These proposals, taken together with the provisions of the Kellogg Pact, provide, I submit, the four pillars of a sound peace structure: First, the renunciation of war as an instrument of national policy; second, a promise of nonaggression; third, consultation in the event of a threat to peace; and fourth, non-interference on our part with such measures of constraint as may be brought against a deliberate violator of peace.

All four are political measures, if you like, as distinguished from technical disarmament measures. However, they are political only in the wider sense of being designed to assist in general pacification and stabilization, of equal benefit to all countries and with no implication of any intervention on our part in controversies between individual states. I should emphasize, moreover, that these four pillars might readily crumble were they to be built on the shifting foundations of unrestricted and competitive armaments. We have therefore insisted that a real limitation and reduction of the instruments of warfare must be an essential concomitant of any such peace program as I have outlined.

I have already indicated that the factors molding our foreign policy toward Europe have led to our support primarily of endeavors of a general and universal nature. While growing out of and adapted to the basic needs of Europe, they are in effect world-wide in scope and application. If we turn our eyes in the opposite direction, toward the Pacific, we find a situation occupying an intermediate stage between our more immediate preoccupation with the issues of the Western Hemisphere and our more generalized participation in transatlantic problems. The greater width of the Pacific is more than compensated for by our possessions in that area and by long-standing historical developments and relationships. I shall not go into the origin of the "open door" and other elements of our traditional Far Eastern policy, but merely point out that this policy is most clearly set forth in a series of connected treaties which set up an integrated system for the maintenance of peace and stability in the Far East and the Pacific. I refer, of course, to the accomplishments of the Washington Conference, which, in their essence, still embody the basic principles we believe in and stand by. The problems dealt with in 1922 were in some respects peculiar to the special situation in the Far East and our relation thereto, notably the emergence of certain territorial questions, the predominance of economic issues, and the emphasis on naval rather than land and air armaments. But the elements common both to our transpacific and transatlantic policies are even more striking: Political and economic stabilization through conference and mutual agreement; cooperation for the maintenance of peace through nonaggression, consultation, and through limitation and reduction of armaments. I endeavored to summarize the basis of our Far Eastern policy when, on March 3, 1934, I expressed the hope, in reply to a message from Foreign Minister Hirota, "that it may be possible for all of the countries which have interests in the Far East to approach every question existing or which may arise between or among them in such spirit and manner that these questions may be regulated or resolved with injury to none and with definite and lasting advantage to all." In other words, a good-neighbor policy in the Orient.

In this brief survey I have endeavored to cover the four major divisions of American foreign policy—Canadian, Latin American, European, and Far Eastern—and have touched upon the varying phases of each. It would be generalizing too much to state that the fundamental object uniting them is the preservation of peace. No nation would ever admit its policy to be or to have been other than one of peace. It is more a question of the means. After all, the Roman Empire knew long periods of peace; but the essence of the

Pax Romana was predominance over wide areas, a peace of inequality based on force. The kind of peace we envisage, and I think it is the kind not only we in the United States but the peoples of all nations, great and small, desire at heart and pray for, is the peace of friends, who feel secure in their independence not through immense armaments, the balance of which must again and again be destroyed by uneven competition, but through the give and take of political and economic cooperation which benefits no one country to the detriment of others but is of equal advantage to all. For what I said in a speech shortly after I became Secretary of State is true fundamentally for all nations: "It is a great satisfaction", I then stated, "to one who is confronted with the tasks devolving upon the Department of State to realize how, in meeting the problems that are our daily portion, the interests of our Government and our people seem so clearly to coincide with the interests of humanity."

44

863.00/1178

Memorandum by the Minister to Austria (Messersmith) Regarding A Conversation With the Ambassador in Germany (Dodd)

[Extract]

BERLIN, March 22, 1935.

I had a talk with the Ambassador this morning and we found ourselves in major agreement on all the subjects discussed.

I mentioned a despatch about the Chinese Minister in Vienna having said that I had told him that there was a Japanese-German understanding, if not alliance. I told him that I had not made such a statement but that I had told the Chinese Minister that in May and June, 1933, I had heard talk in Berlin that the Nazis and Japanese were trying to get together. I told the Ambassador that I had good reason to believe at the time that this was so, but I did not know how far it had gone. He said that he thought this had continued and that he felt that it had gone pretty far and he was not at all sure that there was not a very thorough understanding and perhaps even a very far-reaching one.

I told the Ambassador that I thought if these people stayed in much longer we would have something to reckon with, and that many good men had already been affected. He said this unfortunately was the case. We again went over the situation and agreed that no faith

255

whatever can be laid in the present regime and its promises, and that we are going to suffer unless we recognize what they are really after, and this means unlimited territorial expansion.

G[EORGE] S. M[ESSERSMITH]

45

862.20/800

Memorandum by the Secretary of State Regarding a Conversation With the German Ambassador (Luther)

[WASHINGTON,] March 28, 1935.

The German Ambassador during his call casually stated that he trusted there would be no misunderstanding about the true attitude of the German Government on political and peace questions. He showed no disposition to elaborate, and I then remarked that the German Government at this time had a greater opportunity than any within two generations to make a remarkable showing of leadership with a program that would gradually bring Western Europe to normal political, social and peace relations; that the nations could either take this course or they could continue more or less aloof from each other with more or less misunderstanding of each others true motives, purposes and objectives, with the result that each country would go forward and arm to the teeth and without limit and on an ever-increasing scale, so that at some stage some local incident perchance would ignite the spark that would start a conflagration which in its ultimate effects would not leave a vestige of Western civilization. The Ambassador hurriedly proceeded to disclaim any course on the part of his Government except that of peace. . . . I asked the Ambassador what about the news reports as to the alleged objective of the German Government with respect to the Polish Corridor. He instantly disclaimed and denied as to this. I then referred to the reported objectives, such as the economic union with Austria, the return of Memel, the restoration of certain portions of Czechoslovakia with 3-1/2 million inhabitants, and certain other reported objectives. The Ambassador promptly disclaimed and denied as to each of these and insisted that his Government favored peace. I said, "What about disarmament?" He replied that his Government was and would be willing to disarm on relative equality with other governments. I continued at each stage to repeat as to the almost unprecedented opportunity of his Government for leadership with a program back to normal and peace conditions, and at the same time to emphasize how easy it would be for this opportunity to be lost or thrown away amidst the many difficult and chaotic things that were being said and done or threatened; that it would take a resolute person, strongly bent on the goal of stability in international affairs, political, economic, and peace, if such leadership were to succeed.

C[ORDELL] H[ULL]

46

Department of State pub. 756

Address Delivered by the Secretary of State at New York, June 12, 1935

[Extract]

It is of utmost importance that we seek by every means at our disposal to solidify and make more secure the stability thus far reached and to facilitate continued progress toward an improved international situation. But there are some ominous tendencies present in the world which, if persisted in, cannot fail to bring disaster and to undo whatever progress has thus far been made toward greater world stability. We witness all about us a reckless, competitive building-up of armaments, a recurrence of the mad race which prior to 1914 led the nations of the world headlong to destruction. If persisted in, this course will again plunge the world into disaster. If it remains unchecked, we shall witness national bankruptcies, hopelessly unbalanced budgets, and consequent inevitable inflation, together with the utter destruction of such measure of national stability as has thus far been achieved. The world cannot extricate itself from this relentless circle if it does not stop its extravagant military expenditures. International sanity requires both military and economic disarmament.

Isolationism has been tried and found wanting. It has destroyed 22 billion dollars' worth of international trade. It leaves every nation struggling as best it can to save for itself whatever it can from the general wreckage. The resulting international situation which confronts the world today gives cause for grave concern to every thinking person. We cannot afford, after years of experience, to discount its powerful effect upon peace, economic security, and stable governments everywhere. The issues involved are enormously greater than the petty interests of this or that industry in tariff protection. The explosives packed in the current nationalistic tendencies may result, as they have resulted, in the further disorganization of social and economic fabrics. Facing these threatened dangers, however, I have faith in the great traditions and strength of our American civilization, and I also have faith that statesmanship will, before it is too late, respond to the world crisis and find a workable solution.

47

Department of State pub. 753

Address Delivered by the Secretary of State at Ann Arbor, Michigan, June 17, 1935

In addressing this large graduating class, I feel a peculiar sense of responsibility. For the field of endeavor in which fate has placed me —the conduct of this Nation's foreign relations—is one which perhaps more than any other must affect the lives of the young men and women now leaving their campus in order to assume a share in the burden of carrying our civilization onward. The vast majority of you will not directly participate in the work of the State Department. Some of you will scarcely realize its existence throughout your lives. Others will come in contact with it or its representatives only as a nuisance requiring you to go through all sorts of so-called "red tape" to obtain, at a price, a passport to go abroad, to live abroad, and to come home. A few in this last category will find occasion in foreign lands to call upon our diplomatic or consular representatives abroad to lend a helping hand in carrying on legitimate business operations, or in settling difficulties of one kind or another. Another group, entering into academic life as a profession, will perchance, in the capacity of historians or teachers of international law or government, have occasion to study in further detail—as many of you have already begun during your student days—the organization and functioning of the Department of State.

A small number among you—and I hope it will be sizable—will occupy desks in the granite structure at Washington which houses the State Department and will assist in executing and formulating our country's foreign policy, or will hurdle the Foreign Service examinations—and I believe, when you are faced with them, you will agree they are meant only for those of the highest quality. These latter will find in the diplomatic and consular corps careers giving full play to the creative instinct and permitting them to combine service to the United States with an opportunity of acquiring at first hand a knowledge of foreign peoples and governments.

In speaking of my great responsibility in talking to you, however,

I am thinking of you not so much as future direct beneficiaries or servants of the State Department, but rather as members of the new generation which, whatever your individual occupations, will be profoundly influenced throughout your lives by what my fellow foreign statesmen and I accomplish at this critical juncture in world affairs. I do not mean to imply that the fate of mankind is in the hands of the tribe of foreign ministers. They are, in the first instance, agents of their peoples and cannot run counter to the wills of the nations they represent. What they can and must do is, as far as is humanly possible, to interpret and guide these frequently conflicting and sometimes incompatible wills in ways which will avoid the disaster of war or loss due to economic conflict.

We have passed the lowest depth of our domestic and economic crisis, and there are unmistakable and refreshing signs on every hand that recovery, despite variations now and then, is well under way, but the evidence is overwhelming that the situation in the international field is still deteriorating. If, in keeping with this occasion and the facile optimism many believe it calls for, I should make light of these trends and assure you that they hold out no dangers, I should be belittling the seriousness of the situation. I am not among those who think a new world war inevitable, for if there are undeniable forces driving toward war, there are other powerful forces which are striving for peace, and I would be the last to proclaim that the latter cannot and will not win the day. Nor do I believe that even a major war abroad should engulf this country; for if there is one thing on which the American people is unanimous today, that thing is its desire and determination to remain at peace with other nations—to help them, wherever possible, in maintaining friendship between themselves—but, when and if this should fail, at least to preserve that friendship ourselves. It is one of the tasks of American statesmanship to do what it can to make that wish and determination a reality. But, even assuming the continuance of peace in this continent, any clash abroad would at best so dislocate the slow progress of recovery here that we could not, in the long run, avoid its disastrous effects, just as neutral and belligerent alike are still agonizing in the aftermath of the World War. I cannot, therefore, with a good conscience tell you that as Americans you are immune from the effects of a possible conflict by being far removed from its locus, and that you may look without concern on the darkening clouds around the magic circle of the United States.

There is much loose talk today about self-sufficiency, nationalism, and reduction of foreign contacts to a minimum. I do not know to what extent these theories have made their advent on your campus, yet I feel certain that the great majority here—and certainly those who in their studies have given thought to the question of international relations—will agree with me that there are but two alternatives facing modern civilization: either we go forward to other, greater achievements of material and spiritual culture, with a concomitant growth of every kind of material and spiritual interchange within each nation and as between nations, or we must recognize that our culture has reached its apex and is entering into definite decline and decay. In the latter case—and in that case only—every manner of relationship built up in preceding centuries will become loosened and dissolved and nations will again achieve "self-sufficiency"—the self-sufficiency of barbarism and savagery. This last picture is an extreme, but the directions, to my mind, are clear. And the possibility of a return to the Dark Ages in some form is not, I think, historically excluded. Human history has known such cycles before. Civilizations have been born, have grown, flowered, declined, and ultimately disappeared except insofar as they were absorbed in later cultures. I need not remind you of the rise and fall of past civilizations of Egypt, of Crete, of Babylon, or of Phoenicia. The western world that we know was itself an offspring of the Dark Ages which followed the disruption of the greatest of previous civilizations, that of the Roman Empire. Out of this period of travail there evolved a rebirth of deep moral and spiritual values, a basic idealism which blossomed anew and was the foundation on which our ancestors built our own civilization. I refuse to believe, however, that it is necessary to go through the abyss again in order that our high ideals may be revived and restored; rather, it should be possible without backsliding to advance from this point on and carry our civilization to even greater heights.

We also learn from history that in any epoch of stress and readjustment a small minority of the total population of the world, usually not more than two or three nations at a time, bears aloft the torch of leadership. If such a nation loses the unflinching purpose to lead, if it is content to rest on past achievement, if it expects others to assume its burden, then it does not merely remain static, but a definite period of retrogression sets in. It is not an idle boast when I declare to you that our country, under the guidance and direction of our forbears, has been holding high that torch of leadership. They built up our national civilization on the basis of integrity and hardihood, on the basis of individual initiative coupled with give-and-take for the common good. Throughout the decades there was a driving force that led them inexorably toward their goal, a vision which never let them falter. Hardships were merely obstacles to be overcome. Today, with increasing comforts and opportunities for indolence and ease, there is a danger that we may forget the sacrifices and exertions of the earlier generations. Instead of the physical obstacles that were overcome by our ancestors, we are faced today with a new series of political, social, economic, and moral problems which it is our task to solve without sacrificing either the traditions or the fundamentals of our great democracy.

Throughout the entire world we have been witnessing since the war a growth of distrust in established beliefs and institutions, a disregard of traditional criteria of conduct, and, along with an anarchic rejection of accepted standards, a profound search for new thought forms and ways of living.

Such departures from the past are nothing new; indeed they may be nothing more than the natural stages of evolutionary process. The perennial tendency of each passing generation is to doubt the wisdom of the new ways in which the succeeding generation is seeking to meet its individual problems. But when, as at present, new theories are presented all over the globe with such vigor and persuasion as to enlist the sometimes reasoned, more often fanatical, loyalty of millions, and when such mass movements, far from losing momentum with the passage of time, actually reach the point of attempting to execute their ideals, then we are face to face with one of those critical moments of history in which the human race has reached a crossroads. As I look back through time, I can find few periods to compare with ours in the depth of its contradictions.

Consider for a moment the crisis in what we have come to associate with the term "democracy". Through the past century, the principles of democracy had spread so far that only a few years ago they could be considered the dominant trait of our era. Yet the democratic idea has of late been challenged in one country after another, and several great peoples have seen fit to cast it aside entirely, as undesirable for themselves, in favor of new systems of ideas which they consider superior. First, you have the challenge of communism, involving a frank advocacy of class dictatorship as a means for achieving a social ideal; subsequently, other systems established themselves in a number of countries, each characterized by a conscious rejection of democracy in principle and fact; until today we see four outstanding and rival systems of government struggling for the supremacy of their political philosophy.

In the face of such divergent, but vigorous, attempts in other countries to remold our western civilization, it is natural that we should be reviewing here the various aspects of democracy. I have noticed in recent years a wide-spread questioning among our people, and particularly among the younger generation, not with regard to the foundations of democracy itself—God forbid that we should ever lose the faith in government by the people and for the people— but with regard to some of its more superficial aspects which have been mistakenly taken for integral elements.

In place of stampeding away from the fundamentals of democracy for no better reason than the obsolescence of certain of the methods of its application, our best minds are engaging in a serious effort toward preserving its substance. What I wish to emphasize today, however, is that the self-analysis which is proceeding within the camp of democracy itself, is peculiarly a call to the mind and heart of the young generation. It is an exciting adventure to be crossing, as you are, the threshold between two eras at an age when your minds are still open and your reasons and emotions still adaptable; to assist in the choice of our future course is a task which should fire your imaginations and call forth the best that is in you; and the prospect of living to see the answer to the great question of where our civilization is going, is a privilege for which your elders may well envy you.

The building of our future life in America is, necessarily, in the first instance a task for domestic action. Yet, from all I have said, it is clear that our best efforts are bound to come to naught if the pacific competition between the divergent economic and political systems now wooing the allegiance of mankind should seek a solution through the arbitrament of arms, or, even if it stops short of war, should follow methods which create and preserve ill will or hamper the natural flow of trade so vital to recovery. It is not possible to cloister a nation's foreign policy away from its domestic life. That policy is an essential part of the national being. It is not merely a protector from foreign encroachment and a promoter of interests abroad: it stands as a beacon in the world for the particular type of culture it represents. To a large extent, one nation judges another by its foreign policies.

Just what ultimate modifications in our own foreign policy may emerge from the gradual restatement of democracy which we are now undertaking, I would not be rash enough to predict. From the very nature of international relationships, it is clear that we are not sole masters of the forms they will take, dependent as they are on the interaction of our own desires with those of other countries. I believe, though, that from a brief outline of certain major aspects of our foreign relationships, I may be able to indicate to you certain tendencies. Let me emphasize, however, that the present administration has not broken with any of the basic policies which are the traditions of American democracy. It has merely added here and filed off there and has reinterpreted its principles and practices in harmony with the general modulation of our national thoughts. More particularly, it has had to bear in mind, and continues ceaselessly to bear in mind, that general deterioration in the international situation to which I have already referred.

It is natural, in view of this last factor, that virtually every major element in our foreign policy is directly or indirectly connected with two central objectives of which I spoke at the beginning, namely, to assist in the prevention of war and to insure that, in any event, the United States shall not be involved in war short of having to defend itself against direct aggression.

Before modern students, there is no need to emphasize the importance of economic and trade rivalry as the causation of war. In fact, it is sometimes claimed by critics who hold other views that this factor may have been overstressed in recent years. Be that as it may, the present administration is devoting much effort toward stemming the tide of economic nationalism with its accompanying disastrous throttling of international trade. It is endeavoring, through a series of trade negotiations, authorized by an amendment to the Tariff Act of 1930, to reverse the process of building ever-higher tariff walls and of imposing sundry trade restrictions, and by mutual concessions to stimulate anew the flow of an international exchange of goods and services beneficial to each participant. To date, trade agreements, reducing tariffs on a wide variety of articles, have been signed with five states, and negotiations are being carried on with some dozen additional countries. It is my hope that in time a network of such agreements will stimulate our trade with countries scattered over the whole globe and, through the example they set to others, induce them to conclude similar treaties among themselves, thus breaking the log jam behind which trade and production have been dammed and which is responsible for a larger proportion of world unemployment than the mere percentage of foreign to domestic trade would, at first glance, indicate. The guiding principle of this effort, and one which alone can prevent our modern industrial and commercial civilization from deterioration, is equality in trade, in its rights and in its opportunities.

In the political as opposed to the economic field, I should like to touch by way of example on just a few of our direct relations with foreign nations, for in these the spirit of the administration's foreign policy has found its most concrete embodiment—the spirit which President Roosevelt has defined as that of the "good neighbor". The term is a general one, but it has a well-defined meaning and content, as was clearly indicated at the recent Conference of American States at Montevideo, at which I had the honor to represent the United States. The American delegation went to this conference determined to consider every question raised, not only without bias or prejudice, but with an appreciation of the several points of view represented by the other 20 nations in attendance there. The result of this sympathetic approach was to add impetus to a shift in public opinion throughout Latin America that is one of the most remarkable in recent years. The people of Latin America had come to look upon the United States with a certain suspicion, at times verging on bitterness. They lived in apparent fear of further territorial expansion by the United States, or of intermeddling in their domestic affairs. The reassurance given them by the President in his inaugural message was heightened by the attitude of the American delegation at Montevideo, and particularly the acceptance by this Government of the resolution providing that "No state has the right to intervene in the internal or external affairs of another." This declaration creates a precedent which, in my belief, will never be abandoned.

Hand in hand with the development of our friendly relations with individual nations has gone our effort to assist, without sacrificing traditional principles against political entanglements, in the building and strengthening of a cooperative system of pacific settlement of disputes and security against aggression.

In the field of armaments, we have played a leading role in the long and thus far discouraging effort to bring about a limitation and reduction of instruments of war. We have advocated the abolition of weapons peculiarly suited to destroying fortifications, with a view to increasing security by strengthening the power of defense, as compared with the power of attack. We have pressed for the conclusion of a treaty controlling the manufacture of, and trade in, arms and implements of war. We have stood for the extension of the Washington and London Naval Treaties, which expire next year, or, if this is not possible, of their basic principles and provisions. We have proposed the conclusion of a clear and simple pact of non-aggression, which cuts through a maze of technicalities and singles out as a criterion of aggression the sending of armed forces of whatsoever nature across a nation's frontiers. We have expressed our willingness to consult with other states in case of a threat to peace, with a view to averting conflict. We have in practice associated ourselves with the League of Nations' consultative procedure both in connection with the Sino-Japanese dispute over Manchuria and the Peruvian-Colombian dispute over Leticia. I could go on reciting other evidences of our constructive efforts—but it is less the efforts themselves than their underlying purpose that I am trying to outline to you today.

That these efforts have not given the results we hoped for is due in large measure to the suicidal race in armaments going on throughout the world. Each increase in armament has been met by a further increase, till today the vicious circle is virtually paralyzing all opportunity for permanent productive or creative work. Nations are rapidly bankrupting themselves in this race, and the toll it exacts in national resources is second only to the losses sustained in war. A return to the atmosphere of peace and stability, a return to international sanity, requires that this trend be reversed. The nation that will not play its part, and thus retards our world progress, should be branded. The nation that strives unceasingly, and despite discouragement, for a reduction and limitation of armaments will be found in the vanguard of the march of civilization.

There are certain fundamentals that must govern the life of any community, be it of men or of nations. Among these are justice, humanity, understanding, friendship, and cooperation for the common good. These principles guided the early settlers in Jamestown, the Pilgrim Fathers in Massachusetts, and the early pioneers who crossed the mountains into our great western country. Upon these principles the democracy of the United States was built. It is these principles on which our foreign policy should and will be based. Such a policy will preclude interference in the domestic concerns of others and will cause us to reject any trammels on our independent judgments or decisions, but, at the same time, it will enable us by mutual understanding and cooperation to play an active part in attaining a higher level of civilization for all.

Such is the picture I would leave with you today, as you finish your education and prepare to enter the world of action. Your generation has for solution problems more complex than have faced any preceding generation, and your responsibilities are correspondingly great. If you will meet these problems courageously, yet with understanding; with faith in democracy and the traditions of our past; with a willingness to return to the habits, industry, and hardihood of preceding generations, who never knew the meaning of ease and indolence; with a willingness to rely on yourselves and not admit dependence on any governmental agency for help except in real emergency; and, finally, with a realization that no one country can stand alone, and that each must contribute for the common good—then the future will be yours, and you cannot fail.

48

765.84/870a

The Secretary of State to the Ambassador in Italy (Long)

[Telegram]

WASHINGTON, August 18, 1935—1 p.m.

136. You are instructed to seek an interview at the earliest possible moment with Mussolini and to hand him a copy of the following message which I am sending him at the direction of the President:

"I am asked by the President to communicate to you, in all friendliness and in confidence, a personal message expressing his earnest hope that the controversy between Italy and Ethiopia will be resolved without resort to armed conflict. In this country it is felt both by the Government and by the people that failure to arrive at a peaceful settlement of the present dispute and a subsequent outbreak of hostilities would be a world calamity the consequences of which would adversely affect the interests of all nations."

HULL

49

49 Stat. 1081; 22 U.S.C. 441 note

"Neutrality Act" of August 31, 1935

JOINT RESOLUTION

Providing for the prohibition of the export of arms, ammunition, and implements of war to belligerent countries; the prohibition of the transportation of arms, ammunition, and implements of war by vessels of the United States for the use of belligerent states; for the registration and licensing of persons engaged in the business of manufacturing, exporting, or importing arms, ammunition, or implements of war; and restricting travel by American citizens on belligerent ships during war.

Resolved by the Senate and House of Representatives of the United States of America in Congress assembled, That upon the outbreak or during the progress of war between, or among, two or more foreign states, the President shall proclaim such fact, and it shall thereafter be unlawful to export arms, ammunition, or implements of war from any place in the United States, or possessions of the United States, to any port of such belligerent states, or to any neutral port for transshipment to, or for the use of, a belligerent country.

The President, by proclamation, shall definitely enumerate the arms, ammunition, or implements of war, the export of which is prohibited by this Act.

The President may, from time to time, by proclamation, extend such embargo upon the export of arms, ammunition, or implements of war to other states as and when they may become involved in such war.

Whoever, in violation of any of the provisions of this section, shall export, or attempt to export, or cause to be exported, arms, ammunition, or implements of war from the United States, or any of its possessions, shall be fined not more than $10,000 or imprisoned not more than five years, or both, and the property, vessel, or vehicle containing the same shall be subject to the provisions of sections 1 to 8, inclusive, title 6, chapter 30, of the Act approved June 15, 1917 (40 Stat. 223–225; U. S. C., title 22, secs. 238–245).

In the case of the forfeiture of any arms, ammunition, or implements of war by reason of a violation of this Act, no public or private sale shall be required; but such arms, ammunition, or implements of war shall be delivered to the Secretary of War for such use or disposal thereof as shall be approved by the President of the United States.

When in the judgment of the President the conditions which have caused him to issue his proclamation have ceased to exist he shall revoke the same and the provisions hereof shall thereupon cease to apply.

Except with respect to prosecutions committed or forfeitures incurred prior to March 1, 1936, this section and all proclamations issued thereunder shall not be effective after February 29, 1936.

SEC. 2. That for the purpose of this Act—

(a) The term "Board" means the National Munitions Control Board which is hereby established to carry out the provisions of this Act. The Board shall consist of the Secretary of State, who shall be chairman and executive officer of the Board; the Secretary of the Treasury; the Secretary of War; the Secretary of the Navy; and the Secretary of Commerce. Except as otherwise provided in this Act, or by other law, the administration of this Act is vested in the Department of State;

(b) The term "United States" when used in a geographical sense, includes the several States and Territories, the insular possessions of the United States (including the Philippine Islands), the Canal Zone, and the District of Columbia;

(c) The term "person" includes a partnership, company, association, or corporation, as well as a natural person.

Within ninety days after the effective date of this Act, or upon first engaging in business, every person who engages in the business of manufacturing, exporting, or importing any of the arms, ammunition, and implements of war referred to in this Act, whether as an exporter, importer, manufacturer, or dealer, shall register with the Secretary of State his name, or business name, principal place of business, and places of business in the United States, and a list of the arms, ammunition, and implements of war which he manufactures, imports, or exports.

Every person required to register under this section shall notify the Secretary of State of any change in the arms, ammunition, and implements of war which he exports, imports, or manufactures; and upon such notification the Secretary of State shall issue to such person an amended certificate of registration, free of charge, which shall remain valid until the date of expiration of the original certificate. Every person required to register under the provisions of this section shall pay a registration fee of $500, and upon receipt of such fee the Secretary of State shall issue a registration certificate valid for five years, which shall be renewable for further periods of five years upon the payment of each renewal of a fee of $500.

It shall be unlawful for any person to export, or attempt to export, from the United States any of the arms, ammunition, or implements of war referred to in this Act to any other country or to import, or attempt to import, to the United States from any other country any of the arms, ammunition, or implements of war referred to in this Act without first having obtained a license therefor.

All persons required to register under this section shall maintain, subject to the inspection of the Board, such permanent records of manufacture for export, importation, and exportation of arms, ammunition, and implements of war as the Board shall prescribe.

Licenses shall be issued to persons who have registered as provided for, except in cases of export or import licenses where exportation of arms, ammunition, or implements of war would be in violation of this Act or any other law of the United States, or of a treaty to which the United States is a party, in which cases such licenses shall not be issued.

The Board shall be called by the Chairman and shall hold at least one meeting a year.

No purchase of arms, ammunition, and implements of war shall be made on behalf of the United States by any officer, executive department, or independent establishment of the Government from any person who shall have failed to register under the provisions of this Act.

The Board shall make an annual report to Congress, copies of which shall be distributed as are other reports transmitted to Congress. Such report shall contain such information and data collected by the Board as may be considered of value in the determination of questions connected with the control of trade in arms, ammunition, and implements of war. It shall include a list of all persons required to register under the provisions of this Act, and full information concerning the licenses issued hereunder.

The Secretary of State shall promulgate such rules and regulations with regard to the enforcement of this section as he may deem necessary to carry out its provisions.

The President is hereby authorized to proclaim upon recommendation of the Board from time to time a list of articles which shall be considered arms, ammunition, and implements of war for the purposes of this section.

This section shall take effect on the ninetieth day after the date of its enactment.

Sec. 3. Whenever the President shall issue the proclamation provided for in section 1 of this Act, thereafter it shall be unlawful for any American vessel to carry any arms, ammunition, or implements of war to any port of the belligerent countries named in such proclamation as being at war, or to any neutral port for transshipment to, or for the use of, a belligerent country.

Whoever, in violation of the provisions of this section, shall take, attempt to take, or shall authorize, hire, or solicit another to take any such vessel carrying such cargo out of port or from the jurisdiction of the United States shall be fined not more than $10,000 or imprisoned not more than five years, or both; and, in addition, such vessel, her tackle, apparel, furniture, equipment, and the arms, ammunition, and implements of war on board shall be forfeited to the United States.

When the President finds the conditions which have caused him to issue his proclamation have ceased to exist, he shall revoke his proclamation, and the provisions of this section shall thereupon cease to apply.

Sec. 4. Whenever, during any war in which the United States is neutral, the President, or any person thereunto authorized by him, shall have cause to believe that any vessel, domestic or foreign, whether requiring clearance or not, is about to carry out of a port of the United States, or its possession, men or fuel, arms, ammunition, implements of war, or other supplies to any warship, tender, or supply ship of a foreign belligerent nation, but the evidence is not deemed sufficient to justify forbidding the departure of the vessel as provided for by section 1, title V, chapter 30, of the Act approved June 15, 1917 (40 Stat. [221 [22]]; U. S. C., title 18, sec. 31), and if, in the President's judgment, such action will serve to maintain peace between the United States and foreign nations, or to protect the commercial interests of the United States and its citizens, or to promote the security of the United States, he shall have the power and it shall be his duty to require the owner, master, or person in command thereof, before departing from a port of the United States, or any of its possessions, for a foreign port, to give a bond to the United States, with sufficient sureties, in such amount as he shall deem proper, conditioned that the vessel will not deliver the men, or the cargo, or any part thereof, to any warship, tender, or supply ship of a belligerent nation; and, if the President, or any person thereunto authorized by him, shall find that a vessel, domestic or foreign, in a port of the United States, or one of its possessions, has previously cleared from such port during such war and delivered its cargo or any part thereof to a warship, tender, or supply ship of a belligerent nation, he may prohibit the departure of such vessel during the duration of the war.

SEC. 5. Whenever, during any war in which the United States is neutral, the President shall find that special restrictions placed on the use of the ports and territorial waters of the United States, or of its possessions, by the submarines of a foreign nation will serve to maintain peace between the United States and foreign nations, or to protect the commercial interests of the United States and its citizens, or to promote the security of the United States, and shall make proclamation thereof, it shall thereafter be unlawful for any such submarine to enter a port or the territorial waters of the United States or any of its possessions, or to depart therefrom, except under such conditions and subject to such limitations as the President may prescribe. When, in his judgment, the conditions which have caused him to issue his proclamation have ceased to exist, he shall revoke his proclamation and the provisions of this section shall thereupon cease to apply.

---

[22] Page number omitted in original.

Sec. 6. Whenever, during any war in which the United States is neutral, the President shall find that the maintenance of peace between the United States and foreign nations, or the protection of the lives of citizens of the United States, or the protection of the commercial interests of the United States and its citizens, or the security of the United States requires that the American citizens should refrain from traveling as passengers on the vessels of any belligerent nation, he shall so proclaim, and thereafter no citizen of the United States shall travel on any vessel of any belligerent nation except at his own risk, unless in accordance with such rules and regulations as the President shall prescribe: *Provided, however,* That the provisions of this section shall not apply to a citizen traveling on the vessel of a belligerent whose voyage was begun in advance of the date of the President's proclamation, and who had no opportunity to discontinue his voyage after that date: *And provided further,* That they shall not apply under ninety days after the date of the President's proclamation to a citizen returning from a foreign country to the United States or to any of its possessions. When, in the President's judgment, the conditions which have caused him to issue his proclamation have ceased to exist, he shall revoke his proclamation and the provisions of this section shall thereupon cease to apply.

Sec. 7. In every case of the violation of any of the provisions of this Act where a specific penalty is not herein provided, such violator or violators, upon conviction, shall be fined not more than $10,000 or imprisoned not more than five years, or both.

Sec. 8. If any of the provisions of this Act, or the application thereof to any person or circumstance, is held invalid, the remainder of the Act, and the application of such provision to other persons or circumstances, shall not be affected thereby.

Sec. 9. The sum of $25,000 is hereby authorized to be appropriated, out of any money in the Treasury not otherwise appropriated, to be expended by the Secretary of State in administering this Act.

Approved, August 31, 1935.

50

Press Releases, vol. XIII, p. 162

Statement by President Roosevelt, August 31, 1935

I have given my approval to S.J. Resolution 173—the neutrality legislation which passed the Congress last week.

I have approved this joint resolution because it was intended as an expression of the fixed desire of the Government and the people of the United States to avoid any action which might involve us in war. The purpose is wholly excellent, and this joint resolution will to a considerable degree serve that end.

It provides for a licensing system for the control of carrying arms, et cetera, by American vessels; for the control of the use of American waters by foreign submarines; for the restriction of travel by American citizens on vessels of belligerent nations; and for the embargo of the export of arms, et cetera, to both belligerent nations.

The latter section terminates at the end of February 1936. This section requires further and more complete consideration between now and that date. Here again the objective is wholly good. It is the policy of this Government to avoid being drawn into wars between other nations, but it is a fact that no Congress and no Executive can foresee all possible future situations. History is filled with unforeseeable situations that call for some flexibility of action. It is conceivable that situations may arise in which the wholly inflexible provisions of section I of this act might have exactly the opposite effect from that which was intended. In other words, the inflexible provisions might drag us into war instead of keeping us out. The policy of the Government is definitely committed to the maintenance of peace and the avoidance of any entanglements which would lead us into conflict. At the same time it is the policy of the Government by every peaceful means and without entanglement to cooperate with other similarly minded governments to promote peace.

In several aspects further careful consideration of neutrality needs is most desirable, and there can well be an expansion to include provisions dealing with other important aspects of our neutrality policy which have not been dealt with in this temporary measure.

51

765.84/1101

The Ambassador in Italy (Long) to the Secretary of State

[Telegram : Paraphrase]

ROME, September 10, 1935—6 p.m.
[Received September 10—4: 15 p.m.]

567. In my mind there remains no vestige of doubt that Italy is irrevocably determined to proceed in Africa and that from whatever quarter opposition is offered it will be met by subjected mass attack.

I am convinced from my contacts with the people, from reports of the attitude of the man on the street and from my observation of the antipathy to England on the part of the soldier and the civilian that the whole population, both military and civilian, are in complete accord with Mussolini's policies as they have been developed up to now and as they are prospected for the future. The press in every issue gives additional expression to the national determination to proceed to war and not to tolerate interference from any source.

The Italian plans have developed step by step over a period of many months. Now they find themselves with more than 200,000 men south of the Suez Canal and there are more than three more divisions preparing to go. The withdrawal of those troops would be a defeat and its effect upon the government here a disaster. Hurried on by a gradually approaching domestic economic crisis I have a distinct impression that opposition from England would be welcomed by the Italians as an opportunity for the demonstration of their imaginary and even possible superior strength in the Eastern part of the Mediterranean. Malta is only a few minutes by air from the Italian posts in Sicily, and Cairo, Alexandria, and Port Said are only an hour removed from the Libyan coast.

The Italian press is heaping abuse upon those who have the courage to stand up in Geneva and give expression to thought opposing the Italian aims; it also castigates French and British socialists who dare to speak of sanctions and inveighs against the united opposition of bolshevism and the "piracy of plutocracy", as they designate the Rickett affair, and charges that all of these are joined in a worthless attempt to stop the progress of Italy.

I have the impression that the Italians are quite willing to accept the delay which has been occasioned by the Geneva meetings since they are thus afforded more time for preparation and for the completion of a number of ships they have recently bought for transport purposes, which are now being transformed at Genoa. Likewise, I am equally impressed with the fact that they now find themselves in a position from which a withdrawal is impossible without suffering in effect a defeat. There is every indication of a carefully prepared, well-calculated, hard, cold, and cruel prosecution of preconceived plans by the use of an army and navy which is almost fanatic in idolatry of and devotion to one man and which is worked up to an emotional pitch unique in modern times.

It is my wish that I could send some word in encouragement of the thought that some compromise might be arrived at in Geneva or elsewhere, but it is my firm belief that a compromise is possible only on Mussolini's own terms and that if these terms are not accepted he will proceed to his objectives despite world opinion and in opposition to whatever forces may be raised against him. Military capitulation is the only alternative.

Your attention should be invited at the same time to the lasting effect necessitated by this situation on international situations in Europe and on changing political alignments. The settled friendship between Great Britain and Italy has gone and will not reappear for generations. In the press today is featured the friendly exchange of expressions between Chancelor Hitler and the new Ambassador of Italy to Germany, which presumably is a political warning to France that she must adhere to her alliance with Italy. But whatever arrangements Italy may be able to make with Germany in the future, and it would appear impossible that a reconciliation of their clashing interests could be effected, an entirely new element in the already complicated European situation has been brought about by the changed situation between Italy and England. The British Empire is directly threatened by Italy's action in the eastern Mediterranean and if the latter successfully establishes herself in Ethiopia, the Suez Canal will be almost as important politically to Italy as it is to England. If the Canal assumes its present importance to Italy with 200,000 soldiers south of it, when they achieve their ambition to have 10,000,000 colonists there, it will have a greater importance, and before long there will develop the necessity for an alternate route of communication between Italy and Ethiopia through Libya and across the Sudan which will be part of their efforts to solidify their position in Ethiopia if they accomplish their objective there. Thus the present situation is fraught with dangers from many angles for the future as well as for the present and it is my fear that its reverberations in the international relations of the world will last at least during the life of the present generation unless a decisive military defeat is suffered.

LONG

52

Press Releases, vol. XIII, p. 194

Statement by the Secretary of State, September 12, 1935

In view of the deep concern of this Government and the widespread anxiety of the American people over recent developments which appear to constitute a grave threat to the peace of the world, I consider it desirable to recapitulate the steps thus far taken by this Government in contributing in every practicable way toward a peaceful settlement of the present dispute between Italy and Ethiopia.

On the evening of July 3 the Emperor of Ethiopia summoned the American Chargé d'Affaires *ad interim* at Addis Ababa to the palace and handed the Chargé a communication in which the Emperor stated that he felt it to be his duty to ask the American Government to examine means of securing observance of the Pact of Paris.

The Chargé was instructed to reply to the Emperor as follows:

"I have the honor to acknowledge the receipt of Your Imperial Majesty's note of July 3, 1935, and to inform Your Imperial Majesty that I immediately communicated its contents to my Government. I have been instructed by my Government to reply to your note as follows:

" 'My Government, interested as it is in the maintenance of peace in all parts of the world, is gratified that the League of Nations, with a view to a peaceful settlement, has given its attention to the controversy which has unhappily arisen between your Government and the Italian Government and that the controversy is now in process of arbitration. My Government hopes that, whatever the facts or merits of the controversy may be, the arbitral agency dealing with this controversy may be able to arrive at a decision satisfactory to both of the Governments immediately concerned.

" 'Furthermore, and of great importance, in view of the provisions of the Pact of Paris, to which both Italy and Abyssinia are parties, in common with 61 other countries, my Government would be loath to believe that either of them would resort to other than pacific means as a method of dealing with this controversy or would permit any situation to arise which would be inconsistent with the commitments of the Pact.' "

On July 10, during a call of the Italian Ambassador made at the request of the Secretary of State, the Secretary made to the Ambassador a statement as follows:

"Although we are not familiar with the facts or the merits of the questions at issue between Italy and Ethiopia, we are deeply interested in the preservation of peace in all parts of the world and we are particularly interested in those international arrangements designed to effect the solution of controversies by peaceable means.

"Being convinced that world progress and economic recovery are urgently in need of peaceful conditions, particularly at this time, we feel impelled to impress upon the Italian Ambassador our increasing concern over the situation arising out of Italy's dispute with Ethiopia and our earnest hope that a means may be found to arrive at a peaceful and mutually satisfactory solution of the problem."

On July 11, the Secretary of State conferred with the British and French Ambassadors. He called attention to articles which had appeared in the press wherein there was placed upon the American Government's reply to the Emperor of Ethiopia an interpretation implying that the American Government had abandoned the Kellogg-Briand Pact and the pact therefore was "dead".

The Secretary said he felt this interpretation was entirely contrary to the sense of his note to the Emperor, which had emphasized the principles of the Pact of Paris and had given evidence of this Government's interest in the settlement of this dispute by peaceable means.

On the same day, at his press conference, the Secretary of State pointed out that naturally the American Government, as had frequently been stated previously, is deeply concerned about the preservation of peace in every part of the world and is closely observing conditions and developments.

On July 12, in response to various inquiries of newspaper correspondents, the Secretary of State made a statement as follows:

"The Pact of Paris is no less binding now than when it was entered into by the 63 nations that are parties to it. By form and designation it constitutes a treaty by and among those nations. It is a declaration by the governments of the world that they condemn recourse to war for the solution of international controversies, and renounce it as an instrument of national policy in their relations with one another. Furthermore, it is an agreement and a solemn obligation that the settlement or solution of all disputes or conflicts among nations, of whatever nature or of whatever origin, shall never be sought except by pacific means.

"The United States and the other nations are interested in the maintenance of the pact and the sanctity of the international commitments assumed thereby for the promotion and maintenance of peace among the nations of the world."

On August 1, the President issued a statement as follows:

"At this moment, when the Council of the League of Nations is assembled to consider ways for composing by pacific means the differences that have arisen between Italy and Ethiopia, I wish to voice the hope of the people and the Government of the United States that an amicable solution will be found and that peace will be maintained."

Thereafter, during the month of August, expression of this hope of the people and Government of the United States was communicated in telegrams from the American Government to several other governments.

On September 3, having discovered that an American corporation was a party to a newly granted commercial concession the conclusion of which had added to the perplexities and difficulties confronting the governments and other agencies which are intent upon preservation of peace, the American Government took prompt steps toward removal of this obstacle to peaceful settlement. In connection with that matter, the Secretary of State said at his press conference:

"The central point in the policy of this Government in regard to the Italian and Ethiopian controversy is the preservation of peace—to which policy every country throughout the world is committed by one or more treaties—and we earnestly hope that no nations will, in any circumstances, be diverted from this supreme objective."

Now, this Government feels called upon further to express the attitude of this country.

The Government and people of the United States desire peace. We believe that international controversies can and should be settled by peaceful means. We have signed, along with 62 other nations, including Italy and Ethiopia, a treaty in which the signatories have condemned war as an instrument of national policy and have undertaken, each to all, to settle their disputes by none but pacific means.

Under the conditions which prevail in the world today, a threat of hostilities anywhere cannot but be a threat to the interests—political, economic, legal, and social—of all nations. Armed conflict in any part of the world cannot but have undesirable and adverse effects in every part of the world. All nations have the right to ask that any and all issues, between whatsoever nations, be resolved by pacific means. Every nation has the right to ask that no nations subject it and other nations to the hazards and uncertainties that must inevitably accrue to all from resort to arms by any two.

With good will toward all nations, the American Government asks of those countries which appear to be contemplating armed hostilities that they weigh most solicitously the declaration and pledge given in the Pact of Paris, which pledge was entered into by all the signatories for the purpose of safeguarding peace and sparing the world the incalculable losses and human suffering that inevitably attend and follow in the wake of wars.

53

765.84/1341

The Ambassador in Italy (Long) to the Secretary of State

[Extracts]

No. 1311.
Sir:

Rome, September 13, 1935.
[Received September 23.]

I have the honor to refer to the Italo-Abyssinian difficulty and to attempt some observations thereon as regards its effect upon the present status of European politics and its possible relationship to future alliances.

As was indicated in my despatch No. 1209 of September 12th, our information is that preparations continue for amplification of British forces, both naval and land, in the neighborhood of the Eastern Mediterranean and that the Italian naval and air forces are concentrated. The propaganda which has been developed in the Italian press against England during the last three or four months has been very intensive. The expedition against Abyssinia in itself was not particularly popular in Italy during the fall of 1934 and the winter and spring of 1935. Various attempts were made in the press to attribute to it characteristics of popularity but as a matter of fact the project was not very warmly received by the people. However, as soon as the attack was commenced on England in the Italian papers there was noticeable a distinct change in the attitude of the people. As this propaganda has continued and has increased in intensity, the people have responded to it and today are united, as far as can be judged from the various contacts and reports which come to me, in their entirety and to an extent which is tantamount to a fanatic adherence to Mussolini and his plans, with an antagonism against England which each Italian seems to take personally.

I had occasion to watch Mussolini's review of the Ballila and the Avanguardisti last Sunday evening. Some 20,000 youngsters from the ages of six to eighteen passed before the reviewing stand. Each one carried a rifle with bayonet affixed, was in uniform, and was unusually well drilled. Even the very youngsters showed evidences of personal attachment to the Duce and time after time elicited the applause of the crowd by the rigor of their salutes. In the reviewing stand was the British Military Attaché. There was no open manifestation of antagonism toward him but it was quite noteworthy that among the crowd in front of the stand he was constantly the object of their attention. Time after time groups of three or four would look at him and engage in close conversation and it was equally noteworthy that there was not one single friendly gesture or look in his direction.

When that part of the parade which consisted of the young sailors passed, it was the occasion for a wild outburst of enthusiasm.

I cite this as just one instance. But on every side and from every quarter, one hears the antagonism amongst the people which has been engendered by the propaganda and one becomes definitely conscious of the distinct feeling of hostility toward England.

As it is well known to the Department I will only refer again to my various despatches during the last two years which have carried reports of bitter attacks on other Governments. Noteworthy among them was the attack upon Germany, which commenced shortly after the murder of Dollfuss. There was then the attack upon France in the midst of the Stavisky scandal and aimed at the parliamentary system of government but against France in particular. That was followed by the most bitter campaign against Yugoslavia, preceding the murder of King Alexander and continuing with fitful spasms thereafter. There was then a bitter attack against Switzerland because it closed the border against Italian goods at the time of the imposition of the import restrictions by Italy last winter. In the meantime there have been violent but not such prolonged attacks against Russia and Japan. A few months ago it broke out in all its fury against England, upon which I reported at the time including conversations with the British Ambassador about his intentions in the matter and the conversation I had with Mr. Suvich when the attack commenced in the TEVERE.

The relations of all of these countries and Italy remained strained except in the case of France. The sudden volte-face of Franco-Italian relations occurred last fall and was preparatory to Laval's visit last January, which was such an important incident in modern Italian history. It may be argued from the changed relationship with France, one of extreme friendliness following a state of bitter antagonism, that the press in Italy can also change the attitude of its people toward England and that the all-powerful and omnipresent hand of the Duce can change the sentiment of his people over night from one of bitter antagonism to one of sweet friendship. No doubt there would be some truth in that observation. The press is powerful and the Italian people are volatile. But none of the campaigns except that against Yugoslavia has continued so long or been so bitter and I am reasonably sure that it would be practically impossible to eradicate from the minds of the younger people the personal animosity against England which has been inculcated in their hearts and in their minds. They might, as a matter of stoic obedience, assume a different trend, but the seed that has been planted has had the ground so well cultivated and has been nurtured to such a young growth that it seems impossible in my mind that its influence could be eliminated in a short time and highly improbable that it could be changed to a feeling of friendship in the course of a generation.

But it must not be considered that the effect has been only upon the people of Italy, for the Italian campaign has made a marked impress upon the people of England who are without the scope of Italian propaganda and not subject to its influence.

The effect of this situation is that it has created a relationship between Italy and England which marks the end of their long years of friendly cooperation. It is impossible to conceive today that Italy and England will in the next few years proceed to a friendly cooperation in any degree consonant with that which characterized their relations for the past decades. Even if Italy were willing and the people of Italy could be brought to a realization of the necessity of a changed attitude toward England, the British Government would have difficulty with its own people in establishing close cooperation with the Government which has manifested such bitter antagonism and I might say hostile intentions, and in inducing the British people to reassume their former friendship toward Italians.

So that I am tempted to fear that it will be generations before the situation now existing can be cured and as a corollary to the situation there is the necessity for England and France, or one or the other, in view of the diminishing importance of the League of Nations and the system of collective security, to seek other support from Governments in central and eastern Europe to supplant the reliance they had upon Italy and to establish on a new basis a system of balance.

The Future.

I have dealt up to this point only with the situation as it exists today. I now venture upon the very delicate ground of speculation.

Any consideration of the effects which the present situation will have on the future must be based on one or the other of two premises. The first supposition is that force will be applied to Italy in sufficient strength to stop its bold adventure and to impose upon it a definite defeat at arms. In this case there would no doubt be terrible trouble in Italy. Whether the Fascist regime could continue is quite speculative but even if it did continue it would be with an increasing lack of confidence and with trouble. Nevertheless, in case there was imposed a crushing military defeat, it would leave the eastern Mediterranean and Africa in its present status and would simply place Italy without the pale of friendly association with other nations in Europe.

The other premise is that Italy proceeds to attain her objectives in Ethiopia. In this case there is only trouble for the future. There can be nothing else. Those who consider this to be the high expression of Fascism and the end of their ambitions are entitled to no confidence. If the regime in Italy were successful in this venture it would but embolden them to proceed to other ventures. From time to time in the past Mussolini has made speeches which have been duly reported and commented upon in which he said that he had no European ambitions but that he did have ambitions in Africa and Asia. It was one such speech that caused the changed relationship between Turkey and Italy because Turkey thought that he had ambitions upon some of her territory. There is no doubt in my mind that if he obtains Ethiopia, or even a great part of it, he will proceed to establish himself there and will send millions of colonists. If the Suez Canal assumes an importance as great as it has today when Italy has south of the Canal 250,000 soldiers, how much greater significance would it assume in case Mussolini had south of the Canal 2,500,000 people? The answer in my mind is definite. The Suez Canal would assume a political importance to Italy comparable to its importance to England, and considering the fact that the lease on the Canal ends in about thirty years and England's supposed control over it will terminate in that length of time, it would be the object of competition between the two Governments. It must be conceded that, in circumstances such as I have indicated, with a large Italian population in Ethiopia, it would be necessary to have direct communication with Italy.

An examination of the map will disclose a large Italian colony, Libya, running the entire length of Egypt and most of the length of the Sudan on their western borders. East of the Sudan is Eritrea. With the Italians in Ethiopia they will be also south of the Sudan. An alternative route of communication between the Italian East African colonies and the mother country can be established across the Sudan by joining Ethiopia with Libya. There is no doubt in my mind that shortly after Italy, should she become settled in Ethiopia, would begin a program to establish communications between Libya and Ethiopia. The oasis of Cufra in the southeastern part of Ethiopia has already been largely developed by the Italians as an air base. I shall always regret that when I visited Libya last spring an illness prevented me from accompanying Balbo on an air flight to the oasis of Cufra. But from what I saw and heard even though I was unable to visit Cufra or the other air bases of Italy, I became convinced that extensive preparations had been made in Libya to establish air communications and air bases both along the French border to the west of Libya and along the Egypto-Sudanese eastern border.

The Italian air fleet is only two and a half or three hours from its Sicilian base to Libya; from eastern Libya it is only a short distance by air to Cairo, Alexandria, and Port Said. There is a large Italian colony in Egypt . . . The Italian colony there is subject to a press propaganda similar to that carried on in Italy through the agency of an Italian newspaper there and other organized Fascist groups. It would be very easy for Italy to strike from two directions at the nerve centers at the control of Egypt, i. e., the three cities in the northern part of the country.

So that if you place Italy in control of Ethiopia you have a continuing threat to British control of Egypt and the Suez Canal and a continuing threat to the British Empire as regards its communications to the east. It is also equally true that Italian presence in Ethiopia would threaten British communications with the south by the Italian effort to join up Libya with Ethiopia across the Sudan.

Conclusion.

The inference I draw from it as to the future is that Italy must either be defeated now and prevented in the realization of her ambitions in East Africa, or the trouble will continue on through for a generation as an additional irritation to European politics and an additional menace to world peace. And if she is not defeated now it follows that we will have the menace of a highly organized and militarized state threatening the eastern Mediterranean and from its synchronized bases in Africa challenging the British Empire, with the turmoil it will bring from time to time into international politics through a period of years.

While I realize that this is all speculative, I think the possibilities have a bearing upon the present situation and that they may indicate what we may expect in the way of international relations for some time in the future.

Respectfully yours,

BRECKINRIDGE LONG

54

Press Releases, vol. XIII, p. 255

Statement by President Roosevelt, October 5, 1935

In view of the situation which has unhappily developed between Ethiopia and Italy, it has become my duty under the provisions of the joint resolution of Congress approved August 31, 1935, to issue, and I am today issuing, my proclamation making effective an embargo on the exportation from this country to Ethiopia and Italy of arms, ammunition, and implements of war. Notwithstanding the hope we entertained that war would be avoided, and the exertion of our influence in that direction, we are now compelled to recognize the simple and indisputable fact that Ethiopian and Italian armed forces are engaged in combat, thus creating a state of war within the intent and meaning of the joint resolution.

In these specific circumstances I desire it to be understood that any of our people who voluntarily engage in transactions of any character with either of the belligerents do so at their own risk.

55

765.84/1686

The Secretary of State to the United States Delegation at Geneva

[Telegram: Paraphrase]

[WASHINGTON,] October 9, 1935—9 p.m.

188. For the Minister. Your 325, October 9, 11 a.m. and Gilbert's 448, October 8, 4 p.m. Reports from you and other sources evidence an intention of the League to ask non-League countries to participate in the consideration of the problem of sanctions. We, of course, are not as qualified as others to know whether other non-member states are willing or unwilling to so participate. For ourselves it should be more and more clear that we have used all our influence and support for the preservation of peace; that now we take the position that we are determined that war shall not involve us; that in pursuance of this policy we will not overlook any possible step that would be consistent with our position.

Considering our policy as evidenced by what we have already done and said, with the complete support of American public opinion, we regard it advisable in every respect for the League to understand that definite measures have already been taken by the United States in accordance with our own limitations and policies; that these measures include long steps in restricting commercial and financial transactions with the belligerents; and that we desire to follow our course independently according as circumstances develop. Our course and attitude should be indicated by these measures. With this in mind, it would appear not only unnecessary but at this time inadvisable from the viewpoint of this government to invite us to join in any committee organized to consider sanctions.

It would be useful if you would inform orally and with great discretion the Secretary General and any other appropriate delegation of the sense of the above.

HULL

56

765.84/1847

The Secretary of State to the United States Delegation at Geneva

[Telegram]

[WASHINGTON,] October 17, 1935—6 p.m.

129. Your 508, October 15, 8 p.m. It is important that, if possible, daily newspaper rumors and reports from Europe about the attitude or policy of this Government toward some phase of the Italo-Ethiopian controversy, and especially reports that foreign governments or agencies are just about to inquire of this Government whether it can or will cooperate with foreign Governments or peace agencies in one way or another, shall be minimized to the greatest possible extent. My opinion is that you can anticipate most of these and head them off by casually and unofficially imparting all permissible information relative to our present and prospective course and attitude. Every leading official abroad knows that prior to the outbreak of the war our chief purpose was to aid in preserving peace, whereas after hostilities began our chief object is and will be to avoid being drawn into the war.

The lengthy succession of acts and utterances by this Government in an attempt to preserve peace should be well known in every foreign office and at Geneva. Our numerous steps taken after the outbreak of hostilities primarily and paramountly to keep out of the war, although incidentally and consciously calculated to be very helpful in discouraging a protracted war or a spread of the war, should likewise be well known abroad. This Government preceded others in declaring that a state of war exists, in enforcing embargo on arms, ammunition and implements of war, in refusing Government credit in support of trade transactions, in warning all Americans that any transactions of whatever nature with the belligerent countries would be at their own risk, and that Americans traveling on ships of the belligerent countries would do so at their own risk, and finally in my public statement of October 11 it was made certain that the influence and attitude of this Government under the foregoing policies was definitely to discourage any and all economic transactions between our nationals and those of the belligerent countries. The American public is making a satisfactory response to the policy thus indicated.

Subordinate to this major policy of not being involved in war, this Government is keeping thoroughly alive its definite conviction that it and all nations have a real interest in peace in every part of the world, and hence a special corresponding interest and obligation to contribute to the cause of peace in every practical way consistent with our well known foreign policy of non-involvement or entanglement. The numerous acts and utterances of this Government, both before and after the outbreak of hostilities, offer definite and clear index of the course and attitude of this Government relative to the Italo-Ethiopian controversy in the future.

Foreign Governments and peace agencies are familiar with the extent and limitation of statutory authority of this Government to deal with the various phases of the existing war situation. It must be clear to them by this time that this Government is acting upon its own initiative and proceeding separately and independently of all other Governments or peace organizations. It is also important to keep in mind that in some vital respects the policy of this Government to the extent based upon the discretion of the President is intended primarily to apply to the present specific Italo-Ethiopian situation rather than as an inflexible and permanent policy. The purpose is to meet and deal effectively with conditions and circumstances as they may arise. . . .

HULL

57

Press Releases, vol. XIII, p. 367

Radio Address [23] *of the Secretary of State, November 6, 1935*

Because of the generally unsettled world conditions, and the existence of hostilities between two powers with which we are on terms

---

[23] Delivered by the Under Secretary of State (Phillips).

of friendship, the one phase of our foreign policy uppermost in the minds of our people today is that of neutrality. It is being discussed from the platforms, in the press, and in the streets. It is of concern to our people in every walk of life. They have not forgotten the bitter experiences of the World War, the calamitous effects of which will not be erased from their memories during our present generation. Is it therefore any wonder that they should be concerned regarding our policy of neutrality and the steps that their Government is taking to avoid a repetition of those experiences?

Modern neutrality dates from the latter part of the Middle Ages. Prior to that time neutrality was unknown for the reason that belligerents did not recognize an attitude of impartiality on the part of other powers; under the laws of war observed by the most civilized nations of antiquity, the right of one nation to remain at peace while neighboring nations were at war was not admitted to exist. Efforts made by nations from time to time to adopt an attitude of impartiality were successfully resisted by the belligerents, who proceeded on the theory that any country not an ally was an enemy. No intermediate relation was known to the pagan nations of those earlier times, and hence the term "neutrality" did not exist.

During the sixteenth century, however, neutrality as a concept in international law began to be recognized. In 1625 Hugo Grotius, sometimes referred to as "the father of international law", published his celebrated treatise on the laws of peace and war. While his treatment of the subject of neutrality is brief and necessarily so because of the undeveloped status of the law of his time, he nevertheless recognized the possibility of third parties remaining neutral. He did not, however, have that conception of neutrality to which we have been accustomed in more recent times. He stated that it was the duty of those not engaged in a war "to do nothing whereby he who supports a wicked cause may be rendered more powerful, or whereby the movements of him who wages a just war may be hampered."

Since the days of Grotius, neutrality has passed through several stages of evolution. No nation has done more toward its development than has the United States. In 1794 Congress passed our first neutrality act, temporary in character, covering a variety of subjects. In 1818 permanent legislation on these subjects was passed. This legislation formed the basis of the British act of a similar character of 1819, known as the British Foreign Enlistment Act. Other legislation has been passed by Congress from time to time, including that enacted during the World War—I refer particularly to the act of June 15, 1917—and that enacted as recently as the last session of

Congress—the joint resolution approved August 31, 1935. This last-mentioned resolution, intended to supplement prior legislation, is designed primarily *to keep the United States out of foreign wars.*

Pursuant to this resolution the President has issued two proclamations regarding the war now unhappily existing between Ethiopia and Italy. One of these declared the existence of a state of war within the meaning and intent of section 1 of the resolution, thus bringing into operation the embargo on the shipment of arms, ammunition, and implements of war from the United States to either belligerent, and the other declared that American citizens who travel on vessels of the belligerents shall do so at their own risk.

The effect of issuing the proclamation bringing into operation the embargo on the shipment of arms was automatically to bring into operation the provisions of section 3 of the resolution prohibiting American vessels from carrying arms, ammunition, or implements of war to any port of a belligerent country named in the proclamation, or to any neutral port for transshipment to or for the use of the belligerent country.

Any discussion of the avoidance of war, or of the observance of neutrality in the event of war, would be wholly incomplete if too much stress were laid on the part played in the one or the other by the shipment, or the embargoing of the shipment, of arms, ammunition, and implements of war. The shipment of arms is not the only way and, in fact, is not the principal way by which our commerce with foreign nations may lead to serious international difficulties. To assume that by placing an embargo on arms we are making ourselves secure from dangers of conflict with belligerent countries is to close our eyes to manifold dangers in other directions. The imposition of an arms embargo is not a complete panacea, and we cannot assume that when provision has been made to stop the shipment of arms, which as absolute contraband have always been regarded as subject to seizure by a belligerent, we may complacently sit back with the feeling that we are secure from all danger. Attempts by a belligerent to exercise jurisdiction on the high seas over trade with its enemy, or with other neutral countries on the theory that the latter are supplying the enemy, may give rise to difficulties no less serious than those resulting from the exportation of arms and implements of war. So also transactions of any kind between American nationals and a belligerent may conceivably lead to difficulties of one kind or another between the nationals and that belligerent. Efforts of this Government to extend protection to these nationals might lead to difficulties between the United States and the belligerent. It was with these thoughts in mind that the President issued his timely warning that citizens of the United States who engage in transactions of any character with either belligerent would do so at their own risk.

Every war presents different circumstances and conditions which might have to be dealt with differently both as to time and manner. For these reasons, difficulties inherent in any effort to lay down by legislative enactment inelastic rules or regulations to be applied to every situation that may arise will at once be apparent. The Executive should not be unduly or unreasonably handicapped. There are a number of ways in which discretion could wisely be given the President which are not and could not be seriously controversial. These might well include discretion as to the time of imposing an embargo. Moreover, we should not concentrate entirely on means for remaining neutral and lose sight of other constructive methods of avoiding involvement in wars between other countries. Our foreign policy would indeed be a weak one if it began or ended with the announcement of a neutral position on the outbreak of a foreign war. I conceive it to be our duty and in the interest of our country and of humanity, not only to remain aloof from disputes and conflicts with which we have no direct concern, but also to use our influence in any appropriate way to bring about the peaceful settlement of international differences. Our own interest and our duty as a great power forbid that we shall sit idly by and watch the development of hostilities with a feeling of self-sufficiency and complacency when by the use of our influence, short of becoming involved in the dispute itself, we might prevent or lessen the scourge of war. In short, our policy as a member of the community of nations should be twofold: first, to avoid being brought into a war, and second, to promote as far as possible the interests of international peace and good will. A virile policy tempered with prudent caution is necessary if we are to retain the respect of other nations and at the same time hold our position of influence for peace and international stability in the family of nations.

In summary, while our primary aim should be to avoid involvement in other people's difficulties and hence to lessen our chances of being drawn into a war, we should, on appropriate occasions and within reasonable bounds, use our influence toward the prevention of war and the miseries that attend and follow in its wake. For after all, if peace obtains, problems regarding neutrality will not arise.

58

Press Releases, vol. XIII, p. 375

Address Delivered by President Roosevelt at Arlington National Cemetery, November 11, 1935

The living memory of the World War is close to each of us today. Our thoughts return to great objectives of the past, even as the minds of older men go back to their boyhood's ideals.

We Americans were so placed that we gained a perspective of the great world conflict that was perhaps clearer than that of our fellow men who were closer to the scene of battle. For most of the first 3 years of the war we were not participants; but during the final phase we ourselves engaged on many fronts.

For that reason perhaps we understood, as well as any, the cries that went up—that the world conflict should be made a war to end wars. We were not invaded nor were we threatened with invasion, then or later; but the very distance of our view led us to perceive the dire results of war through days of following peace.

The primary purpose of this Nation is to avoid being drawn into war. It seeks also in every practicable way to promote peace and to discourage war. Except for those few who have placed or who place temporary, selfish gain ahead of national or world peace, the overwhelming mass of American citizens are in hearty accord with these basic policies of our Government, as they are also entirely sympathetic with the efforts of other nations to end war.

That is why we too have striven with great consistency to approve steps to remove the causes of war and to disapprove steps taken by others to commit acts of aggression. We have either led or performed our full part in every important attempt to limit and to reduce armaments. We have sought by definite act and solemn commitment to establish the United States as a good neighbor among nations. We are acting to simplify definitions and facts by calling war "war" when armed invasion and a resulting killing of human beings take place.

But though our course is consistent and clear, it is with disappointment and sorrow that we confess that the world's gain thus far has been small.

I would not be frank with you if I did not tell you that the dangers that confront the future of mankind as a whole are greater to the world and therefore to us than the dangers which confront the people of the United States by and in themselves alone.

Jealousies between nations continue; armaments increase; national ambitions that disturb the world's peace are thrust forward. Most serious of all, international confidence in the sacredness of international contracts is on the wane.

The memory of our hopes of 1917 and 1918 dies with the death of those of us who took part. It is, therefore, your sacred obligation and mine, by conscious effort, to pass that memory on to succeeding generations. A new generation, even in its cradle or still unborn, is coming to the fore. The children in our schools, the young men and women passing through our colleges into productive life, have, unlike us, no direct knowledge of the meaning of war. They are not immune to the glamor of war, to the opportunities to escape from the drabness and worry of hard times at home in the glory and heroism of the arms factory and the battlefield. Fortunately there is evidence on every hand that the youth of America, as a whole, is not trapped by that delusion. They know that elation and prosperity which may come from a new war must lead—for those who survive it—to economic and social collapse more sweeping than any we have experienced in the past. While, therefore, we cannot and must not hide our concern for grave world dangers, and while, at the same time, we cannot build walls around ourselves and hide our heads in the sand, we must go forward with all our strength to stress and to strive for international peace.

In this effort America must and will protect herself. Under no circumstances will this policy of self-protection go to lengths beyond self-protection. Aggression on the part of the United States is an impossibility insofar as the present administration of your Government is concerned. Defense against aggression by others—adequate defense on land, on sea, and in air—is our accepted policy; and the measure of that defense is and will be solely the amount necessary to safeguard us against the armaments of others. The more greatly they decrease their armaments, the more quickly and surely shall we decrease ours.

In many other fields, by word and deed, we are giving example to the world by removing or lowering barriers which impede friendly intercourse. Our soldier and sailor dead call to us across the years to make our lives effective in building constructively for peace. It is fitting that on this Armistice Day I am privileged to tell you that between us and a great neighbor, another act cementing our historic friendship has been agreed upon and is being consummated. Between Canada and the United States exists a neighborliness, a genuine friendship, which for over a century has dispelled every passing rift.

Our two peoples, each independent in themselves, are closely knit by ties of blood and a common heritage; our standards of life are substantially the same; our commerce and our economic conditions rest upon the same foundations. Between two such peoples, if we would build constructively for peace and progress, the flow of intercourse should be mutually beneficial and not unduly hampered. Each has much to gain, by material profit and by increased employment, through the means of enlarged trade, one with the other.

I am, therefore, happy to be able to tell you on Armistice Day that the Canadian Prime Minister and I, after thoughtful discussion of our national problems, have reached a definite agreement which will eliminate disagreements and unreasonable restrictions, and thus work to the advantage of both Canada and the United States.

The power of good example is the strongest force in the world. It surpasses preachments; it excels good resolutions; it is better than agreements unfulfilled.

If we as a nation, by our good example, can contribute to the peaceful well-being of the fellowship of nations, our course through the years will not have been in vain.

We who survive have profited by the good example of our fellow Americans who gave their lives in war. On these surrounding hills of Virginia they rest—thousands upon thousands—in the last bivouac of the dead. Below us, across the river, we see a great Capital of a great Nation.

The past and the present unite in the prayer that America will ever seek the ways of peace, and by her example at home and abroad speed the return of good will among men.

59

740.00/40–½

The Minister in Switzerland (Wilson) to the Secretary of State

[Extract]

BERN, November 13, 1935.

DEAR MR. SECRETARY:

I have reported before, and the impression grows deeper as the days go by, that although Germany is not present at Geneva, none the less it is the concern regarding Germany which is decisively influencing the action of all the European member States today. The States of Europe, while fully realizing and apprehensive of the dangers inherent in Italy's present course, have no real fear of Italy; they are however profoundly afraid of Germany. Hence in their concerted action in the development of the collective idea on the Continent, in the application of sanctions and in their consideration of future eventualities, they are dominated by two thoughts: what will be the effect of such action on Germany and how will analogous action work against Germany when and if necessity calls for it? More than for a solution of the present problem, the setting into operation of the League machine seems to me a trial and test of strength for future possibilities. If I may so phrase it, we are attending a dress rehearsal in which the elements of the piece are carefully inspected for future production, and in which one of the most important props, the British navy in the Mediterranean, is also visible and under scrutiny.

Those who now believe that economic sanctions against Italy will be efficacious also believe, and rejoice thereat, that the machinery of Article 16 of the Covenant has been tried and not found wanting. They do not doubt that this action, if successful, will impress Hitler and that he will come to understand that while the States of Europe are reluctant to intervene in the internal affairs of any country, they will tolerate the existence of a dictator only while he keeps within his own boundaries and refrains from attempts to bully his neighbor. Thus, they contend, at the end of the Italian trouble Hitler should be in a frame of mind to negotiate Germany's international problems and negotiate them reasonably.

Respectfully yours,

HUGH R. WILSON

60

Press Releases, vol. XIII, p. 382

Statement by the Secretary of State, November 15, 1935

In view of the many inquiries that are being asked from time to time with respect to trade with Ethiopia and Italy, I deem it proper again to call attention to the statement by the President on October 5 that he desired it "to be understood that any of our people who voluntarily engage in transactions of any character with either of the belligerents do so at their own risk."

On October 10 I explained that the President's statement was based primarily upon the policy and purpose of keeping this country out of war, and that "it certainly was not intended to encourage transactions with the belligerents." I further explained that "our people might well realize that the universal state of business uncertainty and suspense on account of the war is seriously handicapping business between all countries, and that the sooner the war is terminated the sooner the restoration and stabilization of business in all parts of the world, which is infinitely more important than trade with the belligerents, will be brought about." The President, in a statement on October 30, further emphasized the spirit of this policy.

The American people are entitled to know that there are certain commodities such as oil, copper, trucks, tractors, scrap iron, and scrap steel which are essential war materials, although not actually "arms, ammunition, or implements of war", and that according to recent Government trade reports a considerably increased amount of these is being exported for war purposes. This class of trade is directly contrary to the policy of this Government as announced in official statements of the President and Secretary of State, as it is also contrary to the general spirit of the recent neutrality act.

The administration is closely observing the trend and volume of exports to those countries, and within a few days the Department of Commerce expects to have complete detailed lists of all commodities exported to the belligerents which will enable exact comparison with lists for the same period last year.

61

765.84/2747

Memorandum by the Secretary of State Regarding a Conversation With the Italian Ambassador (Rosso)

[WASHINGTON,] November 22, 1935.

The Italian Ambassador called by his own request and after some preliminary exchanges of the usual nature he said that he called upon instruction of his Government to lay before me two views which his Government supports; that he was not handing me a note or any other formal instrument of writing; that he had reduced to writing the oral conversation that he is proposing to conduct. The Ambassador thereupon proceeded to read to me the typewritten copy of his proposed oral conversation:

"1 – The various official declarations and public statements issued from the Federal Government during the last two months with regard to the Italo-Ethiopian conflict, and particularly the statement of the Secretary of State of November 15, cannot be interpreted otherwise than an extension and aggravation, to the principal detriment of Italy, of the meaning of the Neutrality Act of August 31, 1935.

"Although these declarations and statements apply, formally and theoretically, to both the contending parties, it is well known that their practical result would be actually to impair the freedom of trade only with respect to Italy.

"Such an assumption has been confirmed by the fact that the statement made by the Secretary of State on November 15 specifically mentions certain commodities which Italy has been used to buy in the United States and which, being largely employed for non military purposes, are essential to the needs of the economic and social life of any civilized country.

"We maintain that any measure or policy aiming at, or resulting in, imposing restrictions which actually are detrimental to only one of the contending parties, goes against the spirit of neutrality.

"2 – We maintain also that the above mentioned statement of the Secretary of State is contrary to the letter and the spirit of the Treaty signed between the United States and Italy in 1871—and still in force—which reciprocally guarantees each contracting party a 'complete freedom of commerce and navigation'.

"No justification whatsoever for the limitation of the freedom guaranteed by the Treaty can be found in any international Act dealing with the status of neutrals. Reference is made in this respect to the Hague Convention of 1907.

"Such a limitation, if and when applied, is bound to assume the meaning of a 'sanction' and therefore the positive character of an unfriendly act.

NOVEMBER 22, 1935."

The Ambassador paused briefly here and there in the course of the reading to elaborate with one or two sentences, but they did not change the purport of the instrument of writing. He then indicated his desire to answer any question or listen to any comment I might see fit to offer in case I desired to do so. I addressed the Ambassador and said that, of course, he and his Government should keep in mind all of the essential phases of the situation as it relates to this country; that in all of the past the most cordial and friendly relations have existed between the people of this country and those of Italy; that the people of this country today do not feel personally unfriendly towards the people of Italy, but that they are vigorously and almost wildly against war and are at all hazards in favor of keeping out of the present war; that, if those participating in the war were double cousins and twin brothers of the American people, the people of this country would be just as violently and eternally against the war and in favor of peace and, above all considerations, in favor of keeping away from and out of the war as would be possible. I said that it was in these circumstances and in this highly wrought up state of the public mind of this country that the Neutrality Act of last August was enacted and the Executive Department was directed to pursue the policy of neutrality which it provided; that this mandate of Congress was promptly put into effect when the President declared a state of war to exist between Ethiopia and Italy and declared an embargo on the shipment of arms, ammunition and implements of war to either of the belligerents; that at the time heavy pressure was brought to bear upon the State Department also to include a number of prime and essential war materials out of which finished arms, ammunition and implements of war might be made in large quantities over night; that since that time insistent demands representing large groups of sentiment in this country have been made upon the Executive Department to include these war materials in the embargo issued under the Neutrality Act against arms, ammunition and implements of war. I added, in this connection, that I hoped that the Ambassador and his Government would recall the experience of the people of this country in ways that will shed much light upon the state of mind and the viewpoint of the people and of this Government in accordance with it, and that is that our country sent 2,000,000 men to Europe to fight for Italy and other countries at an enormous cost to this Government and this country; that we likewise loaned Italy much money at the time and afterwards; that we later made almost a nominal settlement with the Italian Government at twenty-five cents on the dollar, all of which, with interest, is due and unpaid, to say nothing of other vast indebtedness in Europe; that I have been besought during past months to demand aggressively, if necessary, payment by the Italian Government of this indebtedness instead of its spending hundreds of millions in this Ethiopian conquest. I said that I had not done so thus far, but until this time I had been willing, on a suitable occasion, to sit down with the Ambassador and seek a satisfactory adjustment of the indebtedness. I then said that with the extremely disastrous and unsatisfactory experience of the American people in going to Europe and aiding Italy and other countries to the extent they did, they are almost wild in their demand that we not only avoid being drawn into the war but that we stay entirely away from the same; that the people of this country are in no state of mind to engage in any activities or steps except those primarily looking towards keeping out of the war and in a secondary or sub-

ordinate sense manifesting proper interest in peace and the short-
ening of the duration of the war in the light of our obligations under
the Kellogg Pact; that it is in this highly wrought up state of mind
of the American people that the Government of Italy now arraigns
this Government upon both a charge of unneutrality and of violating the provisions of the treaty between the United States and Italy
of 1871 pledging complete freedom of commerce and navigation. I
said that these are surprising as well as serious complaints in the
circumstances. I said I might remark here that from the outset
this Government has pursued its own separate, independent course
and initiative with respect to all phases of the controversy between
Ethiopia and Italy; that we have had no agreements whatsoever,
directly or indirectly, with Geneva or London or Paris; that they
did not know of any of the steps this Government had taken until
they read about the same in the press; that this Government believes
that it has been consistent in its course and policies and naturally
feels constrained to adhere to them; that the Government, as stated,
placed in operation its embargoes and at the same time the President warned all Americans against any business or economic contacts with any of the belligerents, except at their own risk. The
President and myself in public statements during the weeks that
followed made it clear that this warning statement of the President was intended, generally, to discourage any business or economic
relationships between our nationals and the belligerents; that nothing further was said by the President, myself or the Government
officials relative to business dealings with the belligerents until some
days ago when the official statistics showed that some five essential
war materials were being exported from this country to belligerents
in abnormal quantities compared with similar shipments during
any recent period, and that I thereupon made a further official statement, in which I said that this class of business was directly contrary to the policy of the Government in opposition to selling war
materials to belligerents, which policy was held and believed to
be strictly within the spirit of the Neutrality Act; that nothing
further has been said by the President or myself with respect to
trade relations between this country and the belligerents. I then
said that the Ambassador must realize that just as soon as the American people discovered that abnormal quantities of essential war
materials were being shipped on an increasing scale to belligerents
without protest but with the silent acquiescence of the proper Government officials, there would probably be a storm of criticism and
a loud demand for the immediate convening of Congress to take

adequate steps in the premises, and that the result scarcely beyond any question would be a swift passage of a drastic act dissolving every possible relationship with the belligerents pending the war. I repeatedly expressed surprise that the Italian Government would make a complaint against this Government in all the circumstances in the severe language that it does. I inquired whether and what the Italian Government had said to Germany in the light of a more sweeping and inflexible prohibition of business relations with the belligerents than this Government has taken. The Ambassador replied that he did not know whether his Government had made any representations to Germany. I commented rather emphatically and stated that I had seen no published account of any complaint whatsoever, and that it was therefore all the more strange to me to read this rather harsh complaint against this Government; that it seemed all the more surprising when both the Ambassador and I know that the bitterest critics of the Executive branch of the Government and the most extreme isolationists who are demanding that all Americans stay entirely away from the war zone do not in the slightest question the integrity of the neutrality policies of this Government as they are being carried out in accordance with the letter or the spirit, or both, of the Neutrality Act. I said that it was really astonishing to find that a government cannot be neutral without being attacked and a demand made to supply war materials to a belligerent under penalty of being charged with an unfriendly act. The Ambassador emphasized the view that the manner in which this Government is conducting its policy of neutrality operates as a discrimination against Italy. I replied that under the law of neutrality in the past any belligerent controlling the high seas was usually at an advantage over its enemy with respect to obtaining goods from neutral countries, that a poor belligerent without means of purchasing and paying for supplies from neutrals was at a disadvantage under the operation of neutrality laws, and likewise where one country has or can produce its military supplies and another is without such facilities or equipment, the latter suffers under the operation of the neutrality law. I then pointed out that, in fact, under the policy this Government is now pursuing neither Italy nor Ethiopia should be securing war materials with the result that both countries are as nearly on a parity in this respect as it is possible for them to be. The charge of discrimination, therefore, does not apply. I repeatedly inquired of the Ambassador why his Government does not sit down with others and work out this difficulty in a peaceful manner. He made very slight and casual comment in reply. The Ambassador sought to emphasize the idea that the attitude of his Government was not fully understood in this country and that it had been misrepresented to a considerable extent. I commented that his Government might well have thought of all of these and other unsatisfactory phases before getting into the war. I stated as emphatically as possible that these trading incidents to which the Italian Government refers and about which it complains are entirely trivial compared with the real problems and deep concern which the Ethiopian-Italian war causes this Government; that the Ambassador must realize the awful repercussions that make their immediate appearance in far and remote parts of the world, but which are calculated to give this nation and perhaps others, including Italy, unimaginable troubles for a generation. The Ambassador immediately indicated that he knew the Far East was in mind. I added that the second condition which is giving this Government immense concern relates to the possible spread of the war to any number of other countries at almost any time with unimaginable troubles and injuries and consequences to this country as well as others; that it is, therefore, all the more deplorable to see the Italian nation moving forward with the war, which it must realize threatens to create these terrific problems and conditions so far-reaching that the imagination cannot grasp their possibilities. I inquired why these considerations were not in the mind of the Italian Government before it went into the war and again reiterated my surprise that the Italian Government, on the contrary, is upbraiding this Government virtually because it is thus so deeply concerned and is striving in every possible way to keep entirely away from and out of the war. I remarked then that the Ambassador well recalls that the President and I pleaded with and almost prayed with Mr. Mussolini to keep out of the war but that he ignored our plea and now seems to expect us to furnish him with war supplies while he prosecutes the war ad libitum. I added that regardless of anything or anybody this nation proposed to stay out of and as far away from the war as possible, and that we feel most deeply the indifference with which the world is subjected to the threat of a general war and with the frightful repercussions in the Far East; that this Government is keeping its attitude flexible under the Neutrality Act and the spirit of that Act which is being carried out in connection with the policy of opposition to the supplying of certain war materials to the belligerents; that if the war should spread, for example, this Government will be in an attitude to take further steps relative to both miscellaneous trade and the five war materials which I recently referred to in a statement opposing their shipment to the belligerents; that this Government cannot think of any course or any precautionary plans short of these, in view of the fact that aeroplane bases, naval bases and submarine bases dot the entire Mediterranean section with the result that almost at any time a conflagration might be touched off; that it is in the light of these dangerous possibilities, which to the American people seem to be probabilities, that this country is almost madly opposed to our Government taking the slightest risk of being drawn into the war by permitting its nationals to trade promiscuously with belligerents in and about this dangerous war zone, especially in essential war materials. I stated that during the past three years I had almost worn myself out physically in an effort to aid in world economic rehabilitation so that Italy and other countries would have an adequate amount of international trade to afford contentment to their respective populations, and that the Ambassador could not begin to imagine the deep disappointment I feel at the effort to renew the practice which all nations have recently undertaken to abandon, relating to that of military aggression by any and all countries at any and all times, and that, of course, if one country is to be allowed to violate this new policy of the pacific settlement of disputes, then every country may do so with consequences that one shudders to contemplate. I pointed out to the Ambassador the fact that the League of Nations organization at Geneva solemnly adjudged an aggressor in this war, while the United States did not; that the Geneva agency seeks to aid Ethiopia, which the United States does not; that the Geneva agency seeks to embargo all imports from Italy, which this Government does not; that this Government, as stated, is pursuing its own separate course without understanding or collaboration with other governments or peace agencies, and that in these circumstances it is not only difficult to understand the Italian complaint but I repeat that it is surprising to contemplate it; that the mere fact that there are some concurring acts on the part of the League of Nations in pursuing sanctions and of the United States in frankly carrying out its policy of neutrality is, in the circumstances, no basis whatever for a charge against the United States of unneutrality and of unfriendliness. This makes a mere coincidence or its absence determine the question of whether the United States is or is not neutral, in the eyes of the Italian Government. In other words, if there were no attempted sanctions at Geneva the United States would be entirely neutral in carrying out its present policies of opposing the sale of war materials to belligerents. I added that when I issued my statement on the 15th of November, about which complaint is now made, I did not know and, in my opinion, no one here knows yet what the League of Nations may or may not do regarding concerted action to curb exports to Italy of oil and other prime war materials, and yet here is a charge that this Government is engaged in an unfriendly act as stated. The Ambassador said that this step, in his opinion, would be taken on the 28th of this month at Geneva. I commented that, of course, that remains to be seen. I inquired of the Ambassador why his Government had not taken $100,000,000 to Ethiopia and brought back a key to the entire Empire instead of expending several hundred million dollars in its military conquest with all of the worry and threat of danger to the balance of the world. He replied that Italy had been attempting for forty years to effect colonizations in Ethiopia, but without success. I repeated that the people of this country are as yet entirely friendly to the Italian people but added that if his note should be made public in the United States, an inflamed public that nobody could control or curb would be almost instantly aroused and that, of course, the pressure of a surprising charge such as he is bringing against this Government will in due time make the American people personally hostile to the people of Italy, and naturally it would endure long in their minds. I took up the complaint of violation by this Government of the treaty of freedom of commerce and navigation of 1871 with Italy and at once stated that I was satisfied that international and all other law makes it possible for either country a party to this commercial treaty to remain neutral in the event the other country becomes involved in war; that it is inconceivable that either Italy or the United States in an ordinary commercial treaty signed away its right to remain neutral in case of war on the part of the other and that that is the precise reason this Government is undertaking to pursue and has no other idea than to pursue it; that, furthermore, with both Italy and America signatories of the Paris Peace Pact with the solemn obligations it imposes upon each, it is not possible to understand how Italy can go to war and announce to the United States Government that despite the Paris Pact it must supply Italy with materials of war under penalty of being guilty of an unfriendly act, as stated. I remarked further, without discussing the merits, that the American people cannot be convinced that the Italian Government is not under most solemn obligations to keep the peace under three or four treaties, and it is incomprehensible to them to find Italy demanding of this Government that to be neutral it must furnish war supplies and that if it fails to do so it is guilty of an unfriendly act. I repeatedly emphasized my great surprise and incomprehension and repeatedly inquired why his Government had not thought of these phases before it went into the war. I finally said that, while entirely satisfied as to the lack of interference of the treaty of 1871 with the present course of this Government, I would, as a matter of courtesy to the Ambassador, again give some further attention to the authorities, although I have no doubt that I have examined them fully and accurately. The Ambassador did not attempt any aggressive utterances and I endeavored throughout the conversation to make the impression upon him that our nation and most other peace loving nations were greatly pained and hurt to find their traditional friends, the Italian people, involved in this war despite the numerous treaties of peace to which the Government is a party, and despite the awful menace to the peace of the world which this war creates.

C[ORDELL] H[ULL]

62

Press Releases, vol. XIII, p. 487

Statement by the Secretary of State, December 5, 1935

In reply to inquiries by press correspondents regarding the "autonomy movement" in North China, Chinese and Japanese activities in relation thereto, and the American Government's attitude, the Secretary of State said:

"There is going on in and with regard to North China a political struggle which is unusual in character and which may have far-reaching effects. The persons mentioned in reports of it are many; the action is rapid and covers a large area; opinions with regard to it vary; what may come of it no one could safely undertake to say; but, whatever the origin, whoever the agents, be what they may the methods, the fact stands out that an effort is being made—and is being resisted— to bring about a substantial change in the political status and condition of several of China's northern Provinces.

"Unusual developments in any part of China are rightfully and necessarily of concern not alone to the Government and people of China but to all of the many powers which have interests in China. For, in relations with China and in China, the treaty rights and the treaty obligations of the 'treaty powers' are in general identical. The United States is one of those powers.

"In the area under reference the interests of the United States are similar to those of other powers. In that area there are located, and our rights and obligations appertain to, a considerable number of American nationals, some American property, and substantial American commercial and cultural activities. The American Government is therefore closely observing what is happening there.

"Political disturbances and pressures give rise to uncertainty and misgiving and tend to produce economic and social dislocations. They make difficult the enjoyment of treaty rights and the fulfillment of treaty obligations.

"The views of the American Government with regard to such matters, not alone in relation to China but in relation to the whole world, are well known. As I have stated on many occasions, it seems to this Government most important in this period of world-wide political unrest and economic instability that governments and peoples keep faith in principles and pledges. In international relations there must be agreements and respect for agreements in order that there may be the confidence and stability and sense of security which are essential to orderly life and progress. This country has abiding faith in the fundamental principles of its traditional policy. This Government adheres to the provisions of the treaties to which it is a party and continues to bespeak respect by all nations for the provisions of treaties solemnly entered into for the purpose of facilitating and regulating, to reciprocal and common advantage, the contacts between and among the countries signatory."

63

794.00/91

Memorandum [24] *by the First Secretary of the United States Embassy In Japan* (*Dickover*)

[TOKYO,] December 23, 1935.

In the course of an extended conversation last evening, Mr. Kurusu [25] said that foreign countries were criticizing the Japanese people for the part Japan was playing in China, but that foreign peoples did not understand what it was all about. . . .

---

[24] Enclosure in despatch 1607 of December 27, 1935 from the Embassy in Japan.

[25] Mr. Saburo Kurusu, Chief of the Bureau of Commercial Affairs, Japanese Foreign Office.

. . . He said that Japan was destined to be the leader of the Oriental civilization and would in course of time be the "boss" of a group comprising China, India, the Netherlands East Indies, etc. (Mr. Kurusu did not say that Japan would conquer and rule these countries, but that Japan would be the "boss". When speaking informally with friends, he uses very colloquial English.) He proceeded to say that the United States will lead the Americas, both North and South. Great Britain is leading the European countries, but Great Britain is degenerating, while the rest of Europe is decadent. Therefore it will end by the United States leading the Occidental civilization, while Japan leads the Oriental civilization.

I asked where Soviet Russia came into the picture. Mr. Kurusu said that the Russians were dreamers and never would "amount to anything". Japan will in the future have its sphere in the Orient, the United States in the Americas, and Great Britain in Europe, Africa and Australia, but the two big nations, the real leaders, will be Japan in the Orient and the United States in the Occident.

I asked Mr. Kurusu how he reconciled this theory with the treaties for collective security which Japan had signed. Mr. Kurusu said that he had always been opposed to Japan's hypocritical attitude toward such things. He said that he had just recently made a speech before a society for the study of international affairs, criticizing his own country for signing agreements which could not be carried out if Japan wanted to progress in this world.

Mr. Kurusu then went on to say that while Japan might lead the Orient and the United States the Occident, they must not fight, as that would be suicidal. They must find some means of getting together. I asked him if he thought that the League of Nations might not be the seed of some sort of future conciliatory medium. He said that it might be, but that the League was too narrow, as it looked to maintaining the *status quo*, whereas nations are not static—they are born, grow up and gradually die. I quoted from Wells' "Outline of History" (first paragraph of Chapter 34) to show that Wells had the same idea. Mr. Kurusu agreed with Wells entirely, and said that he thought that the United States and Japan could work out the solution themselves in time, as both countries were much alike—active, progressive and sensible.

E. R. D[ICKOVER]

64

Press Releases, vol. XIV, p. 11

Address Delivered by President Roosevelt Before the Congress, January 3, 1936

[Extract]

We are about to enter upon another year of the responsibility which the electorate of the United States has placed in our hands. Having come so far, it is fitting that we should pause to survey the ground which we have covered and the path which lies ahead.

On the 4th day of March 1933, on the occasion of taking the oath of office as President of the United States, I addressed the people of our country. Need I recall either the scene or the national circumstances attending the occasion? The crisis of that moment was almost exclusively a national one. In recognition of that fact, so obvious to the millions in the streets and in the homes of America, I devoted by far the greater part of that address to what I called, and the Nation called, critical days within our own borders.

You will remember that on that 4th of March 1933, the world picture was an image of substantial peace. International consultation and wide-spread hope for the bettering of relations between the nations gave to all of us a reasonable expectation that the barriers to mutual confidence, to increased trade, and to the peaceful settlement of disputes could be progressively removed. In fact, my only reference to the field of world policy in that address was in these words: "I would dedicate this Nation to the policy of the good neighbor—the neighbor who resolutely respects himself and, because he does so, respects the rights of others—the neighbor who respects his obligations and respects the sanctity of his agreements in and with a world of neighbors."

In the years that have followed, that sentiment has remained the dedication of this Nation. Among the nations of the great Western Hemisphere the policy of the "good neighbor" has happily prevailed. At no time in the 4½ centuries of modern civilization in the Americas has there existed—in any year, any decade, or any generation in all that time—a greater spirit of mutual understanding, of common helpfulness, and of devotion to the ideals of self-government than exists today in the 21 American republics and their neighbor, the Dominion of Canada. This policy of the "good neighbor" among the Americas is no longer a hope—no longer an objective remaining to be accomplished—it is a fact, active, present, pertinent, and effective.

In this achievement, every American nation takes an understanding part. There is neither war, nor rumor of war, nor desire for war. The inhabitants of this vast area, 250 million strong, spreading more than 8,000 miles from the Arctic to the Antarctic, believe in, and propose to follow, the policy of the "good neighbor". They wish with all their heart that the rest of the world might do likewise.

The rest of the world—ah! there is the rub.

Were I today to deliver an inaugural address to the people of the United States, I could not limit my comments on world affairs to one paragraph. With much regret I should be compelled to devote the greater part to world affairs. Since the summer of that same year of 1933, the temper and the purposes of the rulers of many of the great populations in Europe and in Asia have not pointed the way either to peace or to good will among men. Not only have peace and good will among men grown more remote in those areas of the earth during this period, but a point has been reached where the people of the Americas must take cognizance of growing ill will, of marked trends toward aggression, of increasing armaments, of shortened tempers—a situation which has in it many of the elements that lead to the tragedy of general war.

On those other continents many nations, principally the smaller ones, if left to themselves, would be content with their boundaries and willing to solve within themselves and in cooperation with their neighbors their individual problems, both economic and social. The rulers of those nations, deep in their hearts, follow these peaceful and reasonable aspirations of their peoples. These rulers must remain ever vigilant against the possibility today or tomorrow of invasion or attack by the rulers of other peoples who fail to subscribe to the principles of bettering the human race by peaceful means.

Within those other nations—those which today must bear the primary, definite responsibility for jeopardizing world peace—what hope lies? To say the least, there are grounds for pessimism. It is idle for us or for others to preach that the masses of the people who constitute those nations which are dominated by the twin spirits of autocracy and aggression, are out of sympathy with their rulers, that they are allowed no opportunity to express themselves, that they would change things if they could.

That, unfortunately, is not so clear. It might be true that the masses of the people in those nations would change the policies of their governments if they could be allowed full freedom and full access to the processes of democratic government as we understand them. But they do not have that access: lacking it, they follow blindly and fervently the lead of those who seek autocratic power.

Nations seeking expansion, seeking the rectification of injustices springing from former wars, or seeking outlets for trade, for population, or even for their own peaceful contributions to the progress of civilization, fail to demonstrate that patience necessary to attain reasonable and legitimate objectives by peaceful negotiation or by an appeal to the finer instincts of world justice. They have therefore impatiently reverted to the old belief in the law of the sword, or to the fantastic conception that they, and they alone, are chosen to fulfill a mission and that all the others among the billion and a half of human beings must and shall learn from and be subject to them.

I recognize that these words which I have chosen with deliberation will not prove popular in any nation that chooses to fit this shoe to its foot. Such sentiments, however, will find sympathy and understanding in those nations where the people themselves are honestly desirous of peace but must constantly aline themselves on one side or the other in the kaleidoscopic jockeying for position characteristic of European and Asiatic relations today. For the peace-loving nations, and there are many of them, find that their very identity depends on their moving and moving again on the chessboard of international politics.

I suggested in the spring of 1933 that 85 or 90 percent of all the people in the world were content with the territorial limits of their respective nations and were willing further to reduce their armed forces if every other nation in the world would agree to do likewise.

That is equally true today, and it is even more true today that world peace and world good will are blocked by only 10 or 15 percent of the world's population. That is why efforts to reduce armies have thus far not only failed but have been met by vastly increased armaments on land and in the air. That is why even efforts to continue the existing limits on naval armaments into the years to come show such little current success.

But the policy of the United States has been clear and consistent. We have sought with earnestness in every possible way to limit world armaments and to attain the peaceful solution of disputes among all nations.

We have sought by every legitimate means to exert our moral influence against repression, discrimination, intolerance, and autocracy and in favor of freedom of expression, equality before the law, religious tolerance, and popular rule.

In the field of commerce we have undertaken to encourage a more reasonable interchange of the world's goods. In the field of international finance we have, so far as we are concerned, put an end to "dollar diplomacy", money grabbing, and speculation for the benefit of the powerful and rich, at the expense of the small and the poor.

As a consistent part of a clear policy, the United States is following a twofold neutrality toward any and all nations which engage in wars not of immediate concern to the Americas: First, we decline to encourage the prosecution of war by permitting belligerents to obtain arms, ammunition, or implements of war from the United States; second, we seek to discourage the use by belligerent nations of any and all American products calculated to facilitate the prosecution of a war in quantities over and above our normal exports to them in time of peace.[26]

I trust that these objectives, thus clearly and unequivocally stated, will be carried forward by cooperation between this Congress and the President.

I realize that I have emphasized to you the gravity of the situation which confronts the people of the world. This emphasis is justified because of its importance to civilization and therefore to the United States. Peace is jeopardized by the few and not by the many. Peace is threatened by those who seek selfish power. The world has witnessed similar eras—as in the days when petty kings and feudal barons were changing the map of Europe every fortnight, or when great emperors and great kings were engaged in a mad scramble for colonial empire.

We hope that we are not again at the threshold of such an era. But if face it we must, then the United States and the rest of the Americas can play but one role: through a well-ordered neutrality, to do naught to encourage the contest; through adequate defense, to save ourselves from embroilment and attack; and through example and all legitimate encouragement and assistance, to persuade other nations to return to the ways of peace and good will.

---

[26] In line with the policy enunciated in this sentence a "neutrality" bill containing such a provision was introduced in Congress in January 1936. This proposal was supported by Secretary Hull in testimony before the Senate Committee on Foreign Relations. (Neutrality, Hearings before the Committee on Foreign Relations, United States Senate, 74th Cong., 2d sess., on S. 3474, January 19 to February 5, 1936.)

65

611.41131/140

Memorandum by the Secretary of State Regarding a Conversation With the British Ambassador (Lindsay)

[Extract]

[WASHINGTON,] January 22, 1936.

I emphasized the view that . . . the most incomprehensible circumstance in the whole modern world is the ability of dictators, overnight almost, to stand 35 million Italians and 65 million Germans on their heads and so dominate their mental processes that they arise the next morning and insist on being sent to the first-line trenches without delay.

C[ORDELL] H[ULL]

66

740.00/41–½

The Minister in Switzerland (Wilson) to the Secretary of State

[Extracts]

BERN, January 27, 1936.

DEAR MR. SECRETARY:

The Council session has reached a satisfactory termination with creditable work done in certain items of the agenda. However, the most interesting feature of the session was the revelation of an evolution in the concern with which different questions are regarded. Three months ago the thoughts of the statesmen of Europe were concentrated on Africa; the Abyssinian question was paramount. A month ago a phase of that question, namely the military situation in the Eastern Mediterranean, was the focus of all thought. Today a further evolution has fixed the minds of these men on the intensity of the rearmament of Germany, leading to the realization of the implications throughout the whole of Europe of the return of Germany as a first class military power.

Representations of Great Britain have brought about undertakings in respect to assistance from the Mediterranean Powers which, together with Britain's vigorous military effort, have taken the edge off the apprehension with which a number of Britishers regarded the threat to their strategic position in Egypt and the possibility of an assault by Mussolini. They believe now that time is working for

308

them. They believe that however stout an effort the Italians are making from a military point of view, nevertheless this effort is exceedingly costly, and that the sanctions already in effect are rapidly curtailing Italy's resources and ability to maintain the present effort. Hence they can turn their minds to the question of German rearmament, a question which causes them more profound concern—if not more immediate concern—than a threat by Mussolini.

I cannot conceal from myself the belief that the actual application of an embargo on petroleum by the League States will be dependent largely upon the decision of the United States Congress in respect to the Neutrality legislation. I hope that no step will be taken here which will make the League's action appear to be openly dependent upon ours. A number of the men influential in this matter are convinced that it would be a mistake to do so. Nevertheless, I doubt whether the embargo will be applied by the League States unless they feel that in some way the supply from the United States will not replace that which they cut off. The reverse also appears true. If the United States curtails its shipments, the States of the League will feel it not only expedient, but morally imperative to put on the embargo. Since sending you my cables Nos. 363 and 364, Vasconcellos, the President of the Committee of Eighteen, has come to see me. He believes that while Eden's methods may seem less aggressive, his determination in respect to sanctions has not diminished. I need not recapitulate the arguments for the necessity of the establishment of the oil sanction. Suffice it to say that in the minds of most of the Delegates, it is the test of strength between the League of Nations and Mussolini and must be established as a precedent for use against Germany, if necessity arises.

The extension of the idea of collectivity into a series of military guarantees against the risk involved in the application of sanctions is the most recent step in increasing pressure against the aggressor. It is of the highest importance and cannot fail profoundly to affect the future relationships and political development of Europe. You will remember that Aloisi termed such action a military alliance against Italy in the Mediterranean, and deplored the fact that the League of Nations could be led by England to assume this shape. Germans who have talked to me during this session take an analogous position. They point out that nobody hides the fact that the present action against Italy is in the nature of a rehearsal for action against Germany. They feel convinced that once it has been proved that the League can take the form of a military alliance, the threat of that alliance will be used as a means of coercion against Germany, after this Italian question is liquidated. They recognize that though the phrases used are against Italy, the instrument itself is being forged for eventual use against their own country. Hence the Italians and the Germans are inspired by like apprehension and by like mistrust of what they both deem to be a form of coercion. This in contrast to the League conception, namely, that the military agreements are precautionary only against possible Italian retaliation.

As to whether this manifestation of force in regard to Italy, together with the possibility of such a manifestation in respect to Germany will be effective in bringing Germany to a mood of negotiation is a question of psychological appreciation. Certainly Paul Scheffer of the BERLINER TAGEBLATT, a believer in international co-operative action, makes no secret of his conviction that what he calls a threat of force will have results on Germany completely the opposite of what it is designed to effect. The overwhelming opinion of the representatives of other States here is, however, to the contrary and we can only hope that the future will show that they are right.

There is indisputable evidence of the magnitude and intensity of the German effort in military preparation. There may be question as to the exact stage of the development of this preparation but there is no doubt that it is on a scale to cause alarm and that it proceeds with a rapidity which none of the democratic States can equal. The ability of a dictator to devote practically the entire resources of his country to armament cannot be matched by democratic countries in times of peace. Rightly or wrongly, the idea is becoming prevalent that German rearmament on this scale and in this tempo can be designed only for the purposes of aggression. I believe that in making this statement I am reflecting the profound conviction of most of the statesmen on this Continent.

It seems to be generally believed that there will be no German aggression towards the west. Germany will presumably make every effort not to give Great Britain apprehension as to the Low Countries. Her present policy is predicated on not giving offense to Great Britain. Many French themselves appear to believe that they need fear no attack on their eastern frontier or through Belgium and Holland. If Germany does contemplate aggression, it is generally expected that it will be to the east or down the Danube.

I have gone into this speculation, Mr. Secretary, with no desire to be alarming but because it is a reflection of the type of thought that is occupying the minds of those on the Council. It is the type of thought that has led to a feeling of apprehension which has brought about the conviction that only by an agreement with Germany, both of a political nature and for the limitation of armaments, can a cataclysm be avoided. It is a time in which wisdom and statesmanship are needed on this Continent as never since the end of the War.

I am, my dear Mr. Secretary,

Respectfully yours,

HUGH R. WILSON

67

Press Releases, vol. XIV, p. 162

President Roosevelt to the President of the Argentine Republic (Justo) [27]

THE WHITE HOUSE, January 30, 1936.

MY DEAR MR. PRESIDENT:

The agreement by the Governments of Bolivia and Paraguay upon the peace protocols recently negotiated at Buenos Aires has afforded the Government and people of the United States the deepest gratification, since it has led them to hope that there is now every prospect of a permanent and equitable solution of this tragic controversy, which has continued for so long a period; which has caused the sacrifice of so many lives; and which has placed so crushing a burden of expenditure upon the citizens of the two belligerent nations. I know well with what intimate concern the Government and people of Argentina have followed the course of these hostilities, and their happiness at the termination of the conflict is fully shared by the Government and people of the United States.

I cherish the sincere conviction that the moment has now arrived when the American Republics, through their designated representatives seated at a common council table, should seize this altogether favorable opportunity to consider their joint responsibility and their common need of rendering less likely in the future the outbreak or the continuation of hostilities between them, and by so doing, serve in an eminently practical manner the cause of permanent peace on this Western Continent. If the tragedy of the Chaco can be consid-

---

[27] Practically identical letters were sent at the same time to the Presidents of the other American republics.

ered as having served any useful end, I believe such end will lie in our joint willingness to profit from the experience learned and to exert our common endeavors in guarding against the repetition of such American disasters.

It has seemed to me that the American Governments might for these reasons view favorably the suggestion that an extraordinary inter-American conference be summoned to assemble at an early date, at Buenos Aires, should the Government of the Argentine Republic so desire, or, if not, at some other capital of this Continent, to determine how the maintenance of peace among the American Republics may best be safeguarded—whether, perhaps, through the prompt ratification of all of the inter-American peace instruments already negotiated; whether through the amendment of existing peace instruments in such manner as experience has demonstrated to be most necessary; or perhaps through the creation by common accord of new instruments of peace additional to those already formulated.

These steps, furthermore, would advance the cause of world peace, inasmuch as the agreements which might be reached would supplement and reinforce the efforts of the League of Nations and of all other existing or future peace agencies in seeking to prevent war.

With the conclusion of the Chaco War and with the reestablishment of peace throughout this Continent, there would appear to be offered an opportunity for helpful counsel among our respective governments which may not soon again be presented. Your Excellency's devotion to the maintenance of peace between the American Republics is well known, and I would therefore deeply appreciate such views as Your Excellency may care to express to me, as I would likewise value highly Your Excellency's opinion whether such a special inter-American conference of the American Republics would not in fact prove most beneficial.

I am addressing myself thus personally to Your Excellency, instead of through the usual diplomatic channels, because of my thought that the questions at issue are of such vital concern to the people of this Continent as to warrant a personal interchange of views between the Presidents of the American Republics.

With the expression of my warm regard, believe me, my dear Mr. President,

Faithfully yours,

FRANKLIN D. ROOSEVELT

68

49 Stat. 1152 ; 22 U. S. C. 441 note

"Neutrality Act" of February 29, 1936

JOINT RESOLUTION

Extending and amending the joint resolution (Public Resolution Numbered 67, Seventy-fourth Congress), approved August 31, 1935.

Resolved by the Senate and House of Representatives of the United States of America in Congress assembled, That section 1 of the joint resolution (Public Resolution Numbered 67, Seventy-fourth Congress) approved August 31, 1935, be, and the same hereby is, amended by striking out in the first section, on the second line, after the word "assembled" the following words: "That upon the outbreak or during the progress of war between", and inserting therefor the words: "Whenever the President shall find that there exists a state of war between"; and by striking out the word "may" after the word "President" and before the word "from" in the twelfth line, and inserting in lieu thereof the word "shall"; and by substituting for the last paragraph of said section the following paragraph: "except with respect to offenses committed, or forfeitures incurred prior to May 1, 1937, this section and all proclamations issued thereunder shall not be effective after May 1, 1937."

SEC. 2. There are hereby added to said joint resolution two new sections, to be known as sections 1a and 1b, reading as follows:

"SEC. 1a. Whenever the President shall have issued his proclamation as provided for in section 1 of this Act, it shall thereafter during the period of the war be unlawful for any person within the United States to purchase, sell, or exchange bonds, securities, or other obligations of the government of any belligerent country, or of any political subdivision thereof, or of any person acting for or on behalf of such government, issued after the date of such proclamation, or to make any loan or extend any credit to any such government or person: *Provided,* That if the President shall find that such action will serve to protect the commercial or other interests of the United States or its nationals, he may, in his discretion, and to such extent and under such regulation as he may prescribe, except from the operation of this section ordinary commercial credits and short-time obligations in aid of legal transactions and of a character customarily used in normal peace-time commercial transactions.

"The provisions of this section shall not apply to a renewal or adjustment of such indebtedness as may exist on the date of the President's proclamation.

"Whoever shall violate the provisions of this section or of any regulations issued hereunder shall, upon conviction thereof, be fined not more than $50,000 or imprisoned for not more than five years, or both. Should the violation be by a corporation, organization, or association, each officer or agent thereof participating in the violation may be liable to the penalty herein prescribed.

"When the President shall have revoked his proclamation as provided for in section 1 of this Act, the provisions of this section and of any regulations issued by the President hereunder shall thereupon cease to apply.

"SEC. 1b. This Act shall not apply to an American republic or republics engaged in war against a non-American state or states, provided the American republic is not cooperating with a non-American state or states in such war."

SEC. 3. Section 9 of said joint resolution is amended to read as follows:

"There is hereby authorized to be appropriated from time to time, out of any money in the Treasury not otherwise appropriated, such amounts as may be necessary to carry out the provisions and accomplish the purposes of this Act."

Approved, February 29, 1936.

69

Press Releases, vol. XIV, p. 197

Statement by President Roosevelt, February 29, 1936

By the resolution approved August 31, 1935, a definite step was taken toward enabling this country to maintain its neutrality and avoid being drawn into wars involving other nations. It provided that in the event of the Executive proclaiming the existence of such a war, thereupon an embargo would attach to the exportation of arms, ammunition, and implements of war destined to any belligerent country. It also authorized the Executive to warn citizens of this country against traveling as passengers on the vessels of any belligerent except at their own risk.

By the resolution I have just signed, the operation of the August resolution is extended and strengthened until May 1, 1937. A new and definite step is taken by providing in substance that, when an embargo becomes effective, obligations of any belligerent government issued after the date of the proclamation shall not be purchased or sold in this country, and no loan or credit extended to such government, but with authority to the Executive, if our interests require, to except from the prohibition commercial credits and short-time loans in aid of legal transactions. In addition, it in general exempts the other republics of this hemisphere from the operation of the law.

Following the August enactment promptly on October 5, 1935, I issued a proclamation which made effective the embargo with respect to exportations to Italy and Ethiopia, and I have now issued a new proclamation in order to meet the requirements of the new enactment.

The policies announced by the Secretary of State and myself at the time of and subsequent to the issuance of the original proclamation will be maintained in effect. It is true that the high moral duty I have urged on our people of restricting their exports of essential war materials to either belligerent to approximately the normal peacetime basis has not been the subject of legislation. Nevertheless, it is clear to me that greatly to exceed that basis, with the result of earning profits not possible during peace, and especially with the result of giving actual assistance to the carrying on of war, would serve to magnify the very evil of war which we seek to prevent. This being my view, I renew the appeal made last October to the American people that they so conduct their trade with belligerent nations that it cannot be said that they are seizing new opportunities for profit or that by changing their peacetime trade they give aid to the continuation of war.

70

President Roosevelt to Mrs. William A. Becker, President General, Daughters of the American Revolution [28]

APRIL 20, 1936.

MY DEAR MRS. BECKER:

I had looked forward with pleasure to the opportunity to appear this year before the 45th annual Continental Congress of the Daughters of the American Revolution. You will understand, I am sure, why that is not now possible. I shall be grateful, however, if you will extend my cordial greetings to the officers and delegates assembled.

This Administration, as you know, stands for adequate national defense. It stands, also, for the policy of the good neighbor. These are not contradictory principles. As they are followed by this Administration they represent an expression of the purpose of peace.

---

[28] *The Public Papers and Addresses of Franklin D. Roosevelt* (New York, Random House, 1938), vol. 5, p. 173.

There is much confusion of thought and some unnecessary apprehension on this matter of national defense. There are sincere and patriotic people who have been led to believe that our military and naval establishments are inferior and inadequate. That, so stated, is a totally wrong conclusion. It has been the aim of this Administration to make our national defense efficient and to keep it adequate. Today our defense forces are on a stronger peace-time basis than before. It is our purpose to keep them that way.

There are other equally sincere and patriotic people who look upon our system of national defense as much too large for our needs; an unnecessary expense, a threat, perhaps, to peace. That, too, is a totally wrong conclusion. When we say adequate defense we mean just that. The prospect of a war of aggression has no place in our American policy. It has no place in our military or naval program. We are maintaining a system that will meet our defensive needs. We have no plans for any other kind of system.

Americans generally will agree that some measure of preparedness for defense is necessary. They disagree as to how much is necessary. The policy of the Government on that point is determined by several factors. First of all, it is determined by a very common-sense fact. If we take on any of the obligations of self-protection, it follows that we must take on all the obligations of self-protection. We have, for example, two extensive and widely separated coasts to guard. There would be no sense in a preparedness policy adequate for the defense of only one coast. Defense must be adequate, not sectionally adequate, but nationally adequate.

Now our answer to the question as to what is nationally adequate is not always the same. It changes—is bound to change—with changing international situations. If this were a disarming world it is obvious that our needs would be proportionately decreasing. I regret that today this is not that kind of world. I regret it deeply.

But here we confront the question of disarmament. On that issue our policy is clear. That policy has two elements in it. First, we propose to press, continually, for a limitation of armaments by international agreement. Second, failing to get that, we will make no increase of our own armaments unless other powers by increasing their armaments make increase by us necessary to our national safety.

If progress in armament limitation has been slow, progress in other areas has been rapid. We have stated the principle of the good neighbor as the standard for the conduct of our foreign policy. We have begun the practice of that principle. Already that practice has ushered in a new era of good-will between ourselves and the great Nations of the Americas. One after another we are liquidating the causes of friction and misunderstanding between us. A new confidence has been established. This summer's Pan-American Conference will meet in an atmosphere of unprecedented friendliness. What we have achieved in that one area is a measure of what we desire to achieve through the whole range of our international relationships.

That achievement is wholly consistent with our program of national defense. It is an expression of the very objectives on which our national defense is based.

We have a disinterested, consistent and successful foreign policy. In it we give no thought to a war of aggression on the part of the United States. We stand firmly by our solemn treaty obligations renouncing war as an instrument of national policy.

Very sincerely yours,

FRANKLIN D. ROOSEVELT

71

Press Releases, vol. XIV, p. 486

Statement by the Honorable Norman H. Davis, Chairman of the United States Delegation, London Naval Conference, May 13, 1936 [29]

[Extracts]

A full report of the recent Naval Conference in London and of the treaty which was signed on March 25 last has been made to the President, who in turn has transmitted this to the Senate. I should like, however, to make certain additional observations with regard to the treaty that is now before you for ratification.

At the outset, I must state that there are two regrettable but unavoidable omissions in this treaty. One is that two of the Washington Treaty powers, Japan and Italy, have not yet signed it; the other is that this treaty does not provide for any reduction in total tonnage or for a continuance of the principle of quantitative limitation established by the two previous treaties. The facts are, however, that it was not possible to secure agreement to that effect because all of the naval powers represented at the Conference, with the exception of Great Britain and the United States, refused to enter into a new treaty which continued the limitations and the ratios established by the present treaties. In fact, Japan left the Conference a

---

[29] Before the Committee on Foreign Relations, United States Senate, Hearings on the London Naval Treaty.

few weeks after it began because the other powers were unable to accept as a basis for negotiation the Japanese proposal for a so-called common upper limit which, in effect, was to scrap the present system of naval limitation and, without regard to relative needs and security, to change the present ratio of 5–5–3 to 3–3–3 or 5–5–5. While recognizing Japan's right to equal security, which we believe was achieved under the Washington and London Treaties, it was obviously impossible to accept the Japanese proposal because, owing to the difference in relative needs and vulnerability, naval parity would give to Japan naval superiority.

As it was impossible to agree to continue existing treaties beyond the end of this year, it was necessary, after the Japanese withdrawal from the Conference, for the remaining powers to decide whether to throw up their hands and quit or whether to proceed to the negotiation of such a treaty as might be possible, in order to prevent if possible the chaotic situation that would develop upon the termination of the existing treaties in case there should be nothing to take their place.

Notwithstanding the difficulties that were inherent in this situation, it was decided to continue in conference, with the result that after considerable time and patient effort we succeeded in negotiating a treaty which, while preserving in a modified but practical way the principle of naval limitation, contains new and important provisions which largely offset the omissions.

Although some things which we wanted are not in this treaty, there is nothing in it to which we object. There is, in fact, no single provision of the treaty which is objectionable or unfair to any participating state or to any of the other naval powers, but there is much that should prove to be mutually beneficial. It can thus be hoped that those states who have not yet signed the treaty will readily adhere to its provisions.

When one considers the difficulties which stood in the way of negotiating any treaty whatsoever, and what the situation would be without any treaty at all, it is indeed a source of real satisfaction that we were able to achieve as much as we did. We were indeed fortunate in being able to negotiate a treaty which not only preserves a structure of naval limitation but which establishes a basis for further progress toward naval reduction under more favorable conditions than now exist.

While the new naval treaty is less rigid and less far-reaching than the previous treaties, it has many advantages, and its lack of rigidity may well be one of them. The fact is that the Washington Treaty has been denounced because of its rigidity, and for the same reason the London Treaty could not be renewed, whereas the new treaty, which is more flexible, may be more enduring and prove in the long run to be more practical. At any rate, we have nothing to lose in trying it out, and possibly much to gain.

72

Memorandum by the Secretary of State Regarding a Conversation With the Japanese Ambassador to Great Britain (Yoshida)

[WASHINGTON,] June 12, 1936.

Mr. Yoshida, Japanese Ambassador to England, came in and stated that he was very desirous of promoting better relations and better understanding between our two countries. He said that the one big fact which he wanted the American people to recognize was the immense and rapidly growing population of Japan and the absolute necessity for more territory for their existence in anything like a satisfactory way. He referred to the fact that there was misunderstanding and misapprehension on the part of our people in this respect as it related to Japanese movements in and about China; that this also was probably true as to the British; that the Japanese armaments were not intended for war against any particular country, especially us, but that Japanese naval officials were always undertaking to create additional vacancies and additional room for promotion, etc., etc. I did not tell him that this by itself was not entirely appealing. He expressed an earnest desire for conference, collaboration and, without alliances, such relationships as would work out any questions arising in an amicable and fairly satisfactory way. He expressed his purpose to have a number of conversations with Ambassador Bingham, as well as with the British officials, on these subjects, with the view to the former conversations getting back to me.

In reply, I told Mr. Yoshida that I would speak frankly but in the friendliest possible spirit and say that the impression among many persons in this country was that Japan sought absolute economic domination, first of eastern Asia, and then, of other portions as she might see fit; that this would mean political as well as military domination in the end; that the upshot of the entire movement would be to exclude countries like the United States from trading with all of those portions of China thus brought under the domination or controlling influence so-called of Japan; that this presented a serious question to first-class

319

countries with commercial interests in every part of the world, for the reason that, for instance, my country stood unqualifiedly for the principle of equality of commercial opportunity and industrial right alike in every part of the world; and that it would be strange and impracticable for my country to stand for this doctrine with the announcement always that it qualified same by applying it to only one-half of the world and one-half of the world's population. I remarked that I could say in all candor that this Government had never by the slightest word or intimation suggested to the people or officials of the 20 Latin American countries as to what amount of trade they should conduct with Germany, or Great Britain, or Japan, or any other country.

I continued with the statement that there was no reason, in my judgment, why countries like Japan, the United States and England, could not in the most amicable spirit, and with perfect justice and fairness to each, agree to assert and abide by the worldwide principle of equality in all commercial and industrial affairs, and each country solemnly agree that it would not resort to force in connection with the operation of this rule of equality, and why Governments like the three mentioned could not sit down together and in a spirit of fair dealing and fair play confer and collaborate and not cease until they had found a way for amicable and reasonable adjustments or settlements. I said that this would wipe out and eliminate 90% of all the occasions for friction between the nations. I then repeated what I told him I had stated to Ambassador Saito, which was that neither Japan, the United States, England, nor any other country, would be able for a generation to supply the needed capital of many billions of dollars for the reasonable internal improvements and development of purchasing power in China and similar Asiatic localities; that their purchasing power was down to next to nothing at present; that there was ample room for long years to come for three or four countries like those just mentioned to supply all the capital they would have available, with the result that increased purchasing power would afford markets for most all of what all of the countries combined would have for sale in that part of the world, and that in any event any questions or problems arising in this connection could and should be solved in the same amicable and fair spirit to which I had already referred. I assured the Ambassador more than once of my high opinion and personal regard for his people, and especially his statesmen, and that I was anxious to see all parts of the world develop and go forward with every kind of progress to the fullest extent. He expressed his interest in the views I offered and indicated a disposition to collaborate.

I then carefully and rather fully defined and described the machinery, the policy and the scope, of our present reciprocal trade agreements program, which, I said, related to real international trade recovery to near normal and the restoration of conditions of peace. I added that for more than two years this Government had unselfishly, and at the sacrifice of bilateral trading, been making an earnest fight thus to induce other countries to lower their excessive barriers and permit some 20 billions of dollars of international trade by degrees to be restored. I stated that if and as such increased trade was realized, Japan would receive her substantial share without any effort or contribution on her part, as would other trading countries, and that this would be far more valuable than the limited amount of trade to be secured by purely bilateral bartering and bargaining, such as nations are practicing today, at the expense of triangular and multilateral trade; that we in this country had at the risk of our political situation been carrying forward this broad program; that on account of the opposition sentiment here, it was exceedingly hurtful to the progress of our movement when, at a critical stage as at present, a country like Japan sent in abnormal quantities of highly competitive products to the extent of 20 or 40 or 50% of our domestic production; that this would present a different question in other and ordinary circumstances, but that at this critical stage, as in the recent case of certain cotton textiles and other commodities sent in by Japanese businessmen in unusual quantities, such practice was seriously undermining and jeopardizing the success of our entire program. I stated that I did not desire to be misunderstood; that it was this outside interference at a time when it was extremely dangerous and harmful to the success of the movement on account of the large opposition sentiment in this country; that I felt a trading country like Japan, which would share to the extent of billions of dollars in the world trade which it was proposed to restore by our pending reciprocity program, could well afford to make a slight contribution to the movement by cautioning its nationals to refrain at the psychological moment from seriously embarrassing and handicapping us here by sending in abnormal quantities of competitive products compared with the amount of our domestic production.

I said I could make this plainer by suggesting that if the Argentine were carrying forward our reciprocity program under great difficulties, and just at the critical stage my country should export unusual quantities of beef, wheat, wool and corn in to the Argentine, which, like my own country, produces each of these commodities for export, unquestionably this would seriously endanger the success of such

Argentine trade agreements program. I said that this illustration fitted exactly the present situation between Japan and this country.

The Ambassador stated that he would like for me to remember the difficulties of the businessmen and traders of Japan and the necessity for outside trade.

I assured him that I was keeping this phase specially in mind and then added that if our movement to restore some 20 billions of dollars of world trade should break down tomorrow, as a result of any material number of excessive Japanese imports and their effect on public opinion, Japan instead of getting between 1 and 2 billions of this increased trade then would be confined permanently in the future to such small increases of trade as she might be able to secure by desperate bilateral bargaining and bartering in a world trade situation steadily becoming less in quantity and value. I said that this stated exactly the two courses open and that I would greatly appreciate it if his Government could see more fully these broader phases.

Mr. Yoshida finally ceased to make any comment about the urgent needs of Japanese businessmen, but said that he now understood more fully the viewpoint I had expressed.

C[ordell] H[ull]

73

852.00/2510A

*The Acting Secretary of State (Phillips) to the Diplomatic
And Consular Officers of the United States in Spain* [30]

[Circular telegram]

Washington, August 7, 1936—5 p.m.

While I realize that all of our officers have fully appreciated the necessity for maintaining a completely impartial attitude with regard to the disturbances in Spain, and that such an attitude has at all times been maintained by them, it may be well for them to have a summing up of what this Government's position thus far has been and will continue to be.

It is clear that our Neutrality Law with respect to embargo of arms, ammunition and implements of war has no application in the present situation, since that applies only in the event of war *be-*

---

[30] Text of telegram also sent to Legations of the United States at Lisbon and Tangier.

322

tween or among nations. On the other hand, in conformity with its well-established policy of non-interference with internal affairs in other countries, either in time of peace or in the event of civil strife, this Government will, of course, scrupulously refrain from any interference whatsoever in the unfortunate Spanish situation. We believe that American citizens, both at home and abroad, are patriotically observing this well-recognized American policy.

74

Press Releases, vol. XV, p. 163

Address Delivered by President Roosevelt at Chautauqua, New York, August 14, 1936

As many of you who are here tonight know, I formed the excellent habit of coming to Chautauqua more than 20 years ago. After my inauguration in 1933, I promised Mr. Bestor that during the next 4 years I would come to Chautauqua again; it is in fulfillment of this that I am with you tonight.

A few days ago I was asked what the subject of this talk would be, and I replied that for two good reasons I wanted to discuss the subject of peace: First, because it is eminently appropriate in Chautauqua; and, secondly, because in the hurly-burly of domestic politics it is important that our people should not overlook problems and issues which, though they lie beyond our borders, may, and probably will, have a vital influence on the United States of the future.

Many who have visited me in Washington in the past few months may have been surprised when I have told them that personally and because of my own daily contacts with all manner of difficult situations I am more concerned and less cheerful about international world conditions than about our immediate domestic prospects.

I say this to you not as a confirmed pessimist but as one who still hopes that envy, hatred, and malice among nations have reached their peak and will be succeeded by a new tide of peace and good will. I say this as one who has participated in many of the decisions of peace and war before, during, and after the World War; one who has traveled much, and one who has spent a goodly portion of every 24 hours in the study of foreign relations.

Long before I returned to Washington as President of the United States I had made up my mind that, pending what might be called a more opportune moment on other continents, the United States could best serve the cause of a peaceful humanity by setting an example. That was why on the 4th of March, 1933, I made the following declaration:

"In the field of world policy I would dedicate this nation to the policy of the good neighbor—the neighbor who resolutely respects himself and, because he does so, respects the rights of others—the neighbor who respects his obligations and respects the sanctity of his agreements in and with a world of neighbors."

This declaration represents my purpose; but it represents more than a purpose, for it stands for a practice. To a measurable degree it has succeeded; the whole world now knows that the United States cherishes no predatory ambitions. We are strong; but less powerful nations know that they need not fear our strength. We seek no conquest: we stand for peace.

In the whole of the Western Hemisphere our good-neighbor policy has produced results that are especially heartening.

The noblest monument to peace and to neighborly economic and social friendship in all the world is not a monument in bronze or stone, but the boundary which unites the United States and Canada— 3,000 miles of friendship with no barbed wire, no gun or soldier, and no passport on the whole frontier.

Mutual trust made that frontier. To extend the same sort of mutual trust throughout the Americas was our aim.

The American republics to the south of us have been ready always to cooperate with the United States on a basis of equality and mutual respect, but before we inaugurated the good-neighbor policy there was among them resentment and fear because certain administrations in Washington had slighted their national pride and their sovereign rights.

In pursuance of the good-neighbor policy, and because in my younger days I had learned many lessons in the hard school of experience, I stated that the United States was opposed definitely to armed intervention.

We have negotiated a Pan American convention embodying the principle of nonintervention. We have abandoned the Platt Amendment, which gave us the right to intervene in the internal affairs of the Republic of Cuba. We have withdrawn American marines from Haiti. We have signed a new treaty which places our relations with Panama on a mutually satisfactory basis. We have undertaken a series of trade agreements with other American countries to our mutual commercial profit. At the request of two neighboring republics, I hope to give assistance in the final settlement of the last serious boundary dispute between any of the American nations.

Throughout the Americas the spirit of the good neighbor is a practical and living fact. The 21 American republics are not only living together in friendship and in peace: they are united in the determination so to remain.

To give substance to this determination a conference will meet on December 1, 1936, at the capital of our great southern neighbor, Argentina, and it is, I know, the hope of all chiefs of state of the Americas that this will result in measures which will banish wars forever from this vast portion of the earth.

Peace, like charity, begins at home; that is why we have begun at home. But peace in the western world is not all that we seek.

It is our hope that knowledge of the practical application of the good-neighbor policy in this hemisphere will be borne home to our neighbors across the seas.

For ourselves we are on good terms with them—terms in most cases of straightforward friendship, of peaceful understanding.

But, of necessity, we are deeply concerned about tendencies of recent years among many of the nations of other continents. It is a bitter experience to us when the spirit of agreements to which we are a party is not lived up to. It is an even more bitter experience for the whole company of nations to witness not only the spirit but the letter of international agreements violated with impunity and without regard to the simple principles of honor. Permanent friendships between nations as between men can be sustained only by scrupulous respect for the pledged word.

In spite of all this we have sought steadfastly to assist international movements to prevent war. We cooperated to the bitter end—and it was a bitter end—in the work of the General Disarmament Conference. When it failed we sought a separate treaty to deal with the manufacture of arms and the international traffic in arms. That proposal also came to nothing. We participated—again to the bitter end—in a conference to continue naval limitations, and, when it became evident that no general treaty could be signed because of the objections of other nations, we concluded with Great Britain and France a conditional treaty of qualitative limitations which, much to my regret, already shows signs of ineffectiveness.

We shun political commitments which might entangle us in foreign wars; we avoid connection with the political activities of the League of Nations; but I am glad to say that we have cooperated wholeheartedly in the social and humanitarian work at Geneva. Thus we are a part of the world effort to control traffic in narcotics, to improve international health, to help child welfare, to eliminate double taxation, and to better working conditions and laboring hours throughout the world.

We are not isolationists except insofar as we seek to isolate ourselves completely from war. Yet we must remember that so long as war exists on earth there will be some danger that even the nation which most ardently desires peace may be drawn into war.

I have seen war. I have seen war on land and sea. I have seen blood running from the wounded. I have seen men coughing out their gassed lungs. I have seen the dead in the mud. I have seen cities destroyed. I have seen 200 limping, exhausted men come out of line—the survivors of a regiment of 1,000 that went forward 48 hours before. I have seen children starving. I have seen the agony of mothers and wives. I hate war.

I have passed unnumbered hours, I shall pass unnumbered hours thinking and planning how war may be kept from this nation.

I wish I could keep war from all nations, but that is beyond my power. I can at least make certain that no act of the United States helps to produce or to promote war. I can at least make clear that the conscience of America revolts against war and that any nation which provokes war forfeits the sympathy of the people of the United States.

Many causes produce war. There are ancient hatreds, turbulent frontiers, the "legacy of old, forgotten, far off things, and battles long ago." There are new-born fanaticisms, convictions on the part of certain peoples that they have become the unique depositories of ultimate truth and right.

A dark old world was devastated by wars between conflicting religions. A dark modern world faces wars between conflicting economic and political fanaticisms in which are intertwined race hatreds. To bring it home, it is as if within the territorial limits of the United States, 48 nations with 48 forms of government, 48 customs barriers, 48 languages, and 48 eternal and different verities, were spending their time and their substance in a frenzy of effort to make themselves strong enough to conquer their neighbors or strong enough to defend themselves against their neighbors.

In one field, that of economic barriers, the American policy may be, I hope, of some assistance in discouraging the economic source of war and therefore a contribution toward the peace of the world. The trade agreements which we are making are not only finding outlets for the products of American fields and American factories but are also pointing the way to the elimination of embargoes, quotas, and other devices which place such pressure on nations not possessing great natural resources that to them the price of peace seems less terrible than the price of war.

We do not maintain that a more liberal international trade will stop war, but we fear that without a more liberal international trade war is a natural sequence.

The Congress of the United States has given me certain authority to provide safeguards of American neutrality in case of war.

The President of the United States, who, under our Constitution, is vested with primary authority to conduct our international relations, thus has been given new weapons with which to maintain our neutrality.

Nevertheless—and I speak from a long experience—the effective maintenance of American neutrality depends today, as in the past, on the wisdom and determination of whoever at the moment occupy the offices of President and Secretary of State.

It is clear that our present policy and the measures passed by the Congress would, in the event of a war on some other continent, reduce war profits which would otherwise accrue to American citizens. Industrial and agricultural production for a war market may give immense fortunes to a few men; for the nation as a whole it produces disaster. It was the prospect of war profits that made our farmers in the west plow up prairie land that should never have been plowed but should have been left for grazing cattle. Today we are reaping the harvest of those war profits in the dust storms which have devastated those war-plowed areas.

It was the prospect of war profits that caused the extension of monopoly and unjustified expansion of industry and a price level so high that the normal relationship between debtor and creditor was destroyed.

Nevertheless, if war should break out again in another continent, let us not blink the fact that we would find in this country thousands of Americans who, seeking immediate riches—fools' gold—would attempt to break down or evade our neutrality.

They would tell you—and, unfortunately, their views would get wide publicity—that if they could produce and ship this and that and the other article to belligerent nations the unemployed of America would all find work. They would tell you that if they could extend credit to warring nations that credit would be used in the United States to build homes and factories and pay our debts. They would tell you that America once more would capture the trade of the world.

It would be hard to resist that clamor. It would be hard for many Americans, I fear, to look beyond, to realize the inevitable penalties, the inevitable day of reckoning that comes from a false prosperity. To resist the clamor of that greed, if war should come, would require the unswerving support of all Americans who love peace.

If we face the choice of profits or peace, the Nation will answer—must answer—"we choose peace." It is the duty of all of us to encourage such a body of public opinion in this country that the answer will be clear and for all practical purposes unanimous.

With that wise and experienced man who is our Secretary of State, whose statesmanship has met with such wide approval, I have thought and worked long and hard on the problem of keeping the United States at peace. But all the wisdom of America is not to be found in the White House or in the Department of State; we need the meditation, the prayer, and the positive support of the people of America who go along with us in seeking peace.

No matter how well we are supported by neutrality legislation, we must remember that no laws can be provided to cover every contingency, for it is impossible to imagine how every future event may shape itself. In spite of every possible forethought, international relations involve of necessity a vast uncharted area. In that area safe sailing will depend on the knowledge and the experience and the wisdom of those who direct our foreign policy. Peace will depend on their day-to-day decisions.

At this late date, with the wisdom which is so easy after the event and so difficult before the event, we find it possible to trace the tragic series of small decisions which led Europe into the great war in 1914 and eventually engulfed us and many other nations.

We can keep out of war if those who watch and decide have a sufficiently detailed understanding of international affairs to make certain that the small decisions of each day do not lead toward war, and if, at the same time, they possess the courage to say "no" to those who selfishly or unwisely would let us go to war.

Of all the nations of the world today we are in many ways most singularly blessed. Our closest neighbors are good neighbors. If there are remoter nations that wish us not good but ill, they know that we are strong; they know that we can and will defend ourselves and defend our neighborhood.

We seek to dominate no other nation. We ask no territorial expansion. We oppose imperialism. We desire reduction in world armaments.

We believe in democracy; we believe in freedom; we believe in peace. We offer to every nation of the world the handclasp of the good neighbor. Let those who wish our friendship look us in the eye and take our hand.

75

Press Releases, vol. XV, p. 177

Statement by the Department of State, August 22, 1936

Following is the text of a letter which was addressed to an American manufacturer in response to an inquiry with regard to the policy of this Government concerning the exportation of arms and ammunition to Spain. Similar replies have been made to other oral inquiries on the same subject.

"In reply to your inquiry, I beg to say that the attitude and policy of this Government relative to the question of intervention in the affairs of other sovereign nations has been well known especially since the conclusion of the Montevideo Treaty of 1933.

"For your further information, I enclose a copy of a circular telegraphic instruction which was recently sent to certain consular representatives in Europe and which has not been made public up to the present.[30a]

"I desire to call especial attention to the reference therein to our neutrality laws and to the fact that they have no application in the present Spanish situation, since they apply only in the event of war between or among nations.

"Furthermore, I invite your attention with equal force to the reference, in the same circular instruction, to this Government's well established policy of non-interference with internal affairs in other countries, as well as to the statement that this Government will, of course, scrupulously refrain from any interference whatsoever in the unfortunate Spanish situation. At the same time the Department expressed the opinion that American citizens, both at home and abroad, are patriotically observing this recognized American policy.

"In view of the above, it seems reasonable to assume that the sale of aeroplanes, regarding which you inquire, would not follow the spirit of the Government's policy.

"Very truly yours,

WILLIAM. PHILLIPS
Acting Secretary of State"

[30a] Doc. 73.

Department of State pub. 923

Address Delivered by the Secretary of State at Washington, September 7, 1936

It is a great satisfaction to me to be able to welcome in the name of the Government of the United States the distinguished members of the Third World Power Conference and the Second Congress of the International Commission on Large Dams. I assure you that it affords us genuine pleasure to have you as our guests in the Nation's capital.

The subject of the development and use of power, the harnessing of the forces of nature to make them work for man, is of tremendous and increasing importance. Your meeting here in Washington is convincing proof of that assertion. Engineers in every specialized field, producers of fuel, operators of plants and distributors of power, and prominent Government officials have come here from more than 50 nations for the purpose of meeting together to exchange technical knowledge, experiences, and opinions. Power represents one of the largest single factors in any nation's economic structure; for upon power depend to a large extent industry, transportation, communications, and, to a growing degree, agriculture. And as the uses of power are extended to millions of people throughout the world, the influence upon society of this great expansion must have the careful consideration of us all. Those of you who are concerned with the development of power technology, and those of you who are interested in the organization and use of power resources, have before you almost unlimited opportunities for great service to mankind. Inventive and engineering genius have brought many of the luxuries of two decades ago within the reach of all today. Power and mechanical appliances conceived and produced by men of your training and experience are able to provide an even greater abundance of good things.

But, they also are capable of producing machines of destruction—engines of war. Unfortunately, a vastly disproportionate share of the skill and energy of scientists and statesmen alike is being devoted now, in many parts of the world, to the creation and organization of forces of destruction. Shall we allow this application of genius and energy to be dissipated in the agony of armed conflict, or shall we insist with all the determination at our command that they be employed objectively in the pursuits of peace? Shall the brains of the world be used to lighten the burdens of man, or shall they be used for the grim purposes of war?

The responsibility of maintaining peace in a world fraught with suspicion and fear, and torn by dangerous ambitions and conflicting political philosophies, rests not upon governments alone. This responsibility rests to even greater degree upon the shoulders of the thinking people of each land—people such as you who meet here to consider important matters common to every country. You meet in a spirit of friendly cooperation with no thought of chauvinism or political jealousy. You thus not only make progress in your own field of endeavor; you also advance the cause of peace. And the cause of peace is the cause of civilization: religion, science, culture, and social betterment only go forward in a world without war. Every war of the past has retarded the progress of civilization in direct proportion to the vigor with which it was pursued and the number of days, months, or years it has endured. Yet we find today a lamentable absence of appreciation by many responsible and influential statesmen that these present warlike tendencies can only lead to a world holocaust. Are we in this supposedly enlightened age so stupid that we cannot read this awful lesson of history? I refuse to believe that we are. I am convinced that once this lesson is fully learned by the people of the world, the unanimity of their response will secure to us the blessings of permanent peace.

And it is your duty as well as mine to teach this lesson. The people of the world must learn that war is a cruel mill whose stones are the misled hope of national aggrandizement and the selfish ambitions of unscrupulous persons. The oil and fuel of that mill are furnished by the fear and hate which come from distrust and suspicion. The grain for that mill is the valiant, patriotic youth of the world, ready to carry out the orders of the leaders who are too often reckless or ruthless. The grist from that mill is death—death to youth, death to hope, death to civilization!

Accustomed as you are, as men of science or men of affairs, to deal with tangible things and with exact facts, you are essentially realists. I think the definition of realism as applied to international relations has greatly changed in the recent past. From the end of the World War up to a short time ago, those who labored to bring about the settlement of differences among nations by peaceful means were termed impractical idealists. The realists were those who put no faith in those efforts for the peaceful settlement of international disputes. They refused to believe in the possible effectiveness of this work for peace and held that it was futile to attempt to settle differences between nations except by the judgment of the sword. But today the true realist in international affairs knows that, in the face of present threats, our efforts to devise ways and means of preserving the peace must be redoubled. The true realist is he who knows that the fabric of peace has been worn perilously thin; that if it is again torn asunder by the bloody hands of war it may never be repaired.

I spoke a moment ago of the great responsibility of governments and peoples to preserve the peace. In all history the weight of that responsibility has never been so great as at this hour. The world has countless times in the past known the horror and destruction of war. In each case it has labored back to the sanity of peace, sometimes quickly, sometimes only after long dark years of struggle. But the wars of the past, with the exception of the world conflict which began in 1914, give us no basis for judging the effects of a war of the future. If war comes upon us, it will be fought not alone by uniformed armies and navies but by the entire populations of the countries involved. Airplanes, poison gas, and other modern fighting equipment of which we can only conjecture would make the world a veritable inferno.

A general war now would set loose forces that would be beyond control—forces which might easily bring about a virtual destruction of modern political thought, with all its achievements, and possibly a veritable shattering of our civilization. Our one hope is that the governments and peoples of the world may fully realize the solemn responsibility which rests upon them all, and that realistic envisaging of the inevitable consequences will prevent their flying at each other's throats no matter how great may be their impulses and the fancied incentives. There exists today an unparalleled opportunity for those nations and groups which look forward with clear vision to bring about an early return to sane perspectives and relationships based upon full comprehension that the members of the family of nations must live together amicably and work together in peace or be broken in an utterly destructive misuse of the power and the instruments which, properly used, bear beneficial witness to the amazing constructive capacity of mankind.

I cannot too strongly urge that, with the great capacity which you possess and the influence which you can wield, you, the members of this congress, and your associates in every land, bend your efforts unceasingly toward perfecting programs of methods for the preservation and promotion of peace. I urge that you insist that the products of your constructive thought and efforts be devoted to constructive ends.

Department of State pub. 925

Address Delivered by the Secretary of State at New York,
September 15, 1936

Our foreign relations are largely shaped by the physical geography of our country, the characteristics of our people, and our historical experience. Those who are in charge of the conduct of foreign policy must suit their actions to these underlying facts with due regard to the shifting circumstances of the times. This is particularly true in a democracy, where even in the short run the policies of the government must rest upon the support of the people.

We inhabit a large country which provides the basis for satisfactory and improving conditions of life. We do not seek or threaten the territory or possessions of others. Great oceans lie between us and the powers of Asia and Europe. Though these are now crossed much more quickly and easily than they used to be, they still enable us to feel somewhat protected against physical impacts from abroad. We are a numerous, strong, and active people. We have lived and developed in deep traditions of tolerance, of neighborly friendliness, of personal freedom, and of self-government. We have had long training in the settlement of differences of opinion and interest among ourselves by discussion and compromise. The winds of doctrine that are blowing so violently in many other lands are moderated here in our democratic atmosphere and tradition.

Our contribution must be in the spirit of our own situation and conceptions. It lies in the willingness to be friends but not allies. We wish extensive and mutually beneficial trade relations. We have the impulse to multiply our personal contacts, as shown by the constant American travel abroad. We would share and exchange the gifts which art, the stage, the classroom, and the scientists' and thinkers' study contribute to heighten life and understanding; we have led the world in promoting this sort of interchange among students, teachers, and artists. Our wish that natural human contacts be deeply and fully realized is shown by the great number of international conferences in which we participate, both private and intergovernmental. In such ways we would have our relations grow.

In deciding upon the character of our political relations with the outside world we naturally take into account the conditions prevailing there. These, today, are not tranquil or secure, but on the contrary in many countries are excited and haunted by mutual dread. In less than 20 years events have occurred that have taken away from international agreements their force and reliability as a basis of relations between nations. There appears to have been a great failure of the spirit, and out of this has come a many-sided combat of national ambitions, dogmas, and fears. In many lands the whole national energy has been organized to support absolute aims, far reaching in character but vaguely defined. These flare like a distant fire in the hills, and no one can be sure as to what they mean. There is an increasing acceptance of the idea that the end justifies all means. Under these conditions the individual who questions either means or end is frightened or crushed. For he encounters two controlling rules—compulsory subordination to autocratic will and the ruthless pressure of might. The result is dread and growing confusion.

Behind this lies the knowledge that laboratories and shops are producing instruments which can blow away human beings as though they were mites in a thunder storm, and these instruments have been placed in the hands of an increasing number of young men whom their leaders dedicate to the horrors of war. When Foreign Offices engage in discussion with each other today, they have an inescapable vision of men living in concrete chambers below the earth and concrete and steel forts and tanks upon the earth and operating destructive machines above the earth. They have strained and striven in many negotiations since the war to dispel that vision, but it appears to grow clearer and clearer.

The world waits. You may be sure that in most human hearts there is the steady murmur of prayer that life need not be yielded up in battle and that there may be peace, at least in our time.

It is in these circumstances we must shape our foreign relations. It is also these circumstances that present to us the problem of seeking to achieve a change in the dominant trend that is so full of menace.

I find as I review the line of foreign policy we have followed that we come close to Thomas Jefferson's expression—"peace, commerce, and honest friendship with all nations, entangling alliances with none." It is dangerous to take liberties with the great words of a great man, but I would add—settlement of disputes by peaceful means, renunciation of war as an instrument of national policy.

I think that the term "good neighbor" is an apt description of that policy. We have tried to give full meaning to that term. The good neighbor in any community minds his own essential business and does not willfully disturb the business of others. He mends his fences but does not put up spite fences. He firmly expects that others will not seek to disturb his affairs or dictate to him. He is tolerant, but his toleration does not include those who would introduce discord from elsewhere. He observes his agreements to the utmost of his ability; he adjusts by friendly methods any troubles that arise; he mingles freely in the give and take of life and concerns himself with the community welfare. All of this is in contrast with the hermit who isolates himself, who ignores the community, and, in his resistance to change, decays in a mean and bitter isolation. But the role of the good neighbor is a positive and active one which calls upon the energies, the friendliness, and the self-restraint of man or nation.

In affairs between nations the neighborliness obviously is less direct than between individuals in the local community. Its expression takes the form of just and fair dealings, without encroachment upon the rights of others, or oppression of the weak, or envy of the more fortunate. It contemplates liberal economic relations on the basis of mutual benefit, observance of law, and respect for agreements, and reliance upon peaceful processes when controversies arise.

In the everyday work of the Department of State dealing with critical issues, we have resolutely pursued this course.

We have tried to bring together American opinion and opinion in other countries in a common determination against the use of force for the settlement of disputes or for other national purposes. In that connection we have sought to maintain the vitality of the international agreement to renounce war which was signed by virtually all countries of the world when Mr. Kellogg was Secretary of State. But strong nations have chosen to proceed in disregard of that agreement, and this basis for international trust has thus been greatly impaired. We have tried to soften quarrels between other countries when they have arisen.

At times there has been criticism because we would not depart from our traditional policy and join with other governments in collective arrangements carrying the obligation of employing force, if necessary, in case disputes between other countries brought them into war. That responsibility, carrying direct participation in the political relations of the whole of the world outside, we cannot accept, eager as we are to support means for the prevention of war. For current experience indicates how uncertain is the possibility that we, by our action, could vitally influence the policies or activities of other countries from which war might come. It is for the statesmen to continue their effort to effect security by new agreements which will prove more durable than those that have been broken. This

Government would welcome that achievement. It would be like full light overcoming dense darkness. It is difficult to see how responsible governments can refrain from pushing compromise to its utmost limits to accomplish that result.

Of late we have increased our defense forces substantially. This has appeared essential in the face of the universal increase of armaments elsewhere and the disturbed conditions to which I have alluded. We would not serve the cause of peace by living in the world today without adequate powers of self-defense. We must be sure that in our desire for peace, we will not appear to any other country weak and unable to resist the imposition of force or to protect our just rights. At the same time I would make clear with the utmost emphasis that we stand ready to participate in all attempts to limit armaments by mutual accord and await the day when this may be realized.

I need say little of our relations with our great neighbor Canada. The American people and the Canadian people have lived in unbroken friendship. A new index of that friendship is the trade agreement signed last year. I have had to reckon with a number of attacks on this or that schedule of the agreement. In virtually every instance I have found, and I do not wish to be partisan in this remark, that the criticism represents misjudgment or distortion of the facts. I have watched the malicious attempts of some to juggle a few minor figures in the trade returns in such a way as to prejudice the minds of particular groups against an agreement which was the first step taken within the past half century to enable the American and Canadian peoples to obtain greater mutual benefit from their work and trade.

We have confirmed our good-neighbor policy by our actions in dealing with the American republics to the south of us. This Administration has made it clear that it would not intervene in any of those republics. It has endorsed this principle by signing at the Montevideo Conference the inter-American convention on the rights and duties of states; it has abrogated the Platt Amendment contained in our treaty with Cuba; it has withdrawn the American occupying forces from Haiti; it has negotiated new treaties with Panama, which, while fully safeguarding our rights to protect and operate the Canal, eliminate the rights we previously possessed to interfere in that republic. In all this we have shown that we have no wish to dictate to other countries, that we recognize equality of nations, and that we believe in the possibility of full cooperation between nations. Later this year there will be held in Argentina a conference between

336

the American republics, which has been warmly welcomed, and there is general confidence that further ways can be found to assure the maintenance of peace on this continent.

Certainly the economic troubles that have pressed so hard on the world during these past few years are one of the main causes of the disturbance of spirit and upset of relations that have taken place. This Government has taken the lead in trying to bring about changes in the international trade situation which would improve conditions everywhere. The needs of our own domestic situation have coincided completely with this undertaking. By 1933 a serious emergency had arisen in our trade relationships with other countries. We had repeatedly increased the barriers to the entry of foreign products into this country, and the sale of American goods abroad was being subjected to increasingly drastic retaliation and restriction on the part of other governments. In addition, we had most substantial investments in foreign countries which our previous policy had thrown into great jeopardy. Many branches of American agriculture and industry required a revival of our trade with other countries if they were to escape continued depression, idleness of resources, and unemployment. The other countries had no smaller need.

Under the authority conferred by the Trade Agreements Act of 1934, we have entered into numerous commercial agreements whereby most carefully selected and limited reductions have been made in our own tariffs. In return, we have secured reductions of the barriers imposed against American goods by other countries and assurance of various kinds against the operation of the trade-control systems that have come into existence elsewhere. The vast decline in our foreign trade has ceased. A substantial and steady increase is being recorded. During 1935 our sales abroad exceeded those of 1932, the lowest year, by 671 millions of dollars. The trade records of 1936 to date indicate that this figure will be surpassed. This has been an extremely wholesome factor in the improvement in our own conditions and in building up the world's purchasing power. Our imports of foreign goods have similarly increased, reflecting chiefly the enlarged American demand for raw materials, arising from the improvement of productive activity in the United States and our increased purchasing power.

In the negotiation of these agreements the principle of equality has been maintained in the belief that trade conducted on this basis brings the greatest economic benefit, has the greatest possibilities of expansion, and involves the least conflict. We are vigorously striving to secure similar equality of treatment on the part of other countries with which we have negotiated. In connection with this program we have refused to be drawn into a system of bilateral balancing between pairs of countries because this system is comparatively sterile and requires direct government management of international trade, which soon extends to management of domestic production. At the same time, we have been alert to the problem of protecting our trade interests against the incidental disadvantages that we might suffer from the practice of such a system by other countries.

The trade policy this country is pursuing fits well into our domestic economic situation and policies. I am willing to leave this judgment to the arbitration of facts. Certainly by now it should be clear, even to those engaged in industries that have been the most direct beneficiaries of excessive tariffs, that this alone will not bring them prosperity. It should also be apparent that they can thrive only when other branches of production thrive, including those that habitually dispose of a large part of their products in foreign markets.

The rebuilding of international trade offers a splendid opportunity for governments to improve the conditions of their people and to assure them the necessary means of acquiring the essentials of well-being and the raw materials for production. If this result can be achieved, one of the fertile causes of dissension and possible war would be weakened or removed. The plans and hopes of millions of individuals now appear to have no place except in military formation. An improvement of economic conditions would guarantee another place. Advancement in this direction need not await a solution of all political difficulties. Terms have been found by which advance can be made even in the face of the monetary uncertainty which still exists. A great opportunity awaits great leadership.

In trade interchange baleful elements enter particularly the trade in arms, ammunition, and implements of war. This trade is at present mainly incidental to the preparation for war. However, in some times and circumstances, it may itself be an element in stimulating or provoking war. Therefore, we have established a system requiring full disclosure regarding American trade in this field by placing those engaged in it under a license plan. Whether and to what extent it may be wise to regulate or restrict such trade between ourselves and other nations, for reasons other than the protection of military secrets, is a matter on which we are constantly weighing our current experience. Our existing legal authority is limited. But, as in the present Spanish situation, we assert our influence to the utmost to prevent arms shipped from this country from thwarting national or international efforts to maintain peace or end conflict. But action of that character cannot best be governed by inflexible rule, for, to a large extent, it must be determined in the light of the facts and circumstances of each situation. This much is certain—we are always ready to discourage to the utmost the traffic in arms when required in the interest of peace.

Up to this point I have dealt with the principles of our policies and relationships with other countries when peace prevails. Lately, after a lapse of almost 20 years, we have been called upon to consider with great seriousness the question of what these relationships should be if war were unhappily to occur again among the other great countries of the world. We must squarely face the fact that to stay clear of a widespread major war will require great vigilance, poise, and careful judgment in dealing with such interferences with our peaceful rights and activities as may take place.

Legislation recently passed provides some of the main essentials in a wise anticipatory policy. I have in mind the resolutions of Congress of 1935 and 1936 which, in addition to providing for the licensing of all imports and exports of arms, ammunition, and implements of war, prohibit their shipment to belligerent nations. Those same resolutions prohibit the flotation of loans and the establishment of credits in our market by belligerent countries, and otherwise strengthen our existing neutrality laws. On some of these matters the Congress by law has modified policies formerly pursued by this Government in times of war abroad. There are other vital aspects of this problem which will continue to receive the careful attention and study of the Department of State.

The problems arising during a period of neutrality are so great that they constantly renew in one the determination to spare no reasonable effort to play a full part in the encouragement of the maintenance of peace. We have sought to demonstrate that we are interested in peace everywhere. Surely this endeavor must continue to command our full abilities if war elsewhere can create such difficulties for us, if it can change for the worse the world in which we must live, if it can threaten the civilization with which all of us are concerned.

I cannot believe that the world has completely changed in mentality and desire since those great decades when the principles of liberty and democracy were extending their reign. I believe that this was a natural evolution of our civilization. I do not believe that with the great and growing facilities for education and for personal development people will permanently abandon their individual liberties and political rights. In my judgment it is not a basic defect of democratic institutions that has led to their decline in so many places but rather the onset of weariness, fear, and indifference, which can and must be dispelled. These are the heritage of the last war. They must not be permitted to bring on another.

Let me return to a remark that I made in the beginning—that the direction of our foreign policy must be acceptable to the people. Our task is to formulate out of the wishes and wisdom of a popular democracy a sound foreign policy which will ensure peace and favor progress and prosperity. In the conduct of that task we must be able to distinguish between the sharp voice of excited or prejudiced minorities which may from time to time arise and the fundamental and more lasting welfare of our nation. We must be on guard against the hasty, excited impulse, the quick upsurge of passing emotion.

Satisfactory foreign policy must be able to count upon the qualities of patience, of sympathetic understanding, of steady poise, and of assured inner strength among the people. In the past crises of our history Americans have shown that they possess these qualities in full measure. I do not doubt that they are still present as a firm support. Against the walls of our democratic methods and institutions storms from elsewhere beat violently. Let us avoid flabbiness of spirit, weakness of body, grave dissent within our own numbers, and we shall have nothing to fear from these storms. We must keep before us the knowledge that our democracy was builded on the solid qualities of hardihood, individual self-reliance, full willingness to put general welfare above personal interest in any great matter of national interest, forebearance in every direction, and abiding patriotism. They alone can furnish the necessary assurance that our foreign policy and our foreign relations will continue to bring peace with the whole world and will not fail in that leadership appropriate to a country as great as ours.

78

762.94/113

The Ambassador in Japan (Grew) to the Secretary of State

[Telegram : Paraphrase]

TOKYO, December 4, 1936—1 p.m.
[Received December 4—9:35 a.m.]

251. Embassy's 238, November 23, 6 p.m. The adverse reaction both abroad and in Japan to the recent agreement with Germany seems to have surprised the Japanese Foreign Office, which is trying

in every way to minimize the effect by denying categorically the existence of an understanding in regard to military matters or participation in a Fascist bloc. For the purpose of minimizing the effect of the agreement the Minister for Foreign Affairs held a general press conference on December 3. This is the second conference of this kind which he has called since he took office. Conversations with members of the Diet, Japanese business men and others, as well as views expressed in the press reflect much opposition to the agreement. It appears that there is a feeling that the agreement has engendered an unfortunate suspicion that relations with the United States and Great Britain have thereby been weakened and that Japan should strengthen rather than weaken her relations with those countries.

It is difficult to trace the Japanese leadership which resulted in the agreement. Apparently one of the few active backers of the agreement is the Chief of the Bureau of Military Affairs in the Ministry of War (Isogai). It appears that some of the early conversations took place between the German Ambassador and the Japanese Embassy in London.

According to the description given by the Minister for Foreign Affairs (Arita), the agreement is a kind of police measure providing for a standing commission in Berlin in which an official from the Japanese Home Office will represent Japan. There will be an exchange of information and the Japanese Government will proceed only against Japanese abroad or at home who may engage in communistic propaganda or activities. Arita expressed the hope that other governments may conclude similar agreements and he said that the agreement is aimed against no country.

Foreign diplomatic representatives in Tokyo in general are of the opinion, nevertheless, that the Japanese and German General Staffs have concluded a secret military understanding. Apparently the negotiations were carried on in Berlin by the Japanese Military Attaché there (Major General Oshima) and it is entirely possible that neither the Japanese Ambassador in Berlin nor the Japanese Foreign Office participated directly in the negotiations. Last fall when the German Ambassador to Japan was in Berlin, the German Military Attaché in Tokyo (Colonel Ott) was summoned suddenly to Berlin and returned to Japan a short time before the agreement was signed. Colonel Ott is studiously avoiding conversations with other Military Attachés in Tokyo now.

The British Ambassador feels certain that a secret military agreement exists and he is of the opinion that, as one item of the alleged agreement, an arrangement for the shipment to Manchuria of German arms in payment for various commodities, including soya beans, has been made as a result of the lack of success in carrying out the German Trade Agreement with "Manchukuo".

The Soviet Ambassador is convinced that while the agreement as published is merely a facade to hide a secret agreement for joint action in the event of war with the Soviet Union, this alleged secret agreement is nevertheless aimed also at Great Britain and he insists that an agreement or understanding exists for the division between Germany and Japan in case of war of certain British possessions overseas as well as the Dutch East Indies. The Soviet Ambassador considers the alleged secret pact as part and parcel of Germany's need for colonies and of Japan's southern expansion program. These ideas, although they may be far fetched, are in accord with the perhaps not unreasonable suspicion of Japanese intentions and activities usually held by the Soviet Ambassador, who has informed the American Ambassador that the Soviet Government has indisputable evidence that a military agreement exists. He has informed the British Ambassador that at an opportune moment this evidence might be published.

The Japanese Prime Minister (Hirota) made a significant remark to the American Ambassador to the effect that relations between Germany and Japan would become closer the more communistic activities and the influence of the Comintern spread abroad.

GREW

79

Department of State pub. 1088, p. 82

Address Delivered by the Secretary of State at Buenos Aires,
December 5, 1936 [30b]

The primary purpose of this Conference is to banish war from the Western Hemisphere. In its earnest pursuit of this great undertaking it is necessary at the outset to visualize numerous dangerous conditions and practices in general international affairs to the extent that they bear upon and affect the work of this Conference. It is manifest that every country today is faced with a supreme alternative. Each must play its part in determining whether the world will slip backward toward war and savagery, or whether it can maintain and

---

[30b] At the opening of the Inter-American Conference for the Maintenance of Peace.

will advance the level of civilization and peace. None can escape its responsibility.

The twenty-one American republics cannot remain unconcerned by the grave and threatening conditions in many parts of the world. Our convocation here in Buenos Aires utters this hemisphere's common voice of its interest in, nay, its intense concern over, the determination of this momentous question. The repercussions of wars and preparations for wars have been so universally disastrous that it is now as plain as mathematical truth that each nation in any part of the world is concerned in peace in every part of the world. The nations of all the Americas, through their chosen delegates, have assembled to make careful survey and analysis of all aspects of their responsibilities; to take account of their common duties; and to plan accordingly for the safety and welfare of their peoples.

The Western Hemisphere must now face squarely certain hard realities. For the purpose of our undertaking, we must frankly recognize that for some time the forces of militarism have been in the ascendant in a large part of the world; those of peace have been correspondingly on the decline. We should be lacking in common sense if we ignored the plain fact that the effects of these forces will unavoidably have direct impact upon all of us. We should be lacking in ordinary caution if we fail to counsel together for our common safety and welfare.

It is bad enough when many statesmen and peoples close their minds and memories to the awful lesson taught by the millions of soldiers sacrificed in the World War; the shattered cities, the desolated fields, and all the other material, moral, and spiritual ravages of that conflict. Still worse, that war has brought in its train wounds to man's heart and spirit, national hatreds and fears, the dislocation or destruction of indispensable political and governmental structures, and the collapse or cool abandonment of former high standards of national conduct. The supreme tragedy is completed by the break-down of the commerce of mind and culture, the attempt to isolate the nations of the earth into sealed compartments, all of which have made war a burden not to be endured by mankind.

The delegates of the American nations, meeting here in the face of these grave and threatening world conditions, must realize that mere words will not suffice. From every wise and practical viewpoint, concrete peace planning, peace views, and peace objectives are imperative. We must quicken our words and our hopes into a specific, embracing program to maintain peace. Such a program, adequately implemented, should constitute an armory of peace. It should comprise a structure affording all practical means for safeguarding peace. At a time when many other governments or peoples fail or fear to proclaim and embrace a broad or definite peace plan or movement, while their statesmen are shouting threats of war, it is all the more necessary that we of the Americas must cry out for peace, keep alive the spirit of peace, live by the rules of peace, and forthwith perfect the machinery for its maintenance. Should we fail to make this outstanding contribution, it would be a practical desertion of the cause of peace and a tragic blow to the hopes of humanity.

In meeting this problem, the American republics are in a peculiarly advantageous situation. There are among us no radical differences, no profound mistrusts or deep hatreds. On the contrary we are inspired by the impulse to be constant friends and the determination to be peaceful neighbors.

We recognize the right of all nations to handle their affairs in any way they choose, and this quite irrespective of the fact that their way may be different from our way or even repugnant to our ideas. But we cannot fail to take cognizance of the international aspect of their policies when and to the extent that they may react upon us. I, myself, am unalterably of the view that a policy leading to war may react upon us. In the face of any situation directly leading to war, can we therefore be other than apprehensive?

In sustaining the firm determination that peace must be maintained and that any country whose policies make war likely is threatening injury to all, I believe that the nations of this hemisphere would find themselves in accord with governments elsewhere. I strongly entertain the hope that a united group of American nations may take common action at this Conference further to assure peace among themselves and define their attitude toward war; and that this action may not only demonstrate the happy position of the New World, but, though designed primarily for our own benefit, embody policies of world application and correspond to the views and interests of nations outside this hemisphere.

There is no need for war. There is a practical alternative policy at hand, complete and adequate. It is no exclusive policy aimed at the safety or supremacy of a few, leaving others to struggle with distressful situations. It demands no sacrifices comparable to the advantages which will result to each nation and to each individual.

In these circumstances the representatives of the twenty-one American republics should frankly call the attention of the people of this hemisphere to the possibilities of danger to their future peace and progress and at the same time set forth the numerous steps that can well be undertaken as the most effective means of improving and safeguarding the conditions of permanent peace.

While carefully avoiding any political entanglements, my government strives at all times to cooperate with other nations to every practical extent in support of peace objectives, including reduction or limitation of armaments, the control of traffic in arms, taking the profits out of war, and the restoration of fair and friendly economic relationships. We reject war as a method of settling international disputes and favor such methods as conference, conciliation, and arbitration.

Peace can be partially safeguarded through international agreements. Such agreements, however, must reflect the utmost good faith; this alone can be the guaranty of their significance and usefulness. Contemporary events clearly show that, where mutual trust, good-will, and sincerity of purpose are lacking, pacts or agreements fail; and the world is seized by fear and left to the mercy of the wreckers.

The Conference has the duty of considering all peace proposals of merit. Let me enumerate and briefly discuss eight separate and vitally important principles and proposals for a comprehensive peace program and peace structure. They are not designed to be all-inclusive. In considering them we should be guided by the knowledge that other forces and agencies of peace exist besides those made and to be made on our continents; what we do contemplates no conflict with sincere efforts the world over.

First. I would emphasize the local and unilateral responsibility of each nation carefully to educate and organize its people in opposition to war and its underlying causes. Support must be given to peace, to the most effective policies for its preservation; and, finally, each nation must maintain conditions within its own borders which will permit it to adopt national policies that can be peacefully pursued. More than any other factor, a thoroughly informed and alert public opinion in each country as to the suitable and desirable relationships with other nations and the principles underlying them, enables a government in time of crisis to act promptly and effectively for peace.

The forces of peace everywhere are entitled to function both through governments and through public opinion. The peoples of the world would be far wiser if they expended more of their hard-earned money in organizing the forces of peace and fewer of the present five billion dollars in educating and training their military forces.

Since the time when Thomas Jefferson insisted upon a "decent respect to the opinions of mankind", public opinion has controlled foreign policy in all democracies. It is, therefore, all-important that every platform, every pulpit, and every forum should become constant and active agencies in the great work of education and organization. The limited extent of such highly organized and . intelligent public opinion in support of peace is by far the largest draw-back to any plan to prevent war. Truly the first step is that each nation must thus make itself safe for peace. This, too, develops a common will for freedom, the soil from which peace springs.

People everywhere should be made to know of the peace mechanisms. Even more, there should be brought home to them the knowledge that trade, commerce, finance, debts, communications, have a bearing on peace. The workman at his bench, the farmer on his land, the shopkeeper by his shelves, the clerk at his books, the laborer in factory, plantation, mine, or construction camp, must realize that his work is the work of peace; that to interrupt it for ends of national or personal rapacity is to drive him toward quick death by bayonets, or to slower but not less grievous suffering through economic distress.

In all our countries we have scholars who can demonstrate these facts; let them not be silent. Our churches have direct contact with all groups; may they remember that the peacemakers are the children of God. We have artists and poets who can distil their needed knowledge into trenchant phrase and line; they have work to do. Our great journals on both continents cover the world. Our women are awake; our youth sentient; our clubs and organizations make opinion everywhere. There is a strength here available greater than that of armies. We have but to ask its aid; it will be swift to answer, not only here but in continents beyond the seas.

Second. Indispensable in their influence for peace and well-being are frequent conferences between representatives of the nations and intercourse between their peoples. Collaboration and the exchange of views, ideas, and information are the most effective means of establishing understanding, friendship, and trust. I would again emphasize that any written pacts or agreements not based upon such relationships as these too often exist on paper only. Development of the atmosphere of peace, understanding, and good-will during our sessions here will alone constitute a vast accomplishment.

Third. Any complete program would include safeguarding the nations of this hemisphere from using force, one against the other, through the consummation of all of the five well-known peace agreements, produced in chief part by previous conferences, as well as through the Draft Convention Coordinating the Existing Treaties between the American States and Extending Them in Certain Respects, which the delegation of the United States is presenting for the consideration of this Conference.

In these, virtually all of the essentials of adequate machinery are present. If their operation is somewhat implemented by provisions in the draft proposal I have just mentioned to be considered by this Conference, such machinery would be complete.

The first of these is the Treaty to Avoid and Prevent Conflicts between the American States, which was signed in Santiago in 1923.

The second is the Treaty for the Renunciation of War, known as the Kellogg-Briand pact, or the Pact of Paris, signed at Paris in 1928.

The third is the General Convention of Inter-American Conciliation, signed at Washington in 1929.

The fourth is the General Treaty of Inter-American Arbitration, signed at Washington in 1929.

The fifth is the Anti-War Treaty of Non-Aggression and Conciliation, signed at Rio de Janeiro in 1933.

While the Montevideo Conference in 1933 went on record in favor of the valid execution of these five agreements by each of the twenty-one governments represented, several have not yet completed this ratification. These agreements provide a many-sided and flexible functioning machinery for the adjustment of difficulties that may arise in this hemisphere. A government could not give more tangible proof of its readiness to translate into practicable form its desire to promote and to maintain peace. Swift action by all of us to ratify these agreements should be the natural assertion of our intentions.

Fourth. If war should occur, any peace program must provide for the problem then presented. For the belligerent, there is the ruin and suffering of war. For the neutrals, there is the task of remaining neutral, of not being too disturbed in their own affairs, of not having their own peace imperiled, of working in common to restrict the war and bring it to an end. Can we in this Conference work out for ourselves a common line of policy that might be pursued during a period of neutrality? Some first broad approaches toward that end are, I think, possible. If these are to be sound they must be inspired by the determination to stay at peace. When interests are challenged, when minds are stirred, when entry into war in some particular juncture may appear to offer to some country the chance of national advantage, then determination is needed to retain neutrality. The maintenance of neutrality is an achievement to be attained more readily if undertaken jointly. Such agreement would be a tremendous safeguard for each of us. It might be a powerful means of ending war.

When we have done all that seems to be possible in extending and perfecting an integrated and permanent mechanism for preserving peaceful relations among ourselves, and when we have placed in operation these various instruments, the twenty-one republics of this hemisphere will have given overt expression to the most determined will for peace to be found in the world today. In the face of a weakening elsewhere in the world of reliance on an observance of international agreements, we shall have proclaimed our firm intention that these peaceful instruments shall be the foundation of relations between nations throughout this whole region.

If we can endow peace with certainty, if we can make it glow in our part of the world, then we may indulge the hope that our example will not be in vain.

Fifth. The peoples of this region have a further opportunity. They must make headway with a liberal policy of commerce, which would lower excessive barriers to trade and lessen injurious discriminations as between the trade of different countries. This means the substitution of a policy of economic benefit, good-will, and fair-dealing for one stimulated by greedy and short-sighted calculations of monetary advantage in an impractical isolation. It would have most beneficial effects, both direct and indirect, upon political difficulties and antagonisms.

A thriving international commerce, well-adjusted to the resources and talents of each country, brings benefit to all. It keeps men employed, active, and usefully supplying the wants of others. It leads each country to look upon others as helpful counterparts to itself rather than as antagonists. It opens up to each country, to the extent mutually profitable and desirable, the resources and the organized productive power of other countries; by its benefits small nations with limited territory or resources can have a varied, secure, and prosperous life; it can bring improvement to those who feel their toil too hard and their reward too meager.

Prosperity and peace are not separate entities. To promote one is to promote the other. The economic well-being of peoples is the greatest single protection against civil strife, large armaments, war. Economic isolation and military force go hand in hand; when nations cannot get what they need by the normal processes of trade, they will continue to resort to the use of force. A people employed and in a state of reasonable comfort is not a people among whom class struggles, militarism, and war can thrive. But a people driven to desperation by want and misery is at all times a threat to peace, their conditions an invitation to disorder and chaos, both internal and external.

The intervening years have given added significance to the economic program adopted at the Conference at Montevideo three years ago. That program is today the greatest potential force both for peace and prosperity. Our present Conference should reaffirm and secure action upon this program of economic intelligence.

One feature of the resolutions adopted at Montevideo was the support for the principle of equality of treatment as the basis of acceptable commercial policy. This rule has been followed in a number of commercial agreements that have already been concluded between American nations. Their benefits are already becoming manifest and will continue to grow. We cannot blind ourselves to the fact, however, that at the same time there has taken place even among the American nations a growth in the restrictions upon trade and an extension of discriminatory practices; these have tended to counteract the advantages resulting from the liberalizing terms embodied in other agreements.

I would urge again the wisdom of avoiding discrimination in our commercial policy. The practice of discrimination prevents trade from following the lines which would produce the greatest economic benefits; it inevitably, in the long run, provokes retaliation from those who suffer from discrimination, makes it more difficult for countries eager to pursue a liberal trade policy to secure the fair gains from this policy, and thereby checks the lowering of restrictions. It will not serve our broad and deep aims; on the contrary, if steadily extended, it will lead us into new controversies and difficulties. The Montevideo program offers the only alternative to the present short-sighted, war-breeding bilateral bargaining method of trade, to the exclusion of triangular and multilateral trade, which is being employed in many parts of the world with sterile results.

The ends we seek can best be achieved by the concurrent or concerted action of many countries. Each can exert itself steadfastly amidst the particular circumstances of its economic situation to make its contribution toward the rebuilding of trade. Each can grant new opportunities to others as it receives new opportunities for itself. All are called upon to share in the concurrent or concerted action which is required. Any country which seeks the benefits of the program while avoiding its responsibilities, will in time shut itself off from the benefits. Any country which is tempted or forced by some special calculation to depart from these lines of action and which conveys and seeks special advantage jeopardizes the progress and, perhaps, the very existence of the program. Faithful dealing, without favor, between equal partners will be required to readjust trade along the lines of growth, which is our goal.

Sixth. The Conference must recognize the all-important principle of practical international cooperation to restore many indispensable relationships between nations, for international relationships, in many vital respects, are at a low ebb. The entire international order is severely dislocated. Chaotic conditions in the relations between nations have appeared. Human progress already has slowed down.

Nations in recent years have sought to live a hermit existence by isolating themselves from each other in suspicion and fear. The inevitable result is not unlike that experienced by a community where individuals undertake to live a hermit existence, with the resultant decline and decay of the spiritual, the moral, the educational, and the material benefits and blessings which spring from community organization and effort. The difference, when nations live apart, is that the entire human race in countless instances suffers irreparable injury—political, moral, material, spiritual, and social. Today, for illustration, through lack of comprehension, understanding, and confidence, we see many nations exhausting their material substance and the vitality of their people by piling up huge armaments. We behold others, in their attempted isolation, becoming more indifferent and less considerate toward the rights, privileges, and honest opinions of others. National character and conduct are threatened with utter demoralization. At no distant time we shall see a state of moral and spiritual isolation, bringing with it the condemnation of the world, covering great parts of the earth, unless peoples halt and turn toward a sane course.

Seventh. International law has been in large measure flouted. It should be reestablished, revitalized, and strengthened by general demand. International law protects the peace and security of nations and so safeguards them against maintaining great armaments and wasting their substance in continual readiness for war. Founded upon justice and humanity, the great principles of international law are the source and fountain of the equality, the security, and the very existence of nations. Armies and navies are no permanent substitute. Abandonment of the rule of law would not only leave small or unarmed states at the mercy of the reckless and powerful but would hopelessly undermine all international order. It is inconceivable that the civilized nations would long delay a supreme effort to reestablish that rule of law.

Eighth. Observance of understandings, agreements, and treaties between nations constitutes the foundation of international order.

350

May I say here that this is not a time for crimination or recrimination, nor is such in my mind during this discussion. There must be the fullest patience and forbearance, one country with another, as the nations endeavor to climb back to that high ground of wholesome and elevating relationship of loyalty to the given word, of faithful fair-dealing.

International agreements have lost their force and reliability as a basis of relations between nations. This extremely ominous and fateful development constitutes the most dangerous single phenomenon in the world of today; not international law merely, but that which is higher—moral law—and the whole integrity and honor of governments are in danger of being ruthlessly trampled upon. There has been a failure of the spirit. There is no task more urgent than that of remaking the basis of trusted agreement between nations. They must ardently seek the terms of new agreements and stand behind them with unfailing will. The vitality of international agreements must be restored.

If the solemn rights and obligations between nations are to be treated lightly or brushed aside, the nations of the world will head straight toward international anarchy and chaos. And soon, too, the citizen begins to lower his individual standards of personal, moral, and business conduct to those of his government. Trust in each nation's honor and faith in its given word must be restored by the concerted resolve of all governments.

It is to the interest of everyone that there be an end of treaties broken by arbitrary unilateral action. Peaceful procedure, agreements between the signatories, and mutual understanding must be restored as the means of modifying or ending international agreements.

In the accomplishment of the high aims and purposes of this eight-fold program, the people of every nation have an equal interest. We of this hemisphere have reason to hope that these great objectives may receive the support of all peoples. If peace and progress are to be either maintained or advanced, the time is overripe for renewed effort on each nation's part. There can be no delay. Through past centuries, the human race fought its way up from the low level of barbarism and war to that of civilization and peace. This accomplishment has only been partial, and it may well be but temporary.

It would be a frightful commentary on the human race if, with the awful lesson of its disastrous experience, responsible and civilized governments should now fail.

The nations of this continent should omit no word or act in their attempt to meet the dangerous conditions which endanger peace. Let our actions here at Buenos Aires constitute the most potent possible appeal to peacemakers and warmakers throughout the world.

So only does civilization become real. So only can we rightly ask that universal support which entitles governments to speak for their peoples to the world, not with the voice of propaganda but with that of truth. Having affirmed our faith, we should be remiss if we were to leave anything undone which will tend to assure our peace here and make us powerful for peace elsewhere. In a very real sense, let this continent set the high example of championing the forces of peace, democracy, and civilization.

80

Department of State pub. 1088, p. 227

Declaration of Principles of Inter-American Solidarity And Cooperation, Buenos Aires, December 21, 1936.

The Governments of the American Republics, having considered:

That they have a common likeness in their democratic form of government and their common ideals of peace and justice, manifested in the several Treaties and Conventions which they have signed for the purpose of constituting a purely American system tending towards the preservation of peace, the proscription of war, the harmonious development of their commerce and of their cultural aspirations in the various fields of political, economic, social, scientific and artistic activities;

That the existence of continental interests obliges them to maintain solidarity of principles as the basis of the life of the relations of each to every other American nation;

That Pan Americanism, as a principle of American International Law, by which is understood a moral union of all of the American Republics in defence of their common interests based upon the most perfect equality and reciprocal respect for their rights of autonomy, independence and free development, requires the proclamation of principles of American International Law; and

That it is necessary to consecrate the principle of American solidarity in all non-continental conflicts, especially since those limited to the American Continent should find a peaceful solution by the means established by the Treaties and Conventions now in force or in the instruments hereafter to be executed,

The Inter-American Conference for the Maintenance of Peace

DECLARES:

1. That the American Nations, true to their republican institutions, proclaim their absolute juridical liberty, their unqualified respect for their respective sovereignties and the existence of a common democracy throughout America;

2. That every act susceptible of disturbing the peace of America affects each and every one of them, and justifies the initiation of the procedure of consultation provided for in the Convention for the Maintenance, Preservation and Reestablishment of Peace, signed at this Conference; and

3. That the following principles are accepted by the American community of Nations:

(*a*) Proscription of territorial conquest and that, in consequence, no acquisition made through violence shall be recognized;

(*b*) Intervention by one State in the internal or external affairs of another State is condemned;

(*c*) Forcible collection of pecuniary debts is illegal; and

(*d*) Any difference or dispute between the American nations, whatever its nature or origin, shall be settled by the methods of conciliation, or unrestricted arbitration, or through operation of international justice.

81

50 Stat. 3

Joint Resolution of January 8, 1937

JOINT RESOLUTION

To prohibit the exportation of arms, ammunition, and implements of war from the United States to Spain.

Resolved by the Senate and House of Representatives of the United States of America in Congress assembled, That during the existence of the state of civil strife now obtaining in Spain it shall, from and after the approval of this Resolution be unlawful to export arms, ammunition, or implements of war from any place in the United States, or possessions of the United States, to Spain or to any other foreign country for transshipment to Spain or for use of either of the opposing forces in Spain. Arms, ammunition, or implements of war, the exportation of which is prohibited by this Resolution, are those enumerated in the President's Proclamation No. 2163 of April 10, 1936.

Licenses heretofore issued under existing law for the exportation of arms, ammunition, or implements of war to Spain shall, as to all future exportations thereunder, ipso facto be deemed to be cancelled.

Whoever in violation of any of the provisions of this Resolution shall export, or attempt to export, or cause to be exported either directly or indirectly, arms, ammunition, or implements of war from the United States or any of its possessions, shall be fined not more than ten thousand dollars or imprisoned not more than five years, or both.

When in the judgment of the President the conditions described in this Resolution have ceased to exist, he shall proclaim such fact, and the provisions hereof shall thereupon cease to apply.

Approved, January 8, 1937, at 12.30 p. m.

82

Press Releases, vol. XVI, p. 35

Statement by President Roosevelt, January 8, 1937

In accordance with the provisions of the Navy Appropriation Act of June 3, 1936, I have directed the Navy Department to proceed with the construction of two replacement capital ships. The keels of these ships may be laid in conformity with existing treaties at any time after January 1. Three of our battleships, the *Arkansas*, *Texas*, and *New York*, will be more than 26 years old before these ships can be completed. If we are not to reduce our Navy by obsolescence, the replacement of capital ships can no longer be deferred.

The last Congress made an initial appropriation for "Two Capital ships, as replacement of overage Capital ships, to be undertaken only in event that the President determines as a fact that Capital-ship-replacement construction is commenced by any of the other signatory powers to the Treaty for the Limitation and Reduction of Naval Armaments signed at London April 22, 1930."

On July 29, 1936, Sir Samuel Hoare, First Lord of Admiralty, announced that the orders for two battleships of the 1936 program had been let and stated—

"It is the intention that the keels should be laid at the earliest possible moment permitted by the Washington Naval Treaty; namely in January 1937. In order to achieve this object, it is essential to order the vessels now, and although complete specifications will not be available until October, there is sufficient information available to enable the contractors to prepare for laying down the keels in January next."

On December 12, 1936, France laid the keel of the capital ship *Jean Bart*.

In addition to these three capital ships whose construction has been undertaken since the passage of the Navy Appropriation Act, eight others are under construction in the following countries: Three in France, two in Italy, and three in Germany.

Some time will elapse before bids can be obtained and contracts awarded and additional time will be required for contractors to assemble material before the keels of our two ships can be laid.

83

50 Stat. 121; 22 U.S.C. 441 note

"Neutrality Act" of May 1, 1937

JOINT RESOLUTION

To amend the joint resolution entitled "Joint resolution providing for the prohibition of the export of arms, ammunition, and implements of war to belligerent countries; the prohibition of the transportation of arms, ammunition, and implements of war by vessels of the United States for the use of belligerent states; for the registration and licensing of persons engaged in the business of manufacturing, exporting, or importing arms, ammunition, or implements of war; and restricting travel by American citizens on belligerent ships during war", approved August 31, 1935, as amended.

Resolved by the Senate and House of Representatives of the United States of America in Congress assembled, That the joint resolution entitled "Joint resolution providing for the prohibition of the export of arms, ammunition, and implements of war to belligerent countries; the prohibition of the transportation of arms, ammunition, and implements of war by vessels of the United States for the use of belligerent states; for the registration and licensing of persons engaged in the business of manufacturing, exporting, or importing arms, ammunition, or implements of war; and restricting travel by American citizens on belligerent ships during war", approved August 31, 1935, as amended, is amended to read as follows:

"EXPORT OF ARMS, AMMUNITION, AND IMPLEMENTS OF WAR

"Section 1. (a) Whenever the President shall find that there exists a state of war between, or among, two or more foreign states, the

355

President shall proclaim such fact, and it shall thereafter be unlawful to export, or attempt to export, or cause to be exported, arms, ammunition, or implements of war from any place in the United States to any belligerent state named in such proclamation, or to any neutral state for transshipment to, or for the use of, any such belligerent state.

"(b) The President shall, from time to time, by proclamation, extend such embargo upon the export of arms, ammunition, or implements of war to other states as and when they may become involved in such war.

"(c) Whenever the President shall find that a state of civil strife exists in a foreign state and that such civil strife is of a magnitude or is being conducted under such conditions that the export of arms, ammunition, or implements of war from the United States to such foreign state would threaten or endanger the peace of the United States, the President shall proclaim such fact, and it shall thereafter be unlawful to export, or attempt to export, or cause to be exported, arms, ammunition, or implements of war from any place in the United States to such foreign state, or to any neutral state for transshipment to, or for the use of, such foreign state.

"(d) The President shall, from time to time by proclamation, definitely enumerate the arms, ammunition, and implements of war, the export of which is prohibited by this section. The arms, ammunition, and implements of war so enumerated shall include those enumerated in the President's proclamation Numbered 2163, of April 10, 1936, but shall not include raw materials or any other articles or materials not of the same general character as those enumerated in the said proclamation, and in the Convention for the Supervision of the International Trade in Arms and Ammunition and in Implements of War, signed at Geneva June 17, 1925.

"(e) Whoever, in violation of any of the provisions of this Act, shall export, or attempt to export, or cause to be exported, arms, ammunition, or implements of war from the United States shall be fined not more than $10,000, or imprisoned not more than five years, or both, and the property, vessel, or vehicle containing the same shall be subject to the provisions of sections 1 to 8, inclusive, title 6, chapter 30, of the Act approved June 15, 1917 (40 Stat. 223–225; U. S. C., 1934 ed., title 22, secs. 238–245).

"(f) In the case of the forfeiture of any arms, ammunition, or implements of war by reason of a violation of this Act, no public or private sale shall be required; but such arms, ammunition, or implements of war shall be delivered to the Secretary of War for such use or disposal thereof as shall be approved by the President of the United States.

"(g) Whenever, in the judgment of the President, the conditions which have caused him to issue any proclamation under the authority of this section have ceased to exist, he shall revoke the same, and the provisions of this section shall thereupon cease to apply with respect to the state or states named in such proclamation, except with respect to offenses committed, or forfeitures incurred, prior to such revocation.

"EXPORT OF OTHER ARTICLES AND MATERIALS

"SEC. 2. (a) Whenever the President shall have issued a proclamation under the authority of section 1 of this Act and he shall thereafter find that the placing of restrictions on the shipment of certain articles or materials in addition to arms, ammunition, and implements of war from the United States to belligerent states, or to a state wherein civil strife exists, is necessary to promote the security or preserve the peace of the United States or to protect the lives of citizens of the United States, he shall so proclaim, and it shall thereafter be unlawful, except under such limitations and exceptions as the President may prescribe as to lakes, rivers, and inland waters bordering on the United States, and as to transportation on or over lands bordering on the United States, for any American vessel to carry such articles or materials to any belligerent state, or to any state wherein civil strife exists, named in such proclamation issued under the authority of section 1 of this Act, or to any neutral state for transshipment to, or for the use of, any such belligerent state or any such state wherein civil strife exists. The President shall by proclamation from time to time definitely enumerate the articles and materials which it shall be unlawful for American vessels to so transport.

"(b) Whenever the President shall have issued a proclamation under the authority of section 1 of this Act and he shall thereafter find that the placing of restrictions on the export of articles or materials from the United States to belligerent states, or to a state wherein civil strife exists, is necessary to promote the security or preserve the peace of the United States or to protect the lives or commerce of citizens of the United States, he shall so proclaim, and it shall thereafter be unlawful, except under such limitations and exceptions as the President may prescribe as to lakes, rivers, and inland waters bordering on the United States, and as to transportation on or over land bordering on the United States, to export or transport, or attempt to export or transport, or cause to be exported or transported, from the United States to any belligerent state, or to any state wherein civil strife exists, named in such proclamation issued under the authority of section 1 of this Act, or to any neutral state for transshipment to, or for the use of, any such belligerent state or any such state wherein civil strife exists, any articles or materials whatever until all right, title, and interest therein shall have been transferred to some foreign government, agency, institution, association, partnership, corporation, or national. The shipper of such articles or materials shall be required to file with the collector of the port from which they are to be exported a declaration under oath that there exists in citizens of the United States no right, title, or interest in such articles or materials, and to comply with such rules and regulations as shall be promulgated from time to time by the President. Any such declaration so filed shall be a conclusive estoppel against any claim of any citizen of the United States of right, title, or interest in such articles or materials. Insurance written by underwriters on any articles or materials the export of which is prohibited by this Act, or on articles or materials carried by an American vessel in violation of subsection (a) of this section, shall not be deemed an American interest therein, and no insurance policy issued on such articles or materials and no loss incurred thereunder or by the owner of the vessel carrying the same shall be made a basis of any claim put forward by the Government of the United States.

"(c) The President shall from time to time by proclamation extend such restrictions as are imposed under the authority of this section to other states as and when they may be declared to become belligerent states under proclamations issued under the authority of section 1 of this Act.

"(d) The President may from time to time change, modify, or revoke in whole or in part any proclamations issued by him under the authority of this section.

"(e) Except with respect to offenses committed, or forfeitures incurred, prior to May 1, 1939, this section and all proclamations issued thereunder shall not be effective after May 1, 1939.

"FINANCIAL TRANSACTIONS

"SEC. 3. (a) Whenever the President shall have issued a proclamation under the authority of section 1 of this Act, it shall thereafter be unlawful for any person within the United States to purchase, sell, or exchange bonds, securities, or other obligations of the government of any belligerent state or of any state wherein civil strife exists, named in such proclamation, or of any political sub-division of any such state, or of any person acting for or on behalf of the government of any such state, or of any faction or asserted government within any such state wherein civil strife exists, or of any person acting for or on behalf of any faction or asserted government within any such state wherein civil strife exists, issued after the date of such proclamation, or to make any loan or extend any credit to any such government, political subdivision, faction, asserted government, or person, or to solicit or receive any contribution for any such government, political subdivision, faction, asserted government, or person: *Provided*, That if the President shall find that such action will serve to protect the commercial or other interests of the United States or its citizens, he may, in his discretion, and to such extent and under such regulations as he may prescribe, except from the operation of this section ordinary commercial credits and short-time obligations in aid of legal transactions and of a character customarily used in normal peacetime commercial transactions. Nothing in this subsection shall be construed to prohibit the solicitation or collection of funds to be used for medical aid and assistance, or for food and clothing to relieve human suffering, when such solicitation or collection of funds is made on behalf of and for use by any person or organization which is not acting for or on behalf of any such government, political subdivision, faction, or asserted government, but all such solicitations and collections of funds shall be subject to the approval of the President and shall be made under such rules and regulations as he shall prescribe.

"(b) The provisions of this section shall not apply to a renewal or adjustment of such indebtedness as may exist on the date of the President's proclamation.

"(c) Whoever shall violate the provisions of this section or of any regulations issued hereunder shall, upon conviction thereof, be fined not more than $50,000 or imprisoned for not more than five years, or both. Should the violation be by a corporation, organization, or association, each officer or agent thereof participating in the violation may be liable to the penalty herein prescribed.

"(d) Whenever the President shall have revoked any such proclamation issued under the authority of section 1 of this Act, the provisions of this section and of any regulations issued by the President hereunder shall thereupon cease to apply with respect to the state or states named in such proclamation, except with respect to offenses committed prior to such revocation.

"EXCEPTIONS—AMERICAN REPUBLICS

"SEC. 4. This Act shall not apply to an American republic or republics engaged in war against a non-American state or states, provided the American republic is not cooperating with a non-American state or states in such war.

"NATIONAL MUNITIONS CONTROL BOARD

"SEC. 5. (a) There is hereby established a National Munitions Control Board (hereinafter referred to as the 'Board') to carry out the provisions of this Act. The Board shall consist of the Secretary of State, who shall be chairman and executive officer of the Board, the Secretary of the Treasury, the Secretary of War, the Secretary of the Navy, and the Secretary of Commerce. Except as otherwise provided in this Act, or by other law, the administration of this Act is vested in the Department of State. The Secretary of State shall promulgate such rules and regulations with regard to the enforcement of this section as he may deem necessary to carry out its provisions. The Board shall be convened by the chairman and shall hold at least one meeting a year.

"(b) Every person who engages in the business of manufacturing, exporting, or importing any of the arms, ammunition, or implements of war referred to in this Act, whether as an exporter, importer, manufacturer, or dealer, shall register with the Secretary of State his name, or business name, principal place of business, and places of business in the United States, and a list of the arms, ammunition, and implements of war which he manufactures, imports, or exports.

"(c) Every person required to register under this section shall notify the Secretary of State of any change in the arms, ammunition, or implements of war which he exports, imports, or manufactures; and upon such notification the Secretary of State shall issue to such person an amended certificate of registration, free of charge, which shall remain valid until the date of expiration of the original certificate. Every person required to register under the provisions of this section shall pay a registration fee of $500, unless he manufactured, exported, or imported arms, ammunition, and implements of war to a total sales value of less than $50,000 during the twelve months immediately preceding his registration, in which case he shall pay a registration fee of $100. Upon receipt of the required registration fee, the Secretary of State shall issue a registration certificate valid for five years, which shall be renewable for further periods of five years upon the payment for each renewal of a fee of $500 in the case of persons who manufactured, exported, or imported arms, ammunition, and implements of war to a total sales value of more than $50,000 during the twelve months immediately preceding the renewal, or a fee of $100 in the case of persons who manufactured, exported, or imported arms, ammunition, and implements of war to a total sales value of less than $50,000 during the twelve months immediately preceding the renewal. The Secretary of the Treasury is hereby directed to refund, out of any moneys in the Treasury not otherwise appropriated, the sum of $400 to every person who shall have paid a registration fee of $500 pursuant to this Act, who manufactured, exported, or imported arms, ammunition, and implements of war to a total sales value of less than $50,000 during the twelve months immediately preceding his registration.

"(d) It shall be unlawful for any person to export, or attempt to export, from the United States to any other state, any of the arms, ammunition, or implements of war referred to in this Act, or to import, or attempt to import, to the United States from any other state, any of the arms, ammunition, or implements of war referred to in this Act, without first having obtained a license therefor.

"(e) All persons required to register under this section shall maintain, subject to the inspection of the Secretary of State, or any person or persons designated by him, such permanent records of manufacture for export, importation, and exportation of arms, ammunition, and implements of war as the Secretary of State shall prescribe.

"(f) Licenses shall be issued to persons who have registered as herein provided for, except in cases of export or import licenses where the export of arms, ammunition, or implements of war would be in violation of this Act or any other law of the United States, or of a treaty to which the United States is a party, in which cases such licenses shall not be issued.

"(g) Whenever the President shall have issued a proclamation under the authority of section 1 of this Act, all licenses theretofore issued under this Act shall ipso facto and immediately upon the issuance of such proclamation, cease to grant authority to export arms, ammunition, or implements of war from any place in the United States to any belligerent state, or to any state wherein civil strife exists, named in such proclamation, or to any neutral state for transshipment to, or for the use of, any such belligerent state or any such state wherein civil strife exists; and said licenses, insofar as the grant of authority to export to the state or states named in such proclamation is concerned, shall be null and void.

"(h) No purchase of arms, ammunition, or implements of war shall be made on behalf of the United States by any officer, executive department, or independent establishment of the Government from any person who shall have failed to register under the provisions of this Act.

"(i) The provisions of the Act of August 29, 1916, relating to the sale of ordnance and stores to the Government of Cuba (39 Stat. 619, 643; U. S. C., 1934 ed., title 50, sec. 72), are hereby repealed as of December 31, 1937.

"(j) The Board shall make an annual report to Congress, copies of which shall be distributed as are other reports transmitted to Congress. Such reports shall contain such information and data collected by the Board as may be considered of value in the determination of questions connected with the control of trade in arms, ammunition, and implements of war. The Board shall include in such reports a list of all persons required to register under the provisions of this Act, and full information concerning the licenses issued hereunder.

"(k) The President is hereby authorized to proclaim upon recommendation of the Board from time to time a list of articles which shall be considered arms, ammunition, and implements of war for the purposes of this section.

"AMERICAN VESSELS PROHIBITED FROM CARRYING ARMS TO BELLIGERENT STATES

"SEC. 6. (a) Whenever the President shall have issued a proclamation under the authority of section 1 of this Act, it shall thereafter be unlawful, until such proclamation is revoked, for any American vessel to carry any arms, ammunition, or implements of war to any belligerent state, or to any state wherein civil strife exists, named in such proclamation, or to any neutral state for transshipment to, or for the use of, any such belligerent state or any such state wherein civil strife exists.

"(b) Whoever, in violation of the provisions of this section, shall take, or attempt to take, or shall authorize, hire, or solicit another to take, any American vessel carrying such cargo out of port or from the jurisdiction of the United States shall be fined not more than $10,000, or imprisoned not more than five years, or both; and, in addition, such vessel, and her tackle, apparel, furniture, and equipment, and the arms, ammunition, and implements of war on board, shall be forfeited to the United States.

"USE OF AMERICAN PORTS AS BASE OF SUPPLY

"SEC. 7. (a) Whenever, during any war in which the United States is neutral, the President, or any person thereunto authorized by him, shall have cause to believe that any vessel, domestic or foreign, whether requiring clearance or not, is about to carry out of a port of the United States, fuel, men, arms, ammunition, implements of war, or other supplies to any warship, tender, or supply ship of a belligerent state, but the evidence is not deemed sufficient to justify forbidding the departure of the vessel as provided for by section 1, title V, chapter 30, of the Act approved June 15, 1917 (40 Stat. 217, 221; U. S. C., 1934 ed., title 18, sec. 31), and if, in the President's judgment, such action will serve to maintain peace between the United States and foreign states, or to protect the commercial interests of the United States and its citizens, or to promote the security or neutrality of the United States, he shall have the power and it shall be his duty to require the owner, master, or person in command thereof, before departing from a port of the United States, to give a bond to the United States, with sufficient sureties, in such amount as he shall deem proper, conditioned that the vessel will not deliver the men, or any part of the cargo, to any warship, tender, or supply ship of a belligerent state.

"(b) If the President, or any person thereunto authorized by him, shall find that a vessel, domestic or foreign, in a port of the United States, has previously cleared from a port of the United States during such war and delivered its cargo or any part thereof to a warship, tender, or supply ship of a belligerent state, he may prohibit the departure of such vessel during the duration of the war.

"SUBMARINES AND ARMED MERCHANT VESSELS

"SEC. 8. Whenever, during any war in which the United States is neutral, the President shall find that special restrictions placed on the use of the ports and territorial waters of the United States by the submarines or armed merchant vessels of a foreign state, will serve to maintain peace between the United States and foreign states, or to protect the commercial interests of the United States and its citizens, or to promote the security of the United States, and shall make proclamation thereof, it shall thereafter be unlawful for any such submarine or armed merchant vessel to enter a port or the territorial waters of the United States or to depart therefrom, except under such conditions and subject to such limitations as the President may prescribe. Whenever, in his judgment, the conditions which have caused him to issue his proclamation have ceased to exist, he shall revoke his proclamation and the provisions of this section shall thereupon cease to apply.

"TRAVEL ON VESSELS OF BELLIGERENT STATES

"SEC. 9. Whenever the President shall have issued a proclamation under the authority of section 1 of this Act it shall thereafter be unlawful for any citizen of the United States to travel on any vessel of the state or states named in such proclamation, except in accordance with such rules and regulations as the President shall prescribe: *Provided, however,* That the provisions of this section shall not apply to a citizen of the United States traveling on a vessel whose voyage was begun in advance of the date of the President's proclamation, and who had no opportunity to discontinue his voyage after that date: *And provided further,* That they shall not apply under ninety days after the date of the President's proclamation to a citizen of the United States returning from a foreign state to the United States. Whenever, in the President's judgment, the conditions which have caused him to issue his proclamation have ceased to exist, he shall revoke his proclamation and the provisions of this section shall thereupon cease to apply with respect to the state or states named in such proclamation, except with respect to offenses committed prior to such revocation.

"ARMING OF AMERICAN MERCHANT VESSELS PROHIBITED

"SEC. 10. Whenever the President shall have issued a proclamation under the authority of section 1, it shall thereafter be unlawful, until such proclamation is revoked, for any American vessel engaged in commerce with any belligerent state, or any state wherein civil strife exists, named in such proclamation, to be armed or to carry any armament, arms, ammunition, or implements of war, except small arms and ammunition therefor which the President may deem necessary and shall publicly designate for the preservation of discipline aboard such vessels.

"REGULATIONS

"SEC. 11. The President may, from time to time, promulgate such rules and regulations, not inconsistent with law, as may be necessary and proper to carry out any of the provisions of this Act; and he may exercise any power or authority conferred on him by this Act through such officer or officers, or agency or agencies, as he shall direct.

"GENERAL PENALTY PROVISION

"SEC. 12. In every case of the violation of any of the provisions of this Act or of any rule or regulation issued pursuant thereto where a specific penalty is not herein provided, such violator or violators, upon conviction, shall be fined not more than $10,000, or imprisoned not more than five years, or both.

"DEFINITIONS

"SEC. 13. For the purposes of this Act—

"(a) The term 'United States', when used in a geographical sense, includes the several States and Territories, the insular possessions of the United States (including the Philippine Islands), the Canal Zone, and the District of Columbia.

"(b) The term 'person' includes a partnership, company, association, or corporation, as well as a natural person.

"(c) The term 'vessel' means every description of watercraft (including aircraft) or other contrivance used, or capable of being used, as a means of transportation on, under, or over water.

"(d) The term 'American vessel' means any vessel (including aircraft) documented under the laws of the United States.

"(e) The term 'vehicle' means every description of carriage (including aircraft) or other contrivance used, or capable of being used, as a means of transportation on or over land.

"(f) The term 'state' shall include nation, government, and country.

"SEPARABILITY OF PROVISIONS

"SEC. 14. If any of the provisions of this Act, or the application thereof to any person or circumstance, is held invalid, the remainder of the Act, and the application of such provision to other persons or circumstances, shall not be affected thereby.

"APPROPRIATIONS

"SEC. 15. There is hereby authorized to be appropriated from time to time, out of any money in the Treasury not otherwise appropriated, such amounts as may be necessary to carry out the provisions and accomplish the purposes of this Act."

Approved, May 1, 1937, 6.30 p. m., Central Standard Time.

84

852.00/5953

Memorandum by the Secretary of State Regarding a Conversation With the Italian Ambassador (Suvich)

[Extracts]

[WASHINGTON,] July 6, 1937.

I then launched into the strongest possible discussion of nationalism in its extreme form, carefully distinguishing between sane, practical nationalism within reasonable limits and the extreme type which during the post-war period has constituted the worst disease that could overtake the human family. I repeated my illustration of a community of families, as set forth in a radio address of mine during Foreign Trade Week, in which I pointed out what happened to a family that undertook to live a hermit existence without a single friend among the families of the same community, how it stagnated and steadily became hopelessly decadent. I said, This is the great curse of the world today and threatens civilized nations with still more disastrous effects, unless the nations immediately begin at least to move in a different direction with a definite and sound program. I remarked that our entire program promulgated at Buenos Aires contains a reasonable, practical and most urgent set of principles and policies as the single alternative to the present disastrous course of affairs in Europe,—that is, a peaceful settlement and adjustment and rehabilitation of all worthwhile and indispensable international relationships. I said that it is nobody's fault in particular that after eighteen years the only foundation which Europe presents for a restored international order is the narrowest, cutthroat, troublebreeding method of trading and a wild, runaway race in armaments; but that this is in striking contrast with the program of the 21 American nations, and of several European countries which have approved it in the main, which does provide a solid and permanent foundation for a stable structure of business, of peace, and of government; that the single question is—whether the civilized nations will wait until it is too late before proclaiming and pursuing this practical and constructive course. I elaborated further with my usual arguments in support of this program and especially emphasized the extreme necessity for its support by European countries generally, before too late.

I said, " . . . all of the nations never get fully armed under a policy of rearmament races; one or more always desires longer time to get more fully armed and equipped; and, in the end, an explosion inevitably occurs." I continued, "This is the situation in Europe today. It is to avoid just such a cataclysm that the 21 American nations have offered a program and are pleading to all other civilized nations to embrace it and give it support without a day's delay." ... I said that there was never before such an opportunity for some important country in Europe to furnish leadership with just this sort of a program as I had outlined; that a few addresses proclaiming it and supporting it would result in an amazing awakening of peace and good neighbor sentiment and that a wave of grateful public sentiment would sweep over Europe and over the entire Western World. ... He again came back to the question of the time not being propitious for a movement in support of an alternative program for economic and peace restoration. I replied that if each nation waits until the time is exactly right from its standpoint, then I must again repeat **that the time never would become propitious**; that the experience of recent years in Europe clearly demonstrates this view; that it has not been possible for the nations of Europe to settle any one or two of the 7 or 8 point program involved, or, in other words, the situation is merely drifting amidst increasing turbulence and uproar in Europe, as well as in certain other parts of the world ...

I elaborated here on the general situation in Europe, referring to it as serious and what many would call dangerous. I remarked that either another war or a deep-seated economic panic would be utterly destructive of all that is worthwhile in the affairs of the western world, and yet absolutely nothing in Europe is being done in the way of permanent planning in the direction of peace and general stability. I said that today there are probably 4 million wage-earners in Germany engaged in armament production, who, with their families, comprise 15 to 20 million of the entire German population of 70 million; that relative numbers in the United States, Great Britain, Italy, France, and other countries, are likewise engaged; that within another eighteen months, when the resources of most countries necessary for further increased armaments are exhausted, it would not be humanly possible to find other gainful and productive employment for all the millions and millions and millions of wage-earners now engaged in military production; and that yet, with the roar of the economic and the military Niagara below, now within distinct hearing, and with the certain knowledge that the happening of either catastrophe would be fatal, nations are drifting and drifting and drifting with no broad or permanent or peaceful planning.

I said that it is in these circumstances that this country, as stated before, while taking every precaution to keep aloof from political and military involvements abroad, strongly feels that each civilized country right now has the unshirkable responsibility of making a real contribution to promote peace and normal international relationships; that therefore it and the other American nations are behind the broad economic program and its kindred provisions to which I had referred, and that naturally we are looking longingly to leading countries in Europe to offer a similar contribution to peace and economic well-being; that unless they do awaken and give support to such a program and movement, an economic collapse in Europe within 18 to 24 months is inevitable.

C[ORDELL] H[ULL]

85

793.94/8761

Memorandum by the Secretary of State Regarding a Conversation With the Japanese Ambassador (Saito)

[WASHINGTON,] July 12, 1937.

The Japanese Ambassador called by his own request. He said that he had two things to discuss or to report on—one was that Japan had two ships taking part in the search for Amelia Earhart [31] and that their officials at Hawaii and other points had been instructed to keep closely posted on the search in the hope of being of some help. I thanked him very earnestly for this fine spirit of friendliness and cooperation on the part of his government.

The Ambassador then handed me a manuscript containing six paragraphs or points relative to the Japanese-Chinese military trouble which commenced on July 7th. A copy of the instrument of writing is attached hereto.[31a] The Ambassador read each numbered paragraph for the purpose of any comment I might wish to make. I inquired, when he read the first paragraph, how many troops there were in the Japanese detachment stationed at Fengtai on July 7th. He replied that he did not know but that he supposed it was a hundred or some such number. He said that he imagined this detachment, which was unexpectedly fired upon by Chinese troops, was on the other side of the river from the Chinese troops at the Marco Polo Bridge. When I suggested that Japanese troops had been understood to be camped at various points between the two

---

[31] American aviatrix lost in Pacific Ocean on a round-the-world flight.
[31a] Not printed.

railroads leading into Peking, he said he was not a student of the geography of this locality. He said that these Japanese troops were located in this Chinese area under the same authority that United States guards and those of three or four other countries are at present stationed in Peking and other Chinese cities. I expressed deep regret at the incident during the reading of each paragraph. He said that Chiang Kai-shek is behind the entire movement; that the idea, in the Ambassador's opinion, is to strengthen his prestige in northern China, and especially with certain elements of Chinese who have charged him with being too lax and non-aggressive in his treatment of the Japanese situation. The Ambassador remarked that he still had some hope the matter might be composed, and then added that the Chinese must know that the Japanese could bring their fleet around to the Chinese coast and take complete control of the situation.

At the conclusion of the reading, I specially emphasized with approval the remarks of the Ambassador about the efforts of his government to work out a friendly settlement without war. I elaborated upon the futility of any other course and the awful consequences of war. I said that a great civilized first-class power like Japan not only could afford to exercise general self-restraint in such circumstances but that in the long run it was far better that this should characterize the attitude and policy of his government; that I have been looking forward with increasing encouragement to an early period when our two great nations in particular, while other important countries are hesitating to go forward and in fact are slipping backward fundamentally with respect to their economic and standard-of-living situations, would have the opportunity, as well as the great responsibility, for world leadership with a constructive program like the basic program proclaimed at Buenos Aires [32] for the purpose of restoring and preserving stable conditions of business and of peace, which program I elaborated on; that no two great countries have rarely had such an opportunity in these respects as seems to be ahead for our two countries and that of course it means everything from this viewpoint, as well as others, that serious military operations should not be allowed to get under way; and again I expressed my strongest approval of the disposition and self-restraint which his government is manifesting, judging by the statements of

---

[32] See Department of State Conference Series 33 (pub. 1088), *Report of the Delegation of the United States of America to the Inter-American Conference for the Maintenance of Peace, Buenos Aires, Argentina, December 1–23, 1936* (Washington, Government Printing Office, 1937).

the Ambassador. He said that he would be glad to keep me advised as to any further developments of consequence. I replied that of course this country is greatly interested and greatly concerned in conditions of peace in every part of the world, and that I would welcome anything further in the way of information from time to time, and would be glad to treat in very strictest confidence any confidential information he might care to give me on the subject. I again emphasized the great injury to the victor as well as the vanquished in case of any important war in this day and time, of the great concern of this government for peace everywhere and of my earnest hope that our two countries would soon find themselves in a situation to accentuate a program such as we proclaimed in the main at Buenos Aires. The Ambassador indicated his interest and approval. I concluded by thanking him for his offer to furnish further information.

C[ORDELL] H[ULL]

86

Press Releases, vol. XVII, p. 41

Statement by the Secretary of State, July 16, 1937

I have been receiving from many sources inquiries and suggestions arising out of disturbed situations in various parts of the world.

Unquestionably there are in a number of regions tensions and strains which on their face involve only countries that are near neighbors but which in ultimate analysis are of inevitable concern to the whole world. Any situation in which armed hostilities are in progress or are threatened is a situation wherein rights and interests of all nations either are or may be seriously affected. There can be no serious hostilities anywhere in the world which will not one way or another affect interests or rights or obligations of this country. I therefore feel warranted in making—in fact, I feel it a duty to make—a statement of this Government's position in regard to international problems and situations with respect to which this country feels deep concern.

This country constantly and consistently advocates maintenance of peace. We advocate national and international self-restraint. We advocate abstinence by all nations from use of force in pursuit of policy and from interference in the internal affairs of other nations. We advocate adjustment of problems in international relations by processes of peaceful negotiation and agreement. We advocate faithful observance of international agreements. Upholding the principle of the sanctity of treaties, we believe in modification of provisions of treaties, when need therefor arises, by orderly processes carried out in a spirit of mutual helpfulness and accommodation. We believe in respect by all nations for the rights of others and performance by all nations of established obligations. We stand for revitalizing and strengthening of international law. We advocate steps toward promotion of economic security and stability the world over. We advocate lowering or removing of excessive barriers in international trade. We seek effective equality of commercial opportunity and we urge upon all nations application of the principle of equality of treatment. We believe in limitation and reduction of armament. Realizing the necessity for maintaining armed forces adequate for national security, we are prepared to reduce or to increase our own armed forces in proportion to reductions or increases made by other countries. We avoid entering into alliances or entangling commitments but we believe in cooperative effort by peaceful and practicable means in support of the principles hereinbefore stated.

87

793.94/8952

Memorandum by the Secretary of State Regarding a Conversation With the Japanese Ambassador (Saito)

[WASHINGTON,] July 21, 1937.[33]

The Ambassador of Japan called this morning at my request. After brief preliminaries, I very seriously addressed the Ambassador and said that, of course, he must be fully aware that when two nations comprising 500 million people are engaged in a controversy in which danger of general hostilities appear imminent, this country cannot help but be greatly interested and concerned; that it is in the light of this situation and of the intense desire of this country for peace everywhere that I have been undertaking to confer with the ambassadors from both Japan and China from time to time regarding developments, present and prospective, in the danger zone; that I have approached each government, in a spirit of genuine friendliness and impartiality in an earnest effort to contribute something to the

---

[33] On this day Secretary Hull asked the Chinese Ambassador to call and made to him a statement along the same lines as the one recorded in this memorandum.

cause of peace and to the avoidance of hostilities in the Far East; that, if the Ambassador did not mind, I would be glad to reemphasize the chief points I had referred to in our previous conversations on this general subject and situation; that these included a most earnest appeal to each government, from every possible standpoint, for peace, as well as an earnest expression of the opinion that a war would result in irreparable harm to all governments involved and would prove utterly disastrous, in the present chaotic state of world affairs, to all phases of human welfare and human progress. After elaborating the foregoing views as fully as possible, I then said that I had also brought to the Ambassador's attention the great objective and beneficent purposes of the program adopted at Buenos Aires, including the 8-point pillar of peace proposals in my address at Buenos Aires, and I emphasized the view that such general hostilities now would utterly shatter the future prospects of this broad basic program for improving international relationships and to restore international order and thereby avoiding the opposite trend at present towards international anarchy; that I have been seeking to emphasize to all governments and all nations alike the basic points of this broad Buenos Aires program, and to this end I gave out a statement on last Friday [34] containing these various proposals based originally on the 8-point pillars of peace statement; that I am getting a few of these out each day to various governments for their comment and, I hope, their approval and active cooperation; that I was glad herewith to hand to the Ambassador for his government a copy of this statement of last Friday, in the hope that his government can see its way clear to join with us and other nations in proclaiming the soundness and need of this program, and I added that it would be most pleasing to us if the Government of Japan could and would step up by our side and join in carrying forward this great program, a revival of the principles of which is so much needed by the world today. From the outset of our conversation, the Ambassador from time to time in brief words indicated his approval of what I was saying.

I then said to the Ambassador that I might repeat what I had also said to him at the beginning—that this government is ready and will be most glad at any time to say or do anything, short of mediation which of course requires the agreement of both parties in advance, which might in any way whatever contribute towards composing the present matters of controversy between Japan and China; that this was, of course, said to the Ambassador for his Government;

---

[34] Doc. 86.

and I added that I desired to repeat with emphasis the present, continued attitude of this government of thus being ready and desirous of saying or doing anything that the government or governments concerned might suggest which would be fair and impartial towards all concerned and at the same time calculated to be helpful in restoring thoroughly peaceful relations in the Far East.

I said to the Ambassador that there was another phase of the matter I would like to put before him. I explained that I was anxious that my point of view be completely understood and for this reason I would like to inform the American Ambassadors in Japan and in China of the conversations held here and would like to have those Ambassadors report what I said, just as the Ambassadors of those countries to whom I spoke here would report, to the Japanese and Chinese Governments.

At one stage I asked the Ambassador what the latest developments were. He replied that he knew very little in addition to what had been reported to me by the Japanese Counselor during the past three or four days, except a report about a clash near the Marco Polo Bridge in which the Japanese used artillery only and declined to use their infantry. He said their purpose was to localize the controversy and avoid general hostilities; that he still has hopes that this result may be accomplished; that they are not bringing down troops from Japan proper.

The Ambassador said little throughout the conversation, but sought to make himself agreeable. I emphasized to him that if we did not feel genuinely friendly and impartial towards his country and all concerned I would not be saying some of the things I was saying.

During the course of the conversation, I remarked that I desired to refer specially to an incident of the past two days in which two American women, near their embassy in Peking, were assaulted by Japanese guards. I said that I had remarked to the press, off the record, on yesterday that I had only received newspaper information about this attack upon the American women and I could not comment upon it with accuracy until official information came to me; that in the meantime I assumed and hoped that our Embassy in Peking would take the matter up with the Japanese Government and a settlement, or adjustment, or action satisfactory to all concerned would be brought about. The Ambassador expressed his favorable interest in such action and also his belief that such would be the case. Dr. Hornbeck, who was present, remarked to the Ambassador that similar incidents relating to our nationals or the nationals of other governments have occurred during the past five years and that it would be very helpful to the reputation of the Japanese Government to see to it that their guards would deport and demean themselves in a way to avoid such occurrences. The Ambassador expressed his approval.

C[ORDELL] H[ULL]

88

793.94/9278

The Ambassador in Japan (Grew) to the Secretary of State

[Telegram : Paraphrase]

TOKYO, August 10, 1937—7 p.m.
[Received August 10—2 : 20 p.m.]

254. Department's 140, August 7, 3 p.m.[34a] Today affirmative in-structions were received by the British Chargé.

This afternoon I called upon the Foreign Minister at his home and presented confidentially and informally the United States Government's offer of good offices along the lines of the two points set out in the Department's telegram No. 138 of August 8.[35]

The offer was received by the Foreign Minister in entire friendli-ness. However, he said that there had already been made an opening for negotiations in the conversation at Shanghai yesterday between Ambassador Kawagoe and Kao, Chief of the Asiatic Bureau of the Chinese Foreign Office. The plan of the Japanese for an under-standing between China and Japan was presented to Kao and im-mediately the latter left for Nanking in order to communicate the plan to Chiang Kai-shek. The Foreign Minister said that the complete details of the conversation at Shanghai had not reached him but that war might be avoided if Chiang Kai-shek would reply with some plan (obviously a counter-proposal) which could serve as a basis for negotiations. However, the situation was characterized by the For-eign Minister as critical and he indicated that general hostilities could be prevented only by a favorable and early reply from Chiang Kai-shek.

Foreign Minister Hirota then remarked that if the United States wanted to be helpful the most effective thing it could do would be to persuade Chiang Kai-shek to take prompt action as contemplated in the preceding sentence.

[34a] Not printed.
[35] The two points set out in telegram 138 were the providing of a neutral place for Japanese and Chinese negotiators and assistance in smoothing out dif-ficulties which might arise in negotiations.

Apparently Hirota was reluctant to reveal the plan proposed by Kawagoe even in its general nature except that it included conditions for "good relations" with Manchuria and for the elimination of all anti-Japanese activities in China.

I was requested by the Foreign Minister to consider the fact that an opening for negotiations had been made as strictly confidential. He declared that the press has no information about the nature of the conversation between Kawagoe and Kao.

The British Chargé expects to see the Foreign Minister tomorrow and to take similar action.

The Foreign Minister said that matters had been worsened by the murder recently of a Japanese naval officer in Shanghai. The Japanese navy is observing self-restraint, although it is very angry, in order that the situation in Shanghai be not inflamed. . . .

GREW

89

Press Releases, vol. XVII, p. 166

Press Release Issued by the Department of State on August 23, 1937

At his press conference on August 17, the Secretary of State announced that (1) legislative action to make available funds for purposes of emergency relief necessitated by the situation in the Far East had been asked and that (2) this Government had given orders for a regiment of marines to prepare to proceed to Shanghai. The Secretary then discussed at some length the principles of policy on which this Government was proceeding.

The situation in Shanghai is in many respects unique. Shanghai is a great cosmopolitan center, with a population of over three million, a port which has been developed by the nationals of many countries, at which there have prevailed mutually advantageous contacts of all types and varieties between and among the Chinese and people of almost all other countries of the world. At Shanghai there exists a multiplicity of rights and interests which are of inevitable concern to many countries, including the United States.

In the present situation, the American Government is engaged in facilitating in every way possible an orderly and safe removal of American citizens from areas where there is special danger. Further, it is the policy of the American Government to afford its nationals appropriate protection, primarily against mobs or other uncontrolled elements. For that purpose it has for many years maintained small

375

detachments of armed forces in China, and for that purpose it is sending the present small reinforcement. These armed forces there have no mission of aggression. It is their function to be of assistance toward maintenance of order and security. It has been the desire and the intention of the American Government to remove these forces when performance of their function of protection is no longer called for, and such remains its desire and expectation.

The issues and problems which are of concern to this Government in the present situation in the Pacific area go far beyond merely the immediate question of protection of the nationals and interests of the United States. The conditions which prevail in that area are intimately connected with and have a direct and fundamental relationship to the general principles of policy to which attention was called in the statement of July 16, which statement has evoked expressions of approval from more than 50 governments. This Government is firmly of the opinion that the principle summarized in that statement should effectively govern international relationships.

When there unfortunately arises in any part of the world the threat or the existence of serious hostilities, the matter is of concern to all nations. Without attempting to pass judgment regarding the merits of the controversy, we appeal to the parties to refrain from resort to war. We urge that they settle their differences in accordance with principles which, in the opinion not alone of our people but of most peoples of the world, should govern in international relationships. We consider applicable throughout the world, in the Pacific area as elsewhere, the principles set forth in the statement of July 16. That statement of principles is comprehensive and basic. It embraces the principles embodied in many treaties, including the Washington Conference treaties and the Kellogg-Briand Pact of Paris.

From the beginning of the present controversy in the Far East, we have been urging upon both the Chinese and the Japanese Governments the importance of refraining from hostilities and of maintaining peace. We have been participating constantly in consultation with interested governments directed toward peaceful adjustment. This Government does not believe in political alliances or entanglements, nor does it believe in extreme isolation. It does believe in international cooperation for the purpose of seeking through pacific methods the achievement of those objectives set forth in the statement of July 16. In the light of our well-defined attitude and policies, and within the range thereof, this Government is giving most solicitous attention to every phase of the Far Eastern situation, toward safeguarding the lives and welfare of our people and making effective the policies—especially the policy of peace—in which this country believes and to which it is committed.

This Government is endeavoring to see kept alive, strengthened, and revitalized, in reference to the Pacific area and to all the world, these fundamental principles.

90

793.94/9732

The Secretary of State to the Ambassador in Japan (Grew)

[Telegram : Paraphrase]

WASHINGTON, September 2, 1937—2 p. m.

187. Reference is made to outline in your telegram No. 321 of August 27, 4 p. m.,[36] of the views and estimate of the American Embassy in Japan. I hope that it may be useful for you to have an outline of the general reaction at home to developments taking place and of the Department's present thoughts respecting methods and policy, as a means toward understanding and interpreting the American position.

The United States Government's course, as pursued during recent years in regard to the Far East, has been animated partly by the thought of the advantageousness of encouraging Japanese and Chinese effort at developing toward each other and toward the world attitudes of real cooperativeness. A situation has been produced by the hostilities that have been and are now going on between Japan and China which permits scant hope of any such attitude or practice being reciprocally developed by and between those two countries in the near future.

In view of the methods employed by the Japanese military forces, particularly of their entire lack of responsiveness in their acts to suggestions quietly and patiently made them by the United States and other Governments that reasonable consideration be given by them to the safety, rights, interests, susceptibilities, etc., of individuals and nations which are not parties to the Sino-Japanese conflict, it may be doubted that the elements actually controlling Japan's policies and action value appreciably the friendship of other nations or efforts made by the United States and other Governments to cultivate good will, confidence, and stability in general.

[36] Not printed.

In the current crisis the United States Government has endeavored to follow an absolutely impartial course. It is realized in Washington that hostilities are not likely to be brought to an end by manifestations of disapprobation on moral or legal grounds. It is necessary, however, in shaping the American course, to keep in mind constantly not only the possible serving of that object, not only the possible effects upon Japan, or upon China, or upon both of them, of possible steps, but also the wishes and attitude of the American people, the principles in which the United States believes, the courses which other countries pursue, and various objectives, general and ultimate as well as immediate and particular.

The principles guiding the United States Government were made clear in my statement of July 16, 50 states of the world having since affirmatively expressed themselves in general support thereof. In my subsequent statement of August 23, it is made clear that these principles are regarded as being applicable to the Pacific area. In a well-ordered existence in and of the society of nations, these principles are considered to be fundamental. In their present courses of action it is apparent that neither Japan nor China is acting in accord with these principles, and Japan's course is directly in conflict with many of them.

Of the Japanese feeling that the American course has indicated a desire for fairness and impartiality, I am glad to know. The first solicitude of the United States, however, will have to be, not for the maintenance of unqualified good will by either or both of the combatants toward the United States, but for the welfare of the American people and for the general policies and broad interests of the United States, guided by laws, treaties, public opinion, and other controlling considerations. Your view is shared by me that fundamental American objectives should include (1) the avoidance of involvement and (2) the protection of lives, property, and rights of American citizens. I am in doubt regarding your suggestion that these two objectives might be pursued simultaneously with the third objective, and consequently do not feel that solidifying relations with either combatant nation should be made a definite objective. The United States is opposed to the courses being pursued, particularly Japan's course. We do not desire to injure China or Japan and wish to be a good neighbor to both, but we do not intend to permit the United States to be hampered in making its decisions by especial solicitude lest its actions displease one or the other, or both, of the combatants.

We do not wish the Japanese to entertain any impression that we look upon the Japanese course with less apprehension or disapproval than does the British Government or of condoning in any sense whatever the course which Japan is pursuing.

American public opinion has been outraged by the methods and strategy employed by the combatants, particularly by the Japanese military, and has become gradually more critical of Japan. Last week's events, particularly the circumstances of the Japanese shooting of the British Ambassador in China and the Japanese Prime Minister's statement that the representations of the powers are of little or no importance, have intensified this divergence from the standard of impartiality in popular feeling and thought. Tending to offset this somewhat has been, of course, the Chinese bombing of the liner *President Hoover.*

In addressing the authorities of either side, I do not intend calling names or making threats. I heartily approve of your tactful and dignified manner of conducting approaches to the Japanese Government. However, I wish the Japanese to understand fully that the United States Government is looking with thorough disapproval upon the present manifestation of Japanese foreign policy and upon the methods employed by the Japanese military in pursuit of that policy. I consider it desirable for you not to overlook any opportunity of impressing upon Japanese officials the importance attached by the United States Government to the principles laid down in my statement of July 16 and to the significance of my statement of August 23, and for you to suggest to Japanese officials that Japan, by the course it is pursuing, is destroying the good will of the world and is laying up for itself among the peoples of the world a liability of distrust, suspicion, popular antipathy, and potential ostracism, the liquidation of which would take many, many years of benevolent endeavor by Japan.

The Roosevelt Administration has not repudiated anything in the record of the efforts made on behalf of principles and of peace by the United States Government at the time of the Manchuria affair. We have in the present crisis endeavored to dissuade Japan and China from entering upon and from continuing hostilities; but mediation has not been offered. I am by no means certain that we wish to assume the responsibilities and role of a mediator. I would not desire, at least for the present, to encourage either side to believe or to expect that, after currently rejecting many American suggestions to exercise restraint, they may rely upon the United States Government serving them as a friendly broker whenever it suits their convenience. I would want both sides to feel that. should they desire good will and any form of impartial assistance from the United States, now is the time for evidence by them of appreciation of American policies and methods through being considerate of American legitimate interests and essential solicitudes.

HULL

91

Press Releases, vol. XVII, p. 227

Statement by President Roosevelt, September 14, 1937

Following a conference with the Secretary of State and the Chairman of the United States Maritime Commission, the President today issued the following statement:

"Merchant vessels owned by the Government of the United States will not hereafter, until further notice, be permitted to transport to China or Japan any of the arms, ammunition, or implements of war which were listed in the President's proclamation of May 1, 1937.

"Any other merchant vessels, flying the American flag, which attempt to transport any of the listed articles to China or Japan will, until further notice, do so at their own risk.

"The question of applying the Neutrality Act remains *in statu quo*, the Government policy remaining on a 24-hour basis."

92

793.94/10284

The Secretary of State to the Minister in Switzerland (Harrison)

[Telegram : Paraphrase]

WASHINGTON, September 28, 1937—10 p. m.

7. Reference is made to previous instructions. In my telegram No. 2 of September 24, 6 p. m., the subject under immediate consideration was a step at that time in contemplation by the League of Nations (i. e., to set up a subcommittee of the Assembly Advisory Committee), along with the question whether consideration should be given the Sino-Japanese situation as a matter peculiarly of the Far East or of general world interest and concern. Our view was indicated to you, and I asked you to foster with discretion the view that the entire question should be treated from the viewpoint of general world interest and concern and on the broadest possible basis.

I have telegraphed you more than once my opinion that the League of Nations should decide its own course, that the United States is prepared to consider such concrete proposals as the League may present, and that we do not wish to suggest either the limits or the direction of action to be considered and decided upon by the League.

It is desirable, however, inasmuch as the United States Government associates itself with the League's deliberations through authorizing you to sit with the Assembly Advisory Committe and the subcommittee, that you know of and understand the American Government's thought in connection with any possible contributions you may be able to make toward enabling your associates at Geneva to reach decisions which may have some beneficial practical effect regarding objectives which are common to the United States and to the League's members.

When Japan embarked last July upon military activities in China, the United States Government, which took full account of evidence presented at that time and during the past indicative of Japanese political objectives, on July 16 made public a statement of basic principles which it felt should underlie normal and peaceful international relationships.

The United States Government reiterated more specifically on August 23 in a statement, with especial reference to the armed conflict between Japan and China, certain of the principles comprised in the statement of July 16, and the view was emphasized that these principles applied as well to the Pacific area as elsewhere. Attention was called, *inter alia*, expressly to the Kellogg-Briand Pact and the Nine-Power Treaty. Exception was thus definitely taken to the course followed by Japan.

Moreover, several definite steps have been taken in support of the American position: (1) Direct appeals to Japan and China to desist or refrain from hostilities; (2) repeated statements to both sides regarding the availability to them of good offices should they make any suggestions for resort to conciliation processes; (3) repeated protests to the Japanese Government against aerial bombing of noncombatants and publication in one instance of an American note to the Japanese Government in objection to and condemnation of such bombing and in another instance issuance of a statement today on that subject.

The United States has been approached on several occasions by certain other Governments with suggestions for "joint action," and it has regularly been indicated that, while we believe in and wish to practice cooperation, we are not prepared to take part in joint action, though we will consider the possible taking of parallel action. Whenever possible action which has been thought of also by other governments has been regarded as being intrinsically meritorious, action has been taken, several times prior to and sometimes without parallel action by any other government. In general, it is felt that spontaneous separate action on parallel lines, should two or more governments feel moved thereto anywhere, indicates more strongly serious feeling regarding matters under consideration and is more likely effectively to serve to attain the objectives sought than would inspired joint action.

Japan's military operations have increased in intensity and in extent with the unfolding situation. Charges of Japan's violation of treaty provisions and international law have been amplified by the Chinese Government, and a willingness to resort to conciliation processes has been affirmed by the Chinese. The Japanese have announced, however, their intention to destroy the Chinese will and capacity to resist and actually to overthrow the existing Chinese Government. By declining the League Assembly Advisory Committee's invitation, the Japanese have refused even to consult with other governments with a view to adjusting their difficulties with China.

That the Sino-Japanese situation definitely concerns the world as a whole is our feeling. No longer do the questions involved relate merely to specific provisions of particular treaties being violated; they are questions of international law, of principles of humanity, of war and of peace. Naturally it is true that the questions involve violating agreements, particularly the League of Nations Covenant, the Nine-Power Treaty, and the Kellogg-Briand Pact. But problems of world economy, world humanity, and world security also are involved. I believe that it is not possible on a basis of realism for these questions to be confined to any one forum's consideration or to be brought within the exclusive focus of any one existing agreement. Further, I believe it inexpedient to attempt stating the possible limit of action to be taken by nations desiring peace for the purpose of expressing themselves against activities now being engaged in, as regards the situation under reference, in jeopardy to the security and rights of all nations and in breach of the peace.

In action taken thus far, we feel that the United States has gone further in making efforts calculated to strengthen general principles of world peace and world security and in indicating toward disregard of them disapprobation and disapproval than any other government or group of nations has gone. Therefore, it is felt that other nations might now well direct their efforts to go as far as or further than the United States thus far has gone along these lines.

You are instructed to endeavor with discretion to cultivate thinking along these lines within restricted circles which will respect confidence, at the same time making it clear that the United States does not desire to incite the League of Nations to action and declines to chart a course for its members, whether individually or collectively.

HULL

93

Press Releases, vol. XVII, p. 275

Address Delivered by President Roosevelt at Chicago, October 5, 1937

I am glad to come once again to Chicago and especially to have the opportunity of taking part in the dedication of this important project of civic betterment.

On my trip across the continent and back I have been shown many evidences of the result of common-sense cooperation between municipalities and the Federal Government, and I have been greeted by tens of thousands of Americans who have told me in every look and word that their material and spiritual well-being has made great strides forward in the past few years.

And yet, as I have seen with my own eyes, the prosperous farms, the thriving factories, and the busy railroads—as I have seen the happiness and security and peace which covers our wide land—almost inevitably I have been compelled to contrast our peace with very different scenes being enacted in other parts of the world.

It is because the people of the United States under modern conditions must, for the sake of their own future, give thought to the rest of the world, that I, as the responsible executive head of the Nation, have chosen this great inland city and this gala occasion to speak to you on a subject of definite national importance.

The political situation in the world, which of late has been growing progressively worse, is such as to cause grave concern and anxiety to all the peoples and nations who wish to live in peace and amity with their neighbors.

Some 15 years ago the hopes of mankind for a continuing era of international peace were raised to great heights when more than 60 nations solemnly pledged themselves not to resort to arms in furtherance of their national aims and policies. The high aspirations expressed in the Briand-Kellogg Peace Pact and the hopes for peace thus raised have of late given away to a haunting fear of calamity. The present reign of terror and international lawlessness began a few years ago.

It began through unjustified interference in the internal affairs of other nations or the invasion of alien territory in violation of treaties and has now reached a stage where the very foundations of civilization are seriously threatened. The landmarks and traditions which have marked the progress of civilization toward a condition of law, order, and justice are being wiped away.

Without a declaration of war and without warning or justification of any kind, civilians, including women and children, are being ruthlessly murdered with bombs from the air. In times of so-called peace ships are being attacked and sunk by submarines without cause or notice. Nations are fomenting and taking sides in civil warfare in nations that have never done them any harm. Nations claiming freedom for themselves deny it to others.

Innocent peoples and nations are being cruelly sacrificed to a greed for power and supremacy which is devoid of all sense of justice and humane consideration.

To paraphrase a recent author, "perhaps we foresee a time when men, exultant in the technique of homicide, will rage so hotly over the world that every precious thing will be in danger, every book and picture and harmony, every treasure garnered through two millenniums, the small, the delicate, the defenseless—all will be lost or wrecked or utterly destroyed."

If those things come to pass in other parts of the world let no one imagine that America will escape, that it may expect mercy, that this Western Hemisphere will not be attacked, and that it will continue tranquilly and peacefully to carry on the ethics and the arts of civilization.

If those days come "there will be no safety by arms, no help from authority, no answer in science. The storm will rage till every flower of culture is trampled and all human beings are leveled in a vast chaos."

If those days are not to come to pass—if we are to have a world in which we can breathe freely and live in amity without fear—the peace-loving nations must make a concerted effort to uphold laws and principles on which alone peace can rest secure.

The peace-loving nations must make a concerted effort in opposition to those violations of treaties and those ignorings of humane instincts which today are creating a state of international anarchy and instability from which there is no escape through mere isolation or neutrality.

Those who cherish their freedom and recognize and respect the equal right of their neighbors to be free and live in peace, must work together for the triumph of law and moral principles in order that peace, justice, and confidence may prevail in the world. There must be a return to a belief in the pledged word, in the value of a signed treaty. There must be recognition of the fact that national morality is as vital as private morality.

A bishop wrote me the other day: "It seems to me that something greatly needs to be said in behalf of ordinary humanity against the present practice of carrying the horrors of war to helpless civilians, especially women and children. It may be that such a protest might be regarded by many, who claim to be realists, as futile, but may it not be that the heart of mankind is so filled with horror at the present needless suffering that that force could be mobilized in sufficient volume to lessen such cruelty in the days ahead. Even though it may take twenty years, which God forbid, for civilization to make effective its corporate protest against this barbarism, surely strong voices may hasten the day."

There is a solidarity and interdependence about the modern world, both technically and morally, which makes it impossible for any nation completely to isolate itself from economic and political upheavals in the rest of the world, especially when such upheavals appear to be spreading and not declining. There can be no stability or peace either within nations or between nations except under laws and moral standards adhered to by all. International anarchy destroys every foundation for peace. It jeopardizes either the immediate or the future security of every nation, large or small. It is, therefore, a matter of vital interest and concern to the people of the United States that the sanctity of international treaties and the maintenance of international morality be restored.

The overwhelming majority of the peoples and nations of the world today want to live in peace. They seek the removal of barriers against trade. They want to exert themselves in industry, in agriculture, and in business, that they may increase their wealth through the production of wealth-producing goods rather than striving to produce military planes and bombs and machine guns and cannon for the destruction of human lives and useful property.

In those nations of the world which seem to be piling armament on armament for purposes of aggression, and those other nations which fear acts of aggression against them and their security, a very high proportion of their national income is being spent directly for armaments. It runs from 30 to as high as 50 percent.

The proportion that we in the United States spend is far less—11 or 12 percent.

How happy we are that the circumstances of the moment permit us to put our money into bridges and boulevards, dams and reforestation, the conservation of our soil, and many other kinds of useful works rather than into huge standing armies and vast supplies of implements of war.

I am compelled and you are compelled, nevertheless, to look ahead. The peace, the freedom, and the security of 90 percent of the population of the world is being jeopardized by the remaining 10 percent, who are threatening a breakdown of all international order and law. Surely the 90 percent who want to live in peace under law and in accordance with moral standards that have received almost universal acceptance through the centuries, can and must find some way to make their will prevail.

The situation is definitely of universal concern. The questions involved relate not merely to violations of specific provisions of particular treaties; they are questions of war and of peace, of international law, and especially of principles of humanity. It is true that they involve definite violations of agreements, and especially of the Covenant of the League of Nations, the Briand-Kellogg Pact, and the Nine Power Treaty. But they also involve problems of world economy, world security, and word humanity.

It is true that the moral consciousness of the world must recognize the importance of removing injustices and well-founded grievances; but at the same time it must be aroused to the cardinal necessity of honoring sanctity of treaties, of respecting the rights and liberties of others, and of putting an end to acts of international aggression.

It seems to be unfortunately true that the epidemic of world lawlessness is spreading.

When an epidemic of physical disease starts to spread, the community approves and joins in a quarantine of the patients in order to protect the health of the community against the spread of the disease.

It is my determination to pursue a policy of peace and to adopt every practicable measure to avoid involvement in war. It ought to be inconceivable that in this modern area, and in the face of experience, any nation could be so foolish and ruthless as to run the risk of plunging the whole world into war by invading and violating in contravention of solemn treaties the territory of other nations that have done them no real harm and which are too weak to protect themselves adequately. Yet the peace of the world and the welfare and security of every nation is today being threatened by that very thing.

No nation which refuses to exercise forbearance and to respect the freedom and rights of others can long remain strong and retain the confidence and respect of other nations. No nation ever loses its dignity or good standing by conciliating its differences and by exercising great patience with and consideration for the rights of other nations.

War is a contagion, whether it be declared or undeclared. It can engulf states and peoples remote from the original scene of hostilities. We are determined to keep out of war, yet we cannot insure ourselves against the disastrous effects of war and the dangers of involvement. We are adopting such measures as will minimize our risk of involvement, but we cannot have complete protection in a world of disorder in which confidence and security have broken down.

If civilization is to survive the principles of the Prince of Peace must be restored. Shattered trust between nations must be revived.

Most important of all, the will for peace on the part of peace-loving nations must express itself to the end that nations that may be tempted to violate their agreements and the rights of others will desist from such a cause. There must be positive endeavors to preserve peace.

America hates war. America hopes for peace. Therefore, America actively engages in the search for peace.

94

Press Releases, vol. XVII, p. 284

Press Release Issued by the Department of State on October 6, 1937

The Department of State has been informed by the American Minister to Switzerland of the text of the report adopted by the Advisory Committee of the League of Nations setting forth the Advisory Committee's examination of the facts of the present situation in China and the treaty obligations of Japan. The Minister has further informed the Department that this report was adopted and approved by the Assembly of the League of Nations today, October 6.

Since the beginning of the present controversy in the Far East, the Government of the United States has urged upon both the Chinese and the Japanese Governments that they refrain from hostilities and has offered to be of assistance in an effort to find some means, acceptable to both parties to the conflict, of composing by pacific methods the situation in the Far East.

The Secretary of State, in statements made public on July 16 and August 23, made clear the position of the Government of the United States in regard to international problems and international relationships throughout the world and as applied specifically to the hostilities which are at present unfortunately going on between China and Japan. Among the principles which in the opinion of the Government of the United States should govern international relationships, if peace is to be maintained, are abstinence by all nations from the use of force in the pursuit of policy and from interference in the internal affairs of other nations; adjustment of problems in international relations by process of peaceful negotiation and agreement; respect by all nations for the rights of others and observance by all nations of established obligations; and the upholding of the principle of the sanctity of treaties.

On October 5 at Chicago the President elaborated these principles, emphasizing their importance, and in a discussion of the world situation pointed out that there can be no stability or peace either within nations or between nations except under laws and moral standards adhered to by all; that international anarchy destroys every foundation for peace; that it jeopardizes either the immediate or the future security of every nation, large or small; and that it is therefore of vital interest and concern to the people of the United States that respect for treaties and international morality be restored.

In the light of the unfolding developments in the Far East, the Government of the United States has been forced to the conclusion that the action of Japan in China is inconsistent with the principles which should govern the relationships between nations and is contrary to the provisions of the Nine Power Treaty of February 6, 1922, regarding principles and policies to be followed in matters concerning China, and to those of the Kellogg-Briand Pact of August 27, 1928. Thus the conclusions of this Government with respect to the foregoing are in general accord with those of the Assembly of the League of Nations.

95

793.94 Conference/73C

The Secretary of State to the Honorable Norman H. Davis, United States Delegate to the Conference at Brussels

[Extract]

WASHINGTON, October 18, 1937.

SIR:

A conference having been called of the parties signatory to the Nine Power Treaty signed at Washington February 6, 1922, and the Government of the United States having received and accepted an invitation to participate in this conference, you are to represent the United States.

You will recall that the invitation extended to this Government by the Belgian Government states that the purpose of the conference is "to—examine the situation in the Far East and to study peaceable means of hastening the end of the regrettable conflict which prevails there".

You will in your participation in this conference be guided in general by the outline of principles made public on behalf of this Government by the Secretary of State on July 16, 1937, and the further statement of policy made by the Secretary of State on August 23, 1937.

You will have constantly in mind the character and scope of this country's interest in peace in the Pacific and the Far East as evidenced by the Washington Conference treaties, and especially the rights and interests of the United States under the Nine Power Treaty; the substance and purport of the statement of this Government's position made by the Secretary of State on October 6; also statements relating to foreign policy made by the President in his address at Chicago on October 5 and in his broadcast from Washington on October 12. You will bear in mind that the first objective of the foreign policy of this country is national security, and that consequently we seek to keep peace and to promote the maintenance of peace; that we believe in cooperative effort for the preservation of peace by pacific and practicable means; and that this country has as a signatory of the Pact of Paris of 1928 renounced war as an instrument of national policy and pledged itself to resort for settlement of disputes to none but pacific means. You will bear in mind also that public opinion in the United States has expressed its emphatic determination that the United States keep out of war.

It is the hope of this Government that the conference may be able to achieve results which will contribute toward permanent stability and peace in the Far East. In the concept of this Government, the primary function of the conference is to provide a forum for constructive discussion, to formulate and suggest possible bases of settlement, and to endeavor to bring the parties together through peaceful negotiation.

Very truly yours,

CORDELL HULL

96

Press Releases, vol. XVII, p. 380

Declaration Adopted by the Conference at Brussels
On November 15, 1937

Following is the text of the declaration adopted on November 15, 1937, by the Nine Power Conference at Brussels, Belgium. Italy voted against the declaration, and Norway, Sweden, and Denmark, while endorsing the general principles involved, abstained from voting.

"1. The representatives of the states met at Brussels having taken cognizance of the Japanese Government's reply of November 12, 1937 to the communication addressed to the latter on November 7, 1937 observe with regret that the Japanese Government still contends that the conflict between Japan and China lies outside the scope of the Nine Power Treaty and again declines to enter into an exchange of views for the purpose of endeavoring to achieve a peaceful settlement of that conflict.

"2. It is clear that the Japanese concept of the issues and interests involved in the conflict under reference is utterly different from the concepts of most of the other nations and governments of the world. The Japanese Government insists that as the conflict [is] between Japan and China it concerns those two countries only. Against this the representatives of the states now met at Brussels consider this conflict of concern in fact to all countries party to the Nine Power Treaty of Washington of 1922 and to all countries party to the Pact of Paris of 1928, and of concern in fact to all countries members of the family of nations.

"3. It cannot be denied that in the Nine Power Treaty the parties thereto affirmed it to be their desire to adopt a specified policy designed to stabilize conditions in the Far East and agreed to apply certain specified principles in their relations with China and, in China, with one another; and that in the Pact of Paris the parties agreed 'that the settlement or solution of all disputes or conflicts of whatever nature or of whatever origin they may be which may arise among them shall never be sought except by pacific means.'

"4. It cannot be denied that the present hostilities between Japan and China adversely affect not only the material interests of nearly all nations. These hostilities have brought to some nationals of third countries death, to many nationals of third countries great peril, to property of nationals of third countries widespread destruction, to international communications disruption, to international trade disturbance and loss, to the peoples of all nations a sense of horror and indignation, to all the world feelings of uncertainty and apprehension.

"5. The representatives met at Brussels therefore regard these hostilities and the situation which they have brought about as matters inevitably of concern to the countries which they represent and—more—to the whole world. To them the problem appears not in terms simply of relations between two countries in the Far East but in terms of law, orderly processes, world security and world peace.

"6. The Japanese Government has affirmed in its note of October 27 to which it refers in its note of November 12 that in employing armed force against China it was anxious to 'make China renounce her present policy.' The representatives met at Brussels are moved to point out that there exists no warrant in law for the use of armed force by any country for the purpose of intervening in the internal regime of another country and that general recognition of such a right would avoid a permanent cause of conflict.

"7. The Japanese Government contends that it should be left to Japan and China to proceed to a settlement by and between them alone. But, that a just and lasting settlement could be achieved by such a method cannot be believed.

"Japanese armed forces are present in enormous numbers on Chinese soil and have occupied large and important areas thereof. Japanese authorities have decided in substance that it is Japan's objective to destroy the will and the ability of China to resist the will and the demands of Japan. The Japanese Government affirms that it is China whose actions and attitude are in contravention of the Nine Power Treaty; yet, whereas China is engaged in full and frank discussion of the matter with the other parties to that treaty, Japan refuses to discuss it with any of them. Chinese authorities have repeatedly declared that they will not, in fact that they cannot, negotiate with Japan alone for a settlement by agreement. In these circumstances there is no ground for any belief that, if left to themselves, Japan and China would arrive in the appreciably near future at any solution which would give promise of peace between those two countries, security for the rights and interests of other countries, and political and economic stability in the Far East.

"On the contrary there is every reason to believe that if this matter were left entirely to Japan and China the armed conflict—with attendant destruction of life and property, disorder, uncertainty, instability, suffering, enmity, hatreds, and disturbance to the whole world—would continue indefinitely.

"8. The Japanese Government in their latest communication invite the powers represented at Brussels to make a contribution to the stability of Eastern Asia in accordance with the realities of the situation.

"9. In the view of the representatives of the states met at Brussels, the essential realities of the situation are those to which they draw attention above.

"10. The representatives of the states met at Brussels are firmly of the belief that, for the reasons given above, a just and durable settlement is not to be expected of direct negotiations between the parties. That is why in the communications addressed to the Japanese Government they invited that Government to confer with them or with representatives of a small number of powers to be chosen for that purpose, in the hope that such exchange of views might lead to acceptance of their good offices and thus help towards the negotiation of a satisfactory settlement.

"11. They still believe that if the parties to the conflict would agree to a cessation of hostilities in order to give an opportunity for such a procedure to be tried, success might be achieved. The Chinese Delegation has intimated its readiness to fall in with this procedure. The representatives of the states met at Brussels find it difficult to understand Japan's persistent refusal to discuss such a method.

"12. Though hoping that Japan will not adhere to her refusal the states represented at Brussels must consider what is to be their common attitude in a situation where one party to an international treaty maintains against the views of all the other parties that the action which it has taken does not come within the scope of that treaty, and sets aside provisions of the treaty which the other parties hold to be operative in the circumstances."

97

Press Releases, vol. XVII, p. 399

Declaration Adopted by the Conference at Brussels On November 24, 1937 [36a]

The Nine Power Treaty is a conspicuous example of numerous international instruments by which the nations of the world enunciate certain principles and accept certain self denunciatory rules in their conduct with each other solemnly undertaking to respect the sovereignty of other nations, to refrain from seeking political or economic domination of other nations, and to abstain from interference in their internal affairs.

These international instruments constitute a framework within which international security and international peace are intended to be safeguarded without resort to arms and within which international relationships should subsist on the basis of mutual trust, good will and beneficial trade and financial relations.

It must be recognized that whenever armed force is employed in disregard of these principles the whole structure of international relations based upon the safeguards provided by treaties is disturbed. Nations are then compelled to seek security in ever increasing armaments. There is created everywhere a feeling of uncertainty and insecurity. The validity of these principles cannot be destroyed by force, their universal applicability cannot be denied and indispensability to civilization and progress cannot be gainsaid.

It was in accordance with these principles that this Conference was called in Brussels for the purpose, as set forth in the terms of the invitation issued by the Belgian Government "of examining in conformity with article seven of the Nine Power Treaty, the situation in the Far East and of studying peaceable means of hastening an end of the regrettable conflict which prevails there."

Since its opening session on November 3rd the Conference has continuously striven to promote conciliation and has endeavored to secure the cooperation of the Japanese Government in the hope of arresting hostilities and bringing about a settlement.

[36a] Other documents relating to the proceedings are contained in Department of State Conference Series 37 (pub. 1232), *The Conference of Brussels, November 3–24, 1937, Convened in Virtue of Article 7 of the Nine-Power Treaty of Washington of 1922* (Washington, Government Printing Office, 1938).

The Conference is convinced that force can provide not just and lasting solution for disputes between nations. It continues to believe that it would be to the immediate and the ultimate interest of both parties to the present dispute to avail themselves of the assistance of others in an effort to bring hostilities to an early end as a necessary preliminary to the achievement of a general and lasting settlement. It further believes that a satisfactory settlement cannot be achieved by direct negotiation between the parties to the conflict alone and that only by consultation with other powers principally concerned can there be achieved an agreement the terms of which will be just, generally acceptable and likely to endure.

This Conference strongly reaffirms the principles of the Nine Power Treaty as being among the basic principles which are essential to world peace and orderly progressive development of national and international life.

The Conference believes that a prompt suspension of hostilities in the Far East would be in the best interests not only of China and Japan but of all nations. With each day's continuance of the conflict the loss in lives and property increases and the ultimate solution of the conflict becomes more difficult.

The Conference therefore strongly urges that hostilities be suspended and resort be had to peaceful processes.

The Conference believes that no possible step to bring about by peaceful processes a just settlement of the conflict should be overlooked or omitted.

In order to allow time for participating governments to exchange views and further explore all peaceful methods by which a just settlement of the dispute may be attained consistently with the principles of the Nine Power Treaty and in conformity with the objectives of that treaty the Conference deems it advisable temporarily to suspend its sittings. The conflict in the Far East remains, however, a matter of concern to all of the powers assembled at Brussels—by virtue of commitments in the Nine Power Treaty or of special interest in the Far East—and especially to those most immediately and directly affected by conditions and events in the Far East. Those of them that are parties to the Nine Power Treaty have expressly adopted a policy designed to stabilize conditions in the Far East and, to that end, are bound by the provisions of that treaty, outstanding among which are those of articles 1 and 7.

The Conference will be called together again whenever its chairman or any two of its members shall have reported that they consider that its deliberations can be advantageously resumed.

98

394.115 Panay/92

The Secretary of State to the Ambassador in Japan (Grew)

[Telegram]

WASHINGTON, December 13, 1937—8 p. m.

342. Please communicate promptly to Hirota a note as follows:

"The Government and people of the United States have been deeply shocked by the facts of the bombardment and sinking of the U. S. S. *Panay* and the sinking or burning of the American steamers *Meiping*, *Meian* and *Meisian* [Meihsia] by Japanese aircraft.

The essential facts are that these American vessels were in the Yangtze River by uncontested and incontestable right; that they were flying the American flag; that they were engaged in their legitimate and appropriate business; that they were at the moment conveying American official and private personnel away from points where danger had developed; that they had several times changed their position, moving upriver, in order to avoid danger; and that they were attacked by Japanese bombing planes. With regard to the attack, a responsible Japanese naval officer at Shanghai has informed the Commander-in-Chief of the American Asiatic Fleet that the four vessels were proceeding upriver; that a Japanese plane endeavored to ascertain their nationality, flying at an altitude of three hundred meters, but was unable to distinguish the flags; that three Japanese bombing planes, six Japanese fighting planes, six Japanese bombing planes, and two Japanese bombing planes, in sequence, made attacks which resulted in the damaging of one of the American steamers, and the sinking of the U. S. S. *Panay* and the other two steamers.

Since the beginning of the present unfortunate hostilities between Japan and China, the Japanese Government and various Japanese authorities at various points have repeatedly assured the Government and authorities of the United States that it is the intention and purpose of the Japanese Government and the Japanese armed forces to respect fully the rights and interests of other powers. On several occasions, however, acts of Japanese armed forces have violated the rights of the United States, have seriously endangered the lives of American nationals, and have destroyed American property. In several instances, the Japanese Government has admitted the facts, has expressed regrets, and has given assurances that every precaution will be taken against recurrence of such incidents. In the present case, acts of Japanese armed forces have taken place in complete disregard of American rights, have taken American life, and have destroyed American property both public and private.

In these circumstances, the Government of the United States requests and expects of the Japanese Government a formally recorded expression of regret, an undertaking to make complete and comprehensive indemnifications, and an assurance that definite and specific steps have been taken which will ensure that hereafter American nationals, interests and property in China will not be subjected to attack by Japanese armed forces or unlawful interference by any Japanese authorities or forces whatsoever."

Before seeing Hirota inform your British colleague of intended action and text, but do not thereafter await action by him.

We are informing British Government of this instruction to you.

HULL

99

394.115 Panay/59

The Ambassador in Japan (Grew) to the Secretary of State

[Telegram]

TOKYO, December 14, 1937—6 p. m.
[Received December 14—10 a. m.]

630. 1. At 5 o'clock this afternoon Yoshizawa [37] called on me upon instructions from the Minister for Foreign Affairs and handed me a note of which the following is an informal translation made by the Foreign Office. The translation is accurate in point of substance and corresponds closely to the original Japanese text.

"December 14, 1937.

Monsieur l'Ambassadeur: Regarding the incident of the 12th December in which the United States gunboat *Panay* and three steamers belonging to the Standard Oil Company were sunk by the bombing of the Japanese naval aircraft on the Yangtze River at a point about twenty-six miles above Nanking, I had the honor, as soon as unofficial information of the incident was brought to my knowledge, to request Your Excellency to transmit to the Government of the United States the apologies of the Japanese Government. From the reports subse-

---

[37] Director of the American Bureau of the Japanese Ministry for Foreign Affairs.

quently received from our representatives in China, it has been established that the Japanese naval air force, acting upon information that the Chinese troops fleeing from Nanking were going up the river in steamers, took off to pursue them, and discovered such vessels at the above-mentioned point. Owing to poor visibility, however, the aircraft, although they descended to fairly low altitudes, were unable to discern any mark to show that any one of them was an American ship or man-of-war. Consequently, the United States gunboat *Panay* and the vessels of the Standard Oil Company, being taken for Chinese vessels carrying the fleeing Chinese troops, were bombed and sunk.

While it is clear, in the light of the above circumstances, that the present incident was entirely due to a mistake, the Japanese Government regret most profoundly that it has caused damages to the United States man-of-war and ships and casualties among those on board, and desire to present hereby sincere apologies. The Japanese Government will make indemnifications for all the losses and will deal appropriately with those responsible for the incident. Furthermore, they have already issued strict orders to the authorities on the spot with a view to preventing the recurrence of a similar incident.

The Japanese Government, in the fervent hope that the friendly relations between Japan and the United States will not be affected by this unfortunate affair, have frankly stated as above their sincere attitude which I beg Your Excellency to make known to your Government.

I avail myself, etc., signed Koki Hirota."

2. Yoshizawa then read to me portions of the official Japanese naval report on the disaster the purport of which is that the disaster was not caused by deliberate intention to bomb American vessels but was due to the inability of the aviators to distinguish the nationality of the vessels bombed. I informed Yoshizawa that his explanation does not cover the fact that, notwithstanding information in Japanese hands that foreign vessels were in the neighborhood of Nanking, bombarding and shelling operations by both naval and military forces were carried out without any precautions taken against attack upon foreign vessels. I also pointed out that the bombing and shelling was carried out in the face of repeated assurances that measures had been taken to safeguard against attacks upon American nationals and property.

3. I also stated to Yoshizawa that I had just received instructions to present to the Minister for Foreign Affairs a note from the American Government. I added that, although I appreciated the action of

the Japanese Government in delivering to me its note, I would proceed with the instructions which had been given to me.

4. I am still waiting for an appointment to call on Hirota which I asked for at 4 o'clock.

Repeated to Peiping for Hankow.

GREW

100

793.94Conference/351

Report of the United States Delegate to the Conference at Brussels (Davis)

[Extracts]

DECEMBER 16, 1937.

The Belgian Government "in response to the request of the British Government and with the approval of the American Government" issued to the parties to the Nine Power Treaty an invitation to attend a conference at Brussels for the purpose "of examining in accordance with Article VII of the Nine Power Treaty, the situation in the Far East and to study peaceable methods for hastening the end of the regrettable conflict now taking place there." Also, after consulting other powers to the Treaty, it issued similar invitations to the Soviet Union and Germany.

All parties to the Nine Power Treaty, except Japan, accepted the invitation. Also, the Soviet Union accepted. Japan declined and Germany declined.

By this time it was realized that the task given to the Brussels Conference had been made additionally difficult by the fact that the League and the American Government had already delivered judgment upon Japan's course.

The American Delegate to the Conference received instructions in the form of: a written instruction from the Secretary of State; an informal memorandum; oral instructions given by the President and the Secretary of State at the White House; and oral instructions given by the President at Hyde Park. The general purport of all of these instructions was to the effect that the policy to be followed must be consistent with the principles and provisions of the Nine Power Treaty and the general principles of American foreign policy as laid down especially in public statements of the Secretary of State and the President. There was no provision that any positive methods of pressure should or might be discussed at the Conference; but there was also no express provision that such method should *not* be discussed, provided, however, that previously every effort to bring about mediation had been exhausted. In the written instruction, attention was called not only to the terms of the Belgian Government's invitation but also to statements of the Secretary of State and to the President's address at Chicago of October 5. In the conversations at the White House and at Hyde Park, especially the latter, the President emphasized to the American Delegate the view that if we are to avoid an ultimate serious clash with Japan some practical means must be found to check Japan's career of conquest and to make effective the collective will of those powers which desire that principles of law and order shall prevail and controversies between nations be regulated and settled by peaceful means rather than by use of armed force. The President emphasized the importance of mobilising moral force in all peace-loving nations and suggested a strategy of calling upon Japan repeatedly to come into conference and seek means for desisting from hostilities and submitting the issues between herself and China to peaceful processes of settlement. He suggested that the Conference might be given a prolonged life and that it might be made an agency for informing and educating public opinion by way of bringing to bear upon Japan every moral pressure directed toward bringing about a change in Japan's attitude and policy. Also, he suggested that the Delegation observe closely the trend of public opinion in the United States and take full account thereof. He realized the difficulties before us but hoped that the Conference might nonetheless produce constructive results either in its influence on Japan or in mobilising public opinion.

The outstanding achievements of the Conference were as follows:

1. Exchanging of views, among nineteen governments, enabling the delegates of each—and through them their governments—to obtain knowledge of the attitude and position of the others;

2. Demonstration of the unwillingness of Japan to resort to methods of conciliation;

3. Clarification of the fact that the Japanese continue to insist that the issues between Japan and China are exclusive to those two countries whereas the Conference Powers with the exception of Italy deny this and affirm that the situation is of concern to all of them and in fact to all members of the Family of Nations;

4. Express reaffirmation by the Conference Powers with the exception of Italy of the principles of the Nine Power Treaty.

5. Express serving of notice that the settlement ultimately arrived

at must be consistent with the principles of the Nine Power Treaty and satisfactory to the Conference Powers;

6. Express serving of notice that the Conference Powers will continue to concern themselves with the situation and that the Conference is not ended but is in recess and is subject to re-convocation.

101

Press Releases, vol. XVIII, p. 99

President Roosevelt to the Speaker of the House Of Representatives (Bankhead)

WASHINGTON, January 6, 1938.

MY DEAR MR. SPEAKER:

In response to your request for an expression of my views respecting the proposed resolution calling for a referendum vote as a prerequisite for a declaration of war,[38] I must frankly state that I consider that the proposed amendment would be impracticable in its application and incompatible with our representative form of government.

Our Government is conducted by the people through representatives of their own choosing. It was with singular unanimity that the founders of the Republic agreed upon such free and representative form of government as the only practical means of government by the people.

Such an amendment to the Constitution as that proposed would

---

[38] "Resolved by the Senate and House of Representatives of the United States of America in Congress assembled (two-thirds of each House concurring therein), That the following article is proposed as an amendment to the Constitution of the United States, which shall be valid to all intents and purposes as a part of the Constitution when ratified by the legislatures of three-fourths of the several States.

" 'ARTICLE

" 'SECTION 1. Except in the event of an invasion of the United States or its Territorial possessions and attack upon its citizens residing therein, the authority of Congress to declare war shall not become effective until confirmed by a majority of all votes cast thereon in a Nation-wide referendum. Congress, when it deems a national crisis to exist, may by concurrent resolution refer the question of war or peace to the citizens of the States, the question to cripple any President in his conduct of our foreign relations, and it would encourage other nations to believe that they could violate American rights with impunity.

I fully realize that the sponsors of this proposal sincerely believe that it would be helpful in keeping the United States out of war. I am convinced it would have the opposite effect.

Yours very sincerely,

FRANKLIN D. ROOSEVELT

102

Press Releases, vol. XVIII, p. 100

The Secretary of State to the Chairman of the Committee on Foreign Affairs (McReynolds), House of Representatives

WASHINGTON, January 8, 1938.

DEAR CONGRESSMAN MCREYNOLDS:

In reply to your inquiry I would say that on December 15, 1937, in referring to the Ludlow Resolution, I stated to the press that "from the standpoint of promoting peace and keeping this country out of war, I am unable to see either the wisdom or practicability of this proposal".

The primary objective in the conduct of our foreign affairs is to safeguard the peace of the United States. All American citizens agree alike that this country should be safeguarded against war to the fullest possible extent. It is my judgment that under our present form of government "of the people, by the people, and for the people", our foreign affairs can be conducted far more efficiently from the standpoint of keeping this country out of war than would be at all possible under the operation of any such plan as the Ludlow Resolution proposes. After the fullest consideration I am satisfied that this plan would most seriously handicap the Government in the conduct of our foreign affairs generally, and would thus impair disastrously its ability to safeguard the peace of the American people.

Sincerely yours,

CORDELL HULL

Footnote 38—Continued.

be voted on being, Shall the United States declare war on _____? Congress may otherwise by law provide for the enforcement of this section.' "

This was the so-called "Ludlow Resolution", H.J. Res. 199, 75th Cong., 1st sess.

103

711.62/135

Memorandum by the Secretary of State Regarding a Conversation With the German Ambassador (Dieckhoff)

[WASHINGTON,] January 14, 1938.

The German Ambassador came in upon his own request. He was very prompt to say that he came on his own initiative, and without instructions, to speak very earnestly about the utterances the night before of former Ambassador William E. Dodd, in which among other things he accused Chancellor Hitler of killing as many people in Germany as were killed by Charles II. The Ambassador then launched into a very strong statement about the injury to the relations between our two governments which such an utterance would inevitably cause. The fact, he said, that Dodd had been recognized until recently as Ambassador at Berlin and of his returning here and at once engaging in such serious attacks upon Chancellor Hitler was wholly unjustifiable from every standpoint and would be given more weight by reason of his recently having been ambassador; that, therefore, he felt this Government should say that it disapproved what Dr. Dodd had said. These are the principal points he made. It is possible that I proceeded to talk before he had reached a stage of asking for apologies and regrets, although I cannot say whether this was in his mind. I proceeded to say that, of course, regardless of what might be thought of various forms of government, including this government, we do have under our Constitution and Bill of Rights freedom of speech, from the results of which there is no recourse except under the law of libel and slander, which includes criminal liability; that we who are engaged in the public service in this country are subjected to what we often consider the most outrageous criticisms and insults; that of course the Ambassador knows Dr. Dodd and is acquainted with his ideas and his disposition to give expression to them wherever he goes; that I have very little personal or official influence with Dr. Dodd so far as I was aware, although this latter phase was neither here nor there and was not intended to be a governing or material phase of what I was saying. I then stated that Dr. Dodd, having recently resigned as Ambassador and now being a private citizen, does not in his utterances represent the views of this Government. I then inquired of the Ambassador as to how many men Charles II killed. The Ambassador replied that he did not recall. In fact, neither of us did at the moment. We were not certain that Charles II was especially notorious in this regard.

The Ambassador brought up some phase of the controversy between dictatorships and democracies and indicated his displeasure at the way this debate was being carried on. I said to him that naturally and inevitably the one supreme issue or question is whether the principles which underlie the structure of international law and order shall be preserved or whether the doctrine of force and militarism and aggression and the destruction of all international law and order should prevail; that in support of the first proposal each of the sixty-five nations alike can, with perfect consistency, join in, no matter what their form of government might happen to be. I said this program contemplates that the road to permanent peace is based upon these principles which in turn rest upon the solid foundation of economic restoration.

C[ORDELL] H[ULL]

104

Press Releases, vol. XVIII, p. 190

Message of President Roosevelt to the Congress, January 28, 1938

The Congress knows that for many years this Government has sought in many capitals with the leaders of many Governments to find a way to limit and reduce armaments and to establish at least the probability of world peace.

The Congress is aware also that while these efforts, supported by the hopes of the American people, continue and will continue they have nevertheless failed up to the present time.

We, as a peaceful Nation, cannot and will not abandon active search for an agreement among the nations to limit armaments and end aggression. But it is clear that until such agreement is reached—and I have not given up hope of it—we are compelled to think of our own national safety.

It is with the deepest regret that I report to you that armaments increase today at an unprecedented and alarming rate. It is an ominous fact that at least one-fourth of the world's population is involved in merciless devastating conflict in spite of the fact that most people in most countries, including those where conflict rages, wish to live at peace. Armies are fighting in the Far East and in Europe; thousands of civilians are being driven from their homes and bombed from the air. Tension throughout the world is high.

As Commander-in-Chief of the Army and Navy of the United States it is my constitutional duty to report to the Congress that our national defense is, in the light of the increasing armaments of other nations, inadequate for purposes of national security and requires increase for that reason.

In spite of the well-known fact that the American standard of living makes our ships, our guns, and our planes cost more for construction than in any other nation and that the maintenance of them and of our Army and Navy personnel is more expensive than in any other nation, it is also true that the proportion of the cost of our military and naval forces to the total income of our citizens or to the total cost of our Government is far lower than in the case of any other great nation.

Specifically and solely because of the piling up of additional land and sea armaments in other countries, in such manner as to involve a threat to world peace and security, I make the following recommendations to the Congress:

(1) That there be authorized for the Army of the United States additions to antiaircraft matériel in the sum of $8,800,000 and that of this sum $6,800,000 be appropriated for the fiscal year 1939.

(2) That there be authorized and appropriated for the better establishment of an enlisted reserve for the Army the sum of $450,000.

(3) That there be authorized the expenditure of $6,080,000 for the manufacture of gauges, dies, and other aids to manufacture Army matériel, the sum of $5,000,000 thereof to be expended during the fiscal year 1939.

(4) That the sum of $2,000,000 be authorized and appropriated toward the making up of deficiencies in ammunition for the Army.

(5) That the existing authorized building program for increases and replacements in the Navy be increased by 20 percent.

(6) That this Congress authorize and appropriate for the laying down of two additional battleships and two additional cruisers during the calendar year 1938. This will call for the expenditure of a very small amount of Government funds during the fiscal year 1939.

(7) That the Congress authorize and appropriate a sum not to exceed $15,000,000 for the construction of a number of new types of small vessels, such construction to be regarded as experimental in the light of new developments among navies; and to include the preparation of plans for other types of ships in the event that it may be necessary to construct such ships in the future.

I believe also that the time has come for the Congress to enact legislation aimed at the prevention of profiteering in time of war and the equalization of the burdens of possible war. Such legislation has been the subject for many years of full study in this and previous Congresses.

It is necessary for all of us to realize that the unfortunate world conditions of today have resulted too often in the discarding of those principles and treaties which underlie international law and order, and in the entrance of many new factors into the actual conduct of war.

Adequate defense means that for the protection not only of our coasts but also of our communities far removed from the coast, we must keep any potential enemy many hundred miles away from our continental limits.

We cannot assume that our defense would be limited to one ocean and one coast and that the other ocean and the other coast would with certainty be safe. We cannot be certain that the connecting link—the Panama Canal—would be safe. Adequate defense affects therefore the simultaneous defense of every part of the United States of America.

It is our clear duty to further every effort toward peace but at the same time to protect our Nation. That is the purpose of these recommendations. Such protection is and will be based not on aggression but on defense.

FRANKLIN D. ROOSEVELT

THE WHITE HOUSE,
  January 28, 1938.

105

Press Releases, vol. XVIII, p. 253

*The Secretary of State to the Honorable Louis Ludlow, House
Of Representatives*

WASHINGTON, February 10, 1938.

MY DEAR CONGRESSMAN:

I have your letter of February 9 [7] in which you express yourself as perplexed by "the maze of contradictions and uncertainties" with respect to the problems relating to national defense and peace, and conclude by requesting certain specific information.

I may say that being in possession, as you doubtless are, of the texts of my public statements and published communications which I have made on the subject of our foreign policy and our foreign relations, you should not permit yourself to be disturbed by affirmations from other sources which are contradictory to statements of fact which, as a responsible official, I have repeatedly made. I have in mind especially my statement of principles underlying all international law and order and normal relations between nations, on July 16, 1937; my statement of August 23, 1937; my letter to Senator Smathers of December 13 [*18*], 1937; my letter to the Vice President on January 8, 1938; and numerous statements to the press in addition during the past seven months, setting forth in almost every detail our foreign policy. You will recall that in addition I addressed an executive meeting of some one hundred and fifty Congressmen one evening at the House Office Building on all phases of our foreign policy and invited questions at the conclusion. If you were not present, I am sorry. I have in addition conferred with many Congressmen, as I have with numerous Senators, touching any and every phase of foreign policy in which they expressed the least interest.

Your specific inquiry reads as follows:

"1. Whether all of the ships and auxiliary services provided for in the proposed program are regarded as necessary for defense of our homeland and our possessions, or
"2. Whether the program contemplates the use of some of the units in cooperation with any other nation in any part of the world."

I am glad to have the opportunity to make categorical statements in regard to this matter. First, in my opinion all of the ships and auxiliary services provided for in the proposed program are needed for the national defense of the United States and its possessions. It is the desire of the people and of the Government of the United States that this country be not drawn into or forced into war. It is the duty and the intention of the Administration to make effective so far as lies within its power the desire of the country in this as in other respects. It is the belief of those of us who, with full sense of responsibility, advocate these increases in our naval strength, that the making of these increases will contribute toward attainment of that objective. As you know, in the opinion of the expert technical authorities, our Navy, even with these increases, would not be able to embark upon offensive or aggressive operations overseas. In our foreign policy there is not any disposition or intent to engage in warfare.

We believe, however, that the people of this country desire that the country be respected, that our nationals and our interests abroad be given fair treatment, and that there should prevail in the world conditions of peace, order, and security. This country always has exerted its influence in support of such objectives. We believe that within the limitations of its traditional policies it should continue to do so. If it is prepared and known to be prepared, the likelihood of its being drawn into trouble will either be absent or greatly diminished.

With regard to your second question, I might refer to the letter which I wrote to Senator Pittman under date of February 7 [8], which was read by Senator Pittman in the Senate on February 8. I am glad to repeat or to amplify or in any other possible way restate any of the statements which I have heretofore made public, if by so doing I can be to the least extent helpful to you. For present purposes and in express reply to your question, I may say, the proposed program does not contemplate the use of any of the units in cooperation with any other nation in any part of the world. To be still more specific, I may say that the policy I announced during last August is still being strictly observed; that is that this Government carefully avoids, on the one hand, extreme internationalism with its political entanglements, and, on the other hand, extreme isolation, with its tendency to cause other nations to believe that this nation is more or less afraid; that while avoiding any alliances or entangling commitments, it is appropriate and advisable, when this and other countries have common interests and common objectives, for this Government to exchange information with governments of such other countries, to confer with those governments, and, where practicable, to proceed on parallel lines, but reserving always the fullest freedom of judgment and right of independence of action.

Naturally, we believe that it is a matter of simple common sense for nations which desire peace to cooperate in every satisfactory and practical way toward maintaining peace. If every peaceful nation were to insist on remaining entirely aloof from every other peaceful nation and on pursuing a policy of armament limitation without reference to relative armaments, the inevitable consequence would be that other nations inclined to play lawless roles would thereby be given great encouragement and even assistance toward so doing.

Sincerely yours,

CORDELL HULL

106

Department of State pub. 1146

Address Delivered by the Secretary of State at Washington, March 17, 1938

In the course of the daily press conferences at the Department of State, I have occasion to see many of you and to touch upon day-to-day developments in our foreign relations. Such information as I am able to give you in these conferences must, of necessity, relate to specific questions and, oftentimes, to isolated events. Yet upon you, representatives of the press, rests a heavy responsibility in keeping our people currently and accurately informed on the vital issues which arise in our country's relations with other nations. I welcome, therefore, this opportunity to meet with the members of the National Press Club in the calmer atmosphere of an occasion like the present one, and to discuss with you some of the fundamental conditions and problems presented by our international relations and our foreign policy.

The primary objectives of our foreign policy are the maintenance of the peace of our country and the promotion of the economic, the social, and the moral welfare of our people. Unfortunately, the means of attaining these objectives involve today so many factors of great complexity that their real significance is frequently misunderstood and misinterpreted.

By instinct and tradition our country has been, throughout its history, sincerely devoted to the cause of peace. Within the limitations imposed by time and circumstance we have earnestly sought to discharge our responsibilities as a member of the family of nations in promoting conditions essential to the maintenance of peace. We have consistently believed in the sanctity of treaty obligations and have endeavored to apply this belief in the actual practice of our foreign relations. In common with all other nations we have, since the end of the World War, assumed a solemn obligation not to resort to force as an instrument of national policy. All this gives us a moral right to express our deep concern over the rising tide of lawlessness, the growing disregard of treaties, the increasing reversion to the use of force, and the numerous other ominous tendencies which are emerging in the sphere of international relations.

On July 16, 1937, I issued a public statement setting forth the fundamental principles to which our Government adheres in the formulation of its foreign policy. On behalf of our Government I transmitted a copy of this statement to every government of the world, requesting such comment as each might see fit to offer. To our profound gratification an overwhelming majority of those governments joined in affirming their faith in these vital principles.

The most important of these principles, which are indispensable to a satisfactory international order, are as follows:

Maintenance of peace should be constantly advocated and practiced.

All nations should, through voluntary self-restraint, abstain from use of force in pursuit of policy and from interference in the internal affairs of other nations.

All nations should seek to adjust problems arising in their international relations by processes of peaceful negotiation and agreement.

All nations should uphold the principle of the sanctity of treaties and of faithful observance of international agreements.

Modification of provisions of treaties, when need therefor arises, should be by orderly processes carried out in a spirit of mutual helpfulness and accommodation.

Each nation should respect the rights of others and perform scrupulously its own established obligations; in brief, international law and the spirit which underlies it must be revitalized and strengthened.

Steps should be taken toward promotion of economic security and stability the world over through lowering or removal of barriers to international trade, according of effective equality of commercial opportunity, and application of the principle of equality of commercial treatment.

National armaments should be limited and be progressively reduced; at the same time, realizing the necessity for maintaining armed forces adequate for national security, each nation should to that end be prepared to reduce or increase its own armed forces in proportion as reductions or increases are made by other nations.

Apart from the question of alliances with others, each nation should be prepared to engage in cooperative effort, by peaceful and practicable means, in support of these principles.

The peace and progress of every nation are just as dependent on international law and order, based upon the foregoing principles, as the welfare, stability, and progress of a community are dependent upon domestic law and order, based upon legal, moral, and other recognized standards of conduct. No government faithful to the sacred trust involved in the task of providing for the safety and well-being of its people can disregard these universal principles. Every nation, whatever its form of government, can support them. Every nation must support them, if civilization is to survive. The longer the nations delay acceptance and observance of these fundamental tenets of constructive statesmanship, the graver will be the jeopardy into which all worth-while international relationships will be plunged, and with them the welfare, the happiness, and the civilized existence of all nations.

The crucial issue today is whether these principles will be vitalized and be firmly established as the foundation of an international order or whether international anarchy based on brute force will inundate the world and ultimately sweep away the very bases of civilization and progress. That issue is universal. No more than a community or a nation, can the world base its existence in part on law and in part on lawlessness, in part on order and in part on chaos, in part on processes of peace and in part on methods of violence.

On August 23 I made another public statement reaffirming the principles which should underlie international order, peace, and justice, if the world is to avoid a relapse into another dark night of international anarchy and general retrogression. I called attention again to the fact that if these principles are to be effective they must be universal in their application. This statement was prompted by the fact that the progress and possibilities of armed conflict were becoming more alarming both in the European and the Far Eastern areas and that the basic principles to which I have just referred were being challenged and the doctrine of armed force was gaining supremacy in important regions of the world.

During the early months of the conflict in the Far East I appealed on several occasions, in the name of our Government, to both Japan and China to desist from using armed force and to resort to the well-recognized processes of peaceful settlement for the adjustment of whatever differences existed between them. I said that we would be glad to be of assistance toward facilitating, in any manner that might be practicable and mutually agreeable, resort by them to such processes.

On August 17, and with frequent reiteration thereafter, I stated that we did not intend to abandon our nationals and our interests in China.

From time immemorial it has been the practice of civilized nations to afford protection, by appropriate means and under the rule of reason, to their nationals and their rights and interests abroad. This policy has been pursued by the Government of the United States throughout the existence of our country.

Methods and means of affording protection abroad vary according to the places in which and the circumstances under which protection is called for. In the case of China, where unusual local conditions were such that the protection afforded by local authorities did not suffice to give security against excited and lawless elements, there have occasionally been sent—not by this country alone but by a number of countries—armed forces, to contribute to the affording of such protection as is due under the rules of international law and the provisions of treaties. American forces thus sent to China have at no time had any mission of aggression, and it has been the practice of the American Government to withdraw such forces whenever and as soon as the local situation so develops as to warrant the view that their withdrawal can be effected without detriment to American interests and obligations in general.

In announcing our intention to afford appropriate and reasonable protection to our rights and interests in the Far East, I stated clearly that we are fully determined to avoid the extremes either of internationalism or of isolationism. Internationalism would mean undesirable political involvements; isolationism would either compel us to confine all activities of our people within our own frontiers, with incalculable injury to the standard of living and the general welfare of our people, or else expose our nationals and our legitimate interests abroad to injustice or outrage wherever lawless conditions arise. Steering a sound middle course between these two extremes, we are convinced that a policy of affording appropriate protection—under the rule of reason, in such form as may be best suited to the particular circumstances, and in accordance with the principles we advocate —is imperatively needed to serve our national interest.

Our decision in this matter is based not only on what we firmly believe to be a specific and elementary duty of a government toward its citizens, but also on other and broader considerations. Respect by a country for the rights and interests of others is a visible test of the fulfillment of obligations assumed by virtue of acceptance of international law and of undertakings embodied in negotiated international instruments. It is, therefore, a test of the observance of those fundamental principles of civilized relations among nations, which, if firmly established, provide in themselves the best means of protection against violation and abuse of the legitimate rights and interests of every nation.

To waive rights and to permit interests to lapse in the face of their actual or threatened violation—and thereby to abandon obligations— in any important area of the world, can serve only to encourage disregard of law and of the basic principles of international order, and thus contribute to the inevitable spread of international anarchy throughout the world. For this country, as for any country, to act in such manner *anywhere* would be to invite disregard and violation of its rights and interests *everywhere*, by every nation so inclined, large or small.

To respect the rights of others and to insist that others respect our rights has been the traditional policy of our country. This policy was admirably expressed by James Monroe when, in his message to Congress on December 2, 1823, he said:

"Our policy . . . remains the same: . . . to cultivate friendly relations . . . and to preserve those relations by frank, firm, and manly policy, meeting in all instances the just claims of every power, submitting to injuries from none."

In a world in which the rule of force has not as yet been firmly and surely supplanted by the rule of law, it is the manifest duty of a great nation to maintain armed forces adequate for its national defense. Writing on this subject, which was as vital to our national life 150 years ago as it is today, James Madison said:

"The means of security can only be regulated by the means and the danger of attack. They will, in fact, be ever determined by these rules, and by no others."

It is the duty of the Federal Government to insure the safety of our country and to determine what "means of security" are, at any given moment, needed to provide against "the means and the danger of attack." The responsible heads of our naval establishment offer convincing reasons in support of the program, now before the Congress, to render adequate the means of our national defense. No policy would prove more disastrous than for an important nation to fail to arm adequately when international lawlessness is on the rampage. It is my considered judgment that, in the present state of world affairs, to do less than is now proposed would lay our country open to unpredictable hazards. It would, moreover, seriously restrict our Nation's ability to command, without purpose or occasion for resorting to arms, proper respect for its legitimate rights and interests, the surrender of which would constitute abandonment of the fundamental principles of justice and morality and peace among nations.

The maintenance of these principles that are of concern to all nations alike cannot and should not be undertaken by any one nation alone. Prudence and common sense dictate that, where this and other nations have common interests and common objectives, we should not hesitate to exchange information and to confer with the governments of such other nations and, in dealing with the problems confronting each alike, to proceed along parallel lines—this Government retaining at all times its independence of judgment and freedom of action. For nations which seek peace to assume with respect to each other attitudes of complete aloofness would serve only to encourage, and virtually invite, on the part of other nations lawlessly inclined, policies and actions most likely to endanger peace.

In the present Far Eastern emergency, we have consistently collaborated with other peace-seeking nations in the manner I have just described. I have said often, and I repeat again, that in this collaboration there is not a trace of alliance or involvement of any sort. We have scrupulously followed and we intend to follow the traditional policy of our country not to enter into entangling alliances or involvements with other countries.

When the Brussels Conference was called, this country, as one of the original signatories of the Nine Power Treaty and in accordance with its treaty obligations thus assumed, promptly accepted the invitation to the Conference. Our delegation cooperated fully with the representatives of the other Conference powers in examining the situation in the Far East and exploring methods of bringing about peace by processes of agreement. The Conference made a substantial contribution toward keeping alive principles of world order and of respect for the pledged word. Its declarations placed a new emphasis upon the deep concern of peaceful nations over any developments that threaten the preservation of peace.

In connection with the Far Eastern situation, this Government was confronted with the question of applying the existing neutrality legislation, which was designed primarily to keep our Nation out of war. After mature deliberation the conclusion was reached that in the circumstances attending the controversy in the Far East—a type of circumstances which the authors of the legislation could scarcely have visualized—application of the law would be most likely to endanger the very objectives which the law was designed to promote. Accordingly, exercising the discretion vested in him by the law itself, the President has refrained from putting the provisions of that law into operation. At the same time, in pursuance of our general policy of avoiding unnecessary risks, the President announced, on September 14, 1937, that "Merchant vessels owned by the Government of the United States will not hereafter, until further notice, be permitted to transport to China or Japan any of the arms, ammunition, or implements of war which were listed in the President's proclamation of May 1, 1937," and that "Any other merchant vessels, flying the American flag, which attempt to transport any of the listed articles to China or Japan will, until further notice, do so at their own risk."

Our Government pursues, in relation to every world area alike, a policy of noninterference, with ill will toward no nation and a sincere desire to be friendly with all. At the same time, we endeavor to afford appropriate protection to American citizens and American interests everywhere. During recent months, as throughout the past 150 years, the Government of the United States has sought to exercise moral influence and to cooperate in every practicable way with all peace-seeking nations in support of those basic principles which are indispensable to the promotion and maintenance of stable conditions of peace.

We have affirmed on every possible occasion and have urged upon all nations the supreme need for keeping alive and for practicing sound fundamental principles of relations among civilized nations. We have never entertained and we have not the slightest intention to entertain any such notion as the use of American armed forces for "policing the world." But we equally have not the slightest intention of reversing a tradition of a century and a half by abandoning our deep concern for, and our advocacy of, the establishment everywhere of international order under law, based upon the well-recognized principles to which I have referred. It is our profound conviction that the most effective contribution which we, as a nation sincerely devoted to the cause of peace, can make—in the tragic conditions with which our people, in common with the rest of mankind, are confronted today—is to have this country respected throughout the world for integrity, justice, good will, strength, and unswerving loyalty to principles.

The foregoing is the essence of our foreign policy. The record is an open book. We spare no effort to make known the facts regarding our attitude, our objectives, and our acts. We are always ready to furnish to the members of the Congress essential information. You, gentlemen, have first-hand knowledge of our constant effort to keep the press and the public informed.

There is one thing that we cannot do; and that is, to prepare and to place before every government of the world a detailed chart of the course of policy and action which this country will or will not pursue under any particular set of circumstances. No man, no nation, can possibly foresee all the circumstances that may arise. Moreover, to attempt to make such a detailed chart of future action would merely result in impairing our effectiveness in working for the one objective toward which we constantly strive and on which, I am certain, there is not a vestige of disagreement among the people of our country— the establishment of durable peace.

So strong, indeed, is the desire of this country for peace that many measures have been suggested toward our keeping out of war—some of them in complete disregard of both experience and practicability. It has been urged that we apply the neutrality law automatically in all circumstances, without adequate consideration of the possible consequences of such action for our own peace and for the safety of our citizens. It has been urged that we withdraw precipitately from any part of the world in which violators of international decencies choose to assert themselves. It has even been urged that we change the very basis of our representative form of government in a frantic search for something which the proposers assume would make it more likely that this country avoid war.

I take it for granted that all of us alike are sincere friends of peace. This makes it all the more necessary for every one of us to scrutinize carefully every measure proposed, lest in our attempts to avoid war we imperil the chances of preserving peace.

The problem of the form of government best adapted to this country's needs was one with which the founders of our Republic came to grips in those stirring days when the structure of our independent national existence was being given form and substance. After exhaustive deliberation and discussion they decided upon the system of representative democracy in preference to that of pure democracy as the system through which the people could best safeguard their liberty and promote their national security and welfare. The wisdom of the founders of this Nation in deciding, with conspicuous unanimity, to place the conduct of foreign relations in the hands of the Federal Government has stood the test of generations as providing the most effective means that can be devised for assuring the peace, the security, and the independence of our people.

What warrant is there, in reason or in experience, for the assumption—which underlies such proposals as the plan for a popular referendum on the subject of declaring war—that the Chief Executive and the Congress will be at any time more eager and more likely to embark upon war than would be the general body of citizens to whom they are directly responsible? No President and no Congress have ever carried this country into war against the will of the people. On the other hand, there is not a vestige of doubt that the adoption of a procedure like the referendum plan would hopelessly handicap the Government in the conduct of our foreign relations in general and would thus disastrously impair its ability to safeguard the interests of the Nation, in the forefront among which is that of peace.

Likewise dangerous, from the viewpoint of the preservation of peace, is the proposal that we retire from the Far East, comprising the chief portion of the Pacific area. Unfortunately, many people in this country have wholly misunderstood the position and policy of our Government in relation to that situation. Some have visualized only our trade and investment relationships with China, or our moral and cultural interests there, symbolized by missionary, educational, medical, and similar activities. Some have concentrated their attention solely upon the incidental and exceptional facts of the existence of extraterritoriality and the maintenance of some armed forces to assist in safeguarding our nationals against possible mob violence and similar disorders—special rights which it is our policy to give up and forces which it is our policy to withdraw the moment the unusual conditions disappear.

All these are important. But the interest and concern of the United States—whether in the Far East, in any other part of the Pacific area, in Europe, or anywhere else in the world—are not measured alone by the number of American citizens residing in a particular country, or by the volume of investment and trade, or by exceptional conditions peculiar to the particular area. There is a much broader and more fundamental interest—which is, that orderly processes in international relationships based on the principles to which I have referred be maintained.

As I have already indicated, what is most of all at stake today, throughout the world, is the future of the fundamental principles which must be the foundation of international order as opposed to international anarchy. If we and others were to abandon and surrender these principles in regard to the Pacific area, which is almost one half of the world, we would have to reconcile ourselves to their certain abandonment and surrender in regard to the other half of the world.

It would be absurd and futile for us to proclaim that we stand for international law, for the sanctity of treaty obligations, for nonintervention in internal affairs of other countries, for equality of industrial and commercial rights and opportunities, for limitation and reduction of armaments—but only in one-half of the world, and among one-half of the world's population. The catastrophic developments of recent years, the startling events of the past weeks, offer a tragic demonstration of how quickly the contagious scourge of treaty breaking and armed violence spreads from one region to another.

Those who contend that we can and should abandon and surrender principles in one-half of the world clearly show that they have little or no conception of the extent to which situations and developments in any part of the world of today inevitably affect situations and conditions in other parts of the world. The triumph of this seclusionist viewpoint would inescapably carry the whole world back to the conditions of medieval chaos, conditions toward which some parts of both the eastern and the western worlds are already moving. Such is the fate to which extreme isolationists—isolationists at any price—all those who contend that we should neither protest against abuses nor cooperate with others toward keeping principles alive, those who say that under no circumstances should we insist upon any rights beyond our own territorial waters—such is the fate to which blind extremism of this type would consign this country and the world.

The momentous question—let me repeat—is whether the doctrine of force shall become enthroned once more and bring in its wake, inexorably, international anarchy and a relapse into barbarism; or whether this and other peaceful nations, fervently attached to the principles which underlie international order, shall work unceasingly—singly or in cooperation with each other, as circumstances, their traditional policies and practices, and their enlightened self-interest may dictate—to promote and preserve law, order, morality, and justice as the unshakeable bases of civilized international relations.

We might, if we could reconcile ourselves to such an attitude, turn our backs on the whole problem and decline the responsibility and labor of contributing to its solution. But let us have no illusions as to what such a course of action would involve for us as a nation.

It would mean a break with our past, both internationally and domestically. It would mean a voluntary abandonment of some of the most important things that have made us a great nation. It would mean an abject retreat before those forces which we have, throughout our whole national history, consistently opposed.

It would mean that our security would be menaced in proportion as other nations came to believe that, either through fear or through unwillingness, we did not intend to afford protection to our legitimate national interests abroad, but, on the contrary, intended to abandon them at the first sign of danger. Under such conditions the sphere of our international relationships—economic, cultural, intellectual, and other—would necessarily shrink and shrivel, until we would stand practically alone among the nations, a self-constituted hermit state.

Thrown back upon our own resources, we would find it necessary to reorganize our entire social and economic structure. The process of adaptation to a more or less self-contained existence would mean less production and at higher costs; lower living standards; regimentation in every phase of life; economic distress to wage earners and farmers, and to their families; and the dole, on an ever-increasing scale.

All this we would be doing in pursuit of the notion that by so doing we would avoid war. But would these policies, while entailing such enormous sacrifices and rendering the Nation more and more decadent, really give us any such assurance?

Reason and experience definitely point to the contrary. We may seek to withdraw from participation in world affairs, but we cannot thereby withdraw from the world itself. Isolation is not a means to security; it is a fruitful source of insecurity.

We want to live in a world which is at peace; in which the forces of militarism, of territorial aggression, and of international anarchy in general will become utterly odious, revolting, and intolerable to the conscience of mankind; in which the doctrine of order under law will be firmly established; in which there will no longer be one code of morality, honor, justice, and fair play for the individual in his relations with other individuals, and an entirely different code for governments and nations in their relations with each other. We want to live in a world in which fruitful and constructive international relationships can serve as a medium for disseminating throughout the world the benefits of the material, spiritual, and moral progress of mankind.

To that end we will continue to give full and sincere adherence to the fundamental principles which underlie international order; we will continue to urge universal acceptance and observance of these principles; we will continue, wherever necessary and in every practicable and peaceful way, to cooperate with other nations which are actuated by the same desires and are pursuing the same objectives; we will persevere in appropriate efforts to safeguard our legitimate rights and interests in every part of the world; and we will, while scrupulously respecting the rights of others, insist on their respecting our rights.

To that end we will continue to strive, through our reciprocal trade program and through other economic policies, to restore the normal processes and to expand the volume of mutually beneficial trade among the nations, which is indispensable to an increase of production, employment, purchasing power, and general economic well-being here and everywhere; we will continue to promote peace through economic security and prosperity; we will continue to participate in the numerous international scientific, technical, and other conferences and collaborative efforts, which have been such powerful influences in assisting the stream of new ideas, of new discoveries, of learning and culture, to flow throughout the world; and we will continue to urge other nations to give their support to such policies and efforts.

We believe that a world at peace, with law and justice prevailing, is possible, and that it can be achieved by methods to some of which I have referred. That is the cornerstone of our foreign policy—a policy graphically described by President Roosevelt when he said:

"There must be positive endeavors to preserve peace. America hates war. America hopes for peace. Therefore, America actively engages in the search for peace." [39]

The objectives of our foreign policy are as easy to grasp as they are fundamental. The means we are using to attain these objectives are the only means approved by reason and by experience. For the sake of the best interests of our people, we must maintain our strength, our courage, our moral standards, our influence in world affairs, and our participation in efforts toward world progress and peace. Only by making our reasonable contribution to a firm establishment of a world order based on law can we keep the problem of our own security in true perspective and thus discharge our responsibility to ourselves—to America of today and to America of tomorrow. No other course would be worthy of our past or of the potentialities of this great democracy of which we are all citizens and in whose affairs we all participate.

107

Press Releases, vol. XVIII, p. 578

The Secretary of State to the Chairman of the Committee on Foreign Relations (Pittman), United States Senate

[WASHINGTON,] May 12, 1938.

MY DEAR SENATOR PITTMAN:

I have received your letter of May 3, 1938, enclosing a copy of S.J. Resolution 288 "repealing the Joint Resolution to prohibit the export of arms, ammunition and implements of war from the United States to Spain, approved January 8, 1937, and conditionally raising the embargo against the Government of Spain," and requesting my comment.

In recent years this Government has consistently pursued a course calculated to prevent our becoming involved in war situations. In August, 1936, shortly after the beginning of the civil strife in Spain, it became evident that several of the great powers were projecting themselves into the struggle through the furnishing of arms and war materials and other aid to the contending sides, thus creating a real danger of a spread of the conflict into a European war, with the possible involvement of the United States. That there was such a real danger was realized by every thoughtful observer the world over. Twenty-seven Governments of Europe took special cognizance of that

[39] Doc. 93.

fact in setting up a committee designed to carry out a concerted policy of non-intervention in the conflict. In view of all these special and unusual circumstances, this Government declared its policy of strict non-interference in the struggle and at the same time announced that export of arms from the United States to Spain would be contrary to such policy.

The fundamental reason for the enactment of the Joint Resolution of January 8, 1937, was to implement this policy by legislation. This Joint Resolution was passed in the Senate unanimously and in the House of Representatives by a vote of 406 to 1.

In the form in which it is presented, the proposed legislation, if enacted, would lift the embargo, which is now being applied against both parties to the conflict in Spain, in respect to shipments of arms to one party while leaving in effect the embargo in respect to shipments to the other party. Even if the legislation applied to both parties, its enactment would still subject us to unnecessary risks we have so far avoided. We do not know what lies ahead in the Spanish situation. The original danger still exists. In view of the continued danger of international conflict arising from the circumstances of the struggle, any proposal which at this juncture contemplates a reversal of our policy of strict non-interference which we have thus far so scrupulously followed, and under the operation of which we have kept out of involvements, would offer a real possibility of complications. From the standpoint of the best interests of the United States in the circumstances which now prevail, I would not feel justified in recommending affirmative action on the Resolution under consideration.

Our first solicitude should be the peace and welfare of this country, and the real test of the advisability of making any changes in the statutes now in effect should be whether such changes would further tend to keep us from becoming involved directly or indirectly in a dangerous European situation.

Furthermore, if reconsideration is to be given to a revision of our neutrality legislation, it would be more useful to reconsider it in its broader aspects in the light of the practical experience gained during the past two or three years, rather than to rewrite it piecemeal in relation to a particular situation. It is evident that there is not sufficient time to give study to such questions in the closing days of this Congress.

Sincerely yours,

CORDELL HULL

108

700.00116/360

Memorandum of a Press Conference of the Secretary of State

[Extract]

[WASHINGTON,] June 11, 1938.

At the press conference this morning a correspondent said that there was a report in the morning newspapers to the effect that the Secretary was considering some plan in connection with the bombings, pointed toward discouraging the sale of American bombing planes abroad. Asked whether he could add anything to this report, the Secretary replied that with regard to the British invitation to participate in an investigation of bombings in Spain, the Department had not taken any affirmative action thus far. With regard to the bombing of civilian populations and the probable danger to Americans and American interests in other parts of the world, he said he had made repeated public statements condemning the bombing of civilian populations. He said that he was continuing to maintain that position and to declare to everybody that this Government does condemn the bombing of civilian populations or its material encouragement. He declared that he was saying this abroad and saying it at home to the American people and especially to the manufacturers of bombing planes.

A correspondent inquired whether in the last few days these well-known views had been expressed to the manufacturers of bombing planes. The Secretary said that he was saying these things to the American people just as he had said them for the benefit of other nations, that they had been said frequently in the past and will be said frequently in the future to the American people and to the manufacturers. A correspondent asked whether this meant that the Administration or the Government would frown on all future sales of American airplanes that could be used for bombing purposes or whether the Government would encourage them to pick their customers. The Secretary replied that his public statements condemning the bombing of civilian populations would discourage sales to regions where they would be used to bomb civilian populations.

109

700.00116/375

*The Chief of the Office of Arms and Munitions Control (Green),
Department of State, to One Hundred Forty-eight Persons and
Companies Manufacturing Airplane Parts*

WASHINGTON, July 1, 1938.

As some misunderstanding appears to have arisen as to the purport of the statement made by the Secretary of State in his press conference on June 11 in regard to bombing civilian populations from the air, I am addressing this letter in regard to the matter to all persons and companies registered as manufacturers or exporters of airplanes or aeronautical equipment.

In view of the fact that the Secretary's statement definitely condemned bombing of civilian populations from the air, it should be clear to all concerned that the Government of the United States is strongly opposed to the sale of airplanes or aeronautical equipment which would materially aid or encourage that practice in any countries in any part of the world. Therefore, in view of this policy, the Department would with great regret issue any licenses authorizing exportation, direct or indirect, of any aircraft, aircraft armament, aircraft engines, aircraft parts, aircraft accessories, aerial bombs or torpedoes to countries the armed forces of which are making use of airplanes for attack upon civilian populations.

Should any manufacturer or exporter have already entered into contractual obligations, of which he finds it impossible to divest himself, to sell or export airplanes or aeronautical equipment, for which licenses have been issued or for which he has heretofore intended to apply for licenses, to any country which is engaged in bombing civilian populations from the air, it is suggested that he may wish to inform the Department of the terms of that contract before applying for licenses to export pursuant to it or before exporting under licenses already issued.

Very truly yours,

JOSEPH C. GREEN

110

711.62/160

*Memorandum by the Secretary of State Regarding a Conversation
With the German Ambassador (Dieckhoff)*

[Extracts]

[WASHINGTON,] July 7, 1938.

The German Ambassador called on his own request to say goodby before leaving for Germany where he plans to stay until September. He was affable and agreeable in his personal attitude. I gave him an opportunity to talk if he desired, before saying anything myself. He soon proceeded by stating that the relations between our two countries were not very good when he came here as Ambassador, and that he had come with a special purpose and desire to be instrumental in improving them. He then added that, unfortunately, the relations had not improved but were now worse. . . . I replied that I thoroughly agreed with him that the relations between our two countries had become steadily worse and that they were continuing to grow worse; that I had left the United States Senate in order to come to the State Department and aid the President in the general undertaking of carrying forward a broad basic program to restore world order based on law, with a sound economic foundation; that, when President Roosevelt came into office in 1933, the general international and world situation was becoming fundamentally worse— more chaotic and more nearly anarchistic; that most of the principles governing normal and peaceful international relations and sound economics were being violated and abandoned on a steadily increasing scale; that the doctrine of force, militarism and territorial aggression was being invoked more and more to spread violence throughout the world and to inflict unusual punishments and injuries on people both within and without countries practicing the policy of force; that, in brief, the entire world situation had become dangerous, if not to say desperate, especially from the long viewpoint of the peace and orderly progress of the human race.

I went on to say that, of course, the people of this country utterly abhor many of the practices of the German Government within its own territory and they cannot understand them from any practical viewpoint so far as the future welfare and progress of Germany are concerned. I added that our people generally seem to assume that the German people, having undergone disagreeable experiences during the ten or twelve years following the war, naturally, as opportunities were presented to release them from further restraints, moved entirely over to the opposite extreme, in connection with which they give full vent to their emotions and passions and tolerate acts and practices relating to racial minorities and religions which they would not ordinarily and normally tolerate; that, accordingly, the belief has been definite that these are temporary manifestations and abnormalities and that in due time the German people would swing back to a normal state of mind and normal relations with other governments and with their fellow man; that, in the light of this viewpoint, my Government has been earnestly hoping that the German Government would reach a stage where it would decide to support the program of peace and orderly progress and normal international relations, and the principles underlying the same, which this Government has been striving to keep alive and to aid in advancing. I said that there was only one alternative course—the course of force, militarism and territorial aggression, with all the hurtful and destroying practices and methods that accompany the same; that these inevitably are leading the world backward instead of forward; that this course will, sooner or later, bring on a more or less general war, and in this event that there will scarcely be left a trace of the people who brought it on or those against whom it was waged as well . . .

C[ORDELL] H[ULL]

111

760F.62/1015 .

Memorandum by the Secretary of State Regarding a Conversation With the Canadian Minister (Marler)

[Extract]

[WASHINGTON,] September 21, 1938.

I then stated that since August a year ago I have proceeded here on the theory that Japan definitely contemplates securing domination over as many hundreds of millions of people as possible in eastern Asia and gradually extending her control through the Pacific islands to the Dutch East Indies and elsewhere, thereby dominating in practical effect that one-half of the world; and that she is seeking this objective by any and every kind of means; that at the same time I have gone on the theory that Germany is equally bent on becoming the dominating colossus of continental Europe.

C[ORDELL] H[ULL]

112

Press Releases, vol. XIX, p. 219

Press Release Issued by the Department of State
On September 26, 1938

The President this morning sent the following message direct to the President of Czechoslovakia and the Chancelor of Germany, and through the Secretary of State to the Prime Ministers of Great Britain and France:

"The fabric of peace on the continent of Europe, if not throughout the rest of the world, is in immediate danger. The consequences of its rupture are incalculable. Should hostilities break out the lives of millions of men, women and children in every country involved will most certainly be lost under circumstances of unspeakable horror.

"The economic system of every country involved is certain to be shattered. The social structure of every country involved may well be completely wrecked.

"The United States has no political entanglements. It is caught in no mesh of hatred. Elements of all Europe have formed its civilization.

"The supreme desire of the American people is to live in peace. But in the event of a general war they face the fact that no nation can escape some measure of the consequences of such a world catastrophe.

"The traditional policy of the United States has been the furtherance of the settlement of international disputes by pacific means. It is my conviction that all people under the threat of war today pray that peace may be made before, rather than after, war.

"It is imperative that peoples everywhere recall that every civilized nation of the world voluntarily assumed the solemn obligations of the Kellogg-Briand Pact of 1928 to solve controversies only by pacific methods. In addition, most nations are parties to other binding treaties obligating them to preserve peace. Furthermore, all countries have today available for such peaceful solution of difficulties which may arise, treaties of arbitration and conciliation to which they are parties.

"Whatever may be the differences in the controversies at issue and however difficult of pacific settlement they may be, I am persuaded that there is no problem so difficult or so pressing for solution that it cannot be justly solved by the resort to reason rather than by the resort to force.

"During the present crisis the people of the United States and their Government have earnestly hoped that the negotiations for the adjustment of the controversy which has now arisen in Europe might reach a successful conclusion.

"So long as these negotiations continue so long will there remain the hope that reason and the spirit of equity may prevail and that the world may thereby escape the madness of a new resort to war.

"On behalf of the 130 millions of people of the United States of America and for the sake of humanity everywhere I most earnestly appeal to you not to break off negotiations looking to a peaceful, fair, and constructive settlement of the questions at issue.

"I earnestly repeat that so long as negotiations continue, differences may be reconciled. Once they are broken off reason is banished and force asserts itself.

"And force produces no solution for the future good of humanity.

FRANKLIN D. ROOSEVELT"

113

Press Releases, vol. XIX, p. 223

Press Release Issued by the Department of State
On September 27, 1938

At 3 p. m. on the afternoon of September 27, 1938, the Secretary of State sent the following instruction to all American diplomatic missions accredited to governments from which this Government had not already received messages or which had not already taken action:

"Please call without delay on the Minister of Foreign Affairs or in his absence on the appropriate official, and express the opinion of this Government that the situation in Europe is today so critical, and the consequences of war would be so disastrous, that no step should be overlooked or omitted that might possibly contribute to the maintenance of peace. The President of the United States has already sent an urgent appeal to the Chancellor of the German Reich, the President of Czechoslovakia, and the Prime Ministers of Great Britain and France urging the importance of keeping negotiations alive and seeking a just settlement of the dispute through peaceful means. If the Chief of State or the Government to which you are accredited were at once to send a comparable message to Germany and Czechoslovakia, emphasizing in his own words the supreme importance of foregoing the use of force in settling the dispute now at issue, we feel that the cumulative effect of such an expression of opinion might possibly even at this late date influence the course of events and contribute to the preservation of peace in Europe. Please make it clear that this suggestion on our part does not in any way imply any opinion as to the points of the dispute at issue.

"If the Government to which you are accredited should already have taken such action please express appropriately and with real appreciation of the step taken, the belief of this Government in the cumulative value of this type of international appeal.

"For your information the following is the text of the President's appeal referred to above:

"[Here follows quoted text of the President's appeal as printed in doc. 112.]"

114

760F.62/1238G

President Roosevelt to the Ambassador in Italy (Phillips)

[Telegram]

WASHINGTON, September 27, 1938—3 p.m.

Please convey the following personal and confidential message to Signor Mussolini:

"In view of the tense situation which has arisen in the relations between Germany and Czechoslovakia, I addressed an earnest plea yesterday to the Head of the Government of each of those countries, as well as to the Prime Ministers of Great Britain and France, to continue their efforts to settle their difficulties by negotiation or other peaceable means rather than by resort to force, with its attendant risk of plunging Europe into a general war. Such a conflict would mean the destruction of millions of men, women, and children in Europe, and would threaten the social structure as we know it today.

"While this country has followed a determined policy of refraining from political entanglements, we have always endeavored to further the settlement of international disputes by pacific methods, and we have maintained that war cannot bring about solutions for the future of mankind. I feel sure that you will agree with me as to the destructive and tragic effects of a war in Europe, and I therefore ask whether you would not extend your help in the continuation of the efforts to arrive at an agreement of the questions at issue by negotiation or by other pacific means rather than by resort to force.

FRANKLIN D. ROOSEVELT."

115

Press Releases, vol. XIX, p. 224

President Roosevelt to the Chancelor of Germany (*Hitler*)

[Telegram]

SEPTEMBER 27, 1938.

I desire to acknowledge Your Excellency's reply to my telegram of September 26. I was confident that you would coincide in the opinion I expressed regarding the unforeseeable consequences and the incalculable disaster which would result to the entire world from the outbreak of a European war.

The question before the world today, Mr. Chancellor, is not the question of errors of judgment or of injustices committed in the past. It is the question of the fate of the world today and tomorrow. The world asks of us who at this moment are heads of nations the supreme capacity to achieve the destinies of nations without forcing upon them as a price, the mutilation and death of millions of citizens.

Resort to force in the Great War failed to bring tranquillity. Victory and defeat were alike sterile. That lesson the world should have learned. For that reason above all others I addressed on September 26 my appeal to Your Excellency and to the President of Czechoslovakia and to the Prime Ministers of Great Britain and of France.

The two points I sought to emphasize were, first, that all matters of difference between the German Government and the Czechoslovak Government could and should be settled by pacific methods; and, second, that the threatened alternative of the use of force on a scale likely to result in a general war is as unnecessary as it is unjustifiable. It is, therefore, supremely important that negotiations should continue without interruption until a fair and constructive solution is reached.

My conviction on these two points is deepened because responsible statesmen have officially stated that an agreement in principle has already been reached between the Government of the German Reich and the Government of Czechoslovakia, although the precise time, method and detail of carrying out that agreement remain at issue.

Whatever existing differences may be, and whatever their merits may be—and upon them I do not and need not undertake to pass— my appeal was solely that negotiations be continued until a peaceful settlement is found, and that thereby a resort to force be avoided.

Present negotiations still stand open. They can be continued if you will give the word. Should the need for supplementing them become evident, nothing stands in the way of widening their scope into a conference of all the nations directly interested in the present controversy. Such a meeting to be held immediately—in some neutral spot in Europe—would offer the opportunity for this and correlated questions to be solved in a spirit of justice, of fair dealing, and, in all human probability, with greater permanence.

In my considered judgment, and in the light of the experience of this century, continued negotiations remain the only way by which the immediate problem can be disposed of upon any lasting basis.

Should you agree to a solution in this peaceful manner I am convinced that hundreds of millions throughout the world would recognize your action as an outstanding historic service to all humanity.

Allow me to state my unqualified conviction that history, and the souls of every man, woman, and child whose lives will be lost in the threatened war will hold us and all of us accountable should we omit any appeal for its prevention.

The Government of the United States has no political involvements in Europe, and will assume no obligations in the conduct of the present negotiations. Yet in our own right we recognize our responsibilities as a part of a world of neighbors.

The conscience and the impelling desire of the people of my country demand that the voice of their government be raised again and yet again to avert and to avoid war.

FRANKLIN D. ROOSEVELT

116

611.6231/1055

Memorandum by the Secretary of State Regarding a Conversation With the German Ambassador (Dieckhoff)

[Extracts]

[WASHINGTON] September 28, 1938.

The Ambassador of Germany called on his own request. He said he came in only to let me know that he was back in Washington and at my disposal for the purpose of carrying on suitable relations between our two Governments. I thanked him.

I added that there are varying impressions as to when and whether his Government might change some of its basic policies under the operation of which his Government would not be interested in pursuing the general course of this Government; that some of these reports represent the head of the German Government as seeking general dominion by force; that I was not raising any question as to the truth or falsity of such reports, but only referring to the obstruction which they constitute to the restoration of confidence on the part of bankers and other business people who would ordinarily cooperate with German bankers and business people in a broad way. The Ambassador said he knew about these phases, and he hastily and almost parenthetically denied the world ambitions of Chancellor Hitler. He proceeded in a brief general sentence or two to say that Germany had a right to interests in the Balkan and Danubian countries and there was no ground on which it should be bottled up. I again made some reference to the question of acquiring dominion generally and in a broad way over territory, and he disclaimed as to territory but without explanation or argument. I said that it would be incomprehensible for Europe to commit suicide—all alike. The Ambassador then said that he had talked with Chancellor Hitler and he was taking a genuine interest in this country, its economic and industrial development and policies in particular.

C[ORDELL] H[ULL]

117

Press Releases, vol. XIX, p. 232

Statement by the Secretary of State, September 30, 1938

In response to inquiries at his press conference today, the Secretary of State spoke as follows:

"As to immediate peace results, it is unnecessary to say that they afford a universal sense of relief.

"I am not undertaking to pass upon the merits of the differences to which the Four-Power Pact signed at Munich on yesterday related.

"It is hoped that in any event the forces which stand for the principles governing peaceful and orderly international relations and their proper application should not relax, but redouble, their efforts to maintain these principles of order under law, resting on a sound economic foundation."

118

811.24 Raw Materials/2

The Secretary of State to President Roosevelt

WASHINGTON, October 21, 1938.

MY DEAR MR. PRESIDENT:

I should like to refer to the problem of strategic raw materials, which becomes more and more urgent as time goes on.

Events of the past few weeks have shown so clearly the wisdom of adequate handling of this problem with all possible despatch. They indicated how disturbed sources of supply would be in any general war. They made it clear that countries would undertake to control or to prohibit exports, especially of essential materials. They also indicated the way in which the insurance mechanism would bog down and the movement of supplies be impeded in a hundred and one ways.

You know, of course, that there are insufficient supplies in the United States of a number of raw materials which would be of great strategic importance in the event of a general war, whether or not this nation were involved. This problem has been the subject of a number of bills introduced in Congress. Almost without exception, however, these bills have, in the opinion of the interested executive agencies, been more concerned with certain private interests to be advantaged than with the national welfare and have, on the whole, dealt unwisely or ineffectively with the national problem of strategic materials. Where these bills have come to your attention, you have quite rightly expressed your opposition to them.

This Department has concurred in the view of the War and Navy Departments that it is highly desirable to adopt a national policy with respect to this problem and to secure early and effective action by Congress. I believe that full agreement was reached by the experts of these and other interested departments and executive agencies as a result of a series of conferences last spring. It is my opinion, therefore, that the whole matter is in proper shape to bring before you.

It is our feeling that there should be no further delay in initiating steps which would make available with the greatest possible despatch adequate supplies of the few materials which are of the most critical importance. With these supplies on hand we should have greater freedom in deciding the course of action this Government should take in any given international crisis; without reserve stocks we may be exposed to bargaining by the suppliers of these materials, if indeed we could by any line of policy secure all of the supplies required.

The question of procedure has just been cleared with Secretary Woodring and Acting Secretary Edison, and they join with me in the hope that you will find it convenient in the very near future to discuss the matter briefly, with the three of us, in a general Cabinet session, or in any other manner that you may prefer.

I think you may be interested in glancing at the enclosed résumé of known information regarding the action now being taken by a number of other powers to store up adequate reserves of strategic materials.[39] You will note that this problem is being attacked with vigor not only by the great powers who may be engaged in preparation for war, but also by other powers whose traditional policy is to maintain a position of neutrality.

Faithfully yours,

CORDELL HULL

119

Press Releases, vol. XIX, p. 299

Address Delivered by the Secretary of State at New York, November 1, 1938

As the world relaxes from the tension of last September when the peace of one of its most important regions hung in perilous balance, many observers in this country not unnaturally raise the following question: Has the swift succession of events so altered the world situation that some of the basic policies we have so far pursued have become no longer applicable and need to be discarded or revised in the light of new developments?

This question frequently relates to the outlook for the future of our trade-agreements program and the general prospect of world developments in the field of international commerce. The problem thus presented is of crucial importance for the economic well-being of our country, for our broad national welfare, and for the promotion of peace, which is the primary objective of our foreign policy.

For upwards of 4 years, our country has been carrying out a vigorous and comprehensive program of policy and action in the sphere of international economic relations. The central aim of this program has been the restoration and expansion of healthy and mutually beneficial trade among nations.

---

[39] Not printed.

We embarked upon this program at a time when our country and the whole world were in the grip of a profound economic dislocation. The situation which we faced at the low point of the depression required a combined program of domestic and international action. To combat unemployment, to create conditions of security and well-being for our farmers, workmen, and businessmen, to enable the entire Nation to replace a vista of despair with a prospect of economic and social advancement, it was necessary to restore solvency and stability in our financial structure, to introduce essential reforms in our economic and social organization, to rehabilitate the processes of production and trade, and thus to rebuild the Nation's income. Domestic measures, however necessary and far reaching, would not have alone sufficed to accomplish these vital purposes. They had to be supplemented by a determined effort to repair the shaken and all but shattered structure of international economic relations.

It was clear that the disruption of international commerce had been as much responsible as any other single factor for the advent and the intensity of the great depression. In the course of generations, national economies had become geared to a growing volume of interchange of commodities across national frontiers. Without expanding international trade, the steady rise of living standards—that outstanding characteristic of economic and social progress—would have been impossible. The sharp decline of international commerce, which accompanied the depression, was bound to produce a profound impairment of economic organization and activity within nations and to depress living standards everywhere. There could be no prospect of full and stable recovery, to be followed by sustained prosperity, unless mutually beneficial commerce among nations could be restored to its great role as an indispensable instrument for the promotion of economic welfare within nations.

The trade-agreements program was the principal means which we adopted for attaining this objective. The program was directed toward overcoming the two factors which had been primarily responsible for the collapse of world commerce. The first of these was the trend toward national economic self-sufficiency, toward so-called autarchy. The second was the growing tendency on the part of nations to enter into narrow trade pacts, based upon exclusive treatment for the parties to such arrangements and consequent discrimination against all other nations. Both of these trends produced effects disastrous not only to world trade, but also to the domestic economies of all nations.

The trend toward economic self-sufficiency involved efforts to develop, behind unscalable walls of exaggerated protectionism, the production of natural or synthetic substitutes to replace imports from other regions of the world—no matter at what sacrifices of quality or cost to the consumers. The discriminatory basis of trade served inevitably to divert the currents of commerce from the channels of natural advantage, and thus to cause an irresistible contraction of the total volume of world trade.

By placing upon our statute books the Trade Agreements Act of 1934 and by inaugurating reciprocal trade-agreements negotiations, we announced to the world our willingness to reverse the policy of raising ever higher barriers to trade, which had been pursued by this country for some years with disastrous results. But our offer to reduce, in favor of foreign countries, the excessive barriers to trade represented by some of our tariff rates was made contingent upon the willingness of other countries to reduce in our favor their tariffs and other trade barriers.

In announcing our trade-agreements program, we also proclaimed our determination to continue our firm adherence to the practice of equal treatment, embodied in the unconditional most-favored-nation principle. But here again we announced that we were willing to negotiate reciprocal trade agreements only with such countries as were willing, in turn, to extend to us this type of treatment under the guarantee of that principle.

It was in this reciprocal and eminently equitable manner that we sought to make our attack upon the ruinous practices of exaggerated protectionism and discriminatory treatment and against the dangerous drift toward national economic isolation.

Our decision to make the rule of equal treatment—that is to say, the unconditional most-favored-nation principle in its broad application—the cornerstone of our program was dictated, first of all, by an immediate and practical consideration: in the absence of guarantees of nondiscriminatory treatment, our export trade cannot escape being constantly exposed to unpredictable dangers. But our decision was also dictated by the conviction, derived from the study of universal experience in the field of international commercial relations, that trade among nations can develop and prosper only as all nations can be assured fair dealing and equality of commercial treatment.

Apart from the purely economic aspects of the trade-agreements program, there is another and even more profound reason for the emphasis which we have been placing upon the need for restoring international commerce upon a sound and healthy basis. Many of our citizens must wonder why, being concerned with the conduct of our country's foreign relations, it is necessary for me to devote so much of my time, thought, and effort to economic problems and to questions of foreign trade. It is because I know that without economic security and well-being there can be no social or political stability in national life, and that without economic, social, and political stability and security within nations there can be no peaceful and orderly relations among nations. It is because I know that without expansion of international trade, based upon fair dealing and equal treatment for all, there can be no stability and security either within or among nations. It is because I know that the withdrawal by a nation from orderly trade relations with the rest of the world inevitably leads to regimentation of all phases of national life, to the suppression of human rights, and all too frequently to preparations for war and a provocative attitude toward other nations.

Two opposing tendencies continue to influence the course of international economic relations. One is the effort which we and many other countries are making toward placing such relations upon a sound and constructive basis and thus enabling trade to make its fullest possible contribution to the economic well-being, stability, and peace of all countries. The other is the continuation of policies under which trade—and, therefore, economic welfare—are being sacrificed to such other objectives as vast armaments and the supremacy of force.

In the presence of a persistent operation of this second tendency, it is not difficult to fall prey to despair. It is not difficult to come to the plausible but erroneous belief that, as a result of this tendency, the course of world development must be toward maximum self-sufficiency for each and every country; that trade among nations is doomed to extinction or at best to a precarious existence subject to the arbitrary whim of control authorities; that the principles upon which we have founded our commercial policy have been rendered antiquated and ill-adapted by the apparent implications of the developments which are occurring elsewhere in the world; and that, therefore, no other course of action is open to us than to fall back upon a system of ever-increasing economic isolation.

As I see the world picture, there is no justification in fact for such counsel of despair. The world *is* at a crossroads. *But its power of choice is not lost.*

One of the roads that wind into the future is that of increased reliance upon armed force as an instrument of national policy. So long as the construction of armaments for such a purpose continues to be the center of national effort in some countries, a policy of arming inescapably becomes a universal evil. Other nations find themselves compelled to divert to preparation for self-defense an increasing part of their substance and effort. All this requires—in varying degrees, but in all countries alike—ever greater sacrifice of what mankind universally has regarded as the central objective of civilization and progress—namely, a rising level of national welfare and of the well-being of the individual. All this imposes— again in varying degrees, but in all countries alike—a growth of autarchy, an ever more complete regimentation of national life, an impairment of personal liberty, a lowering of every standard of material, cultural, and spiritual existence. If the nations continue along this road, increasingly strewn with the wreckage of civilized man's most precious possessions, they will be marching toward the final catastrophe of a new world war, the horror and destructiveness of which pass human imagination.

The other of the two roads is that of ever-increasing reliance upon peaceful processes and upon the rule of law and order in the conduct of relations among individuals and among nations. As such reliance becomes more effective, the vast productive forces with which nature, science, and technical skill have endowed mankind, can become released, in greater and greater measure, for the advancement of the human race. As trust in the pledged word and order under law replace the doctrine of armed force and the practice of lawlessness, the human mind can turn once more to the arts of peace, and the human soul can soar once more to ever greater achievements of the spirit.

We in this country are fortunate beyond measure in that we are less immediately affected than are most other nations by the tensions which prevail in other parts of the world. Yet even for us there will be no escape from a dismal outlook if unhappily the rest of the world should choose the road that must lead to another major armed conflict.

Things being as they are, it is undoubtedly our duty to ourselves to render adequate the armed forces needed for our own security and defense. But it is equally our duty to ourselves not to relax by one whit our efforts to exert our maximum influence toward helping mankind to choose the road of peace and justice rather than the road of war.

In no field is effort toward accomplishing this crucial purpose more essential than in that of restoring economic strength, political stability, and social security within nations through a promotion of healthy economic relations among nations. The task is neither easy nor simple. Political antagonisms, national ambitions, the vast armament programs, and many other phases of narrow nationalism present powerful obstacles. But all these obstacles, enormous as they are, will be more readily overcome if there is constantly kept alive the concept of a future for mankind happier than that of an inexorable drift toward economic impoverishment and a military explosion, and if tireless efforts are made to bring about the realization of such a future.

It is my considered judgment that nothing that has occurred in recent years or in recent weeks has served to discredit in any way the principles on the basis of which we are seeking to bring about a restoration of sound economic conditions as a necessary foundation of durable peace. Nothing that has occurred has impaired my profound belief that these principles will sooner or later become firmly established as the foundation of international-commercial relations. The world's need for the translation of these principles, as well as of all other basic principles of peaceful relations among nations, into practical realities is more urgent and more pressing today than it has ever been.

Nor is the present outlook in this respect devoid of hope. In spite of plausible indications and pseudo-logical inferences to the contrary, the drift toward complete national self-sufficiency is far from making ready headway in the world as a whole. While excessive barriers to trade continue to weigh heavily upon international commerce, the major part of world trade is still carried on by countries which are not attempting to be self-contained regardless of cost.

Only a few countries proclaim the attainment of autarchy as their avowed purpose. But these very countries are, at the same time, making desperate efforts to enlarge the volume of their foreign commerce—not only within the limited areas actually or potentially under their immediate influence, but with other parts of the world as well. The striking paradox of the present situation is that in their attempts to find foreign markets and sources of materials indispensable to their national existence, such countries employ methods of forced and artificial stimulation, which inescapably prevent trade from making its full contribution even to their own well-being and economic stability.

As experience accumulates, it becomes increasingly clear that trade methods of this type steadily exhaust the countries which practice them and arouse ever more intense resistance and retaliation on the part of other countries. Whether employed in conjunction with openly proclaimed programs of national or group autarchy or in the absence of avowed desire for self-containment, such methods of trade inevitably defeat themselves. They are, in a full sense, the instruments of destructive economic warfare, adopted by nations in the mistaken belief that they are capable of enhancing national security and strength.

Autarchy and other forms of economic armament create but an illusion of strength and security. They uproot far more than they build. They discourage rather than generate enterprise. By placing impassable barriers to the world flow of material and financial resources, by tending to split up the world into abnormally limited areas of trade relations, they undermine confidence and stability. They make all nations progressively weaker.

The very difficulties which constantly multiply in the application of such policies and methods create powerful pressures in the direction of their abandonment. No nation can prosper or maintain other than a visibly falling standard of living for its population when the world is broken up into air-tight economic compartments.

The program which we advocate offers the only practicable alternative to a drift toward the anarchy of economic warfare, with all its disastrous consequences for the peace and progress of man. Its workability has been demonstrated beyond a shadow of doubt. It can be embraced by all nations alike, without exception, and to the benefit of each and all.

Not by compromising with any of our basic principles, not by joining a retreat to self-imposed poverty of economic isolation, not by attempting to employ the destructive practices of forced trade, can we make our contribution toward rendering brighter and more hopeful the outlook for ourselves and for the world.

Our own best interests and the concern which all of us must feel for the future of the human race imperatively require that, far from abandoning our trade-agreements program, we put redoubled vigor into our efforts to enlarge its scope and its effectiveness. We should not relax, we should intensify our endeavors to influence all nations, by example and by every appropriate means of persuasion open to us, to return to the tested basis of healthy and sound trade, of monetary stability, of financial order and probity—in brief, to that type of international economic relationships which have been incontrovertibly shown by experience to be the only possible foundation of peace, progress, and well-being among mankind.

No nation and no individual can escape a share of responsibility for the fashioning of mankind's choice as to the road which the world will follow. There is nothing more desperately needed today in all countries than clear thinking and a profound sense of national and individual concern for the course of future developments.

120

Press Releases, vol. XIX, p. 338

Statement by President Roosevelt, November 15, 1938

The news of the past few days from Germany has deeply shocked public opinion in the United States. Such news from any part of the world would inevitably produce a similar profound reaction among American people in every part of the Nation.

I myself could scarcely believe that such things could occur in a twentieth-century civilization.

With a view to gaining a first-hand picture of the situation in Germany I asked the Secretary of State to order our Ambassador in Berlin to return at once for report and consultation.

121

Press Releases, vol. XIX, p. 474

"Declaration of Lima" by the Eighth International Conference of American States, December 24, 1938

The Eighth International Conference of American States,
Considering:

That the peoples of America have achieved spiritual unity through the similarity of their republican institutions, their unshakable will for peace, their profound sentiment of humanity and tolerance, and through their absolute adherence to the principles of international law, of the equal sovereignty of states and of individual liberty without religious or racial prejudices;

That on the basis of such principles and will, they seek and defend the peace of the continent and work together in the cause of universal concord;

That respect for the personality, sovereignty, and independence of each American state, constitutes the essence of international order sustained by continental solidarity, which historically has found expression in declarations of various states, or in agreements which were applied, and sustained by new declarations and by treaties in force; that the Inter-American Conference for the Maintenance of Peace, held at Buenos Aires, approved on December 21, 1936, the declaration of the principles of inter-American solidarity and cooperation, and approved, on December 23, 1936, the protocol of nonintervention; the Governments of the American States

Declare:

First. That they reaffirm their continental solidarity and their purpose to collaborate in the maintenance of the principles upon which the said solidarity is based;

Second. That faithful to the above-mentioned principles and to their absolute sovereignty, they reaffirm their decision to maintain them and to defend against all foreign intervention or activity that may threaten them;

Third. And in case the peace, security or territorial integrity of any American republic is thus threatened by acts of any nature that may impair them, they proclaim their common concern and their determination to make effective their solidarity, coordinating their respective sovereign wills by means of the procedure of consultation, established by conventions in force and by declarations of the inter-American conferences, using the measures which in each case the circumstances may make advisable. It is understood that the Governments of the American Republics will act independently in their individual capacity, recognizing fully their juridical equality as sovereign states;

Fourth. That in order to facilitate the consultations established in this and other American peace instruments, the Ministers for Foreign Affairs of the American Republics, when deemed desirable and at the initiative of any one of them, will meet in their several capitals by rotation and without protocolary character. Each government may, under special circumstances or for special reasons, designate a representative as a substitute for its Minister for Foreign Affairs;

Fifth. This declaration shall be known as the "Declaration of Lima."

122

Press Releases, vol. XIX, p. 494

Declaration of American Principles by the Eighth International Conference of American States, December 24, 1938

Declaration of American Principles:

WHEREAS

The need for keeping alive the fundamental principles of relations among nations was never greater than today; and

Each state is interested in the preservation of world order under law, in peace with justice, and in the social and economic welfare of mankind.

The Governments of the American Republics resolve

To proclaim, support and recommend, once again, the following principles, as essential to the achievement of the aforesaid objectives:

1. The intervention of any state in the internal or external affairs of another is inadmissible;

2. All differences of international character should be settled by peaceful means;

3. The use of force as an instrument of national or international policy is proscribed;

4. Relations between states should be governed by the precepts of international law;

5. Respect for and the faithful observance of treaties constitute the indispensable rule for the development of peaceful relations between states, and treaties can only be revised by agreement of the contracting parties;

6. Peaceful collaboration between representatives of the various states and the development of intellectual interchange among their peoples is conducive to an understanding by each of the problems of the other as well as of problems common to all, and makes more readily possible the peaceful adjustment of international controversies;

7. Economic reconstruction contributes to national and international well-being, as well as to peace among nations; and

8. International cooperation is a necessary condition to the maintenance of the aforementioned principles.

LIMA, *December 24, 1938.*

[Here follow signatures.]

123

693.001/510

The Ambassador in Japan (Grew) to the Japanese Minister For Foreign Affairs (Arita)[40]

No. 1153　　　　　　　　　　　　　　TOKYO, December 30, 1938.

EXCELLENCY: Acting under the instructions of my Government I have the honor to address to Your Excellency the following note:

---

[40] Delivered by the Ambassador at 11:30 a.m., December 31, 1938.

The Government of the United States has received and has given full consideration to the reply of the Japanese Government of November 18 to this Government's note of October 6 on the subject of American rights and interests in China.

In the light of facts and experience the Government of the United States is impelled to reaffirm its previously expressed opinion that imposition of restrictions upon the movements and activities of American nationals who are engaged in philanthropic, educational and commercial endeavors in China has placed and will, if continued, increasingly place Japanese interests in a preferred position and is, therefore, unquestionably discriminatory in its effect against legitimate American interests. Further, with reference to such matters as exchange control, compulsory currency circulation, tariff revision, and monopolistic promotion in certain areas of China the plans and practices of the Japanese authorities imply an assumption on the part of those authorities that the Japanese Government or the regimes established and maintained in China by Japanese armed forces are entitled to act in China in a capacity such as flows from rights of sovereignty and further in so acting to disregard and even to declare nonexistent or abrogated the established rights and interests of other countries including the United States.

The Government of the United States expresses its conviction that the restrictions and measures under reference not only are unjust and unwarranted but are counter to the provisions of several binding international agreements, voluntarily entered into, to which both Japan and the United States, and in some cases other countries, are parties.

In the concluding portion of its note under reference, the Japanese Government states that it is firmly convinced that "in the face of the new situation, fast developing in Asia, any attempt to apply to the conditions of today and tomorrow inapplicable ideas and principles of the past neither would contribute toward the establishment of a real peace in East Asia nor solve the immediate issues" and that "as long as these points are understood Japan has not the slightest inclination to oppose the participation of the United States and other Powers in the great work of reconstructing East Asia along all lines of industry and trade."

The Government of the United States in its note of October 6 requested, in view of the oft reiterated assurances proffered by the Government of Japan of its intention to observe the principles of equality of opportunity in its relations with China and in view of Japan's treaty obligations so to do, that the Government of Japan abide by these obligations and carry out these assurances in practice. The Japanese Government in its reply appears to affirm that it is its intention to make its observance of that principle conditional upon an understanding by the American Government and by other governments of a "new situation" and a "new order" in the Far East as envisaged and fostered by Japanese authorities.

Treaties which bear upon the situation in the Far East have within them provisions relating to a number of subjects. In the making of those treaties, there was a process among the parties to them of give and take. Toward making possible the carrying out of some of their provisions, others among their provisions were formulated and agreed upon: toward gaining for itself the advantage of security in regard to certain matters, each of the parties committed itself to pledges of self-denial in regard to certain other matters. The various provisions agreed upon may be said to have constituted collectively an arrangement for safeguarding, for the benefit of all, the correlated principles on the one hand of national integrity and on the other hand of equality of economic opportunity. Experience has shown that impairment of the former of these principles is followed almost invariably by disregard of the latter. Whenever any government begins to exercise political authority in areas beyond the limits of its lawful jurisdiction there develops inevitably a situation in which the nationals of that government demand and are accorded, at the hands of their government, preferred treatment, whereupon equality of opportunity ceases to exist and discriminatory practices, productive of friction, prevail.

The admonition that enjoyment by the nationals of the United States of non-discriminatory treatment in China—a general and well established right—is henceforth to be contingent upon an admission by the Government of the United States of the validity of the conception of Japanese authorities of a "new situation" and a "new order" in East Asia, is, in the opinion of this Government, highly paradoxical.

This country's adherence to and its advocacy of the principle of equality of opportunity do not flow solely from a desire to obtain the commercial benefits which naturally result from the provisions of that principle. They flow from a firm conviction that observance of that principle leads to economic and political stability, which are conducive both to the internal well-being of nations and to mutually beneficial and peaceful relationships between and among nations; from a firm conviction that failure to observe that principle breeds international friction and ill-will, with consequences injurious to all countries, including in particular those countries which fail to observe it; and from an equally firm conviction that observance of that principle promotes the opening of trade channels thereby making available the markets, the raw materials and the manufactured products of the community of nations on a mutually and reciprocally beneficial basis.

The principle of equality of economic opportunity is, moreover, one to which over a long period and on many occasions the Japanese Government has given definite approval. It is one to the observance of which the Japanese Government has committed itself in various international agreements and understandings. It is one upon observance of which by other nations the Japanese Government has of its own accord and upon its own initiative frequently insisted. It is one to which the Japanese Government has repeatedly during recent months declared itself committed.

The people and the Government of the United States could not assent to the establishment at the instance of and for the special purposes of any third country of a regime which would arbitrarily deprive them of the long established rights of equal opportunity and fair treatment which are legally and justly theirs along with those of other nationals.

Fundamental principles such as the principle of equality of opportunity which have long been regarded as inherently wise and just which have been widely adopted and adhered to, and which are general in their application are not subject to nullification by a unilateral affirmation.

With regard to the implication in the Japanese Government's note that the "conditions of today and tomorrow" in the Far East call for a revision of the ideas and principles of the past, this Government desires to recall to the Japanese Government its position on the subject of revision of agreements.

This Government had occasion in the course of a communication delivered to the Japanese Government on April 29, 1934, to express its opinion that "treaties can lawfully be modified or be terminated,—but only by processes prescribed or recognized or agreed upon by the parties to them".

In the same communication this Government also said, "In the opinion of the American people and the American Government, no nation can, without the assent of the other nations concerned, rightfully endeavor to make conclusive its will in situations where there are involved the rights, the obligations and the legitimate interests of other sovereign states". In an official and public statement on

July 16, 1937, the Secretary of State of the United States declared that this Government advocates "adjustment of problems in international relations by processes of peaceful negotiation and agreement".

At various times during recent decades various powers, among which have been Japan and the United States, have had occasion to communicate and to confer with regard to situations and problems in the Far East. In the conducting of correspondence and of conferences relating to these matters, the parties involved have invariably taken into consideration past and present facts and they have not failed to perceive the possibility and the desirability of changes in the situation. In the making of treaties they have drawn up and have agreed upon provisions intended to facilitate advantageous developments and at the same time to obviate and avert the arising of friction between and among the various powers which, having interests in the region or regions under reference, were and would be concerned.

In the light of these facts, and with reference especially to the purpose and the character of the treaty provisions from time to time solemnly agreed upon for the very definite purposes indicated, the Government of the United States deprecates the fact that one of the parties to these agreements has chosen to embark—as indicated both by action of its agents and by official statements of its authorities—upon a course directed toward the arbitrary creation by that power by methods of its own selection, regardless of treaty pledges and the established rights of other powers concerned, of a "new order" in the Far East. Whatever may be the changes which have taken place in the situation in the Far East and whatever may be the situation now, these matters are of no less interest and concern to the American Government than have been the situations which have prevailed there in the past, and such changes as may henceforth take place there, changes which may enter into the producing of a "new situation" and a "new order", are and will be of like concern to this Government. This Government is well aware that the situation has changed. This Government is also well aware that many of the changes have been brought about by the action of Japan. This Government does not admit, however, that there is need or warrant for any one Power to take upon itself to prescribe what shall be the terms and conditions of a "new order" in areas not under its sovereignty and to constitute itself the repository of authority and the agent of destiny in regard thereto.

It is known to all the world that various of the parties to treaties concluded for the purpose of regulating contacts in the Far East and avoiding friction therein and therefrom—which treaties contained, for those purposes, various restrictive provisions—have from time to time and by processes of negotiation and agreement contributed in the light of changed situations toward the removal of restrictions and toward the bringing about of further developments which would warrant in the light of further changes in the situation, further removals of restrictions. By such methods and processes, early restrictions upon the tariff autonomy of all countries in the Far East were removed. By such methods and processes the rights of extraterritorial jurisdiction once enjoyed by Occidental countries in relations with countries in the Far East have been given up in relations with all of those countries except China; and in the years immediately preceding and including the year 1931, countries which still possessed those rights in China including the United States were actively engaged in negotiations—far advanced—looking toward surrender of those rights. All discerning and impartial observers have realized that the United States and others of the "treaty powers" have not during recent decades clung tenaciously to their so-called "special" rights and privileges in countries of the Far East but on the contrary have steadily encouraged the development in those countries of institutions and practices in the presence of which such rights and privileges may safely and readily be given up; and all observers have seen those rights and privileges gradually being surrendered voluntarily through agreement by the Powers which have possessed them. On one point only has the Government of the United States, along with several other governments, insisted: namely, that new situations must have developed to a point warranting the removal of "special" safeguarding restrictions and that the removals be effected by orderly processes.

The Government of the United States has at all times regarded agreements as susceptible of alteration, but it has always insisted that alterations can rightfully be made only by orderly processes of negotiation and agreement among the parties thereto.

The Japanese Government has upon numerous occasions expressed itself as holding similar views.

The United States has in its international relations rights and obligations which derive from international law and rights and obligations which rest upon treaty provisions. Of those which rest on treaty provisions, its rights and obligations in and with regard to China rest in part upon provisions in treaties between the United States and China and in part on provisions in treaties between the United States and several other powers including both China and Japan. These treaties were concluded in good faith for the purpose of safeguarding and promoting the interests not of one only but of all of their signatories. The people and the Government of the United States cannot assent to the abrogation of any of this country's rights or obligations by the arbitrary action of agents or authorities of any other country.

The Government of the United States has, however, always been prepared and is now prepared to give due and ample consideration to any proposals based on justice and reason which envisage the resolving of problems in a manner duly considerate of the rights and obligations of all parties directly concerned by processes of free negotiation and new commitment by and among all of the parties so concerned. There has been and there continues to be opportunity for the Japanese Government to put forward such proposals. This Government has been and it continues to be willing to discuss such proposals, if and when put forward, with representatives of the other powers, including Japan and China, whose rights and interests are involved, at whatever time and in whatever place may be commonly agreed upon.

Meanwhile, this Government reserves all rights of the United States as they exist and does not give assent to any impairment of any of those rights.

I avail myself [etc.] JOSEPH C. GREW

124

H. Doc. 1, 76th Cong., 1st sess.

Address Delivered by President Roosevelt to the Congress, January 4, 1939

[Extract]

In reporting on the state of the Nation, I have felt it necessary on previous occasions to advise the Congress of disturbance abroad and of the need of putting our own house in order in the face of storm signals from across the seas. As this Seventy-sixth Congress opens there is need for further warning.

A war which threatened to envelop the world in flames has been averted, but it has become increasingly clear that peace is not assured.

All about us rage undeclared wars—military and economic. All about us grow more deadly armaments—military and economic. All about us are threats of new aggression—military and economic.

Storms from abroad directly challenge three institutions indispensable to Americans, now as always. The first is religion. It is the source of the other two—democracy and international good faith.

Religion, by teaching man his relationship to God, gives the individual a sense of his own dignity and teaches him to respect himself by respecting his neighbors.

Democracy, the practice of self-government, is a covenant among free men to respect the rights and liberties of their fellows.

International good faith, a sister of democracy, springs from the will of civilized nations of men to respect the rights and liberties of other nations of men.

In a modern civilization, all three—religion, democracy, and international good faith—complement each other.

Where freedom of religion has been attacked, the attack has come from sources opposed to democracy. Where democracy has been overthrown, the spirit of free worship has disappeared. And where religion and democracy have vanished, good faith and reason in international affairs have given way to strident ambition and brute force.

An ordering of society which relegates religion, democracy, and good faith among nations to the background can find no place within it for the ideals of the Prince of Peace. The United States rejects such an ordering and retains its ancient faith.

There comes a time in the affairs of men when they must prepare to defend not their homes alone but the tenets of faith and humanity on which their churches, their governments, and their very civilization are founded. The defense of religion, of democracy, and of good faith among nations is all the same fight. To save one we must now make up our minds to save all.

We know what might happen to us of the United States if the new philosophies of force were to encompass the other continents and invade our own. We, no more than other nations, can afford to be surrounded by the enemies of our faith and our humanity. Fortunate it is, therefore, that in this Western Hemisphere we have, under a common ideal of democratic government, a rich diversity of resources and of peoples functioning together in mutual respect and peace.

That hemisphere, that peace, and that ideal we propose to do our share in protecting against storms from any quarter. Our people and our resources are pledged to secure that protection. From that determination no American flinches.

This by no means implies that the American Republics disassociate themselves from the nations of other continents—*it does not mean* the Americas against the rest of the world. We as one of the Republics reiterate our willingness to help the cause of world peace. We stand on our historic offer to take counsel with all other nations of the world to the end that aggression among them be terminated, that the race of armaments cease and that commerce be renewed.

But the world has grown so small and weapons of attack so swift that no nation can be safe in its will to peace so long as any other single powerful nation refuses to settle its grievances at the council table.

For if any government bristling with implements of war insists on policies of force, weapons of defense give the only safety.

In our foreign relations we have learned from the past what not to do. From new wars we have learned what we must do.

We have learned that effective timing of defense, and the distant points from which attacks may be launched are completely different from what they were 20 years ago.

We have learned that survival cannot be guaranteed by arming after the attack begins—for there is new range and speed to offense.

We have learned that long before any overt military act, aggression begins with preliminaries of propaganda, subsidized penetration, the loosening of ties of good will, the stirring of prejudice, and the incitement to disunion.

We have learned that God-fearing democracies of the world which observe the sanctity of treaties and good faith in their dealings with other nations cannot safely be indifferent to international lawlessness anywhere. They cannot forever let pass, without effective protest, acts of aggression against sister nations—acts which automatically undermine all of us.

Obviously they must proceed along practical, peaceful lines. But the mere fact that we rightly decline to intervene with arms to prevent acts of aggression does not mean that we must act as if there were no aggression at all. Words may be futile, but war is not the only means of commanding a decent respect for the opinions of mankind. There are many methods short of war, but stronger and more effective than mere words, of bringing home to aggressor governments the aggregate sentiments of our own people.

At the very least, we can and should avoid any action, or any lack of action, which will encourage, assist, or build up an aggressor. We have learned that when we deliberately try to legislate neutrality, our neutrality laws may operate unevenly and unfairly—may actually give aid to an aggressor and deny it to the victim. The instinct of self-preservation should warn us that we ought not to let that happen any more.

And we have learned something else—the old, old lesson that probability of attack is mightily decreased by the assurance of an ever ready defense. Since 1931 world events of thunderous import have moved with lightning speed. During these 8 years many of our people clung to the hope that the innate decency of mankind would protect the unprepared who showed their innate trust in mankind. Today we are all wiser—and sadder.

Under modern conditions what we mean by "adequate defense"— a policy subscribed to by all—must be divided into three elements. First we must have armed forces and defenses strong enough to ward off sudden attack against strategic positions and key facilities essential to ensure sustained resistance and ultimate victory. Secondly, we must have the organization and location of those key facilities so that they may be immediately utilized and rapidly expanded to meet all needs without danger of serious interruption by enemy attack.

In the course of a few days I shall send you a special message making recommendations for those two essentials of defense against danger which we cannot safely assume will not come.

If these first two essentials are reasonably provided for, we must be able confidently to invoke the third element, the underlying strength of citizenship—the self-confidence, the ability, the imagination, and the devotion that give the staying power to see things through.

A strong and united nation may be destroyed if it is unprepared against sudden attack. But even a nation well armed and well organized from a strictly military standpoint, may, after a period of time, meet defeat if it is unnerved by self-distrust, endangered by class prejudice, by dissension between capital and labor, by false economy, and by other unsolved social problems at home.

In meeting the troubles of the world we must meet them as one people—with a unity born of the fact that for generations those who have come to our shores, representing many kindreds and tongues, have been welded by common opportunity into a united patriotism. If another form of government can present a united front in its attack on a democracy, the attack must be met by a united democracy. Such a democracy can and must exist in the United States.

A dictatorship may command the full strength of a regimented nation. But the united strength of a democratic nation can be mustered only when its people, educated by modern standards to know what is going on and where they are going, have conviction that they are receiving as large a share of opportunity for development, as large a share of material success and of human dignity, as they have a right to receive.

Our Nation's program of social and economic reform is therefore a part of defense as basic as armaments themselves.

125

H. Doc. 105, 76th Cong., 1st sess.

Message of President Roosevelt to the Congress, January 12, 1939

In my annual message to this Congress I have spoken at some length of the changing world conditions outside of the American Hemisphere which make it imperative that we take immediate steps for the protection of our liberties.

It would be unwise for any of us to yield to any form of hysteria. Nevertheless, regardless of political affiliations, we can properly join in an appraisal of the world situation and agree on the immediate defense needs of the Nation.

It is equally sensational and untrue to take the position that we must at once spend billions of additional money for building up our land, sea, and air forces on the one hand, or to insist that no further additions are necessary on the other.

What needs to be emphasized is the great change which has come over conflicts between nations since the World War ended, and especially during the past 5 or 6 years.

Those of us who took part in the conduct of the World War will remember that in the preparation of the American armies for actual participation in battle, the United States, entering the war on April 6, 1917, took no part whatsoever in any major engagement until the end of May 1918. In other words, while other armies were conducting the actual fighting, the United States had more than a year of absolute peace at home without any threat of attack on this continent, to train men, to produce raw materials, to process them into munitions and supplies and to forge the whole into fighting forces. It is even a matter of record that as late as the autumn of 1918, American armies at the front used almost exclusively French or British artillery and aircraft.

Calling attention to these facts does not remotely intimate that the Congress or the President have any thought of taking part in another war on European soil, but it does show that in 1917 we were not ready to conduct large scale land or air operations. Relatively we are not much more ready to do so today than we were then—and we cannot guarantee a long period, free from attack, in which we could prepare.

I have called attention to the fact that "We must have armed forces and defenses strong enough to ward off sudden attack against strategic positions and key facilities essential to insure sustained resistance and ultimate victory." And I have said, "We must have the organization and location of those key facilities so that they may be immediately utilized and rapidly expanded to meet all needs without danger of serious interruption by enemy attack."

I repeat that "there is new range and speed to offense."

Therefore, it has become necessary for every American to restudy present defense against the possibilities of present offense against us.

Careful examination of the most imperative present needs leads me to recommend the appropriation at this session of the Congress, with as great speed as possible, of approximately $525,000,000, of which sum approximately $210,000,000 would be actually spent from the Treasury before the end of the fiscal year ending June 30, 1940.

The survey indicates that of this sum approximately $450,000,000 should be allocated for new needs of the Army, $65,000,000 for new needs of the Navy, and $10,000,000 for training of civilian air pilots.

The several items will be submitted to the appropriate committees of the Congress by the departments concerned, and I need, therefore, touch only on the major divisions of the total.

In the case of the Army, information from other nations leads us to believe that there must be a complete revision of our estimates for aircraft. The Baker board report of a few years ago is completely out of date. No responsible officer advocates building our air forces up to the total either of planes on hand or of productive capacity equal to the forces of certain other nations. We are thinking in the terms of necessary defenses and the conclusion is inevitable that our existing forces are so utterly inadequate that they must be immediately strengthened.

It is proposed that $300,000,000 be appropriated for the purchase of several types of airplanes for the Army. This should provide a minimum increase of 3,000 planes, but it is hoped that orders placed on such a large scale will materially reduce the unit cost and actually provide many more planes.

Military aviation is increasing today at an unprecedented and alarming rate. Increased range, increased speed, increased capacity of airplanes abroad have changed our requirements for defensive aviation. The additional planes recommended will considerably strengthen the air defenses of the continental United States, Alaska, Hawaii, Puerto Rico, and the Canal Zone. If an appropriation bill can be quickly enacted, I suggest that $50,000,000 of the $300,000,000 for airplanes be made immediately available in order to correct the present lag in aircraft production due to idle plants.

Of the balance of approximately $150,000,000 requested for the Army, I suggest an appropriation of $110,000,000 to provide "critical items" of equipment which would be needed immediately in time of emergency, and which cannot be obtained from any source within the time and quantity desired—matériel such as antiaircraft artillery, semiautomatic rifles, antitank guns, tanks, light and heavy artillery, ammunition, and gas masks. Such purchases would go far to equip existing units of the Regular Army and the National Guard.

I suggest approximately $32,000,000 for "educational orders" for the Army—in other words, to enable industry to prepare for quantity production in an emergency, of those military items which are noncommercial in character and are so difficult of manufacture as to constitute what is known as "bottlenecks" in the problem of procurement.

The balance should be used, I believe, for improving and strengthening the seacoast defenses of Panama, Hawaii, and the continental United States, including the construction of a highway outside the limits of the Panama Canal Zone, important to the defense of the zone.

The estimated appropriation of $65,000,000 for the Navy should be divided into (a) $44,000,000 for the creation or strengthening of Navy bases in both oceans in general agreement with the report of the special board which has already been submitted to the Congress, (b) about $21,000,000 for additional Navy airplanes and air material tests.

Finally, national defense calls for the annual training of additional air pilots. This training should be primarily directed to the essential qualifications for civilian flying. In cooperation with educational institutions, it is believed that the expenditure of $10,000,000 a year will give primary training to approximately 20,000 citizens.

In the above recommendations for appropriations totaling $525,000,000, I have omitted reference to a definite need, which, however, relates to the implementing of existing defenses for the Panama Canal. The security of the Canal is of the utmost importance. The peace garrison now there is inadequate to defend this vital link. This deficiency cannot be corrected with existing forces without seriously jeopardizing the general defense by stripping the continental United States of harbor defense and antiaircraft personnel. The permanent garrison in the Canal Zone should be increased to provide the minimum personnel required to man the antiaircraft and seacoast armament provided for the defense of the Canal. Such personnel cannot be increased until additional housing facilities are provided—and, in the meantime, additional personnel must be trained. I recommend, therefore, an appropriation of $27,000,000 to provide an adequate peace garrison for the Canal Zone and to house it adequately. Five million dollars of this sum should be made available immediately in order that work on necessary construction can be initiated.

All of the above constitutes a well-rounded program, considered by me as Commander in Chief of the Army and Navy, and by my advisors to be a minimum program for the necessities of defense. Every American is aware of the peaceful intentions of the Government and of the people. Every American knows that we have no thought of aggression, no desire for further territory.

Nevertheless, as the Executive head of the Government, I am compelled to look facts in the face. We have a splendid asset in the quality of our manhood. But without modern weapons, and without adequate training, the men, however splendid the type, would be hopelessly handicapped if we were attacked.

The young men of this Nation should not be compelled to take the field with antiquated weapons. It would be economically unsound to provide in time of peace for all the modern equipment needed in a war emergency. But it would be nationally unsound not to provide the critical items of equipment which might be needed for immediate use, and not to provide for facilities for mass production in the event of war.

Devoid of all hysteria, this program is but the minimum of requirements.

I trust, therefore, that the Congress will quickly act on this emergency program for the strengthening of the defense of the United States.

FRANKLIN D. ROOSEVELT

THE WHITE HOUSE,
    January 12, 1939.

126

Press Releases, vol. XX, p. 221

Statement by the Acting Secretary of State (Welles), March 17, 1939

The Government of the United States has on frequent occasions stated its conviction that only through international support of a program of order based upon law can world peace be assured.

This Government, founded upon and dedicated to the principles of human liberty and of democracy, cannot refrain from making known this country's condemnation of the acts which have resulted in the temporary extinguishment of the liberties of a free and independent people with whom, from the day when the Republic of Czechoslovakia attained its independence, the people of the United States have maintained specially close and friendly relations.

The position of the Government of the United States has been made consistently clear. It has emphasized the need for respect for the sanctity of treaties and of the pledged word, and for nonintervention by any nation in the domestic affairs of other nations; and it has on repeated occasions expressed its condemnation of a policy of military aggression.

It is manifest that acts of wanton lawlessness and of arbitrary force are threatening world peace and the very structure of modern civilization. The imperative need for the observance of the principles advocated by this Government has been clearly demonstrated by the developments which have taken place during the past 3 days.

127

Press Releases, vol. XX, p. 261

Statement by the Secretary of State, April 8, 1939

The forcible and violent invasion of Albania is unquestionably an additional threat to the peace of the world. It would be shortsighted not to take notice of this further development.

Any threat to peace seriously concerns all nations and violates the will of all peoples in the world that their governments shall lead them, not toward war, but along paths of peace.

It is scarcely necessary to add that the inevitable effect of this incident, taken with other similar incidents, is further to destroy confidence and to undermine economic stability in every country in the world, thus affecting our own welfare.

128

Press Releases, vol. XX, p. 291

President Roosevelt to the Chancelor of Germany (Hitler)[40]

[Telegram]

THE WHITE HOUSE, April 14, 1939.

You realize I am sure that throughout the world hundreds of millions of human beings are living today in constant fear of a new war or even a series of wars.

[40] The Secretary of State at the same time, at the President's direction, addressed an identical telegram to Premier Benito Mussolini, of Italy.

The existence of this fear—and the possibility of such a conflict—is of definite concern to the people of the United States for whom I speak, as it must also be to the peoples of the other nations of the entire Western Hemisphere. All of them know that any major war, even if it were to be confined to other continents, must bear heavily on them during its continuance and also for generations to come.

Because of the fact that after the acute tension in which the world has been living during the past few weeks there would seem to be at least a momentary relaxation—because no troops are at this moment on the march—this may be an opportune moment for me to send you this message.

On a previous occasion I have addressed you in behalf of the settlement of political, economic, and social problems by peaceful methods and without resort to arms.

But the tide of events seems to have reverted to the threat of arms. If such threats continue, it seems inevitable that much of the world must become involved in common ruin. All the world, victor nations, vanquished nations, and neutral nations will suffer. I refuse to believe that the world is, of necessity, such a prisoner of destiny. On the contrary, it is clear that the leaders of great nations have it in their power to liberate their peoples from the disaster that impends. It is equally clear that in their own minds and in their own hearts the peoples themselves desire that their fears be ended.

It is, however, unfortunately necessary to take cognizance of recent facts.

Three nations in Europe and one in Africa have seen their independent existence terminated. A vast territory in another independent nation of the Far East has been occupied by a neighboring state. Reports, which we trust are not true, insist that further acts of aggression are contemplated against still other independent nations. Plainly the world is moving toward the moment when this situation must end in catastrophe unless a more rational way of guiding events is found.

You have repeatedly asserted that you and the German people have no desire for war. If this is true there need be no war.

Nothing can persuade the peoples of the earth that any governing power has any right or need to inflict the consequences of war on its own or any other people save in the cause of self-evident home defense.

In making this statement we as Americans speak not through selfishness or fear or weakness. If we speak now it is with the voice of strength and with friendship for mankind. It is still clear to me that international problems can be solved at the council table.

It is therefore no answer to the plea for peaceful discussion for one side to plead that unless they receive assurances beforehand that the verdict will be theirs, they will not lay aside their arms. In conference rooms, as in courts, it is necessary that both sides enter upon the discussion in good faith, assuming that substantial justice will accrue to both; and it is customary and necessary that they leave their arms outside the room where they confer.

I am convinced that the cause of world peace would be greatly advanced if the nations of the world were to obtain a frank statement relating to the present and future policy of governments.

Because the United States, as one of the nations of the Western Hemisphere, is not involved in the immediate controversies which have arisen in Europe, I trust that you may be willing to make such a statement of policy to me as the head of a nation far removed from Europe in order that I, acting only with the responsibility and obligation of a friendly intermediary, may communicate such declaration to other nations now apprehensive as to the course which the policy of your Government may take.

Are you willing to give assurance that your armed forces will not attack or invade the territory or possessions of the following independent nations: Finland, Estonia, Latvia, Lithuania, Sweden, Norway, Denmark, The Netherlands, Belgium, Great Britain and Ireland, France, Portugal, Spain, Switzerland, Liechtenstein, Luxemburg, Poland, Hungary, Rumania, Yugoslavia, Russia, Bulgaria, Greece, Turkey, Iraq, the Arabias, Syria, Palestine, Egypt and Iran.

Such an assurance clearly must apply not only to the present day but also to a future sufficiently long to give every opportunity to work by peaceful methods for a more permanent peace. I therefore suggest that you construe the word "future" to apply to a minimum period of assured non-aggression—ten years at the least—a quarter of a century, if we dare look that far ahead.

If such assurance is given by your Government, I will immediately transmit it to the governments of the nations I have named and I will simultaneously inquire whether, as I am reasonably sure, each of the nations enumerated above will in turn give like assurance for transmission to you.

Reciprocal assurances such as I have outlined will bring to the world an immediate measure of relief.

I propose that if it is given, two essential problems shall promptly be discussed in the resulting peaceful surroundings, and in those discussions the Government of the United States will gladly take part.

The discussions which I have in mind relate to the most effective and immediate manner through which the peoples of the world can obtain progressive relief from the crushing burden of armament which is each day bringing them more closely to the brink of economic disaster. Simultaneously the Government of the United States would be prepared to take part in discussions looking towards the most practical manner of opening up avenues of international trade to the end that every nation of the earth may be enabled to buy and sell on equal terms in the world market as well as to possess assurance of obtaining the materials and products of peaceful economic life.

At the same time, those governments other than the United States which are directly interested could undertake such political discussions as they may consider necessary or desirable.

We recognize complex world problems which affect all humanity but we know that study and discussion of them must be held in an atmosphere of peace. Such an atmosphere of peace cannot exist if negotiations are overshadowed by the threat of force or by the fear of war.

I think you will not misunderstand the spirit of frankness in which I send you this message. Heads of great governments in this hour are literally responsible for the fate of humanity in the coming years. They cannot fail to hear the prayers of their peoples to be protected from the foreseeable chaos of war. History will hold them accountable for the lives and the happiness of all—even unto the least.

I hope that your answer will make it possible for humanity to lose fear and regain security for many years to come.

A similar message is being addressed to the Chief of the Italian Government.

FRANKLIN D. ROOSEVELT

129

Press Releases, vol. XX, p. 367

Address Delivered by the Secretary of State at Washington, April 25, 1939

[Extract]

Nations have most frequently resorted to war on the plea that it is the only method open to them for redressing wrongs or the only means left to them of settling international differences. For neither of these purposes is war the best of the remedies available to man, or, in fact, a remedy at all. There is no controversy, no difference that can arise between nations, which could not be settled with far greater benefit to all concerned by the peaceful processes of friendly adjustment than by resort to armed force.

When a nation makes a deliberate resort to armed force, on any plea whatever, it pursues in reality a wholly different objective; it uses war or threat of war as an instrument of a policy of territorial expansion or domination of others. Such nations are the authors of war, the awful cost of which is paid by their own people and by the rest of mankind.

Whenever there are nations in the world which adopt this type of policy, their intentions and actions inevitably set into motion forces of resistance. Terrible as are the realities and consequences of war, sooner or later conditions arise in which peaceful and peace-loving nations prefer armed defense to subjection and slavery.

There is ample room on this earth for the two billion human beings who inhabit it. There are ample known resources of materials and skill to enable all nations to enjoy a high level of economic prosperity and to face a future of continued plenty. There are ample proven resources of mind and soul to enable the whole of mankind to enjoy the blessings of spiritual advancement. But there has never been, and there is not today, room on this earth for a political organization of mankind under which a single nation or a group of nations will enslave and dominate all the others.

No single nation holds a monopoly of material resources needed by all to maintain the modern level of civilized existence. While some nations are more generously endowed than others, none is or can be self-sufficing within its frontiers except at the price of a disastrous decline in the level of satisfaction of its people's wants. In the present stage of civilization and technical progress, the material and spiritual resources of the entire world are available to all nations through mutually beneficial trade and through all those innumerable peaceful and friendly international relationships in every phase of human activity whose capacity to enrich the lives of individuals and of nations has already been convincingly demonstrated. No nation can prosper without adequate access to the resources of the entire world rather than only to those contained within its own frontiers. And such access is possible only on the basis of peaceful international cooperation.

No nation is excluded from participation in the benefits of these precious means of betterment and advancement of mankind, except as it deliberately excludes itself either by short-sighted attempts at national isolation or the even more short-sighted policy of armed aggrandizement. Isolation dooms a people to inescapable impoverishment; armed aggrandizement, under modern conditions of warfare, entails destruction for which no conceivable advantages secured by the conqueror can possibly provide compensation. A nation entering upon either of these ruinous courses inflicts an incalculable injury upon its own people and upon the world as a whole.

The maintenance and improvement of the structure of peaceful international relationships, upon which the entire fabric of our present-day civilization rests, require a willing contribution from every nation. They are impossible unless each nation respects the independence and sovereignty of every other nation; unless each nation scrupulously observes its international obligations and the rules of conduct embodied in the voluntarily accepted provisions of international law; unless each nation is prepared to abstain from resort to armed force as an instrument for the settlement of international differences and controversies and to adjust all such disputes solely by pacific means; unless each nation is willing to place its economic relations with all other nations upon a basis of the greatest practicable, mutually advantageous interchange of goods and services, flowing through the channels of equal economic opportunity and non-discriminatory commercial treatment.

Every thoughtful man today, in every country of the world, is confronted with the inescapable duty of weighing—in the scales of reason, common sense, his own advantage, and the good of his nation—the benefits of living in a world functioning on the basis of the principles I have just enumerated against the prospect of living in a world caught in the stifling net of anguish and suffering engendered by the constant recurrence of war, of preparation for armed hostilities, and of the aftermath of armed conflict.

I, for one, cannot believe that any nation today has irrevocably entered upon a road from which there is no turning save in the direction of a new widespread war. The road to peaceful adjustment of whatever reasonable and legitimate grievances there may exist has always been open and is still open. But upon this road one must travel with a sincere desire for peace, with a firm determination to observe the pledged word once given, with a sense of respect for the dignity of the human soul. I hope with all my heart that at the present fateful juncture of history, all nations will decide to enter upon this road.

Yet so long as some nations continue to arm for conquest, all other nations are confronted with the tragic alternatives of surrender or armed defense. So far as our nation is concerned, the mere posing of the alternatives supplies the answer. We hope devoutly that a negotiated peace before rather than after the senseless arbitrament of war, a peace based on a mutually fair adjustment of outstanding problems, will be the happy lot of mankind in the future which lies immediately ahead. We are prepared to make our appropriate contribution to such a peace. But if our hopes are doomed to disappointment, if, after all, the red flames of war rather than the noonday sun of peace are to illumine our horizon, we are equally prepared to defend successfully our national interests and our cherished institutions.

130

Press Releases, vol. XX, p. 475

The Secretary of State to the Chairman of the Committee on Foreign Relations (Pittman), United States Senate [40]

WASHINGTON, May 27, 1939.

MY DEAR SENATOR PITTMAN:

In harmony with the conversations I have had during recent weeks with you and other members of the appropriate committees of the two houses of Congress with regard to pending legislative proposals for modifying existing peace and neutrality legislation, I wish to offer the following comment.

These proposals are intended to aid in keeping the United States from becoming involved in war. They contemplate, primarily, a state of affairs in which relations in the world have ceased to be peaceful.

Our purpose must be, at all times, to endeavor to foster that state of relations among nations which will maintain the fabric of world peace. In pursuance of that aim we have done, and must do, everything possible within the limits of our traditional policy of noninvolvement in overseas affairs.

In considering the present proposals for legislation, we must keep in mind that, no matter how much we may wish or may try to disassociate ourselves from world events, we cannot achieve disassociation. The simple fact of our existence as a great nation in a world of nations cannot be denied; and the substance of the legislation adopted in this country inevitably influences not only this

---

[40] An identic letter was sent on the same day to Acting Chairman Bloom, Committee on Foreign Affairs, House of Representatives.

country, but also other countries. The problem for us is not whether we shall help any foreign country or any group of foreign countries. Nor is it that of passing judgment upon or interfering in other people's controversies. Rather, it is that of so conducting our affairs and our relations with other peoples, both before and after the outbreak of war elsewhere, that we shall be more, and not less, secure; so that we shall not become parties to controversies; and so that our attitude and actions will encourage other people to avoid, rather than to become engaged in, controversy.

Because of troubled conditions with which we are all familiar, the Congress rightly is now considering the situation which might obtain were a state of war to develop between other nations. In such case the first concern of the United States is its own safety as well as the desire and intent, which all of us resolutely follow, to remain at peace.

In the event of a foreign war, we would be immediately faced with the problem of maintaining our neutrality.

When a war begins, that body of rules for the regulation of international relations which applies in time of peace becomes impaired. Under international law, the belligerent states then acquire certain rights which do not appertain to states at peace; and at the same time states which remain at peace become affected by a body of rules under which they have the rights and obligations of neutrals.

In considering whether legislative restrictions upon our freedom of action can advantageously be maintained or adopted to ensure against our being drawn into war, we should, in my opinion, avoid the error of assuming that provisions which are at the same time rigid and of universal application, will serve our interests satisfactorily in every situation which may arise. The course of world affairs is unpredictable. What we should try to do for the purpose of keeping this country out of war is to enact measures adapted to the safeguarding of our interests in all situations of which we can conceive and at the same time imposing a minimum of abnormal and unnecessary burdens upon our nationals and a minimum of disruption of our peaceful economic life.

I believe it is important that the legislation which may be enacted should conform, so far as possible, to traditional concepts of international law adhered to by this Government. International law requires that the domestic measures adopted by a neutral shall be impartially applied to the contending parties in conflict. It does not require that a neutral nation shall embargo any articles destined for belligerents.

If we go in for embargoes on exports, for the purpose of keeping ourselves out of war, the logical thing to do would be to make our embargo all-inclusive. Modern warfare is no longer warfare between armed forces only: it is warfare between nations in every phase of their national life. Lists of contraband are no longer limited to arms and ammunition and closely related commodities. They include not only those items which contribute toward making warfare possible, but almost every item useful in the life of the enemy nation. A nation at war is no less anxious to keep cotton or petroleum, or, indeed, any useful product, from reaching an enemy nation than it is to keep guns and airplanes from reaching the enemy's armed forces. I doubt whether we can help ourselves to keep out of war by an attempt on our part to distinguish between categories of exports. Yet a complete embargo upon all exports would obviously be ruinous to our economic life. It therefore seems clear that we should have no general and automatic embargo inflexibly and rigidly imposed on any class or group of exports.

Our conclusion that embargo on export of arms is undesirable is not new, and experience has confirmed our belief.

On August 31, 1935, on the occasion of his signing the Neutrality Act of 1935, the President made the following statement:

"The latter section (providing for an embargo of export of arms) terminates at the end of February 1936. This Section requires further and more complete consideration between now and that date. Here again the objective is wholly good. It is the policy of this government to avoid being drawn into wars between other nations, but it is a fact that no Congress and no executive can foresee all possible future situations. History is filled with unforeseeable situations that call for some flexibility of action. It is conceivable that situations may arise in which the wholly inflexible provisions of Section I of this Act might have exactly the opposite effect from that which was intended. In other words, the inflexible provisions might drag us into war instead of keeping us out. The policy of the government is definitely committed to the maintenance of peace and the avoidance of any entanglements which would lead us into conflict. At the same time it is the policy of the government by every peaceful means and without entanglement to cooperate with other similarly minded governments to promote peace."

On November 6, 1935, I made the following statement with respect to neutrality legislation:

"Any discussion of the avoidance of war, or of the observance of neutrality in the event of war, would be wholly incomplete if too much stress were laid on the part played in the one or the other by the shipment, or the embargoing of the shipment, of arms, ammunition and implements of war. . . . To assume that by placing an embargo on arms we are making ourselves secure from dangers of conflict with belligerent countries is to close our eyes to manifold dangers in other directions. . . . we cannot assume that when provision has been made to stop the shipment of arms, which as absolute contraband have always been regarded as subject to seizure by a belligerent, we may complacently sit back with the feeling that we are secure from all danger."

Our involvement in controversies is more likely to arise from destruction of American lives. In this regard we can effectively diminish our risks by keeping our nationals and ships out of areas in which there is special danger. The rights of our nationals under international law may properly be restricted by our own legislation along certain lines for the purpose of avoiding incidents which might involve us in a conflict. In indicating certain restrictions upon the exercise of our rights as a neutral I do not wish to be considered as advocating the abandonment of these, or indeed of any, neutral rights; but there is reasonable ground for restricting at this time the exercise of these rights.

For the reasons heretofore stated, it is my firm conviction that the arms embargo provision of the existing law should be eliminated. I furthermore believe that the most effective legislative contribution at this time toward keeping this country out of war, if war occurs, would be made by enacting or reenacting provisions on lines as follows:

To prohibit American ships, irrespective of what they may be carrying, from entering combat areas;

To restrict travel by American citizens in combat areas;

To provide that the export of goods destined for belligerents shall be preceded by transfer of title to the foreign purchaser;

To continue the existing legislation respecting loans and credits to nations at war;

To regulate the solicitation and collection in this country of funds for belligerents;

To continue the National Munitions Control Board and the system of arms export and import licenses.

Provisions on the suggested lines would, I think, help to keep this country out of war and facilitate our adherence to a position of neutrality. They would make easier our twofold task of keeping this country at peace and avoiding imposition of unnecessary and abnormal burdens upon our citizens.

Sincerely yours,

CORDELL HULL

131

Department of State Bulletin, vol. I, p. 4

Statement by the Secretary of State, July 1, 1939

I am still thoroughly convinced that the six-point peace and neutrality program set forth in my letters to Senator Pittman and Representative Bloom on May 27, 1939,[41] would be far more effective in the interests of peace and in keeping the country out of war than the present embargo law or any equivalent.

This legislative proposal was submitted to the appropriate committees of the two Houses of Congress after lengthy conferences with members of these committees and with other leading Members of Congress of all political persuasions. It was my hope and belief that, while this proposal might not contain all that every individual Member of Congress or every official of the executive branch of the Government wished, it would in the present international exigencies be regarded as desirable by a majority of Congress. Its failure to pass the House by a narrow margin is a matter of regret and disappointment from the standpoint of peace and the best interests of this country in its international relations.

This six-point peace and neutrality proposal is not only best calculated to keep this Nation out of war in the event war comes, but also, what is all-important at this time, best calculated to make a far greater contribution than could the present law or its equivalent toward the discouragement of the outbreak of war. At the same time, while doing this, it would likewise keep this Government and Nation 100 percent within the limits of universally recognized international law.

In these circumstances, I must continue to urge the adoption of this proposal.

132

793.94/15236

Memorandum by the Secretary of State Regarding a Conversation With the Japanese Ambassador (Horinouchi)

[Extracts]

[WASHINGTON,] July 10, 1939.

The Japanese Ambassador came in at my request.

He then referred to a conversation between Ambassador Grew and Foreign Minister Arita, before the Ambassador recently left Tokyo

---

[41] Doc. 130.

for America, in which Mr. Arita had brought up (1) the idea of our two countries exercising their influence toward avoiding war in Europe; (2) the reported apprehension of my Government that the Japanese occupation of the Hainan Islands is part of a plan of permanent military conquest; and (3) my Government's concern about the extent of possible injury and loss of American interests, including American trade, in China, by reason of possible permanent Japanese policies of control. He said he would be interested in anything I might have to say on these points.

Point 3. I said that, taking the last point first, I need not remind him that for six years I had been earnestly pleading with and urging upon his Government the view that there is enough room on this planet for fifteen or eighteen great nations like his and mine, and that by cooperating along progressive and mutually desirable lines, great progress of the entire world population would gradually follow, etc., etc.

Point 2. I said that, on the other hand, while present American interests and rights in the Far East are highly important, the big consideration relates to the question whether all of China and the Pacific islands skirting it is to be Manchuria-ized by Japan, with international law destroyed and treaty observation abolished and all other nations not allowed into that one-half of the world—the door shut and locked by Japan except over preferences for her own citizens. I added that if some one nation is to do this in one-half of the world, some other nation in the other half of the world might undertake to follow the same example, and nothing would be more absurdly impossible for the future progress of the population of the world, including the countries assuming this species of domination, than such attempted course. I proceeded further to say that the Ambassador might suppose an announcement that this hemisphere and a part of Europe would be foreclosed against his country in the sense of being Manchuria-ized, and added that I need not speculate on what his country would think and how it would feel. I said that such efforts at domination, with no facilities for financing and progressive development, and the going forward on such a huge scale, could only result in disaster for all concerned, speaking, of course, from my viewpoint, and that this general idea had been urged by me on his statesmen for six years.

Point 1. As to the question raised with Ambassador Grew by Foreign Minister Arita about the possible cooperation of our two countries to compose the threatened dangers of Europe, I said that the single test of my Government in dealing with other Governments relates to the question of peace; that we consider the preservation of peace so supremely important to the future of all nations that we draw the line between honest, law-abiding, peaceful countries and peoples, without reference to their form of government, on the one hand, and those who are flouting law and order and officially threatening military conquest without limit as to time or extent; that we will work in a friendly spirit with every peaceful nation to promote and preserve peace, without serious thought as to who they are; that while we have not the slightest alliance, or secret or other understandings with any nation on earth, and do not propose to have any, we will keep thoroughly armed and prepared to take care of our interests and rights; that we have, in the spirit I was describing, made every kind and character of plea to the countries of Europe to indicate a willingness for the peaceful settlement and adjustment of their economic and other relations, and we have indicated our readiness to cooperate in every feasible plan to restore international trade and finance to a normal basis; that, notwithstanding these earnest pleas, (which the Japanese Government itself might well have been making, if it has not been doing so, or might well make now and persistently in the future,) nations perhaps could not but take notice that Japan herself is engaged in military operations for purposes of conquest, and that this situation might well call for an ending, if Japan were to exercise her fullest influence along with the United States and other countries in efforts to compose threatened military conquest in other parts of the world.

The Ambassador made no particular comment, except to state that there had been reports in this country to the effect that Japan might enter into a military pact with Germany and Italy, whereas the truth is that his country has no idea of doing so; that Japan, because of its proximity and difficulties with Russia, has been interested in the anti-Comintern policy of certain European states and in working with them against Bolshevism. I replied that, of course, this was primarily the business of his country; that my country . . . abstains from any entanglements or involvements with European countries; that, of course, if Japan desires to tie herself up with the horribly complicated European controversies, so as to make herself immediately involved in any European war, that still was her business primarily; and I might again reiterate that my Government is keeping itself in a detached position, with peace as its supreme objective, and with armaments sufficient for all purposes of security.

C[ORDELL] H[ULL]

Department of State Bulletin, vol. I, p. 43

*Message From President Roosevelt to the Congress, Transmitting
A Statement by the Secretary of State, July 14, 1939*

I am advised that by a vote of twelve to eleven the Senate Committee on Foreign Relations has deferred action on peace and neutrality legislation until the next session of the Congress.

I am appending hereto a statement from the Secretary of State which has my full approval, and which I trust will receive your earnest attention.

It has been abundantly clear to me for some time that for the cause of peace and in the interests of American neutrality and security, it is highly advisable that the Congress at this session should take certain much needed action. In the light of present world conditions, I see no reason to change that opinion.

FRANKLIN D. ROOSEVELT

THE WHITE HOUSE,
July 14, 1939.

[Enclosure]

STATEMENT ON PEACE AND NEUTRALITY BY THE SECRETARY OF
STATE

The cornerstone of the foreign policy of the United States is the preservation of the peace and security of our nation, the strengthening of international law, and the revitalization of international good faith. The foreign policy of this Government may be misinterpreted or it may be misunderstood, but it cannot be destroyed. Peace is so precious and war so devastating that the people of the United States and their Government must not fail to make their just and legitimate contribution to the preservation of peace.

The Congress has pending before it at the present time certain proposals providing for the amendment of the existing so-called neutrality legislation. Some of these proposed changes I regard as necessary to promote the peace and security of the United States.

There is an astonishing amount of confusion and misunderstanding as regards the legislation under consideration, and particularly with regard to the operation of the existing arms embargo.

I shall try to bring out as clearly as I can the important points of agreement and disagreement between those who support the principles contained in the six point peace and neutrality program recommended by the Executive branch of the Government and those who oppose these recommendations.

In substance and in principle both sides of the discussion agree on the following points:

1. Both sides agree that the first concern of the United States must be its own peace and security.

2. Both sides agree that it should be the policy of this Government to avoid being drawn into wars between other nations.

3. Both sides agree that this nation should at all times avoid entangling alliances or involvements with other nations.

4. Both sides agree that in the event of foreign wars this nation should maintain a status of strict neutrality, and that around the structure of neutrality we should so shape our policies as to keep this country from being drawn into war.

On the other hand, the following is the chief essential point of disagreement between those who favor the adoption of the recommendations formulated by the Executive branch of the Government and those who are opposing these recommendations:

The proponents, including the Executive branch of the Government, at the time when the arms embargo was originally adopted called attention to the fact that its enactment constituted a hazardous departure from the principle of international law which recognizes the right of neutrals to trade with belligerents and of belligerents to trade with neutrals. They believe that neutrality means impartiality, and in their view an arms embargo is directly opposed to the idea of neutrality. It is not humanly possible, by enacting an arms embargo, or by refraining from such enactment, to hold the scales exactly even between two belligerents. In either case and due to shifting circumstances one belligerent may find itself in a position of relative advantage or disadvantage. The important difference between the two cases is that when such a condition arises in the absence of an arms embargo on our part, no responsibility attaches to this country, whereas in the presence of an embargo, the responsibility of this country for the creation of the condition is inevitably direct and clear.

There is no theory or practice to be found in international law pertaining to neutrality to the effect that the advantages that any particular belligerent might procure through its geographic location, its superiority on land or at sea, or through other circumstances, should be offset by the establishment by neutral nations of embargoes.

The opposition to the present substitute proposal joins issue on this point, and stands for existing rigid embargo as a permanent part of our neutrality policy. And yet by insisting on an arms embargo in time of war they are, to that extent, for the reasons I have stated, urging not neutrality, but what might well result in actual unneutrality, the serious consequences of which no one can predict.

Those who urge the retention of the present embargo continue to advance the view that it will keep this country out of war,—thereby misleading the American people to rely upon a false and illogical delusion as a means of keeping out of war.

I say it is illogical, because while the trade in "arms, ammunition and implements of war" is at present banned, the trade in equally essential war materials, as well as all the essential materials out of which the finished articles are made can continue. For example, in time of war, we can sell cotton for the manufacture of explosives, but not the explosives; we can sell the steel and copper for cannon and for shells but not the cannon nor the shells; we can continue to sell to belligerents the high-powered fuel necessary for the operation of airplanes, but we are not able to sell the airplanes.

I say it is a false delusion because a continuation of the trade in arms is a clearly recognized and traditional right of the nationals of a neutral country in time of war, subject only to effective blockade and to the right of belligerents to treat any such commodities as contraband. The assertion frequently made that this country has ever engaged or may become engaged in serious controversy solely over the fact that its nationals have sold arms to belligerents is misleading and unsupportable. All available evidence is directly to the contrary. Every informed person knows that arms, as absolute contraband, are subject to seizure by a belligerent and that neither the neutral shipper nor his government has the slightest ground for complaint. There is, therefore, no reason to suppose that the sale of arms may lead to serious controversy between a neutral and a belligerent. Furthermore, under the proposals that have been made American nationals would be divested of all right, title and interest in these and other commodities before they leave our shores and American citizens and ships would be kept out of danger zones. As regards possible complications which might arise as a result of the extension of credits to belligerents or of extraordinary profits accruing to any group of producers in this country, it is wholly within the power of Congress at all times to safeguard the national interest in this respect.

Controversies which would involve the United States are far more likely to arise from the entrance of American ships or American citizens in the danger zones or through the sinking on the high seas of American vessels carrying commodities other than those covered by the arms embargo. In the recommendations formulated by the Executive as a substitute for the present legislation it was especially urged that provisions be adopted which would exclude American nationals and American ships from zones where real danger to their safety might exist and which would divest goods of American ownership, thereby minimizing to the fullest extent the danger of American involvement.

Those of us who support the recommendations formulated for the elimination of the embargo are convinced that the arms embargo plays into the hands of those nations which have taken the lead in building up their fighting power. It works directly against the interests of the peace-loving nations, especially those which do not possess their own munitions plants. It means that if any country is disposed towards conquest, and devotes its energy and resources to establish itself as a superior fighting power, that country may be more tempted to try the fortunes of war if it knows that its less well prepared opponents would be shut off from those supplies which, under every rule of international law, they should be able to buy in all neutral countries, including the United States. It means also that some of those countries which have only limited facilities for the production of arms, ammunition and implements of war are put in a position of increased dependence. During peace-time they would feel the compulsion of shaping their political as well as their economic policy to suit the military strength of others; and during war-time their powers of defense would be limited.

For these reasons those who are supporting the recommendations for the amendment of existing legislation recognize definitely that the present embargo encourages a general state of war both in Europe and Asia. Since the present embargo has this effect its results are directly prejudicial to the highest interests and to the peace and to the security of the United States.

In the present grave conditions of international anarchy and of danger to peace, in more than one part of the world, I profoundly believe that the first great step towards safeguarding this nation from being drawn into war is to use whatever influence it can, compatible with the traditional policy of our country of non-involvement, so as to make less likely the outbreak of a major war. This is a duty placed upon our Government which some may fail to perceive or choose to reject. But it must be clear to every one of us that the outbreak of a general war increases the dangers confronting the United States. This fact cannot be ignored.

I would emphasize that the course proposed through the substitute legislation recommended by the Executive is consistent with the rules of international law and with the policy of our own country over a period of 150 years. The basis for the recommendations made is the firm intention of keeping this country from being drawn into war. If there existed any desire to assist or to injure particular foreign countries this Government would not have been endeavoring persistently, within the limitations of our traditional policy, over a period of many years to do its utmost to avoid the outbreak of a general war. I earnestly hope that the Congress will lend the fullest measure of its cooperation in the endeavor to avoid war in the first place and to place this country in a position of the greatest security possible, should war break out. In the tragic event that peace efforts fail and that a major war occurs, there will be general agreement within the United States that every effort must be exerted to keep this country from being drawn therein.

I must also refer to the impression sedulously created to the effect that the sale of arms, munitions and implements of war by this country is immoral and that on this ground it should be suppressed in time of war.

As a matter of fact almost all sales of arms and ammunition made in recent years by our nationals have been made to governments whose policies have been dedicated to the maintenance of peace, but who have felt the necessity of creating or of augmenting their means of national self-defense, thereby protecting otherwise helpless men, women and children in the event that other powers resort to war. In the face of the present universal danger all countries, including our own, feel the necessity of increasing armament, and small countries in particular are dependent upon countries like the United States which have the capacity to produce armaments. Our refusal to make it possible for them to obtain such means of necessary self-defense in a time of grave emergency, would contribute solely towards making more helpless the law-abiding and peace-devoted peoples of the world. If such action is moral, and if, on the contrary, sales of the means of self-defense for the protection of peaceful and law-abiding peoples are immoral, then a new definition of morality and immorality must be written. This task might be left to the proponents of the arms embargo.

I must also refer to another impression created by propaganda to the effect that the abandonment of the arms embargo would increase power of action on the part of the Executive branch of the Government and conversely that the maintenance of the embargo would serve as an additional check on the powers of the Executive. It is difficult to see how either of these propositions could possibly hold true. An impartial granting of access to American markets to all countries without distinction gives the Executive no additional power to choose among them and to commit this country to any line of policy or action which may lead it either into a dangerous controversy or into war with any foreign power.

The legislative proposals which were recommended to the Congress through the communications which I transmitted to Senator Pittman and to Congressman Bloom on May 27 providing for the safeguarding of our nation to the fullest possible extent from incurring the risks of involvement in war contemplate the elimination of the existing arms embargo and are as follows:

(1) To prohibit American ships from entering combat areas;

(2) To restrict travel by American citizens in combat areas;

(3) To require that goods exported from the United States to belligerent countries shall be preceded by the transfer of title to the foreign purchasers;

(4) To continue the existing legislation respecting loans and credits to belligerent nations;

(5) To regulate the solicitation and collection in this country of funds for belligerents; and

(6) To continue the National Munitions Control Board and the licensing system with respect to the importation and exportation of arms, ammunition, and implements of war.

This six-point program was the best that could be devised after much painstaking thought and study, and after many conferences with members of the Congress, of how best to keep this country out of a conflict should it arise. It rests primarily on the established rules of international law, plus the curtailment of certain rights of our nationals, the exercise of which is permitted under international law but which might lead to controversies with belligerents and eventual involvement in foreign wars.

There has thus been offered as a substitute for the present act a far broader and more effective set of provisions, which in no conceivable sense could breed trouble but which to a far greater extent than the present act would both aid in making less likely a general war, and, while keeping strictly within the limits of neutrality, reduce as far as possible the risk of this nation of being drawn into war if war comes.

In connection with our foreign affairs, I think all must agree that, unless a spirit of collaboration and cooperation characterizes the relations between the Executive and Legislative departments of the Government, the peace and other vital interests of this country will inevitably be jeopardized.

Having spent the best years of my life as a member of the two Houses of Congress, I have the warmest feeling of friendliness toward the membership of, and the greatest respect for, the Legislative Department, and, in that spirit, I earnestly hope for the closest possible cooperation in matters affecting our country's best interests and its security in the present grave international situation.

At this time when critical conditions obtain throughout the greater part of the world I am sure that we are all equally persuaded that while the fullest measure of constructive criticism is helpful and desirable, and is of course most welcome, partisanship should play no part in the determination of the foreign policy of this country.

In the present situation of danger a peaceful nation like ours cannot complacently close its eyes and ears in formulating a peace and neutrality policy, as though abnormal and critical conditions did not exist. The entire question of peace and neutrality at this serious juncture in its possible effects upon the safety and the interest of the United States during coming months is of the utmost importance. This question should, in my judgment, receive full and careful consideration and be acted upon by this Government without unnecessary or undue delay.

CORDELL HULL

134

Department of State Bulletin, vol. I, p. 57

Press Release Issued by the White House on July 18, 1939 [41a]

The President and the Secretary of State maintained the definite position that failure by the Senate to take action now would weaken the leadership of the United States in exercising its potent influence in the cause of preserving peace among other nations in the event of a new crisis in Europe between now and next January.

[41a] Issued after a conference between the President, the Secretary of State, and Senate leaders.

135

711.942/235

The Secretary of State to the Japanese Ambassador (Horinouchi)

WASHINGTON, July 26, 1939.

EXCELLENCY: During recent years the Government of the United States has been examining the treaties of commerce and navigation in force between the United States and foreign countries with a view to determining what changes may need to be made toward better serving the purposes for which such treaties are concluded. In the course of this survey, the Government of the United States has come to the conclusion that the Treaty of Commerce and Navigation between the United States and Japan which was signed at Washington on February 21, 1911, contains provisions which need new consideration. Toward preparing the way for such consideration and with a view to better safeguarding and promoting American interests as new developments may require, the Government of the United States, acting in accordance with the procedure prescribed in Article XVII of the treaty under reference, gives notice hereby of its desire that this treaty be terminated, and, having thus given notice, will expect the treaty, together with its accompanying protocol, to expire six months from this date.

Accept [etc.]   CORDELL HULL

136

Department of State Bulletin, vol. I, p. 158

President Roosevelt to King Victor Emmanuel of Italy [42]

AUGUST 23, 1939.

Again a crisis in world affairs makes clear the responsibility of heads of nations for the fate of their own people and indeed of humanity itself. It is because of traditional accord between Italy and the United States and the ties of consanguinity between millions of our citizens that I feel that I can address Your Majesty in behalf of the maintenance of world peace.

---

[42] Arrangements for Ambassador Phillips to deliver the message to the King in person at Turin, Italy, were made by Premier Mussolini and the Italian Foreign Minister, Ciano. Ambassador Phillips was authorized to give Premier Mussolini a copy of the communication.

It is my belief and that of the American people that Your Majesty and Your Majesty's Government can greatly influence the averting of an outbreak of war. Any general war would cause to suffer all nations whether belligerent or neutral, whether victors or vanquished, and would clearly bring devastation to the peoples and perhaps to the governments of some nations most directly concerned.

The friends of the Italian people and among them the American people could only regard with grief the destruction of great achievements which European nations and the Italian nation in particular have attained during the past generation.

We in America having welded a homogeneous nation out of many nationalities, often find it difficult to visualize the animosities which so often have created crises among nations of Europe which are smaller than ours in population and in territory, but we accept the fact that these nations have an absolute right to maintain their national independence if they so desire. If that be sound doctrine then it must apply to the weaker nations as well as to the stronger.

Acceptance of this means peace, because fear of aggression ends. The alternative, which means of necessity efforts by the strong to dominate the weak, will lead not only to war, but to long future years of oppression on the part of victors and to rebellion on the part of the vanquished. So history teaches us.

On April fourteenth last I suggested in essence an understanding that no armed forces should attack or invade the territory of any other independent nation, and that this being assured, discussions be undertaken to seek progressive relief from the burden of armaments and to open avenues of international trade including sources of raw materials necessary to the peaceful economic life of each nation.

I said that in these discussions the United States would gladly take part. And such peaceful conversations would make it wholly possible for governments other than the United States to enter into peaceful discussions of political or territorial problems in which they were directly concerned.

Were it possible for Your Majesty's Government to formulate proposals for a pacific solution of the present crisis along these lines you are assured of the earnest sympathy of the United States.

The Government of Italy and the United States can today advance those ideals of Christianity which of late seem so often to have been obscured.

The unheard voices of countless millions of human beings ask that they shall not be vainly sacrificed again.

137

Department of State Bulletin, vol. I, p. 157

President Roosevelt to the Chancelor of Germany (Hitler)

[Telegram]

AUGUST 24, 1939.

In the message which I sent to you on April 14 last I stated that it appeared to me that the leaders of great nations had it in their power to liberate their peoples from the disaster that impended, but that unless the effort were immediately made with good will on all sides to find a peaceful and constructive solution of existing controversies, the crisis which the world was confronting must end in catastrophe. Today that catastrophe appears to be very near at hand indeed.

To the message which I sent to you last April I have received no reply, but because of my confident belief that the cause of world peace—which is the cause of humanity itself—rises above all other considerations, I am again addressing myself to you with the hope that the war which impends and the consequent disaster to all peoples everywhere may yet be averted.

I therefore urge with all earnestness—and I am likewise urging the President of the Republic of Poland—that the Governments of Germany and of Poland agree by common accord to refrain from any positive act of hostility for a reasonable and stipulated period, and that they agree likewise by common accord to solve the controversies which have arisen between them by one of the three following methods: first, by direct negotiation; second, by submission of these controversies to an impartial arbitration in which they can both have confidence; or, third, that they agree to the solution of these controversies through the procedure of conciliation, selecting as conciliator or moderator a national of one of the traditionally neutral states of Europe, or a national of one of the American republics which are all of them free from any connection with or participation in European political affairs.

Both Poland and Germany being sovereign governments, it is understood, of course, that upon resort to any one of the alternatives I suggest, each nation will agree to accord complete respect to the independence and territorial integrity of the other.

The people of the United States are as one in their opposition to policies of military conquest and domination. They are as one in rejecting the thesis that any ruler, or any people, possess the right to achieve their ends or objectives through the taking of action which will plunge countless millions of people into war and which will bring distress and suffering to every nation of the world, belligerent and neutral, when such ends and objectives, so far as they are just and reasonable, can be satisfied through processes of peaceful negotiation or by resort to judicial arbitration.

I appeal to you in the name of the people of the United States, and I believe in the name of peace-loving men and women everywhere, to agree to the solution of the controversies existing between your Government and that of Poland through the adoption of one of the alternative methods I have proposed. I need hardly reiterate that should the Governments of Germany and of Poland be willing to solve their differences in the peaceful manner suggested, the Government of the United States still stands prepared to contribute its share to the solution of the problems which are endangering world peace in the form set forth in my message of April 14.

FRANKLIN D. ROOSEVELT

138

Department of State Bulletin, vol. I, p. 158

President Roosevelt to the President of the Polish Republic (Moscicki)

[Telegram]

AUGUST 24, 1939.

The manifest gravity of the existing crisis imposes an urgent obligation upon all to examine every possible means which might prevent the outbreak of general war.

With this in mind, I feel justified in suggesting that certain possible avenues of solution be considered.

The controversy between the Government of Poland and the Government of the German Reich might be made the subject of direct discussion between the two governments.

Should this prove impossible or not feasible, a second avenue might be that of submission of the issues to arbitration.

A third method might be conciliation through a disinterested third party, in which case it would seem appropriate that the parties avail themselves of the services of one of the traditionally neutral states, or a disinterested Republic of the Western Hemisphere wholly removed from the area and issues of the present crisis. Should you determine to attempt solution by any of these methods, you are assured of the earnest and complete sympathy of the United

States and of its people. During the exploration of these avenues, I appeal to you, as I have likewise appealed to the Government of the German Reich, to agree to refrain from any positive act of hostility.

Both Poland and Germany being sovereign governments, it is understood, of course, that upon resort to any one of the alternatives I suggest, each nation will agree to accord complete respect to the independence and territorial integrity of the other.

It is, I think, well known to you that speaking on behalf of the United States I have exerted and will continue to exert every influence in behalf of peace. The rank and file of the population of every nation, large and small, want peace. They do not seek military conquests. They recognize that disputes, claims, and counter claims will always arise from time to time between nations, but that all such controversies without exception can be solved by peaceful procedure if the will on both sides exists so to do.

I have addressed a communication in similar sense to the Chancellor of the German Reich.

FRANKLIN D. ROOSEVELT

139

Department of State Bulletin, vol. I, p. 160

President Roosevelt to the Chancelor of Germany (Hitler)

[Telegram]

AUGUST 25, 1939.

I have this hour received from the President of Poland a reply to the message which I addressed to Your Excellency and to him last night. The text of President Moszicki's reply is as follows:

"I highly appreciate the most important and noble message which Your Excellency was good enough to address to me.

"I would like to emphasize that the Polish Government always considered direct negotiations between governments as the most appropriate method of solving difficulties which may arise between states. We consider this method all the more fitting when adopted between neighboring countries. It was with this principle in view that Poland concluded pacts of nonaggression with Germany and the Union of Soviet Republics.

"We consider likewise the method of conciliation through a third party as disinterested and impartial as Your Excellency to be a just and equitable method in the solution of controversies arising between nations.

"While naturally wishing to avoid even the semblance of availing myself of this occasion to raise the points at issue I nevertheless consider it my duty to point out that in this crisis it is not Poland who is proffering any claims or demanding concessions from any other nation.

"It is therefore only natural that Poland agrees to refrain from any positive act of hostility provided the other party also agrees to refrain from any such act direct or indirect.

"In conclusion may I express my ardent wish that Your Excellency's appeal for peace may contribute towards general appeasement which the people of the world so sorely need to return once more to the blessed path of progress and civilization."

Your Excellency has repeatedly and publicly stated that the ends and the objectives sought by the German Reich were just and reasonable. In his reply to my message the President of Poland has made it plain that the Polish Government is willing, upon the basis set forth in my message, to agree to solve the controversy which has arisen between the Republic of Poland and the German Reich by direct negotiation or through the process of conciliation.

Countless human lives can be yet saved and hope may still be restored that the nations of the modern world may even now construct a foundation for a peaceful and a happier relationship if you and the Government of the German Reich will agree to the pacific means of settlement accepted by the Government of Poland.

All the world prays that Germany, too, will accept.

FRANKLIN D. ROOSEVELT

140

393.112/64

Memorandum by the Secretary of State Regarding a Conversation With the Japanese Ambassador (Horinouchi)

[WASHINGTON,] August 26, 1939.

The Ambassador of Japan called at his own request. He proceeded to refer to the reports, already published in the American press, to the effect that American officials were incorrectly attributing anti-American movements and demonstrations in China to Japanese officials or to their influence in thus instigating the Chinese. The Ambassador handed me the attached paper,[43] which I proceeded to read. I thanked him for the attention his Government had given to this matter and the spirit seemingly prompting his Government to seek to clear it up.

I then said that, having seen in the American press the purpose and nature of his contemplated call on me, I had requested the Far Eastern Division to jot down a list of instances of transgressions by Japanese or due to Japanese influence in China to the detriment and injury of Americans and of American interests. I added that this list of incidents had not been elaborated but that I would proceed to read them. I then read the memorandum prepared by the Far Eastern Division, attached hereto and marked "A".[43] The Ambassador appeared somewhat surprised and at a loss for further comment with regard to this paper. He said he would be pleased to have a copy of it. I replied that I would be glad to request the Far Eastern Division to put it in more elaborate form if possible and to send a copy to him at the Japanese Embassy.

The Ambassador then said that, speaking personally, he might say his Government on yesterday had decided to abandon any further negotiations with Germany and Italy relative to closer relations under the anti-Comintern Pact to which they have been parties for some time. He added that the change in affairs in Europe made this course manifest, and, furthermore, it was plain that his Government would find it important to adopt new foreign policy in more or less respects. I might say that he prefaced this general reference to his country by reiterating his personal desire to clear up any misunderstandings or differences between our two countries and to restore the friendly relations heretofore existing. The Ambassador remarked that he hoped there might come about an adjustment of the Japanese-Chinese situation. He just made this general observation and then he passed on to inquire what I knew or thought about the European situation.

I replied that it was very kaleidoscopic; that just now no one could with any satisfaction predict about developments from day to day; that at this time today the British Cabinet was considering the conversation between Mr. Hitler and the British Ambassador at Berlin on yesterday; that no one knows what their decision may be.

I then referred to his comment about Japan and her purpose to adopt a new foreign policy, and I made observations substantially as follows:

The principles and practices of American policy in regard to the

---

[43] Not printed.

world in general and the Far East in particular are well known to all governments everywhere.

During recent years Japanese authorities and/or agencies have been pursuing courses which come into direct conflict with those principles and policies and which involve disregard of principles of international law and of treaties between the United States and Japan and also multilateral treaties to which the United States and Japan are parties.

The United States has made representations over and over and over again in objection to or protest against overt acts of these types. The Japanese Government has given assurances over and over again that it has regard for the principles and the rules and the provisions involved and that it will show its regard for them,—and over and over Japanese authorities have immediately committed other acts in disregard thereof.

We have clear evidence of inspiration by Japanese authorities of action by agencies thereof hostile not only to occidental nationals and interests in general but to American nationals and interests in particular. These courses of action by Japanese have resulted in arousing against Japan feelings of suspicion and attitudes of opposition on the part of almost all of the other powers which have interests in the Far East, especially in China, including the United States.

It should be evident to Japan that there is something wrong with policies and practices on the part of one nation which arouse antagonism on the part of almost all other nations in contact with that nation.

The United States wishes to have amicable relations with every other country in the world. We have in the past had very friendly relations with every country in the Far East, including Japan. Our policy is a policy of "Live and let live". We seek nowhere any special position; but we seek everywhere equality of opportunity under conditions of fair treatment and security.

The world is being given today new object lessons with regard to the futility of policies wherein nations plan to take advantage of other nations by use of armed force in disregard of moral principles and legal principles and generally accepted axioms of friendly and profitable general international intercourse.

The future of American-Japanese relations lies largely in the hands of Japan. American policy is a policy of friendliness and fair dealing toward all nations. It will not change.

The Ambassador seemed appreciative and this ended the conversation.

C[ORDELL] H[ULL]

141

Department of State Bulletin, vol. I, p. 183

The German Chargé (Thomsen) to the Secretary of State

WASHINGTON, August 31, 1939.

MR. SECRETARY OF STATE:

By order of my Government, I wish to use your kind intermediary for the purpose of stating to the President of the United States that his messages of August 25 and 26 addressed to the German Fuehrer and Reich Chancellor have been greatly appreciated by the latter.

The German Fuehrer and Reich Chancellor has also, on his side, left nothing untried for the purpose of settling the dispute between Germany and Poland in a friendly manner. Even at the last hour he accepted an offer from the Government of Great Britain to mediate in this dispute. Owing to the attitude of the Polish Government, however, all these endeavors have remained without result.

Accept [etc.]   THOMSEN

142

Department of State Bulletin, vol. I, p. 201

Radio Address Delivered by President Roosevelt From Washington, September 3, 1939

Tonight my single duty is to speak to the whole of America.

Until 4:30 this morning I had hoped against hope that some miracle would prevent a devastating war in Europe and bring to an end the invasion of Poland by Germany.

For 4 long years a succession of actual wars and constant crises have shaken the entire world and have threatened in each case to bring on the gigantic conflict which is today unhappily a fact.

It is right that I should recall to your minds the consistent and at times successful efforts of your Government in these crises to throw the full weight of the United States into the cause of peace. In spite of spreading wars I think that we have every right and every reason to maintain as a national policy the fundamental moralities, the teachings of religion, and the continuation of efforts to restore peace—for some day, though the time may be distant, we can be of even greater help to a crippled humanity.

It is right, too, to point out that the unfortunate events of these recent years have been based on the use of force or the threat of force. And it seems to me clear, even at the outbreak of this great war, that the influence of America should be consistent in seeking for humanity a final peace which will eliminate, as far as it is possible to do so, the continued use of force between nations.

It is, of course, impossible to predict the future. I have my constant stream of information from American representatives and other sources throughout the world. You, the people of this country, are receiving news through your radios and your newspapers at every hour of the day.

You are, I believe, the most enlightened and the best informed people in all the world at this moment. You are subjected to no censorship of news; and I want to add that your Government has no information which it has any thought of withholding from you.

At the same time, as I told my press conference on Friday, it is of the highest importance that the press and the radio use the utmost caution to discriminate between actual verified fact on the one hand and mere rumor on the other.

I can add to that by saying that I hope the people of this country will also discriminate most carefully between news and rumor. Do not believe of necessity everything you hear or read. Check up on it first.

You must master at the outset a simple but unalterable fact in modern foreign relations. When peace has been broken anywhere, peace of all countries everywhere is in danger.

It is easy for you and me to shrug our shoulders and say that conflicts taking place thousands of miles from the continental United States, and, indeed, the whole American hemisphere, do not seriously affect the Americas—and that all the United States has to do is to ignore them and go about our own business. Passionately though we may desire detachment, we are forced to realize that every word that comes through the air, every ship that sails the sea, every battle that is fought does affect the American future.

Let no man or woman thoughtlessly or falsely talk of America sending its armies to European fields. At this moment there is being prepared a proclamation of American neutrality. This would have been done even if there had been no neutrality statute on the books, for this proclamation is in accordance with international law and with American policy.

This will be followed by a proclamation required by the existing Neutrality Act. I trust that in the days to come our neutrality can be made a true neutrality.

It is of the utmost importance that the people of this country, with the best information in the world, think things through. The most dangerous enemies of American peace are those who, without well-rounded information on the whole broad subject of the past, the present, and the future, undertake to speak with authority, to talk in terms of glittering generalities, to give to the Nation assurances or prophecies which are of little present or future value.

I myself cannot and do not prophesy the course of events abroad —and the reason is that because I have of necessity such a complete picture of what is going on in every part of the world, I do not dare to do so. And the other reason is that I think it is honest for me to be honest with the people of the United States.

I cannot prophesy the immediate economic effect of this new war on our Nation, but I do say that no American has the moral right to profiteer at the expense either of his fellow citizens or of the men, women, and children who are living and dying in the midst of war in Europe.

Some things we do know. Most of us in the United States believe in spiritual values. Most of us, regardless of what church we belong to, believe in the spirit of the New Testament—a great teaching which opposes itself to the use of force, of armed force, of marching armies, and falling bombs. The overwhelming masses of our people seek peace—peace at home, and the kind of peace in other lands which will not jeopardize peace at home.

We have certain ideas and ideals of national safety, and we must act to preserve that safety today and to preserve the safety of our children in future years.

That safety is and will be bound up with the safety of the Western Hemisphere and of the seas adjacent thereto. We seek to keep war from our firesides by keeping war from coming to the Americas. For that we have historic precedent that goes back to the days of the administration of President George Washington. It is serious enough and tragic enough to every American family in every State in the Union to live in a world that is torn by wars on other continents. Today they affect every American home. It is our national duty to use every effort to keep them out of the Americas.

And at this time let me make the simple plea that partisanship and selfishness be adjourned, and that national unity be the thought that underlies all others.

This Nation will remain a neutral nation, but I cannot ask that every American remain neutral in thought as well. Even a neutral has a right to take account of facts. Even a neutral cannot be asked to close his mind or his conscience.

I have said not once but many times that I have seen war and that I hate war. I say that again and again.

I hope the United States will keep out of this war. I believe that it will. And I give you assurances that every effort of your Government will be directed toward that end.

As long as it remains within my power to prevent, there will be no blackout of peace in the United States.

143

Department of State Bulletin, vol. I, p. 275

Address Delivered by President Roosevelt to the Congress, September 21, 1939

[Extracts]

Since 1931 the use of force instead of the council table has constantly increased in the settlement of disputes between nations—except in the Western Hemisphere, where there has been only one war, now happily terminated.

During these years also the building up of vast armies, navies, and storehouses of war has proceeded abroad with growing speed and intensity. But, during these years, and extending back even to the days of the Kellogg-Briand Pact, the United States has constantly, consistently, and conscientiously done all in its power to encourage peaceful settlements, to bring about reduction of armaments, and to avert threatened wars. We have done this not only because any war anywhere necessarily hurts American security and American prosperity, but because of the more important fact that any war anywhere retards the progress of morality and religion and impairs the security of civilization itself.

For many years the primary purpose of our foreign policy has been that this Nation and this Government should strive to the utmost to aid in avoiding war among other nations. But if and when war unhappily comes, the Government and the Nation must exert every possible effort to avoid being drawn into the war.

The executive branch of the Government did its utmost, within our traditional policy of noninvolvement, to aid in averting the present appalling war. Having thus striven and failed, this Government must lose no time or effort to keep the Nation from being drawn into the war.

In my candid judgment we shall succeed in these efforts.

Beginning with the foundation of our constitutional government in the year 1789, the American policy in respect to belligerent nations, with one notable exception, has been based on international law. Be it remembered that what we call international law has had as its primary objectives the avoidance of causes of war and the prevention of the extension of war.

The single exception was the policy adopted by this Nation during the Napoleonic Wars, when, seeking to avoid involvement, we acted for some years under the so-called Embargo and Non-Intercourse Acts. . . .

Our next deviation by statute from the sound principles of neutrality and peace through international law did not come for 130 years. It was the so-called Neutrality Act of 1935—only 4 years ago—an act continued in force by the joint resolution of May 1, 1937, despite grave doubts expressed as to its wisdom by many Senators and Representatives and by officials charged with the conduct of our foreign relations, including myself. I regret that the Congress passed that act. I regret equally that I signed that act.

On July fourteenth of this year I asked the Congress in the cause of peace and in the interest of real American neutrality and security to take action to change that act.

I now ask again that such action be taken in respect to that part of the act which is wholly inconsistent with ancient precepts of the law of nations—the embargo provisions. I ask it because they are, in my opinion, most vitally dangerous to American neutrality, American security, and American peace.

I seek a greater consistency through the repeal of the embargo provisions and a return to international law. I seek reenactment of the historic and traditional American policy which, except for the disastrous interlude of the Embargo and Non-Intercourse Acts, has served us well for nearly a century and a half.

It has been erroneously said that return to that policy might bring us nearer to war. I give to you my deep and unalterable conviction, based on years of experience as a worker in the field of international peace, that by the repeal of the embargo the United States will more probably remain at peace than if the law remains as it stands today. I say this because with the repeal of the embargo this Government clearly and definitely will insist that American citizens and American ships keep away from the immediate perils of the actual zones of conflict.

Repeal of the embargo and a return to international law are the crux of this issue.

To those who say that this program would involve a step toward war on our part, I reply that it offers far greater safeguards than we now possess or have ever possessed to protect American lives and property from danger. It is a positive program for giving safety. This means less likelihood of incidents and controversies which tend to draw us into conflict, as they did in the last World War. There lies the road to peace!

I should like to be able to offer the hope that the shadow over the world might swiftly pass. I cannot. The facts compel my stating, with candor, that darker periods may lie ahead. The disaster is not of our making; no act of ours engendered the forces which assault the foundations of civilization. Yet we find ourselves affected to the core; our currents of commerce are changing, our minds are filled with new problems, our position in world affairs has already been altered.

In such circumstances our policy must be to appreciate in the deepest sense the true American interest. Rightly considered, this interest is not selfish. Destiny first made us, with our sister nations on this hemisphere, joint heirs of European culture. Fate seems now to compel us to assume the task of helping to maintain in the western world a citadel wherein that civilization may be kept alive. The peace, the integrity, and the safety of the Americas—these must be kept firm and serene. In a period when it is sometimes said that free discussion is no longer compatible with national safety, may you by your deeds show the world that we of the United States are one people, of one mind, one spirit, one clear resolution, walking before God in the light of the living.

144

Department of State Bulletin, vol. I, p. 299

Address Delivered by the Under Secretary of State (Welles)
At Panamá, September 25, 1939

In accordance with the principles of the Convention for the Maintenance, Preservation, and Reestablishment of Peace, the Declaration of Inter-American Solidarity of Buenos Aires, and the Declaration of Lima, the Ministers of Foreign Relations of the American republics or their representatives are meeting here in Panama for the purpose of consultation. Under the terms of the agreements I have cited, this coming together to consult is not an undertaking into which we have entered lightly. We have, on the contrary, agreed and clearly stipulated that the consultation provided for in these agreements shall be undertaken when there exists in the belief of our respective governments a menace to the peace of the continent.

I speak, of course, solely in the name of my own Government, but I venture to assert that the government of every American republic coincides in the opinion that the outbreak of the general war with which the world today is confronted constitutes in very truth a potential menace to the well-being, to the security, and to the peace of the New World. And it is for that reason that we are meeting here in this historic city of Panama. We are today creating a precedent. The Conference for the Maintenance of Peace of Buenos Aires was called, as we all recognize, for the specific purpose of reaching a common understanding while world peace existed as to how the nations of the New World might best safeguard their legitimate interests, and most readily preserve the peace of their own peoples, in the event that war broke out in other parts of the world.

The meeting here assembled is the first and the direct result of the engagements undertaken at the Conference of Buenos Aires.

It is a meeting of the American neighbors to consider, in a moment of grave emergency, the peaceful measures which they may feel it wise to adopt either individually or jointly, so as best to insure their national interests and the collective interests of the nations of the New World.

And it is singularly fitting that this great practical demonstration of inter-American solidarity should be realized in Panama. Every one of us who meets here today will recognize that this assembly constitutes the realization of an ideal—the realization of the vision that Bolívar possessed more than a century ago—an ideal which time and again it had seemed could never be attained. It lies within the power of those of us who have the privilege of representing our governments upon this occasion to insure not only the attainment of that ideal, but also by so doing, to insure the lasting establishment of a peaceful form of practical cooperation and interdependence between equal and sovereign states on a scale which the world has rarely witnessed and which, at this moment, is more than ever imperative.

The purpose for which we meet and the topics which will come up for consideration are clearly set forth in the agenda upon which we have agreed. As my Government envisages it, it is our common desire to take under consideration the complicated question of our rights and duties as neutrals, in view of the outbreak of general war in Europe, with a view to the preservation of the peace of our respective nations and with a view towards obtaining complete respect on the part of all belligerents for our respective sovereignties. It would seem to me desirable, so far as conditions and our untrammeled rights of individual action make it possible, for us in this connection to give some thought to the desirability of our reaching some uniform standards of approach with regard to the steps which we may individually take in determining and in asserting our rights and obligations as neutrals. It would seem to me to be self-evident that should it be possible to attain such an objective, our individual capacity to maintain our sovereign rights unimpaired, as well as our ability to preserve the peace of our continent, would be correspondingly enhanced.

We are further agreed that we will give the fullest consideration to all measures which we may individually or collectively undertake to preserve the American Continent free from conflict and to keep war away from our New World.

Finally, we are agreed that we will undertake to discuss and to consider those practical steps which can most advantageously be undertaken to cushion our national economies from the shock of the war which has broken out and to prevent so far as may be possible that disruption and dislocation of inter-American economic, financial, and commercial intercourse which wrought such havoc during the years of the Great War of 1914–18. We are also in accord that we will give thought to the continuation and expansion of long-range programs for commercial and economic cooperation among our several republics.

In the economic sphere the struggle that is going on confronts us with difficulties of both an immediate and an ultimate character. We are already experiencing dislocations in our usual commerce. Some of the markets for our products will be closed or diminished; others will be greatly changed. We must anticipate difficulties disposing of war-created surpluses in some directions, which will result in lowering prices or in bringing new burdens to our public finances. In other directions we must anticipate an abnormally increased demand which will result in price increases, unexpected gains, and the dangers of expansion on temporary and unstable foundations.

Each of our nations will no doubt determine upon a program aimed to lessen the effects upon its own welfare of these dislocations. But there are many ways in which the American republics can assist each other in the task. We may be able, without undertaking discriminations against the rest of the world, substantially to increase our commerce with one another. Countries which have similar surplus problems may be able to devise temporary arrangements with each other that will ameliorate their situation.

By our concerted effort we may be able to achieve something in the maintenance of our usual trade in staple peace-time commodities with other neutral countries.

We all of us remember only too well the havoc which was occasioned our inter-American economic system after the war broke out in 1914. Inter-American shipping communications were either abandoned or were seriously crippled; the legitimate export trade of many republics—even that to their American neighbors—upon which in great part their national economy depended, was disrupted or destroyed with resultant misery and distress to their respective peoples. It appears to my Government that the opportunity is now afforded for us severally to assure ourselves and each other that this will not occur again.

So far as my own Government is concerned I am authorized to state that so long as the present situation continues, the regular transportation facilities of the shipping lines between the United States and its American neighbors now in operation will not only not be curtailed but will be strengthened and increased whenever such increase may be found to be desirable and feasible.

Financial assistance and cooperation may be developed to tide over short emergency periods and to develop in individual countries new fields of production to replace those temporarily depressed.

I am authorized to state that the United States Government wishes to cooperate with all other American republics in such efforts of each to develop the resources of its country along sound economic and noncompetitive lines. When desired it will assist in making credit available to them through the services and facilities of its privately owned banking system as well as its Government-owned agencies when the latter have funds available for such purposes.

In financing current matters, it is expected that only short-term credits will be requested, but in the purchase of rail and mill equipment, heavy goods, et cetera, longer term credits appropriate to the circumstances will be required. Also, it is of course recognized that war conditions may shift certain international trade markets, and this will need to be taken into account.

My Government likewise recognizes that excessive or unwarranted fluctuations in inter-American exchanges brought about by conditions resulting from the war situation would seriously prejudice beneficial trade between the American republics. It is my hope that our deliberations may result in agreement. To the extent that we sustain bases of commercial policy that are universal in character and leave trade open to all countries on substantially the same terms, and to the extent that our commerce is not dictated by special agreements of an exclusive character, to that extent can we insure that our political independence cannot be subjugated to alien political systems operating through commercial channels.

There is also incumbent upon us the task of keeping vigorous our belief that work and production should be primarily for peaceful welfare. If by our joint effort and strength we keep this continent free from the threat of aggression, we will greatly lessen the need of subordinating our individual productive energies by making preparatory arrangements which may assist in safeguarding against this danger.

These, as I understand them, are the specific and practical measures which we are called upon to consider. They are all of them problems of vital importance to the American republics—problems of the highest and most legitimate self-interest; but we all of us recognize I am sure that however much we may desire to insulate ourselves from the effects of this present conflict, such insulation can be only relative. It cannot in any event do more than mitigate insofar as we are able the disasters which will affect all peoples, belligerent or neutral, as a result of this world calamity.

Beyond these immediate problems produced by the war crisis there are problems which are deeper and more fundamental. We have prospered by regarding our commerce and production as designed to serve, through the exercise of individual initiative, the ends of public welfare and not the ends of political strategy. We shall be faced by the fact that various powerful countries in other parts of the world have now completely converted their own system of trade and production to another basis—making it an instrument of political or ideological ambition. By common determination and cooperation we can do much to avoid having our own purposes dominated by those of others or subordinated to military demands. But, since in these days it is essential to be strong (for we have seen all too often the fate of the weak), we can make every effort to see that our program of defense is of a character that reaffirms our faith in the powers of individual initiative and of free men. We can draw our strength from our liberties and from the contribution of men and women become strong and disciplined under conditions of freedom.

I believe that the time has come when the 21 American republics must state, and state clearly and in no uncertain terms, to all of the belligerents, both as a right of self-protection and as a right inherent in their position as peaceful and independent powers, constituting an entire continent remote from the causes of the hostilities which have broken out, that they cannot agree that their security, their nationals, or their legitimate commercial rights and interests should be jeopardized by belligerent activities in close proximity to the shores of the New World. This assertion of principle, I believe, must be regarded as constituting a declaration of the inalienable right of the American republics to protect themselves, so far as conditions in this modern world make it possible, from the dangers and the repercussions of a war which has broken out thousands of miles from their shores and in which they are not involved.

But in the larger sense, every one of our nations, every one of our fellow citizens, is affected or will be affected by the growing tragedy of this new war.

War spells ruin, waste, torture, and death—not perhaps to the leaders who have wrought it, but to the countless numbers of humble men and women throughout the world who would have none of it. For there is nothing surer in the world today than that the vast mass of the common people everywhere have wanted above all else to prevent the war which has now broken out.

Far removed from the initial scene of hostilities as the peoples of the Americas are, their interests have been jeopardized by the commencement of war. In modern civilization, every country has a natural right that war shall not be loosed upon humanity. This right was subscribed to by every nation of the civilized world in the so-called Pact of Paris, and it is this right, so solemnly subscribed to, that is today being flagrantly violated.

There is no moral justification for any nation to loose war upon humanity when the resort to peaceful procedure for the solution of controversies or of inequities is available.

The only possible road for achieving peace is through cooperation; this implies the juridic equality of every nation and the acceptance of a moral order and of effective international law. It assumes that controversies will be settled by peaceful processes and that all peoples will under these pacific processes cooperate on equal terms with generosity and with justice. It assumes that economic arrangements can be made which are entirely susceptible of satisfying the reasonable needs of any nation for beneficial trade, which will provide access on equal terms to world markets, access on equal terms to raw materials, and which will satisfy the legitimate demand of all nations for those component factors which make for a peaceful life.

There is existing now and at this moment an overwhelming will on the part of the peoples everywhere for peace based on renunciation of force, on justice, and on equality, could it find expression.

It may well be that the facilitation of that means of expression will be determined by the part we play in this Western Hemisphere. We, the American republics, share in common a great heritage—the principles of democratic constitutional government, devotion to justice, respect for the pledged word, love of peace. We have created an American system, an American way of life, which is our chief contribution to world civilization. This way of life we must make every effort to protect, to safeguard, to pass on intact to future generations of our own peoples, and to maintain as an unflinching standard in a world in which each day that passes sees more standards, once believed inviolate, shattered and destroyed.

As the shadows created by the outbreak of this monstrous war darken and spread rapidly across the length and breadth of the world in which we live, the 21 free nations of the New World can still preserve for posterity those ideals and those beliefs which may well constitute the last great hope of the civilization which we have inherited.

Our influence for peace and for the reestablishment of a world order based on morality and on law must be unshaken and secure. To accomplish this we must, and we can, resolutely defend our continent from all menace of aggression, direct or indirect. To do so, we must make every effort to keep alive our liberal commercial policy in our relations with those other nations of the world who are willing to join with us. To do so, we must strengthen and fortify the solidarity of understanding and the identity of individual purpose which bind us closely together. To do so we must rely ever more resolutely upon the principles of freedom and of democracy and upon the ideals of our Christian faith, through which our nations have had their being and only through which can their future rest secure.

145

54 Stat. 4; 22 U.S.C. 441–457, Supp. II, 442–452

Neutrality Act of November 4, 1939

JOINT RESOLUTION

To preserve the neutrality and the peace of the United States and to secure the safety of its citizens and their interests.

Whereas the United States, desiring to preserve its neutrality in wars between foreign states and desiring also to avoid involvement therein, voluntarily imposes upon its nationals by domestic legislation the restrictions set out in this joint resolution; and

Whereas by so doing the United States waives none of its own rights or privileges, or those of any of its nationals, under international law, and expressly reserves all the rights and privileges to which it and its nationals are entitled under the law of nations; and

Whereas the United States hereby expressly reserves the right to repeal, change or modify this joint resolution or any other domestic legislation in the interests of the peace, security or welfare of the United States and its people: Therefore be it

Resolved by the Senate and House of Representatives of the United States of America in Congress assembled,

PROCLAMATION OF A STATE OF WAR BETWEEN FOREIGN STATES

SECTION 1. (a) That whenever the President, or the Congress by concurrent resolution, shall find that there exists a state of war between foreign states, and that it is necessary to promote the security or preserve the peace of the United States or to protect the lives of citizens of the United States, the President shall issue a proclamation naming the states involved; and he shall, from time to time, by proclamation, name other states as and when they may become involved in the war.

(b) Whenever the state of war which shall have caused the President to issue any proclamation under the authority of this section shall have ceased to exist with respect to any state named in such proclamation, he shall revoke such proclamation with respect to such state.

COMMERCE WITH STATES ENGAGED IN ARMED CONFLICT

SEC. 2. (a) Whenever the President shall have issued a proclamation under the authority of section 1 (a) it shall thereafter be unlawful for any American vessel to carry any passengers or any articles or materials to any state named in such proclamation.

(b) Whoever shall violate any of the provisions of subsection (a) of this section or of any regulations issued thereunder shall, upon conviction thereof, be fined not more than $50,000 or imprisoned for not more than five years, or both. Should the violation be by a corporation, organization, or association, each officer or director thereof participating in the violation shall be liable to the penalty herein prescribed.

(c) Whenever the President shall have issued a proclamation under the authority of section 1 (a) it shall thereafter be unlawful to export or transport, or attempt to export or transport, or cause to be exported or transported, from the United States to any state named in such proclamation, any articles or materials (except copyrighted articles or materials) until all right, title, and interest therein shall have been transferred to some foreign government, agency, institution, association, partnership, corporation, or national. Issuance of a bill of lading under which title to the articles or materials to be exported or transported passes to a foreign purchaser unconditionally upon the delivery of such articles or materials to a carrier, shall constitute a transfer of all right, title, and interest therein within the meaning of this subsection. The shipper of such articles or materials shall be required to file with the collector of the port from or through which they are to be exported a declaration under oath that he has complied with the requirements of this subsection with respect to transfer of right, title, and interest in such articles or materials, and that he will comply with such rules and regulations as shall be promulgated from time to time. Any such declaration so filed shall be a conclusive estoppel against any claim of any citizen of the United States of right, title, or interest in such articles or materials, if such citizen had knowledge of the filing of such declaration; and the exportation or transportation of any articles or materials without filing the declaration required by this subsection shall be a conclusive estoppel against any claim of any citizen of the United States of right, title, or interest in such articles or materials, if such citizen had knowledge of such violation. No loss incurred by any such citizen (1) in connection with the sale or transfer of right, title, and interest in any such articles or materials or (2) in connection with the exportation or transportation of any such copyrighted articles or materials, shall be made the basis of any claim put forward by the Government of the United States.

(d) Insurance written by underwriters on articles or materials included in shipments which are subject to restrictions under the provisions of this joint resolution, and on vessels carrying such shipments shall not be deemed an American interest therein, and no insurance policy issued on such articles or materials, or vessels, and no loss incurred thereunder or by the owners of such vessels, shall be made the basis of any claim put forward by the Government of the United States.

(e) Whenever any proclamation issued under the authority of section 1 (a) shall have been revoked with respect to any state the provisions of this section shall thereupon cease to apply with respect to such state, except as to offenses committed prior to such revocation.

(f) The provisions of subsection (a) of this section shall not apply to transportation by American vessels on or over lakes, rivers, and inland waters bordering on the United States, or to transportation by aircraft on or over lands bordering on the United States; and the provisions of subsection (c) of this section shall not apply (1) to such transportation of any articles or materials other than articles listed in a proclamation referred to in or issued under the authority of section 12 (i), or (2) to any other transportation on or over lands bordering on the United States of any articles or materials other than articles listed in a proclamation referred to in or issued under the authority of section 12 (i); and the provisions of subsections (a) and (c) of this section shall not apply to the transportation referred to in this subsection and subsections (g) and (h) of any articles or materials listed in a proclamation referred to in or issued under the authority of section 12 (i) if the articles or materials so listed are to be used exclusively by American vessels, aircraft, or other vehicles in connection with their operation and maintenance.

(g) The provisions of subsections (a) and (c) of this section shall not apply to transportation by American vessels (other than aircraft) of mail, passengers, or any articles or materials (except articles or materials listed in a proclamation referred to in or issued under the authority of section 12 (i)) (1) to any port in the Western Hemisphere south of thirty-five degrees north latitude, (2) to any port in the Western Hemisphere north of thirty-five degrees north latitude and west of sixty-six degrees west longitude, (3) to any port on the Pacific or Indian Oceans, including the China Sea, the Tasman Sea, the Bay of Bengal, and the Arabian Sea, and any other dependent waters of either of such oceans, seas, or bays, or (4) to any port on the Atlantic Ocean or its dependent waters south of thirty degrees north latitude. The exceptions contained in this subsection shall not apply to any such port which is included within a combat area as defined in section 3 which applies to such vessels.

(h) The provisions of subsections (a) and (c) of this section shall not apply to transportation by aircraft of mail, passengers, or any articles or materials (except articles or materials listed in a proclamation referred to in or issued under the authority of section 12 (i)) (1) to any port in the Western Hemisphere, or (2) to any port on the Pacific or Indian Oceans, including the China Sea, the Tasman Sea, the Bay of Bengal, and the Arabian Sea, and any other dependent waters of either of such oceans, seas, or bays. The exceptions contained in this subsection shall not apply to any such port which is included within a combat area as defined in section 3 which applies to such aircraft.

(i) Every American vessel to which the provisions of subsections

(g) and (h) apply, and every neutral vessel to which the provisions of subsection (l) apply, shall, before departing from a port or from the jurisdiction of the United States, file with the collector of customs of the port of departure, or if there is no such collector at such port then with the nearest collector of customs, a sworn statement (1) containing a complete list of all the articles and materials carried as cargo by such vessel, and the names and addresses of the consignees of all such articles and materials, and (2) stating the ports at which such articles and materials are to be unloaded and the ports of call of such vessel. All transportation referred to in subsections (f), (g), (h), and (l) of this section shall be subject to such restrictions, rules, and regulations as the President shall prescribe; but no loss incurred in connection with any transportation excepted under the provisions of subsections (g), (h), and (l) of this section shall be made the basis of any claim put forward by the Government of the United States.

(j) Whenever all proclamations issued under the authority of section 1 (a) shall have been revoked, the provisions of subsections (f), (g), (h), (i), and (l) of this section shall expire.

(k) The provisions of this section shall not apply to the current voyage of any American vessel which has cleared for a foreign port and has departed from a port or from the jurisdiction of the United States in advance of (1) the date of enactment of this joint resolution, or (2) any proclamation issued after such date under the authority of section 1 (a) of this joint resolution; but any such vessel shall proceed at its own risk after either of such dates, and no loss incurred in connection with any such vessel or its cargo after either of such dates shall be made the basis of any claim put forward by the Government of the United States.

(l) The provisions of subsection (c) of this section shall not apply to the transportation by a neutral vessel to any port referred to in subsection (g) of this section of any articles or materials (except articles or materials listed in a proclamation referred to in or issued under the authority of section 12 (i)) so long as such port is not included within a combat area as defined in section 3 which applies to American vessels.

COMBAT AREAS

Sec. 3. (a) Whenever the President shall have issued a proclamation under the authority of section 1 (a), and he shall thereafter find that the protection of citizens of the United States so requires, he shall, by proclamation, define combat areas, and thereafter it shall be unlawful, except under such rules and regulations as may be prescribed, for any citizen of the United States or any American vessel to proceed into or through any such combat area. The combat areas so defined may be made to apply to surface vessels or aircraft, or both.

(b) In case of the violation of any of the provisions of this section by any American vessel, or any owner or officer thereof, such vessel, owner, or officer shall be fined not more than $50,000 or imprisoned for not more than five years, or both. Should the owner of such vessel be a corporation, organization, or association, each officer or director participating in the violation shall be liable to the penalty hereinabove prescribed. In case of the violation of this section by any citizen traveling as a passenger, such passenger may be fined not more than $10,000 or imprisoned for not more than two years, or both.

(c) The President may from time to time modify or extend any proclamation issued under the authority of this section, and when the conditions which shall have caused him to issue any such proclamation shall have ceased to exist he shall revoke such proclamation and the provisions of this section shall thereupon cease to apply, except as to offenses committed prior to such revocation.

AMERICAN RED CROSS

SEC. 4. The provisions of section 2 (a) shall not prohibit the transportation by vessels under charter or other direction and control of the American Red Cross, proceeding under safe conduct granted by states named in any proclamation issued under the authority of section 1 (a), of officers and American Red Cross personnel, medical personnel, and medical supplies, food, and clothing, for the relief of human suffering.

TRAVEL ON VESSELS OF BELLIGERENT STATES

SEC. 5. (a) Whenever the President shall have issued a proclamation under the authority of section 1 (a) it shall thereafter be unlawful for any citizen of the United States to travel on any vessel of any state named in such proclamation, except in accordance with such rules and regulations as may be prescribed.

(b) Whenever any proclamation issued under the authority of section 1 (a) shall have been revoked with respect to any state the provisions of this section shall thereupon cease to apply with respect to such state, except as to offenses committed prior to such revocation.

ARMING OF AMERICAN MERCHANT VESSELS PROHIBITED

Sec. 6. Whenever the President shall have issued a proclamation under the authority of section 1 (a), it shall thereafter be unlawful, until such proclamation is revoked, for any American vessel, engaged in commerce with any foreign state to be armed, except with small arms and ammunition therefor, which the President may deem necessary and shall publicly designate for the preservation of discipline aboard any such vessel.

FINANCIAL TRANSACTIONS

Sec. 7. (a) Whenever the President shall have issued a proclamation under the authority of section 1 (a), it shall thereafter be unlawful for any person within the United States to purchase, sell, or exchange bonds, securities, or other obligations of the government of any state named in such proclamation, or of any political subdivision of any such state, or of any person acting for or on behalf of the government of any such state, or political subdivision thereof, issued after the date of such proclamation, or to make any loan or extend any credit (other than necessary credits accruing in connection with the transmission of telegraph, cable, wireless and telephone services) to any such government, political subdivision, or person. The provisions of this subsection shall also apply to the sale by any person within the United States to any person in a state named in any such proclamation of any articles or materials listed in a proclamation referred to in or issued under the authority of section 12 (i).

(b) The provisions of this section shall not apply to a renewal or adjustment of such indebtedness as may exist on the date of such proclamation.

(c) Whoever shall knowingly violate any of the provisions of this section or of any regulations issued thereunder shall, upon conviction thereof, be fined not more than $50,000 or imprisoned for not more than five years, or both. Should the violation be by a corporation, organization, or association, each officer or director thereof participating in the violation shall be liable to the penalty herein prescribed.

(d) Whenever any proclamation issued under the authority of section 1 (a) shall have been revoked with respect to any state the provisions of this section shall thereupon cease to apply with respect to such state, except as to offenses committed prior to such revocation.

SOLICITATION AND COLLECTION OF FUNDS AND CONTRIBUTIONS

Sec. 8. (a) Whenever the President shall have issued a proclamation under the authority of section 1 (a), it shall thereafter be unlawful for any person within the United States to solicit or receive any contribution for or on behalf of the government of any state named in such proclamation or for or on behalf of any agent or instrumentality of any such state.

(b) Nothing in this section shall be construed to prohibit the solicitation or collection of funds and contributions to be used for medical aid and assistance, or for food and clothing to relieve human suffering, when such solicitation or collection of funds and contributions is made on behalf of and for use by any person or organization which is not acting for or on behalf of any such government, but all such solicitations and collections of funds and contributions shall be in accordance with and subject to such rules and regulations as may be prescribed.

(c) Whenever any proclamation issued under the authority of section 1 (a) shall have been revoked with respect to any state the provisions of this section shall thereupon cease to apply with respect to such state, except as to offenses committed prior to such revocation.

AMERICAN REPUBLICS

Sec. 9. This joint resolution (except section 12) shall not apply to any American republic engaged in war against a non-American state or states, provided the American republic is not cooperating with a non-American state or states in such war.

RESTRICTIONS ON USE OF AMERICAN PORTS

Sec. 10. (a) Whenever, during any war in which the United States is neutral, the President, or any person thereunto authorized by him, shall have cause to believe that any vessel, domestic or foreign, whether requiring clearance or not, is about to carry out of a port or from the jurisdiction of the United States, fuel, men, arms, ammunition, implements of war, supplies, dispatches, or information to any warship, tender, or supply ship of a state named in a proclamation issued under the authority of section 1 (a), but the evidence is not deemed sufficient to justify forbidding the departure of the vessel as provided for by section 1, title V, chapter 30, of the Act approved June 15, 1917 (40 Stat. 217, 221; U. S. C., 1934 edition, title 18, sec. 31), and if, in the President's judgment, such action will serve to maintain peace between the United States and foreign states, or to protect the commercial interests of the United States and its citizens, or to promote the security or neutrality of the United States, he shall have the power, and it shall be his duty to require the owner, master, or person in command thereof, before departing from a port or from the jurisdiction of the United States, to give a bond to the United States, with sufficient sureties, in such amount as he shall deem proper, conditioned that the vessel will not deliver the men, or any fuel, supplies, dispatches, information, or any part of the cargo, to any warship, tender, or supply ship of a state named in a proclamation issued under the authority of section 1 (a).

(b) If the President, or any person thereunto authorized by him, shall find that a vessel, domestic or foreign, in a port of the United States, has previously departed from a port or from the jurisdiction of the United States during such war and delivered men, fuel, supplies, dispatches, information, or any part of its cargo to a warship, tender, or supply ship of a state named in a proclamation issued under the authority of section 1 (a), he may prohibit the departure of such vessel during the duration of the war.

(c) Whenever the President shall have issued a proclamation under section 1 (a) he may, while such proclamation is in effect, require the owner, master, or person in command of any vessel, foreign or domestic, before departing from the United States, to give a bond to the United States, with sufficient sureties, in such amount as he shall deem proper, conditioned that no alien seaman who arrived on such vessel shall remain in the United States for a longer period than that permitted under the regulations, as amended from time to time, issued pursuant to section 33 of the Immigration Act of February 5, 1917 (U. S. C., title 8, sec. 168). Notwithstanding the provisions of said section 33, the President may issue such regulations with respect to the landing of such seamen as he deems necessary to insure their departure either on such vessel or another vessel at the expense of such owner, master, or person in command.

SUBMARINES AND ARMED MERCHANT VESSELS

SEC. 11. Whenever, during any war in which the United States is neutral, the President shall find that special restrictions placed on the use of the ports and territorial waters of the United States by the submarines or armed merchant vessels of a foreign state will serve to maintain peace between the United States and foreign states, or to protect the commercial interests of the United States and its citizens, or to promote the security of the United States, and shall make proclamation thereof, it shall thereafter be unlawful for any such submarine or armed merchant vessel to enter a port or the territorial waters of the United States or to depart therefrom, except under such conditions and subject to such limitations as the President may prescribe. Whenever, in his judgment, the conditions which have caused him to issue his proclamation have ceased to exist, he shall revoke his proclamation and the provisions of this section shall thereupon cease to apply, except as to offenses committed prior to such revocation.

NATIONAL MUNITIONS CONTROL BOARD

SEC. 12. (a) There is hereby established a National Munitions Control Board (hereinafter referred to as the "Board"). The Board shall consist of the Secretary of State, who shall be chairman and executive officer of the Board, the Secretary of the Treasury, the Secretary of War, the Secretary of the Navy, and the Secretary of Commerce. Except as otherwise provided in this section, or by other law, the administration of this section is vested in the Secretary of State. The Secretary of State shall promulgate such rules and regulations with regard to the enforcement of this section as he may deem necessary to carry out its provisions. The Board shall be convened by the chairman and shall hold at least one meeting a year.

(b) Every person who engages in the business of manufacturing, exporting, or importing any arms, ammunition, or implements of war listed in a proclamation referred to in or issued under the authority of subsection (i) of this section, whether as an exporter, importer, manufacturer, or dealer, shall register with the Secretary of State his name, or business name, principal place of business, and places of business in the United States, and a list of the arms, ammunition, and implements of war which he manufactures, imports, or exports.

(c) Every person required to register under this section shall notify the Secretary of State of any change in the arms, ammunition, or implements of war which he exports, imports, or manufactures; and upon such notification the Secretary of State shall issue to such person an amended certificate of registration, free of charge, which shall remain valid until the date of expiration of the original certificate. Every person required to register under the provisions of this section shall pay a registration fee of $100. Upon receipt of the required registration fee, the Secretary of State shall issue a registration certificate valid for five years, which shall be renewable for further periods of five years upon the payment for each renewal of a fee of $100; but valid certificates of registration (including amended certificates) issued under the authority of section 2 of the joint resolution of August 31, 1935, or section 5 of the joint resolution of August 31, 1935, as amended, shall, without payment of any additional registration fee, be considered to be valid certificates of registration issued under this subsection, and shall remain valid for the same period as if this joint resolution had not been enacted.

(d) It shall be unlawful for any person to export, or attempt to export, from the United States to any other state, any arms, ammunition, or implements of war listed in a proclamation referred to in or issued under the authority of subsection (i) of this section, or to import, or attempt to import, to the United States from any other state, any of the arms, ammunition, or implements of war listed in any such proclamation, without first having submitted to the Secretary of State the name of the purchaser and the terms of sale and having obtained a license therefor.

(e) All persons required to register under this section shall maintain, subject to the inspection of the Secretary of State, or any person or persons designated by him, such permanent records of manufacture for export, importation, and exportation of arms, ammunition, and implements of war as the Secretary of State shall prescribe.

(f) Licenses shall be issued by the Secretary of State to persons who have registered as herein provided for, except in cases of export or import licenses where the export of arms, ammunition, or implements of war would be in violation of this joint resolution or any other law of the United States, or of a treaty to which the United States is a party, in which cases such licenses shall not be issued; but a valid license issued under the authority of section 2 of the joint resolution of August 31, 1935, or section 5 of the joint resolution of August 31, 1935, as amended, shall be considered to be a valid license issued under this subsection, and shall remain valid for the same period as if this joint resolution had not been enacted.

(g) No purchase of arms, ammunition, or implements of war shall be made on behalf of the United States by any officer, executive department, or independent establishment of the Government from any person who shall have failed to register under the provisions of this joint resolution.

(h) The Board shall make a report to Congress on January 3 and July 3 of each year, copies of which shall be distributed as are other reports transmitted to Congress. Such reports shall contain such information and data collected by the Board as may be considered of value in the determination of questions connected with the control of trade in arms, ammunition, and implements of war, including the name of the purchaser and the terms of sale made under any such license. The Board shall include in such reports a list of all persons required to register under the provisions of this joint resolution, and full information concerning the licenses issued hereunder, including the name of the purchaser and the terms of sale made under any such license.

(i) The President is hereby authorized to proclaim upon recommendation of the Board from time to time a list of articles which shall be considered arms, ammunition, and implements of war for the purposes of this section; but the proclamation Numbered 2237, of May 1, 1937 (50 Stat. 1834), defining the term "arms, ammunition, and implements of war" shall, until it is revoked, have full force and effect as if issued under the authority of this subsection.

REGULATIONS

SEC. 13. The President may, from time to time, promulgate such rules and regulations, not inconsistent with law, as may be necessary and proper to carry out any of the provisions of this joint resolution; and he may exercise any power or authority conferred on him by this joint resolution through such officer or officers, or agency or agencies, as he shall direct.

UNLAWFUL USE OF THE AMERICAN FLAG

SEC. 14. (a) It shall be unlawful for any vessel belonging to or operating under the jurisdiction of any foreign state to use the flag of the United States thereon, or to make use of any distinctive signs or markings, indicating that the same is an American vessel.

(b) Any vessel violating the provisions of subsection (a) of this section shall be denied for a period of three months the right to enter the ports or territorial waters of the United States except in cases of force majeure.

GENERAL PENALTY PROVISION

SEC. 15. In every case of the violation of any of the provisions of this joint resolution or of any rule or regulation issued pursuant thereto where a specific penalty is not herein provided, such violator or violators, upon conviction, shall be fined not more than $10,000, or imprisoned not more than two years, or both.

DEFINITIONS

SEC. 16. For the purposes of this joint resolution—

(a) The term "United States", when used in a geographical sense, includes the several States and Territories, the insular possessions of the United States (including the Philippine Islands), the Canal Zone, and the District of Columbia.

(b) The term "person" includes a partnership, company, association, or corporation, as well as a natural person.

(c) The term "vessel" means every description of watercraft and aircraft capable of being used as a means of transportation on, under, or over water.

(d) The term "American vessel" means any vessel documented, and any aircraft registered or licensed, under the laws of the United States.

(e) The term "state" shall include nation, government, and country.

(f) The term "citizen" shall include any individual owing allegiance to the United States, a partnership, company, or association composed in whole or in part of citizens of the United States, and any corporation organized and existing under the laws of the United States as defined in subsection (a) of this section.

SEPARABILITY OF PROVISIONS

SEC. 17. If any of the provisions of this joint resolution, or the application thereof to any person or circumstance, is held invalid, the remainder of the joint resolution, and the application of such provision to other persons or circumstances, shall not be affected thereby.

APPROPRIATIONS

SEC. 18. There is hereby authorized to be appropriated from time to time, out of any money in the Treasury not otherwise appropriated, such amounts as may be necessary to carry out the provisions and accomplish the purposes of this joint resolution.

REPEALS

SEC. 19. The joint resolution of August 31, 1935, as amended, and the joint resolution of January 8, 1937, are hereby repealed; but offenses committed and penalties, forfeitures, or liabilities incurred under either of such joint resolutions prior to the date of enactment of this joint resolution may be prosecuted and punished, and suits and proceedings for violations of either of such joint resolutions or of any rule or regulation issued pursuant thereto may be commenced and prosecuted, in the same manner and with the same effect as if such joint resolutions had not been repealed.

SHORT TITLE

SEC. 20. This joint resolution may be cited as the "Neutrality Act of 1939".

Approved, November 4, 1939, 12: 04 p. m.

146

H. Doc. 258, 76th Cong., 3d sess.

Address Delivered by President Roosevelt to the Congress, January 3, 1940

As the Congress reassembles, the impact of wars abroad makes it natural to approach "the state of the Union" through a discussion of foreign affairs.

But it is important that those who hear and read this message should in no way confuse that approach with any thought that our Government is abandoning, or even overlooking, the great significance of its domestic policies.

The social and economic forces which have been mismanaged abroad until they have resulted in revolution, dictatorship, and war are the same as those which we here are struggling to adjust peacefully at home.

You are well aware that dictatorships—and the philosophy of force which justifies and accompanies dictatorships—have originated in almost every case in the necessity for drastic action to improve internal conditions where democratic action for one reason or another has failed to respond to modern needs and modern demands.

It was with farsighted wisdom that the framers of the Constitution brought together in one magnificent phrase three great concepts— "common defense," "general welfare," and "domestic tranquillity."

More than a century and a half later we still believe with them that our best defense is the promotion of our general welfare and domestic tranquillity.

In previous messages to the Congress I have repeatedly warned that, whether we like it or not, the daily lives of American citizens will, of necessity, feel the shock of events on other continents. This is no longer mere theory for it has been definitely proved by the facts of yesterday and today.

To say that the domestic well-being of 130,000,000 Americans is deeply affected by the well-being or the ill-being of the populations of other nations is only to recognize in world affairs the truth we all accept in home affairs.

If in any local unit—a city, county, State, or region—low standards of living are permitted to continue, the level of the civilization of the entire Nation will be pulled downward.

The identical principle extends to the rest of a civilized world. But there are those who wishfully insist, in innocence or ignorance, or both, that the United States of America as a self-contained unit can live happily and prosperously, its future secure, inside a high wall of isolation while, outside, the rest of civilization and the commerce and culture of mankind are shattered.

I can understand the feelings of those who warn the Nation that they will never again consent to the sending of American youth to fight on the soil of Europe. But, as I remember, nobody has asked them to consent—for nobody expects such an undertaking.

The overwhelming majority of our fellow citizens do not abandon in the slightest their hope and expectation that the United States will not become involved in military participation in the war.

I can also understand the wishfulness of those who oversimplify the whole situation by repeating that all we have to do is to mind our own business and keep the Nation out of war. But there is a vast difference between keeping out of war and pretending that this war is none of our business.

We do not have to go to war with other nations, but at least we can strive with other nations to encourage the kind of peace that will lighten the troubles of the world, and by so doing help our own Nation as well.

I ask that all of us everywhere think things through with the single aim of how best to serve the future of our own Nation. I do not mean merely its future relationship with the outside world. I mean its domestic future as well—the work, the security, the prosperity, the happiness, the life of all the boys and girls of the United States, as they are inevitably affected by such world relationships. For it becomes clearer and clearer that the future world will be a shabby and dangerous place to live in—even for Americans to live in—if it is ruled by force in the hands of a few.

Already the crash of swiftly moving events over the earth has made us all think with a longer view. Fortunately, that thinking cannot be controlled by partisanship. The time is long past when any political party or any particular group can curry and capture public favor by labeling itself the "peace party" or the "peace bloc." That label belongs to the whole United States and to every right thinking man, woman, and child within it.

For out of all the military and diplomatic turmoil, out of all the propaganda and counterpropaganda of the present conflicts, there are two facts which stand out and which the whole world acknowledges.

The first is that never before has the Government of the United States done so much as in our recent past to establish and maintain the policy of the good neighbor with its sister nations.

The second is that in almost every nation in the world today there is a true public belief that the United States has been, and will continue to be, a potent and active factor in seeking the reestablishment of peace.

In these recent years we have had a clean record of peace and good will. It is an open book that cannot be twisted or defamed. It is a record that must be continued and enlarged.

So I hope that Americans everywhere will work out for themselves the several alternatives which lie before world civilization, which necessarily includes our own.

We must look ahead and see the possibilities for our children if the rest of the world comes to be dominated by concentrated force alone—even though today we are a very great and a very powerful nation.

We must look ahead and see the effect on our own future if all the small nations throughout the world have their independence snatched from them or become mere appendages to relatively vast and powerful military systems.

We must look ahead and see the kind of lives our children would have to lead if a large part of the rest of the world were compelled to worship the god imposed by a military ruler, or were forbidden to worship God at all; if the rest of the world were forbidden to read and hear the facts—the daily news of their own and other nations—if they were deprived of the truth which makes men free.

We must look ahead and see the effect on our future generations if world trade is controlled by any nation or group of nations which sets up that control through military force.

It is, of course, true that the record of past centuries includes destruction of small nations, enslavement of peoples, and building of empires on the foundation of force. But wholly apart from the greater international morality which we seek today, we recognize the practical fact that with modern weapons and modern conditions, modern man can no longer live a civilized life if we are to go back to the practice of wars and conquests of the seventeenth and eighteenth centuries.

Summing up this need of looking ahead, and in words of common sense and good American citizenship, I hope that we will have fewer American ostriches in our midst. It is not good for the ultimate health of ostriches to bury their heads in the sand.

Only an ostrich would look upon these wars through the eyes of cynicism or ridicule.

Of course, the peoples of other nations have the right to choose their own form of government. But we in this Nation still believe that such choice should be predicated on certain freedoms which we think are essential everywhere. We know that we ourselves will never be wholly safe at home unless other governments recognize such freedoms.

Twenty-one American republics, expressing the will of 250,000,000 people to preserve peace and freedom in this hemisphere are displaying a unanimity of ideals and practical relationships which gives hope that what is being done here can be done on other continents. We in all the Americas are coming to the realization that we can retain our respective nationalities without, at the same time, threatening the national existence of our neighbors.

Such truly friendly relationships, for example, permit us to follow our own domestic policies with reference to our agricultural products, while at the same time we have the privilege of trying to work out mutual assistance arrangements for a world distribution of world agricultural surpluses.

And we have been able to apply the same simple principle to many manufactured products—surpluses of which must be sold in the world export markets if we would continue a high level of production and employment.

For many years after the World War blind economic selfishness in most countries, including our own, resulted in a destructive mine field of trade restrictions which blocked the channels of commerce among nations. This policy was one of the contributing causes of existing wars. It dammed up vast unsalable surpluses, helping to bring about unemployment and suffering in the United States and everywhere else.

To point the way to break up the log jam, our Trade Agreements Act was passed—based upon a policy of equality of treatment among nations and of mutually profitable arrangements of trade.

It is not correct to infer that legislative powers have been transferred from the Congress to the executive branch of the Government. Everybody recognizes that general tariff legislation is a congressional function, but we know that, because of the stupendous task involved in the fashioning and passing of a general law, it is advisable to provide at times of emergency some flexibility to make the general law adjustable to quickly changing conditions.

We are in such a time today. Our present trade-agreement method provides a temporary flexibility and is, therefore, practical in the best sense. It should be kept alive to serve our trade interests—agricultural and industrial—in many valuable ways during the existing wars.

But what is more important, the Trade Agreements Act should be extended as an indispensable part of the foundation of any stable and durable peace.

The old conditions of world trade made for no enduring peace; and when the time comes, the United States must use its influence to open up the trade channels of the world in order that no nation need feel compelled in later days to seek by force of arms what it can well gain by peaceful conference. For this purpose we need the Trade Agreements Act even more than when it was passed.

I emphasize the leadership which this Nation can take when the time comes for a renewal of world peace. Such an influence will be greatly weakened if this Government becomes a dog in the manger of trade selfishness.

The first President of the United States warned us against entangling foreign alliances. The present President of the United States subscribes to and follows that precept.

But trade cooperation with the rest of the world does not violate that precept in any way.

Even as through these trade agreements we prepare to cooperate in a world that wants peace, we must likewise be prepared to take care of ourselves if the world cannot attain peace.

For several years past we have been compelled to strengthen our own national defense. That has created a very large portion of our Treasury deficits. This year, in the light of continuing world uncertainty, I am asking the Congress for Army and Navy increases which are based not on panic but on common sense. They are not as great as enthusiastic alarmists seek. They are not as small as unrealistic persons claiming superior private information would demand.

As will appear in the Annual Budget tomorrow, the only important increase in any part of the Budget is the estimate for national defense. Practically all other important items show a reduction. Therefore, in the hope that we can continue in these days of increasing economic prosperity to reduce the Federal deficit, I am asking the Congress to levy sufficient additional taxes to meet the emergency spending for national defense.

Behind the Army and Navy, of course, lies our ultimate line of defense—"the general welfare" of our people. We cannot report, despite all the progress we have made in our domestic problems—despite the fact that production is back to 1929 levels—that all our problems are solved. The fact of unemployment of millions of men and women remains a symptom of a number of difficulties in our economic system not yet adjusted.

While the number of the unemployed has decreased, while their immediate needs for food and clothing—as far as the Federal Government is concerned—have been largely met, while their morale has been kept alive by giving them useful public work, we have not yet found a way to employ the surplus of our labor which the efficiency of our industrial processes has created.

We refuse the European solution of using the unemployed to build up excessive armaments which eventually result in dictatorships. We encourage an American way—through an increase of national income which is the only way we can be sure will take up the slack. Much progress has been made; much remains to be done.

We recognize that we must find an answer in terms of work and opportunity.

The unemployment problem today has become very definitely a problem of youth as well as of age. As each year has gone by hundreds of thousands of boys and girls have come of working age. They now form an army of unused youth. They must be an especial concern of democratic government.

We must continue, above all things, to look for a solution of their special problem. For they, looking ahead to life, are entitled to action on our part and not merely to admonitions of optimism or lectures on economic laws.

Some in our midst have sought to instill a feeling of fear and defeatism in the minds of the American people about this problem.

To face the task of finding jobs faster than invention can take them away—is not defeatism. To warble easy platitudes that if we will only go back to ways that have failed, everything will be all right—is not courage.

We met a problem of real fear and real defeatism in 1933. We faced the facts—with action, not with words.

The American people will reject the doctrine of fear, confident that in the thirties we have been building soundly a new order of things different from the order of the twenties. In this dawn of the decade of the forties, with our program of social improvement started, we must continue to carry on the processes of recovery so as to preserve our gains and provide jobs at living wages.

There are, of course, many other items of great public interest which could be enumerated in this message—the continued conservation of our natural resources, the improvement of health and of education, the extension of social security to larger groups, the freeing of large areas from restricted transportation discriminations, the extension of the merit system and many others.

Our continued progress in the social and economic field is important not only for the significance of each part of it but for the total effect which our program of domestic betterment has upon that most valuable asset of a nation in dangerous times—its national unity.

The permanent security of America in the present crisis does not lie in armed force alone. What we face is a set of world-wide forces of disintegration—vicious, ruthless, destructive of all the moral, religious, and political standards which mankind, after centuries of struggle, has come to cherish most.

In these moral values, in these forces which have made our Nation great, we must actively and practically reassert our faith.

These words—"national unity"—must not be allowed to become merely a high-sounding phrase, a vague generality, a pious hope, to which everyone can give lip service. They must be made to have real meaning in terms of the daily thoughts and acts of every man, woman, and child in our land during the coming year and the years that lie ahead.

For national unity is, in a very real and deep sense, the fundamental safeguard of all democracy.

Doctrines which set group against group, faith against faith, race against race, class against class, fanning the fires of hatred in men too despondent, too desperate to think for themselves, were used as rabble-rousing slogans on which dictators could ride to power. And once in power they could saddle their tyrannies on whole nations, and on their weaker neighbors.

This is the danger to which we in America must begin to be more alert. For the apologists for foreign aggressors, and equally those selfish and partisan groups at home who wrap themselves in a false mantle of Americanism to promote their own economic, financial, or political advantage, are now trying European tricks upon us, seeking to muddy the stream of our national thinking, weakening us in the face of danger, by trying to set our own people to fighting among themselves. Such tactics are what have helped to plunge Europe into war. We must combat them, as we would the plague, if American integrity and security are to be preserved. We cannot afford to face the future as a disunited people.

We must as a united people keep ablaze on this continent the flames of human liberty, of reason, of democracy, and of fair play as living things to be preserved for the better world that is to come.

Overstatement, bitterness, vituperation, and the beating of drums, have contributed mightily to ill feeling and wars between nations. If these unnecessary and unpleasant actions are harmful in the international field, they are also hurtful in the domestic scene. Peace among ourselves would seem to have some of the advantage of peace between us and other nations. And in the long run history amply demonstrates that angry controversy surely wins less than calm discussion.

In the spirit, therefore, of a greater unselfishness, recognizing that the world—including the United States of America—passes through perilous times, I am very hopeful that the closing session of the Seventy-Sixth Congress will consider the needs of the Nation and of humanity with calmness, tolerance, and cooperative wisdom.

May the year 1940 be pointed to by our children as another period when democracy justified its existence as the best instrument of government yet devised by mankind.

147

Department of State Bulletin, vol. II, p. 335

Statement by President Roosevelt, March 29, 1940

Under Secretary of State Welles has concluded the mission upon which he was sent to Europe and has reported to me and to the Secretary of State.

As I said when the announcement of Mr. Welles' mission was made, Mr. Welles was sent to Europe in order to obtain information with regard to existing conditions. He was neither authorized to make, nor has he made, any commitments involving the Government of the United States, nor was he empowered to offer, and he has not offered, any proposals in the name of this Government. He has not received, nor has he brought back to me, any peace proposals from any source.

The information which he has received from the heads of the governments which he has visited will be of the greatest value to this Government in the general conduct of its foreign relations. As was announced at the time of his departure from the United States, the information communicated to him by the Italian, German, French, and British Governments will be regarded as entirely confidential by this Government. It relates to the views and policies of the European governments mentioned.

I am glad to say that Mr. Welles' mission has likewise resulted, through personal contacts and through the conversations which he held, in a clarification of the relations between the United States and the countries which he visited and will, I believe, assist in certain instances in the development of better understanding and more friendly relations.

Finally, even though there may be scant immediate prospect for the establishment of any just, stable, and lasting peace in Europe, the information made available to this Government as a result of Mr.

Welles' mission will undoubtedly be of the greatest value when the time comes for the establishment of such a peace.

To Mr. Welles go my thanks and full appreciation for carrying out this difficult mission with extraordinary tact and understanding and in accordance with the best American diplomatic traditions.

148

Department of State Bulletin, vol. II, p. 373

Statement by President Roosevelt, April 13, 1940

Force and military aggression are once more on the march against small nations, in this instance through the invasion of Denmark and Norway. These two nations have won and maintained during a period of many generations the respect and regard not only of the American people, but of all peoples, because of their observance of the highest standards of national and international conduct.

The Government of the United States has on the occasion of recent invasions strongly expressed its disapprobation of such unlawful exercise of force. It here reiterates, with undiminished emphasis, its point of view as expressed on those occasions. If civilization is to survive, the rights of the smaller nations to independence, to their territorial integrity, and to the unimpeded opportunity for self-government must be respected by their more powerful neighbors.

149

Department of State Bulletin, vol. II, p. 411

Statement by the Secretary of State, April 17, 1940

I have noted with interest the statement by the Japanese Minister for Foreign Affairs expressing concern on the part of the Japanese Government for the maintenance of the *status quo* of the Netherlands Indies.

Any change in the status of the Netherlands Indies would directly affect the interests of many countries.

The Netherlands Indies are very important in the international relationships of the whole Pacific Ocean. The islands themselves extend for a distance of approximately 3,200 miles east and west astride of the Equator, from the Indian Ocean on the west far into the Pacific Ocean on the east. They are also an important factor in the commerce of the whole world. They produce considerable portions of the world's supplies of important essential commodities such as rubber, tin, quinine, copra, et cetera. Many countries, including the United States, depend substantially upon them for some of these commodities.

Intervention in the domestic affairs of the Netherlands Indies or any alteration of their *status quo* by other than peaceful processes would be prejudicial to the cause of stability, peace, and security not only in the region of the Netherlands Indies but in the entire Pacific area.

This conclusion, based on a doctrine which has universal application and for which the United States unequivocally stands, is embodied in notes exchanged on November 30, 1908, between the United States and Japan in which each of the two Governments stated that its policy was directed to the maintenance of the existing *status quo* in the region of the Pacific Ocean. It is reaffirmed in the notes which the United States, the British Empire, France, and Japan—as parties to the treaty signed at Washington on December 13, 1921, relating to their insular possessions and their insular dominions in the region of the Pacific Ocean—sent to the Netherlands Government on February 4, 1922, in which each of those Governments declared that "it is firmly resolved to respect the rights of the Netherlands in relation to their insular possessions in the region of the Pacific Ocean."

All peaceful nations have during recent years been earnestly urging that policies of force be abandoned and that peace be maintained on the basis of fundamental principles, among which are respect by every nation for the rights of other nations and nonintervention in their domestic affairs, the according of equality of fair and just treatment, and the faithful observance of treaty pledges, with modification thereof, when needful, by orderly processes.

It is the constant hope of the Government of the United States—as it is no doubt that of all peacefully inclined governments—that the attitudes and policies of all governments will be based upon these principles and that these principles will be applied not only in every part of the Pacific area, but also in every part of the world.

150

756.94/65

*Memorandum by the Secretary of State Regarding a Conversation
With the Japanese Ambassador (Horinouchi)*

[WASHINGTON,] April 20, 1940.

The Japanese Ambassador called at his request. He said he came
to discuss the immigration situation as it exists today in the Philippine
legislature. He went over the general facts pertaining to the legislative and to the quota situations and then asked that I urge the Philippine Government to allow Japan, along with all other nations, 1,000
immigrants instead of 500, as contemplated by the amendment to the
bill on its second reading. I first made it clear to the Ambassador
that the Philippine Government has exclusive control over this question of immigration into the Philippine Islands; that this Government, therefore, does not undertake to dictate or otherwise bring
material pressure upon the Philippine officials. I then added that I
would be glad to go into the details of this matter further and somewhat sympathetically and see whether and what might remain to be
properly said by this Government, if anything. The Ambassador
remarked that this Government had more or less jurisdiction over this
matter, according to Dr. Sayre.[44] I corrected this wrong impression
and also brought to his attention that the bill in its entirety would
make possible the admission of about 1,000 Japanese instead of 500
only. I said to him that if anything remained for us to say we would
try to get it off today.

The Ambassador then turned about a time or two in his chair and
said that in regard to the recent statements of Foreign Minister Arita
and of myself in regard to the *status quo* of the Netherlands East
Indies, he thought that our press misinterpreted Minister Arita and
assumed a more or less critical tone. I interrupted him to say that our
press could well have taken the lead given by the Japanese press on the
day of and the day after the statement of Minister Arita, which seemed
to imply the assumption of leadership and special influence in that area
of the world without limitation as to functions and purposes. I said
that it may be possible that the Japanese press misinterpreted Minister
Arita. The Ambassador then said that Minister Arita and I agree
about not disturbing the *status quo* of the Dutch East Indies. I replied in the affirmative and said that the difference between us was

[44] Francis B. Sayre, at that time United States High Commissioner to the
Philippines.

that I placed the matter on a far broader ground than one primarily affecting the interests of Japan in the economic Dutch East Indies situation, and that I need not elaborate upon this except to refer to my statement for full understanding of the position this Government took. In that connection I proceeded to say to the Ambassador that I wished I could get over to him and his Government the fact that there is no more resemblance between our Monroe Doctrine, as we interpret and apply it uniformly since 1823, and the so-called Monroe Doctrine of Japan than there is between black and white. I said our Monroe Doctrine only contemplates steps for our physical safety while the Monroe Doctrine, as practiced by Japan, is seemingly applicable to all other purposes and all objectives, including economic, social, political, et cetera; that thus far the question of a Monroe Doctrine for physical protection has not been needed or invoked by Japan. The Ambassador sought to minimize my description of the Japanese application of their so-called Monroe Doctrine when I reminded him of its application in Manchuria and then, to our great surprise, in China and then implied that it applies economically to the Dutch East Indies.

I said to the Ambassador that his country can trade on absolutely equal terms with mine and with all other nations in every port of every nation in this hemisphere, with a slight modification temporarily in the Cuban trade situation, which grows out of special conditions between the two countries. I again reminded him of my frequent plea to his Government since 1933 to the effect that there should be normal peaceful and other worthwhile relations between important countries in the western world and Japan and China and other countries in the eastern portion. I need not elaborate on the things I have said on this point during past years except to emphasize the great mutual commercial advantages and other extremely valuable advantages in many ways that would follow such a policy of peaceful relationship and mutually cooperative effort. I said if conditions go on as they are, Europe will go bankrupt and cannot get back on its feet until after a long period in the future, while if Asia goes on as she is, both Japan and China will also find themselves bankrupt, while the United States will be greatly handicapped in its normal progress by wholesale bankruptcy in both Europe and Asia. The Ambassador did not seriously dispute this phase of our conversation. He sought to make it appear that Japan was motivated only by innocent purposes, but I said that his Government's formula in this respect does not work out in practice as we have seen from Manchuria, China and other occurrences and experiences; that this is especially true as to economic opportunity.

The Ambassador remarked that we were sending a Consul to Iceland, to which I replied in the affirmative.

He then inquired what new developments there were with respect to Greenland, to which I replied that there were no new developments and no relations about which the slightest question could be raised.

C[ORDELL] H[ULL]

151

740.0011 European War 1939/2691A

President Roosevelt to the Premier of Italy (*Mussolini*) [45]

[Telegram]

98　　　　　　　　　　　　WASHINGTON, April 29, 1940—6 p.m.

MY DEAR SIGNOR MUSSOLINI:

I am requesting my Ambassador in Rome to deliver this message to Your Excellency. Because of the long delays in the transmission of mail, I am conveying to you in this manner a message which under more normal conditions I would have transmitted by means of a personal letter.

During the past days the scope of the conflict in Europe has further widened and two more neutral nations which had done their utmost to avoid involvement in war have been drawn by force into the scene of hostilities.

The people of the United States, as I have already sent you word, have seen with the deepest satisfaction the policy of the Italian Government in exerting every effort to prevent war from spreading to southern and to southeastern Europe. I fully recognize the profound truth of the statement you made recently to my representative, Mr. Welles, that because of Italy's determination to limit, so far as might be possible, the spread of the conflict, more than 200,000,000 of people in the region of the Mediterranean are still at peace.

A further extension of the area of hostilities, which would bring into the war still other nations which have been seeking to maintain their neutrality, would necessarily have farreaching and unforeseeable consequences, not only in Europe, but also in the Near and the Far East, in Africa, and in the three Americas. No man can today predict with assurance, should such a further extension take place, what the ultimate result might be—or foretell what nations, however determined they may today be to remain at peace, might yet eventually find it imperative in their own defense to enter the war.

---

[45] Transmitted in a telegram from the Secretary of State to the Ambassador in Italy (Phillips).

I am, as you know, a realist. As occurs inevitably in every contest, the participants themselves are far less able to predict the eventual outcome of the struggle than the onlookers who are near at hand, and these latter perhaps are not in as good a position to determine which may be the winning side as those onlookers who may be still farther away. By reason of its geographical position, this country has a panoramic view of the existing hostilities in Europe. Because of the many imponderables involved, I see no reason to anticipate that any one nation, or any one combination of nations, can successfully undertake to dominate either the continent of Europe or much less a greater part of the world.

I earnestly hope that the powerful influence of Italy and of the United States—an influence which is very strong so long as they remain at peace—may yet be exercised, when the appropriate opportunity is presented in behalf of the negotiation of a just and stable peace which will permit of the reconstruction of a gravely stricken world.

With the assurance of my highest regard, believe me

Yours very sincerely,

FRANKLIN D. ROOSEVELT

152

740.0011 European War 1939/2691–1/7

The Ambassador in Italy (Phillips) to the Secretary of State

[Telegram : Paraphrase]

[ROME,] May 1, 1940—noon.
[Received May 1—9 a.m.]

301. Your telegram No. 98, April 29, 1940, 6 p.m. This morning at nine-thirty I was received by Mussolini at the Ministry of the Interior. Ciano arrived late and thus was present part of the time. The interview lasted a little over thirty minutes. As I read the message of President Roosevelt to him slowly Mussolini translated it into Italian. That every point was understood by him was clear to me. At the end of the message he took the paper and again read it and while rereading it made observations as follows: The possibility of the three Americas being drawn into the war puzzled him and why they should be he did not understand. Italy, Germany, and Russia did not desire an extension of the war. Germany is not menaced from the Balkans unless a new situation which would indeed be a menace be created by some act of the Allies in the Danubian region or at Salonika. To defeat Russia would be possible in his opinion and

he remarked that he also considered that Germany could not be beaten. After this morning's news of the important victories of Germany in Norway he considers the situation in Scandinavia to be already "liquidated" in Germany's favor. Fifteen countries can now be called upon by Germany for every kind of supplies and he enumerated them to me. In addition the blockade of the Allies was therefore completely ineffective. Apparently with satisfaction he noted the statement of President Roosevelt that he, Roosevelt, was a realist. Mussolini, also being a realist, feels that peace in Europe cannot be considered without recognizing the conditions which had come about as a consequence of the war. Poland had been defeated by Germany and the latter would willingly permit a new independent Polish state to be created without the old boundaries which were completely without justification. Germany was also willing that a new Czechoslovakian state be reestablished. Mussolini hoped that the necessity of a "new geography" would be foreseen by the President as well as the necessity of the liquidation in the first place of all of the political questions and the poisons which now make a peaceful Europe impossible. We can approach the economic problems after the political problems are disposed of. But to tackle the economic problems first would be putting the cart before the horse. He reiterated that a new map of Europe must come into being. His country also had its new position in a reconstituted Europe.

Italy had been formerly an agricultural country and its foreign commerce was not particularly important to her own well-being. At the present time she was a greatly industrialized country. Her large merchant marine was dependent on foreign commerce. Today, however, Italy was a "prisoner within the Mediterranean". This situation was intolerable and as her population increased rapidly she would insist upon getting the free access to the Atlantic Ocean which "under the guns of Gibraltar" she did not now have. He also spoke of the necessity for a change in Italy's favor in regard to the Suez Canal. Answering my question whether these were a new Italy's principal requirements he only said that there were a few other problems with France to be settled but gave no indication of them. Finally he said he would be greatly interested to learn the attitude of President Roosevelt in respect to his observations and also with respect to the new map of Europe. He requested that I thank President Roosevelt cordially for the latter's message and in fact he appeared to be extremely appreciative of it. He expressed himself with calmness and at the same time with decision and appeared to be in good health. It appeared to me that he went out of his way to be friendly.

Ciano was evidently expecting that I would leave a copy of the message with him and seemed disappointed when I told him that I could not do so according to my instructions. Ciano telephoned to me later that through Ambassador Colonna Mussolini would send an answer to President Roosevelt.

PHILLIPS

153

740.0011 European War 1939/2691–¾

The Premier of Italy (Mussolini) to President Roosevelt [46]

[Translation]

[ROME, May 2, 1940.]

1. If two nations, Denmark and Norway, have been involved in the war, the responsibilty does not fall upon Germany, but upon the initiatives of the Allies.

2. Italy's non-belligerency has effectively insured peace for two hundred millions of men, but notwithstanding, Italian merchant traffic is subjected to a constant surveillance that is vexatious and harmful.

3. As far as I know, Germany is opposed to a further extension of the conflict, and Italy likewise. We must learn whether this is also the Franco-British aim.

4. The only European nation that dominates a large part of the world and possesses a monopoly on many basic raw materials is Great Britain. Italy has no programs of that kind, but declares that no peace is possible without the fundamental problems of Italian liberty being settled.

5. As to the repercussions which an extension of the war fronts might have on the three Americas, I call attention to the fact that Italy has never concerned itself with the relations of the American republics with each other and with the United States (thereby respecting the Monroe Doctrine), and might therefore ask for "reciprocity" with regard to European affairs.

6. Whenever conditions permit, and always starting with the recognition of the actual and accomplished facts, Italy is ready to make her contribution to a better order of the world.

MUSSOLINI

---

[46] Delivered at the White House by the Italian Ambassador.

154

Department of State Bulletin, vol. II, p. 494

Address Delivered by President Roosevelt at Washington
May 10, 1940

All of the men and women of this Pan American Scientific Congress have come here tonight with heavy hearts. During the past few years we have seen event follow event, each and every one of them a shock to our hopes for the peaceful development of modern civilization. This very day three more independent nations have been cruelly invaded by force of arms.

In some human affairs the mind of man grows accustomed to unusual actions if they are oft repeated. That is not so in the world happenings of today—and I am proud that it is not so. I am glad that we are shocked and angered by the tragic news from Belgium and the Netherlands and Luxemburg.

The overwhelmingly greater part of the population of the world abhors conquest and war and bloodshed—prays that the hand of neighbor shall not be lifted against neighbor. The whole world has seen attack follow threat on so many occasions and in so many places during these later years. We have come, therefore, to the reluctant conclusion that a continuance of these processes of arms presents a definite challenge to the continuation of the type of civilization to which all of us in the three Americas have been accustomed.

I use this Pan American Scientific Congress as one of many similar illustrations. It is no accident that this meeting takes place in the New World. In fact, this hemisphere is now almost the only part of the earth in which such a gathering can take place. Elsewhere war or politics has compelled teachers and scholars to leave their great calling and to become agents of destruction.

We, and most people in the world, believe in a civilization of construction and not of destruction. We, and most people in the world, believe that men and women have an inherent right to hew out the patterns of their own individual lives, just so long as they as individuals do not harm their fellow beings. We call this by many synonymous terms—individual liberty, civil liberty, democracy.

Until now we permit ourselves by common consent to search for truth, to teach the truth as we see it—and by learning a little here and a little there, and teaching a little here and a little there to allow the normal processes of truth to keep growing for the well-being of our fellow men. In our search and in our teaching we are a part of a great adventure—an exciting adventure—which gives to us a larger satisfaction even than did the adventure of settling the Americas give to our Founding Fathers. We feel that we are building human progress by conquering disease and poverty and discomfort, and by improving science and culture, removing one by one the cruelty, the crudity, and the barbarism of less civilized eras.

In contrast, in other parts of the world, teachers and scholars are not permitted to search for truth lest the truth when made known might not suit the designs of their masters. Too often they are not allowed to teach the truth as they see it, for truth might make men free. They become objects of suspicion if they speak openly, if they show an interest in new truth, for their very tongues and minds are supposed to be mobilized for other ends.

This has not happened in the New World. God willing, it shall not happen in the New World.

At the pan-American conference at Buenos Aires, and again at Lima, we discussed a dim and unpleasant possibility. We feared that other continents might become so involved in wars brought on by the school of destruction that the Americas might have to become the guardian of western culture, the protector of Christian civilization.

In those days it was merely a fear. Today the fear has become a fact.

The inheritance which we had hoped to share with every nation in the world is, for the moment, left largely in our keeping; and it is our compelling duty to guard and enrich that legacy, to preserve it for a world which must be reborn from the ashes of the present disaster.

Today we know that until recent weeks too many citizens of the American republics believed themselves wholly safe—physically and economically and socially—from the impact of the attacks on civilization which are in progress elsewhere. Perhaps this mistaken idea was based on the false teaching of geography—the thought that a distance of several thousand miles from a war-torn Europe gave to us some form of mystic immunity which could never be violated.

Yet, speaking in terms of timetables, in terms of the moving of men and guns and planes and bombs, every acre—every hectare—of the Americas from the Arctic to the Antarctic is closer to the homes of modern conquerors and the scenes of attacks in Europe than was the case in historic efforts to dominate the world in bygone centuries. From the point of view of conquests, it is a shorter distance from the center of Europe to Santiago de Chile than it was for the chariots of

Alexander to roll from Macedonia to Persia. In modern terms it is a shorter distance from Europe to San Francisco than it was for the ships and legions of Caesar to move from Rome to Spain or Britain. Today it is 4 or 5 hours from the Continent of Africa to the Continent of South America, where it was 4 or 5 weeks for the armies of Napoleon to move from Paris to Rome or Paris to Poland.

You who are scientists may be told that you are responsible because of the processes of invention for the annihilation of time and space, but I assure you that it is not the scientists of the world who are responsible, because the objectives which you have had have looked toward closer and more peaceful relations between all nations through the spirit of cooperation and the interchange of knowledge. What has come about has been caused solely by those who would use, and are using, your inventions of peace in a wholly different cause—those who seek to dominate hundreds of millions of people in vast continental areas—those who, if successful in that aim will, we must now admit, enlarge their wild dream to encompass every human being and every mile of the earth's surface.

The great achievements of science and even of art can be used to destroy as well as create; they are only instruments by which men try to do the things they most want to do. If death is desired, science can do that. If a full life is sought, science can do that also. Happily for us that question is solved—for in the New World we live for each other and in the service of a Christian faith.

Is this solution—our solution—permanent or safe if it is solved for us alone? That it seems to me is the most immediate issue that the Americas face. Can we continue our peaceful construction if all the other continents embrace by preference or by compulsion a wholly different principle of life?

Surely it is time for our republics to spread that problem before us in the cold light of day, to analyze it, to ask questions, to demand answers, to use every knowledge, every science we possess, to apply common sense, and especially to act with unanimity and singleness of purpose.

I am a pacifist. You, my fellow citizens of 21 American republics, are pacifists.

But I believe that by overwhelming majorities you and I, in the long run and if it be necessary, will act together to protect and defend by every means our science, our culture, our freedom, and our civilization.

155

740.0011 European War 1939/3004A

President Roosevelt to the Premier of Italy (Mussolini)[47]

[Telegram]

[WASHINGTON,] May 14, 1940—midnight.

I do not know what Your Excellency plans or proposes but reports reaching me from many sources, to the effect that you may be contemplating early entry into the war, have given me great concern.

I send you this appeal as the head of a peaceful nation and as a close friend of twenty other American Republics. All of us in the Americas feel in our hearts that tonight the whole world faces a threat which opposes every teaching of Christ, every philosophy of all the great teachers of mankind over thousands of years.

Forces of slaughter, forces which deny God, forces which seek to dominate mankind by fear rather than by reason seem at this moment to be extending their conquest against a hundred million human beings who have no desire but peace.

You whom the great Italian people call their leader have it in your own hands to stay the spread of this war to another group of 200,-000,000 human souls in the Mediterranean Area.

I have sent word to Your Excellency before that I am a realist. As a realist you also will, I know, recognize that if this war should extend throughout the world it would pass beyond the control of heads of States, would encompass the destruction of millions of lives and the best of what we call the liberty and culture of civilization. And no man, no matter how omniscient, how powerful, can foretell the result either to himself or his own people.

Therefore, I make the simple plea that you, responsible for Italy, withhold your hand, stay wholly apart from any war and refrain from any threat of attack. So only can you help mankind tonight and tomorrow and in the pages of history.

FRANKLIN D. ROOSEVELT

---

[47] Transmitted in a telegram from the Secretary of State to the Ambassador in Italy (Phillips).

156

Department of State Bulletin, vol. II, p. 529

Address Delivered by President Roosevelt to the Congress, May 16, 1940

These are ominous days—days whose swift and shocking developments force every neutral nation to look to its defenses in the light of new factors. The brutal force of modern offensive war has been loosed in all its horror. New powers of destruction, incredibly swift and deadly, have been developed; and those who wield them are ruthless and daring. No old defense is so strong that it requires no further strengthening, and no attack is so unlikely or impossible that it may be ignored.

Let us examine, without self-deception, the dangers which confront us. Let us measure our strength and our defense without self-delusion.

The clear fact is that the American people must recast their thinking about national protection.

Motorized armies can now sweep through enemy territories at the rate of 200 miles a day. Parachute troops are dropped from airplanes in large numbers behind enemy lines. Troops are landed from planes in open fields, on wide highways, and at local civil airports.

We have seen the treacherous use of the "fifth column" by which persons supposed to be peaceful visitors were actually a part of an enemy unit of occupation. Lightning attacks, capable of destroying airplane factories and munition works hundreds of miles behind the lines, are part of the new technique of modern war.

The element of surprise which has ever been an important tactic in warfare has become the more dangerous because of the amazing speed with which modern equipment can reach and attack the enemy's country.

Our own vital interests are widespread. More than ever the protection of the whole American Hemisphere against invasion or control or domination by non-American nations has the united support of the 21 American republics, including the United States. More than ever this protection calls for ready-at-hand weapons capable of great mobility because of the potential speed of modern attack.

The Atlantic and Pacific Oceans were reasonably adequate defensive barriers when fleets under sail could move at an average speed of 5 miles an hour. Even then by a sudden foray it was possible for an opponent actually to burn our National Capitol. Later, the oceans still gave strength to our defense when fleets and convoys propelled by steam could sail the oceans at 15 or 20 miles an hour.

But the new element—air navigation—steps up the speed of possible attack to 200, to 300 miles an hour.

Furthermore, it brings the new possibilities of the use of nearer bases from which an attack or attacks on the American Continents could be made. From the fiords of Greenland it is 4 hours by air to Newfoundland; 5 hours to Nova Scotia, New Brunswick, and Quebec; and only 6 hours to New England.

The Azores are only 2,000 miles from parts of our eastern seaboard, and if Bermuda fell into hostile hands it is a matter of less than 3 hours for modern bombers to reach our shores.

From a base in the outer West Indies, the coast of Florida could be reached in 200 minutes.

The islands off the west coast of Africa are only 1,500 miles from Brazil. Modern planes starting from the Cape Verde Islands can be over Brazil in 7 hours.

And Pará, Brazil, is but 4 flying hours to Caracas, Venezuela; and Venezuela but $2\frac{1}{2}$ hours to Cuba and the Canal Zone; and Cuba and the Canal Zone are $2\frac{1}{4}$ hours to Tampico, Mexico; and Tampico is $2\frac{1}{4}$ hours to St. Louis, Kansas City, and Omaha.

On the other side of the continent, Alaska, with a white population of only 30,000 people, is within 4 or 5 hours of flying distance to Vancouver, Seattle, Tacoma, and Portland. The islands of the southern Pacific are not too far removed from the west coast of South America to prevent them from becoming bases of enormous strategic advantage to attacking forces.

Surely, the developments of the past few weeks have made it clear to all of our citizens that the possibility of attack on vital American zones ought to make it essential that we have the physical, the ready ability to meet those attacks and to prevent them from reaching their objectives.

This means military implements—not on paper—which are ready and available to meet any lightning offensive against our American interest. It means also that facilities for production must be ready to turn out munitions and equipment at top speed.

We have had the lesson before us over and over again—nations that were not ready and were unable to get ready found themselves overrun by the enemy. So-called impregnable fortifications no longer exist. A defense which allows an enemy to consolidate his approach without hindrance will lose. A defense which makes no effective effort to destroy the lines of supplies and communications of the enemy will lose.

An effective defense by its very nature requires the equipment to attack an aggressor on his route before he can establish strong bases within the territory of American vital interests.

Loose talking and thinking on the part of some may give the false impression that our own Army and Navy are not first-rate, or that money has been wasted on them.

Nothing could be further from the truth.

In recent years the defensive power of our Army, Navy, and Marine Corps has been very greatly improved.

The Navy is stronger today than at any time in the Nation's history. Today also a large program of new construction is well under way. Ship for ship, ours are equal to, or better than, the vessels of any foreign power.

The Army likewise is at its greatest peace-time strength. Its equipment in quality and quantity has been greatly increased and improved.

The National Guard and the reserve strength of the two services are better equipped and better prepared than during any other peace-time period.

On the other side of the picture we must visualize the outstanding fact that since the first day of September 1939, every week that has passed has brought new lessons learned from actual combat on land and sea.

I cite examples. Where naval ships have operated without adequate protection by defending aircraft, their vulnerability to air attack has increased. All nations are hard at work studying the need of additional antiaircraft protection.

Several months ago the use of a new type of magnetic mine made many unthinking people believe that all surface ships were doomed. Within a few weeks a successful defensive device against these mines was placed in operation; and it is a fact that the sinkings of merchant ships by torpedo, by mine, or by airplane are definitely much lower than during the similar period in 1915.

Combat conditions have changed even more rapidly in the air. With the amazing progress in the design of planes and engines, the airplane of a year ago is out of date now. It is too slow, it is improperly protected, it is too weak in gun power.

In types of planes, we are not behind the other nations of the world. Many of the planes of the belligerent powers are at this moment not of the latest models. But one belligerent power not only has many more planes than all their opponents combined, but also appears to have a weekly production capacity at the moment that is far greater than that of their opponents.

From the point of view of our own defense, therefore, great additional production capacity is our principal air requisite.

For the permanent record, I ask the Congress not to take any action which would in any way hamper or delay the delivery of American-made planes to foreign nations which have ordered them, or seek to purchase more planes. That, from the point of view of our own national defense, would be extremely short-sighted.

During the past year American production capacity for war planes, including engines, has risen from approximately 6,000 planes a year to more than double that number, due in greater part to the placing of foreign orders.

Our immediate problem is to superimpose on this production capacity a greatly increased additional production capacity. I should like to see this Nation geared up to the ability to turn out at least 50,000 planes a year. Furthermore, I believe that this Nation should plan at this time a program that would provide us with 50,000 military and naval planes.

The ground forces of the Army require the immediate speeding up of last winter's program to procure equipment of all kinds, including motor transport and artillery, including antiaircraft guns and full ammunition supplies. It had been planned to spread these requirements over the next 3 or 4 years. We should fill them at once.

At this time I am asking the immediate appropriation by the Congress of a large sum of money for four primary purposes:

First, to procure the essential equipment of all kinds for a larger and thoroughly rounded-out Army;

Second, to replace or modernize all old Army and Navy equipment with the latest type of equipment;

Third, to increase production facilities for everything needed for the Army and Navy for national defense. We require the ability to turn out quickly infinitely greater supplies;

Fourth, to speed up to a 24-hour basis all existing Army and Navy contracts and all new contracts to be awarded.

I ask for an immediate appropriation of $896,000,000, divided approximately as follows:

1. For the Army $546,000,000
2. For the Navy and Marine Corps 250,000,000
3. To the President to provide for emergencies affecting
   the national security and defense 100,000,000

In addition to the above sum, I ask for authorizations for the Army,

Navy, and Marine Corps to make contract obligations in the further sum of $186,000,000.

And to the President an additional authorization to make contract obligations for $100,000,000.

The total of authorizations is, therefore, $286,000,000.

It is my belief that a large part of the requested appropriation of $100,000,000, and the requested authorization of $100,000,000 to the President will be used principally for the increase of production of airplanes, antiaircraft guns, and the training of additional personnel for these weapons. This would be in addition to the direct estimates for these purposes in the other items requested.

The proposed details of the appropriations and authorizations asked for will be given to the Committees of the Congress.

These estimates do not, of course, duplicate any item now in the pending War and Navy appropriation bills for the year 1941. Nor do they include supplemental or deficiency estimates which may become necessary by reason of pending legislation or shortage of funds under existing programs.

There are some who say that democracy cannot cope with the new techniques of government developed in recent years by a few countries—by a few countries which deny the freedoms which we maintain are essential to our democratic way of life. This I reject.

I know that our trained officers and men know more about fighting and the weapons and equipment needed for fighting than any of us laymen; and I have confidence in them.

I know that to cope with present dangers we must be strong in heart and hand; strong in our faith—strong in faith in our way of living.

I, too, pray for peace—that the ways of aggression and force may be banished from the earth—but I am determined to face the fact realistically that this Nation requires a toughness of moral and physical fiber. Those qualities, I am convinced, the American people hold to a high degree.

Our task is plain. The road we must take is clearly indicated. Our defenses must be invulnerable, our security absolute. But our defense as it was yesterday, or even as it is today, does not provide security against potential developments and dangers of the future.

Defense canot be static. Defense must grow and change from day to day. Defense must be dynamic and flexible, an expression of the vital forces of the Nation and of its resolute will to meet whatever challenge the future may hold. For these reasons, I need hardly assure you that after the adjournment of this session of the Congress, I will not hesitate to call the Congress into special session if at any time the situation of the national defense requires it. The Congress and the Chief Executive constitute a team where the defense of the land is concerned.

Our ideal, our objective is still peace—peace at home and peace abroad. Nevertheless, we stand ready not only to spend millions for defense but to give our service and even our lives for the maintenance of our American liberties.

Our security is not a matter of weapons alone. The arm that wields them must be strong, the eye that guides them clear, the will that directs them indomitable.

These are the characteristics of a free people, a people devoted to the institutions they themselves have built, a people willing to defend a way of life that is precious to them all, a people who put their faith in God.

157

856B.01/22

Memorandum by the Secretary of State Regarding a Conversation With the Japanese Ambassador (Horinouchi)

[WASHINGTON,] May 16, 1940.

The Ambassador of Japan called at his own request. He did not mention the Philippine Immigration Bill, or the reported anti-Japanese disturbances in Peru, or, expressly, the Netherlands Indies, or the status of European armed forces in China. At the beginning of the conversation I made reference to the increased state of war and chaos in other parts of the world and the terrible destructive effects of it in every way, adding that it appeared more and more as if no large country, much less a small country, was safe from some aggressive intervention by force in one way or another, and that about the only thing a nation could do was to arm to the teeth and be ready for any serious interference with its rights and interests by the use of military force or the threat of force. I said that, fortunately, as was shown today in Congress, and as was apparent all over the nation since the more recent invasions of helpless peaceful nations for purposes of their destruction, the American people have now become thoroughly awakened, aroused and alert in regard to any threatened injuries to American rights and interests, and that this was a matter of great gratification to those of us in charge of the foreign affairs of the nation.

The Ambassador then proceeded at great length to question and cross-examine me about the Netherlands West Indies, comprising Curaçao and Aruba. I said that, of course, my Government and the other twenty-one American Republics would not consider for a moment any departure from their traditional policy relating to the safety of this hemisphere, and if that was what the Ambassador had in mind, I could make that statement together with the further statement that as soon as this Government learned of the fact that British and French vessels patrolling the waters near Curaçao and Aruba were offering potential aid to the Netherlands Government in preventing possible sabotage and possible armed expeditions from the mainland intended to seize the governments on one or both of these possessions, . . . this Government proceeded to assemble the facts as expeditiously as possible in regard to the ability of Netherlands guards and citizens in Curaçao and Aruba to protect the islands and their governments from such dangers. I further stated that it was my understanding that the British and French patrols were in no sense interfering with the Netherlands governments on these two islands, but were recognizing the authority of these governments during the brief temporary time deemed necessary to aid in safeguarding against the dangers already mentioned, and that they have made it clear that thereafter their patrols will not offer any guards for additional protection in connection with their continued patrol work, and hence there cannot arise the slightest question of interference with the traditional American policy relating to its own protection from possible dangers from abroad. Furthermore, the Netherlands Government would be expected to send from abroad any additional guards that may later be found to be needed. The Ambassador did not seem to be satisfied with any sort of answer I made. He continued with an increasingly minute cross-examination as it were. I suddenly and emphatically interrupted him and inquired of him if his Government had sent him to me to ask all these detailed questions about a matter of no importance to his Government or to any other government, and if his Government had sent him to go into this almost interminable examination, I desired now to know what the motive and purpose of his Government was for doing so. I said that there would never be any friction between my Government and any other government on account of anything unlawful or unfair that my Government may do, but that it would be due to something unlawful that another government may do. I added that I had devoted most of the past seven years to efforts at understanding and peaceful relations between our two Governments.

I then picked up two or three pages of material which had come in via the news ticker from Tokyo, in which the Japanese Government is reported to be discussing every day or two some phase of the Netherlands East Indies and its supposed special rights in them. I stated that I had not intended to show him this, that it had just come to my desk as the Ambassador came in, but I remarked with emphasis that it had been thought that the Japanese Government and the Governments of the United States, Great Britain and France had each and all repeated recently their prior commitment that each was obligated to respect the *status quo* in the Netherlands East Indies and I had thought that settled the matter as among our four countries, since each country unequivocally pledged itself to respect the *status quo*, but I added that notwithstanding the efforts of many of us to maintain a thorough understanding with the Government of Japan, there was continually coming out of Tokyo additional discussions of the Netherlands East Indies as though the commitment to respect and preserve the *status quo* had not been made. I said that these were news reports and I myself was slow to accredit them, but that the tenor of the reports interfered with the efforts of the Ambassador and myself and others to preserve understanding and fair play and fair treatment between our two countries by causing misunderstanding and increasing hostility on the part of the people in each country. I said that I would make no complaint now about the matter if that was a part of the newspaper policy in Japan. I added finally that my Government strives for peace year in and year out and it desires at all times to avoid controversy, and, therefore, if controversy arises, the fault will not lie at the door of this Government. I said further that in our constant desire and constant effort to promote and preserve peace, both with other countries and among other countries, I hoped that this attitude of ours would not be misunderstood.

The Ambassador undertook in reply to disclaim any purpose of his Government to send him to me to enter into the long examination to which he was subjecting me when interrupted. He then repeated that his Government was entirely satisfied with the situation following the reiteration of the *status quo* in respect to the Netherlands Indies by each of the four governments interested, and that it had no purpose to raise any further controversy in that connection unless perchance the British or French should land troops there to protect them. I remarked that, since my Government was interested, I had made inquiries of the British and the French, and gathered the unequivocal understanding that they had no idea whatever to intervene in the Netherlands East Indies in any way.

The Ambassador then made some reference to the Monroe Doctrine in connection with the West Indies situation, and I replied that I had seemingly in vain sought to point out to his Government that, under the Monroe Doctrine, his country's merchant ships have equal access to every harbor in the Western Hemisphere (not including a special arrangement between the United States and Cuba), while under the policy which his Government is seeking to impose in the Pacific Ocean area, the United States and other countries are to be denied equality of trade and industrial opportunity in every Chinese port, and yet his Government seems to look with complacency on this conflicting situation.

I again brought to his attention the information contained in the news ticker report today from Tokyo, in which Japanese newspapers, as stated, were undertaking to keep alive and emphasize some supposed special interests of Japan in the Netherlands East Indies. I said it seemed very surprising to observe that, after the Japanese Government had undertaken to spread itself out over the huge republic of China, there was an intimation in the news reports that it would not be content unless it extended itself three thousand miles beyond to modestly take in the great archipelago comprising the East Indies, presumably with a view of shutting out all equality of trade opportunities among nations, while Japan would continue to demand equality of trade opportunities in every other part of the world; that there did not exist any selfish or other reason on the part of other nations to interfere in the least with equality of trade opportunities on the part of Japan. The Ambassador again stated that his Government was satisfied about the Netherlands East Indies situation in the light of the renewed promises of each of the three other governments interested, and that they had no plans or purposes to proceed there to attack the Netherlands East Indies. I expressed my satisfaction with his statement, but again reminded him of my difficulty to understand the policy of the Japanese Government or the Japanese press, whichever it was, to continue various lines of discussion indicating a claim to some sort of special interest of Japan in the Netherlands East Indies situation; that in a recent statement, I had set forth rather comprehensively and succinctly the position of this Government that the *status quo* should be respected and preserved by each of the four governments; that the real question presented actually related to the entire Pacific area and that no further elaboration beyond my recent statement on this subject would appear to add to anything I then said.

I still interpret the Ambassador's visit as one under instructions to develop a pretext to support Japan in connection with its plans and purposes toward the Netherlands East Indies.

C[ORDELL] H[ULL]

158

740.0011 European War/3124

The Premier of Italy (Mussolini) to President Roosevelt [48]

[Telegram]

ROME, May 18, 1940.
[Received May 18—10 : 04 a.m.]

379. I reply to the message which you sent me at noon on the fourteenth instant. I understand perfectly the motives by which it was inspired and I consider it worthy of much respect and of the greatest consideration but there are two fundamental motives which cannot escape your spirit of political realism and those are that Italy is and intends to remain allied with Germany and that Italy cannot remain absent at a moment in which the fate of Europe is at stake. I cannot therefore but reconfirm the substance of my first message.

[MUSSOLINI]

159

740.0011 European War 1939/2691–2⁄7A

President Roosevelt to the Premier of Italy (Mussolini) [49]

[Telegram]

WASHINGTON, May 26, 1940—3 p.m.

140. I want to thank you for your courteous reply to my last verbal message to Your Excellency.

Events have been marching swiftly but I still believe that political long range vision favors the limitation of the war to its present areas.

I hope it will be helpful to Your Excellency in keeping war out of the Mediterranean and out of even much wider areas and populations if I make the following suggestions to you:

The people of the United States are greatly concerned by the indications of the past few days which would seem to show that there was an increasing possibility of the extension of the European War to the Mediterranean area.

[48] Transmitted in a telegram from the Ambassador in Italy (Phillips) to the Secretary of State.

[49] Transmitted in a telegram from the Secretary of State to the Ambassador in Italy (Phillips) for immediate, oral communication.

536

I realize fully from your recent messages and from public statements which you have made that the Italian Government desires to obtain readjustments with regard to Italy's position.

If you are willing to inform me of the specific desires of Italy in this regard in order to insure the satisfaction of Italy's legitimate aspirations in that area, I will communicate them to the Governments of Great Britain and of France.

I would take this action in the belief that I am thereby rendering a constructive service at this critical moment with the hope that the cause of peace might thereby be furthered.

Likewise, I would communicate such a message from you with the understanding that if an agreement were arrived at, it would involve an assurance to me by the French and British Governments that such agreement would be faithfully executed by them at the end of the war and that those Governments would welcome Italian participation at any eventual peace conference with a status equal to that of the belligerents; and, finally, that you would in similar fashion assure me that the claims of Italy would be satisfied by the execution of this agreement and that the agreement so reached would avoid the possibility of Italy entering the war.

With the terms which you might be willing to propose or with the counter terms which the French and British Governments might desire to propose I am of course not concerned; nor can I undertake any responsibility other than that indicated. My sole desire in making this suggestion is to make a practical effort towards avoiding the extension of the war.

ROOSEVELT

160

740.0011 European War 1939/2691-¾

The Ambassador in Italy (Phillips) to the Secretary of State

[Telegram : Paraphrase]

ROME, May 27, 1940—1 p.m.
[Received May 27—9 : 55 a.m.]

420. This morning I was received by Ciano at eleven-thirty. I said to him that I had a message of great importance from President Roosevelt, that I had been ordered to deliver it orally to the Duce, but that I would be glad for Ciano to read it for his own information. He answered that the Duce could not receive me but that he, Ciano, would take the message and would make, with my permission, a few notes of

its text. He thereupon did so with care and attention and I did not feel able to press any further the request that I have an interview with Mussolini. After he had finished I asked him if he could let me have some idea of the general nature of the reply. He answered definitely "It would be a no" and proceeded to explain that the position of the Duce was more than the question of realizing the legitimate aspirations of Italy, that Mussolini was resolved to fulfill his obligations under the alliance with Germany. He said that the Duce was not in at that particular moment but would come back later in the day and Ciano promised that as soon as he was in a position to give me the reply he would send for me.

I asked the Foreign Minister if he had full realization of the seriousness and importance of the message of President Roosevelt. He said that he did but that there was nothing that could now change the situation. In addition he said that he could not give me the exact time of Italy's entrance into the war; it would be impossible for a few days and it might not take place for a few weeks but he did say "it will happen soon".

Finally he asked me about the position of the United States. I called his attention to the program of President Roosevelt for a great defensive armament. Ciano only answered that it was his assumption that the United States sympathized with the Allies in the same manner that Italy sympathized with Germany.

The Foreign Minister called for me at one o'clock and informed me that the statements which he had made to me earlier in the day had been confirmed by Mussolini. Ciano declared that it was the desire of Mussolini to keep his "freedom of action" and that the Duce was not disposed to engage in any negotiations which indeed would not be in accordance with the spirit of Fascism. He laid emphasis on the idea that the Duce was responsible for the "fulfillment of an engagement—of words given" and he said in addition "any attempt to prevent Italy from fulfilling her engagements is not well regarded".

PHILLIPS

161

740.0011 European War 1939/2691-3⁄7

The Secretary of State to the Ambassador in Italy (Phillips)

[Telegram]

WASHINGTON, May 30, 1940—6 p.m.

154. By direction of the President you are requested to call on Count Ciano and deliver to him orally the following message for the Chief of Government:

The President has received and has of course given the most thoughtful consideration to the reply conveyed by the Chief of Government to the President's last message.

The President feels compelled in the most friendly manner, but at the same time with the utmost frankness, to lay certain very important considerations before Signor Mussolini.

If the war in Europe is now extended through the entrance of Italy into the war, direct interests of the Government of the United States will be immediately and prejudicially affected. The President has already reminded the Chief of Government of the historic and traditional interests of the United States in the Mediterranean. These interests have been upheld over a period of almost one hundred and fifty years. This Government has never asserted any political interests in Europe, but it has asserted its clearly defined interests of an economic and property character. Through the extension of the war to the Mediterranean region and the inevitable destruction of life and property resulting therefrom, the legitimate interests of the American people will be gravely curtailed and such a possibility cannot be viewed with equanimity by their Government.

An extension of the war into the Mediterranean region will almost unquestionably likewise involve a further extension of the war area in the Near East and in other regions of the world. The President has already stated his belief that such further extension of the war might well bring with it the involvement of countries at present remote from the scene of the hostilities. The President feels it necessary to emphasize that possibility. The social and economic relations between the Americas and the whole of Europe are greater than with any other part of the world. These relations are already gravely disturbed as a result of the present hostilities. In the event that there were any further extension of the war, they would obviously be even more seriously disturbed.

In conclusion, the further extension of the war as a result of Italian participation would at once result in an increase in the rearmament program of the United States itself and in a redoubling of the efforts of the Government of the United States to facilitate in every practical way the securing within the United States by the Allied Powers of all the supplies and matériel which they may require.

Signor Mussolini will recognize that arming on an unprecedented scale in the Americas will make difficult the reduction of armaments in Italy, Europe, and the rest of the world at the conclusion of the present wars. The establishment of normal internal economic and social programs will, therefore, be made infinitely more difficult.

As the Chief of Government well knows, the relations between the Italian and American peoples have always been particularly close and friendly and the President feels sure that the Chief of Government will also recognize that the President has desired and now desires to promote profitable commercial relations between the two countries, as well as a friendly understanding and comprehension of their respective policies and interests between the two Governments. It is for these and the other reasons mentioned that the President believes that entire frankness on his part in these grave moments will be construed by the Chief of Government as an indication of the President's earnest desire to maintain and promote good relations between the two countries.

Please telegraph immediately the reply which may be made to you.

HULL

162

711.94/1517A

The Secretary of State to the Ambassador in Japan (*Grew*)

[Telegram : Paraphrase]

172   WASHINGTON, May 30, 1940—2 p.m.

1. In the light of the course of European events every Government which is not involved in the European war is giving, of course, most serious consideration to the various questions which are raised by developments there. Naturally intensive thought is being given by each such Government to its own national security problems and to questions both long- and short-range of national welfare and national interests in general. Should the present onrush of the Germans be checked and the European war become prolonged the European peoples face a prospect of a long period of economic strain with lowered standards of living, lowered purchasing power, and the continued disruption of normal trade. Should the allies be defeated it will probably be followed by an extension of the German system of economic autarchy to most of Europe and by an effort to extend that system to African and Asian colonial possessions. The result of this would be generally a lowering of living standards and a social deterioration; moreover, in world markets being flooded with cheap goods produced under forced-labor conditions.

2. There is no part of the world which can avoid being affected adversely by either of such developments materializing. The Govern-

540

ment of the United States has hoped, and does hope, that the war's adverse effects may be kept to a minimum and may be made temporary not only in respect to the Americas but also with regard to Asia by an increase of devotion in such areas to the policies and principles which contemplate and call for the lowering or removal of artificial or excessive trade barriers and through the intensification of the efforts of peoples and countries in such areas to protect and advance their national interests on peaceful lines and by peaceful means. Today every country must strengthen its national defense machinery. The people of the United States see that this is necessary and they are going forward strenuously with plans and production which will in a relatively short time make this country far stronger in a military way than it is at present. The United States has no aggressive designs, but it will be ready to defend itself against any aggression which may be undertaken against it. Whatever the results of the European war may be, the United States is very strong in resources and in a relatively short time will probably be more powerful militarily and better organized in the economic field than it has been for many years. It is the firm belief of the people and government of the United States that the general deterioration in the situation which the existing and spreading armed conflicts have brought on can be checked and kept from becoming universal only by determined and enlightened resistance to such deterioration by those nations which have the desire and intention that principles of law, order, justice, and national sovereignty shall survive and the principles of economic freedom prevail.

3. Consideration is being given by various countries which are not yet involved in the European war to the question of whether they will throw in their lot with such countries as Germany which are committed to the use of force for purposes of coercion and conquest or whether they will give their support and adherence to policies and principles of the character to which the United States and a large number of other nations are committed. It is indicated by your reports and by press despatches that the various aspects of that general question are being studied intensively by the Japanese Government. We of course desire to be informed of any significant indications discerned by you regarding the direction in which the thought of the Japanese Government is moving in this matter.

4. We have reviewed your accounts of your various conversations during recent weeks with influential official and non-official Japanese. It is believed that it would be helpful that as the opportune occasion arises you continue to have such conversations with the purpose, among others, of obtaining information and of conveying as of your

own thought whatever among the ideas and statements of fact outlined above you consider would be helpful. Of course it is essential that at all points we guard against the creation of an impression or giving ground for any inference that we have modified or will modify our position of opposition to courses and policies, whether of Japan or any other nation, which entail the attempt to achieve various positive national objectives in international relations by use of force.

HULL

163

H. Doc. 799, 76th Cong., 3d sess.

Message of President Roosevelt to the Congress, May 31, 1940

The almost incredible events of the past 2 weeks in the European conflict, particularly as a result of the use of aviation and mechanized equipment, together with the possible consequences of further developments, necessitate another enlargement of our military program.

No individual, no group, can clearly foretell the future. As long, however, as a possibility exists that not one continent or two continents but all continents may become involved in a world-wide war, reasonable precaution demands that American defense be made more certain.

An investigation into manufacturing resources since my message of May 16, to determine the practicability of placing additional orders with industry for special material, both to provide an early expansion of existing production facilities, and to obtain increased quantities of the special weapons concerned, has caused the War and Navy Departments to submit to me an urgent and new recommendation that increased appropriations and authorizations for the national defense be made before the adjournment of the present Congress.

Over and beyond the acquisition of this actual material is the evident requirement for the immediate creation of additional production facilities to meet possible future emergencies as well as present deficiencies in the making of munitions, such as guns, ammunition, and fire-control equipment. These facilities require a long time to create and to reach quantity production. The increased gravity of the situation indicates that action should be taken without delay.

The problem of defending our national institutions and territorial integrity is no longer a problem for men equipped simply with an indomitable determination. Modern defense requires that this determination be supported by the highly developed machinery of our industrial productive capacity.

542

The expansion of our defense program makes it necessary that we undertake immediately the training and retraining of our people, and especially our young people, for employment in industry and in service in the Army and Navy.

The requirements of industry and the expanded armed forces for persons with experience in mechanical and manual fields are obviously going to be great. We do not have such trained persons in the number that will be required for the tasks that lie ahead of us if our defense is to be assured. We have, therefore, the task of training a large number in the skills and semiskills required by modern production in industry and by a highly mechanized defense force in the Army and Navy. A primary consideration in the training of skills must be, not the existing distribution of workers among skilled fields, but the distribution that would be required if our industrial machine and our defensive forces were fully mobilized.

In the national effort for defense upon which we are now engaged, it is imperative that we make full and effective use of the mighty capacities that lie in our population. Here as yet undeveloped lie the ability and the strength needed in the building up of our armaments to provide a sure industrial foundation for the meeting of any and all defense requirements. Without the full development of these skills, our national defense will be less than it must be in the critical days which lie ahead. Without the full contribution of our people, our defense cannot attain the invulnerability which the Nation demands and which we are determined it shall have.

The one most obvious lesson of the present war in Europe is the value of the factor of speed. There is definite danger in waiting to order the complete equipping and training of armies after a war begins.

Therefore, I suggest the speedy enlargement of the program for equipping and training in the light of our defense needs.

I have instructed the representatives of the War and Navy Departments and also the representatives of the several agencies dealing with the training of young men for noncombatant services to make available to the appropriate committees of the Congress the plans and proposals which they have laid before me.

These plans call for immediate appropriations to carry forward congressional decisions in bills already pending, for immediate appropriations to add to the program, and for authorizations to enter into contracts which it will take some time to complete.

There is a specific recommendation I would make in concluding this message, that before adjournment this Congress grant me the authority to call into active service such portion of the National Guard as may be deemed necessary to maintain our position of neutrality and to safeguard the national defense, this to include authority to call into active service the necessary Reserve personnel.

The amounts involved are large—over a billion dollars—but I believe that for national safety the needs are urgent.

FRANKLIN D. ROOSEVELT

THE WHITE HOUSE,
May 31, 1940.

164

740.0011 European War 1939/2691-4⁄7

The Ambassador in Italy (Phillips) to the Secretary of State

[Telegram : Paraphrase]

ROME, June 1, 1940—1 p.m.
[Received June 1—10 a.m.]

445. My telegram No. 437, May 31, 2 p.m.

I was sent for by Ciano at 12:15 p.m. and he gave me verbally Mussolini's answer to President Roosevelt's message of May 30. Mussolini, in confirming what Ciano told me yesterday, mentioned particularly that already the decision to enter the war had been made. Mussolini does not agree with the views of the President regarding United States' interests in the Mediterranean maintaining that the interest of the United States in that area is the same as that which Italy has, it might be said, in the Caribbean Sea area.

Regarding the statement of the President that participation by Italy in the war would bring about a redoubling of efforts to aid the Allies on the part of the United States, Mussolini indicated that it was our business and of no concern to him. It was thus proven to him, however, that help is actually being given by the United States to the Allies; that America already has "chosen the Allied side". He desires to fulfill on his part his engagements with Germany and does not believe that an enlargement of the Mediterranean war will necessarily be brought about by the intervention of Italy. As that is not the Italian object, to prevent it, Italy will do everything possible.

In conclusion Ciano said that Mussolini preferred not to receive "any further pressure" as this, I was informed, "would only stiffen his attitude". It was added by Ciano that the President's mind is already known to Mussolini, and of Mussolini's mind, the President is doubtless aware by now.

PHILLIPS

165

Department of State Bulletin, vol. II, p. 635

Address Delivered by President Roosevelt at Charlottesville, Virginia, June 10, 1940

I notice by the program that I am asked to address the classes of 1940. I avail myself of that privilege, but I also take this very apt occasion to speak to many other classes, classes that have graduated through all the years, classes that are still in the period of study, classes not alone of the schools of learning of the Nation but classes that have come up through the great schools of experience; in other words a cross section, a cross section just as you who graduate today are a cross section of the Nation as a whole.

Every generation of young men and women in America has questions to ask the world. Most of the time they are the simple but nevertheless difficult questions, questions of work to do, opportunities to find, ambitions to satisfy.

But every now and again in the history of the Republic a different kind of question presents itself—a question that asks, not about the future of an individual or even of a generation, but about the future of the country, the future of the American people.

There was such a time at the beginning of our history—at the beginning of our history as a nation. Young people asked themselves in those days what lay ahead, not for themselves, but for the new United States.

There was such a time again in the seemingly endless years of the War between the States. Young men and young women on both sides of the line asked themselves, not what trades or professions they would enter, what lives they would make, but what was to become of the country they had known.

There is such a time again today. Again today the young men and the young women of America ask themselves with earnestness and with deep concern this same question: "What is to become of the country we know?"

Now they ask it with even greater anxiety than before. They ask, not only what the future holds for this Republic, but what the future holds for all peoples and all nations that have been living under democratic forms of government—under the free institutions of a free people.

It is understandable to all of us, I think, that they should ask this question. They read the words of those who are telling them that the ideal of individual liberty, the ideal of free franchise, the ideal of peace through justice is a decadent ideal. They read the word and hear the boast of those who say that a belief in force—force directed by self-chosen leaders—is the new and vigorous system which will overrun the earth. They have seen the ascendancy of this philosophy of force in nation after nation where free institutions and individual liberties were once maintained.

It is natural and understandable that the younger generation should first ask itself what the extension of the philosophy of force to all the world would lead to ultimately. We see today, for example, in stark reality some of the consequences of what we call the machine age.

Where control of machines has been retained in the hands of mankind as a whole, untold benefits have accrued to mankind. For mankind was then the master; and the machine was the servant.

But, in this new system of force the mastery of the machine is not in the hands of mankind. It is in the control of infinitely small groups of individuals who rule without a single one of the democratic sanctions that we have known. The machine in hands of irresponsible conquerors becomes the master; mankind is not only the servant; it is the victim too. Such mastery abandons with deliberate contempt all of the moral values to which even this young country for more than 300 years has been accustomed and dedicated.

Surely the new philosophy proves from month to month that it could have no possible conception of the way of life or the way of thought of a nation whose origins go back to Jamestown and Plymouth Rock.

And conversely, neither those who spring from that ancient stock nor those who have come hither in later years can be indifferent to the destruction of freedom in their ancestral lands across the sea.

Perception of danger, danger to our institutions, may come slowly or it may come with a rush and a shock as it has to the people of the United States in the past few months. This perception of danger, danger in a world-wide area—it has come to us clearly and overwhelmingly—we perceive the peril in a world-wide arena, an arena that may become so narrowed that only the Americas will retain the ancient faiths.

Some indeed still hold to the now somewhat obvious delusion that we of the United States can safely permit the United States to become a lone island, a lone island in a world dominated by the philosophy of force.

Such an island may be the dream of those who still talk and vote as isolationists. Such an island represents to me and to the overwhelming majority of Americans today a helpless nightmare, the helpless nightmare of a people without freedom; yes, the nightmare of a people lodged in prison, handcuffed, hungry, and fed through the bars from day to day by the contemptuous, unpitying masters of other continents.

It is natural also that we should ask ourselves how now we can prevent the building of that prison and the placing of ourselves in the midst of it.

Let us not hesitate—all of us—to proclaim certain truths. Overwhelmingly we, as a Nation—and this applies to all the other American nations—are convinced that military and naval victory for the gods of force and hate would endanger the institutions of democracy in the western world, and that equally, therefore, the whole of our sympathies lies with those nations that are giving their life blood in combat against these forces.

The people and the Government of the United States have seen with the utmost regret and with grave disquiet the decision of the Italian Government to engage in the hostilities now raging in Europe.

More than 3 months ago the Chief of the Italian Government sent me word that because of the determination of Italy to limit, so far as might be possible, the spread of the European conflict, more than 200 millions of people in the region of the Mediterranean had been enabled to escape the suffering and the devastation of war.

I informed the Chief of the Italian Government that this desire on the part of Italy to prevent the war from spreading met with full sympathy and response on the part of the Government and the people of the United States, and I expressed the earnest hope of this Government and of this people that this policy on the part of Italy might be continued. I made it clear that in the opinion of the Government of the United States any extension of hostilities in the region of the Mediterranean might result in a still greater enlargement of the scene of the conflict, the conflict in the Near East and in Africa, and that if this came to pass no one could foretell how much greater the theater of the war eventually might become.

Again on a subsequent occasion, not so long ago, recognizing that certain aspirations of Italy might form the basis of discussions between the powers most specifically concerned, I offered, in a message addressed to the Chief of the Italian Government, to send to the Governments of France and of Great Britain such specific indications of the desires of Italy to obtain readjustments with regard to her position as the Chief of the Italian Government might desire to transmit through me. While making it clear that the Government of the United States in such an event could not and would not assume responsibility for the nature of the proposals submitted nor for agreements which might thereafter be reached, I proposed that if Italy would refrain from entering the war I would be willing to ask assurances from the other powers concerned that they would faithfully execute any agreement so reached and that Italy's voice in any future peace conference would have the same authority as if Italy had actually taken part in the war, as a belligerent.

Unfortunately, unfortunately to the regret of all of us and to the regret of humanity, the Chief of the Italian Government was unwilling to accept the procedure suggested, and he has made no counterproposal.

This Government directed its efforts to doing what it could to work for the preservation of peace in the Mediterranean area, and it likewise expressed its willingness to endeavor to cooperate with the Government of Italy when the appropriate occasion arose for the creation of a more stable world order, through the reduction of armaments and through the construction of a more liberal international economic system which would assure to all powers equality of opportunity in the world's markets and in the securing of raw materials on equal terms.

I have likewise, of course, felt it necessary in my communications to Signor Mussolini to express the concern of the Government of the United States because of the fact that any extension of the war in the region of the Mediterranean would inevitably result in great prejudice to the ways of life and government and to the trade and commerce of all of the American republics.

The Government of Italy has now chosen to preserve what it terms its "freedom of action" and to fulfill what it states are its promises to Germany. In so doing it has manifested disregard for the rights and security of other nations, disregard for the lives of the peoples of those nations which are directly threatened by this spread of the war; and has evidenced its unwillingness to find the means through pacific negotiations for the satisfaction of what it believes are its legitimate aspirations.

On this tenth day of June 1940, the hand that held the dagger has struck it into the back of its neighbor.

On this tenth day of June 1940, in this University founded by the first great American teacher of democracy, we send forth our prayers and our hopes to those beyond the seas who are maintaining with magnificent valor their battle for freedom.

In our, in our unity, in our American unity, we will pursue two obvious and simultaneous courses; we will extend to the opponents of force the material resources of this Nation and, at the same time, we will harness and speed up the use of those resources in order that we ourselves in the Americas may have equipment and training equal to the task of any emergency and every defense.

All roads leading to the accomplishment of these objectives must be kept clear of obstructions. We will not slow down or detour. Signs and signals call for speed—full speed ahead.

Yes, it is right that each new generation should ask questions. But in recent months the principal question has been somewhat simplified. Once more the future of the Nation, the future of the American people is at stake.

We need not and we will not, in any way, abandon our continuing effort to make democracy work within our borders. Yes, we still insist on the need for vast improvements in our own social and economic life.

But that, that is a component part of national defense itself.

The program unfolds swiftly, and into that program will fit the responsibility and the opportunity of every man and woman in the land to preserve his and her heritage in days of peril.

I call for effort, courage, sacrifice, devotion. Granting the love of freedom, all of these are possible.

And—and the love of freedom is still fierce, still steady in the Nation today.

166

Department of State Bulletin, vol. II, p. 638

The President of the French Council of Ministers (*Reynaud*)
To President Roosevelt [51]

PARIS, June 10, 1940—6 p.m.
[Received 10:13 p.m.]

MR. PRESIDENT: I wish first to express to you my gratitude for the generous aid that you have decided to give us in aviation and armament.

For six days and six nights our divisions have been fighting without one hour of rest against an army which has a crushing superiority in numbers and material. Today the enemy is almost at the gates of Paris.

We shall fight in front of Paris; we shall fight behind Paris; we shall close ourselves in one of our provinces to fight and if we should be driven out of it we shall establish ourselves in North Africa to continue the fight and if necessary in our American possessions.

---

[51] Transmitted in a telegram from the Ambassador in France (Bullitt).

A portion of the government has already left Paris. I am making ready to leave for the front. That will be to intensify the struggle with all the forces which we still have and not to abandon the struggle.

May I ask you, Mr. President, to explain all this yourself to your people to all the citizens of the United States saying to them that we are determined to sacrifice ourselves in the struggle that we are carrying on for all free men.

This very hour another dictatorship has stabbed France in the back. Another frontier is threatened. A naval war will begin.

You have replied generously to the appeal which I made to you a few days ago across the Atlantic. Today this 10th of June 1940 it is my duty to ask you for new and even larger assistance.

At the same time that you explain this situation to the men and women of America, I beseech you to declare publicly that the United States will give the Allies aid and material support by all means "short of an expeditionary force". I beseech you to do this before it is too late. I know the gravity of such a gesture. Its very gravity demands that it should not be made too late.

You said to us yourself on the 5th of October 1937: "I am compelled and you are compelled to look ahead. The peace, the freedom and the security of 90% of the population of the world is being jeopardized by the remaining 10% who are threatening a breakdown of all international order and law.

"Surely the 90% who want to live in peace under law and in accordance with moral standards that have received almost trusty acceptance through the centuries, can and must find some way to make their will prevail."

The hour has now come for these.

PAUL REYNAUD

167

740.0011 European War 1939/3770A

President Roosevelt to the President of the French Council Of Ministers (Reynaud), June 13, 1940 [52]

[Telegram]

Your message of June 10 has moved me very deeply. As I have already stated to you and to Mr. Churchill, this Government is doing everything in its power to make available to the Allied Governments the material they so urgently require, and our efforts to do still more

---

[52] Transmitted in a telegram to the Ambassador in France (Bullitt).

are being redoubled. This is so because of our faith in and our support of the ideals for which the Allies are fighting.

The magnificent resistance of the French and British armies has profoundly impressed the American people.

I am personally particularly impressed by your declaration that France will continue to fight on behalf of democracy even if it means slow withdrawal, even to North Africa and the Atlantic. It is most important to remember that the French and British fleets continue mastery of the Atlantic and other oceans; also to remember that vital materials from the outside world are necessary to maintain all armies.

I am also greatly heartened by what Prime Minister Churchill said a few days ago about the continued resistance of the British Empire and that determination would seem to apply equally to the great French Empire all over the world. Naval power in world affairs still carries the lessons of history, as Admiral Darlan well knows.

168

740.0011 European War 1939/3790

The President of the French Council of Ministers (Reynaud)
To President Roosevelt, June 14, 1940 [53]

[Telegram]

MR. PRESIDENT: I thank you for having published in America the message I sent you on June 10. I told you then that for six days and six nights our troops had been fighting without an hour of respite, and at one against three, with war material five times less powerful.

Four days of bloody fighting have gone by since then. Our army is now cut into several parts. Our divisions are decimated. Generals are commanding battalions. The Reichswehr has just entered Paris. We are going to attempt to withdraw our exhausted forces in order to fight new battles. It is doubtful, since they are at grips with an enemy which is constantly throwing in fresh troops, that this can be accomplished.

At the most tragic hour of its history France must choose.

Will she continue to sacrifice her youth into a hopeless struggle?

Will her Government leave the national territory so as not to give itself up to the enemy and in order to be able to continue the struggle on the sea and in North Africa? Will the whole country then live abandoned abating itself under the shadow of Nazi domination with all that that means for its body and its soul?

---

[53] Transmitted in a telegram from the Ambassador in France (Bullitt).

Or will France ask Hitler for conditions of an armistice?

We can choose the first way, that of resistance only if a chance of victory appears in the distance and if a light shines at the end of the tunnel.

In the present situation in spite of the weakening of the enemy's forces due to the sacrifice of the French army the defeat of England, our loyal ally, left to her own resources, appears possible if not probable.

From that time on France can continue the struggle only if American intervention reverses the situation by making an Allied victory certain.

The only chance of saving the French nation, vanguard of democracies, and through her to save England, by whose side France could then remain with her powerful navy, is to throw into the balance, this very day the weight of American power.

It is the only chance also of keeping Hitler, after he has destroyed France, and then England from attacking America thus renewing the fight of the Horatii against the three Curiatii.

I know that the declaration of war does not depend on you alone.

But I must tell you at this hour, so grave in our history as in yours, that if you cannot give to France in the hours to come the certainty that the United States will come into the war within a very short time, the fate of the world will change. Then you will see France go under like a drowning man and disappear after having cast a last look towards the land of liberty from which she awaited salvation.

PAUL REYNAUD

169

Department of State Bulletin, vol. II, p. 639

President Roosevelt to the President of the French Council Of Ministers (Reynaud)

[Telegram]

JUNE 15, 1940.

I am sending you this reply to your message of yesterday which I am sure you will realize has received the most earnest, as well as the most friendly, study on our part.

First of all, let me reiterate the ever-increasing admiration with which the American people and their Government are viewing the resplendent courage with which the French armies are resisting the invaders on French soil.

I wish also to reiterate in the most emphatic terms that, making every possible effort under present conditions, the Government of the United States has made it possible for the Allied armies to obtain during the weeks that have just passed airplanes, artillery and munitions of many kinds and that this Government so long as the Allied governments continue to resist will redouble its efforts in this direction. I believe it is possible to say that every week that goes by will see additional matériel on its way to the Allied nations.

In accordance with its policy not to recognize the results of conquest of territory acquired through military aggression, the Government of the United States will not consider as valid any attempts to infringe by force the independence and territorial integrity of France.

In these hours which are so heart-rending for the French people and yourself, I send you the assurances of my utmost sympathy and I can further assure you that so long as the French people continue in defense of their liberty which constitutes the cause of popular institutions throughout the world, so long will they rest assured that matériel and supplies will be sent to them from the United States in ever-increasing quantities and kinds.

I know that you will understand that these statements carry with them no implication of military commitments. Only the Congress can make such commitments.

170

740.0011 European War 1939/2691-5⁄7A

The Secretary of State to the Ambassador Near the French Government At Bordeaux (Biddle) [54]

WASHINGTON, June 17, 1940—5 p.m.

3. The President desires that you obtain immediately an interview with Admiral Darlan and subsequently, if possible, with the Minister for Foreign Affairs and state that the views of this Government with regard to the disposition of the French fleet have been made very clear to the French Government on previous occasions. The President desires you to say that in the opinion of this Government, should the French Government, before concluding any armistice with the Germans, fail to see that the fleet is kept out of the hands of her opponents, the French Government will be pursuing a policy which will fatally impair the preservation of the French Empire and the eventual restoration of French independence and autonomy. Further-

---

[51] Transmitted in a telegram to the Consul at Bordeaux.

more, should the French Government fail to take these steps and permit the French fleet to be surrendered to Germany, the French Government will permanently lose the friendship and good-will of the Government of the United States.

Hull

171

740.0011 European War 1939/2691-6⁄7

The Ambassador Near the French Government at Bordeaux (Biddle)
To the Secretary of State

[Telegram]

BORDEAUX, June 18, 1940—noon.
[Received 11:25 p.m.]

20. Your No. 3, June 17, 5 p.m. to Consul and my flash via Press Wireless that message had been delivered to Admiral Darlan.

I called the Minister for Foreign Affairs from the Council of Ministers which is now meeting to consider this and other questions of grave importance. He said that Darlan had already placed your message before the government. He wished to assure me in the name of the government in the most solemn manner that the French fleet would never (repeat never) be surrendered to the enemy: "La question ne se pose pas". He must tell me though that the last sentence of the message had "deeply pained" the French Government (I believe, however, that in spite of this natural feeling the effect thereof was highly salutary at this juncture).

Baudoin added that he could not (repeat not) however, say that the French fleet would join the British fleet; it might be sent overseas or it might be sunk. That question is now before the Council of Ministers. I urged with all possible emphasis that the fleet be moved to safety rather than destroyed.

No reply has yet been received to the request for armistice terms. He said that he understood from the Spanish Government that the answer "might be forthcoming tomorrow".

The Germans are now in the outskirts of Lyons. Herriot tells me the city was bombed last night. The atmosphere of tension and anxiety in Bordeaux is naturally increasing.

BIDDLE

172

Department of State Bulletin, vol. II, p. 681

Press Release Issued by the Department of State on June 19, 1940

The Secretary of State, Mr. Cordell Hull, on June 17 instructed the American Chargé at Berlin and the American Ambassador at Rome to send in writing to the Minister for Foreign Affairs of Germany and to the Minister for Foreign Affairs of Italy, respectively, the following communication in the name of the Government of the United States:

"The Government of the United States is informed that the Government of France has requested of the German Government the terms of an armistice.

"The Government of the United States feels it desirable, in order to avoid any possible misunderstanding, to inform Your Excellency that in accordance with its traditional policy relating to the Western Hemisphere, the United States would not recognize any transfer, and would not acquiesce in any attempt to transfer, any geographic region of the Western Hemisphere from one non-American power to another non-American power.[55]

"I avail myself [etc.]"

---

[55] Subsequently the Senate and the House of Representatives adopted a joint resolution (55 Stat. 133) reading as follows:

Whereas our traditional policy has been to consider any attempt on the part of non-American powers to extend their system to any portion of this hemisphere as dangerous to the peace and safety not only of this country but of the other American republics; and

Whereas the American republics agreed at the Inter-American Conference for the Maintenance of Peace held in Buenos Aires in 1936 and at the Eighth International Conference of American States held in Lima in 1938 to consult with one another in the event that the peace, security, or territorial integrity of any American republic should be threatened; and

Whereas the Meeting of the Foreign Ministers of the American Republics at Panama October 3, 1939, resolved "That in case any geographic region of America subject to the jurisdiction of any non-American state should be obliged to change its sovereignty and there should result therefrom a danger to the security of the American Continent, a consultative meeting such as the one now being held will be convoked with the urgency that the case may require": Therefore be it

Resolved by the Senate and House of Representatives of the United States of America in Congress assembled, (1) That the United States would not recognize any transfer, and would not acquiesce in any attempt to transfer, any geographic region of this hemisphere from one non-American power to another non-American power; and

(2) That if such transfer or attempt to transfer should appear likely, the United States shall, in addition to other measures, immediately consult with the other American republics to determine upon the steps which should be taken to safeguard their common interests.

Approved, April 10, 1941.

The Governments of France, Great Britain, and the Netherlands have been informed in the same sense.

173

Department of State Bulletin, vol. II, p. 683

Address Delivered by the Secretary of State at Harvard University, June 20, 1940

I am deeply conscious of the honor which was conferred on me this morning. I am happy to visit this magnificent campus. From it, throughout our country's national existence, generations of leaders have gone to every corner of the land bearing the torch of truth and of humanity. There is no more fitting site from which to survey the great problems and issues that now confront this Nation.

These are black days for the human race. These are ominous days for us in this country.

There are at work in the world today powerful forces the significance of which no individual and no nation can ignore without falling into a position of the gravest danger and of the utmost jeopardy. These forces are not new in the experience of mankind. They rose on many occasions in the past and, for varying periods and with varying intensity, held sway over human affairs. They spring today from the same source from which they have always sprung in the past—from godless and soulless lust for power which seeks to hold men in physical slavery and spiritual degradation and to displace a system of peaceful and orderly relations among nations by the anarchy of wanton violence and brute force.

Fortunately, these forces have not triumphed in every instance in which they have challenged human freedom and interrupted the advance of civilization. There are times in the lives of individuals and of nations when realization of mortal peril, far from making men recoil in horror and defeat, strengthens and ennobles the soul, gives indomitability to will and to courage, and leads to victory through suffering and sacrifice. History records many heartening instances when in this manner the forces of conquest, violence, and oppression were hurled back, and the onward march of civilized man was resumed.

Never before have these forces flung so powerful a challenge to freedom and civilized progress as they are flinging today. Never before has there been a more desperate need for men and nations who love freedom and cherish the tenets of modern civilization, to gather into an unconquerable defensive force every element of their spiritual and material resources, every ounce of their moral and physical strength.

We, Americans of today, have behind us a century and a half of national existence, to which we point, with justifiable pride, as a successful experiment in democracy and human freedom. That experiment began when a resplendent generation of Americans resolved to stake on its success their lives, their fortunes, and their sacred honor. With unshakable faith in their cause and an unswerving determination to make it prevail, they risked their all for the creation of a nation in which each citizen would have—as his inalienable rights—liberty under law, equality of opportunity, freedom of thought and of conscience. Those Americans believed unreservedly that in a nation founded upon these great principles, the people could enjoy individually a far greater measure of well-being and happiness than is possible under any other form of political and social organization, and could achieve collectively a degree of internal strength and unity of purpose necessary to insure for the Nation itself the inalienable right to manage its own affairs solely by the will of its own people.

A century and a half of active and, at times, tumultuous history have vindicated this faith. The Nation which that generation of Americans founded lives today and has grown great and powerful beyond the fondest dreams of its founders. This has come about because, through the stresses and strains of internal adjustment and external conflict, succeeding generations of Americans have never faltered in their devotion to that faith and have rededicated themselves to it, freely and reverently; because in each generation there was sufficient resoluteness of spirit, tenacity of purpose, moral and physical courage, and capacity for unselfish sacrifice to accept individual and collective responsibility for the preservation of the principles upon which this Nation was founded and upon which it has built its way of life.

Our American history has not been achieved in isolation from the rest of mankind; there is no more dangerous folly than to think that its achievements can be preserved in isolation. It has been a part of a vast movement—in the Old World, as well as the New—which has opened new vistas in the destiny of man; which has carried human progress to new and exalted heights; which has, through scientific attainment, lessened the tyranny over man of the blind forces of nature; which, as never before, has expanded for the human race as a whole the opportunity for freedom of mind and of spirit. To this great stream of new ideas, new attainments, new cultural values, we have made our contribution; and we ourselves, in turn, have been nourished by it.

The massed forces of lust for tyrannical power are directed today against the very bases of the way of life which has come to be the cherished ideal of a preponderant majority of mankind—against the moral, spiritual, social, political, and economic foundations of modern civilization. Nation after nation has been crushed into surrender, overrun and enslaved by the exercise of brute force combined with fraud and guile. And as the dismal darkness descends upon more and more of the earth's surface, as its menacing shadow falls blacker and blacker athwart our continent, the very instinct of self-preservation bids us beware.

We have the power to meet that menace successfully, if we, at this time, face the task which is before us in the same spirit in which former generations of Americans met the crises that confronted them in their times. We need material means of defense. These means we are determined to create, and we are creating them. But more than that is needed.

Men will defend to the utmost only things in which they have complete faith. Those who took part in the struggle by which freedom was won for this Nation would have found its hardships unbearable if they had not been imbued with transcendent faith in the things for which they fought. The task of preserving and defending freedom requires at times as stern and determined a struggle as the task of achieving freedom, and as firm a faith.

No more vital test has ever confronted the American people than that which confronts it today. There are difficult and dangerous times ahead. Our national independence and our cherished institutions are not immune from the challenge of the lust for power that already stalks so much of the earth's surface. Unprecedented effort and heavy sacrifices will be required of us as the price of preserving, for ourselves and for our posterity, the kind of America that has been fostered and preserved for us by the vigilance, courage, and sacrifice of those who preceded us. We shall succeed if we retain unimpaired the most precious heritage which they bequeathed us—an unshakable faith in the everlasting worth of freedom and honor, of truth and justice, of intellectual and spiritual integrity; and an immutable determination to give our all, if need be, for the preservation of our way of life.

Without that faith and that determination, no material means of defense will suffice. With them, we need fear no enemy outside or within our borders.

In times of grave crises, there are always some who fall a prey to doubt and unreasoning fear; some who seek refuge in cynicism and narrow self-interest; some who wrap themselves in the treacherous cloak of complacency. All these are dangers that lie within us. All these impair the faith and weaken the determination without which freedom cannot prevail.

Each and every one of us must search his mind and his heart for these signs of fatal weakness. The stern realities of the crisis which is upon us call, as never before, for vision and for loyalty. They call for all the strength of hand, of mind, and of spirit that we can muster. They call for self-reliance, for self-restraint, for self-imposed and freely accepted discipline. They call for the kind of national unity that can be achieved only by free men, invincible in their resolve that human freedom must not perish. They call for unselfish service today if we are to win through to a secure and bright tomorrow.

A responsibility seldom equalled in gravity and danger rests upon each and every one of us. Neglect or delay in assuming it, willingly and fully, would place in mortal danger our way of life and the sacred cause of human freedom. Were we to fail in that responsibility, we would fail ourselves; we would fail the generations that went before us; we would fail the generations that are to come after us; we would fail mankind; we would fail God.

I am supremely confident that we shall not fail. I am certain that in the minds and hearts of our people still—still—lie welling springs— inexhaustible and indestructible—of faith in the things we cherish, of courage and determination to defend them, of sacrificial devotion, of unbreakable unity of purpose. I am certain that, however great the hardships and the trials which loom ahead, our America will endure and the cause of human freedom will triumph.

174

711.94/1581

Memorandum by the Secretary of State Regarding a Conversation With The British Ambassador (Lothian) and the Australian Minister (Casey)

[Extracts]

[WASHINGTON,] June 28, 1940.

I said that this country has been progressively bringing economic pressure to bear on Japan since last summer, now a year, and I enumerated the different steps and methods, which are familiar to all, and added that our fleet is now somewhere in the Pacific near Hawaii. I said that we have and are doing everything possible short of a serious risk of actual military hostilities to keep the Japanese situation stabilized, and that this course during the past year is the best evidence of our intentions and activities in the future.

As to . . . a joint effort to bring about peace between Japan and China, I explained . . . that this Government would only make two points in that connection, one, the principles underlying the Japanese new order in eastern Asia policy as it is being practiced would need negativing or at least serious modifying, and, second, that no properties or interests of China be offered to Japan by Great Britain or the United States, or, in other words, that we do not make peace with Japan at the expense of China nor at the expense of the principles which were contained in my statement to Japan and 55 other Governments in July, 1937, when Japan moved into China for the purpose of its conquest.

C[ORDELL] H[ULL]

175

Department of State Bulletin, vol. III, p. 3

Statement by the Secretary of State, July 5, 1940

The American Chargé d'Affaires in Berlin has communicated to the Department the text of a note dated July 1, which he has received from the German Minister of Foreign Affairs.

The note in question refers to the note delivered by the American Chargé d'Affairs under instructions of the Government of the United State on June 18, in which this Government informed the Government of the German Reich that it would not recognize any transfer of a geographical region of the Western Hemisphere from one non-American power to another non-American power, and that it would not acquiesce in any attempt to undertake such transfer.

The German Minister of Foreign Affairs states that the Government of the German Reich is unable to perceive for what reason the Government of the United States of America has addressed this communication to the Reich Government. He states that in contrast with other countries, especially in contrast with England and France, Germany has no territorial possessions in the American Continent, and has given no occasion whatever for the assumption that it intends to acquire such possessions, and he asserts that thus insofar as Germany is concerned, the communication addressed to the Reich Government is without object.

The German Minister of Foreign Affairs continues by remarking that in this case the interpretation of the Monroe Doctrine implicit in the communication of the Government of the United States would amount to conferring upon some European countries the right to possess territories in the Western Hemisphere and not to other European countries. He states that it is obvious that such an interpretation would be untenable. He concludes by remarking that apart from this, the Reich Government would like to point out again on this occasion that the nonintervention in the affairs of the American Continent by European nations which is demanded by the Monroe Doctrine can in principle be legally valid only on condition that the American nations for their part do not interfere in the affairs of the European Continent.

The foregoing is the substance of the German note.

I feel that no useful purpose will be served at this time for this Government to undertake to make any further communication to the Government of the German Reich on the subject matter of the communication above quoted.

The fundamental questions involved are entirely clear to all of the peoples of the American republics, and undoubtedly as well to the majority of the governments and peoples in the rest of the world.

The Monroe Doctrine is solely a policy of self-defense, which is intended to preserve the independence and integrity of the Americas. It was, and is, designed to prevent aggression in this hemisphere on the part of any non-American power, and likewise to make impossible any further extension to this hemisphere of any non-American system of government imposed from without. It contains within it not the slightest vestige of any implication, much less assumption, of hegemony on the part of the United States. It never has resembled, and it does not today resemble, policies which appear to be arising in other geographical areas of the world, which are alleged to be similar to the Monroe Doctrine, but which, instead of resting on the sole policies of self-defense and of respect for existing sovereignties, as does the Monroe Doctrine, would in reality seem to be only the pretext for the carrying out of conquest by the sword, of military occupation, and of complete economic and political domination by certain powers of other free and independent peoples.

The Monroe Doctrine has, of course, not the remotest connection with the fact that certain European nations exercise sovereignty over colonies in the Western Hemisphere and that certain other European nations do not. This situation existed before the Monroe Doctrine was proclaimed. The Doctrine did not undertake to interfere with the existing situation, but did announce that further incursions would not be tolerated. It made clear that the future transfer of existing possessions to another non-American state would be regarded as inimical to the interests of this hemisphere. This has become a basic policy of the Government of the United States. As already stated in the communication addressed to the German Government by this Government under date of June 18, the Government of the United States will neither recognize nor acquiesce in the transfer to a non-American power of geographical regions in this hemisphere now possessed by some other non-American power.

The Government of the United States pursues a policy of nonparticipation and of noninvolvement in the purely political affairs of Europe. It will, however, continue to cooperate, as it has cooperated in the past, with all other nations, whenever the policies of such nations make it possible, and whenever it believes that such efforts are practicable and in its own best interests, for the purpose of promoting economic, commercial, and social rehabilitation, and of advancing the cause of international law and order, of which the entire world stands so tragically in need today.

176

Department of State Bulletin, vol. III, p. 36

Statement by the Secretary of State, July 16, 1940

The Secretary of State, in reply to inquiries by press correspondents for comment in regard to reports that, at the instance of the Japanese Government, the British Government would prohibit temporarily the movement of certain commodities through Burma into China over what is known as the Burma Route, said that this Government has a legitimate interest in the keeping open of arteries of commerce in every part of the world and considers that action such as this, if taken, and such as was taken recently in relation to the Indochina railway would constitute unwarranted interpositions of obstacles to world trade.

177

Department of State Bulletin, vol. III, p. 136

Declaration of Reciprocal Assistance and Cooperation for the Defense Of the Nations of the Americas, Habana, July 30, 1940

The Second Meeting of the Ministers of Foreign Affairs of the American Republics

Declares:

That any attempt on the part of a non-American State against the integrity or inviolability of the territory, the sovereignty or the political independence of an American State shall be considered as an act of aggression against the States which sign this declaration.

In case acts of aggression are committed or should there be reason to believe that an act of aggression is being prepared by a non-American nation against the integrity or inviolability of the territory, the sovereign or the political independence of an American nation, the nations signatory to the present declaration will consult among themselves in order to agree upon the measure it may be advisable to take.

All the signatory nations, or two or more of them, according to circumstances, shall proceed to negotiate the necessary complementary agreements so as to organize cooperation for defense and the assistance that they shall lend each other in the event of aggressions such as those referred to in this declaration.

178

Department of State Bulletin, vol. III, p. 103

Statement by the Secretary of State, August 6, 1940

The strong belief of the representatives of the 21 American nations at the recent Habana Meeting was that the military and other sinister activities on the part of some nations in other large areas of the world present real possibilities of danger to the American republics. It was universally recognized that a threat to any important part of the Americas means a threat to each and all of the American nations. It was, therefore, agreed that full and adequate preparations for continental defense could not be taken too soon if the threatened danger from abroad was to be checked and terminated. It was also the unanimous view at Habana that the prompt strengthening of unity and solidarity for the purpose of continental defense and for its implementation by concrete programs supported by the 21 nations was indispensable to the safety, security, peace, and welfare of this hemisphere.

There was general agreement that if the peaceful nations of Europe had thus promptly organized themselves for self-defense on the most effective cooperative basis, the chances are that their situation and that of Europe would be vastly different today. Instead, many of those countries complacently relied upon utterances of peaceful purpose and upon their own neutrality to safeguard them against the mighty forces of invasion, conquest, and destruction. Some of them have been overrun and destroyed by the ruthless invader. Their fate should be a tragic lesson to us.

The vast forces of lawlessness, conquest, and destruction are still moving across the earth like a savage and dangerous animal at large. By their very nature, those forces will not stop unless and until they recognize that there exists unbreakable resistance.

At Habana we forged new instrumentalities of continental defense. These will be of vast importance to our Nation and to every American nation. But there are other and immense tasks still before us.

I would greatly prefer to say that we are safe in this country and in this hemisphere from outside danger. But I am firmly convinced that what is taking place today in many areas of the earth is a relentless attempt to transform the civilized world as we have known it into a world in which lawlessness, violence, and force will reign supreme, as they did a thousand years ago. The people of this country cannot recognize too soon this fact and its overwhelming significance for our national safety and for the maintenance of our national institutions.

The one and only sure way for our Nation to avoid being drawn into serious trouble or actual war by the wild and destructive forces now abroad elsewhere in the world and to command respect for its rights and interests abroad is for our people to become thoroughly conscious of the possibilities of danger, to make up their minds that we must continue to arm, and to arm to such an extent that the forces of conquest and ruin will not dare make an attack on us or on any part of this hemisphere. To this end, each citizen must be ready and willing for real sacrifice of time and of substance and for hard personal service. In the face of terrific problems and conditions, and until the present serious threats and dangers have disappeared, we cannot pursue complacently the course of our customary normal life.

I feel constrained thus to offer my views in the light of what is already a dangerously widespread movement for world conquest and for the destruction of most of the worthwhile things which civilization has given the human race.

179

Department of State Bulletin, vol. III, p. 201

Message of President Roosevelt to the Congress, September 3, 1940

I transmit herewith for the information of the Congress notes exchanged between the British Ambassador at Washington and the Secretary of State on September 2, 1940, under which this Government has acquired the right to lease naval and air bases in Newfoundland, and in the islands of Bermuda, the Bahamas, Jamaica, St. Lucia, Trinidad, and Antigua, and in British Guiana; also a copy of an opinion of the Attorney General dated August 27, 1940, regarding my authority to consummate this arrangement.

The right to bases in Newfoundland and Bermuda are gifts—generously given and gladly received. The other bases mentioned have been acquired in exchange for fifty of our over-age destroyers.

This is not inconsistent in any sense with our status of peace. Still less is it a threat against any nation. It is an epochal and far-reaching act of preparation for continental defense in the face of grave danger.

Preparation for defense is an inalienable prerogative of a sovereign state. Under present circumstances this exercise of sovereign right is essential to the maintenance of our peace and safety. This is the most important action in the reinforcement of our national defense that has been taken since the Louisiana Purchase. Then as now, considerations of safety from overseas attack were fundamental.

The value to the Western Hemisphere of these outposts of security is beyond calculation. Their need has long been recognized by our country, and especially by those primarily charged with the duty of charting and organizing our own naval and military defense. They are essential to the protection of the Panama Canal, Central America, the Northern portion of South America, The Antilles, Canada, Mexico, and our own Eastern and Gulf Seaboards. Their consequent importance in hemispheric defense is obvious. For these reasons I have taken advantage of the present opportunity to acquire them.

FRANKLIN D. ROOSEVELT

[Enclosures]

BRITISH EMBASSY,
Washington, D. C., September 2, 1940.

SIR:

I have the honour under instructions from His Majesty's Principal Secretary of State for Foreign Affairs to inform you that in view of the friendly and sympathetic interest of His Majesty's Government in the United Kingdom in the national security of the United States and their desire to strengthen the ability of the United States to cooperate effectively with the other nations of the Americas in the defence of the Western Hemisphere, His Majesty's Government will secure the grant to the Government of the United States, freely and without consideration, of the lease for immediate establishment and use of

naval and air bases and facilities for entrance thereto and the operation and protection thereof, on the Avalon Peninsula and on the southern coast of Newfoundland, and on the east coast and on the Great Bay
of Bermuda.

Furthermore, in view of the above and in view of the desire of the
United States to acquire additional air and naval bases in the Caribbean
and in British Guiana, and without endeavouring to place a monetary
or commercial value upon the many tangible and intangible rights
and properties involved, His Majesty's Government will make available
to the United States for immediate establishment and use naval and
air bases and facilities for entrance thereto and the operation and
protection thereof, on the eastern side of the Bahamas, the southern
coast of Jamaica, the western coast of St. Lucia, the west coast of
Trinidad in the Gulf of Paria, in the island of Antigua and in British
Guiana within fifty miles of Georgetown, in exchange for naval and
military equipment and material which the United States Government will transfer to His Majesty's Government.

All the bases and facilities referred to in the preceding paragraphs
will be leased to the United States for a period of ninety-nine years,
free from all rent and charges other than such compensation to be
mutually agreed on to be paid by the United States in order to com-
pensate the owners of private property for loss by expropriation or
damage arising out of the establishment of the bases and facilities
in question.

His Majesty's Government, in the leases to be agreed upon, will
grant to the United States for the period of the leases all the rights,
power, and authority within the bases leased, and within the limits of
the territorial waters and air spaces adjacent to or in the vicinity of
such bases, necessary to provide access to and defence of such bases,
and appropriate provisions for their control.

Without prejudice to the above-mentioned rights of the United
States authorities and their jurisdiction within the leased areas, the
adjustment and reconciliation between the jurisdiction of the authorities of the United States within these areas and the jurisdiction of
the authorities of the territories in which these areas are situated,
shall be determined by common agreement.

The exact location and bounds of the aforesaid bases, the necessary
seaward, coast and anti-aircraft defences, the location of sufficient
military garrisons, stores and other necessary auxiliary facilities
shall be determined by common agreement.

His Majesty's Government are prepared to designate immediately experts to meet with experts of the United States for these purposes. Should these experts be unable to agree in any particular situation, except in the case of Newfoundland and Bermuda, the matter shall be settled by the Secretary of State of the United States and His Majesty's Secretary of State for Foreign Affairs.

I have [etc.] LOTHIAN

The Honourable CORDELL HULL,
    Secretary of State of the United States,
        Washington, D.C.

DEPARTMENT OF STATE,
Washington, September 2, 1940.

EXCELLENCY:

I have received your note of September 2, 1940, of which the text is as follows:

[Here follows text of the note printed above.]

I am directed by the President to reply to your note as follows:

The Government of the United States appreciates the declarations and the generous action of His Majesty's Government as contained in your communication which are destined to enhance the national security of the United States and greatly to strengthen its ability to cooperate effectively with the other nations of the Americas in the defense of the Western Hemisphere. It therefore gladly accepts the proposals.

The Government of the United States will immediately designate experts to meet with experts designated by His Majesty's Government to determine upon the exact location of the naval and air bases mentioned in your communication under acknowledgment.

In consideration of the declarations above quoted, the Government of the United States will immediately transfer to His Majesty's Government fifty United States Navy destroyers generally referred to as the twelve hundred-ton type.

Accept [etc.] CORDELL HULL

His Excellency
    The Right Honorable
        THE MARQUESS OF LOTHIAN, C.H.,
            British Ambassador.

180

Department of State Bulletin, vol. III, p. 196

Press Release Issued by the Department of State on September 7, 1940

The Secretary of State on September 6 sent the following instruction to diplomatic missions of the United States in all the other American republics:

"It is desired that you formally notify the Government to which you are accredited that the United States has acquired the right to lease naval and air bases in Newfoundland, and in the islands of Bermuda, the Bahamas, Jamaica, St. Lucia, Trinidad, and Antigua, and in British Guiana.

"The Government of the United States has taken this step to strengthen its ability not only to defend the United States but in order the more effectively to cooperate with the other American republics in the common defense of the hemisphere.

"The resulting facilities at these bases will, of course, be made available alike to all American republics on the fullest cooperative basis for the common defense of the hemisphere and in entire harmony with the spirit of the pronouncements made and the understandings reached at the conferences of Lima, Panama, and Habana."

181

840.51 Frozen Credits/570

Memorandum by the Secretary of State Regarding a Conversation With the French Ambassador (Henry-Haye)

[Extracts]

[WASHINGTON,] September 11, 1940.

The new French Ambassador called to present his credentials and incidentally to have a general discussion regarding several phases of international affairs.

I said that a number of us connected with this Government, including the President, myself and other associates, have for several years pursued the fixed policy of basing all of our utterances and actions on the assumption that Mr. Hitler was out to become the ruthless and utterly destructive conqueror of Europe, and that the Japanese military clique was bent on the same course in the Pacific area from Hawaii to Siam; that from the time Mr. Norman Davis came back from the Disarmament Conference and reported that the German and Italian Governments could no longer be expected to deal seriously with the question of disarmament, he, myself and others have been urging increased armaments here, and this goes back over a four to five-year period.

C[ORDELL] H[ULL]

182

894.00/957

The Ambassador in Japan (Grew) to the Secretary of State

[Extract of telegram ; Paraphrase]

TOKYO, September 12, 1940—9 p.m.

827. [Received September 12—7 p.m.]

2. The circumstances and the situation which led to the exploratory conversations with the former foreign minister and to the recommendations that steps toward the negotiation of a new commercial treaty with Japan be considered obviously have now passed. It is my earnest hope that there will come a time when I shall feel that I am justified in renewing these relations but with the fall of the Yonai cabinet and the radical alteration of the outlook and policy of the present set-up in Japan it would appear to be futile and unwise that we take any further initiative in proposing measures of conciliation at the present time.

3. Whatever the intentions of the present Japanese Government may be there cannot be any doubt that the military and other elements in Japan see in the present world situation a "golden opportunity" to carry their dreams of expansion into effect; the German victories, like strong wine, have gone to their heads; they have believed implicitly until recently in Great Britain's defeat; they have argued that the war will probably be ended in a quick German victory and that Japan's position in Greater East Asia should be consolidated while Germany is still agreeable and before Japan might be robbed of her far-flung control in the Far East by the eventual hypothetical strengthening of the German naval power; although carefully watching the attitude of the United States they have discounted effective opposition on our part. It has been and is doubtful that the saner heads in and out of the government will be able to control these elements.

4. However, now a gradual change can be sensed in the outburst of exhilaration which greeted the inception of the new government. It is beginning to be seen by the Japanese Government, the army, the navy, and the public, that Germany may not defeat Great Britain after all, a possibility which I have constantly emphasized in the plainest language to my Japanese contacts and now, in addition to that dawning realization, they see that Britain and the United States are steadily drawing closer together in mutual defense measures with the American support of the British fleet by the transfer of fifty

destroyers and with our acquisition of naval bases in British Atlantic possessions. Reports are being heard of our rapid construction of a two-ocean Navy and of our consideration of strengthening our Pacific naval bases and they even hear rumors that we will eventually use Singapore. Japanese consciousness is logically being affected by these rumors and developments. They tend on the one hand to emphasize the potential danger facing Japan from the United States and Great Britain eventually acting together in positive action (Japan has long appreciated the danger of combined Anglo-American measures as evidenced by the efforts to avoid the simultaneous irritation of these two countries) or from the United States acting alone. They furnish cogent arguments on the other hand for those Japanese elements who seek political and economic security by securing raw material sources and markets entirely within Japanese control. In regard to Germany, it is beginning to be questioned by the Japanese whether even a victorious Germany would not furnish a new hazard to their program of expansion both in China and in their advance to the south. Meanwhile, an uncertain factor in their calculations is always the future attitude and position of Russia. They are beginning to be concerned by these various considerations. High-powered diplomacy, particularly in the Dutch East Indies, will continue. But the fact that the Japanese military forces could be restrained even temporarily by the government from their plans for a headlong invasion of Indo-China denotes a degree of caution which I have no doubt was influenced partially at least by the American attitude. Until the world situation, particularly the position of the United States, becomes clearer the "nibbling policy" appears likely to continue.

5. I have expressed the opinion in previous communications that American-Japanese relations would be set on a downward curve if sanctions were applied by the United States. It is true that measures are now justified by our new program of national preparedness which need not fall within the category of outright sanctions. On the other hand, the probability must be contemplated that drastic embargoes on such important products as oil, of which a super-abundance is known to be possessed by the United States, would be interpreted by the people and government of Japan as actual sanctions and some form of retaliation might and probably would follow. The risks would depend not so much upon the careful calculations of the Japanese Government as upon the uncalculating "do or die" temper of the army and navy should they impute to the United States the responsibility for the failure of their plans for expansion. It may be that such retaliation would take the form of counter-measures by the

government but it would be more likely that it would be some sudden stroke by the navy or army without the prior authorization or knowledge of the government. These dangers constitute an imponderable element which cannot be weighed with assurance at any given moment. However, it would be short sighted to deny their existence or to formulate policy and adopt measures without fully considering these potential risks and determining the wisdom of facing them squarely.

6. In the following observations I am giving careful consideration to both fundamental purposes of my mission, namely the advancement and protection of American interests and the maintenance of good relations between Japan and the United States. Should these two fundamental purposes conflict the preponderant emphasis to be placed on either one is a matter of high policy which is not within my competency. My object is only to set before the Washington administration the outstanding factors in the situation as viewed from the standpoint of this embassy. Since I have set forth carefully the inevitable hazards which a strong policy involves, I now turn respectfully to the hazards involved in the policy of *laissez faire*.

7. It is impossible in a discussion of the specific question of relations between the United States and Japan to view that problem in its proper perspective unless it is considered part and parcel of the world problem which presents in brief the following aspects: (a) Britain and America are the leaders of a large world-wide group of English-speaking peoples which stand for a "way of life" which today is being threatened appallingly by Italy, Germany, and Japan. . . . The avowed purpose of these powers is the imposition of their will upon conquered peoples by force of arms. In general, the uses of diplomacy are bankrupt in attempting to deal with such powers. Occasionally diplomacy may retard, but it cannot stem the tide effectively. Only by force or the display of force can these powers be prevented from attaining their objectives. Japan is today one of the predatory powers; having submerged all ethical and moral sense she has become unashamedly and frankly opportunist, at every turn seeking to profit through the weakness of others. American interests in the Pacific are definitely threatened by her policy of southward expansion, which is a thrust at the British Empire in the east. (b) Admittedly America's security has depended in a measure upon the British fleet, which has been in turn and could only have been supported by the British Empire. (c) If the support of the British Empire in this her hour of travail is conceived to be in our interest, and most emphatically do I so conceive it, we must strive by every

means to preserve the status quo in the Pacific, at least until the war in Europe has been won or lost. This cannot be done, in my opinion, nor can we further protect our interests properly and adequately merely by the expression of disapproval and carefully keeping a record thereof. Clearly, Japan has been deterred from the taking of greater liberties with American interests only because she respects our potential power; equally is it (clear) that she has trampled upon our rights to an extent in exact ratio to the strength of her conviction that the people of the United States would not permit that power to be used. It is possible that once that conviction is shaken the uses of diplomacy may again become accepted. (d) Therefore, if by firmness we can preserve the status quo in the Pacific until and if Great Britain is successful in the European war, a situation will be faced by Japan which will render it impossible for the present opportunist philosophy to keep the upper hand. Then it might be possible at a moment to undertake a readjustment of the whole problem of the Pacific on a frank, fair, and equitable basis which will be to the lasting benefit of both Japan and America. Until there is in Japan a complete regeneration of thought, a show of force, coupled with the determination that it will be used if necessary, alone can effectively contribute to such an outcome and to our own future security.

8. . . . I believe that in the present outlook and situation we have come to the time when the continuance of restraint and patience by the United States may and will probably lead to developments which will make progressively precarious relations between the United States and Japan. I hope that if the people and the Government of Japan can be led to believe that they are overplaying their hand, eventually there will come about a reverse swing of the pendulum in which it will be possible to reconstruct good relations between the United States and Japan. I consider the alternative to be hopeless. . . .

GREW

183

Department of State Bulletin, vol. III, p. 253

Press Release Issued by the Department of State
On September 23, 1940

In response to inquiries at the press conference today, the Secretary of State said:

"Events are transpiring so rapidly in the Indochina situation that it is impossible to get a clear picture of the minute-to-minute developments. It seems obvious, however, that the *status quo* is being upset and that this is being achieved under duress. The position of the United States in disapproval and in deprecation of such procedures has repeatedly been stated."

___

This Government has not at any time or in any way approved the French concessions to Japan. The attitude of this Government toward developments in French Indochina is as expressed by the Secretary of State this morning and in previous public statements.

184

Department of State Bulletin, vol. III, p. 251

Statement by the Secretary of State, September 27, 1940

The reported agreement of alliance [56] does not, in the view of the Government of the United States, substantially alter a situation which has existed for several years. Announcement of the alliance merely makes clear to all a relationship which has long existed in effect and to which this Government has repeatedly called attention. That such an agreement has been in process of conclusion has been well known for some time, and that fact has been fully taken into account by the Government of the United States in the determining of this country's policies.

___

[56] The following is a tentative translation, as received from the Japanese Ministry for Foreign Affairs on Sept. 27, 1940, of the Tripartite Pact between Japan, Germany, and Italy, signed at Berlin, Sept. 27, 1940 (Dept. of State, file 763.9411/136) :

The Governments of Japan, Germany and Italy, considering it as the condition precedent of any lasting peace that all nations of the world be given each its own proper place, have decided to stand by and co-operate with one another in regard to their efforts in Greater East Asia and the regions of Europe respectively wherein it is their prime purpose to establish and maintain a new order of things calculated to promote mutual prosperity and welfare of the peoples concerned. Furthermore it is the desire of the three Governments to extend cooperation to such nations in other spheres of the world as may be inclined to put forth endeavours along lines similar to their own, in order that their ultimate aspirations for world peace may thus be realized. Accordingly the Governments of Japan, Germany and Italy have agreed as follows:

ARTICLE 1

Japan recognizes and respects the leadership of Germany and Italy in the establishment of a new order in Europe.

185

762.9411/81–½

Memorandum by the Secretary of State Regarding a Conversation With the British Ambassador (Lothian)

[Extracts]

[WASHINGTON,] September 30, 1940.

The British Ambassador called at his request. He invited my comment regarding the significance and probable effect of the recently announced German-Italian-Japanese alliance. I replied that I could better deal with the matter by referring to the views of capable analysts than by expressing an individual opinion. I went on to say that it came about primarily due to Hitler's effort to divert attention from his failure to invade Great Britain and to preserve his prestige by a sensational announcement of something that already existed. Then I merely recited the facts as to the true situation since 1937, up to and including my public statement following the announcement of the German-Japanese-Italian alliance last week. I could best illus-

---

Footnote 56—Continued.

ARTICLE 2

Germany and Italy recognize and respect the leadership of Japan in the establishment of a new order in Greater East Asia.

ARTICLE 3

Japan, Germany and Italy agree to cooperate in their efforts on the aforesaid lines. They further undertake to assist one another with all political, economic and military means when one of the three Contracting Parties is attacked by a power at present not involved in the European War or in the Sino-Japanese Conflict.

ARTICLE 4

With a view to implementing the present Pact, Joint Technical Commissions the members of which are to be appointed by the respective Governments of Japan, Germany and Italy will meet without delay.

ARTICLE 5

Japan, Germany and Italy affirm that the aforesaid terms do not in any way affect the political status which exists at present as between each of the three Contracting Parties and Soviet Russia.

ARTICLE 6

The present Pact shall come into effect immediately upon signature and shall remain in force for ten years from the date of its coming into force.

At proper time before the expiration of the said term the High Contracting Parties shall, at the request of any one of them, enter into negotiations for its removal [*renewal?*].

trate this analysis of the matter by referring to what we have often said about the certainty that Japan would, as a most ordinary precaution, find it necessary to assume that whether or not the United States and Great Britain have express or definite agreements in regard to naval and air bases across the Pacific to and including Singapore, the special relations between these two countries are such that they could overnight easily establish cooperative relations for the mutual use of all of these bases; that, therefore, the relations between Germany, Italy and Japan, each having a common objective of conquering certain areas of the world and each pursuing identical policies of force, devastation and seizure, have been during recent years on a basis of complete understanding and of mutual cooperation for all purposes mutually desirable and reasonably practicable, with the result that the recent announcement was part and parcel of the chain of related events. The Ambassador said that this was the view of himself and his Government.

I then added that I would be interested to make another inquiry, and that is whether and to what extent the British and Dutch Governments and peoples, especially in the South Pacific area, have conferred relative to pooling their defense forces in case of threatened danger from elsewhere, and if so, what are the facts as to the size of such pooled forces, and what size fleet would be necessary to overcome and capture them and the countries they represent.

I then proceeded to say that this Government has pursued a definite and somewhat progressive line of acts and utterances in resisting Japanese aggression and treaty violations during recent years; that these acts and utterances have comprised repeated aid to China, successive moral embargoes, abandonment of the commercial treaty, actual embargoes under law, the sending of our Navy to Hawaii, together with appropriate statements and notes of strong remonstrance against Japanese steps of aggression and constant repetition of the basic principles of world order under law. I added that I did not undertake to predict, much less to make commitments, as to how fast and how far this Government may go in following up the various acts and utterances in which it has been indulging; that, of course, the special desire of this Government is to see Great Britain succeed in the war and that its acts and utterances with respect to the Pacific area would be more or less affected as to time and extent by the question of what course would, on the part of this Government, most effectively and legitimately aid Great Britain in winning the war.

C[ORDELL] H[ULL]

186

811.20(D)Regulations/590

Memorandum by the Secretary of State Regarding a Conversation With the Japanese Ambassador (Horinouchi)

[WASHINGTON,] October 8, 1940.

The Japanese Ambassador called at his request. He first expressed his regret at the unsatisfactory relations existing between our two countries at this time. I replied that, in my opinion, this was not the fault of the Ambassador and myself, who have been untiring in our efforts to promote and preserve satisfactory relations between the United States and Japan.

The Ambassador then said that he was instructed by his Government to hand me a note dated October 7, 1940 (copy attached)[57] relative to our scrap iron and steel embargo which was recently proclaimed.

He read a statement (copy attached)[58] in support of the note mentioned above.

I replied to the effect that I would see what sort of written reply, if any, might be called for.

I then said that I might at this time, and without delay, state that this Government at all times must determine for itself such internal questions as those material to our program of national defense, as we are doing in the instant case, and that it would be impossible for any country engaged in the serious and urgent undertaking of carrying out a program of national defense to allow every other outside nation to come in and pass upon the question of our needs of given commodities; that the embargo, as the Ambassador knows, applies to all nations except Great Britain and the Western Hemisphere. I remarked that for some years this Government had been criticized for not imposing numerous embargoes, primarily from the standpoint of safety and national defense and peace, and that it was only at the height of our national defense preparations that we were imposing a few embargoes on important commodities.

I said that it was really amazing for the Government of Japan, which has been violating in the most aggravating manner valuable American rights and interests throughout most of China, and is doing so in many instances every day, to question the fullest privilege of this Government from every standpoint to impose the proposed scrap iron and

---

[57] Annex 1.
[58] Annex 2.

steel embargo, and that to go still further and call it an unfriendly act was still more amazing in the light of the conduct of the Japanese Government in disregarding all law, treaty obligations and other rights and privileges and the safety of Americans while it proceeded at the same time to seize territory by force to an ever-increasing extent. I stated that of all the countries with which I have had to deal during the past eight years, the Government of Japan has the least occasion or excuse to accuse this Government of an unfriendly act. I concluded with the statement that apparently the theory of the Japanese Government is for all other nations to acquiesce cheerfully in all injuries inflicted upon their citizens by the Japanese policy of force and conquest, accompanied by every sort of violence, unless they are to run the risk of being guilty of an unfriendly act.

The Ambassador again said that he very much regretted the serious differences between our two countries, but that he naturally hoped that trouble may yet be avoided. He added that any Japanese or any American must know that strife between the two countries would be extremely tragic for both alike. To this I replied that, of course, it would be exceedingly unfortunate for such occurrence to take place, but I added that my Government has been patient, extremely patient, and that the Ambassador will bear witness to the long and earnest efforts that he and I have made, and that I have made prior to his coming here, to promote and preserve friendly and satisfactory relations with Japan. I went on to say that we have stood for law and order and treaty observance and justice along with genuine friendliness between our two countries; that it was clear now, however, that those who are dominating the external policies of Japan are, as we here have believed for some years, bent on the conquest by force of all worthwhile territory in the Pacific Ocean area without limit as to extent in the South and in southern continental areas of that part of the world, and that we and all other nations are expected, as stated, to sit perfectly quiet and be cheerful and agreeable, but static, while most of Asia is Manchuria-ized, which would render practically impossible all reasonable or satisfactory relations so far as other nations are concerned; and that corresponding lower levels of existence would be the ultimate lot of the people of most of Asia. The least objection to or taking of issue with Japan with respect to the foregoing matters would be called an unfriendly act, and, as Prime Minister Konoye said recently to the press, it would be the occasion for war so far as Japan was concerned. I added that, of course, if any one country is sufficiently desirous of trouble, it can always find any one of innumerable occasions to start such trouble. In brief, it is not left to the other country to participate in such decision.

The Ambassador undertook to repeat the old line of talk about how fair Japan proposed to be with respect to all rights and privileges of foreign nations within its conquered territory. He agreed that no purpose would be served now to go over the many conversations we have had with respect to these matters. I held up the succession of injuries to American rights and interests in China whenever he referred to the scrap iron embargo.

I reiterated the view that it was unheard of for one country engaged in aggression and seizure of another country, contrary to all law and treaty provisions, to turn to a third peacefully disposed nation and seriously insist that it would be guilty of an unfriendly act if it should not cheerfully provide some of the necessary implements of war to aid the aggressor nation in carrying out its policy of invasion. I made it clear that it is the view of this Government that two nations, one in Europe and one in Asia, are undertaking to subjugate both of their respective areas of the world, and to place them on an international order and on a social basis resembling that of 750 years ago. In the face of this world movement, extending itself from day to day, peaceful and interested nations are to be held up to denunciation and threats if they dare to engage in any lawful acts or utterances in opposition to such wide movements of world conquest.

The Ambassador had little to say. He said virtually nothing in attempted extenuation except that his Government would expect everybody to receive considerate and fair treatment throughout the conquered areas. He emphasized equal treatment, and I replied that when the best interests of other nations in peace and law and order were being destroyed, it was not a matter of any concern as to whether there was discrimination between the nations which were victims of such movements.

C[ORDELL] H[ULL]

[Annex 1]

811.20(D) Regulations/589

The Japanese Embassy to the Department of State, October 7, 1940

No. 235

The Japanese Government has taken note of the regulations governing the exportation of iron and steel scrap, dated September 30,

1940, amending the construction and definition of the term "iron and steel scrap" included in the regulations of July 26, 1940, and the announcement of September 26, 1940 to the effect that, under the new regulations, licenses will be issued to permit shipments to the countries of the Western Hemisphere and Great Britain only.

The above mentioned regulations refer to the Presidential authority derived from the provisions of section 6 of the Act of Congress approved July 2, 1940, entitled "An Act to expedite the strengthening of the national defense", thereby suggesting that it was determined to be necessary in the interest of national defense to curtail the exportation of iron and steel scrap.

In view of the situation of iron and steel scrap markets, the supply and demand of these materials and the volume shipped to Japan, the Japanese Government finds it difficult to concede that this measure was motivated solely by the interest of national defense of the United States.

In the note of the Japanese Ambassador of August 3 the Japanese Government pointed out that the measure announced on July 26, 1940, in regard to the exportation of aviation gasoline, was tantamount to an export embargo as far as countries outside the Western Hemisphere were concerned. Compared to that announcement, the announcement under review may be said to have gone a step further toward discrimination by specifically excluding Great Britain from the virtual embargo.

In view of the fact that Japan has been for some years the principal buyer of American iron and steel scrap, the announcement of the administrative policy, as well as the regulations establishing license system in iron and steel scrap cannot fail to be regarded as directed against Japan, and, as such, to be an unfriendly act.

The Japanese Government hereby protests against the measures taken by the United States Government in connection with the exportation of iron and steel scrap.

[WASHINGTON,] *October 7, 1940.*

[Annex 2]

811.20(D)Regulations/589

The Japanese Embassy to the Department of State [59]

Since iron and steel scrap classified as No. 1 heavy melting scrap was placed under export-licensing system on July 26, 1940, permission

---

[59] This undated statement was handed to the Secretary of State by the Japanese Ambassador on October 8, 1940.

of the United States Government was obtained up to August 19 of the same year for 99 percent of applications for shipments to Japan.

In the light of this fact, the sudden enlargement of the iron and steel scrap licensing system to include all grades of these materials is hardly explicable from the standpoint of national defense, on which the regulation of September 30, 1940, is purported to be based.

The discriminatory feature of the announcement, that licenses will be issued to permit shipments to the countries of the Western Hemisphere and Great Britain only, has created a widespread impression in Japan that it was motivated by a desire to bring pressure upon her.

The fact that the majority of essential articles and materials that Japan desires to import from America is placed under licensing system is causing a feeling of tension among the people of Japan, who naturally presume that the system is intended to be a precursor of severance of economic relations between Japan and the United States.

In view of the high feeling in Japan it is apprehended that, in the event of continuation by the United States Government of the present attitude toward Japan in matters of trade restriction, especially if it ,eads to the imposition of further measures of curtailment, future relations between Japan and the United States will be unpredictable.

It is a matter of course that the Governments of both Japan and the United States should endeavor as best they can to preclude such an eventuality. To this endeavor the Japanese Government will devote itself and trusts that it may have the full co-operation of the United States Government.

187

740.00119 European War 1939/530A

The Secretary of State to the Chargé in France (Matthews)

[Telegram]

WASHINGTON, October 25, 1940—noon.

636. For your information.

The following personal message was delivered yesterday to the French Ambassador from the President with the request that it be transmitted immediately to Marshal Pétain:

"In the opinion of the United States Government the fact that the French Government alleges that it is under duress and consequently cannot act except to a very limited degree as a free agent is in no sense to be considered as justifying any course on the part of the

French Government which would provide assistance to Germany and her allies in their war against the British Empire. The fact that a government is a prisoner of war of another power does not justify such a prisoner in serving its conqueror in operations against its former ally.

The Government of the United States received from the Pétain Government during the first days it held office the most solemn assurances that the French fleet would not be surrendered. If the French Government now permits the Germans to use the French fleet in hostile operations against the British fleet, such action would constitute a flagrant and deliberate breach of faith with the United States Government.

Any agreement entered into between France and Germany which partook of the character above-mentioned would most definitely wreck the traditional friendship between the French and American peoples, would permanently remove any chance that this Government would be disposed to give any assistance to the French people in their distress, and would create a wave of bitter indignation against France on the part of American public opinion.

If France pursued such a policy as that above outlined, the United States could make no effort when the appropriate time came to exercise its influence to insure to France the retention of her overseas possessions."

HULL.

188

Department of State Bulletin, vol. III, p. 331

Address Delivered by the Secretary of State at Washington, October 26, 1940

It is with no light heart that I address you and any others who may be listening tonight on the subject of our international relations. I should be lacking in candor if I did not emphasize the gravity of the present situation.

Only once before in our national existence has as grave a danger from without threatened this Nation as the danger which looms today on the international horizon. That was in the stirring days when the founders of this Republic staked everything on their unshakable conviction that a nation of free men could be established and would endure on the soil of America. Theirs was a struggle and a victory the fruits of which have been the proud inheritance of succeeding generations of Americans for more than a century and a half. These generations, including our own, have enjoyed this inheritance in a world where human freedom, national independence, and order under law were steadily becoming more and more firmly established as a system of civilized relations among nations and among individuals.

Today that system and all peaceful nations, including our own, are gravely menaced. The danger arises out of the plans and acts of a small group of national rulers who have succeeded in transforming their peoples into forceful instruments for widespread domination by conquest.

To understand the significance of this danger and to prepare to meet it successfully we must see clearly the tragic lessons taught by what has occurred since the protagonists of conquest began their march across the earth. I ask you to review with me the whirlwind developments of one of the saddest and most crucial decades in the history of mankind—that of the nineteen-thirties.

I

The opening years of the decade were filled with ominous rumblings of impending disaster. Profound economic dislocation had spread rapidly to every part of the world. It had disrupted international economic relations and was causing untold distress everywhere. The structure of international peace was still intact, but a dangerous breach was opened in it by the Japanese occupation of Manchuria in 1931. That act, universally condemned at the time, proved to be only the beginning of an epidemic of callous disregard of international commitments—probably unparalleled in the annals of history. International discussions for the reduction and limitation of armaments, begun much earlier, were dragging along. Their failure to result in effective agreements was adding to the general feeling of apprehension and insecurity.

These developments were bound to create grave difficulties and grave dangers for our country, as well as for the rest of the world. The problems which they presented imperatively demanded on our part vigorous initiative and leadership in the promotion and defense of the national interest.

Accordingly, in the conduct of foreign policy, this Government directed its efforts to the following objectives: (1) Peace and security for the United States with advocacy of peace and limitation of armament as universal international objectives; (2) support for law, order, justice, and morality and the principle of non-intervention; (3) restoration and cultivation of sound economic methods and relations;

(4) development of the maximum measure of international cooperation; (5) promotion of the security, solidarity, and general welfare of the Western Hemisphere. These basic objectives of a good-neighbor policy represented a sound and practical middle course between the extremes of internationalism and isolation. They have been consistently pursued throughout. The sweep of events has, of course, required the focusing of our attention at different periods upon different problems and different geographic areas.

II

In the early thirties, the relations among the American republics left much to be desired. Elements of mistrust, apprehension, and disunion had to be eliminated if a good-neighbor policy was really to prevail on the American Continent and provide a foundation upon which 21 free and independent American republics could establish peaceful and mutually beneficial relations among themselves and with the rest of the world.

The Seventh International Conference of American States, meeting at Montevideo in December 1933, offered an opportunity for a far-reaching move in this direction. There, a solid foundation was laid for a new structure of inter-American relations built on lines so broad that the entire program of principles was of universal application. At that meeting, the American republics took effective action for the maintenance of inter-American peace, agreed upon non intervention, and adopted an economic program of common benefit based on the rule of equal treatment. During the years which immediately followed, the United States gave tangible proofs of its determination to act in accordance with the newly created system of inter-American relations.

At the same time we inaugurated a new policy in the sphere of economic relations. In the summer of 1934, this country adopted the reciprocal-trade-agreements program, designed to restore and expand international commerce through the reduction of unreasonable trade barriers and the general reestablishment of the rule of equality of commercial treatment. This program proved to be the greatest constructive effort in a world racing toward economic destruction.

In the meantime, other phases of international relations were undergoing further and rapid deterioration. Efforts to achieve international security through the reduction and limitation of armaments were unsuccessful. The long and weary conferences at Geneva during which plan after plan failed of adoption showed that the world was not ready to grasp an opportunity for action which, had it been taken, might have prevented subsequent disasters. This and the notice given by Japan in December 1934 of her intention to terminate the Washington Treaty for the Limitation of Naval Armaments opened the way for a new armament race.

At this juncture, Italy announced her intention to secure control over Ethiopia—by force of arms, if necessary. While there was still a possibility for an amicable settlement of the difficulties between Italy and Ethiopia, the attitude of the Government of the United States was made clear on Sepember 13, 1935, in a statement which read in part as follows:

"Under the conditions which prevail in the world today, a threat of hostilities anywhere cannot but be a threat to the interests—political, economic, legal and social—of all nations. Armed conflict in any part of the world cannot but have undesirable and adverse effects in every part of the world. All nations have the right to ask that any and all issues between whatsoever nations be resolved by pacific means. Every nation has the right to ask that no nations subject it and other nations to the hazards and uncertainties that must inevitably accrue to all from resort to arms by any two."

During the summer of 1935 under the influence of these rapidly unfolding developments threatening the peace of the world the Congress enacted a statute known as the Neutrality Act of 1935. The purpose of this act was to reduce the risks of our becoming involved in war. Unfortunately, it contained as its principal feature the provision for a rigid embargo on export of arms to belligerents. This provision was adopted under the influence of a fallacious concept temporarily accepted by a large number of our people that this country's entrance into the World War had been brought about by the sale of arms to belligerents and the machinations of so-called "international bankers".

It was clear then, and has become even clearer since, that a rigid embargo on export of arms might have an effect the opposite of that which was intended. On the occasion of the signing of the act, the President pointed out that "history is filled with unforeseeable situations" and that conditions might arise in which the wholly inflexible provision for an arms embargo "might drag us into war instead of keeping us out". I myself repeatedly pointed out that in addition to the unforeseeable consequences of the provision itself reliance upon that concept might mean the closing of our eyes to manifold dangers in other directions and from other sources.

By 1938, there was no longer any doubt that the existence of the arms embargo provision was definitely having the effect of making widespread war more likely. Accordingly, early in 1939, the executive branch of the Government urgently recommended to Congress the repeal of that provision. That was finally accomplished, after the outbreak of war in Europe, at a special session of Congress called by the President for that specific purpose.

III

The Italo-Ethiopian war and its attendant circumstances left, in an already shaken Europe, a new condition of intense bitterness and unsettlement. Into that situation, Germany, after three years of intensive military preparation, flung, early in 1936, her first serious challenge to world order under law. The German Government tore up the Treaty of Locarno, into which Germany had freely and voluntarily entered, and proceeded to fortify the Rhineland in violation of the express provisions of that treaty. In the summer of that year, a violent civil conflict flared up in Spain, and that unfortunate country became a battleground of newly emerging power politics.

During this period, the President and I on numerous occasions emphasized the gathering dangers in the world situation. In June 1935, I made the following statement:

"We witness all about us a reckless, competitive building up of armaments, a recurrence of the mad race which prior to 1914 led the nations of the world headlong to destruction. If persisted in, this course will again plunge the world into disaster."

Tragic indeed is the fact that, from the end of 1935, the voice of reason became increasingly drowned by the rising clangor of the furious rearmament by nations preparing for conquest.

We continued our efforts for peace. We continued to carry forward our program of economic restoration through the trade-agreements policy. We intensified the process of strengthening our naval armaments and of improving in other ways our means of defense. Speaking for the Government, I pointed out that we would not serve the cause of peace by not having adequate powers of self-defense; that we must be sure that in our desire for peace we would not appear to any other country unable to protect our just rights.

In view of the imminence of an impending world crisis, we proposed to our sister republics of the Americas, in January 1936, an extraordinary conference to consider the best means of safeguarding the peace of this hemisphere. At this Inter-American Conference for the Maintenance of Peace, convoked at Buenos Aires, the 21 American republics, building on the foundations laid down at Montevideo, adopted for the first time the great principle that a threat from without the continent to the peace of any of them should be regarded by the American republics as a threat to each and every one of them. They established in contractual form the obligation to consult together whenever the peace of the Americas is menaced, either from within or from without.

During the year 1937, while the cauldron of European politics seethed dangerously, the focus of world events again shifted to the Far East. In the summer of that year, Japan struck a further and more extensive blow at China. This new threat to the peace of the world rendered appropriate a restatement of the fundamental aims and principles of the foreign policy of the United States. In a statement issued on July 16, 1937, I set forth those principles. We urged upon all nations the acceptance and observance of those principles. We repeatedly offered to be of assistance toward composing the Chinese-Japanese conflict in accordance with those principles. We participated—and Japan refused to participate—in the Brussels conference of the signatories to the Nine Power Pact, convoked for the purpose of bringing about a peaceful solution of that conflict.

IV

During the year 1938, the focus of events returned to Europe. In March of that year, the armed forces of Germany passed beyond that country's borders, and the annexation of Austria marked the first forcible alteration of the frontiers established in Europe by the treaties of peace. This was followed, within a few months, by an intense crisis, culminating in the Munich conference and the first dismemberment of Czechoslovakia. The darkening shadows of an approaching war deepened over the fields and homes of the European Continent.

It is not necessary for me to dwell in detail on the kaleidoscopic events of the anguished year that preceded the outbreak of the European war, nor of the 14 months we have since lived through. All of us recall the feverish activity in Europe which became a prelude to war and our repeated attempts to influence the contending nations to adjust their differences by pacific means on the basis of justice, equality, and fair-dealing, without recourse to force or threat of force. The tragic and the heroic developments of the war months and the brutal invasion and ruthless extinguishment of the independence and freedom of many countries are too vivid in the minds of all of us to need recapitulation.

The appalling tragedy of the present world situation lies in the fact that peacefully disposed nations failed to recognize in time the true nature of the aims and ambitions which have actuated the rulers of the heavily arming nations. Recoiling from the mere contemplation of the possibility of another widespread war, the peoples of the peaceful nations permitted themselves to be lulled into a false sense of security by the assurances made by these rulers that their aims were limited. This continued even as succeeding events left less and less room for doubt that, behind the screen of these assurances, preparations were being made for new attempts at widespread conquest. To mask still further this monstrous deception, these rulers and their satellites attempted to brand as "war mongers" and "imperialists" all who warned against the clearly emerging dangers, and poured upon them vituperation and abuse.

The United States, together with most other nations, has stood firmly for the basic principles underlying civilized international relations—peace, law, justice, treaty observance, non-intervention, peaceful settlement of differences, and fair-dealing, supported by the fullest practicable measure of international cooperation. The advocacy of these principles has won for us the friendship of all nations, except those which, vaguely describing themselves as the "have-nots" and claiming a superior right to rule over other peoples, are today on the march with great armies, air fleets, and navies to take by force what they say they need or want.

The rulers of these nations have repudiated and violated in every essential respect the long-accepted principles of peaceful and orderly international relations. Merciless armed attack; unrestrained terrorization through slaughter of non-combatant men, women, and children; deceit, fraud, and guile; forced labor; confiscation of property; imposed starvation and deprivations of every sort—all these are weapons constantly used by the conquerors for the invasion and subjugation of other nations.

They adhere to no geographic lines and they fix no time limit on their programs of invasion and destruction. They cynically disregard every right of neutral nations, and, having occupied several such countries, they then proceed to warn all peaceful nations that they must remain strictly neutral until an invading force is actually crossing their borders. They have as a fixed objective the securing of control of the high seas. They threaten peaceful nations with the direst consequences if those nations do not remain acquiescent, while the conquerors are seizing the other continents and most of the seven seas of the earth.

Let no one comfort himself with the delusion that these are mere excesses or exigencies of war, to be voluntarily abandoned when fighting ceases. By deed and by utterance, the would-be conquerors have made it abundantly clear that they are engaged upon a relentless attempt to transform the civilized world as we have known it into a world in which mankind will be reduced again to the degradation of a master-and-slave relationship among nations and among individuals, maintained by brute force.

The hand of crushing assault has struck again and again at peaceful nations, complacent and unprepared in their belief that mere intention on their part to keep peace was an ample shield of security.

There can be nothing more dangerous for our Nation than for us to assume that the avalanche of conquest could under no circumstances reach any vital portion of this hemisphere. Oceans give the nations of this hemisphere no guaranty against the possibility of economic, political, or military attack from abroad. Oceans are barriers but they are also highways. Barriers of distance are merely barriers of time. Should the would-be conquerors gain control of other continents, they would next concentrate on perfecting their control of the seas, of the air over the seas, and of the world's economy; they might then be able with ships and with planes to strike at the communication lines, the commerce, and the life of this hemisphere; and ultimately we might find ourselves compelled to fight on our own soil, under our own skies, in defense of our independence and our very lives.

These are some of the governing facts and conditions of the present-day international situation. These are the dangers which must be recognized. Against these dangers, our policies and measures must provide defense.

V

We are in the presence not of local or regional wars, but of an organized and determined movement for steadily expanding conquest. Against this drive for power no nation and no region is secure save as its inhabitants create for themselves means of defense so formidable that even the would-be conquerors will not dare to raise against them the hand of attack.

The first need for all nations still masters of their own destiny is to create for themselves, as speedily and as completely as possible, impregnable means of defense. This is the staggering lesson of mankind's recent experience.

To meet that need, we are bringing our military, naval, and air establishments to maximum practicable strength. Production of military supplies is being brought to a greater and greater pitch of speed and effectiveness. Wherever necessary for the carrying out of the defense program, export of essential materials is being stringently regulated. Arrangements are being carried forward to provide military and technical training for the youth of this country. We intend to continue and intensify our effort in all these directions.

We are taking measures toward dealing with subversive activities in this country directed from abroad. The experience of many other countries has brought us the shocking realization of the manner in which, and the extent to which, such activities are employed to undermine social and political institutions and to bring about internal disintegration and decay in the countries which they plan to make their victims. We intend to act in this field with unremitting vigor.

We are seeking to advance by every appropriate means the spirit of inter-American solidarity and the system of continental defense. In conformity with the procedure set up at Buenos Aires and Lima, the Panama Consultative Meeting of the Ministers of Foreign Affairs of the American Republics adopted important measures to safeguard the national and collective interests of the American nations, their peace, and their economic security. Last summer they met again, at Habana, to consult with regard to several threats to the peace and security of the Americas, the danger of which, they unanimously agreed, existed. To ward off these threats, they took positive steps to prevent any transfer of sovereignty in the Western Hemisphere from one non-American nation to another, embodied in an international convention and in the Act of Habana. They also agreed upon procedures for combating subversive activities in the American nations and they adopted measures of economic defense and collaboration.

We have concluded an arrangement with Great Britain under which we have acquired long-time leases of eight strategically located naval and air bases which will enable us to create a protective girdle of steel along the Atlantic seaboard of the American Continent—bases which will be available for use by all of the American republics. We are engaged in defense consultations with our neighbors to the south, and we have created facilities for such consultations with Canada. In all these fields, we intend to continue vigorous effort.

We have sought in every appropriate way to discourage conquest and to limit the area of war. We have followed consistently the policy of refusing recognition of territorial changes effected by force or threat of force. We have taken every opportunity to express our concern over threatened changes by force in the existing political status of colonial possessions, disturbance of which would extend the area of hostilities. We have placed under license the funds of invaded countries. In these respects, too, we intend to continue our activities.

We believe that the safety and the primary interests of the United States must be upheld with firmness and resolution—supported by the speediest and fullest possible armament for all defensive purposes. In view of the unprecedented character of menacing developments abroad, we have frankly recognized the danger involved and the increasing need for defense against it. As an important means of strengthening our own defense and of preventing attack on any part of the Western Hemisphere, this country is affording all feasible facilities for the obtaining of supplies by nations which, while defending themselves against barbaric attack, are checking the spread of violence and are thus reducing the danger to us. We intend to continue doing this to the greatest practicable extent. Any contention, no matter from what source, that this country should not take such action is equivalent, in the present circumstances, to a denying of the inalienable right of self-defense.

VI

In our democracy the basic determination of foreign policy rests with the people. As I sense the will of our people today, this Nation is determined that its security and rightful interests shall be safeguarded.

The dangers with which we are confronted are not of our making. We cannot know at what point, or when, we may possibly be attacked. We can, however, be prepared, first, to discourage any thought of assault upon our security and, if any such assault should be attempted, to repel it.

The people of this country want peace. To have peace, we must have security. To have security, we must be strong. These are times that test the fiber of men and of nations.

Our system of defense must, of necessity, be many-sided, because the dangers against which safeguards are imperatively required are manifold. Essential to effective national defense are constant and skilful use of political and economic measures, possession of military weapons, and continuous exercise of wisdom and of high moral qualities. We must have planes and tanks and ships and guns. We must have trained men. We must hold to the ideal of a world in which the rights of all nations are respected and each respects the rights of all; in which principles of law and order and justice and fair-dealing prevail. Above all, we must be a united people—united in purpose and in effort to create impregnable defense.

Thus can we maintain our inheritance. Thus will we continue to make this country's high contribution toward the progress of mankind on the roadway of civilized effort.

189

740.00119 European War 1939/564

The Chargé in France (Matthews) to the Secretary of State

[Telegram]

(PARIS) VICHY, November 1, 1940—5 p.m.
[Received November 2—6:15 p.m.]

872. My telegram No. 861, November 1, 11 a.m.

The Marshal's reply to the President's message was sent off late last night to Ambassador Henry Haye. . . . I quote the text in translation as sent me with a covering Foreign Office note today:

"Reply addressed on November 1, 1940 by Marshal Petain to the message of President Roosevelt.

The Chief of the French State has received the message of President Roosevelt sent to him through the Charge d'Affaires of the United States.

Animated by the desire to preserve the friendship which since the foundation of the United States has bound the French people to the American people, he will refrain from calling attention to what there is in that communication which might make him question the fair attitude (dispositions, equitables) of the American Government. To answer the anxiety of President Roosevelt, he desires to state that the French Government has always preserved its liberty of action and that I knew that he might be surprised at an appraisement as inaccurate as it is unjust. The French Government has declared that the French fleet would never be surrendered and nothing can justify questioning today that solemn undertaking. President Roosevelt speaks of operations directed against the British fleet. He doubtless forgets that as a matter of fact the operations at sea which have taken place as they did in the most unexpected manner were undertaken by the British fleet. Furthermore, England has taken a position against France and against her government which the French people cannot countenance. His Majesty's Government lends its support to Frenchmen, rebels against their country, whose action, thanks to the aid of the British fleet and air force, encourages the unity of her Empire. France—and her Government [having given?] such assurances—will not engage in any unjustified attack

591

but conscious of her duty she will see that her essential interests are honorably respected.

The French Government remains very desirous of maintaining the traditional friendship which unites our two countries and it will strive under all circumstances to avoid misunderstandings or interpretations such as those which doubtless led President Roosevelt to address us this message."

MATTHEWS

190

711.51/145

Memorandum by the Secretary of State Regarding a Conversation With the French Ambassador (Henry-Haye)

[Extract]

[WASHINGTON,] November 4, 1940.

I spoke somewhat in general terms and repeated our frequent statement about the traditional friendship between France and the United States and our anxious desire to preserve in the most genuine manner that spirit of friendliness and of mutual cooperation in every way that might be at all practicable and mutually desirable. I said that the chief trouble seems to be that high-ranking officials in the French Government seem disposed to keep entirely away from this Government in most everything that relates to normal relations, and at the same time to keep extremely close to Hitler and to show every sympathetic interest in his plans and purposes, revealing all the while the utmost antipathy toward Great Britain and the cause for which she is fighting. I stated that this Government has the usual normal relations with all other governments except those at Tokyo, Berlin, Rome and Vichy; that I can always understand readily the attitude of all the other governments and can get legitimate information promptly and voluntarily from all of them with the exception of the four mentioned; that Vichy, along with Tokyo, Berlin and Rome, is just the opposite in its disposition to be frank and friendly. I said that I receive many rumors and reports about the attitude of the Vichy Government contrary to the interests of this country, but nothing direct, and I am obliged to look to other rumors and reports, direct and indirect, coming through the press and through foreign offices in various parts of the wald, in order to get any real grasp of what is actually taking place at Vichy that is calculated seriously to affect this Government. I added that the French Government in adopting this sort of attitude and practice will not get two inches

592

in carrying on its relations with the Government of the United States. The Ambassador said he supposed I referred to Mr. Laval in connection with the foregoing. I remarked that, of course, the Ambassador knew that the definite impression created here and everywhere by Mr. Laval is that he is an extreme partisan of Hitler and Mussolini and very bitter toward Great Britain; that he is reported to favor strongly a permanent rejection of the so-called "old order" in Europe, and the embracing of Hitler's political, social and other policies with totalitarian autarchy a basic part. I said that Mr. Laval had the privilege of becoming an ally and associate of Hitler and the monstrous things for which he stands, but that he must not imagine that this Government does not know what his attitude and purpose are. I added that we propose to be on our guard with respect to acts of the Vichy Government, inspired by Mr. Laval, that are intended to aid by French connivance the military activities of Hitler, such as the supplying of naval and air bases, or other help given by the land, sea or air forces of France; that in any event this Government has had nothing resembling satisfactory information from the French Government about what is really going on that would constitute legitimate information to us from any government at all disposed to be friendly.

I then said that our Government thus far has retained its high regard for Marshal Petain and its anxious desire to be of help to the French people to the fullest practical extent; that this Government recognizes the unfortunate situation of France as a captive nation and it recognizes to the fullest extent the duty of the French Government to conform to the armistice terms along with other functions and requirements of a captive nation, but that in so doing this Government maintains strongly its original position that the French Government has no justification of any sort to render the slightest military aid to Germany; that the French Government has no right in its acts and utterances to go beyond and outside the armistice terms for the purpose of making itself a partisan of Hitler, as between Hitler and non-belligerent countries, such as the United States, unless the French Government intends to abandon its friendly relations with other nations which are antagonistic to Hitler's movements of conquest.

The Ambassador stoutly contended that they had no plan or purpose thus to go beyond their legitimate functions, as I had described them, and he reiterated fairly often the attitude of his Government to the effect that it would not in any circumstances lend aid to the military plans of Hitler. I said that Mr. Laval may think that he can appease Mr. Hitler just as others heretofore have imagined that they could appease him; that that was his affair; that this Government, however, recognizing the great misfortune of the French Government in not pursuing the long-view objectives within sufficient time for its safety, does not propose to trust Hitler for one split second to fall in with any government on a course of appeasement; that the French Government, therefore, should understand the position of this Government and its determination to take no chances. I went on to say that this Government is not remotely thinking about minor considerations between our two Governments, such as freeing some French assets, etc., etc., but that it had a supreme and firm purpose to have no relations with any government, such as that of Vichy, which would give the slightest encouragement to Hitler, either directly or indirectly. It is manifest, therefore, that, if Marshal Petain feels aggrieved at the President's recent message to him,[60] he might well review and take cognizance of Mr. Laval's extreme pro-German plans and efforts, as reported in various ways to this Government, and which have been concealed in the main by the French Government, and only reached this Government to a limited extent, directly or indirectly. I said that there must be a spirit of candor and a willing disposition to confer back and forth with full exchanges of information in a thoroughly accurate and candid manner, so that this Government will know exactly what the Government of France is doing insofar as it relates to possible aid to Hitler over and above the terms of the armistice and the function and duty of a captive of war. I said it would be a mistake for Marshal Petain, knowing what is going on in his Government at the instance of Mr. Laval, to expect good relations between our countries to continue to exist, while he takes exception to any act or utterance of this Government in its strong protest against the reported policies and purposes of Laval.

The Ambassador said that Mr. Laval was merely attempting to procure the release of French prisoners and some other things that would be helpful to France. I said that again there comes up the matter of attempted appeasement of Hitler; that Hitler in the end would do what he pleased with all of his captive nations regardless of whether they offered him gifts and other appeasement considerations; that he would take such nations and then at some future time retake them if his past acts are to be judged fairly; that this again brings back the question of rendering aid to Germany over and above the terms of the armistice, and that the Government of France must

---

[60] See docs. 187 and 189.

understand that this Government is too much concerned about possible future attacks by Hitler to acquiesce in the slightest with acts of the French Government that would aid or encourage Hitler in still wider conquest, especially in the direction of this hemisphere. It is on this broad position that our Government rests its attitude toward France. This applies to Martinique and other possessions. In the case of Martinique, for example, if the French Government is in earnest about the absolute observance of the temporary agreement between officials of this Government and those of the French Government in regard to the status quo of Martinique, there should not be the slightest hesitation on the part of the French Government to give to this Government such assurances as would leave no doubt or uneasiness on the part of this Government, such as removing some of the parts of the ships anchored there, or a large portion of the seamen from the vessels, or to permit American vessels to inspect the properties at any reasonable time, such as the airplanes and the gold. The Ambassador professed to agree entirely and insisted that it should be done. I replied that we would see what happens with respect to all the matters mentioned in our conversation.

C[ORDELL] H[ULL]

191

Department of State Bulletin, vol. III, p. 503

President Roosevelt to King George of Greece, December 5, 1940

I thank Your Majesty for your friendly message which comes at a time when all free peoples are deeply impressed by the courage and steadfastness of the Greek nation.

The American Red Cross has already sent substantial amounts of funds and supplies for the relief of suffering in your country and I am sure that my countrymen will give generously to the new organizations which are being established for the same purpose.

As Your Majesty knows, it is the settled policy of the United States Government to extend aid to those governments and peoples who defend themselves against aggression. I assure Your Majesty that steps are being taken to extend such aid to Greece which is defending itself so valiantly.

FRANKLIN D. ROOSEVELT

192

President Roosevelt to the Appointed Ambassador to France (Leahy)

WASHINGTON, [December 20, 1940.]

MY DEAR ADMIRAL LEAHY:

As Ambassador of the United States near the French Government, you will be serving the United States at a very critical time in the relations between the United States and France. I impose entire confidence in your ability and judgment to meet all situations which may arise. Nevertheless, for your general guidance I feel that I may properly outline some of the basic principles which at present govern the relations of the United States with France.

(1) Marshal Petain occupies a unique position both in the hearts of the French people and in the Government. Under the existing Constitution his word is law and nothing can be done against his opposition unless it is accomplished without his knowledge. In his decrees he uses the royal "we" and I have gathered that he intends to rule.

Accordingly, I desire that you endeavor to cultivate as close relations with Marshal Petain as may be possible. You should outline to him the position of the United States in the present conflict and you should stress our firm conviction that only by defeat of the powers now controlling the destiny of Germany and Italy can the world live in liberty, peace and prosperity; that civilization cannot progress with a return to totalitarianism.

I had reason to believe that Marshal Petian was not cognizant of all of the acts of his Vice Premier and Minister for Foreign Affairs, Monsieur Laval, in his relations with the Germans. There can be no assurance that a similar situation will not exist with the new Foreign Minister. Accordingly, you should endeavor to bring to Marshal Petain's attention such acts done or contemplated in the name of France which you deem to be inimical to the interests of the United States.

(2) I have made it abundantly clear that the policy of this administration is to support in every way practicable those countries which are defending themselves against aggression. In harmony with this principle this Government is affording and will continue to afford to the Government of Great Britain all possible assistance short of war. You may wish from time to time to bring to the attention of Marshal Petain and members of the Government concrete information regarding the American program to this end.

(3) I have been much perturbed by reports indicating that re-sources of France are being placed at the disposal of Germany in a measure beyond that positively required by the terms of the armistice agreement. I have reason to believe that aside from the selfish interests of individuals there is unrequired governmental cooperation with Germany motivated by a belief in the inevitableness of a German victory and ultimate benefit to France. I desire that you endeavor to inform yourself with relation to this question and report fully regarding it.

You should endeavor to persuade Marshal Petain, the members of his Government, and high ranking officers in the military forces with whom you come into contact, of the conviction of this Government that a German victory would inevitably result in the dismemberment of the French Empire and the maintenance at most of France as a vassal state.

(4) I believe that the maintenance of the French fleet free of German control is not only of prime importance to the defense of this hemisphere but is also vital to the preservation of the French Empire and the eventual restoration of French independence and autonomy.

Accordingly, from the moment we were confronted with the imminent collapse of French resistance it has been a cardinal principle of this administration to assure that the French fleet did not fall into German hands and was not used in the furtherance of German aims. I immediately informed the French Government, therefore, that should that Government permit the French fleet to be surrendered to Germany the French Government would permanently lose the friendship and good will of the Government of the United States.

Since that time I have received numerous assurances from those in control of the destiny of France that the French fleet would under no circumstances be surrendered.

On June 18, 1940, Monsieur Paul Baudoin, then Minister for Foreign Affairs, assured Ambassador Biddle "in the name of the French Government in the most solemn manner that the French fleet would never be surrendered to the enemy".

On July 1, 1940, President Le Brun, informed Ambassador Bullitt that "France would under no conditions deliver the fleet to Germany." On the same day Marshal Petain assured Ambassador Bullitt that orders had been issued to every Captain of the French fleet to sink his ship rather than to permit it to fall into German hands, and Admiral Darlan told Ambassador Bullitt that he had "given absolute orders to the officers of his fleet to sink immediately any ship that the Germans should attempt to seize."

When Marshal Petain came into power as Chief of the French State I received renewed and most solemn assurances that the French fleet would not be surrendered to Germany. Vice Premier Laval reiterated these assurances to Mr. Matthews on November 14 when he said that "the French fleet will never fall into the hands of a hostile power."

On November 16 Marshal Petain, when the subject was again raised, told Mr. Matthews: "I have given the most solemn assurances that the French fleet, including the *Jean Bart* and the *Richelieu*, should never fall into Germany's hands. I have given these assurances to your Government. I have given them to the British Government, and even to Churchill personally. I reiterate them now. They will be used to defend French territory and possessions. They will never be used against the British unless we are attacked by them." And most recently Marshal Petain, in a conversation with the present Chargé d'Affaires ad interim, Mr. Murphy, said on December 12: "I hope your President understands that I have kept and will continue to keep the solemn promise I made that the French fleet will be scuttled before it is allowed to fall into German hands."

I feel most strongly that if the French Government after these repeated solemn assurances were to permit the use of the French fleet in hostile operations against the British, such action would constitute a flagrant and deliberate breach of faith to the Government of the United States.

You will undoubtedly associate with high officers of the French Navy. I desire, therefore, that in your relations with such officers, as well as in your conversations with French officials, you endeavor to convince them that to permit the use of the French fleet or naval bases by Germany or to attain German aims, would most certainly forfeit the friendship and good will of the United States and result in the destruction of the French fleet to the irreparable injury of France.

(5) You will undoubtedly be approached from numerous quarters regarding food for the French people.

There is no people on earth who have done more than the American people in relieving the suffering of humanity. The hearts of the American people go out to the people of France in their distress. As you are aware we are continuing our efforts to arrange for the forwarding through the Red Cross of medical supplies and also tinned or powdered milk for children in the unoccupied regions of France. Nevertheless, the primary interest of the American people, and an interest which overshadows all else at the moment, is to see a British victory. The American people are therefore unwilling to take any measure which in the slightest degree will prejudice such a victory. Before the American people would be willing to have influence exerted upon the British Government to permit the shipment of food through the British blockade to France, it would be necessary that the American people be convinced beyond peradventure that such action would not in the slightest assist Germany.

(6) In your discussions regarding the French West Indies and French Guiana you should point out that our sole desire in that region is to maintain the *status quo* and to be assured that neither those possessions nor their resources will ever be used to the detriment of the United States or the American republics. To accomplish this we feel that it is essential that the naval vessels stationed in the ports of those islands or possessions be immobilized and that we have adequate guarantees that the gold which is at present stored in Martinique be not used in any manner which could conceivably benefit Germany in the present struggle.

(7) I have noticed with sympathetic interest the efforts of France to maintain its authority in its North African possessions and to improve their economic status. In your discussions you may say that your Government is prepared to assist in this regard in any appropriate way.

Very sincerely yours,

FRANKLIN D. ROOSEVELT

193

Department of State Bulletin, vol. IV, p. 3

Radio Address Delivered by President Roosevelt From Washington, December 29, 1940

This is not a fireside chat on war. It is a talk on national security; because the nub of the whole purpose of your President is to keep you now, and your children later, and your grandchildren much later, out of a last-ditch war for the preservation of American independence and all of the things that American independence means to you and to me and to ours.

Tonight, in the presence of a world crisis, my mind goes back eight years ago to a night in the midst of a domestic crisis. It was a time when the wheels of American industry were grinding to a full stop, when the whole banking system of our country had ceased to function.

I well remember that while I sat in my study in the White House, preparing to talk with the people of the United States, I had before my eyes the picture of all those Americans with whom I was talking. I saw the workmen in the mills, the mines, the factories; the girl behind the counter; the small shopkeeper; the farmer doing his spring plowing; the widows and the old men wondering about their life's savings.

I tried to convey to the great mass of American people what the banking crisis meant to them in their daily lives.

Tonight, I want to do the same thing, with the same people, in this new crisis which faces America.

We met the issue of 1933 with courage and realism.

We face this new crisis—this new threat to the security of our Nation—with the same courage and realism.

Never before since Jamestown and Plymouth Rock has our American civilization been in such danger as now.

For, on September 27, 1940, by an agreement signed in Berlin, three powerful nations, two in Europe and one in Asia, joined themselves together in the threat that if the United States interfered with or blocked the expansion program of these three nations—a program aimed at world control—they would unite in ultimate action against the United States.

The Nazi masters of Germany have made it clear that they intend not only to dominate all life and thought in their own country, but also to enslave the whole of Europe, and then to use the resources of Europe to dominate the rest of the world.

Three weeks ago their leader stated, "There are two worlds that stand opposed to each other." Then in defiant reply to his opponents, he said this: "Others are correct when they say: 'With this world we cannot ever reconcile ourselves.' . . . I can beat any other power in the world." So said the leader of the Nazis.

In other words, the Axis not merely admits but proclaims that there can be no ultimate peace between their philosophy of government and our philosophy of government.

In view of the nature of this undeniable threat, it can be asserted, properly and categorically, that the United States has no right or reason to encourage talk of peace until the day shall come when there is a clear intention on the part of the aggressor nations to abandon all thought of dominating or conquering the world.

At this moment, the forces of the states that are leagued against all peoples who live in freedom are being held away from our shores. The Germans and Italians are being blocked on the other side of the Atlantic by the British, and by the Greeks, and by thousands of soldiers and sailors who were able to escape from subjugated countries. The Japanese are being engaged in Asia by the Chinese in another great defense.

In the Pacific is our fleet.

Some of our people like to believe that wars in Europe and in Asia are of no concern to us. But it is a matter of most vital concern to us that European and Asiatic war-makers should not gain control of the oceans which lead to this hemisphere.

One hundred and seventeen years ago the Monroe Doctrine was conceived by our Government as a measure of defense in the face of a threat against this hemisphere by an alliance in continental Europe. Thereafter, we stood on guard in the Atlantic, with the British as neighbors. There was no treaty. There was no "unwritten agreement".

Yet, there was the feeling, proven correct by history, that we as neighbors could settle any disputes in peaceful fashion. The fact is that during the whole of this time the Western Hemisphere has remained free from aggression from Europe or from Asia.

Does anyone seriously believe that we need to fear attack while a free Britain remains our most powerful naval neighbor in the Atlantic? Does any one seriously believe, on the other hand, that we could rest easy if the Axis powers were our neighbor there?

If Great Britain goes down, the Axis powers will control the continents of Europe, Asia, Africa, Australasia, and the high seas—and they will be in a position to bring enormous military and naval resources against this hemisphere. It is no exaggeration to say that all of us in the Americas would be living at the point of a gun—a gun loaded with explosive bullets, economic as well as military.

We should enter upon a new and terrible era in which the whole world, our hemisphere included, would be run by threats of brute force. To survive in such a world, we would have to convert ourselves permanently into a militaristic power on the basis of war economy.

Some of us like to believe that even if Great Britain falls, we are still safe, because of the broad expanse of the Atlantic and of the Pacific.

But the width of these oceans is not what it was in the days of clipper ships. At one point between Africa and Brazil the distance is less than from Washington to Denver—five hours for the latest type of bomber. And at the north of the Pacific Ocean, America and Asia almost touch each other.

Even today we have planes which could fly from the British Isles to New England and back without refueling. And the range of the modern bomber is ever being increased.

During the past week many people in all parts of the Nation have told me what they wanted me to say tonight. Almost all of them expressed a courageous desire to hear the plain truth about the gravity of the situation. One telegram, however, expressed the attitude of the small minority who want to see no evil and hear no evil, even though they know in their hearts that evil exists. That telegram begged me not to tell again of the ease with which our American cities could be bombed by any hostile power which had gained bases in this Western Hemisphere. The gist of that telegram was: "Please, Mr. President, don't frighten us by telling us the facts."

Frankly and definitely there is danger ahead—danger against which we must prepare. But we well know that we cannot escape danger, or the fear of it, by crawling into bed and pulling the covers over our heads.

Some nations of Europe were bound by solemn non-intervention pacts with Germany. Other nations were assured by Germany that they need never fear invasion. Non-intervention pact or not, the fact remains that they were attacked, overrun, and thrown into the modern form of slavery at an hour's notice or even without any notice at all. As an exiled leader of one of these nations said to me the other day: "The notice was a minus quantity. It was given to my government two hours after German troops had poured into my country in a hundred places."

The fate of these nations tells us what it means to live at the point of a Nazi gun.

The Nazis have justified such actions by various pious frauds. One of these frauds is the claim that they are occupying a nation for the purpose of "restoring order". Another is that they are occupying or controlling a nation on the excuse that they are "protecting it" against the aggression of somebody else.

For example, Germany has said that she was occupying Belgium to save the Belgians from the British. Would she hesitate to say to any South American country, "We are occupying you to protect you from aggression by the United States"?

Belgium today is being used as an invasion base against Britain, now fighting for its life. Any South American country, in Nazi hands, would always constitute a jumping-off place for German attack on any one of the other republics of this hemisphere.

Analyze for yourselves the future of two other places even nearer to Germany if the Nazis won. Could Ireland hold out? Would Irish freedom be permitted as an amazing exception in an unfree world? Or the islands of the Azores which still fly the flag of Portugal after five centuries? We think of Hawaii as an outpost of defense in the Pacific. Yet, the Azores are closer to our shores in the Atlantic than Hawaii is on the other side.

There are those who say that the Axis powers would never have any desire to attack the Western Hemisphere. This is the same dangerous form of wishful thinking which has destroyed the powers of resistance of so many conquered peoples. The plain facts are that the Nazis have proclaimed, time and again, that all other races are their inferiors and therefore subject to their orders. And most important of all, the vast resources and wealth of this hemisphere constitute the most tempting loot in all the world.

Let us no longer blind ourselves to the undeniable fact that the evil forces which have crushed and undermined and corrupted so many others are already within our own gates. Your Government knows much about them and every day is ferreting them out.

Their secret emissaries are active in our own and neighboring countries. They seek to stir up suspicion and dissension to cause internal strife. They try to turn capital against labor and vice versa. They try to reawaken long slumbering racial and religious enmities which should have no place in this country. They are active in every group that promotes intolerance. They exploit for their own ends our natural abhorrence of war. These trouble-breeders have but one purpose. It is to divide our people into hostile groups and to destroy our unity and shatter our will to defend ourselves.

There are also American citizens, many of them in high places, who, unwittingly in most cases, are aiding and abetting the work of these agents. I do not charge these American citizens with being foreign agents. But I do charge them with doing exactly the kind of work that the dictators want done in the United States.

These people not only believe that we can save our own skins by shutting our eyes to the fate of other nations. Some of them go much further than that. They say that we can and should become the friends and even the partners of the Axis powers. Some of them even suggest that we should imitate the methods of the dictatorships. Americans never can and never will do that.

The experience of the past two years has proven beyond doubt that no nation can appease the Nazis. No man can tame a tiger into a kitten by stroking it. There can be no appeasement with ruthlessness. There can be no reasoning with an incendiary bomb. We know now that a nation can have peace with the Nazis only at the price of total surrender.

Even the people of Italy have been forced to become accomplices of the Nazis; but at this moment they do not know how soon they will be embraced to death by their allies.

The American appeasers ignore the warning to be found in the fate of Austria, Czechoslovakia, Poland, Norway, Belgium, the Netherlands, Denmark, and France. They tell you that the Axis powers are going to win anyway; that all this bloodshed in the world could be saved; and that the United States might just as well throw its influence into the scale of a dictated peace, and get the best out of it that we can.

They call it a "negotiated peace". Nonsense! Is it a negotiated peace if a gang of outlaws surrounds your community and on threat of extermination makes you pay tribute to save your own skins?

Such a dictated peace would be no peace at all. It would be only another armistice, leading to the most gigantic armament race and the most devastating trade wars in history. And in these contests the Americas would offer the only real resistance to the Axis powers.

With all their vaunted efficiency and parade of pious purpose in this war, there are still in their background the concentration camp and the servants of God in chains.

The history of recent years proves that shootings and chains and concentration camps are not simply the transient tools but the very altars of modern dictatorships. They may talk of a "new order" in the world, but what they have in mind is but a revival of the oldest and the worst tyranny. In that there is no liberty, no religion, no hope.

The proposed "new order" is the very opposite of a United States of Europe or a United States of Asia. It is not a government based upon the consent of the governed. It is not a union of ordinary, self-respecting men and women to protect themselves and their freedom and their dignity from oppression. It is an unholy alliance of power and pelf to dominate and enslave the human race.

The British people are conducting an active war against this unholy alliance. Our own future security is greatly dependent on the outcome of that fight. Our ability to "keep out of war" is going to be affected by that outcome.

Thinking in terms of today and tomorrow, I make the direct statement to the American people that there is far less chance of the United States getting into war if we do all we can now to support the nations defending themselves against attack by the Axis than if we acquiesce in their defeat, submit tamely to an Axis victory, and wait our turn to be the object of attack in another war later on.

If we are to be completely honest with ourselves, we must admit there is risk in *any* course we may take. But I deeply believe that the great majority of our people agree that the course that I advocate involves the least risk now and the greatest hope for world peace in the future.

The people of Europe who are defending themselves do not ask us to do their fighting. They ask us for the implements of war, the planes, the tanks, the guns, the freighters, which will enable them to fight for their liberty and our security. Emphatically we must get these weapons to them in sufficient volume and quickly enough, so that we and our children will be saved the agony and suffering of war which others have had to endure.

Let not defeatists tell us that it is too late. It will never be earlier. Tomorrow will be later than today.

Certain facts are self-evident.

In a military sense Great Britain and the British Empire are today the spearhead of resistance to world conquest. They are putting up a fight which will live forever in the story of human gallantry.

There is no demand for sending an American Expeditionary Force outside our own borders. There is no intention by any member of your Government to send such a force. You can, therefore, nail any talk about sending armies to Europe as deliberate untruth.

Our national policy is not directed toward war. Its sole purpose is to keep war away from our country and our people.

Democracy's fight against world conquest is being greatly aided, and must be more greatly aided, by the rearmament of the United States and by sending every ounce and every ton of munitions and supplies that we can possibly spare to help the defenders who are in the front lines. It is no more unneutral for us to do that than it is for Sweden, Russia, and other nations near Germany to send steel and ore and oil and other war materials into Germany every day.

We are planning our own defense with the utmost urgency; and in its vast scale we must integrate the war needs of Britain and the other free nations resisting aggression.

This is not a matter of sentiment or of controversial personal opinion. It is a matter of realistic military policy, based on the advice of our military experts who are in close touch with existing warfare. These military and naval experts and the members of the Congress and the administration have a single-minded purpose—the defense of the United States.

This Nation is making a great effort to produce everything that is necessary in this emergency—and with all possible speed. This great effort requires great sacrifice.

I would ask no one to defend a democracy which in turn would not defend everyone in the Nation against want and privation. The strength of this Nation shall not be diluted by the failure of the Government to protect the economic well-being of all citizens.

If our capacity to produce is limited by machines, it must ever be remembered that these machines are operated by the skill and the stamina of the workers. As the Government is determined to protect the rights of workers, so the Nation has a right to expect that the men who man the machines will discharge their full responsibilities to the urgent needs of defense.

The worker possesses the same human dignity and is entitled to the same security of position as the engineer or manager or owner. For the workers provide the human power that turns out the destroyers, the airplanes, and the tanks.

The Nation expects our defense industries to continue operation without interruption by strikes or lock-outs. It expects and insists that management and workers will reconcile their differences by voluntary or legal means, to continue to produce the supplies that are so sorely needed.

And on the economic side of our great defense program, we are, as you know, bending every effort to maintain stability of prices and with that the stability of the cost of living.

Nine days ago I announced the setting up of a more effective organization to direct our gigantic efforts to increase the production of munitions. The appropriation of vast sums of money and a well-coordinated executive direction of our defense efforts are not in themselves enough. Guns, planes, and ships have to be built in the factories and arsenals of America. They have to be produced by workers and managers and engineers with the aid of machines, which in turn have to be built by hundreds of thousands of workers throughout the land.

In this great work there has been splendid cooperation between the Government and industry and labor.

American industrial genius, unmatched throughout the world in the solution of production problems, has been called upon to bring its resources and talents into action. Manufacturers of watches, of farm implements, linotypes, cash registers, automobiles, sewing machines, lawn mowers, and locomotives are now making fuses, bomb-packing crates, telescope mounts, shells, pistols, and tanks.

But all our present efforts are not enough. We must have more ships, more guns, more planes—more of everything. This can only be accomplished if we discard the notion of "business as usual". This job cannot be done merely by superimposing on the existing productive facilities the added requirements for defense.

Our defense efforts must not be blocked by those who fear the future consequences of surplus plant capacity. The possible consequences of failure of our defense efforts now are much more to be feared.

After the present needs of our defense are past, a proper handling of the country's peacetime needs will require all of the new productive capacity—if not more.

No pessimistic policy about the future of America shall delay the immediate expansion of those industries essential to defense.

I want to make it clear that it is the purpose of the Nation to build now with all possible speed every machine and arsenal and factory that we need to manufacture our defense material. We have the men, the skill, the wealth, and above all, the will.

I am confident that if and when production of consumer or luxury goods in certain industries requires the use of machines and raw materials essential for defense purposes, then such production must yield to our primary and compelling purpose.

I appeal to the owners of plants, to the managers, to the workers, to our own Government employees, to put every ounce of effort into producing these munitions swiftly and without stint. And with this appeal I give you the pledge that all of us who are officers of your Government will devote ourselves to the same whole-hearted extent to the great task which lies ahead.

As planes and ships and guns and shells are produced, your Government, with its defense experts, can then determine how best to use them to defend this hemisphere. The decision as to how much shall be sent abroad and how much shall remain at home must be made on the basis of our over-all military necessities.

We must be the great arsenal of democracy. For us this is an emergency as serious as war itself. We must apply ourselves to our task with the same resolution, the same sense of urgency, the same spirit of patriotism and sacrifice, as we would show were we at war.

We have furnished the British great material support and we will furnish far more in the future.

There will be no "bottlenecks" in our determination to aid Great Britain. No dictator, no combination of dictators, will weaken that determination by threats of how they will construe that determination.

The British have received invaluable military support from the heroic Greek Army and from the forces of all the governments in exile. Their strength is growing. It is the strength of men and women who value their freedom more highly than they value their lives.

I believe that the Axis powers are not going to win this war. I base that belief on the latest and best information.

We have no excuse for defeatism. We have every good reason for hope—hope for peace, hope for the defense of our civilization and for the building of a better civilization in the future.

I have the profound conviction that the American people are now determined to put forth a mightier effort than they have ever yet made to increase our production of all the implements of defense, to meet the threat to our democratic faith.

As President of the United States I call for that national effort. I call for it in the name of this Nation which we love and honor and which we are privileged and proud to serve. I call upon our people with absolute confidence that our common cause will greatly succeed.

194

H. Doc. 1, 77th Cong., 1st sess.

Address Delivered by President Roosevelt to the Congress, January 6, 1941

[Extract]

I address you, the Members of the Seventy-seventh Congress, at a moment unprecedented in the history of the Union. I use the word "unprecedented," because at no previous time has American security been as seriously threatened from without as it is today.

Our national policy is this:

First, by an impressive expression of the public will and without regard to partisanship, we are committed to all-inclusive national defense.

Second, by an impressive expression of the public will and without regard to partisanship, we are committed to full support of all those resolute peoples, everywhere, who are resisting aggression and are thereby keeping war away from our hemisphere. By this support, we express our determination that the democratic cause shall prevail; and we strengthen the defense and security of our own Nation.

Third, by an impressive expression of the public will and without regard to partisanship, we are committed to the proposition that principles of morality and considerations for our own security will never permit us to acquiesce in a peace dictated by aggressors and sponsored by appeasers. We know that enduring peace cannot be bought at the cost of other people's freedom.

In the recent national election there was no substantial difference between the two great parties in respect to that national policy. No issue was fought out on this line before the American electorate. Today, it is abundantly evident that American citizens everywhere are demanding and supporting speedy and complete action in recognition of obvious danger.

Therefore, the immediate need is a swift and driving increase in our armament production.

To change a whole nation from a basis of peacetime production of implements of peace to a basis of wartime production of implements of war is no small task. And the greatest difficulty comes at the beginning of the program, when new tools and plant facilities and new assembly lines and shipways must first be constructed before the actual matériel begins to flow steadily and speedily from them.

The Congress, of course, must rightly keep itself informed at all times of the progress of the program. However, there is certain information, as the Congress itself will readily recognize, which, in the interests of our own security and those of the nations we are supporting, must of needs be kept in confidence.

New circumstances are constantly begetting new needs for our safety. I shall ask this Congress for greatly increased new appropriations and authorizations to carry on what we have begun.

I also ask this Congress for authority and for funds sufficient to manufacture additional munitions and war supplies of many kinds, to be turned over to those nations which are now in actual war with aggressor nations.

Our most useful and immediate role is to act as an arsenal for them as well as for ourselves. They do not need man power. They do need billions of dollars worth of the weapons of defense.

The time is near when they will not be able to pay for them in ready cash. We cannot, and will not, tell them they must surrender, merely because of present inability to pay for the weapons which we know they must have.

I do not recommend that we make them a loan of dollars with which to pay for these weapons—a loan to be repaid in dollars.

I recommend that we make it possible for those nations to continue to obtain war materials in the United States, fitting their orders into our own program. Nearly all of their matériel would, if the time ever came, be useful for our own defense.

Taking counsel of expert military and naval authorities, considering what is best for our own security, we are free to decide how much should be kept here and how much should be sent abroad to our friends who by their determined and heroic resistance are giving us time in which to make ready our own defense.

For what we send abroad, we shall be repaid, within a reasonable time following the close of hostilities, in similar materials, or, at our option, in other goods of many kinds which they can produce and which we need.

Let us say to the democracies: "We Americans are vitally concerned in your defense of freedom. We are putting forth our energies, our resources, and our organizing powers to give you the strength to regain and maintain a free world. We shall send you, in ever-increasing numbers, ships, planes, tanks, guns. This is our purpose and our pledge."

In fulfillment of this purpose we will not be intimidated by the threats of dictators that they will regard as a breach of international law and as an act of war our aid to the democracies which dare to resist their aggression. Such aid is not an act of war, even if a dictator should unilaterally proclaim it so to be.

When the dictators are ready to make war upon us, they will not wait for an act of war on our part. They did not wait for Norway or Belgium or the Netherlands to commit an act of war.

Their only interest is in a new one-way international law, which lacks mutuality in its observance, and, therefore, becomes an instrument of oppression.

The happiness of future generations of Americans may well depend upon how effective and how immediate we can make our aid felt. No one can tell the exact character of the emergency situations that we may be called upon to meet. The Nation's hands must not be tied when the Nation's life is in danger.

We must all prepare to make the sacrifices that the emergency—as serious as war itself—demands. Whatever stands in the way of speed and efficiency in defense preparations must give way to the national need.

A free nation has the right to expect full cooperation from all groups. A free nation has the right to look to the leaders of business, of labor, and of agriculture to take the lead in stimulating effort, not among other groups but within their own groups.

I have called for personal sacrifice. I am assured of the willingness of almost all Americans to respond to that call.

A part of the sacrifice means the payment of more money in taxes. In my Budget message I recommend that a greater portion of this great defense program be paid for from taxation than we are paying today. No person should try, or be allowed, to get rich out of this program; and the principle of tax payments in accordance with ability to pay should be constantly before our eyes to guide our legislation.

If the Congress maintains these principles, the voters, putting patriotism ahead of pocketbooks, will give you their applause.

In the future days, which we seek to make secure, we look forward to a world founded upon four essential human freedoms.

The first is freedom of speech and expression—everywhere in the world.

The second is freedom of every person to worship God in his own way—everywhere in the world.

The third is freedom from want—which, translated into world terms, means economic understandings which will secure to every nation a healthy peacetime life for its inhabitants—everywhere in the world.

The fourth is freedom from fear—which, translated into world terms, means a world-wide reduction of armaments to such a point and in such a thorough fashion that no nation will be in a position to commit an act of physical aggression against any neighbor—anywhere in the world.

That is no vision of a distant millennium. It is a definite basis for a kind of world attainable in our own time and generation. That kind of world is the very antithesis of the so-called new order of tyranny which the dictators seek to create with the crash of a bomb.

To that new order we oppose the greater conception—the moral order. A good society is able to face schemes of world domination and foreign revolutions alike without fear.

Since the beginning of our American history we have been engaged in change—in a perpetual peaceful revolution—a revolution which goes on steadily, quietly adjusting itself to changing conditions—without the concentration camp or the quick-lime in the ditch. The world order which we seek is the cooperation of free countries, working together in a friendly, civilized society.

This Nation has placed its destiny in the hands and heads and hearts of its millions of free men and women; and its faith in freedom under the guidance of God. Freedom means the supremacy of human rights everywhere. Our support goes to those who struggle to gain those rights or keep them. Our strength is in our unity of purpose.

To that high concept there can be no end save victory.

FRANKLIN D. ROOSEVELT

195

Department of State Bulletin, vol. IV, p. 85

Statement by the Secretary of State Before the Committee on Foreign Affairs, House of Representatives, January 15, 1941

We are here to consider a bill designed to promote the defense of the United States. I shall not discuss the technical details of the proposed measure, since that will be done by other departments of the Government more directly concerned with these matters. I shall place before you briefly the controlling facts relating to the manner in which the dangers that now confront this hemisphere and, therefore, this Nation have arisen, and the circumstances which render imperative all possible speed in our preparation for meeting these dangers.

During the past eight years, our Government has striven, by every peaceful means at its disposal, to secure the establishment in the world of conditions under which there would be a reasonable hope for enduring peace. We have proceeded in the firm belief that only if such conditions come to exist will there be a certainty that our country will be fully secure and safely at peace. The establishment of such conditions calls for acceptance and application by all nations of certain basic principles of peaceful and orderly international conduct and relations.

Accordingly, in the conduct of our foreign relations, this Government has directed its efforts to the following objectives: (1) Peace and security for the United States with advocacy of peace and limitation and reduction of armament as universal international objectives; (2) support for law, order, justice, and morality and the principle of non-intervention; (3) restoration and cultivation of sound economic methods and relations, based on equality of treatment; (4) development, in the promotion of these objectives, of the fullest practicable measure of international cooperation; (5) promotion of the security, solidarity, and general welfare of the Western Hemisphere.

Observance and advocacy of the basic principles underlying these policies, and efforts toward their acceptance and application, became increasingly important as three nations, one after another, made abundantly clear, by word and by deed, their determination to repudiate and destroy the very foundations of a civilized world order under law and to enter upon the road of armed conquest, of subjugation of other nations, and of tyrannical rule over their victims.

The first step in this fatal direction occurred in the Far East in 1931 with forceful occupation of Manchuria in contravention of the provisions of the Nine Power Treaty and of the Kellogg-Briand Pact. The equilibrium in the Far East which had been established by the Washington Conference treaties of 1921–1922 became seriously disturbed by the setting up by forceful means in a part of China of a regime under Japanese control under the name of "Manchukuo". This control over Manchuria has been marked by the carrying out of a policy of discrimination which has resulted in forcing out American and other foreign interests.

During the years that followed, Japan went steadily forward in her preparations for expansion by force of arms. In December 1934, she gave notice of her intention to terminate the naval treaty of February 6, 1922. She then proceeded with intensified construction of military and naval armaments, at the same time undertaking, from time to time, limited actions directed toward an extension of her domination over China and involving disregard and destruction of the lawful rights and interests of other countries, including the United States.

In July 1937, the armed forces of Japan embarked upon large-scale military operations against China. Invading forces of more than a million men occupied large areas along the seaboard and in the central provinces. In these areas there were set up puppet regimes which instituted systems of controls and monopolies discriminatory in favor of the interests of the invading country.

It has been clear throughout that Japan has been actuated from the start by broad and ambitious plans for establishing herself in a dominant position in the entire region of the Western Pacific. Her leaders have openly declared their determination to achieve and maintain that position by force of arms and thus to make themselves masters of an area containing almost one half of the entire population of the world. As a consequence, they would have arbitrary control of the sea and trade routes in that region.

Previous experience and current developments indicate that the proposed "new order" in the Pacific area means, politically, domination by one country. It means, economically, employment of the resources of the area concerned for the benefit of that country and to the ultimate impoverishment of other parts of the area and exclusion of the interests of other countries. It means, socially, the destruction of personal liberties and the reduction of the conquered peoples to the role of inferiors.

It should be manifest to every person that such a program for the subjugation and ruthless exploitation by one country of nearly one half of the population of the world is a matter of immense significance, importance, and concern to every other nation wherever located.

Notwithstanding the course which Japan has followed during recent years, this Government has made repeated efforts to persuade the Japanese Government that her best interests lie in the development of friendly relations with the United States and with other countries which believe in orderly and peaceful processes among nations. We have at no time made any threats.

In Europe, the first overt breach of world order was made by Italy, when, in 1935, that country invaded and conquered Ethiopia, in direct contravention of solemnly accepted obligations under the Covenant of the League of Nations and under the Kellogg-Briand Pact. In 1939, Italy seized Albania in violation of unequivocal treaty obligations. In the summer of 1940, she entered the European war on the side of Germany with the openly avowed purpose of participating with that country in a remodeling of the world on the basis of a "new order" founded upon unlimited and unrestricted use of armed force. Finally, without provocation, she has attacked Greece.

Throughout this period, the Government of the United States made known to the Government of Italy its anxious concern over the growing deterioration of peaceful international relationships. Both on the occasion of the Italo-Ethiopian controversy and during the period preceding Italy's entry into the European war, this Government addressed numerous communications to the Government of Italy in an effort to prevent new breaches of world order.

Germany, from the time that Hitler and his associates came to power in 1933, began feverishly to construct vast armaments, while following a program of repeatedly made and repeatedly broken promises as a part of a skillful diplomatic game designed to lull the suspicions of other countries. After employing for several months at the Disarmament Conference in Geneva tactics which have since become a distinct pattern of German policy—further demands as previous demands are met—Germany, in October 1933, rendered impossible any effective international agreement for limitation of armaments by withdrawing from the Disarmament Conference. There then followed nearly six years during which Germany, having determined upon a policy of unlimited conquest, moved inevitably toward the catastrophe of war.

Germany's work of preparation followed two main lines. The first consisted in the creation of armed force. To this end, her entire national economy was transformed into a highly regimented and highly disciplined war economy. Every phase of national activity became harnessed to the requirements of preparation for war. More than half of the national income was expended for military purposes. Foreign trade and foreign payments became rigidly controlled for the same purpose. The production of planes and tanks and guns and all the other countless accessories of a modern war machine became the immediate objective of the whole national effort.

The second line consisted of a series of steps directed toward improving the strategic position of Germany. The first of these was the occupation and fortification of the Rhineland in 1936, in direct violation of the Locarno Treaty, voluntarily entered into by Germany 10 years earlier. Then followed, in rapid succession, the absorption of Austria, in direct violation of pledges given by Hitler to respect the sovereignty and independence of that country; the dismemberment and final seizure of Czechoslovakia, in spite of Hitler's assurances after the seizure of Austria that Germany desired no additional territory in Europe and in violation of a solemn pledge to respect the independence of that country, officially given in October 1938; the annexation of Memel; and finally, on September 1, 1939, a brutal attack upon, and the devastation and partitioning of, Poland.

The period of the war has witnessed the invasion and occupation of Denmark, Norway, Holland, Belgium, and Luxemburg, in violation of the scrupulously observed neutrality of these countries and in contravention, in the cases of some of these countries, of assurances expressly given by Germany of her intention to respect their independence and sovereignty; the invasion and partial occupation of France; the splitting up of Rumania and the German occupation of the remaining portion of that country.

These seizures have been accomplished through a combined use of armed force applied from without and of an almost unbelievable amount of subversive activity from within. Each of the invaded and occupied countries has been subjected to a reign of terror and despotism. By word and by deed, the invaders have made unmistakably clear their determination to impose permanently upon these unfortunate countries a rule of tyranny frequently reminiscent of the worst pages of ancient history.

So long as there seemed to remain even a faint hope of inducing the leaders of Germany to desist from the course which they were following, the Government of the United States neglected no opportunity to make its voice heard in restraint. It went further, and repeatedly offered its assistance in economic readjustments which might promote solution of the existing difficulties by peaceful means. All hope disappeared when the Nazi legions struck at Poland and plunged Europe into a new war.

Since then, it has become increasingly apparent that mankind is today face to face, not with regional wars or isolated conflicts, but with an organized, ruthless, and implacable movement of steadily expanding conquest. We are in the presence of forces which are not restrained by considerations of law or principles of morality; which have fixed no limits for their program of conquest; which have spread over large areas on land and are desperately struggling now to seize control of the oceans as an essential means of achieving and maintaining their conquest of the other continents.

Control of the high seas by law-abiding nations is the key to the security of the Western Hemisphere in the present-day world situation. Should that control be gained by the partners of the Tripartite Pact, the danger to our country, great as it is today, would be multiplied manyfold.

It is frequently said that there can be no danger of an invasion of the New World. It is said: As Germany has not been able to cross the British Channel, how can she cross the Atlantic?

German forces could cross the Channel in an hour's time were it not for the fact that Britain, now thoroughly prepared and well armed, is fighting every hour of the day to prevent that crossing and is fortified with every known device to repel a landing. The 20 miles of water between continental Europe and Britain are under British, not German, control. Were Britain defeated, and were she to lose command of the seas, Germany could easily cross the Atlantic—especially the South Atlantic—unless we were ready and able to do what Britain is doing now. Were the Atlantic to fall into German control, the Atlantic would offer little or no assurance of security.

Under these conditions our national security would require the continuous devotion of a very great part of all our work and wealth for defense production, prolonged universal military service, extremely burdensome taxation, unending vigilance against enemies within our borders, and complete involvement in power diplomacy. These would be the necessities of a condition as exposed as ours would be.

Great Britain is today a veritable fortress. So will this country be when our preparations for armed defense are completed. Most likely, however, it will not be by direct and frontal attack that the would-be invaders will undertake the conquest of this country, if they ever have a chance to embark upon such an enterprise. It is rather to be anticipated that their efforts would first be directed against other portions of this hemisphere more vulnerable than this country, and then against us.

Subversive forces are hard at work in many American countries, seeking to create internal dissension and disunion as a now familiar prelude to armed invasion. Today these forces are held in check and are being steadily eradicated. But the entire situation would change if control of the high seas were to pass into the hands of the would-be attackers. Under such conditions, the difficulties of continental defense would demand from us vastly greater efforts than we are now called upon to envisage.

The most serious question today for this country is whether the control of the high seas shall pass into the hands of powers bent on a program of unlimited conquest. It is in this light, above all, that we should order our present-day thinking and action with respect to the amount of material assistance which our country is prepared to furnish Great Britain.

On no other question of public policy are the people of this country so nearly unanimous and so emphatic today as they are on that of the imperative need, in our own most vital interest, to give Great Britain and other victims of attack the maximum of material aid in the shortest possible space of time. This is so because it is now altogether clear that such assistance to those who resist attack is a vital part of our national self-defense. In the face of the forces of conquest now on the march across the earth, self-defense is and must be the compelling consideration in the determination of wise and prudent national policy.

For us to withhold aid to victims of attack would not result in a restoration of peace. It would merely tend to perpetuate the enslavement of nations already invaded and subjugated and provide an opportunity for the would-be conquerors to gather strength for an attack against us.

The protagonists of the forces against which we are today forging the instrumentalities of self-defense have repudiated in every essential respect the long-accepted principles of peaceful and orderly international relations. They have disregarded every right of neutral nations, even of those to which they themselves had given solemn pledges of inviolability. Their constantly employed weapons for the government of their unfortunate victims are unrestricted terrorization, firing squads, deceit, forced labor, confiscation of property, concentration camps, and deprivations of every sort.

The most scrupulous observance by peaceful countries of legal concepts provides today no security whatever. Many nations which trusted to the integrity of their intentions and the care with which they observed their legal obligations have been destroyed.

I am certain that the day will come again when no nation will have the effrontery and the cynicism to demand that, while it itself scoffs at and disregards every principle of law and order, its intended victims must adhere rigidly to all such principles—until the very moment when its armed forces have crossed their frontiers. But so long as such nations exist, we cannot and must not be diverted—either by their threats or by their hypocritical protests—from our firm determination to create means and conditions of self-defense wherever and in whatever form we find essential to our own security.

The present bill sets up machinery which will enable us to make the most effective use of our resources for our own needs and for the needs of those whom, in our own self-defense, we are determined thus to aid. The great problem of democracy is to organize and to use its strength with sufficient speed and completeness. The proposed legislation is an essential measure for that purpose. This bill will make it possible for us to allocate our resources in ways best calculated to provide for the security of this Nation and of this continent in the complex and many-sided conditions of danger with which we are, and are likely to be, confronted. Above all, it will enable us to do all these things in the speediest possible manner. And, overwhelmingly, speed is our greatest need today.

196

711.94/1935

The Ambassador in Japan (Grew) to the Secretary of State

[Telegram : Paraphrase]

Tokyo, January 27, 1941—6 p.m.
[Received January 27—6 : 38 a.m.]

125. A member of the Embassy was told by my ————— colleague that from many quarters, including a Japanese one, he had heard that a surprise mass attack on Pearl Harbor was planned by the Japanese military forces, in case of "trouble" between Japan and the United States; that the attack would involve the use of all the Japanese military facilities. My colleague said that he was prompted to pass

this on because it had come to him from many sources, although the plan seemed fantastic.

GREW

197

740.0011 European War 1939/8231A

The Secretary of State to the Minister in Yugoslavia (Lane)

[Telegram : Paraphrase]

WASHINGTON, February 9, 1941—10 p.m.

21. In regard to recent discussions of the position of this Government in respect to the developing world situation we desire that you make clear to the Government of Yugoslavia our position as outlined below.

The President said in a recent statement to the Nation, "we are planning our own defense with the utmost urgency and in its vast scale we must integrate the war needs of Britain."

This position continues to be the keystone of the national defense policy of the United States and this effort has been intensified by the developing situation. That Britain will win we are convinced. Already war material production in America has been undertaken on the vast scale indicated and the provision of facilities to meet the requirements of the British will continue until the final victory ever increasingly. On several occasions the President has pointed out that from this policy there can be no deviation as in his own words, "we know now that a nation can have peace with the Nazis only at the price of total surrender."

HULL

198

740.0011 European War 1939/8392A

The Secretary of State to the Minister in Yugoslavia (Lane)

[Telegram]

WASHINGTON, February 14, 1941—7 p.m.

24. My 21, February 9, 10 p.m. In accordance with the President's desire I gave to the Minister of Yugoslavia for transmission to his Government the following message:

"The President at this moment when peaceful nations are seeking a policy to insure their own integrity is convinced that any victory on behalf of the predatory powers even if it only be in the diplomatic field would but pave the way for fresh demands accompanied by threats of force against the very independence of the nation thus menaced. The President also desires it to be realized that the so-called Lend-Lease Bill now before the Congress and which has been passed by the House of Representatives and by the Committee on Foreign Relations of the Senate permits in its present form for the President to supply the materials of war to those nations that are now the victims of aggression or which might be threatened with aggression."

HULL

199

711.94/1987

Memorandum by the Secretary of State Regarding a Conversation With the Japanese Ambassador (Nomura)

[WASHINGTON,] March 8, 1941.

The Japanese Ambassador called at my apartment at the Carlton Hotel by an indirect arrangement based on the equal and joint initiative of himself and myself growing out of his talk with the President in my presence some days ago. I expressed my satisfaction and interest at his coming and he said that he had been watching for an opportunity to talk with me. The idea evidently was that he was seeking to do this without appearing to take the initiative in the conference.

I then said that I was not absolutely certain whether he would come; that at all times most countries have some responsible, fine and capable citizens who are seeking earnestly and patriotically to make their respective contributions to better understanding and other desirable relations between their own and other governments; that in the instant situation I deeply appreciate their purposes and their efforts and have sent word to them to that effect. I have also made it clear that on all official questions and problems between our Governments I can only deal with and through him, the duly authorized Ambassador of Japan, and that much as I appreciate their efforts, this must be the course and attitude of my Government. I made this very definite so that the Ambassador could not misunderstand me. I also said to the Ambassador that I had likewise sent word to these good people from his country that I could not confer with them individually relative to these matters pending between our two Governments unless the Ambassador assumed the responsibility and the initiative to that end; that, in other words, everything must come and go through him, the Ambassador of Japan. He merely bowed each time I referred to the matter without saying anything.

Some casual remark then offered the occasion for me to refer to our program of liberal commercial policy and trade agreements and the extreme need for its adoption by all important nations. I reviewed in some detail the course of extreme nationalism during the post-war period and how each nation had sought to live unto itself, blocking the maximum of imports by arbitrary methods of every kind with the result that the sum total of international trade was far below what the annual increase during the past twenty years should have made it; that the processes of distribution and consumption were hopelessly hobbled and handicapped; that as a result world consumption fell at least twenty billions below what it should have legitimately been; that unemployment correspondingly spread in almost every part of the world, with resultant privations, distress and hunger, so that peoples in many countries became a prey to agitators and those seeking dictatorships while the peaceful nations were stagnant and cursed with large dammed up surpluses of their own with nowhere to sell them. I said it was against this movement of what would ultimately be utter disaster that I and others strove for many years in an effort to prevail on important nations to join in a liberal commercial program for vastly increased production and healthy trade in all parts of the world; but that the movement had been just a little too late for us to prevail, especially on Europe, to get in and actively aid in advancing this movement of economic restoration on a sound healthy basis. I said that we were struggling to get forty nations actively and earnestly behind this movement based on equality of treatment and equality of access to raw materials, so that we could then turn to countries like Germany and Italy and let the forty nations assure them that they would be welcome into this program of trade opportunity and trade equality.

I said that, unfortunately, this sound healthy movement was interrupted by military movements and plans and undertakings; that conquest by force accompanied by virtual military rule of conquered peoples, with all of its elements of semi-barbarism, seemed to effectively block for the time being the movement for peaceful commerce and increased consumption and employment throughout most of the world. I said this policy and this movement of my Government are, of course, well known to every government and every statesman in the world; that in our efforts to ward off any pretext for military adventures for purposes of conquest and arbitrary domination of other nations economically, politically or militarily, we for years strove to the utmost not only to advance and secure the acceptance generally of a sound liberal commercial policy and ever-increasing international trade, but along with it the other fundamentals which underlie all other important relations among civilized nations and with which everyone is familiar; that that was our objectve and our effort; that these efforts conducted vigorously for many years under this Administration were well known to everybody.

I then said that it would be impossible to describe our surprise and deep disappointment to see a number of nations abandon this peaceful course of understanding and adjustment in accordance with basic rules and laws and policies and move straight in the direction of fastening on the world the opposite and opposing policy of military conquest by force, and threat of force, and the adoption of methods of government of the conquered peoples that are a reversion to those extremely and unspeakably vicious methods of arbitrary rulers and despots of many centuries ago.

I said, therefore, that I am glad to have the Ambassador come in in the hope that he may have something definite and systematic in mind that would offer a practical approach to and consideration of the course and attitude of his Government with respect to its present course.

The Ambassador expressed much interest in what I said about attempts to organize the world on a liberal commercial basis and indicated his whole-hearted approval. He said that his Government, like others at times, may have made some mistakes, and he added that all of the people in Japan with very few exceptions, which included extremists, were very much averse to getting into war with the United States; that he had talked with them generally and this included most of the military officials, but not all of them; that Prime Minister Konoye is not one of the latter type, and is not desirous of moving on such a course as I had mentioned and criticized, namely a course of military expansion; that Matsuoka is a politician and the Ambassador smiled and said that he sometimes uses big words. The Ambassador said that the talk of Matsuoka and other statesmen in Japan along the lines I complained of was really for home consumption. The Ambassador then said that his Government would be very glad to effect peace arrangements with China and hoped that at no distant date such terms might be developed as would give consideration to their puppet government and would move Chiang Kai-shek to come into the picture and participate in general peaceful arrangements with China, which the Ambassador emphasized as his country's desire, and which should be on the basis of equality to all nations. In response to inquiries as to further details of the proposed Chinese-Japanese peace or the methods of bringing it about, the Ambassador was silent for the present, but indicated that his adviser, Colonel Iwakuro, is on his way here and that he had intimate details of the whole Chinese-Japanese situation.

The Ambassador then said that it would be well-nigh unthinkable for our two countries to fight each other on account of the destructive effects that would inevitably result in any event. I here spoke and said that my country entertained the same idea about the destructive effects of a military clash between our two countries. I then inquired of the Ambassador whether the military groups in control of his Government could possibly expect important nations like the United States to sit absolutely quiet while two or three nations before our very eyes organized naval and military forces and went out and conquered the balance of the earth, including the seven seas and all trade routes and the other four continents. Could they expect countries like mine to continue to remain complacent as that movement is going on? I inquired further what countries like mine would have to gain by remaining complacent in the face of a movement to substitute force and conquest for law and justice and order and fair dealing and equality. The Ambassador sought to play down the view that such military conquest was really in the mind of his Government and he then said that embargoes by this country were, of course, of increasing concern, and that he did not believe there would be any further military movements unless the policy of increasing embargoes by this country should force his Government, in the minds of those in control, to take further military steps. To this I replied that this is a matter entirely in the hands of his Government for the reason that his Government took the initiative in military expansion and seizures of territory of other countries, thereby creating an increasingly deep concern on the part of my own and other countries as to the full extent of Japanese conquest by force which was contemplated; that my country has not been at fault and none of the nations engaged in conquest have pretended seriously to charge it with any action of omission or commission in relation to the present movement of world conquest by force on the part of some three nations, including Japan. The Ambassador sought here to minimize and mildly to controvert the idea that Japan is engaged in broad unqualified military conquest. I then repeated the terms of the Tripartite Agreement and the public declaration of Hitler and Matsuoka and other high authorities in Japan to the effect that their countries under the Tripartite arrangement were out by military force to establish a new order not for Asia alone, not for Europe alone, but for the world, and a new order under their control. I said that whatever interpretation the Ambassador might give these utterances and military activities in harmony with them thus far, the American people who were long complacent with respect to dangerous international developments have of late become very thoroughly aroused and awakened to what they regard as a matter of most serious concern in relation to movements by Japan and Germany, presumably to take charge of the seas and the other continents for their own personal arbitrary control and pecuniary profit at the expense of the welfare of all of the peoples, who are victims of such a course and of peaceful nations in general. I said, of course, these apprehensions and this tremendous concern will remain and continue so long as Hitler continues his avowed course of unlimited conquest and tyrannical rule and so long as the Japanese Army and Navy increase their occupation by force of other and distant areas on both land and sea, with no apparent occasion to do so other than that of capture and exclusive use of the territory and other interests of other countries. The Ambassador again sought to allay the idea of military conquest on the part of his country, and I again replied with emphasis that as long as Japanese forces were all over China and Japanese troops and airplanes and naval vessels were as far south as Thailand and Indochina and Saigon, accompanied by such threatening declarations as Japanese statesmen are making week after week, there can only be increasing concern by nations who are vitally interested in international affairs both on land and sea as they are also vitally interested in the halt of world conquest by force and barbaric methods of government.

The Ambassador came back again to the desire of his country for peace with China based on equality to all and the hope that it might combine something of their puppet government with Chiang Kaishek's government. I pressed the Ambassador to indicate some further definite ideas he might have in mind about the proper steps to take to approach the whole situation. He did not disagree with me when I spoke of the necessity for acts and utterances by Japan, making it clear that in good faith she was not pursuing or intending to pursue a course of expansion and conquest by force such as had been referred to.

I said that I came from the President who sent his regards and said that he would be only too glad at any time to talk further with the Ambassador just as two old friends would talk, and do so officially and unofficially, or individually at times, if desired by either. I pointed out that such a meeting could be arranged unobtrusively and without publicity, and in a manner permitting the initiative to be shared on a 50-50 basis between him and the President. The Ambassador said he might call on the President the next time; that he would hope to continue these conversations. On two or three occasions I inquired of him whether it was still agreeable to pursue the President's suggestion of talking over and discussing the past relations between our two Governments and the questions that have arisen which call for settlement by mutual agreement. He indicated his favorable disposition in regard to the matter, but not in any specific way as to time or as to officials with whom he might talk.

I referred on one or two occasions to the statement reported to have been made to Mr. Churchill by the Japanese Ambassador in London some days ago to the effect that his Government would not attack Singapore or the Netherlands East Indies, and inquired point-blank what the Ambassador's idea as to this was. In reply to the first inquiry, he was not exceedingly strong in his statement but he did make it fairly definite that he did not believe there would be an attack but added, as heretofore indicated, that if our American embargoes continued to press his Government and the military group in control, they may feel forced to proceed further in a naval or military way. I again said to him that this latter question would not with any consistency or reason arise, in my judgment, because, as already stated to him, the whole responsibility and initiative with respect to military conquest and the departure from laws and treaties and other basic rules of friendly relationship by the Japanese Government rests entirely on that Government.

I again inquired of the Ambassador if he had any further ideas or suggestions which would constitute any plans or purposes for peaceful readjustment additional to that which he had already mentioned in relation to China. The Ambassador did not offer any comment on this except to attempt to convey the impression that later he would give consideration to these further phases.

At an appropriate stage in the conversation I said that the conquest of the world by his country and Germany with the methods of government which were being applied to conquered peoples, all bankrupt, would mean to set not only the world but these very conquering countries back to impossible levels of existence; that the conquering countries themselves would be the losers to an unthinkable extent.

In the course of the conversation I had occasion to remind the Ambassador that few nations were ever on more mutually profitable and genuine friendly relations than our two countries for two generations lasting until about the time of the Coolidge and Hoover Administrations. I said that, speaking in great confidence, when I came to the State Department, one of my greatest ambitions was to work out a mutually satisfactory arrangement with respect to the Quota Limitation Act of 1924, enacted by our Congress, so as to place the whole matter of immigration on an equal or reciprocal basis, which, of course, would have meant that the number of immigrants both ways would be limited, but this basis of equality would settle the feeling that has existed since 1924. He expressed his gratification at this.

I then added that we would get nowhere if the military group should say that they were not expanding in a military way, as they have often said in China, and at the same time go forward with their expansion plans and activities.

The Ambassador also brought up the question about how the doors of trade had been closed against Japan by other countries, including Indochina, and hence the necessity for some steps looking to the comfortable existence of her people. To this I replied by reminding the Ambassador of what I had said at the outset to the effect that during the twenty years of the post-war period under the reign of extreme nationalism in every country alike, all nations had shut their doors to a large extent against each other, that most nations shut their doors against my country as a part of this universal movement of trade and commercial suicide; that, therefore, Japan is not an exception. I then added that it would be an amazing thing to abandon the whole program of economic rehabilitation on peaceful lines and under the principle of equality, to which I have been referring, and turn away to military force and conquest as a substitute.

I inquired whether Matsuoka was going to Berlin and the Ambassador said he did not believe he would go, that he had been invited there at the time of the signing of the Tripartite Pact.

I proceeded to comment on Japan's line of activities and utterances by saying that this country and most other countries only proclaim and practice policies of peaceful international relationships, political, economic, social and cultural. Sometimes the policy to promote these mutually beneficial relationships is proclaimed, such as our good neighbor policy with special reference to Pan America. And yet all of our acts and programs and policies adopted by the twenty-one American nations in their conferences from time to time are made universal in their application, so that Japan and all other nations receive the same equal opportunities for trade and commerce generally throughout the Americas that each of the American nations receives itself. In striking contrast the new order in greater Eastern

Asia is unequivocally believed to be purely a program of military aggression and conquest with entirely arbitrary policies of political, economic and military domination. The Ambassador made no definite promise as to what his Government would do in respect to halting its aggression for purpose of discussions. He did not intimate that it could not and would not do this, no more than he intimated or indicated just what its attitude would be towards the Tripartite Agreement in the future when I definitely brought that phase to his attention in connection with the present and prospective course of the Japanese Government.

During our conversation, I emphasized to the Ambassador that it is the opinion of the President and others of the Administration that the British will beyond any reasonable doubt be able successfully to resist Hitler.

C[ORDELL] H[ULL]

200

55 Stat. 31

"Lend-Lease Act", March 11, 1941

Be it enacted by the Senate and House of Representatives of the United States of America in Congress assembled, That this Act may be cited as "An Act to Promote the Defense of the United States".

SEC. 2. As used in this Act—

(a) The term "defense article" means—

(1) Any weapon, munition, aircraft, vessel, or boat;
(2) Any machinery, facility, tool, material, or supply necessary for the manufacture, production, processing, repair, servicing, or operation of any article described in this subsection;
(3) Any component material or part of or equipment for any article described in this subsection;
(4) Any agricultural, industrial or other commodity or article for defense.

Such term "defense article" includes any article described in this subsection: Manufactured or procured pursuant to section 3, or to which the United States or any foreign government has or hereafter acquires title, possession, or control.

(b) The term "defense information" means any plan, specification, design, prototype, or information pertaining to any defense article.

SEC. 3. (a) Notwithstanding the provisions of any other law, the President may, from time to time, when he deems it in the interest of national defense, authorize the Secretary of War, the Secretary of the Navy, or the head of any other department or agency of the Government—

(1) To manufacture in arsenals, factories, and shipyards under their jurisdiction, or otherwise procure, to the extent to which funds are made available therefor, or contracts are authorized from time to time by the Congress, or both, any defense article for the government of any country whose defense the President deems vital to the defense of the United States.

(2) To sell, transfer title to, exchange, lease, lend, or otherwise dispose of, to any such government any defense article, but no defense article not manufactured or procured under paragraph (1) shall in any way be disposed of under this paragraph, except after consultation with the Chief of Staff of the Army or the Chief of Naval Operations of the Navy, or both. The value of defense articles disposed of in any way under authority of this paragraph, and procured from funds heretofore appropriated, shall not exceed $1,300,000,000. The value of such defense articles shall be determined by the head of the department or agency concerned or such other department, agency or officer as shall be designated in the manner provided in the rules and regulations issued hereunder. Defense articles procured from funds hereafter appropriated to any department or agency of the Government, other than from funds authorized to be appropriated under this Act, shall not be disposed of in any way under authority of this paragraph except to the extent hereafter authorized by the Congress in the Acts appropriating such funds or otherwise.

(3) To test, inspect, prove, repair, outfit, recondition, or otherwise to place in good working order, to the extent to which funds are made available therefor, or contracts are authorized from time to time by the Congress, or both, any defense article for any such government, or to procure any or all such services by private contract.

(4) To communicate to any such government any defense information, pertaining to any defense article furnished to such government under paragraph (2) of this subsection.

(5) To release for export any defense article disposed of in any way under this subsection to any such government.

(b) The terms and conditions upon which any such foreign government receives any aid authorized under subsection (a) shall be those which the President deems satisfactory, and the benefit to the United States may be payment or repayment in kind or property, or any other direct or indirect benefit which the President deems satisfactory.

(c) After June 30, 1943, or after the passage of a concurrent resolution by the two Houses before June 30, 1943, which declares that the powers conferred by or pursuant to subsection (a) are no longer necessary to promote the defense of the United States, neither the President nor the head of any department or agency shall exercise any of the powers conferred by or pursuant to subsection (a); except that until July 1, 1946, any of such powers may be exercised to the extent necessary to carry out a contract or agreement with such a foreign government made before July 1, 1943, or before the passage of such concurrent resolution, whichever is the earlier.

(d) Nothing in this Act shall be construed to authorize or to permit the authorization of convoying vessels by naval vessels of the United States.

(e) Nothing in this Act shall be construed to authorize or to permit the authorization of the entry of any American vessel into a combat area in violation of section 3 of the Neutrality Act of 1939.

Sec. 4. All contracts or agreements made for the disposition of any defense article or defense information pursuant to section 3 shall contain a clause by which the foreign government undertakes that it will not, without the consent of the President, transfer title to or possession of such defense article or defense information by gift, sale, or otherwise, or permit its use by anyone not an officer, employee, or agent of such foreign government.

Sec. 5. (a) The Secretary of War, the Secretary of the Navy, or the head of any other department or agency of the Government involved shall, when any such defense article or defense information is exported, immediately inform the department or agency designated by the President to administer section 6 of the Act of July 2, 1940 (54 Stat. 714), of the quantities, character, value, terms of disposition, and destination of the article and information so exported.

(b) The President from time to time, but not less frequently than once every ninety days, shall transmit to the Congress a report of operations under this Act except such information as he deems incompatible with the public interest to disclose. Reports provided for under this subsection shall be transmited to the Secretary of the Senate or the Clerk of the House of Representatives, as the case may be, if the Senate or the House of Representatives, as the case may be, is not in session.

Sec. 6. (a) There is hereby authorized to be appropriated from time to time, out of any money in the Treasury not otherwise appropriated, such amounts as may be necessary to carry out the provisions and accomplish the purposes of this Act.

(b) All money and all property which is converted into money received under section 3 from any government shall, with the approval of the Director of the Budget, revert to the respective appropriation or appropriations out of which funds were expended with respect to the defense article or defense information for which such consideration is received, and shall be available for expenditure for the purpose for which such expended funds were appropriated by law, during the fiscal year in which such funds are received and the ensuing fiscal year; but in no event shall any funds so received be available for expenditure after June 30, 1946.

SEC. 7. The Secretary of War, the Secretary of the Navy, and the head of the department or agency shall in all contracts or agreements for the disposition of any defense article or defense information fully protect the rights of all citizens of the United States who have patent rights in and to any such article or information which is hereby authorized to be disposed of and the payments collected for royalties on such patents shall be paid to the owners and holders of such patents.

SEC. 8. The Secretaries of War and of the Navy are hereby authorized to purchase or otherwise acquire arms, ammunition, and implements of war produced within the jurisdiction of any country to which section 3 is applicable, whenever the President deems such purchase or acquisition to be necessary in the interests of the defense of the United States.

SEC. 9. The President may, from time to time, promulgate such rules and regulations as may be necessary and proper to carry out any of the provisions of this Act; and he may exercise any power or authority conferred on him by this Act through such department, agency, or officer as he shall direct.

SEC. 10. Nothing in this Act shall be construed to change existing law relating to the use of the land and naval forces of the United States, except insofar as such use relates to the manufacture, procurement, and repair of defense articles, the communication of information and other noncombatant purposes enumerated in this Act.

SEC. 11. If any provision of this Act or the application of such provision to any circumstance shall be held invalid, the validity of the remainder of the Act and the applicability of such provision to other circumstances shall not be affected thereby.

Approved, March 11, 1941.

201

Department of State Bulletin, vol. IV, p. 277

Address Delivered by President Roosevelt at Washington, March 15, 1941

This dinner of the White House Correspondents' Association is unique. It is the first one at which I have made a speech in all these eight years. It differs from the press conferences that you and I hold twice a week. You cannot ask me any questions; and everything I have to say is word for word "*on* the record".

For eight years you and I have been helping each other. I have been trying to keep you informed of the news of Washington and of the nation and of the world from the point of view of the Presidency. You, more than you realize it, have been giving me a great deal of information about what the people of this country are thinking.

In our press conferences, as at this dinner tonight, we include reporters representing papers and news agencies of many other lands. To most of them it is a matter of constant amazement that press conferences such as ours can exist in any nation in the world.

That is especially true in those lands where freedoms do not exist—where the purposes of our democracy and the characteristics of our country and of our people have been seriously distorted.

Such misunderstandings are not new. I remember that in the early days of the first World War the German Government received solemn assurances from their representatives in the United States that the people of America were disunited; that they cared more for peace at any price than for the preservation of ideals and freedom; that there would even be riots and revolutions in the United States if this Nation ever asserted its own interests.

Let not dictators of Europe and Asia doubt our unanimity now.

Before the present war broke out on September 1, 1939, I was more worried about the future than many people—most people. The record shows I was not worried enough.

That, however, is water over the dam. Do not let us waste time reviewing the past or fixing or dodging the blame for it. History cannot be rewritten by wishful thinking. We, the American people, are writing new history today.

The big news story of this week is this: The world has been told that we, as a united nation, realize the danger which confronts us—and that to meet that danger our democracy has gone into action.

We know that although Prussian autocracy was bad enough, Naziism is far worse.

Nazi forces are not seeking mere modifications in colonial maps or in minor European boundaries. They openly seek the destruction of all elective systems of government on every continent—including our own; they seek to establish systems of government based on the regimentation of all human beings by a handful of individual rulers who have seized power by force.

These men and their hypnotized followers call this a new order. It is not new. It is not order. For order among nations presupposes something enduring—some system of justice under which individuals, over a long period of time, are willing to live. Humanity will never permanently accept a system imposed by conquest and based on slavery.

These modern tyrants find it necessary to their plans to eliminate all democracies—eliminate them one by one. The nations of Europe, and indeed we ourselves, did not appreciate that purpose. We do now. The process of the elimination of the European nations proceeded according to plan through 1939 and 1940, until the schedule was shot to pieces by the unbeatable defenders of Britain.

The enemies of democracy were wrong in their calculations for a very simple reason. They were wrong because they believed that democracy could not adjust itself to the terrible reality of a world at war.

They believed that democracy, because of its profound respect for the rights of men, would never arm itself to fight.

They believed that democracy, because of its will to live at peace with its neighbors, could not mobilize its energies even in its own defense.

They know now that democracy can still remain democracy, and speak, and reach conclusions, and arm itself adequately for defense.

From the bureaus of propaganda of the Axis powers came the confident prophecy that the conquest of our country would be "an inside job"—a job accomplished not by overpowering invasion from without, but by disrupting confusion and disunion and moral disintegration from within.

Those who believed that knew little of our history. America is not a country which can be confounded by the appeasers, the defeatists, the backstairs manufacturers of panic. It is a country which talks out its problems in the open, where any man can hear them.

We have just now engaged in a great debate. It was not limited to the halls of Congress. It was argued in every newspaper, on every wave length—over every cracker barrel in the land. It was finally settled and decided by the American people themselves.

The decisions of our democracy may be slowly arrived at. But when that decision is made, it is proclaimed not with the voice of any one man but with the voice of 130 millions. It is binding on all of us. And the world is no longer left in doubt.

This decision is the end of any attempts at appeasement in our land; the end of urging us to get along with the dictators; the end of compromise with tyranny and the forces of oppression.

The urgency is *now*.

We believe firmly that when our production output is in full swing, the democracies of the world will be able to prove that dictatorships cannot win.

But, now, the time element is of supreme importance. Every plane, every other instrument of war, old and new, which we can spare now, we will send overseas. That is commonsense strategy.

The great task of this day, the deep duty which rests upon us is to move products from the assembly lines of our factories to the battle lines of democracy—Now!

We can have speed and effectiveness if we maintain our existing unity. We do not have and never will have the false unity of a people browbeaten by threats and misled by propaganda. Ours is a unity which is possible only among free men and women who recognize the truth and face reality with intelligence and courage.

Today, at last, ours is not a partial effort. It is a total effort and that is the only way to guarantee ultimate safety.

Beginning a year ago, we started the erection of hundreds of plants and we started the training of millions of men.

Then, at the moment the aid-to-democracies bill was passed we were ready to recommend the seven-billion-dollar appropriation on the basis of capacity production as now planned.

The articles themselves cover the whole range of munitions of war and of the facilities for transporting them.

The aid-to-democracies bill was agreed to by both Houses of the Congress last Tuesday afternoon. I signed it one half hour later. Five minutes later I approved a list of articles for immediate shipment. Many of them are on their way. On Wednesday, I recommended an appropriation for new material to the extent of seven billion dollars; and the Congress is making patriotic speed in making the appropriation available.

Here in Washington, we are thinking in terms of speed, and speed now. And I hope that that watchword will find its way into every home in the Nation.

We shall have to make sacrifices—every one of us. The final extent of those sacrifices will depend upon the speed with which we act—Now!

I must tell you tonight in plain language what this undertaking means to you—to your daily life.

Whether you are in the armed services; whether you are a steel worker or a stevedore; a machinist or a housewife; a farmer or a banker; a storekeeper or a manufacturer—to all of you it will mean sacrifice in behalf of country and your liberties. You will feel the impact of this gigantic effort in your daily lives. You will feel it in a way which will cause many inconveniences.

You will have to be content with lower profits from business because obviously your taxes will be higher.

You will have to work longer at your bench or your plow or your machine.

Let me make it clear that the Nation is calling for the sacrifice of some privileges but not for the sacrifice of fundamental rights. Most of us will do that willingly. That kind of sacrifice is for the common national protection and welfare; for our defense against the most ruthless brutality in history; for the ultimate victory of a way of life now so violently menaced.

A half-hearted effort on our part will lead to failure. This is no part-time job. The concepts of "business as usual" and "normalcy" must be forgotten until the task is finished. This is an all-out effort—nothing short of all-out effort will win.

We are now dedicated, from here on, to a constantly increasing tempo of production—a production greater than we now know or have ever known before—a production that does not stop and should not pause.

And so, tonight, I am appealing to the heart and to the mind of every man and every woman within our borders who loves liberty. I ask you to consider the needs of our Nation at this hour and to put aside all personal differences until our victory is won.

The light of democracy must be kept burning. To the perpetuation of this light, each must do his own share. The single effort of one individual may seem very small. But there are 130 million individuals over here. There are many more millions in Britain and elsewhere bravely shielding the great flame of democracy from the blackout of barbarism. It is not enough for us merely to trim the wick or polish the glass. The time has come when we must provide the fuel in ever-increasing amounts to keep the flame alight.

There will be no divisions of party or section or race or nationality or religion. There is not one among us who does not have a stake in the outcome of the effort in which we are now engaged.

A few weeks ago I spoke of four freedoms—freedom of speech and expression, freedom of every person to worship God in his own way, freedom from want, freedom from fear. They are the ultimate stake. They may not be immediately attainable throughout the world but humanity does move toward those ideals through democratic processes. If we fail—if democracy is superseded by slavery—then those four freedoms or even the mention of them will become forbidden things. Centuries will pass before they can be revived.

By winning now, we strengthen their meaning, we increase the stature of mankind and the dignity of human life.

There is a vast difference between the word "loyalty" and the word "obedience". Obedience can be obtained and enforced in a dictatorship by the use of threat and extortion or it can be obtained by a failure on the part of government to tell the truth to its citizens.

Loyalty is different. It springs from the mind that is given the facts, that retains ancient ideals and proceeds without coercion to give support to its own government.

That is true in England and in Greece and in China and in the United States today. And in many other countries millions of men and women are praying for the return of a day when they can give that kind of loyalty.

Loyalty cannot be bought. Dollars alone will not win this war. Let us not delude ourselves as to that.

Today, nearly a million and a half American citizens are hard at work in our armed forces. The spirit and the determination of these men of our Army and Navy are worthy of the highest traditions of our country. No better men ever served under Washington, or John Paul Jones, or Grant, or Lee, or Pershing. That is a boast, I admit—but it is not an idle one.

Upon the national will to sacrifice and to work depends the output of our industry and our agriculture.

Upon that will depends the survival of the vital bridge across the ocean—the bridge of ships which carry the arms and food for those who are fighting the good fight.

Upon that will depends our ability to aid other nations which may determine to offer resistance.

Upon that will may depend practical assistance to people now living in nations which have been overrun, should they find the opportunity to strike back in an effort to regain their liberties.

This will of the American people will not be frustrated either by threats from powerful enemies abroad or by small, selfish groups or individuals at home.

The determination of America must not be obstructed by war profiteering.

It must not be obstructed by unnecessary strikes of workers, by short-sighted management, or by deliberate sabotage.

For, unless we win, there will be no freedom for either management or labor.

Wise labor leaders and wise business managers will realize how necessary it is to their own existence to make common sacrifice for this great common cause.

There is no longer the slightest question or doubt that the American people recognize the extreme seriousness of the present situation. That is why they have demanded, and got, a policy of unqualified, immediate, all-out aid for Britain, Greece, China, and for all the governments in exile whose homelands are temporarily occupied by the aggressors.

From now on that aid will be increased—and yet again increased—until total victory has been won.

The British are stronger than ever in the magnificent morale which has enabled them to endure all the dark days and the shattered nights of the past 10 months. They have the full support and help of Canada, and the other dominions, of the rest of their Empire, and non-British people throughout the world who still think in terms of the great freedoms.

The British people are braced for invasion whenever the attempt may come—tomorrow—next week—next month.

In this historic crisis, Britain is blessed with a brilliant and great leader in Winston Churchill. But, no one knows better than Mr. Churchill himself, that it is not alone his stirring words and valiant deeds which give the British their superb morale. The essence of that morale is in the masses of plain people who are completely clear in their minds about the one essential fact—that they would rather die as free men than live as slaves.

These plain people—civilians as well as soldiers and sailors and airmen—women and girls as well as men and boys—are fighting in the front line of civilization, and they are holding that line with a fortitude which will forever be the pride and the inspiration of all free men on every continent and on every island of the sea.

The British people and their Grecian allies need ships. From America, they will get ships.

They need planes. From America, they will get planes.

They need food. From America, they will get food.

They need tanks and guns and ammunition and supplies of all kinds. From America, they will get tanks and guns and ammunition and supplies of all kinds.

China likewise expresses the magnificent will of millions of plain people to resist the dismemberment of their Nation. China, through the Generalissimo, Chiang Kai-shek, asks our help. America has said that China shall have our help.

Our country is going to be what our people have proclaimed it must be—the arsenal of democracy.

Our country is going to play its full part.

And when dictatorships disintegrate—and pray God that will be sooner than any of us now dares to hope—then our country must continue to play its great part in the period of world reconstruction.

We believe that the rallying cry of the dictators, their boasting about a master-race, will prove to be pure stuff and nonsense. There never has been, there isn't now, and there never will be, any race of people fit to serve as masters over their fellowmen.

The world has no use for any nation which, because of size or because of military might, asserts the right to goose-step to world power over other nations or other races. We believe that any nationality, no matter how small, has the inherent right to its own nationhood.

We believe that the men and women of such nations, no matter what size, can, through the processes of peace, serve themselves and serve the world by protecting the common man's security; improve the standards of healthful living; provide markets for manufacture and for agriculture. Through that kind of peaceful service every nation can increase its happiness, banish the terrors of war, and abandon man's inhumanity to man.

Never, in all our history, have Americans faced a job so well worthwhile. May it be said of us in the days to come that our children and our children's children rise up and call us blessed.

202

740.0011 European War 1939/9531

*Memorandum by the Acting Secretary of State (Welles) Regarding
A Conversation With the Soviet Ambassador (Oumansky)*

[WASHINGTON,] March 20, 1941.

After the conclusion of the general conference with the Soviet Ambassador this afternoon, I asked the Ambassador to remain in order
that I might talk with him alone for a few minutes. The Ambassador
asked if I had any further information in confirmation of what I stated
to him secretly in our last interview, namely, that this Government
believed that Germany was planning to attack the Soviet Union. I
said that I had additional information in confirmation of that report.

S[UMNER] W[ELLES]

203

740.0011 European War 1939/9720A

The Secretary of State to the Minister in Bulgaria (Earle) [60]

[Telegram : Paraphrase]

WASHINGTON, April 5, 1941—1 p.m.

35. In your discretion please use your good offices to the end that the
Bulgarian Government may understand how support given acts of
aggression against Yugoslavia is bound to be regarded in the United
States. Our every effort is now being exerted under existing law to
assist the nations which are defending their integrity and intelligence
against aggression.

Presumably you are using all information reaching you from the
United States (including *Radio Bulletin*) to emphasize the scope of
our national determination.

HULL

204

Statement by the Secretary of State, April 6, 1941 [60a]

The barbaric invasion of Yugoslavia and the attempt to annihilate
that country by brute force is but another chapter in the present
planned movement of attempted world conquest and domination.

[60] Similar telegrams, *mutatis mutandis*, were sent to the missions in Hungary
and Rumania.

[60a] Issued after consultation with the President.

Another small nation has been assaulted by the forces of aggression and is further proof that there are no geographical limitations or bounds of any kind to their movement for world conquest.

The American people have the greatest sympathy for the nation which has been thus so outrageously attacked and we follow closely the valiant struggle the Yugoslav people are making to protect their homes and preserve their liberty.

This Government with its policy of helping those who are defending themselves against would-be conquerors is now proceeding as speedily as possible to send military and other supplies to Yugoslavia.

205

740.0011 European War 1939/9955B

The Secretary of State to the Minister in Portugal (Fish)[61]

[Telegram : Paraphrase]

WASHINGTON, April 10, 1941—6 p.m.

197. I wish to emphasize, at this crucial period in the struggle against totalitarian world aggression, the obligation resting upon every representative of the United States abroad to contribute to the success of that struggle in every way within his power. It has been made abundantly clear by the people and government of the United States that we do not intend to stand on the sidelines but that on the contrary we do intend to play our part in resistance against the forces of aggression. Therefore it is incumbent upon every representative of the United States and in fact upon every American citizen who is abroad to reflect in his own conduct and in his conversations with those with whom he may come in contact the absolute determination of his country and his government to see this thing through to a successful conclusion.

The President relies upon you to make clear to the military and civil leaders of the government and of public opinion in Portugal the scope of our national effort and determination to resist aggression. I have confidence that you will not lose any opportunity in conversations with such leaders, and by every other means at your disposal, to bring home repeatedly the significance of our position and to stress that we are absolutely convinced that the forces of aggression will be checked

---

[61] Similar telegrams were sent to the missions in Spain, Finland, and Sweden.

and defeated. You need have no hesitancy in expressing in the strongest terms our convictions and our determination.

I desire that you immediately bring these considerations to the attention of the members of your staff, as well as all consular officers under your jurisdiction. Every effort should be made at the same time to see that such authoritative statements of our position as the declarations of President Roosevelt in his March 15 speech are given the widest circulation possible. It is our conviction that at this time a forceful continuous presentation of our position and of the scope of our national effort to resist aggression will have a salutary effect upon public and official opinion in such countries as Portugal which not yet have been drawn directly into the war, and will be of great assistance in counteracting the cumulative effect of totalitarian propaganda.

HULL

206

[Extract]

Department of State Bulletin, vol. IV, p. 443

Statement by the Department of State, April 10, 1941

The Department of State announced April 10 the signing on April 9, 1941 of an agreement between the Secretary of State, acting on behalf of the Government of the United States of America, and the Danish Minister, Henrik de Kauffmann, acting on behalf of His Majesty the King of Denmark in his capacity as sovereign of Greenland.

The agreement recognizes that as a result of the present European war there is danger that Greenland may be converted into a point of aggression against nations of the American Continent, and accepts the responsibility on behalf of the United States of assisting Greenland in the maintenance of its present status.

The agreement, after explicitly recognizing the Danish sovereignty over Greenland, proceeds to grant to the United States the right to locate and construct airplane landing fields and facilities for the defense of Greenland and for the defense of the American Continent.

The circumstances leading up to the agreement are as follows.

On April 9, 1940 the German Army invaded and occupied Denmark, and that occupation continues. In condemning this invasion President Roosevelt said [see doc. 148].

This invasion at once raised questions as to the status of Greenland, which has been recognized as being within the area of the

Monroe Doctrine. The Government of the United States announces its policy of maintenance of the *status quo* in the Western Hemisphere.

On May 3, 1940 the Greenland Councils, meeting at Godhavn, adopted a resolution in the name of the people of Greenland reaffirming their allegiance to King Christian X of Denmark, and expressed the hope that so long as Greenland remained cut off from the mother country, the Government of the United States would continue to keep in mind the exposed position of the Danish flag in Greenland and of the native and Danish population of Greenland. The Government of the United States expressed its willingness to assure that the needs of the population of Greenland would be taken care of.

On July 25, 1940, the consultation of American Foreign Ministers at Habana declared that any attempt on the part of a non-American state against the integrity or inviolability of the territory, the sovereignty, or the political independence of an American state should be considered an act of aggression, and that they would cooperate in defense against any such aggression. In a further declaration, known as the Act of Habana, it declared that the status of regions in this continent belonging to European powers was a subject of deep concern to all of the governments of the American republics.

During the summer of 1940 German activity on the eastern coast of Greenland became apparent. Three ships proceeding from Norwegian territory under German occupation arrived off the coast of Greenland, ostensibly for commercial or scientific purposes; and at least one of these ships landed parties nominally for scientific purposes, but actually for meteorological assistance to German belligerent operations in the north Atlantic. These parties were eventually cleared out. In the late fall of 1940, air reconnaissance appeared over East Greenland under circumstances making it plain that there had been continued activity in that region.

On March 27, 1941, a German bomber flew over the eastern coast of Greenland and on the following day another German war plane likewise reconnoitered the same territory. Under these circumstances it appeared that further steps for the defense of Greenland were necessary to bring Greenland within the system of hemispheric defense envisaged by the Act of Habana.

The Government of the United States has no thought in mind save that of assuring the safety of Greenland and the rest of the American Continent, and Greenland's continuance under Danish sovereignty. The agreement recognizes explicitly the full Danish sovereignty over Greenland. At the same time it is recognized that so long as Denmark remains under German occupation the Government in Denmark cannot exercise the Danish sovereign powers over Greenland under the Monroe Doctrine, and the agreement therefore was signed between the Secretary of State and the Danish Minister in Washington, acting as representative of the King of Denmark in his capacity as sovereign of Greenland, and with the concurrence of the Governors of Greenland.

The step is taken in furtherance of the traditional friendliness between Denmark and the United States. The policy of the United States is that of defending for Denmark her sovereignty over Greenland, so that she may have a full exercise of it as soon as the invasion is ended. The agreement accordingly provides that as soon as the war is over and the danger has passed, the two Governments shall promptly consult as to whether the arrangements made by the present agreement shall continue or whether they shall then cease.

TEXT OF THE AGREEMENT

Whereas:

ONE. After the invasion and occupation of Denmark on April 9, 1940 by foreign military forces, the United Greenland Councils at their meeting at Godhavn on May 3, 1940 adopted in the name of the people of Greenland a resolution reiterating their oath of allegiance to King Christian X of Denmark and expressing the hope that, for as long as Greenland remains cut off from the mother country, the Government of the United States of America will continue to hold in mind the exposed position of the Danish flag in Greenland, of the native Greenland and Danish population, and of established public order; and

Two. The Governments of all of the American Republics have agreed that the status of regions in the Western Hemisphere belonging to European powers is a subject of deep concern to the American Nations, and that the course of military events in Europe and the changes resulting from them may create the grave danger that European territorial possessions in America may be converted into strategic centers of aggression against nations of the American Continent; and

THREE. Defense of Greenland against attack by a non-American power is essential to the preservation of the peace and security of the American Continent and is a subject of vital concern to the United States of America and also to the Kingdom of Denmark; and

FOUR. Although the sovereignty of Denmark over Greenland is fully recognized, the present circumstances for the time being prevent the Government in Denmark from exercising its powers in respect of Greenland.

Therefore,

The undersigned, to wit: CORDELL HULL, Secretary of State of the United States of America, acting on behalf of the Government of the United States of America, and HENRIK DE KAUFFMANN, Envoy Extraordinary and Minister Plenipotentiary of His Majesty the King of Denmark at Washington, acting on behalf of His Majesty the King of Denmark in His capacity as sovereign of Greenland, whose authorities in Greenland have concurred herein, have agreed as follows:

ARTICLE I

The Government of the United States of America reiterates its recognition of and respect for the sovereignty of the Kingdom of Denmark over Greenland. Recognizing that as a result of the present European war there is danger that Greenland may be converted into a point of aggression against nations of the American Continent, the Government of the United States of America, having in mind its obligations under the Act of Habana signed on July 30, 1940, accepts the responsibility of assisting Greenland in the maintenance of its present status.

ARTICLE II

It is agreed that the Government of the United States of America shall have the right to construct, maintain and operate such landing fields, seaplane facilities and radio and meteorological installations as may be necessary for the accomplishment of the purposes set forth in Article I.

ARTICLE III

The grants of the rights specified in Article II shall also include the right to improve and deepen harbors and anchorages and the approaches thereto, to install aids to navigation by air and by water, and to construct roads, communication services, fortifications, repair and storage facilities, and housing for personnel, and generally, the right to do any and all things necessary to insure the efficient operation, maintenance and protection of such defense facilities as may be established.

ARTICLE IV

The landing fields, seaplane, harbor and other defense facilities that may be constructed and operated by the Government of the United

States of America under Articles II and III will be made available to the airplanes and vessels of all the American Nations for purposes connected with the common defense of the Western Hemisphere.

ARTICLE V

It is agreed that the Government of the United States of America shall have the right to lease for such period of time as this Agreement may be in force such areas of land and water as may be necessary for the construction, operation and protection of the defense facilities specified in Articles II and III. In locating the aforesaid defense areas, the fullest consideration consistent with military necessity shall be given to the welfare, health and economic needs of the native population of Greenland. It is agreed, however, that since the paramount objective sought is the early attainment of an adequate defense establishment in Greenland, the utilization of any area deemed by the Government of the United States of America to be needed for this purpose shall not be delayed pending the reaching of an agreement upon the precise terms of a formal lease. A description of such areas, by metes and bounds, and a statement of the purpose for which they are needed shall in each case be communicated to the Danish authorities in Greenland as soon as practicable, and the negotiation of a formal lease shall be undertaken within a reasonable period of time thereafter.

ARTICLE VI

The Kingdom of Denmark retains sovereignty over the defense areas mentioned in the preceding articles. So long as this Agreement shall remain in force, the Government of the United States of America shall have exclusive jurisdiction over any such defense area in Greenland and over military and civilian personnel of the United States, and their families, as well as over all other persons within such areas except Danish citizens and native Greenlanders, it being understood, however, that the Government of the United States may turn over to the Danish authorities in Greenland for trial and punishment any person committing an offense within a defense area, if the Government of the United States shall decide not to exercise jurisdiction in such case. The Danish authorities in Greenland will take adequate measures to insure the prosecution and punishment in case of conviction of all Danish citizens, native Greenlanders, and other persons who may be turned over to them by the authorities of the United States, for offenses committed within the said defense areas.

ARTICLE VII

It is agreed that the Government of the United States of America shall have the right to establish and maintain postal facilities and commissary stores to be used solely by military and civilian personnel of the United States, and their families, maintained in Greenland in connection with the Greenland defense establishment. If requested by the Danish authorities in Greenland, arrangements will be made to enable persons other than those mentioned to purchase necessary supplies at such commissary stores as may be established.

ARTICLE VIII

All materials, supplies and equipment for the construction, use and operation of the defense establishment and for the personal needs of military and civilian personnel of the United States, and their families, shall be permitted entry into Greenland free of customs duties, excise taxes, or other charges, and the said personnel, and their families, shall also be exempt from all forms of taxation, assessments or other levies by the Danish authorities in Greenland.

ARTICLE IX

The Government of the United States of America will respect all legitimate interests in Greenland as well as all the laws, regulations and customs pertaining to the native population and the internal administration of Greenland. In exercising the rights derived from this Agreement the Government of the United States will give sympathetic consideration to all representations made by the Danish authorities in Greenland with respect to the welfare of the inhabitants of Greenland.

ARTICLE X

This Agreement shall remain in force until it is agreed that the present dangers to the peace and security of the American Continent have passed. At that time the modification or termination of the Agreement will be the subject of consultation between the Government of the United States of America and the Government of Denmark. After due consultation has taken place, each party shall have the right to give the other party notice of its intention to terminate the Agreement, and it is hereby agreed, that at the expiration of twelve months after such notice shall have been received by either party from the other this Agreement shall cease to be in force.

Signed at Washington in duplicate, in the English and Danish languages, both texts having equal force, this 9th day of April, nineteen hundred and forty-one.

[SEAL]   CORDELL HULL
         Secretary of State
            of the United States of America

[SEAL]   HENRIK KAUFFMANN
         Envoy Extraordinary and Minister
           Plenipotentiary of His Majesty
              the King of Denmark at Washington

EXCHANGE OF NOTES BETWEEN THE SECRETARY OF STATE AND THE MINISTER OF DENMARK

DEPARTMENT OF STATE,
Washington, April 7, 1941.

SIR:

I have the honor to refer to the informal conversations which you have had with officers of the Department of State during which the concern of the Government of the United States was expressed over the effect of recent military developments, particularly affecting Greenland, upon the maintenance of the peace and security of the United States and the rest of the American Continent.

You are also aware of the interest of the Government of the United States in maintaining unimpaired the safety of Greenland and the sovereignty of Denmark over that island. My Government has continuously had in mind the desire expressed by the United Greenland Councils at their meeting at Godhavn on May 3, 1940 that the Government of the United States of America would continue to hold in mind the exposed position of the Danish flag in Greenland and of the native Greenland and Danish population of the island.

My Government has taken note of the unusual situation in which Greenland now finds itself. The Kingdom of Denmark is at present under occupation by a foreign army. The Government of the United States has condemned that invasion as a violation of Danish sovereign rights, and has repeatedly expressed its friendly concern and its most earnest hope for the complete and speedy liberation of Denmark. Although the Government of the United States fully recognizes the sovereignty of the Kingdom of Denmark over Greenland, it is unhappily clear that the Government in Denmark is not in a position to exercise sovereign power over Greenland so long as the present military occupation continues.

Greenland is within the area embraced by the Monroe Doctrine and by the Act of Havana, with which you are familiar, and its defense against attack by a non-American power is plainly essential to the preservation of the peace and security of the American continent, and of the traditional policies of this Government respecting the Western Hemisphere.

My Government has consequently proposed measures for the adequate defense of Greenland consistent with the obligations of the United States under the Act of Havana signed on July 30, 1940. In doing so it is animated by sentiments of the completest friendliness for Denmark, and believes that by taking these steps it is safeguarding the eventual re-establishment of the normal relationship between Greenland and the Kingdom of Denmark.

I have the honor to enclose a draft of the proposed agreement relating to the defense of Greenland, which I believe embodies the ideas agreed upon in the course of our various conversations.

Accept [etc.]   CORDELL HULL

_____

ROYAL DANISH LEGATION,
Washington, D. C., April 9, 1941.

SIR:

I have received your note of the seventh instant concerning the defense of Greenland together with a draft of a proposed agreement regarding the same subject.

It is with appreciation that I note your renewed assurance that, although the present circumstances prevent the Government in Denmark for the time being from exercising its powers in respect of Greenland, your Government fully recognizes the Sovereignty of the Kingdom of Denmark over the island. At the same time I wish to convey to you my feelings of gratitude for the expression of friendly concern of your Government and its earnest hope for the complete and speedy liberation of Denmark.

I share your view that the proposed agreement, arrived at after an open and friendly exchange of views, is, under the singularly unusual circumstances, the best measure to assure both Greenland's present safety and the future of the island under Danish Sovereignty.

Furthermore, I am of the opinion that the terms of the agreement protect, as far as possible, the interests of the native population of Greenland whose welfare traditionally has been the paramount aim of Denmark's policy in Greenland.

I, therefore, shall accept and sign the agreement as proposed, acting on behalf of His Majesty, the King of Denmark, in His capacity of Sovereign over Greenland, whose authorities in Greenland have concurred herein.

I avail [etc.] HENRIK KAUFFMANN

207

Department of State Bulletin, vol. IV, p. 491

Address Delivered by the Secretary of State at Washington, April 24, 1941

FELLOW MEMBERS AND GUESTS OF THE AMERICAN SOCIETY OF INTERNATIONAL LAW: On the occasion of this our thirty-fifth annual meeting I shall undertake to discuss briefly certain acute phases of the world situation which are of vital interest to all of us.

We are in the midst of desperately serious days which involve all peoples and all nations. Unfortunately, many people fail to grasp the nature of this world-wide crisis and its meaning to our country.

Too many people assume that the present struggle is merely an ordinary regional war, and that when it comes to an end the side which is victorious will collect indemnities but otherwise leave the defeated nations more or less as they were before the conflict began. This assumption would prove entirely erroneous should the aggressor powers be the winners. As waged by them this is not an ordinary war. It is a war of assault by these would-be conquerors, employing every method of barbarism, upon nations which cling to their right to live in freedom and which are resisting in self-defense.

The would-be conquerors propose to take unto themselves every part of every conquered nation: the territory, the sovereignty, the possessions of every such nation. They propose to make the people of each conquered nation into serfs; to extinguish their liberties, their rights, their law, and their religion. They systematically uproot everything that is high and fine in life.

Such is the movement which is extending rapidly throughout the world.

If experience shows anything, it shows that no nation anywhere has the slightest reason to feel that it will be exempted from attack by the invader, any more than, in a town overrun by bandits, the wealthiest citizen might expect to be free from attack.

Every thinking man can answer the question for himself by simply calling the roll of the wretched victims of world-aggression who are now in a condition of semi-slavery and whose every hope of again enjoying the blessings of civilization depends only on the defeat or failure of the movement of conquest. So it is in Austria, Czechoslovakia, Poland, Norway, Denmark, Holland, Belgium, Albania, Luxemburg, France, Rumania, Hungary, Bulgaria, Yugoslavia. Many right-thinking people have not been able to conceive that this would happen. To them it has seemed incredible. Yet the physical facts are now before our very eyes, and the agony of the period through which the world is passing is marked by the most terrible events. As the armies of invasion move on, they bring with them blasted houses, families driven out to starve, civilian dead in the fields. When fighting is over, the administration of the invader offers no relief. Homes are plundered; families are separated; churches are closed; food is denied; semi-slavery is introduced. Military frightfulness is merely replaced by civilian terror. Every resource of organized fiendishness is set to work to subjugate and cow the individual and to use the conquered territory as a springboard for new aggressions.

The conclusion is plain. Now, after some 15 nations have lost everything that makes life worth living, it is high time that the remaining free countries should arm to the fullest extent and in the briefest time humanly possible and act for their self-preservation.

Some among us, doubtless with the best of intentions, still contend that our country need not resist until armed forces of an invader shall have crossed the boundary line of this hemisphere. But this merely means that there would be no resistance by the hemisphere, including the United States, until the invading countries had acquired complete control of the other four continents and of the high seas, and thus had obtained every possible strategic advantage, reducing us to the corresponding disadvantage of a severely handicapped defense. This is an utterly short-sighted and extremely dangerous view.

Events have shown beyond possible question that the safety of this hemisphere and of this country calls for resistance wherever resistance will be most effective. In my judgment our safety and security require that, in accordance with the declared policy of the legislative and executive branches of the Government, aid must be supplied without hesitation to Great Britain and those other countries that are resisting the sweep of the general conflagration. This policy means, in practical application, that such aid must reach its destination in the shortest of time and in maximum quantity. So ways must be found to do this.

You and I are familiar with the questions sometimes raised when we speak of aid to other nations. Why, it is asked, should we interest ourselves in the defense of other countries? Surely the answer is terribly clear.

Those nations that are making resistance are primarily seeking to save themselves, their homes, and their liberties. Great Britain for instance is acting primarily for her own safety. The United States, both in its direct defense effort and in the aid which it extends to the resisting nations, is likewise acting primarily for its own safety. As safety for the nations that are offering resistance means security for us, aid to them is an essential part of our own defense. Every new conquest makes available to the aggressor greater resources for use against the remaining free peoples. Our aid to the resisting nations is not the mere crusading of a world-benefactor. It is based on the definite knowledge that every free nation anywhere is a bastion of strength to all the remaining free peoples everywhere.

Sometimes the same confusion of thought is expressed in a different question. Why, it is asked, should we care who wins? Is not this merely the traditional and recurrent struggle for power? Does it make any difference to America? What difference does it make to America?

It makes a fateful difference. In a world which was, in the main, devoted to the cause of peace and in which no nation had designs upon the Western Hemisphere, we could, perhaps, take a detached attitude. But evidence has been piling up over several years which makes it perfectly plain that one group of powers actually does have designs both upon the New World and upon the principles, the possessions, and the way of life that are ours. All the military movements and official acts and utterances of these powers have confirmed the knowledge that we too are included in their plans for world domination. Our freedom and our wealth inevitably make us magnets for their machine of force.

Yes, it makes a difference who wins—the difference between whether we stand with our backs to the wall with the other four continents against us and the high seas lost, alone defending the last free territories on earth, or whether we keep our place in an orderly world.

Again, it is asked, How are we in danger? Are not these idle fears? Since one warring nation cannot successfully invade Britain across 20 miles of the English Channel how can any nation invade us from across three thousand miles of the Atlantic?

The reason why the English Channel has not been successfully crossed is that the British have maintained control of that Channel.

Forty million determined Britons in a heroic resistance have converted their island into a huge armed base out of which proceeds a steady stream of sea and air power. It is not water that bars the way. It is the resolute determination of British sea power and British arms. Were the control of the seas by the resisting nations lost, the Atlantic would no longer be an obstacle—rather, it would become a broad highway for a conqueror moving westward. Our protection would be enormously lessened.

Those Americans who, in effect, are saying that a British defeat would not matter to us, signally overlook the fact that the resulting delivery of the high seas to the invader would create colossal danger to our own national defense and security. The breadth of the sea may give us a little time. It does not give us safety. Safety can only come from our ability, in conjunction with other peace-loving nations, to prevent any aggressor from attaining control of the high seas.

Some, hoping that this crisis may end, ask whether some sort of peace cannot be made—a peace that will end the struggle in Europe and that will permit us to resume our normal life. I wish this were possible. But one obstinate fact stands in the way. One of the contending groups not only does not wish peace, as we understand peace, but literally does not believe in peace. That group uses the word, it is true—as it was used by the aggressor at the time of the Munich arrangement in 1938. Peace to that group is merely a convenient cloak for a continuing undeclared, under-cover war, as France and many other nations to their misery have discovered. Behind the deceptive protection of the word "peace" the rulers of that group accumulate vast striking-forces. They infiltrate shock troops disguised as peaceful travelers and businessmen. They set up organizations for spying, sabotage, and propaganda. They endeavor to sow hatred and discord. They use every tool of economic attack, bribery, corruption, and local disturbance to weaken the countries with which they are at "peace", until a military movement can easily complete the task of subjugation. That kind of peace is nothing more than a trap—a trap into which many nations fell in earlier phases of this movement for world conquest when its true nature was not understood. Indeed, the dictator nations make no secret of their plans. They scornfully state their ideas, arrogantly confident that the law-abiding nations will not take them seriously—until it is too late successfully to resist them.

Finally, there are those who sometimes wonder whether aid to freedom-loving nations and a vigorous policy of defending our interests will not irritate some aggressor into attacking us. This theory assumes that a lawless invader will become "irritated" if its intended victim dares to defend itself at the most effective stage. Under this theory, the only way to avoid giving such "irritation" is to submit.

No nation is going to attack us merely because it is our policy to defend ourselves. Neither, for that matter, are any aggressors going to let us alone merely because we attempt to placate them. In the philosophy of the conquerors, an attack is justified whenever and wherever it looks easy and convenient and serves their purposes. There is no possible safeguarding our security, except by solid strength, placed when and where it is most effective.

The best, indeed the only way, of allaying the fears and doubts and questions of those who are in anxiety is for us, one hundred and thirty millions of Americans, to rise in our might and proceed as one man in the Herculean task of equipping this Nation to the fullest for its self-defense. These preparations should not be for a month or for a year, but they must continue as long as our safety is threatened.

The countries that have set about to impose their rule upon the world have turned their backs upon all the ordinary peacetime ways of work and living. They dreamed of force, they have created force, and they are now using it to the full. In their preparations and in their warfare they have demanded everything of their peoples. Ordinary family life, leisure, personal enjoyment, pursuit of private interest—all of these have been swept aside. Everything has been given over to the creation and use to the utmost of force.

For us, the task of safeguarding our security requires the full, continuous, patriotically inspired effort of each and every one of us. The energies of those who control the operation of our factories and their machines, together with the labor of those who make and operate the machines, must be devoted to the attainment of maximum production. Each and all must work with a sense that what they do or do not do is important in determining whether this country shall be secure. Every part of our vast productive machine that can serve to produce military supplies must be put to that purpose. The desire to continue ordinary ways of business must yield to the needs of the crisis. Individuals and groups have no right at this time to think or act primarily in terms of their personal interest to the detriment of the general national good.

What we do in the production of the fighting instruments needed by ourselves and by the free countries of the world now becomes a measure of our intelligence.

There are those who are too easily discouraged when the news is temporarily unfavorable. Powerful propaganda machines endeavor to spread that discouragement. It is not the tradition of those who love liberty to yield to discouragement. That is not the American tradition. Our country owes its place in history to the fact that the people become more resolute and determined as danger and difficulty increase.

There can be no temporizing with lawlessness or with disregard for the elemental rights of nations and peoples.

Although the task is huge, though time is pressing, and though the struggle may continue for a long time, I am confident that at the end there will come a better day. We are at work not only at the task of insuring our own safety but also at the task of creating ultimate conditions of peace with justice. We can help to lay a firm foundation for the independence, the security, and the returning prosperity of the members of the family of nations. I have absolute faith in the ultimate triumph of the principles of humanity, translated into law and order, by which freedom and justice and security will again prevail.

208

711.94/2086

Memorandum by the Secretary of State Regarding a Conversation With the Japanese Ambassador (Nomura)

[WASHINGTON,] May 11, 1941.

The Japanese Ambassador called at my hotel apartment at his request. He promptly proceeded to say that his Government had instructed him to hand me certain documents, of which the attached are copies.[62] He had still another document, which he said was prepared by his Government and which constituted a part of the written material that he was instructed to deliver to me. The latter document, he stated, was not correctly translated in certain respects, and he added that he would withhold it until the translation was perfected tomorrow, when it would be sent to me in proper form.

I thanked him for coming in and then very clearly and slowly said to him in effect that, in accordance with our past conversations, I was receiving these documents in a purely unofficial way with a

---

[62] These documents were returned upon request to the Japanese Ambassador on May 12, before complete copies had been made.

view to examining them and ascertaining whether they, accompanied by any suggestions or proposals of our own made in the same unofficial and informal manner, would or might afford a basis for a step in negotiations. I added that, in these circumstances, either Government could deal with any rumors or reports about negotiations by truthfully saying that no negotiations have been instituted; that the rumors or reports on this subject could at the most only relate to a casual reference or remark made at some time by representatives of the United States or Japan regarding some phase of the relations existing between our two Governments, et cetera, et cetera. The Ambassador agreed entirely to the foregoing.

I then inquired whether Matsuoka would conduct the negotiations at Tokyo. The Ambassador replied that he would, but that the Army, the Navy and Konoye would participate in the work of carrying on the negotiations, although Konoye did not make it a habit of interfering materially in such work of the Foreign Office. I said that Matsuoka was, of course, a politician and that he had recently been quoted as making, in a purely gratuitous way, numerous unfriendly remarks about the United States, as well as announcing ideas and doctrines diametrically opposed to most of the fundamental principles set out in the document which the Ambassador prepared some weeks ago, and with the contents of which we were all familiar. I added that, in these circumstances, there will be real difficulty to persuade even my associates of the absolute dependability of Matsuoka's acts and utterances. I said that I mentioned this in order that the Ambassador would fully understand my difficulties in more respects than one. The Ambassador not only did not take issue with anything I said, but I felt that he was really in harmony with the statements I made about Matsuoka.

The Ambassador then said that Japan was very desirous of keeping war out of the Pacific. I remarked very emphatically that many people in this country strongly believe that Japan's real purpose was to secure cooperation to aid her in getting out of China and her disastrous Chinese campaign and that this point would be uppermost in the minds of many and it was one of the most important to be guarded against. The Ambassador said he realized that that would be an exceedingly important matter to be made clear. I emphasized this point a number of times in the conversation.

I then inquired as to whether there were any definite plans in the mind of his Government in regard to when the Japanese troops would come out of China, and what assurances, if any, there were that they would actually come out under a mutually satisfactory arrangement.

654

The Ambassador did not know so much about this, but felt it could and would be worked out to the satisfaction of both sides. I said this would, of course, be a vitally important point for determination.

I asked the Ambassador whether his Government had in mind any method of giving absolute assurances that it would not use either force or threat of force for purposes of conquest in the southeastern area of the Pacific or other countries. The Ambassador had nothing special to offer on this point except to say that his Government had no purpose to use force or threat of force in this entire southeastern area.

I spoke generally then and said that, if his Government really desires a settlement of the Pacific situation on a basis of peace and genuine friendliness, there should be no serious difficulty about the matter; that he and his Government know the relations existing between this country and South America, which offer equal opportunity, politically, economically and every other way, to all countries alike, including the United States and Japan; that my Government treats the smallest countries in this hemisphere, such as Haiti, on a basis of absolute equality in every sense with the largest countries, such as Brazil and the Argentine. I then inquired why it was that Japan, with ample capacity and standing to command influence and recognition, both at home and abroad, persists in an effort to use such high-sounding phrases as the "new order in greater east Asia" and variations of this slogan. I added that, unless Japan uses this slogan not as embodying the principles of law, justice, equality and non-intervention, but as a cloak under which Japan would continue her policy of conquest by force, there was absolutely no reason why this trouble-making slogan should be persistently flaunted before the peaceful and sovereign nations, and that Japan could get all of the benefits from contacts with other nations without this slogan that the United States gets from its association with South American countries without such slogan, and, therefore, I cannot understand why Japan persisted in using it. The Ambassador had little comment to make, but did not take issue with what I said. He emphasized from time to time that his country desired to keep war out of the Pacific, and that it did not intend to use force in the South Sea area.

I again repeated that we were profoundly convinced that Hitler and Hitlerism will prove not only a scourge to other parts of the world, as it has in Europe, but that it will be applied to Japan herself just as quickly as it was applied to friendly countries in Europe who trusted Hitler and his previous guarantees of friendship, safety and freedom from attack and invasion.

I took advantage of a remark of the Ambassador to the effect that it would be an incalculable loss to both Japan and the United States, as well as to civilization, if our two countries should become engaged in war, by saying that unless the civilization of the world is to run the great risk of being destroyed anyhow by the world movements of Hitler, it will require all of the united efforts of civilized nations like Japan, the United States and Great Britain to shape the course of the world in a different direction, and that steps looking towards the gradual development of basic programs both for the transition and the post-war periods cannot be taken too soon. The Ambassador, of course, agreed to this.

In conclusion, I reemphasized that this Government is determined that Hitler shall not get control of the seas and that we would feel obliged without the slightest hesitation to resist to a successful conclusion such efforts on his part whether one year, five years or ten years should be involved. The Ambassador again bowed and smiled approvingly without saying anything. I said that, in these circumstances, with things moving so rapidly, no one could tell, as I remarked to him in our previous conversations, what any day might bring forth. I then repeated my former statement to him that, since Hitler avows his movement to be one of world control, and hence of conquest by force, this country does not propose to commit suicide, as so many countries in continental Europe did, by trusting Hitler and by waiting until it was too late to resist; that we propose to resist, when and where such resistance would be most effective, whether within our own boundaries or on the high seas or in aid of such countries as Great Britain, and that such resistance would be to the maximum extent within the minimum of time, and that this in its very nature would constitute necessary self-defense against an avowed world-wide aggressor, and in no sense could be construed as an act of offense, much less aggression, in the light of the world nature of the movement of aggression on Hitler's part.

C[ordell] H[ull]

209

711.94/2086

Draft Proposal Handed by the Japanese Ambassador (Nomura) To the Secretary of State on May 12, 1941

CONFIDENTIAL MEMORANDUM AGREED UPON BETWEEN THE GOVERNMENT OF THE UNITED STATES OF AMERICA AND THE GOVERNMENT OF JAPAN

The Governments of the United States and of Japan accept joint responsibility for the initiation and conclusion of a general agreement disposing the resumption of our traditional friendly relations.

Without reference to specific causes of recent estrangement, it is the sincere desire of both Governments that the incidents which led to the deterioration of amicable sentiment among our peoples should be prevented from recurrence and corrected in their unforeseen and unfortunate consequences.

It is our present hope that, by a joint effort, our nations may establish a just peace in the Pacific; and by the rapid consummation of an entente cordiale [*amicable understanding*], arrest, if not dispel, the tragic confusion that now threatens to engulf civilization.

For such decisive action, protracted negotiations would seem ill-suited and weakening. Both Governments, therefore, desire that adequate instrumentalities should be developed for the realization of a general agreement which would bind, meanwhile, both Governments in honor and in act.

It is our belief that such an understanding should comprise only the pivotal issues of urgency and not the accessory concerns which could be deliberated at a conference and appropriately confirmed by our respective Governments.

Both Governments presume to anticipate that they could achieve harmonious relations if certain situations and attitudes were clarified or improved; to wit:

1. The concepts of the United States and of Japan respecting international relations and the character of nations.
2. The attitude of both Governments toward the European War.
3. The relations of both nations toward the China Affair.
4. Commerce between both nations.
5. Economic activity of both nations in the Southwestern Pacific area.
6. The policies of both nations affecting political stabilization in the Pacific area.

Accordingly, we have come to the following mutual understanding:—

I. The concepts of the United States and of Japan respecting international relations and the character of nations.

The Governments of the United States and of Japan jointly acknowledge each other as equally sovereign states and contiguous Pacific powers.

Both Governments assert the unanimity of their national policies as directed toward the foundation of a lasting peace and the inauguration of a new era of respectful confidence and cooperation among our peoples.

Both Governments declare that it is their traditional, and present, concept and conviction that nations and races compose, as members of a family, one household; each equally enjoying rights and admitting responsibilities with a mutuality of interests regulated by peaceful processes and directed to the pursuit of their moral and physical welfare, which they are bound to defend for themselves as they are bound not to destroy for others; they further admit their responsibilities to oppose the oppression or exploitation of backward nations.

Both governments are firmly determined that their respective traditional concepts on the character of nations and the underlying moral principles of social order and national life will continue to be preserved and never transformed by foreign ideas or ideologies contrary to these moral principles and concepts.

II. *The attitude of both Governments toward the European War.*

The Governments of the United States and Japan make it their common aim to bring about the world peace; they shall therefore jointly endeavour not only to prevent further extension of the European War but also speedily to restore peace in Europe.

The Government of Japan maintains that its alliance with the Axis Powers was, and is, defensive and designed to prevent the nations which are not at present directly affected by the European War from engaging in it.

The Government of Japan maintains that its obligations of military assistance under the Tripartite Pact between Japan, Germany and Italy will be applied in accordance with the stipulation of Article 3 of the said Pact.

The Government of the United States maintains that its attitude toward the European War is, and will continue to be, directed by no such aggressive measures as to assist any one nation against another. The United States maintains that it is pledged to the hate of war, and accordingly, its attitude toward the European War is, and will continue to be, determined solely and exclusively by considerations of the protective defense of its own national welfare and security.

III. *The relations of both nations toward the China Affair.*

The Government of the United States, acknowledging the three principles as enunciated in the Konoe Statement and the principles set forth on the basis of the said three principles in the treaty with the Nanking Government as well as in the Joint Declaration of Japan, Manchoukuo and China and relying upon the policy of the Japanese Government to establish a relationship of neighborly friendship with

China, shall forthwith request the Chiang Kai-shek régime to negotiate peace with Japan.

IV. Commerce between both nations.

When official approbation to the present Understanding has been given by both Governments, the United States and Japan shall assure each other to mutually supply such commodities as are, respectively, available or required by either of them. Both Governments further consent to take necessary steps to the resumption of normal trade relations as formerly established under the Treaty of Commerce and Navigation between the United States and Japan.

V. Economic activity of both nations in the Southwestern Pacific area.

Having in view that the Japanese expansion in the direction of the Southwestern Pacific area is declared to be of peaceful nature, American cooperation shall be given in the production and procurement of natural resources (such as oil, rubber, tin, nickel) which Japan needs.

VI. The policies of both nations affecting political stabilization in the Pacific area.

a. The Governments of the United States and Japan jointly guarantee the independence of the Philippine Islands on the condition that the Philippine Islands shall maintain a status of permanent neutrality. The Japanese subjects shall not be subject to any discriminatory treatment.

b. Japanese immigration to the United States shall receive amicable consideration—on a basis of equality with other nationals and freedom from discrimination.

Addendum.

The present Understanding shall be kept as a confidential memorandum between the Governments of the United States and of Japan.

The scope, character and timing of the announcement of this Understanding will be agreed upon by both Governments.

[Annex]

ORAL EXPLANATION FOR PROPOSED AMENDMENTS TO THE ORIGINAL DRAFT [63]

II. Par. 2.

Attitude of Both Governments toward the European War.

Actually the meaning of this paragraph is virtually unchanged

---

[63] This refers to an earlier draft which was never officially presented to the Government of the United States.

but we desire to make it clearer by specifying a reference to the Pact. As long as Japan is a member of the Tripartite Pact, such stipulation as is mentioned in the Understanding seems unnecessary.

If we must have any stipulation at all, in addition, it would be important to have one which would clarify the relationship of this Understanding to the aforementioned Pact.

III.

China Affair.

The terms for China-Japan peace as proposed in the original Understanding differ in no substantial way from those herein affirmed as the "principles of Konoe." Practically, the one can be used to explain the other.

We should obtain an understanding, in a separate and secret document, that the United States would discontinue her assistance to the Chiang Kai-shek régime if Chiang Kai-shek does not accept the advice of the United States that he enter into negotiations for peace.

If, for any reason, the United States finds it impossible to sign such a document, a definite pledge by some highest authorities will suffice.

The three principles of Prince Konoe as referred to in this paragraph are:

 1. Neighborly friendship;
 2. Joint defense against communism;
 3. Economic cooperation—by which Japan does not intend to exercise economic monopoly in China nor to demand of China a limitation in the interests of Third Powers.

The following are implied in the aforesaid principles:

 1. Mutual respect of sovereignty and territories;
 2. Mutual respect for the inherent characteristics of each nation cooperating as good neighbors and forming a Far Eastern nucleus contributing to world peace;
 3. Withdrawal of Japanese troops from Chinese territory in accordance with an agreement to be concluded between Japan and China;
 4. No annexation, no indemnities;
 5. Independence of Manchoukuo.

III.

Immigration to China.

The stipulation regarding large-scale immigration to China has been deleted because it might give an impression, maybe a mistaken impression, to the Japanese people who have been offended by the past immigration legislation of the United States, that America is now taking a dictating attitude even toward the question of Japanese immigration in China.

Actually, the true meaning and purpose of this stipulation is fully understood and accepted by the Japanese Government.

IV.

Naval, Aerial and Mercantile Marine Relations.

(*a*) and (*c*) of this section have been deleted not because of disagreement but because it would be more practical, and possible, to determine the disposition of naval forces and mercantile marine after an understanding has been reached and relations between our two countries improved; and after our present China commitments are eliminated. Then we will know the actual situation and can act accordingly.

Courtesy visit of naval squadrons.

This proposal, (*b*) of IV. might better be made a subject of a separate memorandum. Particular care must be taken as to the timing, manner and scope of carrying out such a gesture.

V.

Gold Credit.

The proposal in the second paragraph of V. has been omitted for the same reasons as suggested the omission of paragraphs (*a*) and (*c*).

VI.

Activity in Southwestern Pacific Area.

The words, in the first paragraph, "without resorting to arms" have been deleted as inappropriate and unnecessarily critical. Actually, the peaceful policy of the Japanese Government has been made clear on many occasions in various statements made both by the Premier and the Foreign Minister.

VIII.

Political Stabilization in the Pacific Area.

As the paragraph (*a*) implying military and treaty obligation would require, for its enactment, such a complicated legislative procedure in both countries, we consider it inappropriate to include this in the present Understanding.

Paragraph (*b*) regarding the independence of the Philippine Islands has been altered for the same reason.

In paragraph (*c*) the words "and to the Southwestern Pacific Area" have been omitted because such questions should be settled, as necessity arises, through direct negotiation with the authorities in the Southwestern areas by the Governments of the United States and of Japan respectively.

Conference.

The stipulation for holding a Conference has been deleted. We consider that it would be better to arrange, by an exchange of letters, that a conference between the President and the Premier or between suitable representatives of theirs will be considered when both the United States and Japan deem it useful to hold such a conference after taking into due consideration the effect resulting from the present Understanding.

Announcement.

In regard to the statement to be issued on the successful conclusion of the present Understanding a draft will be prepared in Tokio and cabled to Washington for the consideration of the United States Government.

210

Department of State Bulletin, vol. IV, p. 647

Radio Address Delivered by President Roosevelt From Washington, May 27, 1941

I am speaking tonight from the White House in the presence of the Governing Board of the Pan American Union, the Canadian Minister, and their families. The members of this Board are the ambassadors and ministers of the American republics in Washington. It is appropriate that I do this. Now, as never before, the unity of the American republics is of supreme importance to each and every one of us and to the cause of freedom throughout the world. Our future independence is bound up with the future independence of all of our sister republics.

The pressing problems that confront us are military problems. We cannot afford to approach them from the point of view of wishful thinkers or sentimentalists. What we face is cold, hard fact.

The first and fundamental fact is that what started as a European war has developed, as the Nazis always intended it should develop, into a world war for world-domination.

Adolf Hitler never considered the domination of Europe as an end in itself. European conquest was but a step toward ultimate goals in all the other continents. It is unmistakably apparent to all of us that, unless the advance of Hitlerism is forcibly checked now, the Western Hemisphere will be within range of the Nazi weapons of destruction.

For our own defense we have accordingly undertaken certain obviously necessary measures.

First, we joined in concluding a series of agreements with all the other American republics. This further solidified our hemisphere against the common danger.

And then, a year ago, we launched, and are successfully carrying out, the largest armament-production program we have ever undertaken.

We have added substantially to our splendid Navy, and we have mustered our manpower to build up a new Army which is already worthy of the highest traditions of our military service.

We instituted a policy of aid for the democracies—the nations which have fought for the continuation of human liberties.

This policy had its origin in the first month of the war, when I urged upon the Congress repeal of the arms-embargo provisions in the Neutrality Law. In that message of September 1939, I said, "I should like to be able to offer the hope that the shadow over the world might swiftly pass. I cannot. The facts compel my stating, with candor, that darker periods may lie ahead."

In the subsequent months, the shadows deepened and lengthened. And the night spread over Poland, Denmark, Norway, Holland, Belgium, Luxemburg, and France.

In June 1940, Britain stood alone, faced by the same machine of terror which had overwhelmed her allies. Our Government rushed arms to meet her desperate needs.

In September 1940, an agreement was completed with Great Britain for the trade of 50 destroyers for 8 important off-shore bases.

In March 1941, the Congress passed the Lend-Lease Bill and an appropriation of seven billion dollars to implement it. This law realistically provided for material aid "for the government of any country whose defense the President deems vital to the defense of the United States".

Our whole program of aid for the democracies has been based on hard-headed concern for our own security and for the kind of safe and civilized world in which we wish to live. Every dollar of material we send helps to keep the dictators away from our own hemisphere. Every day that they are held off gives us time to build more guns and tanks and planes and ships.

We have made no pretense about our own self-interest in this aid. Great Britain understands it—and so does Nazi Germany.

And now—after a year—Britain still fights gallantly, on a "far-flung battle line". We have doubled and redoubled our vast production, increasing, month by month, our material supply of tools of war for ourselves and Britain and China—and eventually for all the democracies.

The supply of these tools will not fail—it will increase.

With greatly augmented strength, the United States and the other American republics now chart their course in the situation of today.

Your Government knows what terms Hitler, if victorious, would impose. They are, indeed, the only terms on which he would accept a so-called "negotiated" peace.

Under those terms, Germany would literally parcel out the world—hoisting the swastika itself over vast territories and populations and setting up puppet governments of its own choosing, wholly subject to the will and the policy of a conqueror.

To the people of the Americas, a triumphant Hitler would say, as he said after the seizure of Austria, and after Munich, and after the seizure of Czechoslovakia: "I am now completely satisfied. This is the last territorial readjustment I will seek." And he would of course add: "All we want is peace, friendship, and profitable trade relations with you in the New World."

And were any of us in the Americas so incredibly simple and forgetful as to accept those honeyed words, what would then happen?

Those in the New World who were seeking profits would be urging that all that the dictatorships desired was "peace". They would oppose toil and taxes for more American armament. Meanwhile, the dictatorships would be forcing the enslaved peoples of their Old World conquests into a system they are even now organizing—to build a naval and air force intended to gain and hold and be master of the Atlantic and the Pacific as well.

They would fasten an economic stranglehold upon our several nations. Quislings would be found to subvert the governments in our republics; and the Nazis would back their fifth columns with invasion, if necessary.

I am not speculating about all this. I merely repeat what is already in the Nazi book of world-conquest. They plan to treat the Latin American nations as they are now treating the Balkans. They plan then to strangle the United States of America and the Dominion of Canada.

The American laborer would have to compete with slave labor in the rest of the world. Minimum wages, maximum hours? Nonsense! Wages and hours would be fixed by Hitler. The dignity and power and standard of living of the American worker and farmer would be gone. Trade unions would become historical relics and collective bargaining a joke.

Farm income? What happens to all farm surpluses without any foreign trade? The American farmer would get for his products exactly what Hitler wanted to give. He would face obvious disaster and complete regimentation.

Tariff walls—Chinese walls of isolation—would be futile. Freedom to trade is essential to our economic life. We do not eat all the food we can produce; we do not burn all the oil we can pump; we do not use all the goods we can manufacture. It would not be an American wall to keep Nazi goods out; it would be a Nazi wall to keep us in.

The whole fabric of working life as we know it—business, manufacturing, mining, agriculture—all would be mangled and crippled under such a system. Yet to maintain even that crippled independence would require permanent conscription of our manpower; it would curtail the funds we could spend on education, on housing, on public works, on flood control, on health. Instead, we should be permanently pouring our resources into armaments; and, year in and year out, standing day and night watch against the destruction of our cities.

Even our right of worship would be threatened. The Nazi world does not recognize any God except Hitler; for the Nazis are as ruthless as the Communists in the denial of God. What place has religion which preaches the dignity of the human being, of the majesty of the human soul, in a world where moral standards are measured by treachery and bribery and fifth columnists? Will our children, too, wander off, goose-stepping in search of new gods?

We do not accept, and will not permit, this Nazi "shape of things to come". It will never be forced upon us if we act in this present crisis with the wisdom and the courage which have distinguished our country in all the crises of the past.

The Nazis have taken military possession of the greater part of Europe. In Africa they have occupied Tripoli and Libya, and they are threatening Egypt, the Suez Canal, and the Near East. But their plans do not stop there, for the Indian Ocean is the gateway to the East.

They also have the armed power at any moment to occupy Spain and Portugal; and that threat extends not only to French North Africa and the western end of the Mediterranean, but also to the Atlantic fortress of Dakar, and to the island outposts of the New World—the Azores and Cape Verde Islands.

The Cape Verde Islands are only seven hours' distance from Brazil by bomber or troop-carrying planes. They dominate shipping routes to and from the South Atlantic.

The war is approaching the brink of the Western Hemisphere itself. It is coming very close to home.

Control or occupation by Nazi forces of any of the islands of the Atlantic would jeopardize the immediate safety of portions of North and South America and of the island possessions of the United States and of the ultimate safety of the continental United States itself.

Hitler's plan of world-domination would be near its accomplishment today, were it not for two factors: One is the epic resistance of Britain, her Colonies, and the great Dominions, fighting not only to maintain the existence of the Island of Britain, but also to hold the Near East and Africa. The other is the magnificent defense of China, which will, I have reason to believe, increase in strength. All of these, together, prevent the Axis from winning control of the seas by ships and aircraft.

The Axis powers can never achieve their objective of world-domination unless they first obtain control of the seas. This is their supreme purpose today; and to achieve it, they must capture Great Britain.

They could then have the power to dictate to the Western Hemisphere. No spurious argument, no appeal to sentiment, and no false pledges like those given by Hitler at Munich, can deceive the American people into believing that he and his Axis partners would not, with Britain defeated, close in relentlessly on this hemisphere.

But if the Axis powers fail to gain control of the seas, they are certainly defeated. Their dreams of world-domination will then go by the board; and the criminal leaders who started this war will suffer inevitable disaster.

Both they and their people know this—and they are afraid. That is why they are risking everything they have, conducting desperate attempts to break through to the command of the ocean. Once they are limited to a continuing land war, their cruel forces of occupation will be unable to keep their heel on the necks of the millions of innocent, oppressed peoples on the continent of Europe; and in the end, their whole structure will break into little pieces. And the wider the Nazi land effort, the greater the danger.

We do not forget the silenced peoples. The masters of Germany—those, at least, who have not been assassinated or escaped to free soil—have marked these peoples and their children's children for slavery. But those people, spiritually unconquered: Austrians, Czechs, Poles, Norwegians, Dutch, Belgians, Frenchmen, Greeks, Southern Slavs—yes, even those Italians and Germans who themselves have been enslaved—will prove to be a powerful force in disrupting the Nazi system.

Yes, all freedom—meaning freedom to live, and not freedom to conquer and subjugate other peoples—depends on freedom of the seas. All of American history—North, Central, and South American history—has been inevitably tied up with those words "freedom of the seas".

Since 1799, when our infant Navy made the West Indies and the Caribbean and the Gulf of Mexico safe for American ships; since 1804 and 1805 when we made all peaceful commerce safe from the depredations of the Barbary pirates; since the War of 1812, which was fought for the preservation of sailors' rights; since 1867, when our sea power made it possible for the Mexicans to expel the French Army of Louis Napoleon, we have striven and fought in defense of freedom of the seas—for our own shipping, for the commerce of our sister republics, for the right of all nations to use the highways of world trade—and for our own safety.

During the first World War we were able to escort merchant ships by the use of small cruisers, gunboats, and destroyers; and this type of convoy was effective against submarines. In this second World War, however, the problem is greater, because the attack on the freedom of the seas is now fourfold: first, the improved submarine; second, the much greater use of the heavily armed raiding cruiser or hit-and-run battleship; third, the bombing airplane, which is capable of destroying merchant ships seven or eight hundred miles from its nearest base; and fourth, the destruction of merchant ships in those ports of the world which are accessible to bombing attack.

The battle of the Atlantic now extends from the icy waters of the North Pole to the frozen continent of the Antarctic. Throughout this huge area, there have been sinkings of merchant ships in alarming and increasing numbers by Nazi raiders or submarines. There have been sinkings even of ships carrying neutral flags. There have been sinkings in the South Atlantic, off West Africa and the Cape Verde Islands; between the Azores and the islands off the American coast; and between Greenland and Iceland. Great numbers of these sinkings have been actually within the waters of the Western Hemisphere.

The blunt truth is this—and I reveal this with the full knowledge of the British government: the present rate of Nazi sinkings of merchant ships is more than three times as high as the capacity of British shipyards to replace them; it is more than twice the combined British and American output of merchant ships today.

We can answer this peril by two simultaneous measures: First, by speeding up and increasing our great ship-building program; and second, by helping to cut down the losses on the high seas.

Attacks on shipping off the very shores of land which we are determined to protect, present an actual military danger to the Americas. And that danger has recently been heavily underlined by the presence in Western Hemisphere waters of Nazi battleships of great striking-power.

Most of the supplies for Britain go by a northerly route, which comes close to Greenland and the nearby island of Iceland. Germany's heaviest attack is on that route. Nazi occupation of Iceland or bases in Greenland would bring the war close to our continental shores because they are stepping-stones to Labrador, Newfoundland, Nova Scotia, and the northern United States, including the great industrial centers of the North, East, and the Middle West.

Equally, the Azores and the Cape Verde Islands, if occupied or controlled by Germany, would directly endanger the freedom of the Atlantic and our own physical safety. Under German domination they would become bases for submarines, warships, and airplanes raiding the waters which lie immediately off our own coasts and attacking the shipping in the South Atlantic. They would provide a springboard for actual attack against the integrity and independence of Brazil and her neighboring republics.

I have said on many occasions that the United States is mustering its men and its resources only for purposes of defense—only to repel attack. I repeat that statement now. But we must be realistic when we use the word "attack"; we have to relate it to the lightning speed of modern warfare.

Some people seem to think that we are not attacked until bombs actually drop on New York or San Francisco or New Orleans or Chicago. But they are simply shutting their eyes to the lesson we must learn from the fate of every nation that the Nazis have conquered.

The attack on Czechoslovakia began with the conquest of Austria. The attack on Norway began with the occupation of Denmark. The attack on Greece began with occupation of Albania and Bulgaria. The attack on the Suez Canal began with the invasion of the Balkans and North Africa. The attack on the United States can begin with the domination of any base which menaces our security—north or south.

Nobody can foretell tonight just when the acts of the dictators will ripen into attack on this hemisphere and us. But we know enough by now to realize that it would be suicide to wait until they are in our front yard.

When your enemy comes at you in a tank or a bombing plane, if you hold your fire until you see the whites of his eyes, you will never know what hit you. Our Bunker Hill of tomorrow may be several thousand miles from Boston.

Anyone with an atlas and a reasonable knowledge of the sudden striking-force of modern war, knows that it is stupid to wait until a probable enemy has gained a foothold from which to attack. Old-fashioned common sense calls for the use of a strategy which will prevent such an enemy from gaining a foothold in the first place.

We have, accordingly, extended our patrol in north and south Atlantic waters. We are steadily adding more and more ships and planes to that patrol. It is well known that the strength of the Atlantic Fleet has been greatly increased during the past year, and is constantly being built up.

These ships and planes warn of the presence of attacking raiders, on the sea, under the sea, and above the sea. The danger from these raiders is greatly lessened if their location is definitely known. We are thus being forewarned; and we shall be on our guard against efforts to establish Nazi bases closer to our hemisphere.

The deadly facts of war compel nations, for simple self-preservation, to make stern choices. It does not make sense, for instance, to say, "I believe in the defense of all the Western Hemisphere", and in the next breath to say, "I will not fight for that defense until the enemy has landed on our shores". And if we believe in the independence and integrity of the Americas, we must be willing to fight to defend them just as much as we would to fight for the safety of our own homes.

It is time for us to realize that the safety of American homes even in the center of our country has a definite relationship to the continued safety of homes in Nova Scotia or Trinidad or Brazil.

Our national policy today, therefore, is this:

First, we shall actively resist wherever necessary, and with all our resources, every attempt by Hitler to extend his Nazi domination to the Western Hemisphere, or to threaten it. We shall actively resist his every attempt to gain control of the seas. We insist upon the vital importance of keeping Hitlerism away from any point in the world which could be used and would be used as a base of attack against the Americas.

Second, from the point of view of strict naval and military necessity, we shall give every possible assistance to Britain and to all who, with Britain, are resisting Hitlerism or its equivalent with force of arms. Our patrols are helping now to insure delivery of the needed supplies to Britain. All additional measures necessary to deliver the goods will be taken. Any and all further methods or combination of methods, which can or should be utilized, are being devised by our military and naval technicians, who, with me, will work out and put into effect such new and additional safeguards as may be needed.

The delivery of needed supplies to Britain is imperative. This can be done; it must be done; it will be done.

To the other American nations—20 republics and the Dominion of Canada—I say this: The United States does not merely propose these purposes, but is actively engaged today in carrying them out.

I say to them further: You may disregard those few citizens of the United States who contend that we are disunited and cannot act.

There are some timid ones among us who say that we must preserve peace at any price—lest we lose our liberties forever. To them I say: Never in the history of the world has a nation lost its democracy by a successful struggle to defend its democracy. We must not be defeated by the fear of the very danger which we are preparing to resist. Our freedom has shown its ability to survive war, but it would never survive surrender. "The only thing we have to fear is fear itself."

There is, of course, a small group of sincere, patriotic men and women whose real passion for peace has shut their eyes to the ugly realities of international banditry and to the need to resist it at all costs. I am sure they are embarrassed by the sinister support they are receiving from the enemies of democracy in our midst—the Bundists and Fascists and Communists and every group devoted to bigotry and racial and religious intolerance. It is no mere coincidence that all the arguments put forward by these enemies of democracy—all their attempts to confuse and divide our people and to destroy public confidence in our Government—all their defeatist forebodings that Britain and democracy are already beaten—all their selfish promises that we can "do business" with Hitler—all of these are but echoes of the words that have been poured out from the Axis bureaus of propaganda. Those same words have been used before in other countries—to scare them, to divide them, to soften them up. Invariably, those same words have formed the advance guard of physical attack.

Your Government has the right to expect of all citizens that they take loyal part in the common work of our common defense— take loyal part from this moment forward.

I have recently set up the machinery for civilian defense. It will rapidly organize, locality by locality. It will depend on the organized effort of men and women everywhere. All will have responsibilities to fulfil.

Defense today means more than merely fighting. It means morale, civilian as well as military; it means using every available resource; it means enlarging every useful plant. It means the use of a greater American common sense in discarding rumor and distorted statement. It means recognizing, for what they are, racketeers and fifth columnists, who are the incendiary bombs of the moment.

All of us know that we have made very great social progress in recent years. We propose to maintain that progress and strengthen it. When the Nation is threatened from without, however, as it is today, the actual production and transportation of the machinery of defense must not be interrupted by disputes between capital and capital, labor and labor, or capital and labor. The future of all free enterprise—of capital and labor alike—is at stake.

This is no time for capital to make, or be allowed to retain, excess profits. Articles of defense must have undisputed right-of-way in every industrial plant in the country.

A nation-wide machinery for conciliation and mediation of industrial disputes has been set up. That machinery must be used promptly—and without stoppage of work. Collective bargaining will be retained, but the American people expect that impartial recommendations of our Government services will be followed both by capital and by labor.

The overwhelming majority of our citizens expect their Government to see that the tools of defense are built; and for the very purpose of preserving the democratic safeguards of both labor and management, this Government is determined to use all of its power to express the will of its people and to prevent interference with the production of materials essential to our Nation's security.

Today the whole world is divided between human slavery and human freedom—between pagan brutality and the Chrisitian ideal.

We choose human freedom—which is the Christian ideal.

No one of us can waver for a moment in his courage or his faith.

We will not accept a Hitler-dominated world. And we will not accept a world, like the post-war world of the 1920's, in which the seeds of Hitlerism can again be planted and allowed to grow.

We will accept only a world consecrated to freedom of speech and expression—freedom of every person to worship God in his own way—freedom from want—and freedom from terrorism.

Is such a world impossible of attainment?

Magna Charta, the Declaration of Independence, the Constitution of the United States, the Emancipation Proclamation, and every other milestone in human progress—all were ideals which seemed impossible of attainment, yet they were attained.

As a military force, we were weak when we established our independence, but we successfully stood off tyrants, powerful in their day, who are now lost in the dust of history.

Odds meant nothing to us then. Shall we now, with all our potential strength, hesitate to take every single measure necessary to maintain our American liberties?

Our people and our Government will not hesitate to meet that challenge.

As the President of a united and determined people, I say solemnly:

We reassert the ancient American doctrine of freedom of the seas.

We reassert the solidarity of the 21 American republics and the Dominion of Canada in the preservation of the independence of the hemisphere.

We have pledged material support to the other democracies of the world—and we will fulfil that pledge.

We in the Americas will decide for ourselves whether and when and where our American interests are attacked or our security threatened.

We are placing our armed forces in strategic military position.

We will not hesitate to use our armed forces to repel attack.

We reassert our abiding faith in the vitality of our constitutional republic as a perpetual home of freedom, of tolerance, and of devotion to the Word of God.

Therefore, with profound consciousness of my responsibilities to my countrymen and to my country's cause, I have tonight issued a proclamation that an unlimited national emergency exists and requires the strengthening of our defense to the extreme limit of our national power and authority.

The Nation will expect all individuals and all groups to play their full parts without stint and without selfishness and without doubt that our democracy will triumphantly survive.

I repeat the words of the Signers of the Declaration of Independence—that little band of patriots, fighting long ago against overwhelming odds, but certain, as are we, of ultimate victory: "With a firm reliance on the protection of Divine Providence, we mutually pledge to each other our lives, our fortunes, and our sacred honor."

211

Department of State Bulletin, vol. IV, p. 681

Statement by the Secretary of State at a Press Conference, June 5, 1941

We have received some preliminary reports from Ambassador Leahy. Frankly we are very much concerned about the situation which seems to be growing up. As you know, we have throughout our history been sympathetic to the true aspirations of France. We have fought beside her. Her cause has been our cause. The principles of free, representative government by the people have been the bases of the democratic institutions of both of our countries.

In her present difficult situation we have given concrete evidence of our sympathetic friendship and thought for the well-being of the French people and the French Empire.

We have continued to maintain full and friendly diplomatic relations with the French Government at Vichy and have received its emissaries freely in this country. We have given the fullest and most sympathetic consideration to financial problems connected with the maintenance of French establishments, not only in this hemisphere but in the Far East, both diplomatic and semi-official services.

We have, through Admiral Leahy, the American Ambassador at Vichy, consistently conveyed to the French Government our understanding of the difficulties of their position and our determination to be of every assistance we could in solving their problems for the ultimate benefit of the French people. We have made clear to the French Government that a basic policy of this Government was to aid Great Britain in her defense against those same forces of conquest which had invaded and are subjugating France.

We have aided in the furnishing of foodstuffs for unoccupied France, and children's supplies are now being distributed through the American Red Cross, and we had planned the continuation of these services.

We have facilitated the passage of ships from this hemisphere to France's African colonies.

We have collaborated with the other American republics as well as with the French Government in safeguarding the welfare and maintaining the integrity of the French possessions in the Western Hemisphere.

In collaboration with the French Government we have arranged for the maintenance of the economic stability of the French North African territories by providing facilities for increasing trade and the purchase from us of commodities urgently needed by the people of North Africa with a view to maintaining their previous status as an integral part of the French Empire.

Happily, whenever such action was necessary, Ambassador Leahy has been able to assure the Vichy Government that this Nation had no other interest in any territories of the French Empire than their preservation for the French people.

We have given the most sympathetic consideration to the financial problems arising out of the freezing of French funds.

It has been the determined policy of this Government to continue friendly and helpful cooperation with France in the present difficult situation, in which its action is restricted and limited by the terms of its armistice with Germany and Italy. This policy has been based upon assurances by the French Government that there was no intention on its part to exceed the strict limitations imposed by those terms.

It would seem scarcely believable that the French Government at Vichy should adopt the policy of collaboration with other powers for the purpose of aggression and oppression, despite indications appearing in our preliminary reports. Such action would not only be yielding priceless rights and interests beyond the requirements of a harsh armistice but it would at once place France in substantial political and military subservience and would also make her, in part, the instrument of aggression against many other peoples and nations. This could only be utterly inimical to the just rights of other countries, to say nothing of its ultimate effects on the liberties, the true interests, and the welfare of the people of France.

We are therefore undertaking as speedily as possible to assemble every material fact and circumstance calculated to shed light on this alleged course of the French Government.

212

Department of State Bulletin, vol. IV, p. 741

Message of President Roosevelt to the Congress, June 20, 1941

I am under the necessity of bringing to the attention of the Congress the ruthless sinking by a German submarine on May 21 of an American ship, the *Robin Moor*, in the South Atlantic Ocean (25°40′ West, 6°10′ North) while the vessel was on the high seas en route to South Africa.

According to the formal depositions of survivors the vessel was sunk within 30 minutes from the time of the first warning given by the Commander of the submarine to an officer of the *Robin Moor*.

The submarine did not display its flag, and the Commander did not announce its nationality.

The *Robin Moor* was sunk without provision for the safety of the passengers and crew.

It was sunk despite the fact that its American nationality was admittedly known to the Commander of the submarine and that its nationality was likewise clearly indicated by the flag and other markings.

The sinking of this American ship by a German submarine flagrantly violated the right of United States vessels freely to navigate the seas subject only to a belligerent right accepted under international law. This belligerent right, as is known to the German Government, does not include the right deliberately to sink a merchant vessel, leaving the passengers and crew to the mercies of the elements. On the contrary the belligerent is required to place the passengers and crew in places of safety.

The passengers and crew of the *Robin Moor* were left afloat in small lifeboats from approximately two to three weeks when they were accidentally discovered and rescued by friendly vessels. This chance rescue does not lessen the brutality of casting the boats adrift in mid-ocean.

The total disregard shown for the most elementary principles of international law and of humanity brands the sinking of the *Robin Moor* as the act of an international outlaw.

The Government of the United States holds Germany responsible for the outrageous and indefensible sinking of the *Robin Moor*. Full reparation for the losses and damages suffered by American nationals will be expected from the German Government.

Our Government believes that freedom from cruelty and inhuman treatment is a natural right. It is not a grace to be given or withheld at the will of those temporarily in a position to exert force over defenseless people.

Were this incident capable of being regarded apart from a more general background, its implications might be less serious—but it must be interpreted in the light of a declared and actively pursued policy of frightfulness and intimidation which has been used by the German Reich as an instrument of international policy.

The present leaders of the German Reich have not hesitated to engage in acts of cruelty and many other forms of terror against the innocent and the helpless in other countries, apparently in the belief that methods of terrorism will lead to a state of affairs permitting the German Reich to exact acquiescence from the nations victimized.

This Government can only assume that the Government of the German Reich hopes through the commission of such infamous acts of cruelty to helpless and innocent men, women, and children to intimidate the United States and other nations into a course of nonresistance to German plans for universal conquest—a conquest based upon lawlessness and terror on land and piracy on the sea.

Such methods are fully in keeping with the methods of terrorism hitherto employed by the present leaders of the German Reich in the policy which they have pursued toward many other nations subsequently victimized.

The Government of the German Reich may however be assured that the United States will neither be intimidated nor will it acquiesce in the plans for world-domination which the present leaders of Germany may have.

We are warranted in considering whether the case of the *Robin Moor* is not a step in a campaign against the United States analogous to campaigns against other nations. We cannot place reliance on official declarations to the contrary.

Like statements, declarations, and even solemn pledges have been forthcoming in respect of many nations, commencing with the statement that the Government of the German Reich considered its territorial aspirations satisfied when it seized Austria by force. Evidence that the Government of the German Reich continues to plan further conquest and domination is convincing, and, indeed, scarcely disputed.

Viewed in the light of the circumstances the sinking of the *Robin Moor* becomes a disclosure of policy as well as an example of method. Heretofore, lawless acts of violence have been preludes to schemes of land conquest. This one appears to be a first step in assertion of the supreme purpose of the German Reich to seize control of the high seas, the conquest of Great Britain being an indispensable part of that seizure.

Its general purpose would appear to be to drive American commerce from the ocean wherever such commerce was considered a disadvantage to German designs; and its specific purpose would appear to be interruption of our trade with all friendly countries.

We must take it that notice has now been served upon us that no American ship or cargo on any of the seven seas can consider itself immune from acts of piracy. Notice is served on us, in effect, that the German Reich proposes so to intimidate the United States that we would be dissuaded from carrying out our chosen policy of helping Britain to survive.

In brief, we must take the sinking of the *Robin Moor* as a warning to the United States not to resist the Nazi movement of world conquest. It is a warning that the United States may use the high seas of the world only with Nazi consent.

Were we to yield on this we would inevitably submit to world-domination at the hands of the present leaders of the German Reich.

We are not yielding and we do not propose to yield.

213

711.94/2162–11/44

Draft Proposal Handed by the Secretary of State to the Japanese Ambassador (Nomura)

[WASHINGTON,] June 21, 1941.

The Governments of the United States and of Japan accept joint responsibility for the initiation and conclusion of a general agreement of understanding as expressed in a joint declaration for the resumption of traditional friendly relations.

Without reference to specific causes of recent estrangement, it is the sincere desire of both Governments that the incidents which led to the deterioration of amicable sentiment between their countries should be prevented from recurrence and corrected in their unforeseen and unfortunate consequences.

It is our earnest hope that, by a cooperative effort, the United States and Japan may contribute effectively toward the establishment and preservation of peace in the Pacific area and, by the rapid consummation of an amicable understanding, encourage world peace and arrest, if not dispel, the tragic confusion that now threatens to engulf civilization.

For such decisive action, protracted negotiations would seem ill-suited and weakening. Both Governments, therefore, desire that adequate instrumentalities should be developed for the realization of a general understanding which would bind, meanwhile, both Governments in honor and in act.

It is the belief of the two Governments that such an understanding should comprise only the pivotal issues of urgency and not the accessory concerns which could be deliberated later at a conference.

Both Governments presume to anticipate that they could achieve harmonious relations if certain situations and attitudes were clarified or improved; to wit:

1. The concepts of the United States and of Japan respecting international relations and the character of nations.
2. The attitudes of both Governments toward the European war.
3. Action toward a peaceful settlement between China and Japan.
4. Commerce between both nations.
5. Economic activity of both nations in the Pacific area.
6. The policies of both nations affecting political stabilization in the Pacific area.
7. Neutralization of the Philippine Islands.

Accordingly, the Government of the United States and the Government of Japan have come to the following mutual understanding and declaration of policy:

I. The concepts of the United States and of Japan respecting international relations and the character of nations.

Both governments affirm that their national policies are directed toward the foundation of a lasting peace and the inauguration of a new era of reciprocal confidence and cooperation between our peoples.

Both Governments declare that it is their traditional, and present, concept and conviction that nations and races compose, as members of a family, one household living under the ideal of universal concord through justice and equity; each equally enjoying rights and admitting responsibilities with a mutuality of interests regulated by peaceful processes and directed to the pursuit of their moral and physical welfare, which they are bound to defend for themselves as they are bound not to destroy for others; they further admit their responsibilities to oppose the oppression or exploitation of other peoples.

Both Governments are firmly determined that their respective traditional concepts on the character of nations and the underlying moral principles of social order and national life will continue to be preserved and never transformed by foreign ideas or ideologies contrary to those moral principles and concepts.

II. The attitudes of both Governments toward the European war.

The Government of Japan maintains that the purpose of the Tripartite Pact was, and is, defensive and is designed to contribute to the prevention of an unprovoked extension of the European war.

The Government of the United States maintains that its attitude toward the European hostilities is and will continue to be determined solely and exclusively by considerations of protection and self-defense: its national security and the defense thereof.

NOTE (There is appended a suggested draft of an exchange of letters as a substitute for the Annex and Supplement on the Part of the Government of the United States on this subject which constituted a part of the draft of May 31, 1941. . . .)

III. Action toward a peaceful settlement between China and Japan.

The Japanese Government having communicated to the Government of the United States the general terms within the framework of which the Japanese Government will propose the negotiation of a peaceful settlement with the Chinese Government, which terms are declared by the Japanese Government to be in harmony with the Konoe principles regarding neighborly friendship and mutual respect of sovereignty and territories and with the practical application of those principles, the President of the United States will suggest to the Government of China that the Government of China and the Government of Japan enter into a negotiation on a basis mutually advantageous and acceptable for a termination of hostilities and resumption of peaceful relations.

NOTE (The foregoing draft of Section III is subject to further discussion of the question of cooperative defense against communistic activities, including the stationing of Japanese troops in Chinese territory, and the question of economic cooperation between China and Japan. With regard to suggestions that the language of Section III be changed, it is believed that consideration of any suggested change can most advantageously be given after all the points in the annex relating to this section have been satisfactorily worked out, when the section and its annex can be viewed as a whole.)

IV. Commerce between both nations.

When official approbation to the present understanding has been given by both Governments, the United States and Japan shall assure each other mutually to supply such commodities as are, respectively, available and required by either of them. Both Governments further consent to take necessary steps to resume normal trade relations as formerly established under the Treaty of Commerce and Navigation between the United States and Japan. If a new commercial treaty is desired by both Governments, it would be negotiated as soon as possible and be concluded in accordance with usual procedures.

V. Economic activity of both nations in the Pacific area.

On the basis of mutual pledges hereby given that Japanese activity and American activity in the Pacific area shall be carried on by peaceful means and in conformity with the principle of non-discrimination in international commercial relations, the Japanese Government and the Government of the United States agree to cooperate each with the other toward obtaining non-discriminatory access by Japan and by the United States to commercial supplies of natural resources (such as oil, rubber, tin, nickel) which each country needs for the safeguarding and development of its own economy.

VI. The policies of both nations affecting political stabilization in the Pacific area.

Both Governments declare that the controlling policy underlying this understanding is peace in the Pacific area; that it is their fundamental purpose, through cooperative effort, to contribute to the maintenance and the preservation of peace in the Pacific area; and that neither has territorial designs in the area mentioned.

VII. Neutralization of the Philippine Islands.

The Government of Japan declares its willingness to enter at such time as the Government of the United States may desire into negotiation with the Government of the United States with a view to the conclusion of a treaty for the neutralization of the Philippine Islands, when Philippine independence shall have been achieved.

[Annex 1]

ANNEX AND SUPPLEMENT ON THE PART OF THE JAPANESE GOVERNMENT

III. Action toward a peaceful settlement between China and Japan.

The basic terms as referred to in the above section are as follows:
1. Neighborly friendship.
2. (Cooperative defense against injurious communistic activities—including the stationing of Japanese troops in Chinese territory.) Subject to further discussion.
3. (Economic cooperation.) Subject to agreement on an exchange of letters in regard to the application to this point of the principle of non-discrimination in international commercial relations.
4. Mutual respect of sovereignty and territories.
5. Mutual respect for the inherent characteristics of each nation cooperating as good neighbors and forming an East Asian nucleus contributing to world peace.
6. Withdrawal of Japanese armed forces from Chinese territory as promptly as possible and in accordance with an agreement to be concluded between Japan and China.

7. No annexation.
8. No indemnities.
9. Amicable negotiation in regard to Manchoukuo.

[Annex 2]

ANNEX AND SUPPLEMENT ON THE PART OF THE GOVERNMENT OF THE UNITED STATES

IV. Commerce between both nations.

It is understood that during the present international emergency Japan and the United States each shall permit export to the other of commodities in amounts up to the figures of usual or pre-war trade, except, in the case of each, commodities which it needs for its own purposes of security and self-defense. These limitations are mentioned to clarify the obligations of each Government. They are not intended as restrictions against either Government; and, it is understood, both Governments will apply such regulations in the spirit dominating relations with friendly nations.

[Annex 3]

SUGGESTED EXCHANGE OF LETTERS BETWEEN THE SECRETARY OF STATE AND THE JAPANESE AMBASSADOR

The Secretary of State to the Japanese Ambassador:

EXCELLENCY: In Section II of the Joint Declaration which was entered into today on behalf of our two Governments, statements are made with regard to the attitudes of the two Governments toward the European war. During the informal conversations which resulted in the conclusion of this Joint Declaration I explained to you on a number of occasions the attitude and policy of the Government of the United States toward the hostilities in Europe and I pointed out that this attitude and policy were based on the inalienable right of self-defense. I called special attention to an address which I delivered on April 24 setting forth fully the position of this Government upon this subject.

I am sure that you are fully cognizant of this Government's attitude toward the European war but in order that there may be no misunderstanding I am again referring to the subject. I shall be glad to receive from you confirmation by the Government of Japan that, with regard to the measures which this nation may be forced to adopt in defense of its own security, which have been set forth as indicated, the Government of Japan is not under any commitment which would require Japan to take any action contrary to or destructive of the fundamental objective of the present agreement, to establish and to preserve peace in the Pacific area.

Accept [etc.]

The Japanese Ambassador to the Secretary of State:

EXCELLENCY: I have received your letter of June—.

I wish to state that my Government is fully aware of the attitude of the Government of the United States toward the hostilities in Europe as explained to me by you during our recent conversations and as set forth in your address of April 24. I did not fail to report to my Government the policy of the Government of the United States as it had been explained to me, and I may assure you that my Government understands and appreciates the attitude and position of the Government of the United States with regard to the European war.

I wish also to assure you that the Government of Japan, with regard to the measures which the Government of the United States may be forced to adopt in defense of its own security, is not under any commitment requiring Japan to take any action contrary to or destructive of the fundamental objective of the present agreement.

The Government of Japan, fully cognizant of its responsibilities freely assumed by the conclusion of this agreement, is determined to take no action inimical to the establishment and preservation of peace in the Pacific area.

Accept [etc.] .

[Annex 4]

SUGGESTED LETTER TO BE ADDRESSED BY THE SECRETARY OF STATE TO THE JAPANESE AMBASSADOR IN CONNECTION WITH THE JOINT DECLARATION

EXCELLENCY: In the informal conversations which resulted in the conclusion of a general agreement of understanding between our two Governments, you and your associates expressed fully and frankly views on the intentions of the Japanese Government in regard to applying to Japan's proposed economic cooperation with China the principle of non-discrimination in international commercial relations. It is believed that it would be helpful if you could be so good as to confirm the statements already expressed orally in the form of replies on the following points:

1. Does the term "economic cooperation" between Japan and China contemplate the granting by the Government of China to the Japanese Government or its nationals of any preferential or monopolistic rights

which would discriminate in favor of the Japanese Government and Japanese nationals as compared with the Government and nationals of the United States and of other third countries? Is it contemplated that upon the inauguration of negotiations for a peaceful settlement between Japan and China the special Japanese companies, such as the North China Development Company and the Central China Promotion Company and their subsidiaries, will be divested, in so far as Japanese official support may be involved, of any monopolistic or other preferential rights that they may exercise in fact or that may inure to them by virtue of present circumstances in areas of China under Japanese military occupation?

2. With regard to existing restrictions upon freedom of trade and travel by nationals of third countries in Chinese territory under Japanese military occupation, could the Japanese Government indicate approximately what restrictions will be removed immediately upon the entering into by the Government of Chungking of negotiations with the Government of Japan and what restrictions will be removed at later dates, with an indication in each case in so far as possible of the approximate time within which removal of restrictions would be effected?

3. Is it the intention of the Japanese Government that the Chinese Government shall exercise full and complete control of matters relating to trade, currency and exchange? Is it the intention of the Japanese Government to withdraw and to redeem the Japanese military notes which are being circulated in China and the notes of Japanese-sponsored regimes in China? Can the Japanese Government indicate how soon after the inauguration of the contemplated negotiations arrangements to the above ends can in its opinion be carried out?

It would be appreciated if as specific replies as possible could be made to the questions above listed.

Accept [etc.]

214

Department of State Bulletin, vol. IV, p. 755

Statement by the Acting Secretary of State (Welles) at a Press Conference, June 23, 1941

If any further proof could conceivably be required of the real purposes and projects of the present leaders of Germany for world-domination, it is now furnished by Hitler's treacherous attack upon Soviet Russia.

We see once more, beyond peradventure of doubt, with what intent the present Government of Germany negotiates "non-aggression pacts". To the leaders of the German Reich sworn engagements to refrain from hostile acts against other countries—engagements regarded in a happier and in a civilized world as contracts to the faithful observance of which the honor of nations themselves was pledged—are but a symbol of deceit and constitute a dire warning on the part of Germany of hostile and murderous intent. To the present German Government the very meaning of the word "honor" is unknown.

This Government has often stated, and in many of his public statements the President has declared, that the United States maintains that freedom to worship God as their consciences dictate is the great and fundamental right of all peoples. This right has been denied to their peoples by both the Nazi and the Soviet Governments. To the people of the United States this and other principles and doctrines of communistic dictatorship are as intolerable and as alien to their own beliefs as are the principles and doctrines of Nazi dictatorship. Neither kind of imposed overlordship can have or will have any support or any sway in the mode of life or in the system of government of the American people.

But the immediate issue that presents itself to the people of the United States is whether the plan for universal conquest, for the cruel and brutal enslavement of all peoples, and for the ultimate destruction of the remaining free democracies, which Hitler is now desperately trying to carry out, is to be successfully halted and defeated.

That is the present issue which faces a realistic America. It is the issue at this moment which most directly involves our own national defense and the security of the New World in which we live.

In the opinion of this Government, consequently, any defense against Hitlerism, any rallying of the forces opposing Hitlerism, from whatever source these forces may spring, will hasten the eventual downfall of the present German leaders, and will therefore redound to the benefit of our own defense and security.

Hitler's armies are today the chief dangers of the Americas.

215

740.0011 European War 1939/14615

Statement Handed by the Ambassador in Japan (Grew) to Mr. Tomohiko Ushiba, Private Secretary of the Japanese Prime Minister (Prince Konoye) [64]

From a variety of sources reports are reaching the Government of the United States that it is the intention of the Japanese Government to enter upon hostilities against the Soviet Union.

As is well known to the Japanese Government, the maintenance and preservation of peace in the area of the Pacific has been the earnest desire of the American Government, which has contributed its greatest efforts to the achievement of that high purpose.

From statements made in recent months by the Japanese Ambassador in Washington, Admiral Nomura, to the Secretary of State, Mr. Hull, in the course of conversations between them, as well as from the utterances of responsible Japanese officials, the Government of the United States has derived the hope that it was also the desire of the Government of Japan to maintain and preserve peace in the area of the Pacific. The reports which are now reaching the American Government are so completely contrary to those statements and utterances that the Government of the United States finds it very difficult to believe in the truth of those reports.

Should Japan enter upon a course of military aggression and conquest it stands to reason that such action would render illusory the cherished hope of the American Government, which it understood was shared by the Japanese Government, that peace in the Pacific area, far from being further upset, might now indeed be strengthened and made more secure.

It is the earnest hope of the Government of the United States that the reports of Japan's decision to enter upon hostilities against the Soviet Union are not based upon fact, and an assurance to that effect from His Excellency the Prime Minister of Japan would be deeply appreciated by the Government of the United States.

TOKYO, *July 6, 1941.*

---

[64] Message sent on July 4 by the Secretary of State at the specific request of the President for delivery to His Excellency the Prime Minister of Japan, Prince Fumimaro Konoye.

216

Department of State Bulletin, vol. V, p. 15

Message of President Roosevelt to the Congress, July 7, 1941

I am transmitting herewith for the information of the Congress a message I received from the Prime Minister of Iceland on July first and the reply I addressed on the same day to the Prime Minister of Iceland in response to this message.

In accordance with the understanding so reached, forces of the United States Navy have today arrived in Iceland in order to supplement, and eventually to replace, the British forces which have until now been stationed in Iceland in order to insure the adequate defense of that country.

As I stated in my message to the Congress of September third last regarding the acquisition of certain naval and air bases from Great Britain in exchange for certain over-age destroyers, considerations of safety from overseas attack are fundamental.

The United States cannot permit the occupation by Germany of strategic outposts in the Atlantic to be used as air or naval bases for eventual attack against the Western Hemisphere. We have no desire to see any change in the present sovereignty of those regions. Assurance that such outposts in our defense-frontier remain in friendly hands is the very foundation of our national security and of the national security of every one of the independent nations of the New World.

For the same reason substantial forces of the United States have now been sent to the bases acquired last year from Great Britain in Trinidad and in British Guiana in the south in order to forestall any pincers movement undertaken by Germany against the Western Hemisphere. It is essential that Germany should not be able successfully to employ such tactics through sudden seizure of strategic points in the south Atlantic and in the north Atlantic.

The occupation of Iceland by Germany would constitute a serious threat in three dimensions:

> The threat against Greenland and the northern portion of the North American Continent, including the Islands which lie off it.
> The threat against all shipping in the north Atlantic.
> The threat against the steady flow of munitions to Britain—which is a matter of broad policy clearly approved by the Congress.

It is, therefore, imperative that the approaches between the

Americas and those strategic outposts, the safety of which this country regards as essential to its national security, and which it must therefore defend, shall remain open and free from all hostile activity or threat thereof.

As Commander-in-Chief I have consequently issued orders to the Navy that all necessary steps be taken to insure the safety of communications in the approaches between Iceland and the United States, as well as on the seas between the United States and all other strategic outposts.

This Government will insure the adequate defense of Iceland with full recognition of the independence of Iceland as a sovereign state.

In my message to the Prime Minister of Iceland I have given the people of Iceland the assurance that the American forces sent there would in no way interfere with the internal and domestic affairs of that country, and that immediately upon the termination of the present international emergency all American forces will be at once withdrawn, leaving the people of Iceland and their Government in full and sovereign control of their own territory.

FRANKLIN D. ROOSEVELT

THE WHITE HOUSE,
  July 7, 1941.

[Enclosures]

MESSAGE SENT BY THE PRIME MINISTER OF ICELAND
TO THE PRESIDENT OF THE UNITED STATES

In a conversation of June 24th, the British Minister explained that British forces in Iceland are required elsewhere. At the same time he stressed the immense importance of adequate defense of Iceland. He also called my attention to the declaration of the President of the United States to the effect that he must take all necessary measures to ensure the safety of the Western Hemisphere—one of the President's measures is to assist in the defense of Iceland—and that the President is therefore prepared to send here immediately United States troops to supplement and eventually to replace the British force here. But that he does not consider that he can take this course except at the invitation of the Iceland Government.

After careful consideration of all the circumstances the Iceland Government, in view of the present state of affairs, admit that this measure is in accordance with the interest of Iceland, and therefore are ready to entrust the protection of Iceland to United States on the following conditions:

1. United States promise to withdraw all their military forces—

land, air, and sea—from Iceland immediately on conclusion of present war.

2. United States further promise to recognize the absolute independence and sovereignty of Iceland and to exercise their best efforts with those powers which will negotiate the peace treaty at the conclusion of the present war in order that such treaty shall likewise recognize the absolute independence and sovereignty of Iceland.

3. United States promise not to interfere with Government of Iceland neither while their armed forces remain in this country nor afterwards.

4. United States promise to organize the defense of the country in such a way as to insure the greatest possible safety for the inhabitants themselves and assure that they suffer minimum disturbance from military activities, these activities being carried out in consultation with Iceland authorities as far as possible. Also because of small population of Iceland and consequent danger to nation from presence of a numerous army, great care must be taken that only picked troops are sent here. Military authorities should be also instructed to keep in mind that Icelanders have been unarmed for centuries and are entirely unaccustomed to military discipline and conduct of troops towards the inhabitants of the country should be ordered accordingly.

5. United States undertake defense of the country without expense to Iceland and promise compensation for all damage occasioned to the inhabitants by their military activities.

6. United States promise to further interests of Iceland in every way in their power, including that of supplying the country with sufficient necessities, of securing necessary shipping to and from the country and of making in other respects favorable commercial and trade agreements with it.

7. Iceland Government expects that declaration made by President in this connection will be in agreement with these promises on the part of Iceland, and Government would much appreciate its being given the opportunity of being cognizant with wording of this declaration before it is published.

8. On the part of Iceland it is considered obvious that if United States undertake defense of the country it must be strong enough to meet every eventuality and particularly in the beginning it is expected that as far as possible effort will be made to prevent any special danger in connection with changeover. Iceland Government lays special stress on there being sufficient airplanes for defensive purposes wherever they are required and they can be used as soon as decision is made for United States to undertake the defense of the country.

This decision is made on the part of Iceland as an absolutely free and sovereign state and it is considered as a matter of course that United States will from the beginning recognize this legal status of the country, both states immediately exchanging diplomatic representatives.

MESSAGE SENT BY THE PRESIDENT OF THE UNITED STATES IN RESPONSE TO A MESSAGE FROM THE PRIME MINISTER OF ICELAND

I have received your message in which you have informed me that after careful consideration of all the circumstances, the Iceland Government, in view of the present state of affairs, admits that the sending to Iceland of United States troops to supplement and eventually to replace the present British forces there would be in accordance with the interests of Iceland and that, therefore, the Iceland Government is ready to entrust the protection of Iceland to the United States on the following considerations:

1. United States promise to withdraw all their military forces— land, air, and sea—from Iceland immediately on conclusion of present war.

2. United States further promise to recognize the absolute independence and sovereignty of Iceland and to exercise their best efforts with those powers which will negotiate the peace treaty at the conclusion of the present war in order that such treaty shall likewise recognize the absolute independence and sovereignty of Iceland.

3. United States promise not to interfere with Government of Iceland neither while their armed forces remain in this country nor afterwards.

4. United States promise to organize the defense of the country in such a way as to ensure the greatest possible safety for the inhabitants themselves and assure that they suffer minimum disturbance from military activities; these activities being carried out in consultation with Iceland authorities as far as possible. Also because of small population of Iceland and consequent danger to nation from presence of a numerous army, great care must be taken that only picked troops are sent here. Military authorities should be also instructed to keep in mind that Icelanders have been unarmed for centuries and are entirely unaccustomed to military discipline and conduct of troops towards the inhabitants of the country should be ordered accordingly.

5. United States undertake defense of the country without expense to Iceland and promise compensation for all damage occasioned to the inhabitants by their military activities.

6. United States promise to further interests of Iceland· in every way in their power, including that of supplying the country with sufficient necessities, of securing necessary shipping to and from the country and of making in other respects favorable commercial and trade agreements with it.

7. Iceland Government expect that declaration made by President in this connection will be in agreement with these promises on the part of Iceland, and Government would much appreciate its being given the opportunity of being cognizant with wording of this declaration before it is published.

8. On the part of Iceland it is considered obvious that if United States undertake defense of the country it must be strong enough to meet every eventuality and particularly in the beginning it is expected that as far as possible efforts will be made to prevent any special danger in connection with change-over. Iceland Government lays special stress on there being sufficient airplanes for defensive purposes wherever they are required and they can be used as soon as decision is made for United States to undertake the defense of the country.

You further state that this decision is made on the part of Iceland as an absolutely free and sovereign state and that it is considered as a matter of course that the United States will from the beginning recognize the legal status of Iceland, both states immediately exchanging diplomatic representatives.

I take pleasure in confirming to you hereby that the conditions set forth in your communication now under acknowledgment are fully acceptable to the Government of the United States and that these conditions will be observed in the relations between the United States and Iceland. I may further say that it will give me pleasure to request of the Congress its agreement in order that diplomatic representatives may be exchanged between our two countries.

It is the announced policy of the Government of the United States to undertake to join with the other nations of the Western Hemisphere in the defense of the New World against any attempt at aggression. In the opinion of this Government, it is imperative that the integrity and independence of Iceland should be preserved because of the fact that any occupation of Iceland by a power whose only too clearly apparent plans for world conquest include the domination of the peoples of the New World would at once directly menace the security of the entire Western Hemisphere.

It is for that reason in response to your message, the Government of the United States will send immediately troops to supplement and eventually to replace the British forces now there.

The steps so taken by the Government of the United States are taken in full recognition of the sovereignty and independence of Iceland and with the clear understanding that American military or naval forces sent to Iceland will in no wise interfere in the slightest degree with the internal and domestic affairs of the Icelandic people; and with the further understanding that immediately upon the termination of the present international emergency, all such military and naval forces will be at once withdrawn leaving the people of Iceland and their Government in full sovereign control of their own territory.

The people of Iceland hold a proud position among the democracies of the world, with a historic tradition of freedom and of individual liberty which is more than a thousand years old. It is, therefore, all the more appropriate that in response to your message, the Government of the United States, while undertaking this defensive measure for the preservation of the independence and security of the democracies of the New World should at the same time be afforded the privilege of cooperating in this manner with your Government in the defense of the historic democracy of Iceland.

I am communicating this message, for their information, to the governments of all of the other nations of the Western Hemisphere.

217

740.0011 European War 1939/14615

Statement Handed by the Japanese Minister for Foreign Affairs (Matsuoka) to the Ambassador in Japan (Grew), July 8, 1941

MESSAGE IN REPLY SENT BY H.I.M.'S FOREIGN MINISTER AT THE REQUEST OF THE PRIME MINISTER FOR DELIVERY TO THE PRESIDENT OF THE U.S.A., DATED JULY 7TH, SHOWA 16

[Translation]

At a time like this all sorts of rumours are abundantly bred not only in Japan but in all countries.

It is hardly necessary to state that the prevention of the European War from spreading to the regions of Greater East Asia and the maintenance and preservation of peace in the area of the Pacific have always been the sincere and genuine desire of the Japanese Government which have consistently contributed their earnest efforts toward achieving that high purpose.

The Japanese Government wish to state, in reply to the last paragraph of the Message, that they have not so far considered the possibility of joining the hostilities against the Soviet Union. The position of the Japanese Government vis-à-vis the Soviet-Axis war was made clear in the Oral statement of July 2nd, 1941 of H. I. M.'s Foreign Minister to the Soviet Ambassador in Tokyo. One can do no better than attach hereto a copy of this Oral statement for the President's perusal in order to bring home the course of policy Japan has been compelled to pursue in the present circumstances. Of course, it is understood that the American Government will treat it as strictly confidential. Incidentally, the Japanese Government would like to avail themselves of this opportunity for definitely ascertaining whether it is really the intention of the President or the American Government to intervene in the European war as they are naturally and very deeply concerned at the prospect, disturbed as they sincerely are, by reports reaching them from a variety of sources.

[Annex]

ORAL STATEMENT HANDED BY H.I.M.'S FOREIGN MINISTER TO THE SOVIET AMBASSADOR IN TOKYO ON JULY 2, 1941

[Translation]

I take pleasure in informing Your Excellency that Japan necessarily feels deep concern with the German-Soviet war that has unfortunately broken out. To be frank, Japan finds herself in the most awkward position faced with the war between Germany and Italy, her allies, on one hand, and the U. S. S. R. on the other, with whom she has but recently begun to improve relations in sincere desire to promote and maintain good neighbourliness. Japan is, therefore, most anxious to see the termination of the hostilities at the earliest possible date, earnestly wishing that they may at least be confined to regions not immediately adjacent to the Far East where she possesses vital interests.

The Japanese Government take this opportunity to state that they do not at present feel compelled to modify their policy towards the U. S. S. R. except to the extent of their natural desire not to give rise to misunderstandings to their allies. It is their sincere hope that they will be able to pursue a course of policy carefully calculated at once to serve their own interests and to preserve the spirit of mutual trust among the allies, while maintaining good relations with the U. S. S. R. I need hardly add that their Excellencies, Messieurs Stalin and Molotoff, may rest assured that I will do my best but that future developments will largely decide if the Japanese Government can consistently abide by this policy.

TOKYO, *July 2, 1941.*

218

711.94/2176–½

*Memorandum by the Acting Secretary of State (Welles) Regarding
A Conversation With the Japanese Ambassador (Nomura)*

[WASHINGTON,] July 23, 1941.

The Japanese Ambassador called to see me this afternoon at his request.

Admiral Nomura commenced the conversation by saying that as soon as he had received from Mr. Wakasugi the report of his conversation with me two days ago, he had immediately returned to Washington in order to speak with me personally.

The Ambassador then commenced his exposition, which I did not interrupt until he had concluded.

The Ambassador said that he had now received from press reports, but not as yet officially, information that the Japanese Government had concluded with the Vichy Government an agreement whereunder the Japanese Government would send military forces to occupy certain portions of southern Indochina. The Ambassador said that he understood this agreement entailed no violation of the inherent sovereignty of French Indochina. He stated that I was well aware of the critical economic situation of Japan and of the great difficulty which Japan had in procuring raw materials, particularly food supplies, from abroad. He stressed the question of lack of fertilizer which Japan had been accustomed to importing from Germany and said that consequently additional rice must be imported from abroad. He stated that Japan was now importing a million tons of rice a year from Indochina. He went on to say that one of the two reasons for the step taken was to assure to Japan an uninterrupted source of supply of rice and other food stuffs, which Indochina afforded, as well as an uninterrupted supply of other raw materials which they required from that region. He stated that Japan believed that de Gaullist French agents were stirring up trouble in southern Indochina and that of course there were many Chinese agitators in that region and the Japanese Government feared that at some time in the near future a situation might develop which would cut off Japan's supplies from those territories.

The Ambassador then said that the second reason for the occupation undertaken was the need for military security. He stated that Japan believed that certain foreign powers were bent upon a policy of encirclement of Japan and that the step taken was purely a precautionary measure in the nature of a safeguard.

The two situations which the Ambassador had set forth above, he stated, had occasioned great "uneasiness" to Japan.

The Ambassador then said that from the tone of the press in this country and from observations which had been made to him by various Americans in whom he placed reliance, these recent developments were creating a condition of great excitement and perturbation in the United States. He said that of course the question of the measures which the United States might take was something which the United States alone could determine, but he urged most urgently that this Government should not "reach hasty conclusions" and should permit a little time to elapse in the hope that a friendly adjustment between Japan and the United States might be found. He said that any measures restricting oil exports to Japan would undoubtedly inflame Japanese public opinion exceedingly and he hoped, in view of his own belief that friendly relations could be maintained between the two countries, that full consideration might be given to his views in this connection.

The Ambassador concluded his exposition by saying that one of the first messages he had received from the new Cabinet was an urgent instruction to him to press for an understanding with the United States along the lines he had been discussing with Secretary Hull. These instructions, he said, were not as yet given to him in full detail but made it completely clear that the new Government fully supported the policies which he had been representing throughout the course of the conversations.

He said that I would of course realize that "third powers" were doing everything within their power to prevent the reaching of an agreement with the United States. He expressed the hope that this Government would bear this fact fully in mind in reaching any decisions it might contemplate.

I replied to the Ambassador that in view of his statement to me that Mr. Wakasugi had fully reported his conversation with me to the Ambassador, I felt I need not cover the same ground again in my conversation with the Ambassador this afternoon. I said that I had made it clear to Mr. Wakasugi that if the Japanese Government was now determined to pursue a policy diametrically opposed to the policy laid down by the Japanese Ambassador in his conversation with Secretary Hull as the policy which would result from the reaching of an agreement with the United States, this Government must reconsider its own position in the matter.

I said it was very clear to this Government that any agreement which Japan might have reached with the Vichy Government could only have been reached as a result of pressure brought to bear upon the Vichy Government by Berlin. Since that was the case in our judgment, the reaching of this agreement by Japan could only be regarded as offering assistance to Hitler in his obvious policy of world conquest and of world domination, which, I emphasized, in the opinion of the United States, would, if successful, prove equally deleterious to Japan and to the United States.

The Ambassador had referred to the desire of Japan, by occupying Indochina, to assure itself of supplies of food and raw materials from that territory. I said that if the agreement which Secretary Hull and the Ambassador had been discussing were concluded, the Ambassador must fully realize that a far greater measure of economic security would be afforded Japan since the whole agreement was predicated upon equal economic opportunity and equal economic security for all of the nations directly concerned in the Pacific region. With regard to the statement made by the Ambassador that the measure taken was in the nature of a military precaution, I inquired as to what possible justification there could be for such a step on the part of Japan when the Japanese Government had been fully informed through the Ambassador by Secretary Hull, of the policy of this Government in the Pacific, which was a policy of the maintenance of peace, of non-aggression and of the refusal to carry out any policy of conquest or of physical force. I said the policy of this Government was the reverse of a policy of encirclement or of a policy which would constitute any threat to Japan. Furthermore, I said, this Government was equally confident that the policy of Great Britain constituted no menace to Japan and that if an agreement of the kind which had been under discussion were concluded, the United States would have been joined, together with Japan, in support of the underlying principles for which this Government stood, by the Governments of Great Britain, of the Dominions, of the Netherlands, and, I was confident, by the Government of China as well.

I said the Ambassador could hardly expect me to take seriously the Ambassador's statement that Japan was concerned by the activities of Chinese agitators or de Gaullist sympathizers in southern Indochina. I said I believed we could both agree to pass that by without further reference.

I said I thought the time had now come to speak with the complete frankness which the Ambassador would expect from a member of his own naval profession and I would consequently take the liberty of doing so. I said that the movement now undertaken by Japan could only be regarded by the United States as having two probable purposes, neither of which purpose this Government could ignore.

First, the United States could only assume that the occupation of Indochina by Japan constituted notice to the United States that the Japanese Government intended to pursue a policy of force and of conquest, and, second, that in the light of these acts on the part of Japan, the United States, with regard to its own safety in the light of its own preparations for self-defense, must assume that the Japanese Government was taking the last step before proceeding upon a policy of totalitarian expansion in the South Seas and of conquest in the South Seas through the seizure of additional territories in that region.

This Government could not see that there was any fact or factual theory upon which Japan could possibly fill Indochina with Japanese military and other forces for purposes of defending Japan. The only consequent alternative was to regard the occupation of Indochina by Japan as being undertaken because of the Japanese realization of its value to Japan for purposes of offense against the South Sea area.

I said that in view of all of these considerations, which I believed I had set forth very clearly to the Ambassador, I was now in a position where I must tell him, at the request of Secretary Hull, that the latter could not see that there was any basis now offered for the pursuit of the conversations in which he and the Ambassador had been engaged. This Government, in the opinion of Secretary Hull, had made it thoroughly clear to the Government of Japan that it was entirely ready to go forward with Japan on the basis of peaceful adjustment of the relations between the two countries in accordance with the principles and policies set forth in the agreement which it had been proposed should be concluded. This Government had already shown the utmost measure of patience in its dealings with Japan—and at this stage the Ambassador emphatically nodded his head—and had been prepared, as I had emphasized to Mr. Wakasugi, to continue to be patient in the event that the Government of Japan had required time in order to deal with its own public opinion but had at the same time refrained from embarking upon measures which were fundamentally opposed to the principles which both parties here in Washington had been endeavoring to establish. I repeated again that in the judgment of the United States if such an agreement had been reached, the Government of Japan would have obtained an infinitely greater amount of security, both military and economic, than it could obtain through its embarkation upon a policy of conquest by force.

The Ambassador then said that he fully realized that this Government had been exceedingly patient. He urged that it continue, at least for a short time, to be patient and he said most emphatically that he was willing to assure me that if the agreement which had been under discussion had been concluded, the present steps would not have been taken by the present Government of Japan. He said he felt that the procrastination which had taken place—and for this he did not attempt to place the blame—had been responsible for the creation of conditions with which the new Government was confronted when it took office and from which it could not immediately free itself.

The Ambassador concluded by saying that he would report to Tokyo what I had said.

I concluded the interview by saying that I was happy to say that Secretary Hull was now almost completely restored to health and that he hoped he would be able to return to Washington in the near future and in such event I was sure that he himself would wish to talk again with the Ambassador.

The Ambassador gave me the impression of being greatly disturbed and sincerely concerned by the possibility that a situation might now develop which would make utterly impossible any understanding between the two countries. His manner was exceedingly conciliatory throughout the interview and when he spoke about his hope that the United States would not reach "hasty conclusions", he said three or four times that, of course, he had no right to interfere or to give the impression that he was intervening in the decisions which might be made by this country, but that he made the remark solely because of his belief that a friendly adjustment could still be found.

S[UMNER] W[ELLES]

Department of State Bulletin, vol. V, p. 71

Statement by the Acting Secretary of State (*Welles*), *July 24, 1941*

It will be recalled that in 1940 the Japanese Government gave expression on several occasions to its desire that conditions of disturbance should not spread to the region of the Pacific, with special references to the Netherlands East Indies and French Indochina. This desire was expressly concurred in by many other governments, including the Government of the United States. In statements by this Government, it was made clear that any alteration in the existing status of such areas by other than peaceful processes could not but be prejudicial to the security and peace of the entire Pacific area and that this conclusion was based on a doctrine which has universal application.

On September 23, 1940, referring to the events then rapidly happening in the Indochina situation, the Secretary of State stated that it seemed obvious that the existing situation was being upset and that the changes were being achieved under duress. Present developments relating to Indochina provide clear indication that further changes are now being effected under duress.

The present unfortunate situation in which the French Government of Vichy and the French Government of Indochina find themselves is, of course, well known. It is only too clear that they are in no position to resist the pressure exercised upon them.

There is no doubt as to the attitude of the Government and people of the United States toward acts of aggression carried out by use or threat of armed force. That attitude has been made abundantly clear.

By the course which it has followed and is following in regard to Indochina, the Japanese Government is giving clear indication that it is determined to pursue an objective of expansion by force or threat of force.

There is not apparent to the Government of the United States any valid ground upon which the Japanese Government would be warranted in occupying Indochina or establishing bases in that area as measures of self-defense.

There is not the slightest ground for belief on the part of even the most credulous that the Governments of the United States, of Great Britain, or of the Netherlands have any territorial ambitions in Indochina or have been planning any moves which could have been regarded as threats to Japan. This Government can, therefore, only conclude that the action of Japan is undertaken because of the estimated value to Japan of bases in that region primarily for purposes of further and more obvious movements of conquest in adjacent areas.

In the light of previous developments, steps such as are now being taken by the Government of Japan endanger the peaceful use by peaceful nations of the Pacific. They tend to jeopardize the procurement by the United States of essential materials such as tin and rubber which are necessary for the normal economy of this country and the consummation of our defense program. The purchase of tin, rubber, oil, or other raw materials in the Pacific area on equal terms with other nations requiring these materials has never been denied to Japan. The steps which the Japanese Government has taken also endanger the safety of other areas of the Pacific, including the Philippine Islands.

The Government and people of this country fully realize that such developments bear directly upon the vital problem of our national security.

220

711.94/2177

Memorandum by the Acting Secretary of State (Welles)

[WASHINGTON,] July 24, 1941.

At the request of the Japanese Ambassador, the President received the Ambassador for an off-the-record conference in the Oval Room at the White House at five o'clock this afternoon. At the President's request, Admiral Stark and I were present.

At the outset of the conference the President made approximately the following statement to the Ambassador. The President said, referring to a talk [64] which he had made this morning to a home defense group under the leadership of Mayor LaGuardia, that for more than two years the United States had been permitting oil to be exported from the United States to Japan. He said that this had been done because of the realization on the part of the United States that if these oil supplies had been shut off or restricted the Japanese Government and people would have been furnished with an incentive or a pretext for moving down upon the Netherlands East Indies in order to assure themselves of a greater oil supply than that which, under present conditions, they were able to obtain. The United States had been pursuing this policy primarily for the purpose of doing its utmost to play its full part in making the effort to preserve peace in the

---

[64] See doc. 221.

Pacific region. At the present time, the President said, the Ambassador undoubtedly knew that there was a very considerable shortage in the oil supply in the eastern part of the United States and the average American man and woman were unable to understand why, at a time when they themselves were asked to curtail their use of gasoline oil, the United States Government should be permitting oil supplies to continue to be exported to Japan when Japan during these past two years had given every indication of pursuing a policy of force and conquest in conjunction with the policy of world conquest and domination which Hitler was carrying on. The average American citizen could not understand why his Government was permitting Japan to be furnished with oil in order that such oil might be utilized by Japan in carrying on her purposes of aggression. The President said that if Japan attempted to seize oil supplies by force in the Netherlands East Indies, the Dutch would, without the shadow of a doubt, resist, the British would immediately come to their assistance, war would then result between Japan, the British and the Dutch, and, in view of our own policy of assisting Great Britain, an exceedingly serious situation would immediately result. It was with all of these facts in mind, the President said, that notwithstanding the bitter criticism that had been leveled against the Administration and against the Department of State, the President up to now had permitted oil to be shipped by Japan from the United States.

The President then went on to say that this new move by Japan in Indochina created an exceedingly serious problem for the United States. He said that, as I had stated to the Ambassador yesterday, insofar as assuring itself that it could obtain foodstuffs and raw materials from Indochina, Japan, of course, had it reached an agreement with the United States along the terms of the discussions between Secretary Hull and the Ambassador, would have been afforded far greater assurances of obtaining such supplies on equal terms with any other nation. More than that, the President said, the cost of any military occupation is tremendous and the occupation itself is not conducive to the production by civilians in occupied countries of food supplies and raw materials of the character required by Japan. Had Japan undertaken to obtain the supplies she required from Indochina in a peaceful way, she not only would have obtained larger quantities of such supplies, but would have obtained them with complete security and without the draining expense of a military occupation. Furthermore, from the military standpoint, the President said, surely the Japanese Government could not have in reality the slightest belief that China, Great Britain, the Netherlands or the United States had any territorial designs on Indochina nor were in the slightest degree providing any real threats of aggression against Japan. This Government, consequently, could only assume that the occupation of Indochina was being undertaken by Japan for the purpose of further offense and this created a situation which necessarily must give the United States the most serious disquiet.

The President said that he had been following in complete detail the conversations which had been progressing between Secretary Hull and the Ambassador and that he was confident that the Ambassador would agree that the policies now undertaken in Indochina by the Japanese Government were completely opposed to the principles and the letter of the proposed agreement which had been under discussion.

At this point the Ambassador took out of his pocket two sheets of notes which he had prepared and asked the President's permission to refer to them in order to make a statement of his Government's position.

In this exposition the Ambassador covered exactly the same ground which he had covered in his conversation with me last night.

The only points of difference were that at the outset of the conversation, the Ambassador very clearly and emphatically stated that the move by Japan into Indochina was something which he personally deplored and with which he personally was not in agreement.

After the Ambassador had made this exposition, the President said that he had been glad to learn that the new Foreign Minister, Admiral Toyoda, was an intimate friend of the Ambassador. The Ambassador replied that that was the fact; that they both had grown up in the same surroundings and that the relationship between them was very close.

The President then said that he had a proposal to make to the Ambassador which had occurred to him just before the Ambassador had come in and which he had not had time to talk over with me before making his proposal to the Ambassador.

The President said that it might be too late for him to make this proposal but he felt that no matter how late the hour might be, he still wished to seize every possible opportunity of preventing the creation of a situation between Japan and the United States which could only give rise to serious misunderstandings between the two peoples. The President stated that if the Japanese Government would refrain from occupying Indochina with its military and naval forces, or, had such steps actually been commenced, if the Japanese

Government would withdraw such forces, the President could assure the Japanese Government that he would do everything within his power to obtain from the Governments of China, Great Britain, the Netherlands, and of course the United States itself a binding and solemn declaration, provided Japan would undertake the same commitment, to regard Indochina as a neutralized country in the same way in which Switzerland had up to now been regarded by the powers as a neutralized country. He stated that this would imply that none of the powers concerned would undertake any military act of aggression against Indochina and would refrain from the exercise of any military control within or over Indochina. He would further endeavor to procure from Great Britain and the other pertinent powers a guarantee that so long as the present emergency continued, the local French authorities in Indochina would remain in control of the territory and would not be confronted with attempts to dislodge them on the part of de Gaullist or Free French agents or forces.

If these steps were taken, the President said, Japan would be given solemn and binding proof that no other power had any hostile designs upon Indochina and that Japan would be afforded the fullest and freest opportunity of assuring herself of the source of food supplies and other raw materials in Indochina which she was seeking to secure.

The Ambassador then reiterated concisely and quite clearly what the President had suggested. He then made some statement which was not quite clear to the effect that such a step would be very difficult at this time on account of the face-saving element involved on the part of Japan and that only a very great statesman would reverse a policy at this time.

The President then mentioned the fact that in the United States the belief was apparent that such policies as those which Japan was now pursuing were due to German pressure upon Japan. To this the Ambassador reacted by saying that Japan was, of course, an independent country and that while such pressure might be exercised, decisions on the policy she was pursuing were solely her own and no one else had any responsibility for them. The President then said that one thing the Japanese Government did not understand as clearly as this Government was the fact that Hitler was bent upon world domination and not merely the domination of Europe or of Africa. The President said that if Germany succeeded in defeating Russia and dominating Europe and then dominating Africa, there wasn't the slightest question in his mind that Germany thereafter would turn her attention to the Far East and likewise to the Western Hemisphere, and that while such a development might not

702

take place for many years, perhaps even ten years, the laws of chance made it easily possible that in such contingency, the navies of Japan and of the United States would be cooperating together against Hitler as the common enemy. The President reemphasized his belief that what Hitler had in mind was complete domination of the entire world.

To this the Ambassador replied that he would like to quote an old Chinese proverb in which he had great faith, namely, "He who continuously brandishes the sword eventually kills himself."

The Ambassador said that he would immediately report his conversation to his Government in Tokyo. He seemed to be very much impressed with what the President had said but I did not gather from his reactions that he was in any sense optimistic as to the result.

S[UMNER] W[ELLES]

221

Department of State Bulletin, vol. V, p. 72

Informal Remarks of President Roosevelt to the Volunteer Participation Committee, Washington, July 24, 1941

[Extract]

There are lots of thing that people don't quite understand. You are an information bureau to all of them. And I will give you the example.

Here on the East Coast you have been reading that the Secretary of the Interior, as Oil Administrator, is faced with the problem of not enough gasoline to go around in the East Coast, and how he is asking everybody to curtail their consumption of gasoline. All right. Now I am—I might be called—an American citizen, living in Hyde Park, N. Y. And I say, "That's a funny thing. Why am I asked to curtail my consumption of gasoline when I read in the papers that thousands of tons of gasoline are going out from Los Angeles—West Coast—to Japan; and we are helping Japan in what looks like an act of aggression?"

All right. Now the answer is a very simple one. There is a world war going on, and has been for some time—nearly two years. One of our efforts, from the very beginning, was to prevent the spread of that world war in certain areas where it hadn't started. One of those areas is a place called the Pacific Ocean—one of the largest areas of the earth. There happened to be a place in the South Pacific where we had to get a lot of things—rubber, tin, and so forth and so on—down in the Dutch Indies, the Straits Settlements, and Indochina. And we had to help get the Australian surplus of meat and wheat, and corn, for England.

It was very essential, from our own selfish point of view of defense, to prevent a war from starting in the South Pacific. So our foreign policy was—trying to stop a war from breaking out down there. At the same time, from the point of view of even France at that time—of course, France still had her head above water—we wanted to keep that line of supplies from Australia and New Zealand going to the Near East—all their troops, all their supplies that they have maintained in Syria, North Africa, and Palestine. So it was essential for Great Britain that we try to keep the peace down there in the South Pacific.

All right. And now here is a nation called Japan. Whether they had at that time aggressive purposes to enlarge their empire southward, they didn't have any oil of their own up in the north. Now, if we cut the oil off, they probably would have gone down to the Dutch East Indies a year ago, and you would have had war.

Therefore, there was—you might call—a method in letting this oil go to Japan, with the hope—and it has worked for two years—of keeping war out of the South Pacific for our own good, for the good of the defense of Great Britain, and the freedom of the seas.

You people can help to enlighten the average citizen who wouldn't hear of that, or doesn't read the papers carefully, or listen to the radio carefully, to understand what some of these apparent anomalies mean. So, on the information end, I think you have got just as great a task as you have in the actual organization work.

222

Department of State Bulletin, vol. V, p. 73

Statement Issued by the White House on July 26, 1941

In view of the unlimited national emergency declared by the President, he issued, on July 26, an Executive order freezing Japanese assets in the United States in the same manner in which assets of various European countries were frozen on June 14, 1941. This measure, in effect, brings all financial and import and export trade transactions in which Japanese interests are involved under the control of the Government and imposes criminal penalties for violation of the order.

This Executive order, just as the order of June 14, 1941, is designed among other things to prevent the use of the financial facilities of the United States and trade between Japan and the United States in ways harmful to national defense and American interests, to prevent the liquidation in the United States of assets obtained by duress or conquest, and to curb subversive activities in the United States.

At the specific request of Generalissimo Chiang Kai-shek, and for the purpose of helping the Chinese Government, the President has, at the same time, extended the freezing control to Chinese assets in the United States. The administration of the licensing system with respect to Chinese assets will be conducted with a view to strengthening the foreign trade and exchange position of the Chinese Government. The inclusion of China in the Executive Order, in accordance with the wishes of the Chinese Government, is a continuation of this Government's policy of assisting China.

223

711.94/2244–3/11

Oral Statement Handed by the Japanese Ambassador (Nomura) To the Secretary of State on August 6, 1941

The purport and nature of the measures taken by the Japanese Government in effecting a joint defense of French Indo-China has already been explained by the Japanese Foreign Minister to the United States Ambassador in Tokio as well as by myself to the President and the Acting Secretary of State. To summarise, the measures are of entirely peaceful character and for self-defense, and an intervention by any third Power would be wholly unwarranted. They were absolutely necessary in order to prevent from getting beyond control the Japanese public opinion which had been dangerously aroused because of the successive measures taken by the United States, Great Britain and Netherlands East Indies against Japan, and consequently in order to preserve peace in the Pacific.

As the United States Government has nevertheless manifested certain anxiety over the situation in regard to French Indo-China, the Japanese Government, with a view to dispelling any such misgiving, has instructed me to transmit a proposal and to enter into negotiations in strict confidence and on an "off record" basis. The proposal is intended to serve as a reply in a way to the suggestion made by the President on July 24 during his conversation with me, and to provide a fresh basis for Japanese-American understanding on which informal conversations have been carried on during the past months. I have to add that any accord of views which may result from the present negotiations is to be incorporated in the general formula for the adjustment of the relations between our two countries.

At all events, the Japanese Government is convinced that it is more than ever necessary to examine calmly and with a spirit of understanding toward the standpoint of each other the diverse causes which have been responsible for the strained relations between Japan and the United States, and to endeavor for the removal and alleviation of such causes and conditions as will upset the military, political and economic equilibrium that should normally exist between the two countries. The Japanese Government believes that its views in this respect are fully shared by the Government of the United States.

[WASHINGTON,] *August 6, 1941.*

[Annex]

PROPOSAL BY THE JAPANESE GOVERNMENT HANDED BY THE JAPANESE AMBASSADOR (NOMURA) TO THE SECRETARY OF STATE ON AUGUST 6, 1941

I. The Japanese Government undertakes:—

(A) that, in order to remove such causes as might constitute a menace of a military character to the United States, it will not further station its troops in the Southwestern Pacific areas except French Indo-China and that the Japanese troops now stationed in French Indo-China will be withdrawn forthwith on the settlement of the China Incident, and

(B) that, in order to remove such causes as might constitute a menace of political and military character to the Philippine Islands, the Japanese Government will guarantee the neutrality of the islands at an opportune time on the condition that Japan and the Japanese subjects will not be placed in any discriminatory positions as compared with other countries and their nationals including the United States and its nationals, and

(C) that, in order to remove such causes as might be responsible for the instability of the economic relations between Japan and the United States,[65] the Japanese Government will cooperate with the Government of the United States in the production and procurement of such natural resources as are required by the United States.

---

[65] On August 7, 1941 the Japanese Embassy requested that a correction be made at this point by the insertion of three words, omitted through a typographical error, as follows: "in East Asia".

II. The Government of the United States undertakes:—

(A) that, in order to remove such causes as might constitute a direct menace of military character to Japan or to her international communications, the Government of the United States will suspend its military measures in the Southwestern Pacific areas, and also that, upon a successful conclusion of the present conversations, it will advise the Governments of Great Britain and of the Netherlands to take similar steps, and

(B) that, in order to remove such causes as might be responsible for military, political and economic friction between Japan and the United States, the Government of the United States will cooperate with the Japanese Government in the production and procurement of natural resources as are required by Japan in the Southwestern Pacific areas, especially in the Netherlands East Indies, and

(C) that, in conjunction with the measures as set forth in (B) above, the Government of the United States will take steps necessary for restoring the normal relations of trade and commerce which have hitherto existed between Japan and the United States, and

(D) that, in view of the undertaking by the Japanese Government as set forth in I. (A) above, the Government of the United States will use its good offices for the initiation of direct negotiations between the Japanese Government and the Chiang Kai-shek régime for the purpose of a speedy settlement of the China Incident, and that the Government of the United States will recognise a special status of Japan in French Indo-China even after the withdrawal of Japanese troops from that area.

[WASHINGTON,] *August 6, 1941.*

224

711.94/2244–4/11

Memorandum[66] *Regarding a Conversation Between the Secretary Of State and the Japanese Ambassador (Nomura)*

[WASHINGTON,] August 8, 1941.

The Japanese Ambassador called at the Secretary's request.

The Secretary handed the Japanese Ambassador a document marked strictly confidential and dated August 8, 1941[67] in reply to the proposal of the Japanese Government contained in the docu-

[66] Prepared by Joseph W. Ballantine, Division of Far Eastern Affairs.
[67] Doc. 225.

ment handed by the Japanese Ambassador to the Secretary on August 6. The Secretary suggested that the Ambassador might care to glance over the document.

The Japanese Ambassador read the document and stated that he understood its import. He said that the Japanese Government was very desirous of adjusting relations with the United States and was anxious to find means of doing so. He asked whether it might not be possible for the responsible heads of the two Governments to meet, say in Honolulu, as was suggested in the original Japanese proposal presented to us, with a view to discussing means whereby an adjustment could be brought about.

The Secretary said that if an understanding of the nature which the Secretary and the Ambassador had been discussing for these last several months had been reached the two countries by now would have been able to go forward along a course of peace and of mutual benefit. The Secretary went on to say that this Government had been prepared to be patient and to move gradually and to be of all possible help it could to the Japanese Government in order to enable the Japanese Government to assert control over all groups in Japan so that the Japanese Government as a whole and public opinion could be brought into line to support policies such as those which the Ambassador and the Secretary had in mind. The Secretary pointed out that while this Government was proceeding along this patient course the Secretary had, at a time when he was recuperating from illness in the country, received word of measures taken by the Japanese Government which made it clear that those elements in the Japanese Government which favored peaceful courses had lost control and that accordingly he had directed officers of the Department to inform the Japanese Ambassador that, in the opinion of this Government, the measures now taken by the Japanese Government had served to remove the basis for an understanding such as the Ambassador and he had had in mind. Thus, the Secretary said, the understanding which the Secretary and the Ambassador had hoped to reach and which he felt that they had nearly reached failed of realization.

The Secretary went on to say that the Japanese press was being constantly stimulated to speak of encirclement of Japan by the United States. He said that today he had told press correspondents that there is no occasion for any nation in the world that is law-abiding and peaceful to become encircled by anybody except itself. The Secretary said that while in Japan the press was being officially inspired in ways calculated to inflame public opinion this

Government was not treating Japan in any such way but was doing all that it could to deprecate agitation.

The Ambassador replied that he thought that the efforts being made to inspire the press in Japan were motivated purely by a desire to invigorate the Japanese people and were not inconsistent with a sincere desire on the part of the Japanese Government to improve relations with the United States.

He asked whether what the Secretary had said could be taken as the Secretary's reply to the suggestion he had made for a meeting of the responsible heads of the two Governments.

The Secretary went over once more the points which he had previously brought out and suggested that, in the light of what he had said and of the reply which he had handed the Ambassador, it remained with the Japanese Government to decide whether it could find means of shaping its policies accordingly and then endeavor to evolve some satisfactory plan.

225

711.94/2244–4/11

Document Handed by the Secretary of State to the Japanese Ambassador (Nomura)

[WASHINGTON,] August 8, 1941.

The President's proposal was that, if the Japanese Government would refrain from occupying Indochina or establishing bases there with its military and naval forces, or, in case such steps had already actually been begun, would withdraw such forces, the President would do everything in his power to obtain from the Chinese Government, the British Government and the Netherland Government, and the Government of the United States would of course itself give, a binding and solemn declaration, provided the Japanese Government would make the same commitment to regard French Indochina as a "neutralized" country in the same way in which Switzerland had up to now been regarded by the powers as a neutralized country; that such a binding and solemn declaration on the part of each of the Governments mentioned would imply that none of these Governments would undertake any military act of aggression against French Indochina and that each of those Governments would refrain from the exercise of any military control within or over French Indochina. The President's proposal contemplated further that the Government of the United States would endeavor to obtain from Great Britain and the other interested powers a guarantee that, so long as the present emergency continues, the local French authorities in Indochina would remain undisturbed in control of the territory of French Indochina. Subsequently, the President's proposal with regard to French Indochina was extended to include Thailand as well, and the Japanese Government was informed that, should the Japanese Government accept the proposal of the President and abandon its present course with regard to French Indochina, the President would request of the other Governments which he had mentioned in connection with his proposal concerning French Indochina the same declaration and guarantee with regard to Thailand.

The Government of the United States feels that its views in regard to a broad understanding which would be calculated to establish and maintain peace in the Pacific area to the benefit of each and every country concerned in that area have been made abundantly clear in various official utterances and acts and in the course of the long series of conversations which the Secretary of State has had during recent months with the Japanese Ambassador. It feels that the Japanese Government is well aware of its attitude, of what it is able and willing to do, and of what it cannot do. It therefore feels that the proposals advanced in the document handed to the Secretary by the Japanese Ambassador on August 6 are lacking in responsiveness to the suggestion made by the President, the specifications of which have been for convenience of reference reiterated above.

226

740.0011 Pacific War/460

Memorandum by the Secretary of State Regarding a Conversation With the British Ambassador (Halifax)

[Extract]

[WASHINGTON,] August 9, 1941.

The Ambassador made some inquiry about the amount of aid this Government might give in case Singapore or the Dutch East Indies should be attacked. I replied that I myself have visualized the problem and issue in a broader way and that issue is presented by the plan of the Japanese to invade by force the whole of the Indian Ocean and the islands and continents adjacent thereto, isolating China, sailing across probably to the mouth of the Suez Canal, to the Persian Gulf oil area, to the Cape of Good Hope area, thereby blocking by a military despotism the trade routes and the supply sources to the British. I added that this broad military occupation would perhaps be more damaging to British defense in Europe than any other step short of the German crossing of the Channel. I said that this Government visualizes these broad conditions and the problem of resistance which they present; that the activities of this Government in the way of discouraging this Japanese movement and of resistance will be more or less affected by the British defensive situation in Europe and hence by the question of the number of American naval vessels and other American aid that may be needed by Great Britain at the same time. I said that in the event of further Japanese movements south this Government and the British Government should naturally have a conference at once and this Government would then be able to determine more definitely and in detail its situation pertaining to resistance, in the light of the statement I had just made.

C[ORDELL] H[ULL]

227

Department of State Bulletin, vol. V, p. 134

Joint Message of President Roosevelt and Prime Minister Churchill To Joseph Stalin, President of the Soviet of People's Commissars Of the Union of Soviet Socialist Republics, August 15, 1941

We have taken the opportunity afforded by the consideration of the report of Mr. Harry Hopkins on his return from Moscow to consult together as to how best our two countries can help your country in the splendid defense that you are making against the Nazi attack. We are at the moment cooperating to provide you with the very maximum of supplies that you most urgently need. Already many shiploads have left our shores and more will leave in the immediate future.

We must now turn our minds to the consideration of a more long term policy, since there is still a long and hard path to be traversed before there can be won that complete victory without which our efforts and sacrifices would be wasted.

The war goes on upon many fronts and before it is over there may be further fighting fronts that will be developed. Our resources though immense are limited, and it must become a question as to where and when those resources can best be used to further the greatest extent our common effort. This applies equally to manufactured war supplies and to raw materials.

The needs and demands of your and our armed services can only be determined in the light of the full knowledge of the many factors which must be taken into consideration in the decisions that we make. In order that all of us may be in a position to arrive at speedy decisions as to the apportionment of our joint resources, we suggest that we prepare for a meeting to be held at Moscow, to which we would send high representatives who could discuss these matters directly with you. If this conference appeals to you, we want you to know that pending the decisions of that conference we shall continue to send supplies and material as rapidly as possible.

We realize fully how vitally important to the defeat of Hitlerism is the brave and steadfast resistance of the Soviet Union and we feel therefore that we must not in any circumstances fail to act quickly and immediately in this matter on planning the program for the future allocation of our joint resources.

FRANKLIN D. ROOSEVELT
WINSTON S. CHURCHILL

228

711.94/2184

Memorandum by the Secretary of State

[WASHINGTON,] August 17, 1941.

The Ambassador of Japan called to see the President at the latter's request. Following some few exchanges of preliminary remarks, the President then became serious and proceeded to refer to the strained relations between our two countries. He referred to the Ambassador's visit to me and the latter's request for a reopening of the conversations between our two Governments. The President commented briefly on the policies and principles that this Government has been standing for in its relations with Japan, and he made some contrast to Japan's opposite course of conquest by force, et cetera. He concluded by saying that our attitude of opposition to Japan's course has been made well known, and that the next move is now up to Japan. The President inquired of the Ambassador if he had anything in mind to say in connection with the situation. Thereupon the Ambassador drew out of his pocket an instruction which he said was from his Government, in which the Japanese Government set forth some generalities and asserted very earnestly that it desired to see peaceful relations preserved between our two countries; that Prince Konoye feels so seriously and so earnestly about preserving such relations that he would be disposed to meet the President midway, geographically speaking, between our two countries and sit down together and talk the matter out in a peaceful spirit.

The President thereupon said that this Government should really bring the matters between the two Governments literally up to date and that he would, therefore, offer certain observations about the position of this Government; he added that he regretted the necessity of so doing but that he had no other recourse. The President said he had dictated what he was about to say and that he would read it to the Ambassador and then hand him the written instrument containing the oral conversation. This the President proceeded to do as follows:

[Here follows text of the oral statement printed *infra*.]

The President, after some little delay in the conversation so as to set apart the first statement which he read to the Ambassador, then proceeded to turn to the Ambassador's request to the Secretary of State and to himself for a resumption of the conversations. The President made further references to Japan's opposing course of conquest by force and bitter denunciation of this country by the Japanese Government-controlled press and then coming to the request for a reopening of the conversations he repeated our former statements to the Japanese Government that, of course, we could not think of reopening the conversations if the Japanese Government is to continue its present movement of force and conquest supported by its bitter press campaign against this country.

Thereupon the President proceeded to read to the Ambassador the following statement, which is self-explanatory:

[Here follows text of the statement printed on p. 715.]

The Ambassador received each paper in writing and said he would communicate both to his Government. He reiterated from time to time that his Government was very desirous of preserving peaceful relations between the two countries and he took no issue with the President relative to the reasons set forth by this Government for discontinuing conversations with Japan.

C[ordell] H[ull]

———

ORAL STATEMENT HANDED BY PRESIDENT ROOSEVELT TO THE JAPANESE AMBASSADOR (NOMURA) ON AUGUST 17, 1941

During past months the Governments of the United States and of Japan, through the Secretary of State and the Japanese Ambassador in Washington, have engaged in protracted conversations directed toward exploring the possibility of reaching a sound basis for negotiations between the two countries relative to the maintenance of peace with order and justice in the Pacific. The principles and policies which were under discussion in these conversations precluded pursuit by either Government of objectives of expansion by force or by threat of force.

On July 24 last the President of the United States informed the Japanese Government through the Japanese Ambassador in Washington that he was willing to suggest to the Governments of Great Britain, of The Netherlands and of China that they make a binding and solemn declaration that they had no aggressive intentions with regard to Indochina and that they would agree that the markets and raw materials of Indochina should be available to all Powers on equal terms. The President stated further that he would be willing to suggest to the Powers mentioned that they undertake this declaration, in which the United States would be willing to join, upon the understanding that the Government of Japan would be disposed to make a similar declaration and would be further disposed to withdraw its military and naval forces from Indochina.

Notwithstanding these efforts, the Government of Japan has continued its military activities and its disposals of armed forces at various points in the Far East and has occupied Indochina with its military, air and naval forces.

The Government of the United States is in full sympathy with the desire expressed by the Japanese Government that there be provided a fresh basis for amicable and mutually profitable relations between our two countries. This Government's patience in seeking an acceptable basis for such an understanding has been demonstrated time and again during recent years and especially during recent months. This Government feels at the present stage that nothing short of the most complete candor on its part, in the light of evidence and indications which come to it from many sources, will at this moment tend to further the objectives sought.

Such being the case, this Government now finds it necessary to say to the Government of Japan that if the Japanese Government takes any further steps in pursuance of a policy or program of military domination by force or threat of force of neighboring countries, the Government of the United States will be compelled to take immediately any and all steps which it may deem necessary toward safeguarding the legitimate rights and interests of the United States and American nationals and toward insuring the safety and security of the United States.

STATEMENT HANDED BY PRESIDENT ROOSEVELT TO THE JAPANESE AMBASSADOR (NOMURA) ON AUGUST 17, 1941

Reference is made to the question which the Japanese Ambassador raised on August 8 during a conversation with the Secretary of State whether it might not be possible for the responsible heads of the Japanese Government and the Government of the United States to meet with a view to discussing means whereby an adjustment in relations between the United States and Japan might be brought about. The thought of Prince Konoe and of the Japanese Government in offering this suggestion is appreciated.

Reference is made also to the desire expressed by the Japanese Ambassador during a call on the Secretary of State on August 16 that there be resumed the informal conversations which had been in progress between the two Governments toward ascertaining whether there existed a basis for negotiations relative to a peaceful settlement covering the entire Pacific situation.

When the Japanese Ambassador brought up these suggestions, the Secretary of State reminded the Ambassador that the Government of the United States had shown great patience and had been prepared to continue in that course of patience so long as the Japanese Government manifested a desire to follow courses of peace. It was pointed out to the Ambassador that while proceeding along this course this Government had received reports indicating clearly that the Japanese Government was adopting courses directly the opposite of those on which the recent conversations between the Ambassador and the Secretary of State had been predicated. It was pointed out also that the Japanese press was being constantly stimulated to speak of encirclement of Japan by the United States and was being officially inspired in ways calculated to inflame public opinion. The Secretary of State made it clear that he did not see how conversations between the two Governments could usefully be pursued or proposals be discussed while Japanese official spokesmen and the Japanese press contended that the United States was endeavoring to encircle Japan and carried on a campaign against the United States.

On two occasions officers of the Department of State, pursuant to instructions from the Secretary of State, called on the Japanese Ambassador to indicate concern over the reports that Japan intended to acquire by force or threat of force military and naval bases in French Indochina. Subsequently, on July 21 and July 23 the Acting Secretary of State raised with the Japanese Minister and with the Japanese Ambassador the question of Japan's intentions with regard to French

Indochina and pointed out that the Government of the United States could only assume that the occupation by Japan of French Indochina or the acquisition of military and naval bases in that area constituted notice to the United States that Japan had taken by forceful means a step preparatory to embarking on further movements of conquest in the South Pacific area. The Acting Secretary pointed out further that this new move on Japan's part was prejudicial to the procurement by the United States of essential raw materials and to the peace of the Pacific, including the Philippine Islands.

The Government of the United States accordingly had no alternative but to inform the Japanese Ambassador that, in the opinion of this Government, the measures then being taken by the Japanese Government had served to remove the basis for further conversations relative to a peaceful settlement in the Pacific area.

Informal discussions between the Japanese Government and the Government of the United States directed toward ascertaining whether there existed a basis for negotiations relative to a peaceful settlement covering the entire Pacific situation would naturally envisage the working out of a progressive program attainable by peaceful methods. It goes without saying that no proposals or suggestions affecting the rights and privileges of either the United States or Japan would be considered except as they might be in conformity with the basic principles to which the United States has long been committed. The program envisaged in such informal discussions would involve the application in the entire Pacific area of the principle of equality of commercial opportunity and treatment. It would thus make possible access by all countries to raw materials and to all other essential commodities. Such a program would envisage cooperation by all nations of the Pacific on a voluntary and peaceful basis toward utilizing all available resources of capital, technical skill, and progressive economic leadership for the purpose of building up not only their own economies but also the economies of regions where productive capacity can be improved. The result would be to increase the purchasing power of the nations and peoples concerned, to raise standards of living, and to create conditions conducive to the maintenance of peace. If such a program based upon peaceable and constructive principles were to be adopted for the Pacific and if thereafter any of the countries or areas within the Pacific were menaced, the policy of aiding nations resisting aggression would continue to be followed by this Government and this Government would cooperate with other nations in extending assistance to any country threatened.

Under such a program for the Pacific area Japan would, in the opinion of the Government of the United States, attain all the objectives which Japan affirms that it is seeking. This program would not enable any country to extend its military or political control over other peoples or to obtain economic rights of a definitely monopolistic or preferential character. In those cases where the production and distribution of essential commodities are vested in monopolies, the Government of the United States would expect to use its influence to see that all countries are given a fair share of the distribution of the products of such monopolies and at a fair price.

If the Japanese Government is seeking what it affirms to be its objectives, the Government of the United States feels that the program above outlined is one that can be counted upon to assure Japan satisfaction of its economic needs and legitimate aspirations with much greater certainty than could any other program.

In case the Japanese Government feels that Japan desires and is in position to suspend its expansionist activities, to readjust its position, and to embark upon a peaceful program for the Pacific along the lines of the program and principles to which the United States is committed, the Government of the United States would be prepared to consider resumption of the informal exploratory discussions which were interrupted in July and would be glad to endeavor to arrange a suitable time and place to exchange views. The Government of the United States, however, feels that, in view of the circumstances attending the interruption of the informal conversations between the two Governments, it would be helpful to both Governments, before undertaking a resumption of such conversations or proceeding with plans for a meeting, if the Japanese Government would be so good as to furnish a clearer statement than has yet been furnished as to its present attitude and plans, just as this Government has repeatedly outlined to the Japanese Government its attitude and plans.

229

H. Doc. 358, 77th Cong., 1st sess.

Message of President Roosevelt to the Congress, August 21, 1941, Embodying Text of the Atlantic Charter

Over a week ago I held several important conferences at sea with the British Prime Minister. Because of the factor of safety to British, Canadian, and American ships, and their personnel, no prior announcement of these meetings could properly be made.

At the close, a public statement by the Prime Minister and the

President was made. I quote it for the information of the Congress and for the record:

"The President of the United States and the Prime Minister, Mr. Churchill, representing His Majesty's Government in the United Kingdom, have met at sea.

"They have been accompanied by officials of their two Governments, including high-ranking officers of their military, naval, and air services.

"The whole problem of the supply of munitions of war, as provided by the Lease-Lend Act, for the armed forces of the United States, and for those countries actively engaged in resisting aggression, has been further examined.

"Lord Beaverbrook, the Minister of Supply of the British Government, has joined in these conferences. He is going to proceed to Washington to discuss further details with appropriate officials of the United States Government. These conferences will also cover the supply problems of the Soviet Union.

"The President and the Prime Minister have had several conferences. They have considered the dangers to world civilization arising from the policies of military domination by conquest upon which the Hitlerite government of Germany and other governments associated therewith have embarked, and have made clear the steps which their countries are respectively taking for their safety in the face of these dangers.

"They have agreed upon the following joint declaration:

"Joint declaration of the President of the United States of America and the Prime Minister, Mr. Churchill, representing His Majesty's Government in the United Kingdom, being met together, deem it right to make known certain common principles in the national policies of their respective countries on which they base their hopes for a better future for the world.

"First, their countries seek no aggrandizement, territorial or other;

"Second, they desire to see no territorial changes that do not accord with the freely expressed wishes of the peoples concerned;

"Third, they respect the right of all peoples to choose the form of government under which they will live; and they wish to see sovereign rights and self-government restored to those who have been forcibly deprived of them;

"Fourth, they will endeavor, with due respect for their existing obligations, to further the enjoyment by all states, great or small, victor or vanquished, of access, on equal terms, to the trade and to the raw materials of the world which are needed for their economic prosperity;

"Fifth, they desire to bring about the fullest collaboration between all nations in the economic field with the object of securing, for all, improved labor standards, economic advancement, and social security;

"Sixth, after the final destruction of the Nazi tyranny, they hope to see established a peace which will afford to all nations the means of dwelling in safety within their own boundaries, and which will afford assurance that all the men in all the lands may live out their lives in freedom from fear and want;

"Seventh, such a peace should enable all men to traverse the high seas and oceans without hindrance;

"Eighth, they believe that all of the nations of the world, for realistic as well as spiritual reasons, must come to the abandonment of the use of force. Since no future peace can be maintained if land, sea, or air armaments continue to be employed by nations which threaten, or may threaten, aggression outside of their frontiers, they believe, pending the establishment of a wider and permanent system of general security, that the disarmament of such nations is essential. They will likewise aid and encourage all other practicable measures which will lighten for peace-loving peoples the crushing burden of armaments.

FRANKLIN D. ROOSEVELT

WINSTON S. CHURCHILL"

The Congress and the President having heretofore determined, through the Lend-Lease Act, on the national policy of American aid to the democracies which East and West are waging war against dictatorships, the military and naval conversations at these meetings made clear gains in furthering the effectiveness of this aid.

Furthermore, the Prime Minister and I are arranging for conferences with the Soviet Union to aid it in its defense against the attack made by the principal aggressor of the modern world—Germany.

Finally, the declaration of principles at this time presents a goal which is worth while for our type of civilization to seek. It is so clear-cut that it is difficult to oppose in any major particular without automatically admitting a willingness to accept compromise with nazi-ism; or to agree to a world peace which would give to nazi-ism domination over large numbers of conquered nations. Inevitably such a peace would be a gift to nazi-ism to take breath—armed breath—for a second war to extend the control over Europe and Asia, to the American Hemisphere itself.

It is perhaps unnecessary for me to call attention once more to the utter lack of validity of the spoken or written word of the Nazi government.

It is also unnecessary for me to point out that the declaration of principles includes, of necessity, the world need for freedom of religion and freedom of information. No society of the world organized under the announced principles could survive without these freedoms which are a part of the whole freedom for which we strive.

230

711.94/2227

Memorandum by the Secretary of State

[WASHINGTON,] August 28, 1941.

The Ambassador of Japan called on the President at the former's request. The Secretary of State was present. The Ambassador expressed his usual appreciation of certain courtesies and considerations shown him and his Government.

He then handed to the President a communication from the Prince Premier of Japan to the President of the United States (copy attached). The President read it with interest and complimented the tone and spirit of it.

The President then spoke somewhat as he did at the last meeting a week ago Sunday about the idea suggested by the Japanese Prime Minister of a personal meeting between the President and the Prime Minister at as early a date as possible for the purpose of having a frank discussion of all important affairs existing between the two countries. The President again spoke of the difficulty of going as far as Hawaii and elaborated on the reasons why it would be difficult to get away for twenty-one days. He then turned to Juneau, Alaska, as a meeting place, which would only require some fourteen or fifteen days, allowing for a three or four days conversation with the Japanese Prime Minister. The only point raised by the Ambassador in this connection was that the conversation be held as early as possible.

The Ambassador then handed to the President a communication from his Government in reply to the communication of the President to the Japanese Government, dated August 17, 1941 (copy attached). The President expressed his keen interest to get this reply and proceeded to read it. At two or three stages he stopped to comment briefly and, as he stated each time, study would later, of course, be given to the subject. For example, he remarked that there was nothing in the note to prevent the Japanese from reinforcing their Army and Navy in the Indochina area while the conversations were going on, even though there was no advance whatever by the Japanese forces. At another point he injected some oral comment to the effect that Japan is in no possible danger from Russia at the present time and he emphasized this very strongly. At still another point he referred critically to the Japanese oil complaints and their baseless nature. He then reminded the Ambassador that under the oil quota allowed Japan by this Government, Japan was in a position to have a number of tankers loaded with oil and transported to Japan if and when it so desired.

At the conclusion of the reading of the communication, the President said to the Ambassador that he could say to his Government that he considered this note a step forward and that he was very hopeful. He then added that he would be keenly interested in having three or four days with Prince Konoye, and again he mentioned Juneau.

C[ORDELL] H[ULL]

[Annexes]

THE JAPANESE PRIME MINISTER (PRINCE KONOYE) TO
PRESIDENT ROOSEVELT

I deeply appreciate the courtesy of Your Excellency in delivering personally to Ambassador Nomura the reply of the United States Government to the proposal of the Japanese Government regarding a meeting between Your Excellency and myself.

In the face of universal warlike turmoil Japan and the United States are the last two major Powers who hold the key to international peace. That the two nations should fall in the worst of relations at this time would mean not only a disaster in itself, but also the collapse of world civilization. Japan is solicitous for the maintenance of the peace of the Pacific and the peace of the world and she desires therefore to improve Japanese-American relations.

The present deterioration of the Japanese-American relations is largely due, I feel, to a lack of understanding which has led to mutual suspicions and misapprehensions, and also encouraged the machinations and maneuvers of Third Powers.

Without first eliminating such causes, it is impossible to expect adjustment of Japanese-American relations. This is why I wish to meet Your Excellency personally for a frank exchange of views.

The preliminary informal conversations, disrupted July last, were quite appropriate both in spirit and content. But the idea of continuing those conversations and to have their conclusion confirmed by the responsible heads of the two Governments does not meet the need of the present situation which is developing swiftly and may produce unforeseen contingencies.

I consider it, therefore, of urgent necessity that the two heads of the Governments should meet first to discuss from a broad standpoint all important problems between Japan and America covering the entire Pacific area, and to explore the possibility of saving the situation. Adjustment of minor items may, if necessary, be left to negotiations between competent officials of the two countries, following the meeting.

Such is my aim in making the present proposal. I sincerely hope my views in this regard are fully understood and reciprocated by Your Excellency.

Because of the nature of the meeting as stated above, I would prefer that it will take place as soon as possible.

[TOKYO,] *August 27, 1941.*

STATEMENT BY THE JAPANESE GOVERNMENT HANDED BY THE JAPANESE AMBASSADOR (NOMURA) TO PRESIDENT ROOSEVELT ON AUGUST 28, 1941

The Japanese Government has received the communication conveyed by the Secretary of State and the President of the United States to the Japanese Ambassador on August 17, 1941. The Japanese Government desires to state its views as follows:

The Japanese Government profoundly regrets that despite the pledge it has given heretofore as well as its repeated explanations concerning Japan's actions and measures in the foreign field, the United States Government continues to entertain misgivings.

The United States Government mentions certain situations and measures which it regards as inimical to a peaceful settlement in the Pacific area. In an atmosphere of world crisis and international confusion, it is sometimes difficult to ascertain when an event is a cause and when it is a consequence.

When a nation is obstructed in the path of natural and peaceful development or when the means of its existence is threatened, not only is it imperative that that nation should take defensive measures, but it is also required to do so for the maintenance of a just peace. This was the motivating policy of the Japanese Government.

Meanwhile, the United States had taken certain measures which could be interpreted in Japan as indicative of a continuing unfriendly pressure at variance with the then current amicable conversations.

The United States Government certainly regards some of its actions as merely counter-measures against Japan's policy and procedures which were considered as conflicting with American interests and principles. On the other hand, to the Japanese Government those procedures were determined by considerations of self-protection for meeting national requirements or removing environmental and political obstacles against national security.

With admirable modesty of mind, the Government of the United States has seemed frequently unaware that its words and policies are automatically weighted with the immense power of America's accomplished facts, natural endowment and potential might. The President of the United States, and the Secretary of State, in their own unquestioning adherence to the ways of peaceful procedures, might find it difficult to believe that other nations, anywhere, could consider themselves threatened by the United States.

Yet, as long as there is lacking the assuagement of that possible threat, there will be some less favorably endowed (especially in essential resources) who will feel compelled to consider defensively their relations with the United States.

In consequence, the Japanese Government welcomes the invitation by the Government of the United States to an exchange of views in regard to basic policies and attitudes as the foundation of an understanding that will condition lasting and extensive peace in the Pacific area. For such peace, the Government of Japan is ready: for such a united effort toward a peaceful settlement covering the entire Pacific situation the Government of Japan, like the Government of the United States, would be proud to make sacrifices.

Japan's measure in Indo-China was intended to accelerate the settlement of the China Incident; and at the same time it was calculated to remove all menace to the peace of the Pacific and to secure to Japan an equitable supply of essential materials. It was a measure of self-defense the Japanese Government felt obliged to take. But the Japanese Government has no intention of threatening thereby other countries.

Therefore, the Japanese Government is prepared to withdraw its troops from Indo-China as soon as the China Incident is settled or a just peace is established in East Asia.

Furthermore, in order to remove all possible doubt in this regard, the Japanese Government reaffirms herewith its repeated declaration that its present action in Indo-China is not a preparatory step for military advance into neighboring territories. The Japanese Government believes the above pledge will suffice to clarify also Japan's intentions toward Thailand.

As regards Soviet-Japanese relations, the Japanese Government declares likewise that Japan will take no military action as long as the Soviet Union remains faithful to the Soviet-Japanese neutrality treaty and does not menace Japan or Manchoukuo or take any action contrary to the spirit of the said treaty. On the other hand, the Japanese Government sincerely hope that the United States Government will avoid any action that might give rise to a fear of menace to Japan through collaboration with the Soviet Union.

In a word, the Japanese Government has no intention of using, without provocation, military force against any neighboring nation.

Quite properly, discussions between the Japanese Government and the Government of the United States directed toward ascertaining if there existed a basis for negotiations for a peaceful settlement covering the entire situation,—such discussions would naturally envisage the working out of a progressive program, obtainable by peaceful methods. The Japanese Government shares fully that view with the Government of the United States.

It is also stated by the United States Government that no proposals or suggestions affecting the rights and privileges of either the United States or Japan would be considered except as these might be in conformity with the basic principles to which the United States has long been committed. The fundamental national policy long cherished by the Japanese Government is again in full agreement on that point.

Regarding the principles and directives set forth in detail by the American Government and envisaged in the informal conversations as constituting a program for the Pacific area, the Japanese Government wishes to state that it considers these principles and the practical application thereof, in the friendliest manner possible, are the prime requisites of a true peace and should be applied not only in the Pacific area but throughout the entire world. Such a program has long been desired and sought by Japan itself.

The Japanese Government now confidently hopes that from the larger viewpoint of a constructive world peace, and in the light of the current international situation, past differences may be merged in an agreement of principles and a cooperative effort based on order and justice. The meeting of the responsible heads of our respective Governments would confirm and give such sanction to our purposes that peace in the Pacific would be instituted by that meeting.

231

711.94/2244–8/11

Memorandum [68] *Regarding a Conversation Between the Secretary Of State and the Japanese Ambassador (Nomura)*

[WASHINGTON,] August 28, 1941.

The Japanese Ambassador called by appointment made at his re-

[68] Prepared by Joseph W. Ballantine.

quest at the Secretary's apartment. He expressed his appreciation for the Secretary's having arranged to have the Ambassador see the President that morning. The Ambassador said that he felt much encouraged from his interview with the President to hope for a successful outcome of our common effort to bring about an improvement in the relations between the two countries, and he added that he has telegraphed a full account of that interview to his Government.

The Ambassador said that it was his personal opinion that the suggestion of the President that the meeting between the President and the Japanese Prime Minister be held at Juneau would be agreeable to his Government and that the Prime Minister would probably proceed thither by a Japanese warship, making the journey in about ten days. The Ambassador thought that the Prime Minister would be assisted by a staff of about twenty persons, of whom five each would be from the Foreign Office, the Army, the Navy and the Japanese Embassy at Washington. The Ambassador thought that the inclusion of army and navy representatives in the delegation would be especially beneficial in view of the responsibility which they would share for the settlement reached. He said his Government was very anxious that the meeting be held at the earliest possible moment in view of the efforts of a third country and fifth columnists in Japan, who are now behind a press campaign against the United States, to disturb Japanese-American relations. He suggested the period between September 21 and 25 as suitable. He said that the question of publicity was something which the two Governments should agree upon, and that involved in the question of timing of any announcement was the fact that the Prime Minister would necessarily have to leave Tokyo about five days before the President left Washington.

The Secretary said that he would refer these points to the President for his consideration.

The Secretary then pointed out to the Ambassador the desirability of there being reached in advance of the proposed meeting an agreement in principle on the principal questions which were involved in a settlement of Pacific questions between the two nations. He dwelt upon the serious consequences from the point of view of both Governments which would ensue if the meeting failed to result in an agreement as a consequence of issues arising which could not be resolved, and he expressed the view that the meeting should therefore have as its purpose the ratification of essential points already agreed to in principle. The Secretary pointed out that in the conversations which had taken place last spring difficulties had been encountered in regard to certain fundamental points which had caused delays which finally culminated in Japan's taking action contrary to the spirit which had animated both the Ambassador and himself in those conversations. The Secretary also pointed out that it would be unfortunate if now, while one half of the Japanese Government was disposed to go along a course of peace the other half should be pulling in the opposite direction.

The Ambassador reviewed the points in regard to which difficulties had been encountered in the conversations, namely: (1) Japan's relations to the Axis, (2) the question of the retention of Japanese troops in North China and Inner Mongolia, and (3) the question of the application of the principle of nondiscrimination in international commercial relations. He noted that only in regard to the question of the retention of Japanese troops in North China, concerning which he had no information that his Government had modified its attitude, did he anticipate real difficulty. He observed that with regard to Japan's relations with the Axis there should be no difficulties, as the Japanese people regarded their adherence to the Axis as merely nominal and as he could not conceive of his people being prepared to go to war with the United States for the sake of Germany. He said he thought our attitude in regard to self-protection was entirely reasonable. The only difficulty that he saw was that to ask that Japan give a blank check for action that the United States might take against Germany in the name of self-defense was equivalent to asking for a nullification of the Tripartite Pact.

The Secretary commented that the Japanese Government had entered into the Tripartite Pact at a most critical moment in our efforts to extend aid to England, and Japan's action therefore was given particular emphasis in this country. In addition, Mr. Matsuoka kept reasserting gratuitously Japan's alignment with the Axis. The Secretary said he felt that unless something was done to counteract the effect upon the American people, it might prove a source of serious embarrassment to the President upon his return from the proposed meeting. The Secretary went on to refer to the actual situation in our relations with Germany, to the fact that although no shooting is taking place we are maintaining patrols all the way to Iceland.

The Japanese Ambassador said that with regard to the China question it was the idea of the Japanese Government that we exercise our good offices in bringing the Chinese and Japanese together leaving China and Japan to reach a direct settlement among themselves whereas the United States Government desired to discuss with Japan the basic terms on which peace was to be concluded.

The Secretary said that we were involved in this matter through

Japan's requesting this Government to exercise its good offices. In order to exercise such good offices it was necessary for us to have the confidence and friendship of the Chinese Government before and after exercising those good offices. We could not, he said, propose that the Chinese negotiate with Japan until we knew what the basic terms were which Japan intended to propose and it can be imagined what a difficult situation would be created if, after a meeting between Prince Konoye and the President, an explosion should take place in China as a result of dissatisfaction with the results of that meeting. The Secretary explained further that we could not now afford to have the Chinese think that we were ignoring their interests in going ahead with any arrangements and that it was our idea to help the Japanese achieve the purpose of establishing friendship with China on a solid basis. In this way the Secretary said we could work together, Japan and the United States, in order to make the most of the potentialities of the 500,000,000 people of China as a trading nation.

The Ambassador commented that of course the China question was a very important matter but in view of the wide-spread press comments to the effect that the situation had now come to a show-down between Japan and the United States were there not other questions pending between the United States and Japan even apart from the China question which could be disposed of at the meeting with a view to tiding over a critical situation.

The Secretary replied that it was quite true that there were these other questions but that the China question was one of the pivotal questions underlying relations between the United States and Japan and if this question remained unsettled to the satisfaction of all there would remain the roots of future instability and trouble. The Ambassador said that he recognized the soundness of what the Secretary said especially in view of the French Indochina situation. Mr. Ballantine said he assumed that what the Ambassador had reference to was the Japanese assurance that they would withdraw their troops from French Indochina as soon as the China affair was settled.

The Ambassador then recapitulated briefly what the Secretary had said, namely, that the Secretary considers that there should be an agreement in principle on the outstanding questions of importance prior to the holding of the meeting, that the meeting would serve the purpose of ratifying agreement in principle already reached, that the Secretary considered that the Chinese question was one of the pivotal subjects calling for settlement, and that this Government in exercising its good offices between China and Japan would have to consider the basic terms on which Japan proposed to negotiate. The Secretary said that this represented his views. The Ambassador said that he recognized that what the Secretary said was quite reasonable. The Ambassador had misgivings as to how far the Japanese Government could go on account of the internal political difficulties in Japan. He said, however, that Prince Konoye was a man of great courage and was prepared to assume great risks in bringing to a successful conclusion an effort to improve relations.

232

711.94/2267

Memorandum by the Secretary of State

[WASHINGTON,] September 3, 1941.

At the request of the President, the Japanese Ambassador called at the White House this afternoon. The President proceeded at once to read the written oral statement (copy attached) which had been prepared in reply to the communication recently sent to the President by the Japanese Prime Minister. He emphasized certain points as he read. He particularly emphasized the fact that he appreciated the difficulties of Prince Konoye in connection with the Japanese internal situation, but he added that he has difficulties here which he hopes that Prince Konoye and his Government would appreciate. The President referred to his recent conversations with Prime Minister Churchill, especially that portion relating to plebiscites at the end of the war as the best means of settling many differences and as the soundest policy of dealing with conditions existing between different races. He cited several instances existing at the end of the World War, which were effectively dealt with by plebiscites.

The President then proceeded to read his letter to Prime Minister Konoye, a copy of which is hereto attached. The Ambassador inquired if the President was still favorable to a conference and the President replied that he was, but that it was very important to settle a number of these questions beforehand, if the success of the conference was to be safeguarded to the extent warranted by the holding of such a meeting. It was also emphasized that if and when we had secured sufficient assurances from the Japanese Government that it stands earnestly for all of the principles which this Government has been proclaiming as applicable to the Pacific area, it would be necessary for us to discuss the matter fully with the British, the Chinese and the Dutch, since there is no other way to effect a suitable peaceful settlement for the Pacific area; that any settlement must be on a basis that will restore confidence and friendliness among the nations concerned; in no other way can a suitable economic structure be rebuilt for that area. The Ambassador seemed to appreciate this viewpoint. Both the President and I repeatedly emphasized the necessity for his Government to clarify its position on the question of abandoning a policy of force and conquest and on three fundamental questions concerning which difficulties had been encountered in our discussion of the Japanese proposal of May twelfth and the discussion of which we had not pursued after the Japanese went into Indochina. The Ambassador said that Prince Konoye, while preferring to go to Hawaii, would be disposed to go to any place in the Pacific where there was suitable anchorage.

The Ambassador then proceeded to say that he had a despatch from Tokyo referring to the fact that certain elements of opposition to the proposals of the Prime Minister existed and were active in their opposition. He said that the Government, however, is determined to overcome such opposition. He stated that a meeting between the President and the Prime Minister would enable Japan to overcome these disagreements at home and that the opposition would gradually get in line with the Government. He said that Konoye thinks that he and the President can discuss the three questions which were left untouched when the Japanese went into Indochina in July, mainly the question relating to the complete evacuation of Japanese troops from China, the question of non-discrimination in commerce, et cetera, et cetera, and the Tripartite Pact.

It was made clear to the Ambassador that several days should be consumed by his Government both in clarifying and stating strongly its position on the principles already referred to and their application so far as China is concerned, and also that their Government should by word and act in every way possible devote some time at once to the education and organization of public opinion in support of the proposals for a peaceful settlement, as already set forth.

C[ORDELL] H[ULL]

[Annexes]

ORAL STATEMENT HANDED BY PRESIDENT ROOSEVELT TO THE
JAPANESE AMBASSADOR (NOMURA) ON SEPTEMBER 3, 1941

Reference is made to the proposal of the Japanese Government communicated on August 28, 1941, by the Japanese Ambassador to the President of the United States that there be held as soon as possible a meeting between the responsible heads of the Government of Japan and of the Government of the United States to discuss important problems between Japan and the United States covering the entire Pacific area in an endeavor to save the situation and to the reply of the President of the United States, in which the President assured the Prime Minister of the readiness of the Government of the United States to move as rapidly as possible toward the consummation of arrangements for such a meeting and suggested that there be held preliminary discussion of important questions that would come up for consideration in the meeting. In further explanation of the views of the Government of the United States in regard to the suggestion under reference observations are offered, as follows:

On April 16, at the outset of the informal and exploratory conversations which were entered into by the Secretary of State with the Japanese Ambassador, the Secretary of State referred to four fundamental principles which this Government regards as the foundation upon which all relations between nations should properly rest. These four fundamental principles are as follows:

1. Respect for the territorial integrity and the sovereignty of each and all nations.
2. Support of the principle of non-interference in the internal affairs of other countries.
3. Support of the principle of equality, including equality of commercial opportunity.
4. Non-disturbance of the *status quo* in the Pacific except as the *status quo* may be altered by peaceful means.

In the subsequent conversations the Secretary of State endeavored to make it clear that in the opinion of the Government of the United States Japan stood to gain more from adherence to courses in harmony with these principles than from any other course, as Japan would thus best be assured access to the raw materials and markets which Japan needs and ways would be opened for mutually beneficial cooperation with the United States and other countries, and that only upon the basis of these principles could an agreement be reached which would be effective in establishing stability and peace in the Pacific area.

The Government of the United States notes with satisfaction that in the statement marked "Strictly Confidential" which was communicated by the Japanese Ambassador to the President of the United States on August 28 there were given specific assurances of Japan's peaceful intentions and assurances that Japan desires and seeks a program for the Pacific area consistent with the principles to which the Government of the United States has long been committed and which were set forth in detail in the informal conversations already referred to. The Government of the United States understands that the assurances which the Japanese Government has given in that statement exclude any policy which would seek political expansion or the acquisition of economic rights, advantages or preferences by force.

The Government of the United States is very desirous of collaborating in efforts to make effective in practice the principles to which the Japanese Government has made reference. The Government of the United States believes that it is all-important that preliminary precautions be taken to insure the success of any efforts which the Governments of Japan and of the United States might make to collaborate toward a peaceful settlement. It will be recalled that in the course of the conversations to which reference has already been made, the Secretary of State on June 21, 1941, handed the Japanese Ambassador a document marked "Oral, Unofficial and Without Commitment" which contained a redraft of the Japanese Government's proposal of May 12, 1941. It will be recalled further that in oral discussion of this draft it was found that there were certain fundamental questions with respect to which there were divergences of view between the two Governments, and which remained unreconciled at the time the conversations were interrupted in July. The Government of the United States desires to facilitate progress toward a conclusive discussion, but believes that a community of view and a clear agreement upon the points above-mentioned are essential to any satisfactory settlement of Pacific questions. It therefore seeks an indication of the present attitude of the Japanese Government with regard to the fundamental questions under reference.

It goes without saying that each Government in reaching decisions on policy must take into account the internal situation in its own country and the attitude of public opinion therein. The Government of Japan will surely recognize that the Government of the United States could not enter into any agreement which would not be in harmony with the principles in which the American people—in fact all nations that prefer peaceful methods to methods of force—believe.

The Government of the United States would be glad to have the reply of the Japanese Government on the matters above set forth.

PRESIDENT ROOSEVELT'S REPLY TO THE JAPANESE PRIME MINISTER (PRINCE KONOYE), HANDED TO THE JAPANESE AMBASSADOR (NOMURA) ON SEPTEMBER 3, 1941

I have read with appreciation Your Excellency's message of August 27, which was delivered to me by Admiral Nomura.

I have noted with satisfaction the sentiments expressed by you in regard to the solicitude of Japan for the maintenance of the peace of the Pacific and Japan's desire to improve Japanese-American relations.

I fully share the desire expressed by you in these regards, and I wish to assure you that the Government of the United States, recognizing the swiftly-moving character of world events, is prepared to proceed as rapidly as possible toward the consummation of arrangements for a meeting at which you and I can exchange views and endeavor to bring about an adjustment in the relations between our two countries.

In the statement which accompanied your letter to me reference was made to the principles to which the Government of the United States has long been committed and it was declared that the Japanese Government "considers these principles and the practical application thereof, in the friendliest manner possible, are the prime requisites of a true peace and should be applied not only in the Pacific area but throughout the entire world" and that "such a program has long been desired and sought by Japan itself".

I am very desirous of collaborating with you in efforts to make these principles effective in practice. Because of my deep interest in this matter I find it necessary that I constantly observe and take account of developments both in my own country and in Japan which have a bearing upon problems of relations between our two countries. At this particular moment I cannot avoid taking cognizance of indications of the existence in some quarters in Japan of concepts which, if widely entertained, would seem capable of raising obstacles to successful collaboration between you and me along the line which I am sure we both earnestly desire to follow. Under these circumstances, I feel constrained to suggest, in the belief that you will share my view, that it would seem highly desirable that we take precaution, toward ensuring that our proposed meeting shall prove a success, by endeavoring to enter immediately upon preliminary discussion of the fundamental and essential questions on which we seek agreement. The questions which I have in mind for such preliminary discussions involve practical application of the principles fundamental to achievement and maintenance of peace which are mentioned with more of specification in the statement accompanying your letter. I hope that you will look favorably upon this suggestion.

233

711.94/2624

Memorandum by the Ambassador in Japan (Grew)[69]

[Tokyo,] September 6, 1941.

This evening the Prime Minister invited me to dine at a private house of a friend. Only Mr. Dooman and Mr. Ushiba, the Prime Minister's private secretary, were also present. The conversation lasted for three hours and we presented with entire frankness the fundamental views of our two countries. The Prime Minister requested that his statements be transmitted personally to the President in the belief that they might amplify and clarify the approach through diplomatic channels which he had made in Washington through Admiral Nomura. The following is a brief summary of the salient points as they emerged in the course of our discussion.

1. Prince Konoye, and consequently the Government of Japan, conclusively and wholeheartedly agree with the four principles enunciated by the Secretary of State as a basis for the rehabilitation of relations between the United States and Japan.

2. Prince Konoye recognizes that the responsibility is his for the present regrettable state of relations between our two countries but, with appropriate modesty as to his personal capabilities, he likewise recognizes that only he can cause the desired rehabilitation to come about. In the event of failure on his part no succeeding Prime Minister, at least during his own lifetime, could achieve the results desired. Prince Konoye is therefore determined to spare no effort, despite all elements and factors opposing him, to crown his present endeavors with success.

3. The Prime Minister hopes that as a result of the commitments which the Japanese Government is prepared to assume as communicated to me by Admiral Toyoda, a rational basis has been established for a meeting between the President and himself. The Prime Minister, however, is cognizant of the fact that certain points may need clarification and more precise formulation, and he is confident that the divergencies in view can be reconciled to our mutual satisfaction, particularly by reason of the favorable disposition on the part of Japanese naval and military leaders who have not only subscribed to his proposals but who will also be represented at the suggested meeting. The Prime Minister stated that both the Ministers of War and of the Navy have given their full agreement to his proposals to the United States.

---

[69] Reported by Ambassador Grew in a telegram of September 6.

4. The reports which the Prime Minister has received from the Japanese Ambassador concerning the latter's conversations with the President and the Secretary have led the Prime Minister to think that the Administration in Washington entertains serious doubts as to the strength of the present Cabinet and that the Administration is not certain that in the event that the Cabinet should adopt a peaceful program it could successfully resist the attacks of opposing elements. Prince Konoye told me that from the inception of the informal talks in Washington he had received the strongest concurrence from the responsible chiefs of both the Army and the Navy. Only today he had conferred with the Minister of War who had promised to send a full General to accompany the Prime Minister to the meeting with the President; the Minister of the Navy had agreed that a full Admiral should accompany the Prime Minister. Prince Konoye added in confidence that he expected that the representative of the Navy would probably be Admiral Yoshida, a former Minister of the Navy. In addition the Premier would be accompanied by the Vice Chiefs of Staff of the Army and the Navy and other high ranking officers of the armed services who are in entire accord with his aims. He admitted that there are certain elements within the armed forces who do not approve his policies, but he voiced the conviction that since he had the full support of the responsible chiefs of the Army and Navy it would be possible for him to put down and control any opposition which might develop among those elements.

5. Prince Konoye repeatedly stressed the view that time is of the essence. It might take half a year to a year to work out all the details of the complete settlement and since resentment is daily mounting in Japan over the economic pressure being exerted by other countries, he could not guarantee to put into effect any such program of settlement six months or a year from now. He does, however, guarantee that at the present time he can carry with him the Japanese people to the goal which he has selected and that should difficulties be encountered in working out the details of the commitments which he may assume, these difficulties can be overcome satisfactorily because of the determined intention of his Government to see to it that its present efforts are fully successful.

6. In the course of our discussion I outlined in general terms the bitter lessons of the past to our Government as the result of the failure of the Japanese Government to honor the promises given to me by former Japanese Ministers for Foreign Affairs apparently in all sincerity, as a result of which the Government of the United States had at long last concluded that it must place its reliance on

actions and facts and not on Japanese promises or assurances. The Prime Minister did not attempt to refute this statement but stressed the fact that his Government now wished to bring about a thorough-going reconstruction of American-Japanese relations and he assured me that any commitments which he would undertake would bear no resemblance to the "irresponsible" assurances which we had received in the past and that such commitments if given would be observed. The Prime Minister concluded his presentation of this point by giving me to understand that given the will the way can be found.

7. Prince Konoye stated that should the President desire to communicate any kind of suggestion to him personally and confidentially he would be glad to arrange subsequent secret meetings with me, but he expressed the earnest hope that in view of the present internal situation in Japan the projected meeting with the President could be arranged with the least possible delay. Prince Konoye feels confident that all problems and questions at issue can be disposed of to our mutual satisfaction during the meeting with the President, and he ended our conversation with the statement that he is determined to bring to a successful conclusion the proposed reconstruction of relations with the United States regardless of cost or personal risk.

J[OSEPH] C. G[REW]

234

711.94/2344–7/25

Draft Proposal Handed by the Japanese Ambassador (Nomura) To the Secretary of State on September 6, 1941 [70]

The Government of Japan undertakes:

(*a*) that Japan is ready to express its concurrence in those matters which were already tentatively agreed upon between Japan and the United States in the course of their preliminary informal conversations;

(*b*) that Japan will not make any military advancement from French Indo-China against any of its adjoining areas, and likewise will not, without any justifiable reason, resort to military action against any regions lying south of Japan;

(*c*) that the attitudes of Japan and the United States towards the European War will be decided by the concepts of protection and self-defense, and, in case the United States should participate in the Euro-

---

[70] This proposal was also handed to the Ambassador in Japan (Grew) by the Japanese Minister for Foreign Affairs (Toyoda) on September 4, 1941.

pean War, the interpretation and execution of the Tripartite Pact by Japan shall be independently decided;

(*d*) that Japan will endeavour to bring about the rehabilitation of general and normal relationship between Japan and China, upon the realization of which Japan is ready to withdraw its armed forces from China as soon as possible in accordance with the agreements between Japan and China;

(*e*) that the economic activities of the United States in China will not be restricted so long as pursued on an equitable basis;

(*f*) that Japan's activities in the Southwestern Pacific Area will be carried on by peaceful means and in accordance with the principle of non-discrimination in international commerce, and that Japan will coöperate in the production and procurement by the United States of natural resources in the said area which it needs;

(*g*) that Japan will take measures necessary for the resumption of normal trade relations between Japan and the United States, and in connection with the above-mentioned, Japan is ready to discontinue immediately the application of the foreigners' transactions control regulations with regard to the United States on the basis of reciprocity.

The Government of the United States undertakes:

(*a*) that, in response to the Japanese Government's commitment expressed in point (*d*) referred to above, the United States will abstain from any measures and actions which will be prejudicial to the endeavour by Japan concerning the settlement of the China Affair;

(*b*) that the United States will reciprocate Japan's commitment expressed in point (*f*) referred to above;

(*c*) that the United States will suspend any military measures in the Far East and in the Southwestern Pacific Area;

(*d*) that the United States will immediately [upon settlement] reciprocate Japan's commitment expressed in point (*g*) referred to above by discontinuing the application of the so-called freezing act with regard to Japan and further by removing the prohibition against the passage of Japanese vessels through the Panama Canal.

235

Department of State Bulletin, vol. V, p. 193

Radio Address Delivered by President Roosevelt From Washington, September 11, 1941

The Navy Department of the United States has reported to me that on the morning of September fourth the United States destroyer *Greer*, proceeding in full daylight towards Iceland, had reached a point southeast of Greenland. She was carrying American mail to Iceland. She was flying the American flag. Her identity as an American ship was unmistakable.

She was then and there attacked by a submarine. Germany admits that it was a German submarine. The submarine deliberately fired a torpedo at the *Greer*, followed later by another torpedo attack. In spite of what Hitler's propaganda bureau has invented, and in spite of what any American obstructionist organization may prefer to believe, I tell you the blunt fact that the German submarine fired first upon this American destroyer without warning, and with deliberate design to sink her.

Our destroyer, at the time, was in waters which the Government of the United States had declared to be waters of self-defense—surrounding outposts of American protection in the Atlantic.

In the north, outposts have been established by us in Iceland, Greenland, Labrador, and Newfoundland. Through these waters there pass many ships of many flags. They bear food and other supplies to civilians; and they bear matériel of war, for which the people of the United States are spending billions of dollars, and which, by congressional action, they have declared to be essential for the defense of their own land.

The United States destroyer, when attacked, was proceeding on a legitimate mission.

If the destroyer was visible to the submarine when the torpedo was fired, then the attack was a deliberate attempt by the Nazis to sink a clearly identified American warship. On the other hand, if the submarine was beneath the surface and, with the aid of its listening devices, fired in the direction of the sound of the American destroyer without even taking the trouble to learn its identity—as the official German communiqué would indicate—then the attack was even more outrageous. For it indicates a policy of indiscriminate violence against any vessel sailing the seas—belligerent or non-belligerent.

This was piracy—legally and morally. It was not the first nor the last act of piracy which the Nazi Government has committed against the American flag in this war. Attack has followed attack.

A few months ago an American-flag merchant ship, the *Robin Moor*, was sunk by a Nazi submarine in the middle of the South Atlantic, under circumstances violating long-established international law and every principle of humanity. The passengers and the crew were forced into open boats hundreds of miles from land, in direct violation of international agreements signed by the Government of Germany. No apology, no allegation of mistake, no offer of reparations has come from the Nazi Government.

In July 1941, an American battleship in North American waters was followed by a submarine which for a long time sought to maneuver itself into a position of attack. The periscope of the submarine was clearly seen. No British or American submarines were within hundreds of miles of this spot at the time, so the nationality of the submarine is clear.

Five days ago a United States Navy ship on patrol picked up three survivors of an American-owned ship operating under the flag of our sister Republic of Panama—the S. S. *Sessa*. On August seventeenth, she had been first torpedoed without warning and then shelled, near Greenland, while carrying civilian supplies to Iceland. It is feared that the other members of her crew have been drowned. In view of the established presence of German submarines in this vicinity, there can be no reasonable doubt as to the identity of the attacker.

Five days ago, another United States merchant ship, the *Steel Seafarer* was sunk by a German aircraft in the Red Sea two hundred and twenty miles south of Suez. She was bound for an Egyptian port.

Four of the vessels sunk or attacked flew the American flag and were clearly identifiable. Two of these ships were warships of the American Navy. In the fifth case, the vessel sunk clearly carried the flag of Panama.

In the face of all this, we Americans are keeping our feet on the ground. Our type of democratic civilization has outgrown the thought of feeling compelled to fight some other nation by reason of any single piratical attack on one of our ships. We are not becoming hysterical or losing our sense of proportion. Therefore, what I am thinking and saying does not relate to any isolated episode.

Instead, we Americans are taking a long-range point of view in regard to certain fundamentals and to a series of events on land and on sea which must be considered as a whole—as a part of a world pattern.

It would be unworthy of a great nation to exaggerate an isolated incident or to become inflamed by some one act of violence. But it would be inexcusable folly to minimize such incidents in the face of evidence which makes it clear that the incident is not isolated but part of a general plan.

The important truth is that these acts of international lawlessness are a manifestation of a design which has been made clear to the American people for a long time. It is the Nazi design to abolish the freedom of the seas and to acquire absolute control and domination of the seas for themselves.

For with control of the seas in their own hands, the way can become clear for their next step—domination of the United States and the Western Hemisphere by force. Under Nazi control of the seas, no merchant ship of the United States or of any other American republic would be free to carry on any peaceful commerce, except by the condescending grace of this foreign and tyrannical power. The Atlantic Ocean which has been, and which should always be, a free and friendly highway for us would then become a deadly menace to the commerce of the United States, to the coasts of the United States, and to the inland cities of the United States.

The Hitler Government, in defiance of the laws of the sea and of the recognized rights of all other nations, has presumed to declare, on paper, that great areas of the seas—even including a vast expanse lying in the Western Hemisphere—are to be closed, and that no ships may enter them for any purpose, except at peril of being sunk. Actually they are sinking ships at will and without warning in widely separated areas both within and far outside of these far-flung pretended zones.

This Nazi attempt to seize control of the oceans is but a counterpart of the Nazi plots now being carried on throughout the Western Hemisphere—all designed toward the same end. For Hitler's advance guards—not only his avowed agents but also his dupes among us—have sought to make ready for him footholds and bridgeheads in the New World, to be used as soon as he has gained control of the oceans.

His intrigues, his plots, his machinations, his sabotage in this New World are all known to the Government of the United States. Conspiracy has followed conspiracy.

Last year a plot to seize the Government of Uruguay was smashed by the prompt action of that country, which was supported in full by her American neighbors. A like plot was then hatching in Argentina, and that Government has carefully and wisely blocked it at every point. More recently, an endeavor was made to subvert the Government of Bolivia. Within the past few weeks the discovery was made of secret air-landing fields in Colombia, within easy range of the Panama Canal. I could multiply instances.

To be ultimately successful in world-mastery, Hitler knows that he must get control of the seas. He must first destroy the bridge of ships which we are building across the Atlantic, over which we shall continue to roll the implements of war to help destroy him and all his works in the end. He must wipe out our patrol on sea and in the air. He must silence the British Navy.

It must be explained again and again to people who like to think of the United States Navy as an invincible protection, that this can be true only if the British Navy survives. That is simple arithmetic.

For if the world outside the Americas falls under Axis domination, the shipbuilding facilities which the Axis powers would then possess in all of Europe, in the British Isles, and in the Far East would be much greater than all the shipbuilding facilities and potentialities of all the Americas—not only greater but two or three times greater. Even if the United States threw all its resources into such a situation, seeking to double and even redouble the size of our Navy, the Axis powers, in control of the rest of the world, would have the man-power and the physical resources to outbuild us several times over.

It is time for all Americans of all the Americas to stop being deluded by the romantic notion that the Americas can go on living happily and peacefully in a Nazi-dominated world.

Generation after generation, America has battled for the general policy of the freedom of the seas. That policy is a very simple one— but a basic, fundamental one. It means that no nation has the right to make the broad oceans of the world, at great distance from the actual theater of land war, unsafe for the commerce of others.

That has been our policy, proved time and time again, in all our history.

Our policy has applied from time immemorial—and still applies— not merely to the Atlantic but to the Pacific and to all other oceans as well.

Unrestricted submarine warfare in 1941 constitutes a defiance—an act of aggression—against that historic American policy.

It is now clear that Hitler has begun his campaign to control the seas by ruthless force and by wiping out every vestige of international law and humanity.

His intention has been made clear. The American people can have no further illusions about it.

No tender whisperings of appeasers that Hitler is not interested in the Western Hemisphere, no soporific lullabies that a wide ocean protects us from him can long have any effect on the hard-headed, far-sighted, and realistic American people.

Because of these episodes, because of the movements and operations of German warships, and because of the clear, repeated proof that the present Government of Germany has no respect for treaties or for international law, that it has no decent attitude toward neutral nations or human life—we Americans are now face to face not with abstract theories but with cruel, relentless facts.

This attack on the *Greer* was no localized military operation in the North Atlantic. This was no mere episode in a struggle between two nations. This was one determined step towards creating a permanent world system based on force, terror, and murder.

And I am sure that even now the Nazis are waiting to see whether the United States will by silence give them the green light to go ahead on this path of destruction.

The Nazi danger to our Western World has long ceased to be a mere possibility. The danger is here now—not only from a military enemy but from an enemy of all law, all liberty, all morality, all religion.

There has now come a time when you and I must see the cold, inexorable necessity of saying to these inhuman, unrestrained seekers of world-conquest and permanent world-domination by the sword—"You seek to throw our children and our children's children into your form of terrorism and slavery. You have now attacked our own safety. You shall go no further."

Normal practices of diplomacy—note-writing—are of no possible use in dealing with international outlaws who sink our ships and kill our citizens.

One peaceful nation after another has met disaster because each refused to look the Nazi danger squarely in the eye until it actually had them by the throat.

The United States will not make that fatal mistake.

No act of violence or intimidation will keep us from maintaining intact two bulwarks of defense: first, our line of supply of matériel to the enemies of Hitler; and second, the freedom of our shipping on the high seas.

No matter what it takes, no matter what it costs, we will keep open the line of legitimate commerce in these defensive waters.

We have sought no shooting war with Hitler. We do not seek it now. But neither do we want peace so much that we are willing to pay for it by permitting him to attack our naval and merchant ships while they are on legitimate business.

I assume that the German leaders are not deeply concerned by what we Americans say or publish about them. We cannot bring about the downfall of Nazism by the use of long-range invective.

But when you see a rattlesnake poised to strike, you do not wait until he has struck before you crush him.

These Nazi submarines and raiders are the rattlesnakes of the Atlantic. They are a menace to the free pathways of the high seas. They are a challenge to our sovereignty. They hammer at our most precious rights when they attack ships of the American flag—symbols of our independence, our freedom, our very life.

It is clear to all Americans that the time has come when the Americas themselves must now be defended. A continuation of attacks in our own waters, or in waters which could be used for further and greater attacks on us, will inevitably weaken American ability to repel Hitlerism.

Do not let us split hairs. Let us not ask ourselves whether the Americas should begin to defend themselves after the fifth attack, or the tenth attack, or the twentieth attack.

The time for active defense is now.

Do not let us split hairs. Let us not say—"We will only defend ourselves if the torpedo succeeds in getting home, or if the crew and the passengers are drowned."

This is the time for prevention of attack.

If submarines or raiders attack in distant waters, they can attack equally well within sight of our own shores. Their very presence in any waters which America deems vital to its defense constitutes an attack.

In the waters which we deem necessary for our defense, American naval vessels and American planes will no longer wait until Axis submarines lurking under the water, or Axis raiders on the surface of the sea, strike their deadly blow—first.

Upon our naval and air patrol—now operating in large number over a vast expanse of the Atlantic Ocean—falls the duty of maintaining the American policy of freedom of the seas—now. That means, very simply and clearly, that our patrolling vessels and planes will protect all merchant ships—not only American ships but ships of any flag—engaged in commerce in our defensive waters.

They will protect them from submarines; they will protect them from surface raiders.

This situation is not new. The second President of the United States, John Adams, ordered the United States Navy to clean out European privateers and European ships of war which were infesting the Caribbean and South American waters, destroying American commerce.

The third President of the United States, Thomas Jefferson, ordered the United States Navy to end the attacks being made upon American ships by the corsairs of the nations of North Africa.

My obligation as President is historic; it is clear; it is inescapable.

It is no act of war on our part when we decide to protect the seas which are vital to American defense. The aggression is not ours. Ours is solely defense.

But let this warning be clear. From now on, if German or Italian vessels of war enter the waters the protection of which is necessary for American defense they do so at their own peril.

The orders which I have given as Commander-in-Chief to the United States Army and Navy are to carry out that policy—at once.

The sole responsibility rests upon Germany. There will be no shooting unless Germany continues to seek it.

That is my obvious duty in this crisis. That is the clear right of this sovereign nation. That is the only step possible, if we would keep tight the wall of defense which we are pledged to maintain around this Western Hemisphere.

I have no illusions about the gravity of this step. I have not taken it hurriedly or lightly. It is the result of months and months of constant thought and anxiety and prayer. In the protection of your Nation and mine it cannot be avoided.

The American people have faced other grave crises in their history—with American courage and American resolution. They will do no less today.

They know the actualities of the attacks upon us. They know the necessities of a bold defense against these attacks. They know that the times call for clear heads and fearless hearts.

And with that inner strength that comes to a free people conscious of their duty and of the righteousness of what they do, they will—with Divine help and guidance—stand their ground against this latest assault upon their democracy, their sovereignty, and their freedom.

711.94/2624

Document Handed by the Japanese Minister for Foreign Affairs (Toyoda) to the Ambassador in Japan (Grew), September 22, 1941

TEXT OF BASIC JAPANESE TERMS OF PEACE WITH CHINA

1. Neighborly friendship.
2. Respect for sovereignty and territorial integrity.
3. Cooperative defense between Japan and China.

Cooperation between Japan and China for the purposes of preventing communistic and other subversive activities which may constitute a menace to the security of both countries and of maintaining the public order in China.

Stationing of Japanese troops and naval forces in certain areas in the Chinese territory for a necessary period for the purposes referred to above and in accordance with the existing agreements and usages.

4. Withdrawal of Japanese armed forces.

The Japanese armed forces which have been dispatched to China for carrying out the China Affairs will be withdrawn from China upon the settlement of the said Affairs, excepting those troops which come under point 3.

5. Economic cooperation.

(*a*) There shall be economic cooperation between Japan and China, having the development and utilization of essential materials for national defense in China as its principal objective.

(*b*) The preceding paragraph does not mean to restrict any economic activities by third Powers in China so long as they are pursued on an equitable basis.

6. Fusion of the Chiang Kai-shek regime and the Wang Ching-wei Government.
7. No annexation.
8. No indemnities.
9. Recognition of Manchoukuo.

237

711.94/2344–18½₅

Memorandum [72] *Regarding a Conversation Between the Secretary of State and the Japanese Ambassador* (*Nomura*)

[WASHINGTON,] September 23, 1941.

The Japanese Ambassador called at his request at the Secretary's apartment. The Ambassador read from notes an oral statement substantially the same as that contained in Tokyo's 1497, September 22, 8 p.m.[73] He then handed to the Secretary two papers, copies of which are attached hereto. One of these papers was headed "Basic Terms of Peace between Japan and China" [74] and the other marked "Strictly Confidential" was captioned "Reply to the American Communication of September 10, 1941. Delivered to the American Ambassador by the Japanese Foreign Minister in Tokyo September 13".[75]

The Ambassador said that what he had now placed before us was a full expression of what the Japanese Government desired to say to us and that the question of anything further by way of clarification in regard to Japan's relations to the Tripartite Pact might best be left to the proposed meeting between the heads of our two Governments. He hoped that this Government would be able as soon as possible to give a reply to the Japanese Government's proposals. The Secretary replied that we would, of course, study the papers which the Japanese Ambassador had given us as expeditiously as possible with a view to making a reply. He asked the Ambassador what the Ambassador's impressions were in regard to the situation.

The Ambassador replied that of course he understood very well the position of the American Government and he also appreciated the difficulties in the domestic situation in Japan. He said his hope was, however, that if we should proceed to have a meeting it would have a psychological effect in Japan in setting Japan on a new course. The Secretary referred to suggestions he had previously made of the desirability of the Japanese Government's being allowed time to assert control of public opinion and thus attain support for a liberal program such as we had discussed in our conversations. He asked the Ambassador whether the Ambassador thought that a meeting between the heads of states would contribute more to setting Japan upon a new course than the taking of the steps which the

---

[72] Prepared by Joseph W. Ballantine.
[73] Not printed.
[74] For text of terms, see doc. 236.
[75] Not printed.

Secretary had suggested. The Ambassador said that he had not failed to communicate to his Government the Secretary's suggestion and he thought that the Japanese Government had already taken steps in that direction and that these steps had produced good results. He said that, as he had noted on previous occasions, perhaps not more than one-tenth of one percent of the Japanese people desired war with the United States, although of course if ordered to go to war the Japanese people would be ready. He felt that the holding of a meeting such as suggested would be of great value in counteracting the influence of the pro-Axis elements in the Japanese Government and in providing support for those elements desiring peaceful relations with the United States.

The Secretary brought up again the great opportunity that was now presented for Japan and the United States to work together along peaceful and progressive lines and he said he could not emphasize too much his view that by following such a course both countries would stand to gain more than through any other course. He referred to the fact that for the last ten years the youth in Germany had received no other training than for war and that no country could benefit from the staggering burden of armaments that warlike policies were imposing upon the world. The Ambassador said that he fully shared the Secretary's views on these points.

The Secretary went on to say that as this country had been following courses of peace and was committed to these courses there was very little that we could offer Japan in the way of bargaining. He then repeated that he would give careful and expeditious study to the papers which the Japanese Ambassador had presented and would communicate with the Ambassador as soon as possible.

238

711.94/2344–2⅖, enclosure 1

Document Handed by the Japanese Ambassador (Nomura) to the Secretary of State on September 27, 1941

The Governments of Japan and of the United States accept joint responsibility for the initiation and conclusion of a general agreement of understanding as expressed in a joint declaration for the resumption of traditional friendly relations.

Without reference to specific causes of recent estrangement, it is the sincere desire of both Governments that the incidents which led to the deterioration of the amicable sentiment between their countries should be prevented from recurrence and corrected in their unforeseen and unfortunate consequences.

It is the earnest hope of both Governments that, by a cooperative effort, Japan and the United States may contribute effectively toward the establishment and preservation of peace in the Pacific area and, by the rapid consummation of an amicable understanding, encourage world peace and arrest, if not dispel, the tragic confusion that now threatens to engulf civilization.

For such decisive action, protracted negotiations would seem ill-suited and weakening. Both Governments, therefore, desire that adequate instrumentalities should be developed for the realization of a general understanding which would bind, meanwhile, both Governments in honor and in act.

It is the belief of both Governments that such an understanding should comprise only the pivotal issues of urgency and not the accessory concerns which could be deliberated later at a conference.

Both Governments presume to anticipate that they could achieve harmonious relations if certain situations and attitudes were clarified or improved; to wit:

1. The concepts of Japan and of the United States respecting international relations and the character of nations.
2. The attitudes of both Governments toward the European War.
3. Action toward a peaceful settlement between Japan and China.
4. Commerce between both nations.
5. Economic problems in the Southwestern Pacific area.
6. The policies of both nations affecting political stabilization in the Pacific area.

Accordingly, the Government of Japan and the Government of the United States have come to the following mutual understanding and declaration of policy:

I. The concepts of Japan and of the United States respecting international relations and the character of nations.

Both Governments affirm that their national policies are directed toward the foundation of a lasting peace and the inauguration of a new era of reciprocal confidence and cooperation between the peoples of both countries.

Both Governments declare that it is their traditional, and present, concept and conviction that nations and races compose, as members of a family, one household living under the ideal of universal concord through justice and equity; each equally enjoying rights and admitting responsibilities with a mutuality of interests regulated by peaceful processes and directed to the pursuit of their moral and physical welfare, which they are bound to defend for themselves as they are bound not to destroy for others; they further admit their responsibilities to oppose the oppression or exploitation of other peoples.

Both Governments are firmly determined that their respective traditional concepts on the character of nations and the underlying moral principles of social order and national life will continue to be preserved and never transformed by foreign ideas or ideologies contrary to those moral principles and concepts.

III. The attitudes of both Governments toward the European War.

Both Governments maintain it their common aim to bring about peace in the world, and, when an opportune time arrives, they will endeavor jointly for the early restoration of world peace.

With regard to developments of the situation prior to the restoration of world peace, both Governments will be guided in their conduct by considerations of protection and self-defense; and, in case the United States should participate in the European War, Japan would decide entirely independently in the matter of interpretation of the Tripartite Pact between Japan, Germany and Italy, and would likewise determine what actions might be taken by way of fulfilling the obligations in accordance with the said interpretation.

III. Action toward a peaceful settlement between Japan and China.

Both Governments, taking cognizance of the fact that the settlement of the China Affair has a vital bearing upon the peace of the entire Pacific area and consequently upon that of the world, will endeavor to expedite a rapid realization of the settlement of the said Affair.

The Government of the United States, recognizing the effort and the sincere desire on the part of the Japanese Government concerning the peaceful settlement of the China Affair will, with the intention of facilitating the realization of the settlement, render its good offices in order that the Chungking Government may promptly enter into negotiations with the Government of Japan for a termination of hostilities and a resumption of peaceful relations, and will refrain from resorting to any measures and actions which might hamper the measures and efforts of the Government of Japan directed toward the settlement of the China Affair.

The Government of Japan maintains that the basic general terms of peace for the settlement of the China Affair will be in harmony with the principles embodied in the Konoye statement, and those agreements between Japan and China and those matters which have been put into effect in accordance with the said statement; that the economic cooperation between Japan and China will be carried on by peaceful means and in conformity with the principle of non-discrimination in the international commercial relations and also with the principle of especially close relationship which is natural between neighboring countries; and that the economic activities of third Powers in China will not be excluded so long as they are pursued on an equitable basis.

NOTE: There is appended a draft of the basic terms of peace between Japan and China.[77]

IV. Commerce between Japan and the United States.

Both Governments agree to take without delay measures necessary for resuming normal trade relations between the two countries.

Both Governments guarantee each other that they will, as the first of the measures envisaged in the preceding paragraph, discontinue immediately the measures of freezing assets now being enforced, and that they will supply mutually such commodities as are, respectively, available and required by either of them.

V. Economic problems in the Southwestern Pacific area.

Both Governments mutually pledge themselves that the economic activities of Japan and the United States in the Southwestern Pacific area shall be carried on by peaceful means and in conformity with the principle of non-discrimination in the international commercial relations in pursuance of the policy stated in the preceding paragraph, both Governments agree to cooperate each with the other towards the creation of conditions of international trade and international investment under which both countries will have a reasonable opportunity to secure through the trade process the means of acquiring those goods and commodities which each country needs for the safeguarding and development of its own economy.

Both Governments will amicably cooperate for the conclusion and execution of agreements with the Powers concerned in regard to the production and supply, on the basis of non-discrimination, of such specific commodities as oil, rubber, nickel, and tin.

VI. The policies of both nations affecting political stabilization in the Pacific area.

Both Governments, taking cognizance of the fact that it is a matter of vital importance to stabilize promptly the situation in the South-

---

[77] Doc. 236.

western Pacific area, undertake not to resort to any measures and actions which may jeopardize such stabilization. The Government of Japan will not make any armed advancement, using French Indo-China as a base, to any adjacent area thereof (excluding China), and, upon the establishment of an equitable peace in the Pacific area, will withdraw its troops which are now stationed in French Indo-China.

The Government of the United States will alleviate its military measures in the Southwestern Pacific area.

Both Governments declare that they respect the sovereignty and territorial integrity of Thailand and Netherland East Indies, and that they are prepared to conclude an agreement concerning the neutralization of the Philippine Islands when its independence will have been achieved.

The Government of the United States guarantees non-discriminatory treatment of the Japanese nationals in the Philippine Islands.

239

711.94/2344—2½₂₅

Memorandum [78] *Regarding a Conversation Between the Secretary Of State and the Japanese Ambassador (Nomura)*

[WASHINGTON,] September 29, 1941.

The Japanese Ambassador called at his request at the Secretary's apartment. He handed the Secretary a document (copy of which is attached hereto) containing the gist of what the Foreign Minister said in his conversations with the American Ambassador at Tokyo on September 27.

The Ambassador said with an apparent touch of embarrassment that he was very well aware of the attitude of this Government and had made this Government's position very clear to his own Government, and that notwithstanding this his Government had instructed him to press for an answer on the Japanese Government's proposal. The Ambassador added that he had been asked by his Government to seek a further meeting with the President, but that the Ambassador realized the situation here and that was why he was laying the matter before the Secretary.

The Secretary replied that, as the Ambassador knew, the President's brother-in-law had died last week, that the President went to Hyde Park over the weekend, and that consequently the Secretary

---

[78] Prepared by Joseph W. Ballantine.

had not been able to see the President for the last three or four days. The Secretary said, however, that he expected to see the President today. The Secretary went on to say that he expected to be able to give the Ambassador within two or three days a memorandum having a bearing upon the Japanese Government's proposal. The Secretary pointed out that just as the Japanese Government had its difficulties we had our difficulties, that the whole effort of our conversations had been to narrow the gap between our respective views, and that we had felt that time was necessary in order to enable the Japanese Government to educate its public opinion to accept a broad-gauge program such as we advocated.

The Ambassador commented that he himself was in favor of a broad-gauge program, but that he knew very well the psychology within the Japanese Army. He said that even the highest-ranking generals had a simplicity of mind which made it difficult for them to see why, as they saw the situation, when the United States should be asserting leadership on the American continent with the Monroe Doctrine the United States should want to interfere with Japan's assuming leadership on the Asiatic continent. The Secretary asked why the Japanese Government could not educate the generals. The Ambassador replied that this would take twenty years.

The Secretary then asked whether the Japanese public as a whole desired a speedy settlement of the conflict with China. The Ambassador replied that for the last two or three years the Japanese public desired such a settlement but felt that under existing circumstances they had no alternative to continuing fighting. The Secretary observed that there have been a number of our marine guards who did not want to leave China and he supposed that in the case of the Japanese occupationary forces there were many who would not like to be recalled. The Ambassador laughed and replied that this was quite true, and he observed that when an Army general in China was clothed with the authority of a viceroy, naturally he did not welcome the prospect of being shorn of that authority.

The Ambassador, in reply to a further question by the Secretary, stated that he believed that the Japanese Government was in a stronger position internally than it had been, but that, nevertheless, in his own personal opinion, he judged that if nothing came of the proposal for a meeting between the chiefs of our two Governments it might be difficult for Prince Konoye to retain his position and that Prince Konoye then would be likely to be succeeded by a less moderate leader. He suggested that this was one reason why the Japanese Government desired to move as speedily as possible. The

Secretary repeated that we would expect to communicate with the Japanese Ambassador in two or three days.

STATEMENT HANDED BY THE JAPANESE AMBASSADOR (NOMURA) TO THE SECRETARY OF STATE ON SEPTEMBER 29, 1941

Gist of What the Foreign Minister Said in His Conversation With the American Ambassador at the Foreign Office, Tokyo, September 27, 1941

1. The war in Europe, involving many major Powers, has spread to the Atlantic. Fortunately, it has not yet touched the Pacific Ocean, where the key to peace or war lies in the hands of Japan and the United States. Should these two countries go to war, it would mean the destruction of world civilization and a dire calamity to mankind.

In recent times various events have occurred in rapid succession, tending to destroy the friendly relations between the two countries.

An adjustment of Japanese-American relations at this time and the enhancement of the friendship of the two countries will redound not only to the benefit of Japan and America but also to the cause of world peace. The Japanese Government seeks such adjustment not solely for the sake of the two countries but also for the purpose of paving the way for a general peaceful settlement throughout the world.

2. For the past two months since my appointment as Foreign Minister I have striven night and day toward obtaining an amicable settlement between Japan and America. It is also with the same purpose in view that Prince Konoye himself has decided to come to the front and proposed a meeting with President Roosevelt.

3. Japan is bound in alliance with Germany and Italy. The very idea that the Head of my Government should meet the President of the United States is liable to give rise to misunderstandings regarding Japan's ties with those two countries. Such a step would entail really a great sacrifice on the part of the Japanese Government. Moreover, from Japan's domestic standpoint, it will be an event unprecedented in history for the Prime Minister to go out of the country on a diplomatic mission. This fact alone should be a sufficient testimony to the sincerity of the Japanese Government in its desire for an adjustment of Japanese-American relations and for the preservation of peace in the Pacific.

4. If there are those who would interpret Japan's attitude as an

indication not of her solicitude for peace but of her submission to American pressure, they are grossly mistaken. Eager as we are for peace, we will not bow under the pressure of another country, nor do we want peace at any price. It is a characteristic trait of our people to repel, rather than to submit to, external pressure. I repeat this point in view of certain comments that have appeared in American newspapers, although I am told they are showing nowadays signs of moderation.

5. Japanese-American relations are so complex and complicated that they are not capable of being adjusted at one stroke. The proposed meeting of the heads of the two Governments may not succeed in effecting a general solution of all difficulties. However, this meeting is bound to have a vast political significance. Moreover, it is certain that at least those problems yet to be settled (assuming that there will remain such problems) that had been the subject of our negotiations by cable will be readily solved at the conference. It will mark an epochal turn for good in Japanese-American relations. The American Government has already agreed in principle to the proposed meeting between Prince Konoye and President Roosevelt. Should it fail to take place there will never be another opportunity combined with such an auspicious setting for such a conference. Besides, the repercussions of the failure might be most unfortunate.

6. The policy and aims of my Government have been fully communicated to the American Government. A resumé of these, put in the form of the American Draft Understanding of June 21, 1941, has also been submitted to Your Excellency. I trust that the views of my Government are being given careful consideration by the American Government.

7. On our side, the ship to carry the Prime Minister is ready. The members of his suite including a full General and a full Admiral have been privately appointed. The party is prepared to depart at any moment.

8. In the circumstances such as I have described, the Japanese Government is now anxiously looking forward to receiving a reply from the American Government at the earliest date possible. As I have spoken to Your Excellency at our last meeting, any further delay—especially after today's anniversary of the Tripartite Pact—would put my Government in a very delicate position.

Furthermore, the climatic conditions in the Northern Pacific and the vicinity of the Alaskan coast are likely to become unfavorable for the proposed meeting.

9. Time, as I have often said, is a vital factor from both internal and international viewpoints. The decision must be made as soon as possible. So I desire to ask for the most speedy and sincere consideration of the American Government.

I may add that, as regards the date for the meeting, October 10–15 will suit the Japanese Government.

Finally, by way of a conclusion, I should like to say that negotiations of this sort require sincerity and mutual confidence. I need not dwell on the character, the convictions and faith of Prince Konoye as well as his political position, all of which are well known to Your Excellency. Without Prince Konoye and the present Cabinet under him, an opportunity for Japanese-American *rapprochement* is likely to be lost for some time to come. I wish to emphasize again the urgent necessity of having the proposed meeting at the earliest possible date.

240

711.94/2406–1/11

Memorandum [79] Regarding a Conversation Between the Secretary Of State and the Japanese Ambassador (Nomura)

[WASHINGTON,] October 2, 1941.

The Ambassador called at the Secretary's apartment at the request of the Secretary. The Secretary handed the Ambassador a strictly confidential statement [80] containing the views of this Government with respect to the Japanese Government's proposals.

After the Ambassador had read the statement the Secretary invited the Japanese Ambassador to comment. The Ambassador said that he feared that his Government would be disappointed because of its very earnest desire to hold the meeting. He said he wished to assure the Secretary that he was convinced that the Japanese Government was entirely sincere in this matter and had no ulterior purpose. He added, however, that in view of the difficulties of the internal situation in Japan he did not think his Government could go further at this time. The Secretary replied that he was fully convinced of the sincerity of the Prime Minister and others in the Japanese Government. He said that so far as this Government was concerned we had our difficulties, too; that we had to meet the objections of critics; and that in view of past developments it was not possible in one day to remove their misgivings. For this reason, as the Secretary had often re-

[79] Prepared by Joseph W. Ballantine.
[80] Doc. 241.

marked, we felt it necessary to have an agreement that would speak for itself: one that would on the face of it make manifest the purposes of both Governments consistently to pursue courses of peace. The Ambassador referred to a press report that he had seen yesterday of a speech by a member of the American Cabinet in which there was a reference to bringing about the defeat of Japan. His comment implied that such statements would have a bad effect in Japan as it would be assumed that what a member of the Cabinet said represented the views of the administration. He said that certain persons in Japan might have made unfortunate statements, but he did not think that such persons were members of the Cabinet and that anything a member of the Japanese Cabinet might say would be taken as representing the views of the Japanese Government.

The Secretary referred to the fact that all the time the Ambassador and he were holding conversations in regard to our proposed understanding Mr. Matsuoka was making public statements of a character inconsistent with the spirit of those conversations. He noted that the Ambassador had continued their conversations despite those statements.

The Secretary went on to say that we had felt that we could not proceed through indirect courses to attain the objects which our two Governments are seeking, that we must proceed directly, and that no patchwork arrangement would meet the situation of establishing peace in the Pacific area. It was for that reason the Secretary felt that we should endeavor to reach a meeting of minds on essential points before holding the proposed meeting. We had no desire whatever, he emphasized, to cause any delay. The Secretary further pointed out that we had tried the effects of both secrecy and of publicity and that we already were able to gauge public reaction to the proposed understanding between the two Governments as a result of our letting it be known that informal and exploratory conversations were proceeding. Thus the important thing for us now was to endeavor to reach a meeting of minds on essentials in order to insure the success of any meeting that we might hold.

As the Ambassador did not appear to understand the foregoing point made to him, Mr. Ballantine repeated in Japanese what the Secretary had said.

The Ambassador said that he felt that the only point on which he anticipated difficulty in the two Governments reaching an agreement was in regard to the question of retention of Japanese troops in China. He thought that, with regard to the question of non-discrimination, the Japanese Government would meet us. The Secretary emphasized that in his opinion no country would stand to gain more than Japan from the general universal application of the principle. The Secretary added that he would like to give the Ambassador a report of the Lima Conference containing the resolutions adopted in regard to economic matters and he suggested that the Japanese Government might be interested in adopting similar policies in the Far East. The Ambassador said that Japanese present-day thought with respect to regional economic blocs was the result of circumstances, that is to say, of measures taken by other countries such as the Empire preferences introduced at Ottawa. The Secretary replied that he had been fighting such measures as those taken at Ottawa and he would like to have Japan join with the United States in fighting for liberal economic policies.

In conclusion, the Ambassador commented that he thought that the Konoye Cabinet was in a comparatively strong position and that he did not anticipate that there was a likelihood of reactionary groups coming into power. He repeated his conviction that the Konoye Cabinet was extremely desirous of reaching an agreement with the United States.

241

711.94/2340a

Oral Statement Handed by the Secretary of State to the Japanese Ambassador (Nomura)

[WASHINGTON,] October 2, 1941.

Reference is made to the proposals of the Japanese Government communicated on September 6, 1941, by the Japanese Ambassador to the Secretary of State, and to statements relating thereto subsequently communicated to this Government by the Japanese Government.

Thoughtful study has been given to the communications to which reference is made, and in connection with that study careful review has been made of other communications previously received from the Japanese Government on the same subject. On the basis of this study observations are offered as follows:

The Government of the United States welcomed, as affording a possible opportunity for furthering the broad-gauge objectives and principles of a program of peace, the Japanese Government's suggestions made through its Ambassador here in the early part of August that there be held a meeting of the responsible heads of the Japanese Government and of the Government of the United States to discuss means for bringing about an adjustment of relations between the United States and Japan and that there be resumed the informal conversations which had been in progress between the two countries to ascertain whether there existed a basis for negotiations relative to a peaceful settlement covering the entire Pacific situation.

Accordingly, in the reply made by the President on August 17, 1941, to the Japanese Ambassador the view was expressed that such informal conversations would naturally envisage the working out of a progressive program attainable by peaceful means; that such a program would involve the application in the entire Pacific area of the principle of equality of commercial opportunity and treatment, thus making possible access by all countries to raw materials and to all other essential commodities, and there were described the advantages which would flow to all countries, including Japan from the adoption of such a program. In conclusion, it was stated that if the Japanese Goverment were in position to embark upon a peaceful program for the Pacific along the lines of the program and principles to which the United States is committed, this Government would be prepared to consider resumption of the informal exploratory discussions and would be glad to endeavor to arrange a suitable time and place to exchange views.

In the light of the broad purposes and fundamental principles which this Government holds, it was gratifying to the President and the Government of the United States to receive the message of the Prime Minister and the statement of the Government of Japan on August 28, 1941, containing statements expressing Japan's desire and intent to pursue courses of peace in harmony with the fundamental principles to which the people and Government of the United States are committed. In its statement the Japanese Government gave, with some qualifications, broad assurances of its peaceful intent, including a comprehensive assurance that the Japanese Government has no intention of using without provocation military force against any neighboring nation. The Japanese Government declared that it supported the program and principles which had been briefly outlined by the President not only as applicable to the Pacific area but also as a program for the entire world.

The Government of the United States, while desiring to proceed as rapidly as possible with consideration of arrangements for a meeting between the heads of state, felt it desirable, in order to assure that that meeting would accomplish the objectives in view, to clarify the interpretation of certain principles and the practical application thereof to concrete problems in the Pacific area. It has not been the purpose of this Government to enter into a discussion of details; this

Government has felt, however, that the clarification sought would afford a means of expediting our effort to arrive at a meeting of minds.

On September 3, 1941, the President in giving reply to the Japanese Ambassador expressed the earnest desire of the Government of the United States to collaborate in efforts to make effective in practice the principles to which the Japanese Government made reference. The President reiterated the four principles regarded by this Government as the foundation upon which relations between nations should properly rest. Those principles are:

1. Respect for the territorial integrity and the sovereignty of each and all nations.
2. Support of the principle of non-interference in the internal affairs of other countries.
3. Support of the principle of equality, including equality of commercial opportunity.
4. Non-disturbance of the *status quo* in the Pacific except as the *status quo* may be altered by peaceful means.

The President pointed out that in order to bring about any satisfactory settlement of Pacific questions it was highly important to reach a community of view and a clear agreement upon certain points with respect to which fundamental differences of opinion between our two Governments had developed in the informal conversations; and the President requested an indication of the present attitude of the Japanese Government with regard to those fundamental questions.

On September 6, the Prime Minister of Japan in a conversation with the American Ambassador at Tokyo stated that he subscribed fully to the four principles above mentioned.

The foregoing developments and assurances, together with other statements made by the Japanese Government, seemed to justify this Government in concluding that the Japanese Government might be expected to adhere to and to give practical application to a broad progressive program covering the entire Pacific area. It was therefore a source of disappointment to the Government of the United States that the proposals of the Japanese Government presented by the Japanese Ambassador on September 6, 1941, which the Japanese Government apparently intended should constitute a concrete basis for discussions, appeared to disclose divergence in the concepts of the two Governments. That is to say, those proposals and the subsequent explanatory statements made in regard thereto serve, in the opinion of this Government, to narrow and restrict not only the application of the principles upon which our informal conversations already referred to had been based but also the various assurances given by the Japanese Government of its desire to move along with the United States in putting into operation a broad program looking to the establishment and maintenance of peace and stability in the entire Pacific area.

As has already been said, the various broad assurances given by the Japanese Premier and the Japanese Government are highly gratifying. In putting forward its attitude of peaceful intent toward other nations, the Japanese Government qualified its assurances with certain phrases the need for which is not easily understood. It is difficult to conceive of there developing under present circumstances in any of the territories neighboring French Indochina, in Thailand or in the Soviet Union any aggressive threat or provocation to Japan. The inalienable right of self-defense is of course well recognized by all nations and there could arise in some minds a question as to just what the Japanese Government has in view in circumscribing its assurances of peaceful intent with what would seem to be unnecessary qualifying phrases.

In the informal conversations there was tentatively arrived at a formula in regard to economic policy (Section V of the draft understanding), which provided that Japanese activity and American activity in the Pacific area shall be carried on by peaceful means and in conformity with the principle of non-discrimination in international commercial relations. In the Japanese Government's proposals of September 6 and in subsequent communications from the Japanese Government the commitments contained in that formula were restricted to the countries of the Southwest Pacific area (not the Pacific area as a whole). In reference to China, the Japanese Government states that it will respect the principle of non-discrimination, but the explanation given in regard to this point would seem to be open to the implication that the Japanese Government has in mind some limitation upon the application of this principle occasioned by reasons of Japan's geographical propinquity to China.

Obviously, it would not be likely to serve the purposes affirmed by the Japanese Government or by this Government if either the United States or Japan were to pursue one course or policy in certain areas while at the same time pursuing an opposite course or policy in other areas.

This Government has noted the views of the Japanese Government in support of its desire to station troops for an indeterminate period in certain areas of China. Entirely apart from the question of the reasons for such a proposal, the inclusion of such a provision in the proposed terms of a peaceful settlement between Japan and China at a time when Japan is in military occupation of large areas in China is open to certain objections. For example, when a country in military occupation of territory of another country proposes to the second country the continued stationing of troops of the first country in certain areas as a condition for a peaceful settlement and thus for the withdrawal of the occupationary forces from other areas, such procedure would seem to be out of keeping with the progressive and enlightened courses and principles which were discussed in the informal conversations and thus would not, in the opinion of this Government, make for peace or offer prospects of stability.

It is believed that a clear-cut manifestation of Japan's intention in regard to the withdrawal of Japanese troops from China and French Indochina would be most helpful in making known—in particular to those who might be inclined to be critical—Japan's peaceful intentions and Japan's desire to follow courses calculated to establish a sound basis for future stability and progress in the Pacific area.

With reference to the attitude of each country toward the European war, this Government has noted with appreciation the further step taken by the Japanese Government to meet the difficulties inherent in this aspect of the relations between the two countries. It is believed that it would be helpful if the Japanese Government could give further study to the question of possible additional clarification of its position.

In the exchanges of views which have taken place between the two Governments in an effort to reach an agreement in principle upon fundamental questions in order to prepare the ground for the proposed meeting of the responsible chiefs of government, this Government has endeavored to make clear that what it envisages is a comprehensive program calling for the application uniformly to the entire Pacific area of liberal and progressive principles. From what the Japanese Government has so far indicated in regard to its purposes this Government derives the impression that the Japanese Government has in mind a program which would be circumscribed by the imposition of qualifications and exceptions to the actual application of those principles.

If this impression is correct, can the Japanese Government feel that a meeting between the responsible heads of government under such circumstances would be likely to contribute to the advancement of the high purposes which we have mutually had in mind?

As already stated, this Government welcomed the assurances contained in the statement of the Japanese Government which accompanied the Japanese Prime Minister's message to the President of the United States that the Japanese Government subscribed to the principles which have long been advocated by this Government as the only sound basis for stable international relations. This Government believes that renewed consideration of these fundamental principles may be helpful in our effort to seek a meeting of minds in regard to the essential questions on which we seek agreement and thus lay a firm foundation for a meeting between the responsible heads of the two Governments. The subject of the meeting proposed by the Prime Minister and the objectives sought have engaged, and continue to engage, the close and active interest of the President of the United States, and it is the President's earnest hope that discussion of the fundamental questions may be so developed that such a meeting can be held. It is also the President's hope that the Japanese Government shares the conviction of this Government that, if the Governments of Japan and of the United States are resolved to give those principles practical and comprehensive application, the two Governments can work out a fundamental rehabilitation of the relations between the United States and Japan and contribute to the bringing about of a lasting peace with justice, equity and order in the whole Pacific area.

242

Department of State Bulletin, vol. V, p. 257

Message of President Roosevelt to the Congress, October 9, 1941

It is obvious to all of us that world conditions have changed violently since the first American Neutrality Act of 1935. The Neutrality Act of 1939 was passed at a time when the true magnitude of the Nazi attempt to dominate the world was visualized by few persons. We heard it said, indeed, that this new European war was not a real war, and that the contending armies would remain behind their impregnable fortifications and never really fight. In this atmosphere the Neutrality Act seemed reasonable. But so did the Maginot Line.

Since then—in these past two tragic years—war has spread from continent to continent; very many nations have been conquered and enslaved; great cities have been laid in ruins; millions of human beings have been killed, soldiers and sailors and civilians alike. Never before has such widespread devastation been visited upon God's earth and God's children.

The pattern of the future—the future as Hitler seeks to shape it— is now as clear and as ominous as the headlines of today's newspapers.

Through these years of war we Americans have never been neutral in thought. We have never been indifferent to the fate of Hitler's victims. And, increasingly, we have become aware of the peril to ourselves, to our democratic traditions and institutions, to our country, and to our hemisphere.

We have known what victory for the aggressors would mean to us. Therefore, the American people, through the Congress, have taken important and costly steps to give great aid to those nations actively fighting against Nazi-Fascist domination.

We know that we could not defend ourselves in Long Island Sound or in San Francisco Bay. That would be too late. It is the American policy to defend ourselves wherever such defense becomes necessary under the complex conditions of modern warfare.

Therefore, it has become necessary that this Government should not be handicapped in carrying out the clearly announced policy of the Congress and of the people. We must face the truth that the Neutrality Act requires a complete reconsideration in the light of known facts.

The revisions which I suggest do not call for a declaration of war any more than the Lend-Lease Act called for a declaration of war. This is a matter of essential defense of American rights.

In the Neutrality Act are various crippling provisions. The repeal or modification of these provisions will not leave the United States any less neutral than we are today, but will make it possible for us to defend the Americas far more successfully, and to give aid far more effectively against the tremendous forces now marching towards conquest of the world.

Under the Neutrality Act we established certain areas as zones of combat into which no American-flag ships could proceed. Hitler proclaimed certain far larger areas as zones of combat into which any neutral ship, regardless of its flag or the nature of its cargo, could proceed only at its peril. We know now that Hitler recognizes no limitation on any zone of combat in any part of the seven seas. He has struck at our ships and at the lives of our sailors within the waters of the Western Hemisphere. Determined as he is to gain domination of the entire world, he considers the entire world his own battlefield.

Ships of the United States and of other American republics continue to be sunk, not only in the imaginary zone proclaimed by the Nazis in the North Atlantic, but also in the zoneless South Atlantic.

I recommend the repeal of section 6 of the act of November 4, 1939, which prohibits the arming of American-flag ships engaged in foreign commerce.

The practice of arming merchant ships for civilian defense is an old one. It has never been prohibited by international law. Until 1937 it had never been prohibited by any statute of the United States. Through our whole history American merchant vessels have been armed whenever it was considered necessary for their own defense.

It is an imperative need now to equip American merchant vessels with arms. We are faced not with the old type of pirates but with the modern pirates of the sea who travel beneath the surface or on the surface or in the air destroying defenseless ships without warning and without provision for the safety of the passengers and crews.

Our merchant vessels are sailing the seas on missions connected with the defense of the United States. It is not just that the crews of these vessels should be denied the means of defending their lives and their ships.

Although the arming of merchant vessels does not guarantee their safety, it most certainly adds to their safety. In the event of an attack by a raider they have a chance to keep the enemy at a distance until help comes. In the case of an attack by air, they have at least a chance to shoot down the enemy or keep the enemy at such height that it cannot make a sure hit. If it is a submarine, the armed merchant ship compels the submarine to use a torpedo while submerged—and many torpedoes thus fired miss their mark. The submarine can no longer rise to the surface within a few hundred yards and sink the merchant ship by gunfire at its leisure.

Already we take many precautions against the danger of mines— and it seems somewhat incongruous that we have authority today to "degauss" our ships as a protection against mines, whereas we have no authority to arm them in protection against aircraft or raiders or submarines.

The arming of our ships is a matter of immediate necessity and extreme urgency. It is not more important than some other crippling provisions in the present act, but anxiety for the safety of our crews and of the almost priceless goods that are within the holds of our ships leads me to recommend that you, with all speed, strike the prohibition against arming our ships from the statute books.

There are other phases of the Neutrality Act to the correction of which I hope the Congress will give earnest and early attention. One of these provisions is of major importance. I believe that it is essential to the proper defense of our country that we cease giving the definite assistance which we are now giving to the aggressors. For, in effect, we are inviting their control of the seas by keeping our ships out of the ports of our own friends.

It is time for this country to stop playing into Hitler's hands, and to unshackle our own.

DOCUMENTS

A vast number of ships are sliding into the water from the American shipbuilding ways. We are lending them to the enemies of Hitlerism and they are carrying food and supplies and munitions to belligerent ports in order to withstand Hitler's juggernaut.

Most of the vital goods authorized by the Congress are being delivered. Yet many of them are being sunk; and as we approach full production requiring the use of more ships now being built it will be increasingly necessary to deliver American goods under the American flag.

We cannot, and should not, depend on the strained resources of the exiled nations of Norway and Holland to deliver our goods, nor should we be forced to masquerade American-owned ships behind the flags of our sister republics.

I earnestly trust that the Congress will carry out the true intent of the Lend-Lease Act by making it possible for the United States to help to deliver the articles to those who are in a position effectively to use them. In other words, I ask for congressional action to implement congressional policy. Let us be consistent.

I would not go back to the earlier days when private traders could gamble with American life and property in the hope of personal gain, and thereby embroil this country in some incident in which the American public had no direct interest. But today, under the controls exercised by the Government, no ship and no cargo can leave the United States, save on an errand which has first been approved by governmental authority. And the test of that approval is whether the exportation will promote the defense of the United States.

I cannot impress too strongly upon the Congress the seriousness of the military situation that confronts all of the nations that are combating Hitler.

We would be blind to the realities if we did not recognize that Hitler is now determined to expend all the resources and all the mechanical force and manpower at his command to crush both Russia and Britain. He knows that he is racing against time. He has heard the rumblings of revolt among the enslaved peoples—including the Germans and Italians. He fears the mounting force of American aid. He knows that the days in which he may achieve total victory are numbered.

Therefore, it is our duty, as never before, to extend more and more assistance and ever more swiftly to Britain, to Russia, to all peoples and individuals fighting slavery. We must do this without fear or favor. The ultimate fate of the Western Hemisphere lies in the balance.

I say to you solemnly that if Hitler's present military plans are brought to successful fulfilment, we Americans shall be forced to fight in defense of our own homes and our own freedom in a war as costly and as devastating as that which now rages on the Russian front.

Hitler has offered a challenge which we as Americans cannot and will not tolerate.

We will not let Hitler prescribe the waters of the world on which our ships may travel. The American flag is not going to be driven from the seas either by his submarines, his airplanes, or his threats.

We cannot permit the affirmative defense of our rights to be annulled and diluted by sections of the Neutrality Act which have no realism in the light of unscrupulous ambition of madmen.

We Americans have determined our course.

We intend to maintain the security and the integrity and the honor of our country.

We intend to maintain the policy of protecting the freedom of the seas against domination by any foreign power which has become crazed with a desire to control the world. We shall do so with all our strength and all our heart and all our mind.

243

Department of State Bulletin, vol. V, p. 307

Statement by the Secretary of State Before the Committee on Foreign Relations, United States Senate, October 21, 1941

The progress of events, and particularly of military and naval operations beyond and on the seas, makes it advisable and urgent that the Congress grant full authority to take certain measures which are plainly essential for the defense of the United States. It is imperative now to exercise what Elihu Root in 1914 called "the right of every sovereign state to protect itself by preventing a condition of affairs in which it will be too late to protect itself".

Such a condition of affairs now impends. Unless it is promptly dealt with, efforts at self-defense may come too late.

The paramount principle of national policy is the preservation of the safety and security of the Nation. The highest right flowing from that principle is the right of self-defense. That right must now be invoked. The key to that defense under present conditions is to prevent Hitler from gaining control of the seas.

On October 26, 1940, I said:

"Should the would-be conquerors gain control of other continents, they would next concentrate on perfecting their control of the seas, of the air over the seas, and of the world's economy; they might then be able with ships and with planes to strike at the communication lines, the commerce, and the life of this hemisphere; and ultimately we might find ourselves compelled to fight on our own soil, under our own skies, in defense of our independence and our very lives."

In the year which has ensued, Hitler and his satellites have extended their military occupation to most of the Continent of Europe. They are already seeking control of the sea. They have attacked American vessels, contrary to all law, in widely separated areas; particularly they are now trying to sever the sea lanes which link the United States to the remaining free peoples. Hitler under his policy of intimidation and frightfulness has in effect given notice that American lives and American ships, no less than the lives and ships of other nations, will be destroyed if they are found in most of the north Atlantic Ocean. In the presence of threats and acts by an outlaw nation, there arises the right, and there is imposed the duty, of prompt and determined defense. Our ships and men are legitimately sailing the seas. The outlaw who preaches and practices indiscriminate, terroristic attack in pursuit of world-conquest is estopped to invoke any law if law-abiding nations act to defend themselves.

The conviction that the Atlantic approaches to the Western Hemisphere are under attack no longer rests on inference. The attack is continuous; there is reason to believe that it will steadily increase in strength and intensity.

When the Neutrality Act of 1939 was passed, we went far in foregoing the exercise of certain rights by our citizens in time of foreign war. This was for the purpose of avoiding incidents such as those that confronted our Government during the first World War as a result of unrestricted German-submarine warfare. But there was no waiving of our right to take the fullest measures needed for self-defense on land and sea if the tide of conquest should move in our direction.

The tide has so moved. The course of the present war has altered the picture completely. Certain provisions of the existing legislation under the changed circumstances now handicap our necessary work of self-defense and stand squarely in the way of our national safety.

The Congress has recognized the change in circumstances and has passed the Lend-Lease Act. It thereby determined that the efforts of those nations which are actively resisting aggression are important and necessary to the safety of the United States. It approved, as a necessary measure of defense, the fullest support to nations which are in the front line of resistance to a movement of world-conquest more ruthless in execution and more hideous in effects than any other such movement of all time. An indispensable part of our policy must be resolute self-defense on the high seas, and this calls especially for protection of shipping on open sea lanes.

One of the greatest mistakes that we could possibly make would be to base our policy upon an assumption that we are secure, when, if the assumption should prove erroneous, the fact of having so acted would lay us completely open to hostile invasion.

When American ships are being wantonly and unlawfully attacked with complete disregard of life and property, it is absurd to forego any legitimate measures that may be helpful toward self-defense. It is especially absurd to continue to tie our hands by a provision of law which prohibits arming our merchant vessels for their own defense.

I repeat, the highest duty of this Government is to safeguard the security of our Nation. The basic consideration is that measures and methods of defense shall be made effective when and where needed. They are now needed especially on the high seas and in those areas which must be preserved from invasion if the full tide of the movement of world-conquest is not to beat at our gates.

It would be little short of criminal negligence to proceed on the hope that some happy chance or chances will save us from a fate like that which has befallen so many other countries in the world. We cannot run away from a situation which can only be dealt with by the firm measures of a people determined and prepared to resist. It is worse than futile to read the war news from overseas and conclude that each temporary check to the would-be world-conqueror relieves us of the need to provide fully for our own national defense.

I am convinced that in the interest of our national security the passage of the pending bill to repeal section 6 of the Neutrality Act is both urgent and important. Inasmuch as section 2 is not under consideration I will offer no comment except to say that in my judgment section 2 should be repealed or modified.

244

Department of State Bulletin, vol. V, p. 341

Address Delivered by President Roosevelt at Washington,
October 27, 1941

Five months ago tonight I proclaimed to the American people the existence of a state of unlimited emergency.

Since then much has happened. Our Army and Navy are temporarily in Iceland in the defense of the Western Hemisphere.

Hitler has attacked shipping in areas close to the Americas throughout the Atlantic.

Many American-owned merchant ships have been sunk on the high seas. One American destroyer was attacked on September fourth. Another destroyer was attacked and hit on October seventeenth. Eleven brave and loyal men of our Navy were killed by the Nazis.

We have wished to avoid shooting. But the shooting has started. And history has recorded who fired the first shot. In the long run, however, all that will matter is who fired the last shot.

America has been attacked. The U.S.S. *Kearny* is not just a Navy ship. She belongs to every man, woman, and child in this Nation.

Illinois, Alabama, California, North Carolina, Ohio, Louisiana, Texas, Pennsylvania, Georgia, Arkansas, New York, Virginia—those are the home States of the honored dead and wounded of the *Kearny*. Hitler's torpedo was directed at every American, whether he lives on our seacoasts or in the innermost part of the Nation, far from the seas and far from the guns and tanks of the marching hordes of would-be conquerors of the world.

The purpose of Hitler's attack was to frighten the American people off the high seas—to force us to make a trembling retreat. This is not the first time he has misjudged the American spirit. That spirit is now aroused.

If our national policy were to be dominated by the fear of shooting, then all of our ships and those of our sister republics would have to be tied up in home harbors. Our Navy would have to remain respectfully—abjectly—behind any line which Hitler might decree on any ocean as his own dictated version of his own war zone.

Naturally we reject that absurd and insulting suggestion. We reject it because of our own self-interest, our own self-respect, and our own good faith. Freedom of the seas is now, as it has always been, the fundamental policy of this Government.

Hitler has often protested that his plans for conquest do not extend across the Atlantic Ocean. His submarines and raiders prove otherwise. So does the entire design of his new world-order.

For example, I have in my possession a secret map made in Germany by Hitler's government—by the planners of the new world-order. It is a map of South America and a part of Central America as Hitler proposes to reorganize it. Today in this area there are 14 separate countries. The geographical experts of Berlin, however, have ruthlessly obliterated all existing boundary lines and have divided South America into five vassal states, bringing the whole continent under their domination. And they have also so arranged it that the territory of one of these new puppet states includes the Republic of Panama and our great life line—the Panama Canal.

This map makes clear the Nazi design not only against South America but against the United States itself.

Your Government has in its possession another document made in Germany by Hitler's government. It is a detailed plan, which, for obvious reasons, the Nazis did not wish to publicize just yet, but which they are ready to impose on a dominated world—if Hitler wins. It is a plan to abolish all existing religions—Protestant, Catholic, Mohammedan, Hindu, Buddhist, and Jewish alike. The property of all churches will be seized by the Reich. The cross and all other symbols of religion are to be forbidden. The clergy are to be forever silenced under penalty of the concentration camps, where even now so many fearless men are being tortured because they placed God above Hitler.

In the place of the churches of our civilization, there is to be set up an International Nazi Church—a church which will be served by orators sent out by the Nazi government. In the place of the Bible, the words of *Mein Kampf* will be imposed and enforced as Holy Writ. And in place of the cross of Christ will be put two symbols—the swastika and the naked sword.

The God of Blood and Iron will take the place of the God of Love and Mercy.

These grim truths which I have told you of the present and future plans of Hitlerism will of course be hotly denied tomorrow in the controlled press and radio of the Axis Powers. And some Americans will continue to insist that Hitler's plans need not worry us—and that we should not concern ourselves with anything that goes on beyond rifle shot of our own shores.

The protestations of these American citizens—few in number—will, as usual, be paraded with applause through the Axis press and radio during the next few days, in an effort to convince the world that the majority of Americans are opposed to their duly chosen Government, and in reality are only waiting to jump on Hitler's bandwagon when it comes this way.

The motive of such Americans is not the point at issue. The fact is that Nazi propaganda continues in desperation to seize upon such isolated statements as proof of American disunity.

The Nazis have made up their own list of modern American heroes. It is, fortunately, a short list. I am glad that it does not contain my name.

All of us Americans, of all opinions, are faced with the choice between the kind of world we want to live in and the kind of world which Hitler and his hordes would impose upon us.

None of us wants to burrow under the ground and live in total darkness like a comfortable mole.

The forward march of Hitlerism can be stopped—and it will be stopped.

Very simply and very bluntly—we are pledged to pull our own oar in the destruction of Hitlerism.

And when we have helped to end the curse of Hitlerism we shall help to establish a new peace which will give to decent people everywhere a better chance to live and prosper in security and in freedom and in faith.

Each day that passes we are producing and providing more and more arms for the men who are fighting on actual battlefronts. That is our primary task.

And it is the Nation's will that these vital arms and supplies of all kinds shall neither be locked up in American harbors nor sent to the bottom of the sea. It is the Nation's will that America shall deliver the goods. In open defiance of that will, our ships have been sunk and our sailors have been killed.

I say that we do not propose to take this lying down.

Our determination not to take it lying down has been expressed in the orders to the American Navy to shoot on sight. Those orders stand.

Furthermore, the House of Representatives has already voted to amend part of the Neutrality Act of 1939, today outmoded by force of violent circumstances. The Senate Committee on Foreign Relations has also recommended elimination of other hamstringing provisions in that act. That is the course of honesty and of realism.

Our American merchant ships must be armed to defend themselves against the rattlesnakes of the sea.

Our American merchant ships must be free to carry our American goods into the harbors of our friends.

Our American merchant ships must be protected by our American Navy.

It can never be doubted that the goods will be delivered by this Nation, whose Navy believes in the tradition of "Damn the torpedoes; full speed ahead!"

Our national will must speak from every assembly line in our vast industrial machine. Our factories and our shipyards are constantly expanding. Our output must be multiplied.

It cannot be hampered by the selfish obstruction of a small but dangerous minority of industrial managers who hold out for extra profits or for "business as usual". It cannot be hampered by the selfish obstruction of a small but dangerous minority of labor leaders who are a menace to the true cause of labor itself, as well as to the Nation as a whole.

The lines of our essential defense now cover all the seas, and to meet the extraordinary demands of today and tomorrow our Navy grows to unprecedented size. Our Navy is ready for action. Indeed, units of it in the Atlantic patrol are in action. Its officers and men need no praise from me.

Our new Army is steadily developing the strength needed to withstand the aggressors. Our soldiers of today are worthy of the proudest traditions of the United States Army. But traditions cannot shoot down dive bombers or destroy tanks. That is why we must and shall provide, for every one of our soldiers, equipment and weapons—not merely as good but better than that of any other army on earth. And we are doing that right now.

For this—and all of this—is what we mean by total national defense.

The first objective of that defense is to stop Hitler. He can be stopped and can be compelled to dig in. And that will be the beginning of his downfall, because dictatorship of the Hitler type can live only through continuing victories—increasing conquests.

The facts of 1918 are proof that a mighty German Army and a tired German people can crumble rapidly and go to pieces when they are faced with successful resistance.

Nobody who admires qualities of courage and endurance can fail to be stirred by the full-fledged resistance of the Russian people. The Russians are fighting for their own soil and their own homes. Russia needs all kinds of help—planes, tanks, guns, medical supplies, and other aids—toward the successful defense against the invaders. From the United States and from Britain she is getting great quantities of those essential supplies. But the needs of her huge army will continue—and our help and British help will have to continue!

The other day the Secretary of State of the United States was asked by a Senator to justify our giving aid to Russia. His reply was: "The answer to that depends on how anxious a person is to stop and destroy the march of Hitler in his conquest of the world. If he were anxious enough to defeat Hitler, he would not worry about who was helping to defeat him."

Upon our American production falls the colossal task of equipping our own armed forces and helping to supply the British, the Russians, and the Chinese. In the performance of that task we dare not fail. And we will not fail.

It has not been easy for us Americans to adjust ourselves to the shocking realities of a world in which the principles of common humanity and common decency are being mowed down by the firing squads of the Gestapo. We have enjoyed many of God's blessings. We have lived in a broad and abundant land, and by our industry and productivity we have made it flourish.

There are those who say that our great good fortune has betrayed us—that we are now no match for the regimented masses who have been trained in the Spartan ways of ruthless brutality. They say that we have grown fat and flabby and lazy—and that we are doomed.

But those who say that know nothing of America or of American life.

They do not know that this land is great because it is a land of endless challenge. Our country was first populated, and it has been steadily developed, by men and women in whom there burned the spirit of adventure and restlessness and individual independence which will not tolerate oppression.

Ours has been a story of vigorous challenges which have been accepted and overcome—challenges of uncharted seas, of wild forests and desert plains, of raging floods and withering drought, of foreign tyrants and domestic strife, of staggering problems—social, economic, and physical; and we have come out of them the most powerful nation—and the freest—in all of history.

Today in the face of this newest and greatest challenge, we Americans have cleared our decks and taken our battle stations. We stand ready in the defense of our Nation and the faith of our fathers to do what God has given us the power to see as our full duty.

245

711.94/2408

The Ambassador in Japan (Grew) to the Secretary of State

[Telegram : Paraphrase]

Tokyo, November 3, 1941—3 p.m.
[Received 4 : 19 p.m.[81]]

1736.

(1) I refer a leading article from the Tokyo *Nichi Nichi* of November 1 (reported in my telegram No. 1729 of that date [82]), with

---

[81] Telegram in seven sections.
[82] Not printed.

a banner headline declaring "Empire Approaches Its Greatest Crisis" and introducing a despatch from New York with a summary of a statement the Japanese Embassy reportedly gave to the *New York Times* regarding the need of ending the United States-Japanese economic war. Both the article and the *Nichi Nichi* editorial (see my telegram of November 1, 7 p. m.[82a]) are believed to be close reflections of Japanese sentiments at present.

(2) I also refer to my various telegraphic reports during several months past analyzing the factors affecting policy in Japan and I have nothing to add thereto nor any substantial revision to make thereof. A conclusive estimate may be had of Japan's position through the application to the existing situation and the immediate future of the following points:

(*a*) It is not possible for Japan to dissociate either Japan or the conflict with China from the war in Europe and its fluctuations.

(*b*) In Japan political thought ranges from medieval to liberal ideas and public opinion is thus a variable quantity. The impact of events and conditions beyond Japan may determine at any given time which school of thought shall predominate. (In the democracies, on the other hand, owing to a homogeneous body of principles which influence and direct foreign policy and because methods instead of principles are more likely to cause differences of opinion, public opinion is formed differently.) For example, in Japan the pro-Axis elements gained power following last year's German victories in Western Europe; then Japanese doubt of ultimate German victory was created by Germany's failure to invade the British Isles, this factor helping to reinforce the moderate elements; and finally Germany's attack on the Soviet Union upset the expectation of continued Russo-German peace and made the Japanese realize that those who took Japan into the Tripartite Alliance had misled Japan.

(*c*) An attempt to correct the error of 1940 may be found in the efforts to adjust Japanese relations with the United States and thereby to lead the way to conclusion of peace with China, made by Prince Konoye and promised by the Tojo Cabinet. If this attempt fails, and if success continues to favor German arms, a final, closer Axis alinement may be expected.

(*d*) I and my staff have never been convinced by the theory that Japan's collapse as a militaristic power would shortly result

---

[82a] Not printed.

from the depletion and the eventual exhaustion of Japan's financial and economic resources, as propounded by many leading American economists. Such forecasts were unconsciously based upon the assumption that a dominant consideration would be Japan's retention of the capitalistic system. The outcome they predicted has not transpired, although it is true that the greater part of Japan's commerce has been lost, Japanese industrial production has been drastically curtailed, and Japan's national resources have been depleted. Instead, there has been a drastic prosecution of the process to integrate Japan's national economy, lacking which there might well have occurred the predicted collapse of Japan. What has happened to date therefore does not support the view that continuation of trade embargoes and imposition of a blockade (proposed by some) can best avert war in the Far East.

(3) I call your attention, in this regard, to my telegram No. 827, September 12, 1940 [83] (which reported the "golden opportunity" seen by Japanese army circles for expansion as a consequence of German triumphs in Europe). I sent this telegram under circumstances and at a time when it appeared unwise and futile for the United States to adopt conciliatory measures. The strong policy recommended in that telegram was subsequently adopted by the United States. This policy, together with the impact of world political events upon Japan brought the Japanese Government to the point of seeking conciliation with the United States. If these efforts fail, I foresee a probable swing of the pendulum in Japan once more back to the former Japanese position or even farther. This would lead to what I have described as an all-out, do-or-die attempt, actually risking national hara-kiri, to make Japan impervious to economic embargoes abroad rather than to yield to foreign pressure. It is realized by observers who feel Japanese national temper and psychology from day to day that, beyond peradventure, this contingency not only is possible but is probable.

(4) If the fiber and temper of the Japanese people are kept in mind, the view that war probably would be averted, though there might be some risk of war, by progressively imposing drastic economic measures is an uncertain and dangerous hypothesis upon which to base considered United States policy and measures. War would not be averted by such a course, if it is taken, is our own view. However, each view is only opinion, and, accordingly, to postu-

[83] Doc. 182.

late the correctness of either one and to erect a definitive policy thereon would, in the belief of the Embassy, be contrary to American national interests. It would mean putting the cart before the horse. The primary point to be decided apparently involves the question whether war with Japan is justified by American national objectives, policies, and needs in the case of failure of the first line of national defense, namely, diplomacy, since it would be possible only on the basis of such a decision for the Roosevelt administration to follow a course which would be divested as much as possible of elements of uncertainty, speculation, and opinion. I doubt not that such a decision, irrevocable as it might well prove to be, already has been debated fully and adopted, because the sands are running fast.

(5) You will realize that, in the above discussion of this grave, momentous subject, I am not in touch with the intentions and thoughts of the Administration thereon, and I do not at all mean to imply that Washington is pursuing an undeliberated policy. Nor do I intend to advocate for a single moment any "appeasement" of Japan by the United States or recession in the slightest degree by the United States Government from the fundamental principles laid down as a basis for the conduct and adjustment of international relations, American relations with Japan included. There should be no compromise with principles, though methods may be flexible. My purpose is only to ensure against the United States becoming involved in war with Japan because of any possible misconception of Japan's capacity to rush headlong into a suicidal struggle with the United States. While national sanity dictates against such action, Japanese sanity cannot be measured by American standards of logic. We have no need to be over concerned respecting the bellicose tone and substance at present of the Japanese press (which in the past several years has attacked the United States intensely in recurrent waves), but underestimating Japan's obvious preparations to implement a program in the event the alternative peace program fails, would be short-sighted. Similarly it would be short-sighted for American policy to be based upon the belief that Japanese preparations are no more than saber rattling, merely intended to give moral support to the high pressure diplomacy of Japan. Japan may resort with dangerous and dramatic suddenness to measures which might make inevitable war with the United States.

GREW

246

711.94/2540–3⁄25

Document Handed by the Japanese Ambassador (Nomura)
To the Secretary of State on November 7, 1941

[Tentative translation]

DISPOSITION OF JAPANESE FORCES

(A) Stationing of Japanese forces in China and the withdrawal
thereof:

With regard to the Japanese forces that have been despatched to China in connection with the China Affair, those forces in specified areas in North China and Mengchiang (Inner Mongolia) as well as in Hainan-tao (Hainan Island) will remain to be stationed for a certain required duration after the restoration of peaceful relations between Japan and China. All the rest of such forces will commence withdrawal as soon as general peace is restored between Japan and China, and the withdrawal will proceed according to separate arrangements between Japan and China and will be completed within two years with the firm establishment of peace and order.

(B) Stationing of Japanese forces in French Indo-China and the
withdrawal thereof:

The Japanese Government undertakes to guarantee the territorial sovereignty of French Indo-China. The Japanese forces at present stationed there will be withdrawn as soon as the China Affair is settled or an equitable peace is established in East Asia.

PRINCIPLE OF NON-DISCRIMINATION

The Japanese Government recognizes the principle of non-discrimination in international commercial relations to be applied to all the Pacific areas, inclusive of China, on the understanding that the principle in question is to be applied uniformly to the rest of the entire world as well.

247

Press release, Navy Department

Address Delivered by the Secretary of the Navy (Knox) at Providence,
November 11, 1941

Armistice Day this year is an obvious anomaly. It was established a legal holiday to commemorate the beginnings of peace with Germany. Now, twenty-three years later, we gather not to celebrate peace with Germany, but to dedicate one of the greatest air bases on the American Continent—the air base in neighboring Quonset. That great base, and many others like it, have been created and equipped to meet a threat to our security which proceeds from the same Germany which signed the Armistice in 1918.

This time, Germany does not fight alone. This time, she has allies and associates. The Axis powers have been for years engaged in conquest, by force, of neighboring states. Their moves of conquest have been characterized by methods that have violated every principle of honor, justice and righteousness. Gradually, this movement of conquest has broadened until it has produced hostilities in all parts of the world save only the Western Hemisphere.

It was instinctive and inevitable that the sympathies and the support of the American people should have been extended, from the outset, to the victims of this plan for world-wide dominion by force of arms. At the beginning of the war, the American people, while reprobating, instinctively, those who were responsible for plunging the world into the horrors of war, hoped that we might escape involvement. We sought in every way open to us to give aid to those who strove to prevent an outbreak of war, both in the Far East and in Europe. We employed every ounce of persuasion and influence we possessed to halt the unmistakable trend toward hostilities. When, nevertheless, hostilities began, the American people, both unofficially and officially, through their elected representatives, disclosed unmistakably, our sympathy for the nations whose rights were trampled under foot by ruthless, would-be conquerors, and our hatred of both the methods and acts of the aggressors.

Almost from the outset, it became plain that the world was confronted with no mere local war involving the extension of the boundaries of the aggressor nations at the expense of their neighbors, but rather, what we were witnessing—what was actually in progress, was a well defined plan and purpose to establish, by force of arms, a worldwide dominion to be shared by the three major powers that comprised the Axis. As affairs progressed and this purpose became more plain and obvious, alarm grew among our people and we moved from mere expressions of sympathy to measures of actual aid to those nations which were fighting the Axis and striving to preserve their independence. This change was initiated by the repeal of the Arms Embargo, a feature of the so-called Neutrality Act. This enabled us to sell supplies and munitions to those who could come to our ports and pay cash for their purchases. This step met with the instant and overwhelming approval of the public.

A few months later, when the submarine sinkings threatened Britain with starvation and defeat, we exchanged fifty destroyers for a half-dozen island bases in the Atlantic. This action met with the instant approval of the American people.

The war went on, and nation after nation fell before the armored might of the conquering Nazis, until England stood almost alone in all of Europe, and China driven from her coast to the deep interior, fought desperately against frightful odds. Then, to our everlasting credit, and because of our growing alarm, we decided to erase the dollar sign from our help to these two gallant survivors of world-wide blitzkreig, and prompted by the President and supported by over-whelming majorities in both houses of Congress, we placed the whole resources of our huge industrial plant on a lease or lend basis primarily to England and China, but also to other nations fighting the cause of Freedom. This likewise met with instant popular approval, and Congress swiftly implemented the Lease-Lend Act by the appropriation of billions of dollars.

By the terms of the Lease-Lend Act, we also opened our shipyards, both government owned and privately owned, for the repair of British Men-of-War.

China came to us in her need and we first loaned her millions of dollars, and then made available to her supplies under the Lease-Lend Law.

Finally, as the piratical activities of Axis submarines came nearer and nearer to our shores, we expanded our Atlantic bases to include Greenland and Iceland. Again, in an unmistakable way, the American public indicated its approval.

From this point on, both by word and by act, the Axis powers made plain that the scope of their conquest included not alone the lands of Europe and Asia, but control of the high seas as well. To emphasize and implement this purpose, attacks began to be made upon our ships at sea, and, acting under the most obvious necessity for self-defense, we provided our merchant ships with naval protection against this form of piracy, extending that protection as far as Iceland in the Atlantic.

Here, we have the general outlines of the picture presented on this 11th day of November, Armistice Day.

The national House of Representatives has already repealed the provision of our Neutrality Law which forbade the arming of our merchant ships. The Senate of the United States last Friday, not only repealed that same section of the Law, but likewise, repealed the provision that forbade us to enter belligerent ports or combat zones on the high seas. Within forty-eight hours, it is confidently expected that the House will concur in the Senate action. Thus, at last, we will have freed our hands. For what? For self-defense! Self-defense, a primary instinct of men and nations alike!

We are facing a group of nations who are endeavoring to divide the earth among themselves. They have made it plain that if we are to live in the world that they are trying to create by the most ghastly methods that men have ever employed in conquest, we must adjust our methods of living, our way of life, to theirs. They have left no doubt that if we are to live in the midst of this world ruled under this new order of Totalitarianism which always means by military force, we must do business on terms which they will dictate by such military force. The whole thing is not only repugnant to every instinct we possess, but acquiescence in such a demand would destroy the institutions of government and the principles of self rule which we hold dearer than life itself.

This is the somber outline of what the world looks like twenty-three years after we celebrated an armistice that we hoped would end all war and usher in a lasting era of peace.

My friends, we meet here in the presence of grave dangers. It is impossible to overemphasize them or exaggerate them. We are not only confronted with the necessity of extreme measures of self-defense in the Atlantic, but we are likewise faced with grim possibilities on the other side of the world—on the far side of the Pacific. Just what the morrow may hold for us in that quarter of the globe, no one may say with certainty. The only thing we can be sure of is that the Pacific, no less than the Atlantic, calls for instant readiness for defense. In the Pacific area, no less than in Europe, interests which are vital to our national security are seriously threatened.

In an hour of great danger, the American people expect and deserve a frank disclosure of pertinent facts relating to any such danger that threatens. The very act of facing the truth—the courageous confronting of the facts, unadorned—is itself a great steadier. Honest facing of facts, pleasant or unpleasant, creates courage and fortifies resolution. Evasion of the facts, or refusal to face the facts, is the greatest corrupter of courage and resolution.

In the last few years, the efforts this government has made to maintain amicable relations with the Japanese have been long-suffering and patient to a degree almost unmatched in the history of international relations. We have cooperated with every liberal and peace-loving element in Japan, and we are still ready to cooperate with those elements. We have been patient while, repeatedly, our rights have been violated. We have continued to permit supplies to go to Japan although we could very well have stopped them on the just and truthful ground that we needed such supplies for our own defense. We have felt that in the interests of peace we must be tolerant and take risks. But there comes a time in the life of every man, and every nation, when principles cannot be sacrificed, and when vital and essential rights can no longer be ignored; a time when to go further would mean that our liberality and forbearance would be misunderstood. We are moved and actuated in the Pacific, no less than in the Atlantic, solely by considerations of self-defense.

Our people must understand that grave questions are about to be decided—that the hour of decision is here. There must be clear realization that we will not shrink from or seek to evade the staggering responsibilities of these days. Our country has been made what it is by the courage, the resolution and the sacrifice of our forbears. We shall meet the danger of our times as they met theirs: with heads up, shoulders squared and eyes straight to the front, seeking only to protect that which is our own and coveting not one thing which is another's.

I have every confidence that we shall not fail in this hour of trial.

If I had ever had any doubts they would have been swept away by such achievements as you Rhode Islanders have accomplished at Quonset. This huge base will be one of the most important links in our chain of air defenses. It was planned and built in record time—a fine example of American skill and initiative. Only the close cooperation of the builders, the workers and government made such an achievement possible. Quonset stands today a symbol of the American spirit. It is a symbol also of the ever increasing importance of air activity to sea power. Yesterday it was enough if our fleets ruled the surface of the seas: today we must control the air above the oceans as well. Quonset and our other bases will ensure that we do so.

But we must look beyond our present preparations. Indeed we must look beyond the victory which we all know lies ahead. In the last great struggle we won the war but lost the peace. We must make sure that this does not occur again. And there is no better time for us to consider how we can avoid the mistakes of the past peace settlement than Armistice Day, when our thoughts inevitably turn back to the sacrifices made twenty-three years ago.

What then are the conditions upon which we can hope to build an enduring post-war peace settlement? First of all, it must not be a peace of revenge.

In our treatment of individuals we have learned that punishment of the erring is not enough. Today we try to reform the criminal and, what is even more important, to remove the conditions which led him to a life of crime. If this is good logic for the relation of society to the individual, it is even better logic for the relation of international society to individual nations which have been led into criminal activity.

But we have less altruistic reasons for not imposing a peace of punishment. Vengeance breeds revenge. The loser in each war plots vengeance against the victor; and in his turn, when he becomes the victor, imposes harsh punishment upon the conquered. Thus the vicious circle continues. War breeds vengeance. Vengeance breeds hatred. Hatred breeds revenge. Revenge breeds war. The circle must be broken if peace is ever to come either to Europe or to any other part of the world. The whole weight of the United States must be thrown upon the side of making a peace, not of revenge but of justice and righteousness.

But it is not enough merely to avoid the colossal error of a peace based upon revenge. We must take positive action to build a world free of the forces which drive men to war. This action should be both political and economic.

Political autonomy must go hand in hand with economic unity. Many of Europe's post-war difficulties arose from the fact that in freeing the minorities of the Austrian-Hungarian empire politically we broke up the economic unity of the Danube Basin. The succession states were allowed to set up a multitude of trade barriers which hindered the free interchange of goods between the manufacturing and agricultural sections of Eastern Europe. In doing this, the succession states were merely following the example of the great powers of the world. Indeed, the post-war era saw economic nationalism grow to the point where it undermined the economic structure of the world.

And in this folly it must be admitted, to our shame, the United States took the leading part. Looking back at it now, the idea that we could base an economic policy upon a plan of selling as much as possible, while buying as little as possible, seems ridiculous. It is too much to hope that these delusions will not again find advocates in the future. But we must see to it that they never again are taken seriously as a basis for our economy. Free interchange of goods, and free access to raw materials must be the cornerstone of any new world to come. The great powers—and that includes the United States and the British Empire—which dominate the material resources of the earth, must see to it that the rest of the nations get a fair share of them. This is vital to prevent any future demagogue from preaching a crusade of the "have not" nations against the "haves". And it is also vital for those nations who themselves already possess these raw materials. For if there is one thing the world has learned in the experience of the past twenty years, it is that no enduring world order can survive half poor and half rich. The world is an economic whole. It is as ridiculous to believe that a depression in one country is no concern of other nations as it would be to believe that a cancer in the hand will not eventually concern the legs and the head and eventually the heart itself.

The third basic point on which we must base any new order is the assumption by the United States of the position of world leadership to which its material resources and stable government call it. Nature abhors a vacuum as much in politics as in physics. If those to whom leadership would naturally fall evade the responsibility other nations will immediately grasp it. And if we turn our backs on world affairs, what right will we have to complain if these affairs are not managed to our satisfaction? No world order can possibly succeed if the strongest and richest nation refuses to accept any responsibility for making it succeed. If those four freedoms of which we proudly boast—freedom of speech, freedom of religion, freedom of assembly, freedom of press—really mean anything to us we have a tremendous responsibility to see to it that the other peoples of the world have an opportunity to share in them.

And, finally, any world order which we attempt to establish after the present war must rest upon more than scraps of paper. To the unthinking it may seem a paradox that a peaceful world must rest ultimately on a basis of force. Actually, of course, the paradox is more apparent than real. All stable society rests ultimately upon force. There will always be those elements who seek to acquire by force, or fraud, those things which they are unable to gain honestly. This is as true of nations as of individuals. In both cases, the more readily all the members of the community recognize their personal responsibility to use force on behalf of public order the less likely they are to be called upon to do so. In frontier days, for example, there was a strong tendency toward personal isolationism. If a man was shot down the street it was none of your business. Naturally, violence became more and more common until it was impossible for the community to endure it longer. The law-abiding members of the town rose in wrath, fought it out with the criminals, and restored order with a hempen halter. The community was preserved because its members were willing to risk their lives to suppress those who would destroy it. Once this willingness was established, it was no longer necessary to form mass posses. A single constable was enough to keep the peace. But he could do it only because the full force of the community was behind him, ready to back him up should his authority be challenged.

The same is true of nations. Because the great peace-loving powers of the earth were unwilling in the past to risk a single ship or a single man to enforce peace, they face today the loss of vast armadas and huge armies. In some cases they have lost independence itself and are now undergoing an agonizing reduction to slavery. We must establish some sort of international order in which the entire community of nations will move as one against any country which deliberately invokes bloodshed to achieve aggressive purposes.

And it is here that the United States will find its place in the world to come after the war. Sea power, the ability to say who shall and who shall not pass over the wide oceans, will be an indispensable element of the force necessary to maintain an orderly world. Here is why the growth of our sea and air power has a significance far beyond the present need. The great air field at Quonset today carries our defenses a thousand miles out to sea. Tomorrow it may be a key point in a world force whose task will be to try to banish war from the earth.

There are those who say that it is too soon to begin thinking about the world to come after the war. There are those who will say that the task of helping to establish an orderly world is too great for America to accomplish. I think they both are wrong. It cannot be too early to begin to plan a world of peace and order. These very plans are vital to our victory. If we are to conquer Fascism we must offer the peoples of the earth some alternative to the recurring terror and bloodshed which have been their lot in the past. We must show that we too can plan for the future—and plan more successfully and more enduringly than any paranoiac of the Nazi brain trust.

And neither do I believe this task too great for America to accomplish. We have always been a nation of dreamers. And our dreams have been the dreams of giants. It was a mad dream which sent Columbus half way across the world, facing unknown terrors to search for a land which all the "hard headed" people of his time knew did not exist. It was a dream of a great united nation in the New World which carried Washington, Jefferson and Adams through the dark days of the Revolution when all the "realistic" observers knew that the settlements in North America could never be more than a few colonies scattered along the coast. The men and women who crossed the mountains, the prairies and the deserts to build a nation across the length and breadth of the continents—they were dreamers. They were dreamers who built great railroads and vast dams and huge mills. They were all dreamers—but they were all Americans, and they made their dreams come true. We, too, must be dreamers if we wish ever to escape the present nightmare of world hatred, war, cruelty and death. And we must be Americans—willing to work to make our dreams come true. I believe in America. And I believe in Americans. I believe we will not fail to build a better world when the opportunity is offered. We dare not.

248

Department of State Bulletin, vol. V, p. 391

Address Delivered by the Under Secretary of State (Welles)
At Washington, November 11, 1941

Twenty-three years ago today, Woodrow Wilson addressed the Congress of the United States in order to inform the representatives of the American people of the terms of the Armistice which signalized the victorious conclusion of the first World War.

That day marked, as he then said, the attainment of a great objective: the opportunity for the setting up of "such a peace as will satisfy the longing of the whole world for disinterested justice, embodied in settlements which are based upon something much better and much more lasting than the selfish competitive interests of powerful states".

Less than five years later, shrouded in the cerements of apparent defeat, his shattered body was placed in the grave beside which we now are gathered.

He was laid to rest amid the apathy of the many and amid the sneers of those of his opponents who had, through appeal to ignorance, to passion, and to prejudice, temporarily persuaded the people of our country to reject Wilson's plea that the influence, the resources, and the power of the United States be exercised for their own security and for their own advantage, through our participation in an association of the free and self-governed peoples of the world.

And yet, when we reflect upon the course of the years that have since intervened, how rarely in human history has the vision of a statesman been so tragically and so swiftly vindicated.

Only a score of years have since elapsed, and today the United States finds itself in far greater peril than it did in 1917. The waves of world-conquest are breaking high both in the East and in the West. They are threatening, more nearly each day that passes, to engulf our own shores.

Beyond the Atlantic a sinister and pitiless conqueror has reduced more than half of Europe to abject serfdom. It is his boast that his system shall prevail even unto the ends of the earth.

In the Far East the same forces of conquest under a different guise are menacing the safety of all nations that border upon the Pacific.

Were these forces to prevail, what place in such a world would there be for the freedoms which we cherish and which we are passionately determined to maintain?

Because of these perils we are arming ourselves to an extent to which we have never armed ourselves before. We are pouring out billions upon billions of dollars in expenditures, not only in order that we may successfully defend ourselves and our sister nations of the Western Hemisphere but also, for the same ends, in order to make available the weapons of defense to Great Britain, to Russia, to China, and to all the other nations that have until now so bravely fought back the hordes of the invaders. And in so doing we are necessarily diverting the greater part of our tremendous productive capacity into channels of destruction, not those of construction, and we are piling up a debt-burden which will inevitably affect the manner of life and diminish the opportunity for progressive advancement of our children and of our children's children.

But far graver than that—for the tides are running fast—our people realize that at any moment war may be forced upon us, and if it is, the lives of all of us will have to be dedicated to preserving the freedom of the United States and to safeguarding the independence of the American people, which are more dear to us than life itself.

The heart-searching question which every American citizen must ask himself on this day of commemoration is whether the world in which we have to live would have come to this desperate pass had the United States been willing in those years which followed 1919 to play its full part in striving to bring about a new world-order based on justice and on "a steadfast concert for peace".

Would the burdens and the dangers which the American people might have had to envisage through that "partnership of democratic nations" which Woodrow Wilson then urged upon them, have represented even an infinitesimal portion of the burdens and the dangers with which they are now confronted?

Solely from the standpoint of the interest of the American people themselves, who saw straight and who thought straight 20 years ago? Was it Woodrow Wilson when he pled with his fellow Americans to insure the safety and the welfare of their country by utilizing the influence and the strength of their great Nation in joining with the other peace-loving powers of the earth in preventing the outgrowth of those conditions which have made possible this new world-upheaval? Or was it that group of self-styled, "practical, hard-headed Americans", who jeered at his idealism, who loudly proclaimed that our very system of government would be destroyed if we raised our voice in the determination of world-affairs, and who refused to admit that our security could be even remotely jeopardized if the whole of the rest of the earth was plunged into the chaos of world-anarchy?

A cycle in human events is about to come to its end.

The American people after full debate, in accordance with their democratic institutions, have determined upon their policy. They are pledged to defend their freedom and their ancient rights against every form of aggression, and to spare no effort and no sacrifice in bringing to pass the final defeat of Hitlerism and all that which that evil term implies.

We have no doubt of the ultimate victory of the forces of liberty and of human decency. But we cannot know, we cannot yet foresee, how long and how hard the road may be which leads to that new day when another armistice will be signed.

And what will come to pass thereafter?

Three months ago the President of the United States and the Prime Minister of the United Kingdom signed and made public a new charter "on which they base their hopes for a better future for the world".

The principles and the objectives set forth in that joint declaration gave new hope and new courage to millions of people throughout the earth. They saw again more clearly the why and the wherefore of this ghastly struggle. They saw once more the gleam of hope on the horizon—hope for liberty; freedom from fear and want; the satisfaction of their craving for security.

These aspirations of human beings everywhere cannot again be defrauded. Those high objectives set forth in the Charter of the Atlantic must be realized. They must be realized, quite apart from every other consideration, because of the fact that the individual interest of every man and woman in the United States will be advanced consonantly with the measure in which the world where they live is governed by right and by justice, and the measure in which peace prevails.

The American people thus have entered the Valley of Decision.

Shall we as the most powerful Nation of the earth once more stand aloof from all effective and practical forms of international concert, wherein our participation could in all human probability insure the maintenance of a peaceful world in which we can safely live?

Can we afford again to refrain from lifting a finger until gigantic forces of destruction threaten all of modern civilization, and the raucous voice of a criminal paranoiac, speaking as the spokesman for these forces from the cellar of a Munich beer hall, proclaims as his set purpose the destruction of our own security, and the annihilation of religious liberty, of political liberty, and of economic liberty throughout the earth?

The decision rests solely with the people of the United States—the power is theirs to determine the kind of world of the future in which they would live. Is it conceivable that, in enlightened self-interest, they could once more spurn that opportunity?

When the time for the making of that great decision is at hand, I believe that they will turn again for light and for inspiration to the ideals of that great seer, statesman, patriot, and lover of his fellow men—Woodrow Wilson—whose memory we here today revere.

Then, again, they will remember that great cause he once held up before their eyes—"A universal dominion of right by such a concert of free peoples as shall bring peace and safety to all nations and make the world itself at last free."

249

55 Stat. 764

Joint Resolution To Repeal Sections 2, 3, and 6 of the Neutrality Act Of 1939, and for Other Purposes

Resolved by the Senate and House of Representatives of the United States of America in Congress assembled, That section 2 of the Neutrality Act of 1939 (relating to commerce with States engaged in armed conflict), and section 3 of such Act (relating to combat areas), are hereby repealed.

SEC. 2. Section 6 of the Neutrality Act of 1939 (relating to the arming of American vessels) is hereby repealed; and, during the unlimited national emergency proclaimed by the President on May 27,

1941, the President is authorized, through such agency as he may designate, to arm, or to permit or cause to be armed, any American vessel as defined in such Act. The provisions of section 16 of the Criminal Code (relating to bonds from armed vessels on clearing) shall not apply to any such vessel.

Approved, November 17, 1941, 4:30 p.m., E.S.T.

250

711.94/2447

The Ambassador in Japan (Grew) to the Secretary of State

[Telegram : Paraphrase]

Токуо, November 17, 1941—8 p.m.
[Received November 17—2:09 p.m.]

1814. Referring to Embassy's previous telegram No. 1736 of November 3, 3 p.m., final sentence, and emphasizing the need to guard against sudden Japanese naval or military actions in such areas as are not now involved in the Chinese theater of operations. I take into account the probability of the Japanese exploiting every possible tactical advantage, such as surprise and initiative. Accordingly you are advised of not placing the major responsibility in giving prior warning upon the Embassy staff, the naval and military attachés included, since in Japan there is extremely effective control over both primary and secondary military information. We would not expect to obtain any information in advance either from personal Japanese contacts or through the press; the observation of military movements is not possible by the few Americans remaining in the country, concentrated mostly in three cities (Tokyo, Yokohama, Kobe); and with American and other foreign shipping absent from adjacent waters the Japanese are assured of the ability to send without foreign observation their troop transports in various directions. Japanese troop concentrations were reported recently by American consuls in Manchuria and Formosa, while troop dispositions since last July's general mobilization have, according to all other indications available, been made with a view to enabling the carrying out of new operations on the shortest possible notice either in the Pacific southwest or in Siberia or in both.

We are fully aware that our present most important duty perhaps is to detect any premonitory signs of naval or military operations likely in areas mentioned above and every precaution is being taken to guard against surprise. The Embassy's field of naval or military observation is restricted almost literally to what could be seen with the naked eye, and this is negligible. Therefore, you are advised, from an abundance of caution, to discount as much as possible the likelihood of our ability to give substantial warning.

GREW

251

711.94/2466

Memorandum by the Secretary of State

[WASHINGTON,] November 17, 1941.

I accompanied Ambassador Nomura and Ambassador Saburo Kurusu to the White House in order that the latter might be received by the President.

Following several minutes of an exchange of courtesies and formalities, the President brought up the more serious side by referring to the misunderstandings and matters of difference between our countries and made clear the desire of this country, and he accepted the statement of the Japanese Ambassador that it was the desire of Japan equally, to avoid war between our two countries and to bring about a settlement on a fair and peaceful basis so far as the Pacific area was concerned.

Ambassador Kurusu proceeded with one line of remarks that he kept up during the conversation and that was that we must find ways to work out an agreement to avoid trouble between our two countries. He said that all the way across the Pacific it was like a powder keg, and again he repeated that some way must be found to adjust the situation.

Ambassador Kurusu made some specious attempt to explain away the Tripartite Pact. I replied in language similar to that which I used in discussing this matter with Ambassador Nomura on November fifteenth, which need not be repeated here. I made it clear that any kind of a peaceful settlement for the Pacific area, with Japan still clinging to her Tripartite Pact with Germany, would cause the President and myself to be denounced in immeasurable terms and the peace arrangement would not for a moment be taken seriously while all the countries interested in the Pacific would redouble their efforts to arm against Japanese aggression. I emphasized the point about the Tripartite Pact and self-defense by saying that when Hitler starts on a march of invasion across the earth with ten million soldiers and thirty thousand airplanes with an official announcement that he is out for unlimited invasion objectives, this country from that time was in danger and that danger has grown each week until this minute. The result was that this country with no other motive except self-defense has recognized that danger, and has proceeded thus far to defend itself before it is too late; and that the Government of Japan says that it does not know whether this country is thus acting in self-defense or not. This country feels so profoundly the danger that it has committed itself to ten, twenty-five or fifty billions of dollars in self-defense; but when Japan is asked about whether this is self-defense, she indicates that she has no opinion on the subject—I said that I cannot get this view over to the American people; that they believe Japan must know that we are acting in self-defense and, therefore, they do not understand her present attitude. I said that he was speaking of their political difficulties and that I was thus illustrating some of our difficulties in connection with this country's relations with Japan.

The President remarked that some time ago he proclaimed a zone around this hemisphere, 300 miles out in the sea in some places and 1,100 miles in others. The President added that this was self-defense.

I then said that Ambassador Nomura and I have been proceeding on the view that the people of the United States and Japan alike are a proud and great people and there is no occasion for either to attempt to bluff the other and we would not consider that bluffing enters into our conversations, which are of genuine friendliness.

The President brought out a number of illustrations of our situation and the Japanese situation as it relates to Germany and our self-defense which serve to emphasize our position and to expose the sophistry of the Japanese position.

Ambassador Kurusu said that Germany had not up to this time requested Japan to fight; that she was serving a desirable purpose without doing so,—this must have meant that she was keeping the American and British Navies, aircraft, et cetera, diverted.

The further question of whether the United States is on the defensive in the present Pacific situation came up by some general discussion in reference to that situation by Ambassador Kurusu, and the President and I made it clear that we were not the aggressors in the Pacific but that Japan was the aggressor.

At another point I said that the belief in this country is that the Japanese formula of a new order in greater East Asia is but another name for a program to dominate entirely, politically, economically, socially and otherwise by military force all of the Pacific area; that this would include the high seas, the islands and the continents and would place every other country at the mercy of very arbitrary military rule just as the Hitler program does in Europe and the Japanese in China. The Ambassador made no particular comment.

There was some effort by Ambassador Kurusu to defend their plan of not bringing the troops out of China. Placing the Japanese on the defensive, the President said that the question ought to be worked out in a fair way considering all of the circumstances and relative merits of the matters involved; and that at a suitable stage, while we know that Japan does not wish us to mediate in any way, this Government might, so to speak, introduce Japan and China to each other and tell them to proceed with the remaining or detailed adjustments, the Pacific questions having already been determined.

Ambassador Kurusu strongly stated that it would be most difficult to bring all the troops out of China at once.

Ambassador Kurusu said that we, of course, desired to bring up both sides of matters existing between our two countries and he said that we would recall that when the Japanese went into Shantung during the World War, this Government insisted that she get out. I replied that my own country opposed a policy of this seizure of new territory by any country to the fullest extent of its ability to do so; that it declined to take a dollar of compensation or a foot of territory for itself; that it insisted that the world must turn over a new leaf in this respect or nations would be fighting always for territory and under modern methods of war would soon destroy and utterly impoverish each other; that in any event his country fared well in this respect.

The question of our recent proposal on commercial policy was brought up by us and Ambassador Kurusu said he had not examined it and that he had forgotten much of the technical side of commercial policy since he was in the Foreign Office. The President made very pertinent and timely reference to the destructive nature of armaments and the still more destructive effects of a permanent policy of armaments which always means war, devastation and destruction. He emphasized the point that there is from the long-term point of view no difference of interest between our two countries and no occasion, therefore, for serious differences.

All in all, there was nothing new brought out by the Japanese Ambassador and Ambassador Kurusu. Ambassador Kurusu constantly made the plea that there was no reason why there should be serious differences between the two countries and that ways must be found to solve the present situation. He referred to Prime Minister Tojo as being very desirous of bringing about a peaceful adjustment notwithstanding he is an Army man. The President expressed his interest and satisfaction to hear this. The President frequently parried the remarks of Ambassador Nomura and also of Ambassador Kurusu, especially in regard to the three main points of difference between our two countries. There was no effort to solve these questions at the conference. The meeting broke up with the understanding that I would meet the Japanese representatives tomorrow morning.

C[ORDELL] H[ULL]

252

711.94/2540–18⅗₃₅

Memorandum [84] *Regarding a Conversation Between the Secretary Of State, the Japanese Ambassador (Nomura), and Mr. Kurusu*

[WASHINGTON,] November 18, 1941.

The Japanese Ambassador and Mr. Kurusu called on the Secretary, by appointment made at their request, at the Department.

After some preliminary remarks the Secretary took up the question of Japan's relations with the Axis. He pointed out that the public would place their own interpretation upon the implications of a situation wherein on the one hand Japan had an agreement with us and on the other was in an alliance with the Axis powers. He said that our people do not trust Hitler and furthermore we feel that it would be inevitable that Hitler would eventually, if he was successful, get around to the Far East and double-cross Japan. The Secretary cited the instance when Germany, after having concluded an anti-Comintern pact with Japan had surprised Japan later on by entering into a non-aggression pact with Russia and finally went back on the non-aggression pact by attacking Russia. The Secretary said that he presumed Japan did not know in advance what Germany's intentions were any more than we did. The Secretary expressed great doubt that any agreement into which we entered with Japan while Japan at the same time had an alliance with Hitler would carry the confidence of our people and he emphasized that we would have to have a clear-cut agreement making self-evident our peaceful purpose, for otherwise there would be a redoubled effort by all nations to strengthen their armaments. He

---

[84] Prepared by Joseph W. Ballantine.

pointed out that we are coming out of the Philippines in 1946 and that we are now bringing our marines out of China and in this way we are trying to make a contribution to the establishment of a peaceful world based on law and order. He said that this is what we want to work out with Japan; that we had nothing to offer in the way of bargaining except our friendship. Our commercial program was one, he said, calling for a maximum production and distribution of goods. The Secretary pointed out also that we are even now engaged in efforts to induce the British Empire to reduce its Empire preferences. He said that what we desire is to put our people back to work in a way that can never be accomplished through permitting armies to overrun countries. The Secretary observed that many Japanese spokesmen had spoken of Japan's desire to have a controlling influence in Eastern Asia, but the only kind of controlling influence which was worth anything was one that could not be achieved or maintained by the sword. He dwelt briefly upon what we have accomplished in South America through our peaceful policies and through renouncing the employment of gunboats and armed forces. The Secretary made it clear that we recognized that under present emergency conditions we cannot carry out to perfection our commercial policy which must be modified to meet war conditions, but we can at least establish the principles. The Secretary said, going back to the situation with regard to Japan's relations with the Axis, that a difficult situation was created thereby as far as our public was concerned—as, for example, when telegrams of congratulations were sent to Hitler by Japanese leaders when he commits some atrocity.

The Japanese Ambassador observed that the United States and Russia were not pursuing parallel courses and yet we are aligned with Russia at the present time. He also said he appreciated very well the relations we had developed with South America but that, although Japan would like to imitate us, Japan was not in a position to be so magnanimous—as, for example, in the matter of extending substantial lend-lease aid to other countries. . . . The Secretary then added that he frankly did not know whether anything could be done in the matter of reaching a satisfactory agreement with Japan; that we can go so far but rather than go beyond a certain point it would be better for us to stand and take the consequences. The Ambassador then said that Japan is now hard-pressed and that the Secretary was well aware of how desirous Japan was to reach some agreement with the United States.

Mr. Kurusu said that he had served five years as Director of the

Commercial Bureau of the Japanese Foreign Office and that he was familiar with the developments in Japan's commercial policy. He said that the situation with respect to the Empire preferences was one of the factors which had influenced Japan to go into the Axis camp. He said that the United States was an economically powerful country and that the United States was, therefore, in a much better position than was Japan to enter into commercial bargaining. Furthermore, Japan was much more dependent than was the United States upon foreign trade. He felt that what the two Governments should now do would be to achieve something to tide over the present abnormal situation. He referred, for example, to the exchange control situation which had been developed in Japanese-occupied China and expressed the view that that situation could not be done away with in a short time. He said that perhaps after the war was over it might be possible to adopt a more liberal policy but that he was unable to promise anything on the part of his Government. The Secretary asked whether Japan could not now agree in principle on commercial policy. Mr. Kurusu made no direct reply but went on to say that in the early years of American intercourse in the Far East our main interest was in commerce and not religious and cultural activities; that we had pursued a course of idealism, but with American occupation of the Philippines the situation changed somewhat and the United States tied itself in with the European concert of nations.

Turning to the question of the Tripartite Pact, Mr. Kurusu said that he could not say that Japan would abrogate the Tripartite Pact but that Japan might do something which would "outshine" the Tripartite Pact.

The Secretary pointed out that unless peacefully minded nations now start their program of reconstruction it will be impossible to get such a program started later on because the selfish elements would get control of the situation and prevent the materialization of a liberal policy. Therefore, he said it was necessary to get the fundamental principles established so that we might begin to enable the peaceful forces, which were now demoralized, to assert a leadership. Unless we pursue such a course, the Secretary noted, we shall not be able to obtain the confidence of peacefully minded people when the time for putting into effect a reconstruction program arrives. Mr. Kurusu asked whether the Secretary had a concrete formula for dealing with Japan's relations with the Axis alliance. The Secretary made it clear that this was a matter for Japan to work out. He said that if we could get a peaceful program firmly established, Hitler ought to be asked not to embarrass us too much. He asked whether Japan could not work it out in some way which would be convincing to the American people. He said that if it goes the wrong way every peaceful nation will redouble its defensive efforts. The Secretary emphasized again that the public would be confused in regard to a survival of a relationship between Japan and the Axis while Japan had an agreement with the United States.

The Ambassador asked whether it was not important now to make some understanding to save the situation. The Secretary said he agreed but that he felt that the Tripartite Pact was inconsistent with the establishment of an understanding.

Mr. Kurusu asked what could the Secretary suggest. The Secretary said that if we mix the Tripartite Pact with an agreement with the United States it will not be possible to get many people to follow us. The Secretary said that the question arises whether Japanese statesmen desire to follow entirely peaceful courses with China or whether they desire to face two ways. The Secretary went on to say that if the Japanese should back away from adopting a clear-cut position with regard to commercial policy, with regard to a course in China consistent with peaceful principles and with regard to Japanese relations to the European war this would leave us in an indefensible position in regard to the proposed agreement. We would have to say that the Japanese Government is unable to get its politicians into line.

The Ambassador repeated that the situation in Japan was very pressing and that it was important to arrest a further deterioration of the relations between the two countries. He suggested that if this situation could now be checked an atmosphere would develop when it would be possible to move in the direction of the courses which this Government advocated. He pointed out that big ships cannot turn around too quickly, that they have to be eased around slowly and gradually.

The Secretary replied that if we should sit down and write an agreement permeated with the doctrine of force it would be found that each country would be entirely distrustful and would be piling up armaments, as countries cannot promote peace so long as they are tied in in any way with Hitler.

Mr. Kurusu pointed out that a comprehensive solution cannot be worked out immediately, that he could make no promises. He said that our freezing regulations had caused impatience in Japan and a feeling that Japan had to fight while it still could. If we could come to some settlement now, he said, it would promote an atmosphere which would be conducive to discussing fundamentals. The Secretary asked if he did not think that something could be worked out on the Tripartite Pact. The Ambassador said that he desired to emphasize that Japan would not be a cat's-paw for Germany, that Japan's purpose in entering into the Tripartite alliance was to use it for Japan's own purposes, that Japan entered the Tripartite Pact because Japan felt isolated. The Secretary observed that it would be difficult to get public opinion in this country to understand the situation as Mr. Kurusu had described it.

He then asked what the Ambassador had in mind in regard to the Chinese situation and whether the Japanese stood for no annexations, no indemnities, respect for China's sovereignty, territorial integrity and the principle of equality. The Ambassador replied in the affirmative.

The Secretary then said that while he had made this point already clear to the Ambassador he wished to make it clear also to Mr. Kurusu, that whereas the Japanese Government desired to consider our talks negotiations rather than exploratory conversations, the Secretary felt that without having first reached a real basis for negotiations, he was not in a position to go to the British or the Chinese or the other governments involved, as these governments had a rightful interest in these problems. Mr. Kurusu tried to get the Secretary to specify in just which problems each of the respective governments were interested but the Secretary said that he had not yet, for manifest reasons, discussed these problems with these other governments and anything that he might say would be just an assumption on his part. Mr. Kurusu then said that under such circumstances United States-Japanese relations would be at the mercy of Great Britain and China. The Secretary replied that he believed and must repeat that we must have something substantial in the way of a basis for an agreement to take to these governments for otherwise there would be no point in talking to them. Mr. Kurusu said that the situation was so pressing that it might get beyond our control. The Secretary agreed that that was true but he pointed out that the fact that Japan's leaders keep announcing programs based upon force adds to our difficulties. He said he would like to leave the Hitler situation to the Japanese Government for consideration.

Turning to the China situation the Secretary asked how many soldiers the Japanese wanted to retain in China. The Ambassador replied that possibly 90 per cent would be withdrawn. The Secretary asked how long the Japanese intended to keep that remaining 10 per cent in China. The Ambassador did not reply directly to this but he invited attention to the fact that under the existing Boxer

Protocol Japan was permitted to retain troops in the Peiping and Tientsin area. The Secretary pointed out that the question of the Japanese troops in China was one in which there were many elements of trouble. American interests even had suffered severely from the actions of the Japanese forces and we had a long list of such instances. The Secretary made mention of the great patience this Government had exercised in the presence of this situation. He said the situation was one in which the extremists seemed to be looking for trouble and he said that it was up to the Japanese Government to make an extra effort to take the situation by the collar. He said also that the United States and Japan had trusted each other in the past, that the present situation was one of Japan's own making and it was up to the Japanese Government to find some way of getting itself out of the difficulty in which it had placed itself. The Secretary went on to say that the situation was now exceptionally advantageous for Japan to put her factories to work in producing goods which are needed by peaceful countries if only the Japanese people could get war and invasion out of mind. The Ambassador said that our conversations had been protracted and if the American Government could only give the Japanese some hope with regard to the situation it might be helpful. He added that our country was great and strong. The Secretary replied that our Government has not made any threats and he has exercised his influence throughout to deprecate bellicose utterances in this country. He added that the Japanese armed forces in China do not appear to realize whose territory they are in and that the people in this country say that Hitler proposes to take charge of one-half of the world and Japan proposes to take charge of the other half and if they should succeed what would there be left for the United States? Mr. Kurusu suggested that Japan would have to move gradually in China, that one step might lead to another and that what was important now was to do something to enable Japan to change its course. The Secretary asked what was in Mr. Kurusu's mind. In reply to a suggestion that it was felt in Japanese circles that we have been responsible for delay the Secretary pointed out that we could more rightly accuse the Japanese of delays, that he had met with the Japanese Ambassador promptly every time the latter had asked for a meeting and had discussed matters fully with him. The Secretary added that when Japan's movement into Indochina in July took place this had caused an interruption of our conversations and it was then that the Secretary could no longer defend the continued shipments of petroleum products to Japan, especially as for the past year he had been under severe criticism in this country for not having cut off those shipments. Mr. Kurusu asked whether we wanted the *status quo ante* to be restored or what we expected Japan to do. The Secretary replied that if the Japanese could not do anything now on those three points—getting troops out of China, commercial policy and the Tripartite agreement—he could only leave to Japan what Japan could do. The Secretary said that it is our desire to see Japan help furnish a world leadership for a peaceful program and that he felt that Japan's long-swing interests were the same as our interests. The Ambassador said that he realized that our Government was suspicious of the Japanese Government but he wished to assure us that Japan wanted to settle the China affair notwithstanding the fact that Japan desired to keep a few troops in China for the time being. The Secretary then asked again what the Japanese had in mind. Mr. Kurusu said that it was Japan's intention to withdraw Japanese troops from French Indochina as soon as a just Pacific settlement should be reached and he pointed out that the Japanese Government took the Burma Road situation very seriously. The Secretary asked, if there should be a relaxation of freezing, to what extent would that enable Japan to adopt peaceful policies. He explained that what he had in mind was to enable the peaceful leaders in Japan to get control of the situation in Japan and to assert their influence. The Ambassador said that our position was unyielding and that it was Japan's unyielding attitude toward Chiang Kai-shek which had stiffened Chinese resistance against Japan. He asked whether there was any hope of a solution—some small beginning toward the realization of our high ideals. The Secretary replied that if we do not work out an agreement that the public trusts the arming of nations will go on; that the Japanese Government has a responsibility in the matter as it has created the conditions we are trying to deal with. The Ambassador then suggested the possibility of going back to the status which existed before the date in July when, following the Japanese move into southern French Indochina, our freezing measures were put into effect. The Secretary said that if we should make some modifications in our embargo on the strength of a step by Japan such as the Ambassador had mentioned we do not know whether the troops which have been withdrawn from French Indochina will be diverted to some equally objectionable movement elsewhere. The Ambassador said that what he had in mind was simply some move toward arresting the dangerous trend in our relations. The Secretary said that it would be difficult for him to get this Government to go a long way in removing the embargo unless this Government believed that Japan was definitely started on a peaceful course and had renounced purposes of conquest. The Ambassador said that the Japanese were tired of fighting China and that Japan would go as far as it could along a first step. The Secretary said that he would consult with the British and the Dutch to see what their attitude would be toward the suggestion offered by the Japanese Ambassador. In reply to a question by the Secretary the Ambassador replied that the Japanese Government was still studying the questions of commercial policy involved in our proposal of November 15. He said he assumed that what we had in mind was a program for dealing with the situation after the war. The Secretary replied in the affirmative, so far as the full operation of a sound program is concerned, but added that it should now be agreed upon as to principles.

When asked by the Secretary as to when the Ambassador would like to confer with us again the Ambassador said that he would get in touch with his Government and would communicate to the Secretary through Mr. Ballantine.

253

711.94/2540–22⁄₃₅

Memorandum [85] *Regarding a Conversation Between the Secretary Of State, the Japanese Ambassador (Nomura), and Mr. Kurusu*

[WASHINGTON,] November 20, 1941.

The Japanese Ambassador and Mr. Kurusu called at their request at the Department. Mr. Kurusu said that they had referred to their Government the suggestion which the Ambassador had made at a previous meeting in regard to a return to the status which prevailed prior to the Japanese move into south Indochina last July, and said that they had anticipated that the Japanese Government might perceive difficulty in moving troops out of Indochina in short order, but that nevertheless the Japanese Government was now prepared to offer a proposal on that basis. He said, however, that the proposal represented an amplification of the Ambassador's suggestion. He then read the proposal to the Secretary which was as follows:

[Here follows text of the proposal printed as doc. 254.]

The Secretary said that he would later examine the proposal, and that he would give sympathetic study to the proposal speaking generally, but that the comments which he was about to make were not directed specifically to the proposal but to the general situation. The

---

[85] Prepared by Joseph W. Ballantine.

Secretary said that Japan had it in its power at any moment to put an end to the present situation by deciding upon an all-out peaceful course; that at any moment Japan could bring to an end what Japan chose to call encirclement. He said that we want to have Japan develop public opinion in favor of a peaceful course. Mr. Kurusu said that if we could alleviate the situation by adopting a proposal such as the Japanese Government had just made it would help develop public opinion. The Ambassador said that the Japanese Government was clearly desirous of peace and that it was trying to show this peaceful purpose by relieving the pressure on Thailand which adoption of the proposal would accomplish.

The Secretary asked what the Ambassador thought would be the public reaction in this country if we were to announce tomorrow that we had decided to discontinue aid to Great Britain. He said that in the minds of the American people the purposes underlying our aid to China were the same as the purposes underlying aid to Great Britain; that the American people believed that there was a partnership between Hitler and Japan aimed at enabling Hitler to take charge of one-half of the world and Japan of the other half; and that the fact of the Tripartite Alliance and the continual harping by Japanese leaders upon slogans of the Nazi type such as "new order in East Asia" and "co-prosperity sphere" served to strengthen the public in their belief. What was therefore needed, the Secretary pointed out, was the manifestation by Japan of a clear purpose to pursue peaceful courses.

The Ambassador replied that there was no doubt of Japan's desire for peace, as this was clear from the eagerness of the Japanese Government to reach a settlement of the China affair—and indeed adoption of the Japanese Government's proposal that he had just presented was designed to bring about speedy settlement of the China affair. He said that the Japanese people after four years of fighting were jaded and that the slogans to which the Secretary had made reference were intended to encourage the Japanese people to push on to victory.

The Secretary said that we of course are anxious to help work this matter out for if we should get into trouble everybody was likely to get hurt.

Mr. Kurusu said that if we could go ahead with the present proposal the Japanese idea would be that we could go on working at fundamentals. He said that Japan has never pledged itself to a policy of expansion. The Secretary observed that the Chinese might have an answer to that point. The Secretary said that our people desired to avoid a repetition in east Asia of what Hitler was doing in Europe;

that our people oppose the idea of a "new order" under military control. He said also that the public in this country thinks that Japan is chained to Hitler. Mr. Kurusu asked how Japan could eradicate such a belief as Japan could not abrogate the Tripartite Pact. The Secretary said that he did not want to be disagreeable, but he felt he must observe that Japan did not talk that way about the Nine Power Treaty. Mr. Kurusu said something about the Nine Power Treaty being twenty years old and being outmoded. The Secretary said that of course he did not wish to argue the matter. He said that when the Japanese complained about our helping China the public in this country wonders what is underneath the Comintern Pact. He emphasized that Japan is doing this country tremendous injury in the Pacific; that Japanese statesmen ought to understand that we are helping China for the same reason that we are helping Britain; that we are afraid of the military elements led by Hitler. He added that the methods adopted by the Japanese military leaders in China were not unlike Hitler's methods. The Ambassador asked how we could save the situation at this juncture. The Secretary replied that he agreed upon the urgent importance of saving it, but he asked whether the Ambassador thought that the Japanese statesmen could tone down the situation in Japan. Mr. Kurusu said, with reference to the fifth point in the Japanese proposal, that he did not know whether his Government would agree but he thought that that point might be interpreted to mean that American aid to China would be discontinued as from the time that negotiations were started. The Secretary made no comment on that point but noted that in the last few days there had been marked subsidence in warlike utterances emanating from Tokyo, and he felt that it was indeed a great tribute to the Ambassador and Mr. Kurusu that so much had been accomplished in this direction within a short space of two days as he felt sure that it was their efforts which had brought this about. He said that if so much had been accomplished within the course of two days, much more could be accomplished in the course of a longer period.

No time was set for the next meeting.

254

711.94/2540—22⅖₅

Draft Proposal Handed by the Japanese Ambassador (Nomura)
To the Secretary of State on November 20, 1941

1. Both the Governments of Japan and the United States undertake not to make any armed advancement into any of the regions in

the South-eastern Asia and the Southern Pacific area excepting the part of French Indo-China where the Japanese troops are stationed at present.

2. The Japanese Government undertakes to withdraw its troops now stationed in French Indo-China upon either the restoration of peace between Japan and China or the establishment of an equitable peace in the Pacific area.

In the meantime the Government of Japan declares that it is prepared to remove its troops now stationed in the southern part of French Indo-China to the northern part of the said territory upon the conclusion of the present arrangement which shall later be embodied in the final agreement.

3. The Government of Japan and the United States shall co-operate with a view to securing the acquisition of those goods and commodities which the two countries need in Netherlands East Indies.

4. The Governments of Japan and the United States mutually undertake to restore their commercial relations to those prevailing prior to the freezing of the assets.

The Government of the United States shall supply Japan a required quantity of oil.

5. The Government of the United States undertakes to refrain from such measures and actions as will be prejudicial to the endeavors for the restoration of general peace between Japan and China.

255

711.94/2540–27⅗5

Memorandum [86] *Regarding a Conversation Between the Secretary Of State, the Japanese Ambassador* (*Nomura*), *and Mr. Kurusu*

[WASHINGTON,] November 22, 1941.

The Japanese Ambassador and Mr. Kurusu called at the Secretary's apartment by appointment made at the request of the Ambassador. The Secretary said that he had called in the representatives of certain other governments concerned in the Pacific area and that there had been a discussion of the question of whether things (meaning Japanese peaceful pledges, et cetera) could be developed in such a way that there could be a relaxation to some extent of freezing. The Secretary said that these representatives were interested in the sug-

---

[86] Prepared by Joseph W. Ballantine.

gestion and there was a general feeling that the matter could all be settled if the Japanese could give us some satisfactory evidences that their intentions were peaceful.

The Secretary said that in discussing the situation with the representatives of these other countries he found that there had arisen in their minds the same kind of misgivings that had troubled him in the course of the conversations with the Japanese Ambassador. He referred to the position in which the Japanese Government had left the Ambassador and the Secretary as they were talking of peace when it made its move last July into Indochina. He referred also to the mounting oil purchases by Japan last Spring when the conversations were in progress, to the fact that he had endured public criticism for permitting those shipments because he did not wish to prejudice a successful outcome to the conversations and to the fact that that oil was not used for normal civilian consumption.

The Secretary went on to say that the Japanese press which is adopting a threatening tone gives him no encouragement and that no Japanese statesmen are talking about a peaceful course, whereas in the American press advocacy of a peaceful course can always get a hearing. He asked why was there not some Japanese statesman backing the two Ambassadors by preaching peace. The Secretary pointed out that if the United States and other countries should see Japan coming along a peaceful course there would be no question about Japan's obtaining all the materials she desired; that the Japanese Government knows that.

The Secretary said that while no decisions were reached today in regard to the Japanese proposals he felt that we would consider helping Japan out on oil for civilian requirements only as soon as the Japanese Government could assert control of the situation in Japan as it relates to the policy of force and conquest. He said that if the Ambassador could give him any further assurances in regard to Japan's peaceful intentions it would help the Secretary in talking with senators and other persons in this country.

Mr. Kurusu said it was unfortunate that there had been a special session of the Diet at this time, as the efforts of the Government to obtain public support had brought out in sharp relief the abnormal state of the present temper of the Japanese people who had been affected by four years of war and by our freezing measures.

The Secretary asked to what extent in the Ambassador's opinion did the firebrand attitude prevail in the Japanese army. Mr. Kurusu said that it took a great deal of persuasion to induce the army to abandon a position once taken, but that both he and the Ambassador had been pleasantly surprised when the Japanese army acceded to their suggestion in regard to offering to withdraw the Japanese troops from southern Indochina. He said he thought this was an encouraging sign, but that nevertheless the situation was approaching an explosive point.

The Secretary asked whether it was not possible for a Japanese statesman now to come out and say that Japan wanted peace; that while there was much confusion in the world because of the war situation Japan would like to have a peace which she did not have to fight for to obtain and maintain; that the United States says it stands for such ideas; and that Japan might well ask the United States for a show-down on this question.

The Ambassador said he did not have the slightest doubt that Japan desired peace. He then cited the popular agitation in Japan following the conclusion of the peace settlement with Russia in 1905, as pointing to a difficulty in the way of publicly backing a conciliatory course.

The Secretary asked whether there was any way to get Japanese statesmen to approach the question before us with real appreciation of the situation with which we are dealing including the question of finding a way to encourage the governments of other powers concerned in the Pacific area to reach some trade arrangement with Japan. He pointed out that Japan's Indochina move, if repeated, would further give a spurt to arming and thus undo all the work that he and the Ambassador had done. He suggested that if the United States and the other countries should supply Japan with goods in moderate amounts at the beginning those countries would be inclined to satisfy Japan more fully later on if and as Japan found ways in actual practice of demonstrating its peaceful intentions. He said that one move on Japan's part might kill dead our peace effort, whereas it would be easy to persuade the other countries to relax their export restrictions if Japan would be satisfied with gradual relaxation.

Mr. Kurusu said that at best it would take some time to get trade moving. The Secretary replied that he understood this but that it would be difficult to get other countries to understand until Japan could convince those countries that it was committed to peaceful ways. Mr. Kurusu said that some immediate relief was necessary and that if the patient needed a thousand dollars to effect a cure an offer of three hundred dollars would not accomplish the purpose. The Secretary commented that if the Japanese Government was as weak as to need all that had been asked for, nothing was likely to save it.

Mr. Kurusu said that Japan's offer to withdraw its forces from southern Indochina would set a reverse movement in motion.

The Secretary said that the Japanese were not helping as they should help in the present situation in which they had got themselves but were expecting us to do the whole thing.

Mr. Kurusu asked what was the idea of the American Government.

The Secretary replied that although the Japanese proposal was addressed to the American Government he had thought it advisable to see whether the other countries would contribute and he found that they would like to move gradually. The effect of an arrangement between these countries and Japan would be electrifying by showing that Japan had committed herself to go along a peaceful course.

Mr. Kurusu asked what Japan could do. The Secretary replied that if, for example, he should say that he agreed to enter into a peaceful settlement provided that there should be occasional exceptions and qualifications he could not expect to find peaceful-minded nations interested.

The Secretary then asked whether his understanding was correct that the Japanese proposal was intended as a temporary step to help organize public opinion in Japan and that it was intended to continue the conversations looking to the conclusion of a comprehensive agreement. Mr. Kurusu said yes.

Mr. Kurusu asked whether the Secretary had any further suggestions. The Secretary replied that he did not have in mind any suggestions and that he did not know what amounts of exports the various countries would be disposed to release to Japan. He said that Japan made the situation very difficult, for if Japan left her forces in Indochina, whether in the north, east, south or west, she would be able to move them over night, and that therefore this would not relieve the apprehensions of neighboring countries. The British, for example, would not be able to move one warship away from Singapore.

The Ambassador argued that it would take many days to move troops from northern Indochina to southern Indochina, and he stated that the Japanese desired the troops in northern Indochina in order to bring about a settlement with China. He said that after the settlement of the China affair Japan promised to bring the troops out of Indochina altogether.

The Secretary emphasized again that he could not consider this, that also uneasiness would prevail as long as the troops remained in Indochina, and commented that Japan wanted the United States to do all the pushing toward bringing about a peaceful settlement; that they should get out of Indochina.

Mr. Kurusu observed that the Japanese Foreign Minister had told

Ambassador Grew that we seemed to expect that all the concessions should be made by the Japanese side.

The Secretary rejoined that Mr. Kurusu had overlooked the fact that in July the Japanese had gone into Indochina. He added that the United States had remained from the first in the middle of the road, that it was the Japanese who had strayed away from the course of law and order, and that they should not have to be paid to come back to a lawful course.

Mr. Kurusu said that this country's denunciation of the commercial treaty had caused Japan to be placed in a tight corner.

The Secretary observed that Japan had cornered herself; that we had been preaching for the last nine years that militarism was sapping everybody and that if the world were to be plunged into another war there would not be much left of the people anywhere. He said that in 1934 he had told Ambassador Saito that Japan was planning an overlordship in East Asia. The Secretary added that he had tried to persuade Hitler that participation by him in a peaceful course would assure him of what he needed. The Secretary said it was a pity that Japan could not do just a few small peaceful things to help tide over the situation.

Mr. Kurusu asked what the Secretary meant. The Secretary replied that the major portion of our fleet was being kept in the Pacific and yet Japan asked us not to help China. He said we must continue to aid China. He said it was little enough that we were actually doing to help China. The Ambassador commented that our moral influence was enabling Chiang to hold out.

The Secretary said that a peaceful movement could be started in thirty or forty days by moving gradually, and yet Japan pushed everything it wanted all at once into its proposal. The Ambassador explained that Japan needed a quick settlement and that its psychological value would be great.

The Secretary said that he was discouraged, that he felt that he had rendered a real contribution when he had called in the representatives of the other countries, but that he could only go a certain distance. He said he thought nevertheless that if this matter should move in the right way peace would become infectious. He pointed also to the danger arising from blocking progress by injecting the China matter in the proposal, as the carrying out of such a point in the Japanese proposal would effectually prevent the United States from ever successfully extending its good offices in a peace settlement between Japan and China. He said this could not be considered now.

There then ensued some further but inconclusive discussion of the troop situation in Indochina, the Secretary still standing for withdrawal, after which the Ambassador reverted to the desire of the Japanese Government to reach a quick settlement and asked whether we could not say what points in the Japanese proposal we would accept and what points we desired to have modified.

The Secretary emphasized that there was no way in which he could carry the whole burden and suggested that it would be helpful if the Japanese Government could spend a little time preaching peace. He said that if the Japanese could not wait until Monday [87] before having his answer there was nothing he could do about it as he was obliged to confer again with the representatives of the other governments concerned after they had had an opportunity to consult with their governments. He repeated that we were doing our best, but emphasized that unless the Japanese were able to do a little there was no use in talking.

The Ambassador disclaimed any desire to press the Secretary too hard for an answer, agreed that the Secretary had always been most considerate in meeting with the Ambassador whenever an appointment had been requested, and said that the Japanese would be quite ready to wait until Monday.

The Secretary said he had in mind taking up with the Ambassador sometime a general and comprehensive program which we had been engaged in developing and which involved collaboration of other countries.

The Ambassador said that the Japanese had in mind negotiating a bilateral agreement with us to which other powers could subsequently give their adherence.

256

711.94/2504

Memorandum [88] *Regarding a Conversation Between the Secretary Of State, the Japanese Ambassador (Nomura), and Mr. Kurusu*

[WASHINGTON,] November 26, 1941.

The Japanese Ambassador and Mr. Kurusu called by appointment at the Department. The Secretary handed each of the Japanese copies of an outline of a proposed basis of an agreement between the United States and Japan [89] and an explanatory oral statement.[90]

---

[87] November 24, 1941.
[88] Prepared by Joseph W. Ballantine.
[89] Doc. 257.
[90] Doc. 258.

After the Japanese had read the documents, Mr. Kurusu asked whether this was our reply to their proposal for a *modus vivendi.* The Secretary replied that we had to treat the proposal as we did, as there was so much turmoil and confusion among the public both in the United States and in Japan. He reminded the Japanese that in the United States we have a political situation to deal with just as does the Japanese Government, and he referred to the fire-eating statements which have been recently coming out of Tokyo, which he said had been causing a natural reaction among the public in this country. He said that our proposed agreement would render possible practical measures of financial cooperation, which, however, were not referred to in the outline for fear that this might give rise to misunderstanding. He also referred to the fact that he had earlier in the conversations acquainted the Ambassador of the ambition that had been his of settling the immigration question but that the situation had so far prevented him from realizing that ambition.

Mr. Kurusu offered various depreciatory comments in regard to the proposed agreement. He noted that in our statement of principles there was a reiteration of the Stimson doctrine. He objected to the proposal for multilateral non-aggression pacts and referred to Japan's bitter experience of international organizations, citing the case of the award against Japan by the Hague tribunal in the Perpetual Leases matter. He went on to say that the Washington Conference Treaties had given a wrong idea to China, that China had taken advantage of them to flaunt Japan's rights. He said he did not see how his Government could consider paragraphs (3) and (4) of the proposed agreement and that if the United States should expect that Japan was to take off its hat to Chiang Kai-shek and propose to recognize him Japan could not agree. He said that if this was the idea of the American Government he did not see how any agreement was possible.

The Secretary asked whether this matter could not be worked out.

Mr. Kurusu said that when they reported our answer to their Government it would be likely to throw up its hands. He noted that this was a tentative proposal without commitment, and suggested that it might be better if they did not refer it to their Government before discussing its contents further informally here.

The Secretary suggested that they might wish to study the documents carefully before discussing them further. He repeated that we were trying to do our best to keep the public from becoming uneasy as a result of their being harangued. He explained that in the light of all that has been said in the press, our proposal was as far as we would go at this time in reference to the Japanese proposal; that there was so much confusion among the public that it was necessary to bring about some clarification; that we have reached a stage when the public has lost its perspective and that it was therefore necessary to draw up a document which would present a complete picture of our position by making provision for each essential point involved.

The Secretary then referred to the oil question. He said that public feeling was so acute on that question that he might almost be lynched if he permitted oil to go freely to Japan. He pointed out that if Japan should fill Indochina with troops our people would not know what lies ahead in the way of a menace to the countries to the south and west. He reminded the Japanese that they did not know what tremendous injury they were doing to us by keeping immobilized so many forces in countries neighboring Indochina. He explained that we are primarily out for our permanent futures, and the question of Japanese troops in Indochina affects our direct interests.

Mr. Kurusu reverted to the difficulty of Japan's renouncing its support of Wang Ching-wei. The Secretary pointed out that Chiang Kai-shek had made an outstanding contribution in bringing out national spirit in China and expressed the view that the Nanking regime had not asserted itself in a way that would impress the world. Mr. Kurusu agreed with what the Secretary had said about Chiang, but observed that the question of the standing of the Nanking regime was a matter of opinion. His arguments on this as well as on various other points were specious, and unconvincing.

The Ambassador took the occasion to observe that sometimes statesmen of firm conviction fail to get sympathizers among the public; that only wise men could see far ahead and sometimes suffered martyrdom; but that life's span was short and one could only do his duty. The Ambassador then asked whether there was no other possibility and whether they could not see the President.

The Secretary replied that he had no doubt that the President would be glad to see them at any time.

Mr. Kurusu said that he felt that our response to their proposal could be interpreted as tantamount to meaning the end, and asked whether we were not interested in a *modus vivendi*.

The Secretary replied that we had explored that. Mr. Kurusu asked whether it was because the other powers would not agree; but the Secretary replied simply that he had done his best in the way of exploration.

The Ambassador when rising to go raised the question of publicity. The Secretary replied that he had it in mind to give the press something of the situation tomorrow, and asked what the Ambassador thought. The Ambassador said that they did not wish to question the Secretary's right to give out what he desired in regard to the American proposal. The Ambassador said he would like to have Mr. Wakasugi call on Mr. Ballantine on Thursday to discuss further details.

257

711.94/2504

Document Handed by the Secretary of State to the Japanese Ambassador (Nomura)

WASHINGTON, November 26, 1941.

OUTLINE OF PROPOSED BASIS FOR AGREEMENT BETWEEN THE UNITED STATES AND JAPAN

SECTION I

Draft Mutual Declaration of Policy

The Government of the United States and the Government of Japan both being solicitous for the peace of the Pacific affirm that their national policies are directed toward lasting and extensive peace throughout the Pacific area, that they have no territorial designs in that area, that they have no intention of threatening other countries or of using military force aggressively against any neighboring nation, and that, accordingly, in their national policies they will actively support and give practical application to the following fundamental principles upon which their relations with each other and with all other governments are based:

(1) The principle of inviolability of territorial integrity and sovereignty of each and all nations.

(2) The principle of non-interference in the internal affairs of other countries.

(3) The principle of equality, including equality of commercial opportunity and treatment.

(4) The principle of reliance upon international cooperation and conciliation for the prevention and pacific settlement of controversies and for improvement of international conditions by peaceful methods and processes.

The Government of Japan and the Government of the United States have agreed that toward eliminating chronic political instability, preventing recurrent economic collapse, and providing a basis for peace, they will actively support and practically apply the following principles in their economic relations with each other and with other nations and peoples:

(1) The principle of non-discrimination in international commercial relations.

(2) The principle of international economic cooperation and abolition of extreme nationalism as expressed in excessive trade restrictions.

(3) The principle of non-discriminatory access by all nations to raw material supplies.

(4) The principle of full protection of the interests of consuming countries and populations as regards the operation of of international commodity agreements.

(5) The principle of establishment of such institutions and arrangements of international finance as may lend aid to the essential enterprises and the continuous development of all countries and may permit payments through processes of trade consonant with the welfare of all countries.

Section II

Steps To Be Taken by the Government of the United States and by the Government of Japan

The Government of the United States and the Government of Japan propose to take steps as follows:

1. The Government of the United States and the Government of Japan will endeavor to conclude a multilateral non-aggression pact among the British Empire, China, Japan, the Netherlands, the Soviet Union, Thailand and the United States.

2. Both Governments will endeavor to conclude among the American, British, Chinese, Japanese, the Netherland and Thai Governments an agreement whereunder each of the Governments would pledge itself to respect the territorial integrity of French Indochina and, in the event that there should develop a threat to the territorial integrity of Indochina, to enter into immediate consultation with a view to taking such measures as may be deemed necessary and advisable to meet the threat in question. Such agreement would provide also that each of the Governments party to the agreement would not seek or accept preferential treatment in its trade or economic relations with Indochina and would use its influence to obtain for each of the signatories equality of treatment in trade and commerce with French Indochina.

3. The Government of Japan will withdraw all military, naval, air and police forces from China and from Indochina.

811

4. The Government of the United States and the Government of Japan will not support—militarily, politically, economically—any government or regime in China other than the National Government of the Republic of China with capital temporarily at Chungking.

5. Both Governments will give up all extraterritorial rights in China, including rights and interests in and with regard to international settlements and concessions, and rights under the Boxer Protocol of 1901.

Both Governments will endeavor to obtain the agreement of the British and other governments to give up extraterritorial rights in China, including rights in international settlements and in concessions and under the Boxer Protocol of 1901.

6. The Government of the United States and the Government of Japan will enter into negotiations for the conclusion between the United States and Japan of a trade agreement, based upon reciprocal most-favored-nation treatment and reduction of trade barriers by both countries, including an undertaking by the United States to bind raw silk on the free list.

7. The Government of the United States and the Government of Japan will, respectively, remove the freezing restrictions on Japanese funds in the United States and on American funds in Japan.

8. Both Governments will agree upon a plan for the stabilization of the dollar-yen rate, with the allocation of funds adequate for this purpose, half to be supplied by Japan and half by the United States.

9. Both Governments will agree that no agreement which either has concluded with any third power or powers shall be interpreted by it in such a way as to conflict with the fundamental purpose of this agreement, the establishment and preservation of peace throughout the Pacific area.

10. Both Governments will use their influence to cause other governments to adhere to and to give practical application to the basic political and economic principles set forth in this agreement.

258

711.94/2504

Oral Statement Handed by the Secretary of State to the Japanese Ambassador (Nomura)

WASHINGTON, November 26, 1941.

The representatives of the Government of the United States and of the Government of Japan have been carrying on during the past several months informal and exploratory conversations for the purpose of arriving at a settlement if possible of questions relating to the entire Pacific area based upon the principles of peace, law and order and fair dealing among nations. These principles include the principle of inviolability of territorial integrity and sovereignty of each and all nations; the principle of non-interference in the internal affairs of other countries; the principle of equality, including equality of commercial opportunity and treatment; and the principle of reliance upon international cooperation and conciliation for the prevention and pacific settlement of controversies and for improvement of international conditions by peaceful methods and processes.

It is believed that in our discussions some progress has been made in reference to the general principles which constitute the basis of a peaceful settlement covering the entire Pacific area. Recently the Japanese Ambassador has stated that the Japanese Government is desirous of continuing the conversations directed toward a comprehensive and peaceful settlement in the Pacific area; that it would be helpful toward creating an atmosphere favorable to the successful outcome of the conversations if a temporary *modus vivendi* could be agreed upon to be in effect while the conversations looking to a peaceful settlement in the Pacific were continuing. On November 20 the Japanese Ambassador communicated to the Secretary of State proposals in regard to temporary measures to be taken respectively by the Government of Japan and by the Government of the United States, which measures are understood to have been designed to accomplish the purposes above indicated.

The Government of the United States most earnestly desires to contribute to the promotion and maintenance of peace and stability in the Pacific area, and to afford every opportunity for the continuance of discussions with the Japanese Government directed toward working out a broad-gauge program of peace throughout the Pacific area. The proposals which were presented by the Japanese Ambassador on November 20 contain some features which, in the opinion of this Government, conflict with the fundamental principles which form a part of the general settlement under consideration and to which each Government has declared that it is committed. The Government of the United States believes that the adoption of such proposals would not be likely to contribute to the ultimate objectives of ensuring peace under law, order and justice in the Pacific area, and it suggests that further effort be made to resolve our divergences of views in regard to the practical application of the fundamental principles already mentioned.

With this object in view the Government of the United States offers for the consideration of the Japanese Government a plan of a broad but simple settlement covering the entire Pacific area as one practical exemplification of a program which this Government envisages as something to be worked out during our further conversations.

The plan therein suggested represents an effort to bridge the gap between our draft of June 21, 1941 and the Japanese draft of September 25 by making a new approach to the essential problems underlying a comprehensive Pacific settlement. This plan contains provisions dealing with the practical application of the fundamental principles which we have agreed in our conversations constitute the only sound basis for worthwhile international relations. We hope that in this way progress toward reaching a meeting of minds between our two Governments may be expedited.

259

711.94/2507

Memorandum by the Secretary of State

[WASHINGTON,] November 27, 1941.

The two Japanese Ambassadors called at their request. The President opened the conversation with some reference to German international psychology. Ambassador Nomura then said that they were disappointed about the failure of any agreement regarding a *modus vivendi*. The President proceeded to express the grateful appreciation of himself and of this Government to the peace element in Japan which has worked hard in support of the movement to establish a peaceful settlement in the Pacific area. He made it clear that we were not overlooking for a moment what that element has done and is ready still to do. The President added that in the United States most people want a peaceful solution of all matters in the Pacific area. He said that he does not give up yet although the situation is serious and that fact should be recognized. He then referred to the conversations since April which have been carried on here with the Japanese Ambassador in an attempt to deal with the difficulties. The President added that some of these difficulties at times have the effect of a cold bath on the United States Government and people, such as the recent occupation of Indochina by the Japanese and recent movements and utterances of the Japanese slanting wholly in the direction of conquest by force and ignoring the whole question of a peaceful settlement and the principles underlying it. The President then made the following points:

(1) We have been very much disappointed that during the course of these very important conversations Japanese leaders have continued to express opposition to the fundamental principles of peace and order which constitute the central spirit of the conversations which we have been carrying on. This attitude on the part of Japanese leaders has naturally created an atmosphere both in this country and abroad which has added greatly to the difficulty of making mutually satisfactory progress in the conversations.

(2) We have been very patient in our dealing with the whole Far Eastern situation. We are prepared to continue to be patient if Japan's courses of action permit continuance of such an attitude on our part. We still have hope that there may be worked out a peaceful settlement in the entire Pacific area of the character we have been discussing. The temper of public opinion in this country has become of such a character and the big issues at stake in the world today have become so sharply outlined that this country cannot bring about any substantial relaxation in its economic restrictions unless Japan gives this country some clear manifestation of peaceful intent. If that occurs, we can also take some steps of a concrete character designed to improve the general situation.

(3) We remain convinced that Japan's own best interests will not be served by following Hitlerism and courses of aggression, and that Japan's own best interests lie along the courses which we have outlined in the current conversations. If, however, Japan should unfortunately decide to follow Hitlerism and courses of aggression, we are convinced beyond any shadow of doubt that Japan will be the ultimate loser.

The President emphasized that the leaders in Japan had obstructed this whole movement involved in the conversations here. He said that having been in war for four years the Japanese people need to have a peace tempo; that war does not help us nor would it help Japan.

Ambassador Kurusu proceeded to say that he had been here for ten days in an endeavor to discuss and develop a peaceful arrangement; that the trouble was not with the fundamentals so much as with their application. Referring to a recent remark of the President about introducing Japan and China, Kurusu asked to know who would request the President to introduce these two governments. The President promptly replied "both sides". He then gave an illustration of his dealing with some strike conditions when neither side desired to request the Mediation Board to bring up the matter but were anxious, without saying so, for the President to do so. I referred to the 250,000 carpetbaggers that had gone into north China following the army and said that they had seized other peoples' rights and properties and located there as the carpetbaggers had done in the south after the Civil War and added that they had no rights over there and ought to give up the property they took from other people and get out.

The President, referring to the efforts of Japan to colonize countries that they conquer, said that Germany would completely fail because she did not have enough top people to govern the fifteen or more conquered countries in Europe and that this would cause Germany to fail in her present movements; that second class people cannot run fifteen captured countries.

The President further referred to the matter of encirclement that Japan has been alleging. He pointed out that the Philippines were being encircled by Japan so far as that is concerned.

I made it clear that unless the opposition to the peace element in control of the Government should make up its mind definitely to act and talk and move in a peaceful direction, no conversations could or would get anywhere as has been so clearly demonstrated; that everyone knows that the Japanese slogans of co-prosperity, new order in East Asia and a controlling influence in certain areas, are all terms to express in a camouflaged manner the policy of force and conquest by Japan and the domination by military agencies of the political, economic, social and moral affairs of each of the populations conquered; and that so long as they move in that direction and continue to increase their cultural relations, military and otherwise with Hitler through such instruments as the Anti-Comintern Pact and the Tripartite Pact, et cetera, et cetera, there could not be any real progress made on a peaceful course.

C[ordell] H[ull]

260

711.94/2539

Memorandum by the Secretary of State Regarding a Conversation With the British Ambassador (Halifax)

[Extract]

[Washington,] November 29, 1941.

I expressed the view that the diplomatic part of our relations with Japan was virtually over and that the matter will now go to the officials of the Army and the Navy with whom I have talked and to whom I have given my views for whatever they are worth. Speaking in great confidence, I said that it would be a serious mistake for our country and other countries interested in the Pacific situation to make plans of resistance without including the possibility that Japan may move suddenly and with every possible element of surprise and spread out over considerable areas and capture certain positions and posts before the peaceful countries interested in the Pacific would have time to confer and formulate plans to meet these new conditions; that this would be on the theory that the Japanese recognize that their course of unlimited conquest now renewed all along the line probably is a desperate gamble and requires the utmost boldness and risk.

I also said to the Ambassador that a calm deliberate Japanese Government would more than ever desire to wait another thirty days to see whether the German Army is driven out of Russia by winter. I added that the extremist fire-eating elements in Japan, who have preached a general forward movement supported by the Army and Navy have influenced a vast portion of the Japanese public to clamor for such a movement, would probably take no serious notice of the Russian-German situation, but would go forward in this desperate undertaking which they have advocated for some time; that at least it would be a mistake not to consider this possibility as entirely real, rather than to assume that they would virtually halt and engage in some movements into Thailand and into the Burma Road while waiting the results on the Russian front.

C[ORDELL] H[ULL]

261

711.94/2594–⅛

Memorandum [91] *Regarding a Conversation Between the Secretary Of State, the Japanese Ambassador (Nomura), and Mr. Kurusu*

[WASHINGTON,] December 1, 1941.

The Japanese Ambassador and Mr. Kurusu called at their request at the Department. Mr. Kurusu said that he noted that the President was returning to Washington in advance of his schedule and inquired what the reason for this was. The Secretary indicated that one of the factors in the present situation was the loud talk of the Japanese

---

[91] Prepared by Joseph W. Ballantine.

Prime Minister. The Secretary added that the Prime Minister seemed to be in need of advice which would deter him from indulging in such talk at a time when the Ambassador was here talking about good relations. The Secretary then asked the Japanese how they felt about the general trend in the world situation, especially the situation in Libya and Russia. The Japanese Ambassador replied to the effect that their attention had been largely engrossed in the situation as between the United States and Japan. The Secretary observed that from our point of view we felt much interest in and were very much encouraged about the news from Libya and Russia and it looked as if we might be turning the corner into a more favorable situation.

The Ambassador and Mr. Kurusu endeavored to convince the Secretary that in this country we seem to take a more serious view of the Japanese Prime Minister's utterances than was warranted. Mr. Kurusu said that what the Prime Minister had done was nothing more than a ten-minute broadcast. The Secretary pointed out that a broadcast was all the more effective. Mr. Kurusu said that the Prime Minister had been misquoted and asked whether we had heard anything from Ambassador Grew. The Secretary replied that we had heard nothing from Ambassador Grew and that we felt that the Associated Press was reliable and that we should give credence to its reports of what the Prime Minister said. Mr. Kurusu said that Japanese news services did not always correctly translate statements into English.

The Secretary said that he had been talking peace for nine months with the Japanese Ambassador, both of them acting in entire good faith. He said that during all the time that Matsuoka was holding forth on the Tripartite Alliance and engaging in general bluster, the Secretary had ignored all of that. Then while the talks were in progress last July the Japanese moved suddenly into Indochina without any advance notice to this Government, and possibly the Ambassador was not informed of the Japanese Government's intention in advance. Then, too, the Secretary said, the Japanese press had been conducting a blustering campaign against the United States. The Secretary said that this Government had no idea of trying to bluff Japan and he saw no occasion for Japan's trying to bluff us, and he emphasized that there is a limit beyond which we cannot go further and that one of these days we may reach a point when we cannot keep on as we are.

Mr. Kurusu said that the Japanese Government had been very much surprised at the reaction in this country to the Prime Minister's statements and he would see to it that the Secretary was given a correct translation of the Prime Minister's statements. He said he hoped we would get something from Ambassador Grew. He then said that he was pleased to inform the Secretary that the document we had given them on November 26 had been communicated to the Japanese Government, that the Japanese Government is giving the case study, and that within a few days the Japanese Government's observation thereon would be communicated to us. He then said that the Japanese Government believed that the proposal which they submitted to us on November 20 was equitable and that full consideration had been given therein to the points of view taken by both sides in the conversations; that the Japanese Government finds it difficult to understand the position taken by the Government of the United States; and that the proposal which we had communicated to them seemed to fail to take cognizance of the actual conditions in the Far East. He said that his Government directed him to inquire what was the ultimate aim of the United States in the conversations and to request this Government to make "deep reflection of this matter". Mr. Kurusu said that the Japanese offer to withdraw its troops from southern Indochina still stands; that Japan has shown its extreme desire to promote a peaceful settlement.

The Secretary replied that we had to take into account the bellicose utterances emanating from Tokyo and that never would there be possible any peaceful arrangements if such arrangements have to be based upon principles of force. He pointed out that the methods the Japanese are using in China are similar to those which are being adopted by Hitler to subjugate Europe. The Secretary said that he had called attention to that during the progress of our conversations and that we cannot lose sight of the movement by Hitler to seize one-half of the world. He said that we believe that the Japanese militarists are moving in a similar direction to seize the other half of the earth, and that this Government cannot yield to anything of that kind. He explained that this is why we desire to work things out in a way that would promote peace, stability and prosperity and that this is why he has thus far made no complaint, notwithstanding the fact that the Japanese press has heaped filthy abuse on this country.

The Ambassador expressed the view that as a matter of fact there is not much difference between Japan's idea of a co-prosperity sphere and Pan-Americanism, except that Japanese methods may be more primitive. He denied that it was Japan's purpose to use force. The Secretary asked whether, when the Japanese Government was moving on the territory of other countries, inch by inch by force, the

Ambassador thought that this was a part of our policy. The Ambassador replied that Japan was motivated by self-defense in the same way as Britain had been motivated by her acts, for example, in Syria; that Japan needed rice and other materials at a time when she was being shut off by the United States and other countries and she had no alternative but to endeavor to obtain access to these materials.

The Secretary observed that the Japanese are saying that the United States has no right to interfere with what Japan is doing in eastern Asia; that when the Japanese keep their troops in Indochina this constitutes a menace to the South Sea area, irrespective of where in Indochina the troops are stationed; that the stationing of these troops in Indochina is making it necessary for the United States and its friends to keep large numbers of armed forces immobilized in east Asia, and in this way Japan's acts were having the effect of aiding Hitler. The Secretary reminded the Ambassador that he had made it clear to the Ambassador that we could not sit still while such developments were taking place.

The Ambassador commented that today war is being conducted through the agency of economic weapons, that Japan was being squeezed, and that Japan must expand to obtain raw materials. The Secretary pointed out that we were selling Japan oil until Japan suddenly moved into Indochina; that he could not defend such a situation indefinitely; and that the United States would give Japan all she wanted in the way of materials if Japan's military leaders would only show that Japan intended to pursue a peaceful course. The Secretary emphasized that we do not propose to go into partnership with Japan's military leaders; that he has not heard one whisper of peace from the Japanese military, only bluster and blood-curdling threats. The Secretary added that he had been subjected to very severe criticism for his policy of patience but that he would not mind if only the Japanese Government could back him up.

The Secretary went on to enumerate various points in the Japanese proposal of November 20. He reminded the Ambassador that on November 22 he had promptly told the Ambassador that we could not sell oil to the Japanese Navy, although we might be prepared to consider the release of some oil for civilian purposes. He made it clear that this Government was anxious to help settle the China affair if the Japanese could reach a settlement in accordance with the basic principles which we had discussed in our conversations, and that under such circumstances we would be glad to offer our good offices. The Secretary went on to say that under existing circumstances, when Japan was tied in with the Tripartite Pact, Japan might just as well ask us to cease aiding Britain as to cease aiding China. He emphasized again that we can't overlook Japan's digging herself into Indochina, the effect of which is to create an increasing menace to America and her friends; that we can't continue to take chances on the situation; and that we will not allow ourselves to be kicked out of the Pacific. The Secretary called attention to reports that we have received from the press and other sources of heavy Japanese troop movements into Indochina and endeavored to make it clear that, when a large Japanese army is anywhere in Indochina, we have to give that situation all the more attention when Japanese statesmen say that they will drive us out of east Asia. He pointed out that we cannot be sure what the Japanese military leaders are likely to do, that we do not know where the Japanese Army intends to land its forces, and that for this reason we cannot sit still but will have to puzzle these things out in some way. The Secretary explained that this situation had been very painful to him and he did not know whether the Ambassador could do anything in the matter of influencing the Japanese Government. Mr. Kurusu said that he felt it was a shame that nothing should come out of the efforts which the conversations of several months had represented. He said he felt that the two sides had once been near an agreement except for two or three points, but that our latest proposals seem to carry the two sides further away than before.

The Secretary pointed out that every time we get started in the direction of progress the Japanese military does something to overturn us. The Secretary expressed grave doubts whether we could now get ahead in view of all the threats that had been made. He pointed out that the acts of the Japanese militarists had effectively tied the hands of the Ambassadors and he did not know whether the Ambassadors could succeed in having anything accomplished toward untying their hands. Mr. Kurusu brought up again his contention made on previous occasions that China had taken advantage of the Washington Conference treaties to flaunt Japan, and commented that if we don't look out China will sell both the United States and Japan down the river. The Secretary observed that he has been plowing through various contradictions in Japanese acts and utterances. He pointed out that the Japanese had been telling us that if something quick is not done something awful was about to happen; that they kept urging upon the Secretary the danger of delay, and kept pressing the Secretary to do something. He said that in view of all the confusion, threats and pressure, he had been brought to the stage where he felt that something must be done to clear the foggy atmosphere; that his conclusion was that he must bring us back to fundamentals; and that these fundamentals were embodied in the proposal which we had offered the Japanese on November 26. He said that we have stood from the first on the points involved in this proposal. He pointed out that everything that Japan was doing and saying was in precisely the opposite direction from the course we have been talking about in our conversations, and that these should be reversed by his government before we can further seriously talk peace.

Mr. Kurusu endeavored to make some lame apology for the direct military mind of the Japanese Army and commented that General Tojo was in position to control the situation. The Secretary asked what possibility there was of peace-minded people coming out in Japan and expressing themselves. He expressed doubt whether anybody in Japan would be free to speak unless he preached conquest. The Ambassador commented that the Japanese people are not talking about conquest. The Secretary pointed out that we all understand what are the implications of such terms as "controlling influence", "new order in east Asia", and "co-prosperity sphere". The Secretary observed that Hitler was using similar terms as synonyms for purposes of conquest. The Secretary went on to say that there was no reason for conflict between the United States and Japan, that there was no real clash of interests. He added that Japan does not have to use a sword to gain for herself a seat at the head of the table. He pointed out that equality of opportunity is in our opinion the key to the future peace and prosperity of all nations.

Mr. Kurusu disclaimed on the part of Japan any similarity between Japan's purposes and Hitler's purposes. The Ambassador pointed out that wars never settle anything and that war in the Pacific would be a tragedy, but he added that the Japanese people believe that the United States wants to keep Japan fighting with China and to keep Japan strangled. He said that the Japanese people feel that they are faced with the alternative of surrendering to the United States or of fighting. The Ambassador said that he was still trying to save the situation. The Secretary said that he has practically exhausted himself here, that the American people are going to assume that there is real danger to this country in the situation, and that there is nothing he can do to prevent it.

The Ambassadors said that they understood the Secretary's position in the light of his statements and they would report the matter to the Japanese Government with a view to seeing what could be done.

711.94/2594–⅝

Memorandum [92] *Regarding a Conversation Between the Under Secretary of State* (*Welles*), *the Japanese Ambassador* (*Nomura*), *and Mr. Kurusu*

[WASHINGTON,] December 2, 1941.

The Under Secretary said that the Secretary was absent from the Department because of a slight indisposition and that the President had therefore asked Mr. Welles to request the Japanese Ambassador and Mr. Kurusu to call to receive a communication which the President wished to make to them. Mr. Welles then read to Their Excellencies the following statement (a copy of which was handed to the Ambassador):

"I have received reports during the past days of continuing Japanese troop movements to southern Indochina. These reports indicate a very rapid and material increase in the forces of all kinds stationed by Japan in Indochina.

"It was my clear understanding that by the terms of the agreement—and there is no present need to discuss the nature of that agreement—between Japan and the French Government at Vichy that the total number of Japanese forces permitted by the terms of that agreement to be stationed in Indochina was very considerably less than the total amount of the forces already there.

"The stationing of these increased Japanese forces in Indochina would seem to imply the utilization of these forces by Japan for purposes of further aggression, since no such number of forces could possibly be required for the policing of that region. Such aggression could conceivably be against the Philippine Islands; against the many islands of the East Indies; against Burma; against Malaya or either through coercion or through the actual use of force for the purpose of undertaking the occupation of Thailand. Such new aggression would, of course, be additional to the acts of aggression already undertaken against China, our attitude towards which is well known, and has been repeatedly stated to the Japanese Government.

"Please be good enough to request the Japanese Ambassador and Ambassador Kurusu to inquire at once of the Japanese Government what the actual reasons may be for the steps already taken, and what I am to consider is the policy of the Japanese Government as demon-

---

[92] Prepared by Joseph W. Ballantine.

strated by this recent and rapid concentration of troops in Indochina. This Government has seen in the last few years in Europe a policy on the part of the German Government which has involved a constant and steady encroachment upon the territory and rights of free and independent peoples through the utilization of military steps of the same character. It is for that reason and because of the broad problem of American defense that I should like to know the intention of the Japanese Government."

The Japanese Ambassador said that he was not informed by the Japanese Government of its intentions and could not speak authoritatively on the matter but that of course he would communicate the statement immediately to his Government. Mr. Kurusu said that, in view of Japan's offer of November 20 to transfer all its forces from southern Indochina to northern Indochina, it was obvious no threat against the United States was intended. Both Mr. Kurusu and the Ambassador endeavored to explain that owing to lack of adequate land communication facilities in Indochina a rapid transfer of forces from northern to southern Indochina for purposes of aggression against countries neighboring southern Indochina could not be easily effected. Mr. Kurusu asked whether the reports to which the President referred were from our authorities. Mr. Welles said that he was not in position to say any more on that point than was contained in the statement.

The Ambassador said that it appeared to him that the measures which Japan was taking were natural under the circumstances, as the strengthening of armaments and of military dispositions by one side naturally leads to increasing activity by the other side. Mr. Welles stated that, as the Japanese Ambassador must be fully aware, this Government has not had any aggressive intention against Japan. The Ambassador said that, while he did not wish to enter into a debate on the matter, he wished to point out that the Japanese people believe that economic measures are a much more effective weapon of war than military measures; that they believe they are being placed under severe pressure by the United States to yield to the American position; and that it is preferable to fight rather than to yield to pressure. The Ambassador added that this was a situation in which wise statesmanship was needed; that wars do not settle anything; and that under the circumstances some agreement, even though it is not satisfactory, is better than no agreement at all.

Mr. Welles pointed out that the settlement which we are offering

Japan is one which would assure Japan of peace and the satisfaction of Japan's economic needs much more certainly than any other alternative which Japan might feel was open to her.

Mr. Kurusu said that having just recently arrived from Japan he could speak more accurately of the frame of mind which is prevalent in Japan than could the Ambassador. He dwelt briefly upon the reaction which has been caused in Japan by our freezing measures and he said that this produces a frame of mind which has to be taken into account.

Mr. Welles pointed out that, as the Ambassadors must fully understand, there is a frame of mind in this country also which must be taken into account, and that frame of mind is produced by the effect of four years of the measures taken by Japan in China causing the squeezing out of American interests in Japanese-occupied areas. Mr. Kurusu then repeated what he had said two or three times previously about the effect of the Washington Conference treaties upon China which had caused China to flaunt Japan's rights. He said that in view of the actual situation in the Far East there were points in our proposal of November 26 which the Japanese Government would find it difficult to accept. Mr. Welles asked whether we may expect shortly a reply from the Japanese Government on our proposal. The Ambassador replied in the affirmative, but said that it might take a few days in view of the important questions which it raised for the Japanese Government. Mr. Kurusu expressed the hope that the American Government would exercise cool judgment in its consideration of questions under discussion between the two Governments. Mr. Welles said that we are asking for cool judgment on the part of Japanese statesmen.

Then Mr. Kurusu said that the Japanese felt that we had made real progress in our discussions and that the Japanese Government had been hopeful of being able to work out with us some settlement of the three outstanding points on which our draft of June 21 and the Japanese draft of September 25 had not been reconciled. He asked whether the Secretary would be willing to consider resuming our efforts to reconcile our differences on those three points, in view of all the progress that had been made, instead of approaching the problem from a new angle as we had done in our latest proposal which seemed to the Japanese Government to require a completely fresh start.

Mr. Welles said that our proposal of November 26 represented an effort to restate our complete position, as it has always stood. He said, however, that he would be glad to refer to the Secretary Mr. Kurusu's suggestion.

263

711.94/2594–6⁄8

Memorandum [93] *Regarding a Conversation Between the Secretary Of State, the Japanese Ambassador (Nomura), and Mr. Kurusu*

[WASHINGTON,] December 5, 1941.

The Japanese Ambassador and Mr. Kurusu called at their request at the Department. The Ambassador handed to the Secretary a paper which he said was the Japanese Government's reply to the President's inquiry in regard to Japanese troops in French Indochina. The paper reads as follows:

[Here follows text of the statement printed on p. 828.]

The Secretary read the paper and asked whether the Japanese considered that the Chinese were liable to attack them in Indochina. He said, so Japan has assumed the defensive against China. He said that he had heard that the Chinese are contending that their massing troops in Yunnan was in answer to Japan's massing troops in Indochina. Mr. Kurusu said that that is all that they have received from their Government in regard to this matter. The Ambassador said that as the Chinese were eager to defend the Burma Road he felt that the possibility of a Chinese attack in Indochina as a means of preventing Japan's attacking the Burma Road from Indochina could not be excluded.

The Secretary said that he had understood that Japan had been putting forces into northern Indochina for the purpose of attacking China from there. He said that he had never heard before that Japan's troop movements into northern Indochina were for the purpose of defense against Chinese attack. The Secretary added that it was the first time that he knew that Japan was on the defensive in Indochina.

The Ambassador said that the Japanese are alarmed over increasing naval and military preparations of the ABCD powers in the southwest Pacific area, and that an airplane of one of those countries had recently flown over Formosa. He said that our military men are very alert and enterprising and are known to believe in the principle that offense is the best defense. The Secretary asked whether the Ambassador's observations applied to defensive measures we are taking against Hitler. The Ambassador replied that he did not say that, but that it was because of Japan's apprehensions in regard to the situation that they had made their November 20 proposal.

---

[93] Prepared by Joseph W. Ballantine.

The Secretary asked whether, if the Chinese are about to attack Japan in Indochina, this would not constitute an additional reason for Japan to withdraw her armed forces from Indochina. The Secretary said that he would be glad to get anything further which it might occur to the Japanese Government to say to us on this matter.

The Ambassador said that the Japanese Government was very anxious to reach an agreement with this Government and Mr. Kurusu said that the Japanese Government felt that we ought to be willing to agree to discontinue aid to China as soon as conversations between China and Japan were initiated. The Secretary pointed out that when the Japanese bring that matter up it brings up the matter of the aid Japan is giving to Hitler. He said that he did not see how Japan could demand that we cease giving aid to China while Japan was going on aiding Hitler. Mr. Kurusu asked in what way was Japan aiding Hitler. The Secretary replied that, as he had already made clear to the Japanese Ambassador, Japan was aiding Hitler by keeping large forces of this country and other countries immobilized in the Pacific area. (At this point the Ambassador uttered *sotto voce* an expression in Japanese which in the present context means "this isn't getting us anywhere".) The Secretary reminded the Ambassador of what the Secretary had said to the Ambassador on this point on November 22 as well as on our unwillingness to supply oil to Japan for the Japanese Navy which would enable Japan to operate against us in the southern Pacific and also on our attitude toward continuing aid to China. The Ambassador said that he recalled that the Secretary had said that he would almost incur the danger of being lynched if he permitted oil to go to Japan for her navy. The Ambassador said that he believed that if the Secretary would explain that giving of oil to Japan had been prompted by the desirability of reaching a peaceful agreement such explanation would be accepted. The Secretary replied that senators and others are not even now desisting from criticizing the Secretary for the course that he had hitherto taken.

The Secretary then recapitulated the three points on which he had orally commented to the Japanese Ambassador on November 22, with reference to the Japanese proposal of November 20, namely one, our difficulty with reference to the Japanese request that we discontinue aid to China, two, our feeling that the presence of large bodies of Japanese troops anywhere in Indochina caused among neighboring countries apprehensions for their security, and, three, public attitude in this country toward supplying Japan with oil for military and naval needs. He asked the Ambassador whether he had not set forth clearly his position on these points to the Ambassador on November 22. The Ambassador agreed.

The Ambassador said that this Government blames Japan for its move into Indochina but that if Indochina was controlled by other powers it would be a menace to Japan. The Secretary replied that as the Ambassador was aware we could solve matters without delay if only the Japanese Government would renounce courses of force and aggression. The Secretary added that we were not looking for trouble but that at the same time we were not running away from menaces.

Mr. Kurusu said that he felt that if we could only come to an agreement on temporary measures we could then proceed with our exploration of fundamental solutions. He said that such a fundamental agreement would necessarily take time and that what was needed now was a temporary expedient. The Secretary replied that the Japanese were keeping the situation confused by a malignant campaign conducted through the officially controlled and inspired press which created an atmosphere not conducive to peace. The Secretary said that we knew the Japanese Government could control the press and that therefore we did not understand what the motives are of the higher officials of the Japanese Government in promoting such a campaign. Mr. Kurusu said that on the American side we were not free from injurious newspaper propaganda. He said that for example there was the case of a newspaper report of the Secretary's interview with the press which created an unfortunate impression in Japan. The Secretary replied that he had been seeing for months and months that Japanese officials and the Japanese press had been proclaiming slogans of a bellicose character and that while all this was going on he had kept silent. He pointed out that now he was being jumped on by the Japanese if he said a single word in regard to his Government's principles. Mr. Kurusu then referred to a press report casting aspersions on Kurusu to the effect that he had been sent here to check on the Ambassador, et cetera, et cetera. The Secretary replied that he had heard only good reports in regard to Mr. Kurusu and the Ambassador. At this point the Ambassador and Mr. Kurusu took their leave after making the usual apologies for taking so much of the Secretary's time when he was busy.

STATEMENT HANDED BY THE JAPANESE AMBASSADOR (NOMURA) TO THE SECRETARY OF STATE ON DECEMBER 5, 1941

Reference is made to your inquiry about the intention of the Japanese Government with regard to the reported movements of Japanese troops in French Indo-china. Under instructions from Tokyo I wish to inform you as follows:

As Chinese troops have recently shown frequent signs of movements along the northern frontier of French Indo-china bordering on China, Japanese troops, with the object of mainly taking precautionary measures, have been reinforced to a certain extent in the northern part of French Indo-china. As a natural sequence of this step, certain movements have been made among the troops stationed in the southern part of the said territory. It seems that an exaggerated report has been made of these movements. It should be added that no measure has been taken on the part of the Japanese Government that may transgress the stipulations of the Protocol of Joint Defense between Japan and France.

264

740.0011 Pacific War/856

President Roosevelt to Emperor Hirohito of Japan [94]

[WASHINGTON,] December 6, 1941.

Almost a century ago the President of the United States addressed to the Emperor of Japan a message extending an offer of friendship of the people of the United States to the people of Japan. That offer was accepted, and in the long period of unbroken peace and friendship which has followed, our respective nations, through the virtues of their peoples and the wisdom of their rulers have prospered and have substantially helped humanity.

Only in situations of extraordinary importance to our two countries need I address to Your Majesty messages on matters of state. I feel I should now so address you because of the deep and far-reaching emergency which appears to be in formation.

Developments are occurring in the Pacific area which threaten to deprive each of our nations and all humanity of the beneficial influence of the long peace between our two countries. These developments contain tragic possibilities.

The people of the United States, believing in peace and in the

---

[94] This message was transmitted in telegram 818, Dec. 6, 1941, 9 p.m., to the Ambassador in Japan (Grew), under instructions to communicate the President's message to the Japanese Emperor in such manner as deemed most appropriate by the Ambassador and at the earliest possible moment, addressed to "His Imperial Majesty, the Emperor of Japan". The telegram added that the press was being informed that the President was dispatching a message to the Emperor.

right of nations to live and let live, have eagerly watched the conversations between our two Governments during these past months. We have hoped for a termination of the present conflict between Japan and China. We have hoped that a peace of the Pacific could be consummated in such a way that nationalities of many diverse peoples could exist side by side without fear of invasion; that unbearable burdens of armaments could be lifted for them all; and that all peoples would resume commerce without discrimination against or in favor of any nation.

I am certain that it will be clear to Your Majesty, as it is to me, that in seeking these great objectives both Japan and the United States should agree to eliminate any form of military threat. This seemed essential to the attainment of the high objectives.

More than a year ago Your Majesty's Government concluded an agreement with the Vichy Government by which five or six thousand Japanese troops were permitted to enter into Northern French Indochina for the protection of Japanese troops which were operating against China further north. And this Spring and Summer the Vichy Government permitted further Japanese military forces to enter into Southern French Indochina for the common defense of French Indochina. I think I am correct in saying that no attack has been made upon Indochina, nor that any has been contemplated.

During the past few weeks it has become clear to the world that Japanese military, naval and air forces have been sent to Southern Indo-China in such large numbers as to create a reasonable doubt on the part of other nations that this continuing concentration in Indo-China is not defensive in its character.

Because these continuing concentrations in Indo-China have reached such large proportions and because they extend now to the southeast and the southwest corners of that Peninsula, it is only reasonable that the people of the Philippines, of the hundreds of Islands of the East Indies, of Malaya and of Thailand itself are asking themselves whether these forces of Japan are preparing or intending to make attack in one or more of these many directions.

I am sure that Your Majesty will understand that the fear of all these peoples is a legitimate fear in as much as it involves their peace and their national existence. I am sure that Your Majesty will understand why the people of the United States in such large numbers look askance at the establishment of military, naval and air bases manned and equipped so greatly as to constitute armed forces capable of measures of offense.

It is clear that a continuance of such a situation is unthinkable.

None of the peoples whom I have spoken of above can sit either indefinitely or permanently on a keg of dynamite.

There is absolutely no thought on the part of the United States of invading Indo-China if every Japanese soldier or sailor were to be withdrawn therefrom.

I think that we can obtain the same assurance from the Governments of the East Indies, the Governments of Malaya and the Government of Thailand. I would even undertake to ask for the same assurance on the part of the Government of China. Thus a withdrawal of the Japanese forces from Indo-China would result in the assurance of peace throughout the whole of the South Pacific area.

I address myself to Your Majesty at this moment in the fervent hope that Your Majesty may, as I am doing, give thought in this definite emergency to ways of dispelling the dark clouds. I am confident that both of us, for the sake of the peoples not only of our own great countries but for the sake of humanity in neighboring territories, have a sacred duty to restore traditional amity and prevent further death and destruction in the world.

FRANKLIN D. ROOSEVELT

265

711.94/2594–⅞

Memorandum [95] *Regarding a Conversation Between the Secretary Of State, the Japanese Ambassador (Nomura), and Mr. Kurusu*

[WASHINGTON,] December 7, 1941.

The Japanese Ambassador asked for an appointment to see the Secretary at 1:00 p.m.,[96] but later telephoned and asked that the appointment be postponed to 1:45 as the Ambassador was not quite ready. The Ambassador and Mr. Kurusu arrived at the Department at 2:05 p.m. and were received by the Secretary at 2:20.

The Japanese Ambassador stated that he had been instructed to deliver at 1:00 p.m. the document which he handed the Secretary, but that he was sorry that he had been delayed owing to the need of more time to decode the message. The Secretary asked why he had

---

[95] Prepared by Joseph W. Ballantine.

[96] The Japanese attack on Pearl Harbor, Hawaii, took place on December 7, 1941, at 1:20 p.m., Washington time (7:50 a.m., Honolulu time), which was December 8, 3:20 a.m., Tokyo time. On December 8 at 6 a.m., Tokyo time (December 7, 4 p.m., Washington time), the Japanese imperial headquarters announced that war began as of "dawn" on that date.

specified one o'clock. The Ambassador replied that he did not know but that that was his instruction.

The Secretary said that anyway he was receiving the message at two o'clock.

After the Secretary had read two or three pages he asked the Ambassador whether this document was presented under instructions of the Japanese Government. The Ambassador replied that it was. The Secretary as soon as he had finished reading the document turned to the Japanese Ambassador and said,

"I must say that in all my conversations with you (the Japanese Ambassador) during the last nine months I have never uttered one word of untruth. This is borne out absolutely by the record. In all my fifty years of public service I have never seen a document that was more crowded with infamous falsehoods and distortions—infamous falsehoods and distortions on a scale so huge that I never imagined until today that any Government on this planet was capable of uttering them."

The Ambassador and Mr. Kurusu then took their leave without making any comment.

A copy of the paper which was handed to the Secretary by the Japanese Ambassador is attached.

[Annex]

MEMORANDUM HANDED BY THE JAPANESE AMBASSADOR (NOMURA) TO THE SECRETARY OF STATE AT 2:20 P.M. ON DECEMBER 7, 1941

1. The Government of Japan, prompted by a genuine desire to come to an amicable understanding with the Government of the United States in order that the two countries by their joint efforts may secure the peace of the Pacific Area and thereby contribute toward the realization of world peace, has continued negotiations with the utmost sincerity since April last with the Government of the United States regarding the adjustment and advancement of Japanese-American relations and the stabilization of the Pacific Area.

The Japanese Government has the honor to state frankly its views concerning the claims the American Government has persistently maintained as well as the measures the United States and Great Britain have taken toward Japan during these eight months.

2. It is the immutable policy of the Japanese Government to insure the stability of East Asia and to promote world peace and thereby to enable all nations to find each its proper place in the world.

Ever since China Affair broke out owing to the failure on the part of China to comprehend Japan's true intentions, the Japanese Government has striven for the restoration of peace and it has consistently exerted its best efforts to prevent the extension of war-like disturbances. It was also to that end that in September last year Japan concluded the Tripartite Pact with Germany and Italy.

However, both the United States and Great Britain have resorted to every possible measure to assist the Chungking régime so as to obstruct the establishment of a general peace between Japan and China, interfering with Japan's constructive endeavours toward the stabilization of East Asia. Exerting pressure on the Netherlands East Indies, or menacing French Indo-China, they have attempted to frustrate Japan's aspiration to the ideal of common prosperity in cooperation with these regions. Furthermore, when Japan in accordance with its protocol with France took measures of joint defence of French Indo-China, both American and British Governments, willfully misinterpreting it as a threat to their own possessions, and inducing the Netherlands Government to follow suit, they enforced the assets freezing order, thus severing economic relations with Japan. While manifesting thus an obviously hostile attitude, these countries have strengthened their military preparations perfecting an encirclement of Japan, and have brought about a situation which endangers the very existence of the Empire.

Nevertheless, to facilitate a speedy settlement, the Premier of Japan proposed, in August last, to meet the President of the United States for a discussion of important problems between the two countries covering the entire Pacific area. However, the American Government, while accepting in principle the Japanese proposal, insisted that the meeting should take place after an agreement of view had been reached on fundamental and essential questions.

3. Subsequently, on September 25th the Japanese Government submitted a proposal based on the formula proposed by the American Government, taking fully into consideration past American claims and also incorporating Japanese views. Repeated discussions proved of no avail in producing readily an agreement of view. The present cabinet, therefore, submitted a revised proposal, moderating still further the Japanese claims regarding the principal points of difficulty in the negotiation and endeavoured strenuously to reach a settlement. But the American Government, adhering steadfastly to its original assertions, failed to display in the slightest degree a spirit of conciliation. The negotiation made no progress.

Therefore, the Japanese Government, with a view to doing its utmost for averting a crisis in Japanese-American relations, submitted on November 20th still another proposal in order to arrive at an equitable solution of the more essential and urgent questions which, simplifying its previous proposal, stipulated the following points:

(1) The Governments of Japan and the United States undertake not to dispatch armed forces into any of the regions, excepting French Indo-China, in the Southeastern Asia and the Southern Pacific area.

(2) Both Governments shall cooperate with the view to securing the acquisition in the Netherlands East Indies of those goods and commodities of which the two countries are in need.

(3) Both Governments mutually undertake to restore commercial relations to those prevailing prior to the freezing of assets.

The Government of the United States shall supply Japan the required quantity of oil.

(4) The Government of the United States undertakes not to resort to measures and actions prejudicial to the endeavours for the restoration of general peace between Japan and China.

(5) The Japanese Government undertakes to withdraw troops now stationed in French Indo-China upon either the restoration of peace between Japan and China or the establishment of an equitable peace in the Pacific Area; and it is prepared to remove the Japanese troops in the southern part of French Indo-China to the northern part upon the conclusion of the present agreement.

As regards China, the Japanese Government, while expressing its readiness to accept the offer of the President of the United States to act as "introducer" of peace between Japan and China as was previously suggested, asked for an undertaking on the part of the United States to do nothing prejudicial to the restoration of Sino-Japanese peace when the two parties have commenced direct negotiations.

The American Government not only rejected the above-mentioned new proposal, but made known its intention to continue its aid to Chiang Kai-shek; and in spite of its suggestion mentioned above, withdrew the offer of the President to act as so-called "introducer" of peace between Japan and China, pleading that time was not yet ripe for it. Finally on November 26th, in an attitude to impose upon the Japanese Government those principles it has persistently maintained, the American Government made a proposal totally ignoring Japanese claims, which is a source of profound regret to the Japanese Government.

4. From the beginning of the present negotiation the Japanese Government has always maintained an attitude of fairness and moderation, and did its best to reach a settlement, for which it made all possible concessions often in spite of great difficulties. As for the China question which constituted an important subject of the negotiation, the Japanese Government showed a most conciliatory attitude. As for the principle of non-discrimination in international commerce, advocated by the American Government, the Japanese Government expressed its desire to see the said principle applied throughout the world, and declared that along with the actual practice of this principle in the world, the Japanese Government would endeavour to apply the same in the Pacific Area including China, and made it clear that Japan had no intention of excluding from China economic activities of third powers pursued on an equitable basis. Furthermore, as regards the question of withdrawing troops from French Indo-China, the Japanese Government even volunteered, as mentioned above, to carry out an immediate evacuation of troops from Southern French Indo-China as a measure of easing the situation.

It is presumed that the spirit of conciliation exhibited to the utmost degree by the Japanese Government in all these matters is fully appreciated by the American Government.

On the other hand, the American Government, always holding fast to theories in disregard of realities, and refusing to yield an inch on its impractical principles, caused undue delay in the negotiation. It is difficult to understand this attitude of the American Government and the Japanese Government desires to call the attention of the American Government especially to the following points:

1. The American Government advocates in the name of world peace those principles favorable to it and urges upon the Japanese Government the acceptance thereof. The peace of the world may be brought about only by discovering a mutually acceptable formula through recognition of the reality of the situation and mutual appreciation of one another's position. An attitude such as ignores realities and imposes one's selfish views upon others will scarcely serve the purpose of facilitating the consummation of negotiations.

Of the various principles put forward by the American Government as a basis of the Japanese-American Agreement, there are some which the Japanese Government is ready to accept in principle, but in view of the world's actual conditions, it seems only a utopian ideal on the part of the American Government to attempt to force their immediate adoption.

Again, the proposal to conclude a multilateral non-aggression pact between Japan, United States, Great Britain, China, the Soviet Union, the Netherlands and Thailand, which is patterned after the old concept of collective security, is far removed from the realities of East Asia.

2. The American proposal contained a stipulation which states— "Both Governments will agree that no agreement, which either has concluded with any third power or powers, shall be interpreted by it in such a way as to conflict with the fundamental purpose of this agreement, the establishment and preservation of peace throughout the Pacific area." It is presumed that the above provision has been proposed with a view to restrain Japan from fulfilling its obligations under the Tripartite Pact when the United States participates in the War in Europe, and, as such, it cannot be accepted by the Japanese Government.

The American Government, obsessed with its own views and opinions, may be said to be scheming for the extension of the war. While it seeks, on the one hand, to secure its rear by stabilizing the Pacific Area, it is engaged, on the other hand, in aiding Great Britain and preparing to attack, in the name of self-defense, Germany and Italy, two Powers that are striving to establish a new order in Europe. Such a policy is totally at variance with the many principles upon which the American Government proposes to found the stability of the Pacific Area through peaceful means.

3. Whereas the American Government, under the principles it rigidly upholds, objects to settle international issues through military pressure, it is exercising in conjunction with Great Britain and other nations pressure by economic power. Recourse to such pressure as a means of dealing with international relations should be condemned as it is at times more inhumane than military pressure.

4. It is impossible not to reach the conclusion that the American Government desires to maintain and strengthen, in coalition with Great Britain and other Powers, its dominant position it has hitherto occupied not only in China but in other areas of East Asia. It is a fact of history that the countries of East Asia for the past hundred years or more have been compelled to observe the *status quo* under the Anglo-American policy of imperialistic exploitation and to sacrifice themselves to the prosperity of the two nations. The Japanese Government cannot tolerate the perpetuation of such a situation since it directly runs counter to Japan's fundamental policy to enable all nations to enjoy each its proper place in the world.

The stipulation proposed by the American Government relative to French Indo-China is a good exemplification of the above-mentioned

American policy. Thus the six countries,—Japan, the United States, Great Britain, the Netherlands, China and Thailand,—excepting France, should undertake among themselves to respect the territorial integrity and sovereignty of French Indo-China and equality of treatment in trade and commerce would be tantamount to placing that territory under the joint guarantee of the Governments of those six countries. Apart from the fact that such a proposal totally ignores the position of France, it is unacceptable to the Japanese Government in that such an arrangement cannot but be considered as an extension to French Indo-China of a system similar to the Nine Power Treaty structure which is the chief factor responsible for the present predicament of East Asia.

5. All the items demanded of Japan by the American Government regarding China such as wholesale evacuation of troops or unconditional application of the principle of non-discrimination in international commerce ignored the actual conditions of China, and are calculated to destroy Japan's position as the stabilizing factor of East Asia. The attitude of the American Government in demanding Japan not to support militarily, politically or economically any régime other than the régime at Chungking, disregarding thereby the existence of the Nanking Government, shatters the very basis of the present negotiation. This demand of the American Government falling, as it does, in line with its above-mentioned refusal to cease from aiding the Chungking régime, demonstrates clearly the intention of the American Government to obstruct the restoration of normal relations between Japan and China and the return of peace to East Asia.

5. In brief, the American proposal contains certain acceptable items such as those concerning commerce, including the conclusion of a trade agreement, mutual removal of the freezing restrictions, and stabilization of yen and dollar exchange, or the abolition of extra-territorial rights in China. On the other hand, however, the proposal in question ignores Japan's sacrifices in the four years of the China Affair, menaces the Empire's existence itself and disparages its honour and prestige. Therefore, viewed in its entirety, the Japanese Government regrets that it cannot accept the proposal as a basis of negotiation.

6. The Japanese Government, in its desire for an early conclusion of the negotiation, proposed simultaneously with the conclusion of the Japanese-American negotiation, agreements to be signed with Great Britain and other interested countries. The proposal was accepted by the American Government. However, since the American Government has made the proposal of November 26th as a re-

sult of frequent consultation with Great Britain, Australia, the Netherlands and Chungking, and presumably by catering to the wishes of the Chungking régime in the questions of China, it must be concluded that all these countries are at one with the United States in ignoring Japan's position.

7. Obviously it is the intention of the American Government to conspire with Great Britain and other countries to obstruct Japan's efforts toward the establishment of peace through the creation of a new order in East Asia, and especially to preserve Anglo-American rights and interests by keeping Japan and China at war. This intention has been revealed clearly during the course of the present negotiation. Thus, the earnest hope of the Japanese Government to adjust Japanese-American relations and to preserve and promote the peace of the Pacific through cooperation with the American Government has finally been lost.

The Japanese Government regrets to have to notify hereby the American Government that in view of the attitude of the American Government it cannot but consider that it is impossible to reach an agreement through further negotiations.

[WASHINGTON,] *December 7, 1941.*

266

740.0011 Pacific War/891

The Ambassador in Japan (Grew) to the Secretary of State

[Telegram : Paraphrase]

TOKYO, December 8, 1941—1 p.m.
[Received December 10—6:23 a.m.]

1910. Embassy's 1906 of December 8.

At seven this morning the Foreign Minister asked that I call at his official residence. There he handed to me a memorandum of today's date.[96a] The Foreign Minister said it had been transmitted to Washington for the Japanese Ambassador to present this morning to you (Washington time, evening of December 7). The Foreign Minister said that the Japanese Emperor desired this memorandum to be considered as his reply to the message of President Roosevelt.

The following oral statement was then made to me by the Foreign Minister:

[96a] Annex to doc. 265.

"His Majesty has expressed his gratefulness and appreciation for the cordial message of the President. He has graciously let known his wishes to the Foreign Minister to convey the following to the President as a reply to the latter's message:

"Some days ago, the President made inquiries regarding the circumstances of the augmentation of Japanese forces in French Indochina to which His Majesty has directed the Government to reply. Withdrawal of Japanese forces from French Indochina constitutes one of the subject matters of the Japanese-American negotiations. His Majesty has commanded the Government to state its views to the American Government also on this question. It is, therefore, desired that the President will kindly refer to this reply.

"Establishment of peace in the Pacific, and consequently of the world, has been the cherished desire of His Majesty for the realization of which he has hitherto made his Government to continue its earnest endeavors. His Majesty trusts that the President is fully aware of this fact".

GREW

267

Department of State Bulletin, vol. V, p. 474

Address Delivered by President Roosevelt to the Congress, December 8, 1941

Yesterday, December 7, 1941—a date which will live in infamy—the United States of America was suddenly and deliberately attacked by naval and air forces of the Empire of Japan.

The United States was at peace with that Nation and, at the solicitation of Japan, was still in conversation with its Government and its Emperor looking toward the maintenance of peace in the Pacific. Indeed, one hour after Japanese air squadrons had commenced bombing in Oahu, the Japanese Ambassador to the United States and his colleague delivered to the Secretary of State a formal reply to a recent American message. While this reply stated that it seemed useless to continue the existing diplomatic negotiations, it contained no threat or hint of war or armed attack.

It will be recorded that the distance of Hawaii from Japan makes it obvious that the attack was deliberately planned many days or even weeks ago. During the intervening time the Japanese Government has deliberately sought to deceive the United States by false statements and expressions of hope for continued peace.

The attack yesterday on the Hawaiian Islands has caused severe damage to American naval and military forces. Very many American lives have been lost. In addition American ships have been reported torpedoed on the high seas between San Francisco and Honolulu.

Yesterday the Japanese Government also launched an attack against Malaya.

Last night Japanese forces attacked Hong Kong.

Last night Japanese forces attacked Guam.

Last night Japanese forces attacked the Philippine Islands.

Last night the Japanese attacked Wake Island.

This morning the Japanese attacked Midway Island.

Japan has, therefore, undertaken a surprise offensive extending throughout the Pacific area. The facts of yesterday speak for themselves. The people of the United States have already formed their opinions and well understand the implications to the very life and safety of our Nation.

As Commander in Chief of the Army and Navy I have directed that all measures be taken for our defense.

Always will we remember the character of the onslaught against us.

No matter how long it may take us to overcome this premeditated invasion, the American people in their righteous might will win through to absolute victory.

I believe I interpret the will of the Congress and of the people when I assert that we will not only defend ourselves to the uttermost but will make very certain that this form of treachery shall never endanger us again.

Hostilities exist. There is no blinking at the fact that our people, our territory, and our interests are in grave danger.

With confidence in our armed forces—with the unbounded determination of our people—we will gain the inevitable triumph—so help us God.

I ask that the Congress declare that since the unprovoked and dastardly attack by Japan on Sunday, December 7, a state of war has existed between the United States and the Japanese Empire.

268

55 Stat. 795

Joint Resolution Declaring That a State of War Exists Between The Imperial Government of Japan and the Government And the People of the United States and Making Provisions To Prosecute the Same

Whereas the Imperial Government of Japan has committed unprovoked acts of war against the Government and the people of the United States of America: Therefore be it

Resolved by the Senate and House of Representatives of the United States of America in Congress assembled, That the state of war between the United States and the Imperial Government of Japan which has thus been thrust upon the United States is hereby formally declared; and the President is hereby authorized and directed to employ the entire naval and military forces of the United States and the resources of the Government to carry on war against the Imperial Government of Japan; and, to bring the conflict to a successful termination, all of the resources of the country are hereby pledged by the Congress of the United States.

Approved, December 8, 1941, 4:10 p.m., E.S.T.

269

740.0011 Pacific War/877

The Ambassador in Japan (Grew) to the Secretary of State

[Telegram]

Tokyo, undated [97]
[Received December 10, 1941—2:35 a. m.]

The following note was received yesterday: "Ministry of Foreign Affairs, Tokyo, December 8, 1941. Excellency, I have the honor to inform Your Excellency that there has arisen a state of war between Your Excellency's country and Japan beginning today. I avail, et cetera. Signed Shigenori Togo, Minister for Foreign Affaires."

GREW

---

[97] This telegram apparently was dispatched from Tokyo on December 9 through the Japanese Foreign Office after the Embassy had been placed incommunicado.

DOCUMENTS

270

Department of State Bulletin, vol. V, p. 476

*Radio Address Delivered by President Roosevelt From Washington,
December 9, 1941*

The sudden criminal attacks perpetrated by the Japanese in the
Pacific provide the climax of a decade of international immorality.

Powerful and resourceful gangsters have banded together to make
war upon the whole human race. Their challenge has now been
flung at the United States of America. The Japanese have treacherously violated the long-standing peace between us. Many American
soldiers and sailors have been killed by enemy action. American
ships have been sunk; American airplanes have been destroyed.

The Congress and the people of the United States have accepted
that challenge.

Together with other free peoples, we are now fighting to maintain
our right to live among our world neighbors in freedom and in
common decency, without fear of assault.

I have prepared the full record of our past relations with Japan,
and it will be submitted to the Congress. It begins with the visit
of Commodore Perry to Japan 88 years ago. It ends with the visit
of two Japanese emissaries to the Secretary of State last Sunday, an
hour after Japanese forces had loosed their bombs and machine guns
against our flag, our forces, and our citizens.

I can say with utmost confidence that no Americans today or a
thousand years hence need feel anything but pride in our patience
and our efforts through all the years toward achieving a peace in
the Pacific which would be fair and honorable to every nation, large
or small. And no honest person, today or a thousand years hence,
will be able to suppress a sense of indignation and horror at the
treachery committed by the military dictators of Japan, under the
very shadow of the flag of peace borne by their special envoys in our
midst.

The course that Japan has followed for the past 10 years in Asia
has paralleled the course of Hitler and Mussolini in Europe and
Africa. Today, it has become far more than a parallel. It is collaboration so well calculated that all the continents of the world,
and all the oceans, are now considered by the Axis strategists as one
gigantic battlefield.

In 1931, Japan invaded Manchukuo—without warning.

In 1935, Italy invaded Ethiopia—without warning.

In 1938, Hitler occupied Austria—without warning.

In 1939, Hitler invaded Czechoslovakia—without warning.

Later in 1939, Hitler invaded Poland—without warning.

In 1940, Hitler invaded Norway, Denmark, Holland, Belgium, and Luxembourg—without warning.

In 1940, Italy attacked France and later Greece—without warning.

In 1941, the Axis Powers attacked Yugoslavia and Greece and they dominated the Balkans—without warning.

In 1941, Hitler invaded Russia—without warning.

And now Japan has attacked Malaya and Thailand—and the United States—without warning.

It is all of one pattern.

We are now in this war. We are all in it—all the way. Every single man, woman, and child is a partner in the most tremendous undertaking of our American history. We must share together the bad news and the good news, the defeats and the victories—the changing fortunes of war.

So far, the news has all been bad. We have suffered a serious set-back in Hawaii. Our forces in the Philippines, which include the brave people of that Commonwealth, are taking punishment, but are defending themselves vigorously. The reports from Guam and Wake and Midway Islands are still confused, but we must be prepared for the announcement that all these three outposts have been seized.

The casualty lists of these first few days will undoubtedly be large. I deeply feel the anxiety of all families of the men in our armed forces and the relatives of people in cities which have been bombed. I can only give them my solemn promise that they will get news just as quickly as possible.

This Government will put its trust in the stamina of the American people, and will give the facts to the public as soon as two conditions have been fulfilled: first, that the information has been definitely and officially confirmed; and, second, that the release of the information at the time it is received will not prove valuable to the enemy directly or indirectly.

Most earnestly I urge my countrymen to reject all rumors. These ugly little hints of complete disaster fly thick and fast in wartime. They have to be examined and appraised.

As an example, I can tell you frankly that until further surveys are made, I have not sufficient information to state the exact damage which has been done to our naval vessels at Pearl Harbor. Admittedly the damage is serious. But no one can say how serious until we know how much of this damage can be repaired and how quickly the necessary repairs can be made.

I cite as another example a statement made on Sunday night that a Japanese carrier had been located and sunk off the Canal Zone. And when you hear statements that are attributed to what they call "an authoritative source", you can be reasonably sure that under these war circumstances the "authoritative source" was not any person in authority.

Many rumors and reports which we now hear originate with enemy sources. For instance, today the Japanese are claiming that as a result of their one action against Hawaii they have gained naval supremacy in the Pacific. This is an old trick of propaganda which has been used innumerable times by the Nazis. The purposes of such fantastic claims are, of course, to spread fear and confusion among us, and to goad us into revealing military information which our enemies are desperately anxious to obtain.

Our Government will not be caught in this obvious trap—and neither will our people.

It must be remembered by each and every one of us that our free and rapid communication must be greatly restricted in wartime. It is not possible to receive full, speedy, accurate reports from distant areas of combat. This is particularly true where naval operations are concerned. For in these days of the marvels of radio it is often impossible for the commanders of various units to report their activities by radio, for the very simple reason that this information would become available to the enemy and would disclose their position and their plan of defense or attack.

Of necessity there will be delays in officially confirming or denying reports of operations, but we will not hide facts from the country if we know the facts and if the enemy will not be aided by their disclosure.

To all newspapers and radio stations—all those who reach the eyes and ears of the American people—I say this: you have a most grave responsibility to the Nation now and for the duration of this war.

If you feel that your Government is not disclosing enough of the truth, you have every right to say so. But—in the absence of all the facts, as revealed by official sources—you have no right to deal out unconfirmed reports in such a way as to make people believe they are gospel truth.

Every citizen, in every walk of life, shares this same responsibility. The lives of our soldiers and sailors—the whole future of this Nation—depend upon the manner in which each and every one of us fulfils his obligation to our country.

Now a word about the recent past—and the future. A year and a half has elapsed since the fall of France, when the whole world first realized the mechanized might which the Axis nations had been building for so many years. America has used that year and a half to great advantage. Knowing that the attack might reach us in all too short a time, we immediately began greatly to increase our industrial strength and our capacity to meet the demands of modern warfare.

Precious months were gained by sending vast quantities of our war material to the nations of the world still able to resist Axis aggression. Our policy rested on the fundamental truth that the defense of any country resisting Hitler or Japan was in the long run the defense of our own country. That policy has been justified. It has given us time, invaluable time, to build our American assembly lines of production.

Assembly lines are now in operation. Others are being rushed to completion. A steady stream of tanks and planes, of guns and ships, of shells and equipment—that is what these 18 months have given us.

But it is all only a beginning of what has to be done. We must be set to face a long war against crafty and powerful bandits. The attack at Pearl Harbor can be repeated at any one of many points in both oceans and along both our coast lines and against all the rest of the hemisphere.

It will not only be a long war, it will be a hard war. That is the basis on which we now lay all our plans. That is the yardstick by which we measure what we shall need and demand; money, materials, doubled and quadrupled production—ever-increasing. The production must be not only for our own Army and Navy and Air Forces. It must reinforce the other armies and navies and air forces fighting the Nazis and the war-lords of Japan throughout the Americas and the world.

I have been working today on the subject of production. Your Government has decided on two broad policies.

The first is to speed up all existing production by working on a seven-day-week basis in every war industry, including the production of essential raw materials.

The second policy, now being put into form, is to rush additions to the capacity of production by building more new plants, by adding to old plants, and by using the many smaller plants for war needs.

Over the hard road of the past months, we have at times met obstacles and difficulties, divisions and disputes, indifference and callous-ness. That is now all past—and, I am sure, forgotten.

The fact is that the country now has an organization in Washing-ton built around men and women who are recognized experts in their own fields. I think the country knows that the people who are actually responsible in each and every one of these many fields are pulling to-gether with a teamwork that has never before been excelled.

On the road ahead there lies hard work—gruelling work—day and night, every hour and every minute.

I was about to add that ahead there lies sacrifice for all of us.

But it is not correct to use that word. The United States does not consider it a sacrifice to do all one can, to give one's best to our Nation, when the Nation is fighting for its existence and its future life.

It is not a sacrifice for any man, old or young, to be in the Army or the Navy of the United States. Rather is it a privilege.

It is not a sacrifice for the industrialist or the wage-earner, the farmer or the shopkeeper, the trainman or the doctor, to pay more taxes, to buy more bonds, to forego extra profits, to work longer or harder at the task for which he is best fitted. Rather is it a privilege.

It is not a sacrifice to do without many things to which we are accustomed if the national defense calls for doing without.

A review this morning leads me to the conclusion that at present we shall not have to curtail the normal articles of food. There is enough food for all of us and enough left over to send to those who are fighting on the same side with us.

There will be a clear and definite shortage of metals of many kinds for civilian use, for the very good reason that in our increased pro-gram we shall need for war purposes more than half of that portion of the principal metals which during the past year have gone into articles for civilian use. We shall have to give up many things entirely.

I am sure that the people in every part of the Nation are pre-pared in their individual living to win this war. I am sure they will cheerfully help to pay a large part of its financial cost while it goes on. I am sure they will cheerfully give up those material things they are asked to give up.

I am sure that they will retain all those great spiritual things without which we cannot win through.

I repeat that the United States can accept no result save victory, final and complete. Not only must the shame of Japanese treachery be wiped out, but the sources of international brutality, wherever they exist, must be absolutely and finally broken.

In my message to the Congress yesterday I said that we "will make very certain that this form of treachery shall never endanger us again." In order to achieve that certainty, we must begin the great task that is before us by abandoning once and for all the illusion that we can ever again isolate ourselves from the rest of humanity.

In these past few years—and, most violently, in the past few days—we have learned a terrible lesson.

It is our obligation to our dead—it is our sacred obligation to their children and our children—that we must never forget what we have learned.

And what we all have learned is this:

There is no such thing as security for any nation—or any individual—in a world ruled by the principles of gangsterism.

There is no such thing as impregnable defense against powerful aggressors who sneak up in the dark and strike without warning.

We have learned that our ocean-girt hemisphere is not immune from severe attack—that we cannot measure our safety in terms of miles on any map.

We may acknowledge that our enemies have performed a brilliant feat of deception, perfectly timed and executed with great skill. It was a thoroughly dishonorable deed, but we must face the fact that modern warfare as conducted in the Nazi manner is a dirty business. We don't like it—we didn't want to get in it—but we are in it, and we're going to fight it with everything we've got.

I do not think any American has any doubt of our ability to administer proper punishment to the perpetrators of these crimes.

Your Government knows that for weeks Germany has been telling Japan that if Japan did not attack the United States, Japan would not share in dividing the spoils with Germany when peace came. She was promised by Germany that if she came in she would receive the complete and perpetual control of the whole of the Pacific area—and that means not only the Far East, not only all of the islands in the Pacific, but also a stranglehold on the west coast of North, Central, and South America.

We also know that Germany and Japan are conducting their military and naval operations in accordance with a joint plan. That plan considers all peoples and nations which are not helping the Axis powers as common enemies of each and every one of the Axis powers.

That is their simple and obvious grand strategy. That is why the

American people must realize that it can be matched only with similar grand strategy. We must realize for example that Japanese successes against the United States in the Pacific are helpful to German operations in Libya; that any German success against the Caucasus is inevitably an assistance to Japan in her operations against the Dutch East Indies; that a German attack against Algiers or Morocco opens the way to a German attack against South America.

On the other side of the picture, we must learn to know that guerilla warfare against the Germans in Serbia helps us; that a successful Russian offensive against the Germans helps us; and that British successes on land or sea in any part of the world strengthen our hands.

Remember always that Germany and Italy, regardless of any formal declaration of war, consider themselves at war with the United States at this moment just as much as they consider themselves at war with Britain and Russia. And Germany puts all the other republics of the Americas into the category of enemies. The people of the hemisphere can be honored by that.

The true goal we seek is far above and beyond the ugly field of battle. When we resort to force, as now we must, we are determined that this force shall be directed toward ultimate good as well as against immediate evil. We Americans are not destroyers—we are builders.

We are now in the midst of a war, not for conquest, not for vengeance, but for a world in which this Nation, and all that this Nation represents, will be safe for our children. We expect to eliminate the danger from Japan, but it would serve us ill if we accomplished that and found that the rest of the world was dominated by Hitler and Mussolini.

We are going to win the war and we are going to win the peace that follows.

And in the dark hours of this day—and through dark days that may be yet to come—we will know that the vast majority of the members of the human race are on our side. Many of them are fighting with us. All of them are praying for us. For, in representing our cause, we represent theirs as well—our hope and their hope for liberty under God.

271

Department of State Bulletin, vol. V, p. 475

Message of President Roosevelt to the Congress, December 11, 1941

On the morning of December eleventh, the Government of Germany, pursuing its course of world-conquest, declared war against the United States.

The long known and the long expected has thus taken place. The forces endeavoring to enslave the entire world now are moving towards this hemisphere.

Never before has there been a greater challenge to life, liberty, and civilization.

Delay invites greater danger. Rapid and united effort by all of the peoples of the world who are determined to remain free will insure a world victory of the forces of justice and of righteousness over the forces of savagery and of barbarism.

Italy also has declared war against the United States.

I therefore request the Congress to recognize a state of war between the United States and Germany, and between the United States and Italy.

FRANKLIN D. ROOSEVELT

272

55 Stat. 796

Joint Resolution Declaring That a State of War Exists Between The Government of Germany and the Government and the People of the United States and Making Provision To Prosecute The Same

Whereas the Government of Germany has formally declared war against the Government and the people of the United States of America: Therefore be it

Resolved by the Senate and House of Representatives of the United States of America in Congress assembled, That the state of war between the United States and the Government of Germany which has thus been thrust upon the United States is hereby formally declared; and the President is hereby authorized and directed to employ the entire naval and military forces of the United States and the resources of the Government to carry on war against the Government of Germany; and, to bring the conflict to a successful termination, all of the resources of the country are hereby pledged by the Congress of the United States.

Approved, December 11, 1941, 3:05 p.m., E.S.T.

55 Stat. 797

Joint Resolution Declaring That a State of War Exists Between The Government of Italy and the Government and the People Of the United States and Making Provision To Prosecute the Same

Whereas the Government of Italy has formally declared war against the Government and the people of the United States of America: Therefore be it

Resolved by the Senate and House of Representatives of the United States of America in Congress assembled, That the state of war between the United States and the Government of Italy which has thus been thrust upon the United States is hereby formally declared; and the President is hereby authorized and directed to employ the entire naval and military forces of the United States and the resources of the Government to carry on war against the Government of Italy; and, to bring the conflict to a successful termination, all of the resources of the country are hereby pledged by the Congress of the United States.

Approved, December 11, 1941, 3:06 p.m., E.S.T.

274

Department of State Bulletin, vol. VI, p. 3

Declaration by United Nations, January 1, 1942

A JOINT DECLARATION BY THE UNITED STATES OF AMERICA, THE UNITED KINGDOM OF GREAT BRITAIN AND NORTHERN IRELAND, THE UNION OF SOVIET SOCIALIST REPUBLICS, CHINA, AUSTRALIA, BELGIUM, CANADA, COSTA RICA, CUBA, CZECHOSLOVAKIA, DOMINICAN REPUBLIC, EL SALVADOR, GREECE, GUATEMALA, HAITI, HONDURAS, INDIA, LUXEMBOURG, NETHERLANDS, NEW ZEALAND, NICARAGUA, NORWAY, PANAMA, POLAND, SOUTH AFRICA, YUGOSLAVIA.

The Governments signatory hereto,

Having subscribed to a common program of purposes and principles embodied in the Joint Declaration of the President of the United States of America and the Prime Minister of the United Kingdom of Great Britain and Northern Ireland dated August 14, 1941, known as the Atlantic Charter,[98]

---

[98] See doc. 229.

Being convinced that complete victory over their enemies is essential to defend life, liberty, independence and religious freedom, and to preserve human rights and justice in their own lands as well as in other lands, and that they are now engaged in a common struggle against savage and brutal forces seeking to subjugate the world, *Declare:*

(1) Each Government pledges itself to employ its full resources, military or economic, against those members of the Tripartite Pact and its adherents with which such government is at war.

(2) Each Government pledges itself to cooperate with the Governments signatory hereto and not to make a separate armistice or peace with the enemies.

The foregoing declaration may be adhered to by other nations which are, or which may be, rendering material assistance and contributions in the struggle for victory over Hitlerism.[99]

Done at WASHINGTON, *January First, 1942.*

> The United States of America
>   by FRANKLIN D. ROOSEVELT
>
> The United Kingdom of Great Britain
> and Northern Ireland
>   by WINSTON CHURCHILL
>
> On behalf of the Government of the
> Union of Soviet Socialist Republics
>   MAXIM LITVINOFF, *Ambassador*
>
> National Government of the Republic of China
>   TSE VUNG SOONG, *Minister for Foreign Affairs*
>
> The Commonwealth of Australia
>   by R. G. CASEY
>
> The Kingdom of Belgium
>   by Cte R. v. d. STRATEN
>
> Canada
>   by LEIGHTON McCARTHY

---

[99] During 1942 the Declaration was adhered to by Mexico, the Commonwealth of the Philippines, and Ethiopia; in the first four months of 1943, it was adhered to by Iraq, Brazil, and Bolivia.

DOCUMENTS

The Republic of Costa Rica
   by LUIS FERNANDEZ

The Republic of Cuba
   by AURELIO F. CONCHESO

Czechoslovak Republic
   by V. S. HURBAN

The Dominican Republic
   by J. M. TRONCOSO

The Republic of El Salvador
   by C. A. ALFARO

The Kingdom of Greece
   by CIMON P. DIAMANTOPOULOS

The Republic of Guatemala
   by ENRIQUE LOPEZ-HERRARTE

La Republique d'Haiti
   par FERNAND DENNIS

The Republic of Honduras
   by JULIAN R. CACERES

India
   GIRJA SHANKAR BAJPAI

The Grand Duchy of Luxembourg
   by HUGUES LE GALLAIS

The Kingdom of the Netherlands
   A. LOUDON

Signed on behalf of the Government of the
Dominion of New Zealand
   by FRANK LANGSTONE

The Republic of Nicaragua
   by LEON DEBAYLE

852

DOCUMENTS

The Kingdom of Norway
by W. MUNTHE DE MORGENSTIERNE

The Republic of Panama
by JAEN GUARDIA

The Republic of Poland
by JAN CIECHANOWSKI

The Union of South Africa
by RALPH W. CLOSE

The Kingdom of Yugoslavia
by CONSTANTIN A. FOTITCH

INDEX

INDEX

Albania, Italian invasion of, 64, 455.

Alliance of Germany, Italy, and Japan. See Tripartite Pact.

Amau, Eiji (Director of Intelligence Bureau, Japanese Foreign Office), China, foreign assistance to (statement, April 1934), 18, 19, 214.

American republics:
Buenos Aires Conference (1936), 41, 61, 311, 342, 352, 366.
Habana Conference (1940), 82, 562, 563.
Lima Conference (1938), 61, 439, 440, 756.
Montevideo Conference (1933), 25, 61, 195, 199.
Panamá Conference (1939), 70, 488.

American Solidarity Declaration (1938), 61, 439.

Anti-Comintern Pact, Germany, Japan, and Italy, 40, 84, 92, 340, 481.

Armistice (1940), France and Germany, 78, 96, 553, 554.

Arms embargo:
European war, proclamation, 69.
Hull, Secretary, letters and statements to Congress (Apr. 5 and May 17, 1933, May 12, 1938, May 27 and July 14 1939), 7, 23, 37, 66, 67, 177, 183, 419, 461, 465, 468, 474.
Italian-Ethiopian conflict, proclamation, 31, 283, 287.
Proposed legislation (1933), 23, 177, 183.
Roosevelt, President, statement regarding (Aug. 31, 1935), 25, 271; message to Congress (July 14, 1939), 66, 468; press release (July 18, 1939), 67, 474; address to Congress (Sept. 21, 1939), 69, 486.
Spain, joint resolution (Jan. 8, 1937), 37, 322, 329, 353.
U.S. neutrality acts, 25, 31, 33, 35, 49, 66, 69, 266, 271, 313, 314, 355, 380, 484; repeal of, 70, 116, 487, 494, 506, 761, 765, 787.

"Arsenal of democracy" address by President Roosevelt, 87, 599.

Atlantic, Battle of the, 106, 113, 115, 662, 737.

Atlantic Charter (Aug. 14, 1941), 111, 151, 717.

Austria, German invasion of, 56.

Axis powers (see also Anti-Comintern Pact; Tripartite Pact; and the individual countries):
Aggressive policies of, 3.
Japan, pro-Axis elements in, 134, 746.
Japanese alignment with, 122.
Menace to world, 87, 106, 114, 149, 599, 666, 740, 845.
U.S. war with, 147, 149, 150, 839, 841, 842, 848, 849, 850.

Battleships, U.S. construction of, 44, 354.

Belgium, German invasion of, 75, 523.

Bolivia, boundary dispute with Paraguay, 26.

Brussels Conference (1937), 50–52, 389, 390, 393, 398.

Buenos Aires Conference (1936), 41, 61, 311, 342, 352, 366.

Bulgaria:
German aggression against Yugoslavia, instructions to U.S. Minister, 103, 638.
Tripartite Pact, adherence to, 103.

Burma Road:
Closing (July 18, 1940), 94, 562.
Reopening (Oct. 17, 1940), 95.

Casey, Richard C. (Australian Minister to U.S.), Japanese aggression, conversation with Secretary Hull and Lord Lothian (June 28, 1940), 94, 559.

Chamberlain, Neville (Prime Minister of Great Britain), conferences with Hitler, 58.

China (see also Hull; Manchuria; Roosevelt; Sino-Japanese war):
"Autonomy movement" in North China, Japanese attempt to promote, 38; Hull statement regarding (Dec. 5, 1935), 38, 301.
Civilians, bombing by Japan, 89, 421, 422.
Foreign assistance to, Japan's attitude, 18, 19, 214.
Japanese attack on (1937)—
Hull and Horinouchi conversations (1939), 91, 92, 465, 480.

857

INDEX

864